LoserPalooza

Other Books by Darby Conley

The Dog Is Not a Toy (House Rule #4)

Fuzzy Logic: Get Fuzzy 2

Groovitude: A Get Fuzzy Treasury

The Get Fuzzy Experience: Are You Bucksperienced

I Would Have Bought You a Cat, But . . .

Blueprint for Disaster

Bucky Katt's Big Book of Fun

Say Cheesy

Scrum Bums

LoserPalooza
A GET FUZZY Treasury

by Darby Conley

**Andrews McMeel
Publishing, LLC**

Kansas City

Get Fuzzy is distributed internationally by United Feature Syndicate, Inc.

Loserpalooza copyright © 2007 by Darby Conley. All rights reserved. Printed in the United States of America. No part of this book may be used or reproduced in any manner whatsoever without written permission except in the case of reprints in the context of reviews. For information, write Andrews McMeel Publishing, LLC, an Andrews McMeel Universal company, 4520 Main Street, Kansas City, Missouri 64111.

07 08 09 10 11 BAM 10 9 8 7 6 5 4 3 2 1

ISBN-13: 978-0-7407-5709-9

ISBN-10: 0-7407-5709-1

Library of Congress Control Number: 2006939078

Get Fuzzy can be viewed on the Internet at

www.comics.com/getfuzzy.

--- **ATTENTION: SCHOOLS AND BUSINESSES** ---

Andrews McMeel books are available at quantity discounts with bulk purchase for educational, business, or sales promotional use. For information, please write to: Special Sales Department, Andrews McMeel Publishing, LLC, 4520 Main Street, Kansas City, Missouri 64111.

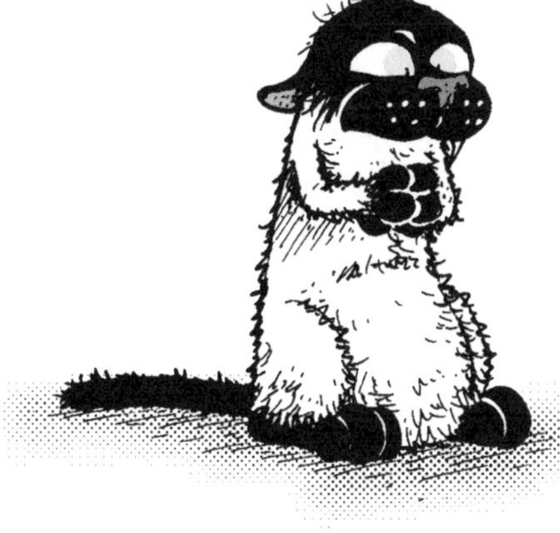

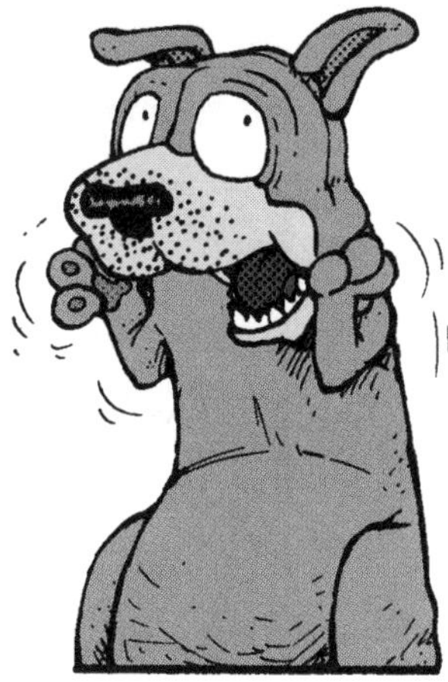

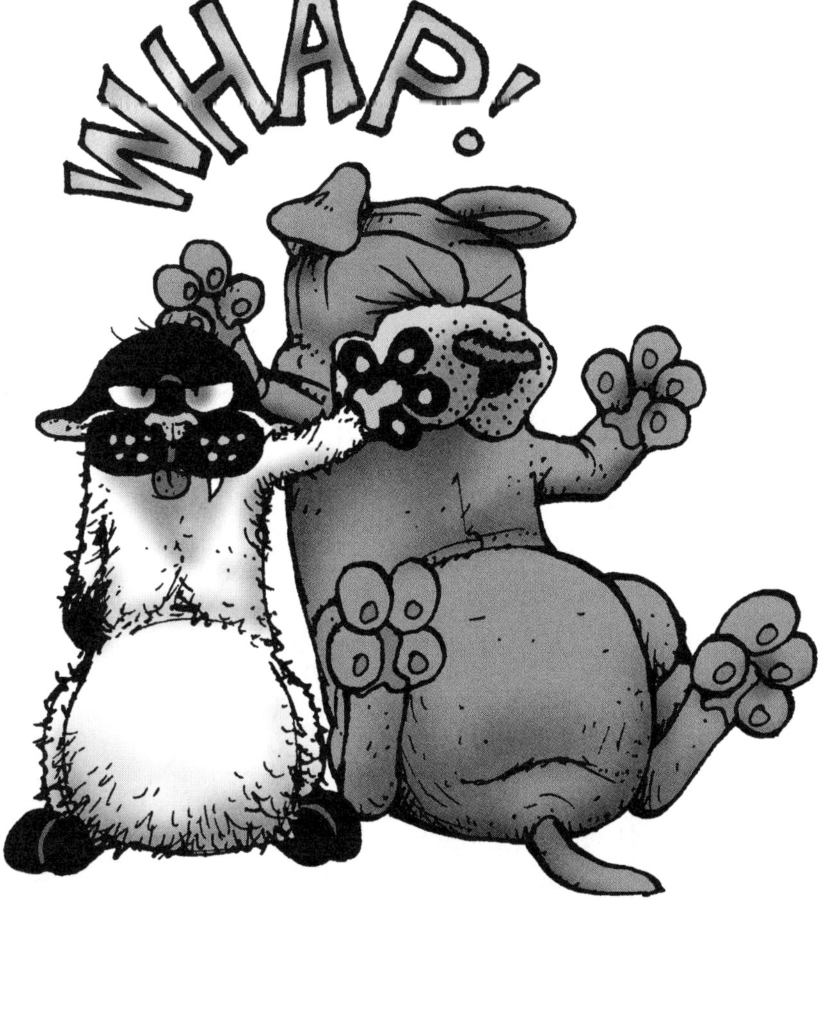
WHAP!

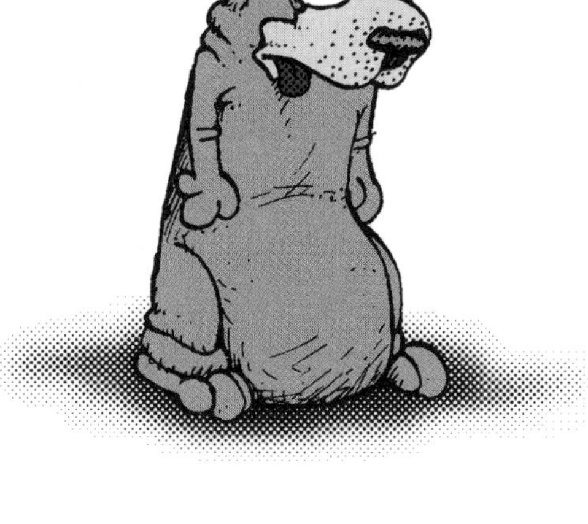

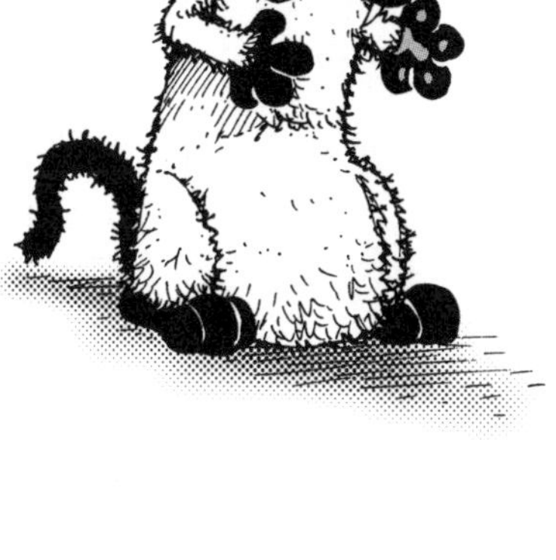

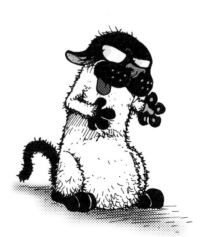

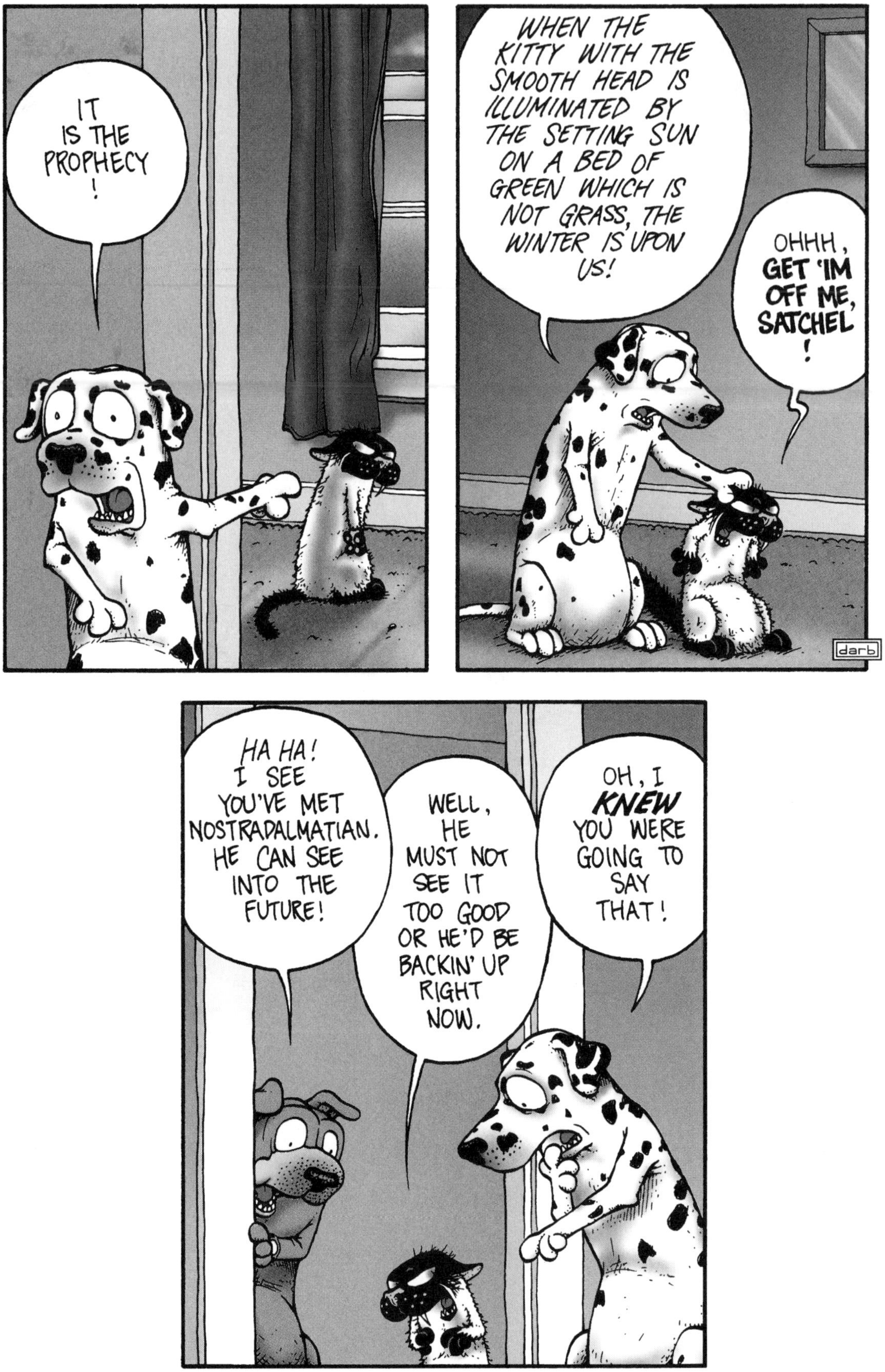
IT IS THE PROPHECY!
WHEN THE KITTY WITH THE SMOOTH HEAD IS ILLUMINATED BY THE SETTING SUN ON A BED OF GREEN WHICH IS NOT GRASS, THE WINTER IS UPON US!
OHHH, GET 'IM OFF ME, SATCHEL!
darb
HA HA! I SEE YOU'VE MET NOSTRADALMATIAN. HE CAN SEE INTO THE FUTURE!
WELL, HE MUST NOT SEE IT TOO GOOD OR HE'D BE BACKIN' UP RIGHT NOW.
OH, I KNEW YOU WERE GOING TO SAY THAT!

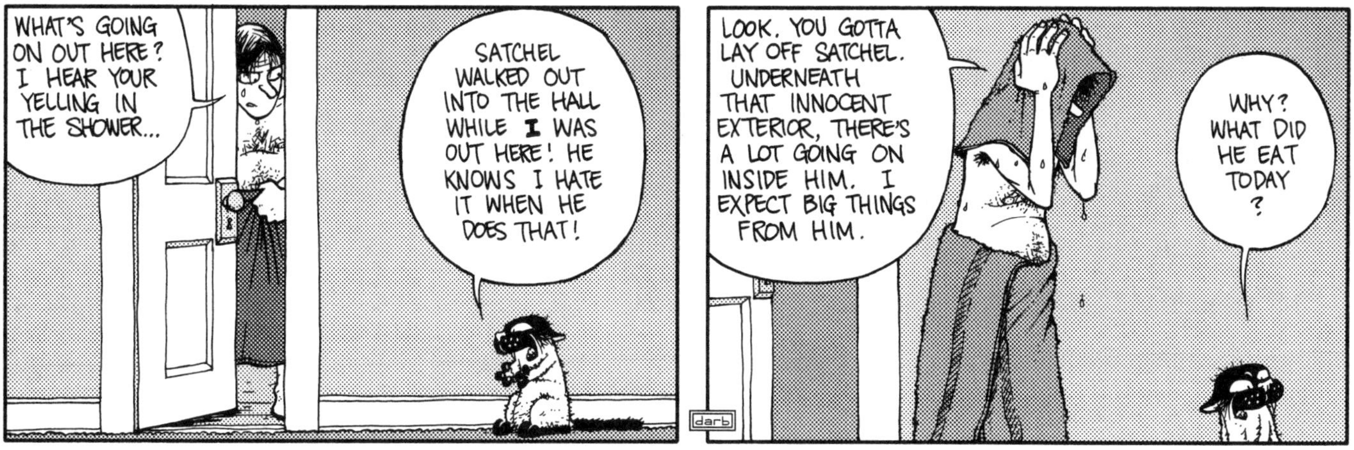
WHAT'S GOING ON OUT HERE? I HEAR YOUR YELLING IN THE SHOWER...
SATCHEL WALKED OUT INTO THE HALL WHILE I WAS OUT HERE! HE KNOWS I HATE IT WHEN HE DOES THAT!
darb
LOOK. YOU GOTTA LAY OFF SATCHEL. UNDERNEATH THAT INNOCENT EXTERIOR, THERE'S A LOT GOING ON INSIDE HIM. I EXPECT BIG THINGS FROM HIM.
WHY? WHAT DID HE EAT TODAY?

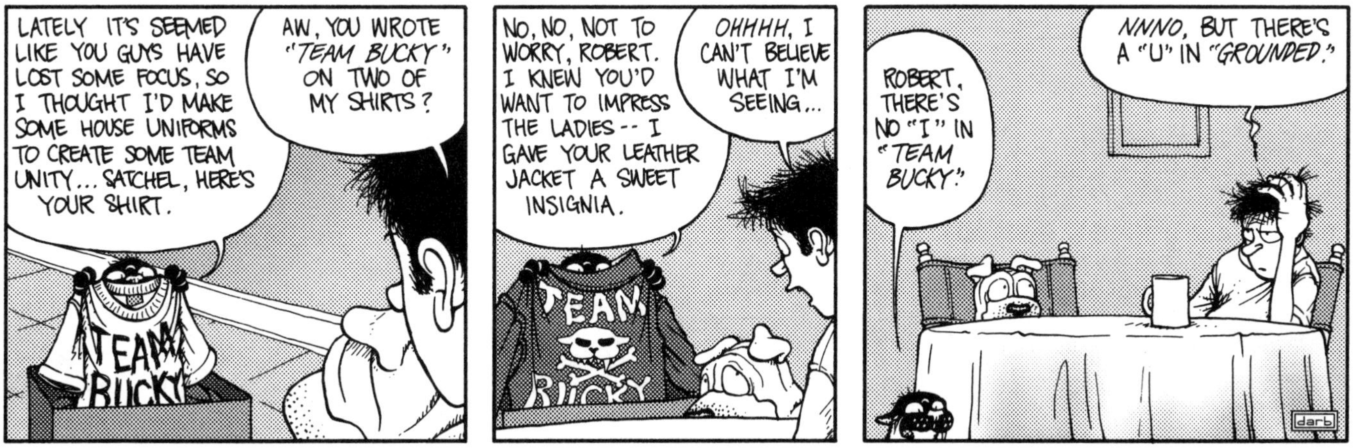
LATELY IT'S SEEMED LIKE YOU GUYS HAVE LOST SOME FOCUS, SO I THOUGHT I'D MAKE SOME HOUSE UNIFORMS TO CREATE SOME TEAM UNITY... SATCHEL, HERE'S YOUR SHIRT.
AW, YOU WROTE "*TEAM BUCKY*" ON TWO OF MY SHIRTS?
TEAM BUCKY
NO, NO, NOT TO WORRY, ROBERT. I KNEW YOU'D WANT TO IMPRESS THE LADIES -- I GAVE YOUR LEATHER JACKET A SWEET INSIGNIA.
OHHHH, I CAN'T BELIEVE WHAT I'M SEEING...
ROBERT, THERE'S NO "I" IN "*TEAM BUCKY*."
NNNO, BUT THERE'S A "U" IN "*GROUNDED*."
darb

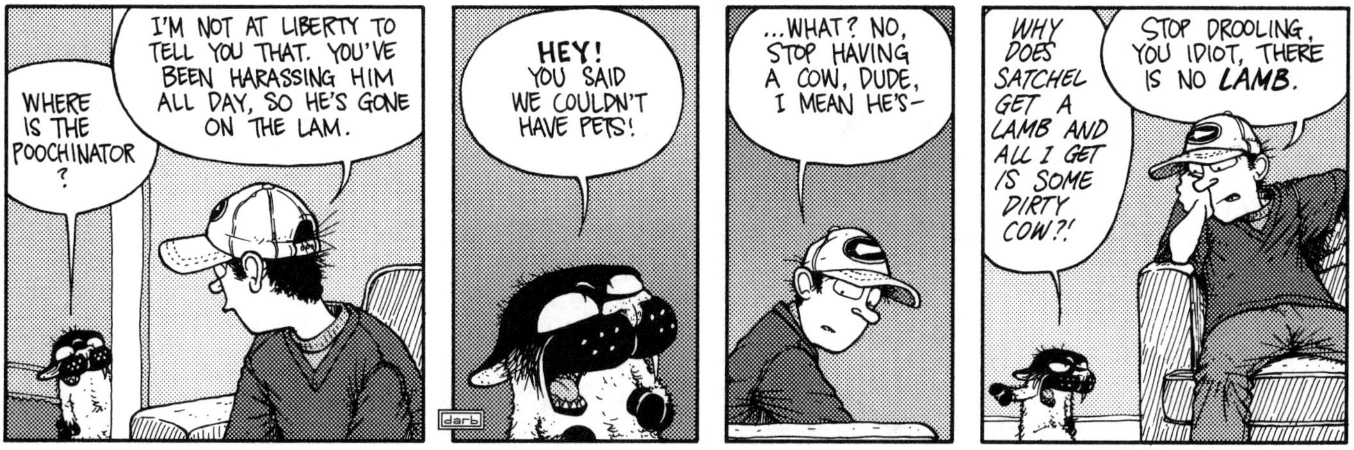
WHERE IS THE POOCHINATOR?
I'M NOT AT LIBERTY TO TELL YOU THAT. YOU'VE BEEN HARASSING HIM ALL DAY, SO HE'S GONE ON THE LAM.
darb
HEY! YOU SAID WE COULDN'T HAVE PETS!
...WHAT? NO, STOP HAVING A COW, DUDE, I MEAN HE'S—
WHY DOES SATCHEL GET A LAMB AND ALL I GET IS SOME DIRTY COW?!
STOP DROOLING, YOU IDIOT, THERE IS NO **LAMB**.

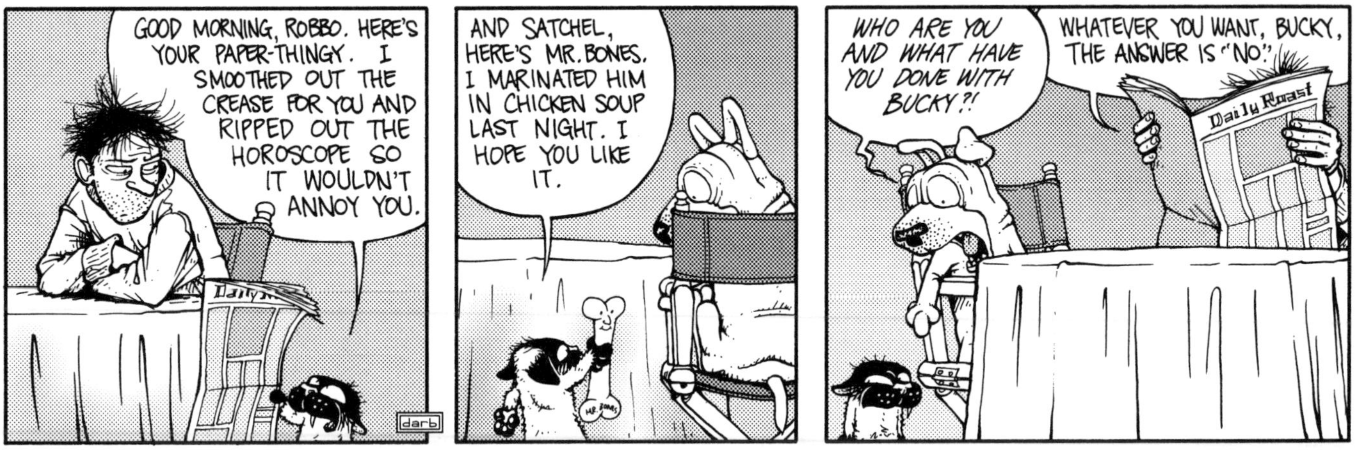
GOOD MORNING, ROBBO. HERE'S YOUR PAPER-THINGY. I SMOOTHED OUT THE CREASE FOR YOU AND RIPPED OUT THE HOROSCOPE SO IT WOULDN'T ANNOY YOU.
AND SATCHEL, HERE'S MR. BONES. I MARINATED HIM IN CHICKEN SOUP LAST NIGHT. I HOPE YOU LIKE IT.
WHO ARE YOU AND WHAT HAVE YOU DONE WITH BUCKY?!
WHATEVER YOU WANT, BUCKY, THE ANSWER IS "NO."
Daily Roast

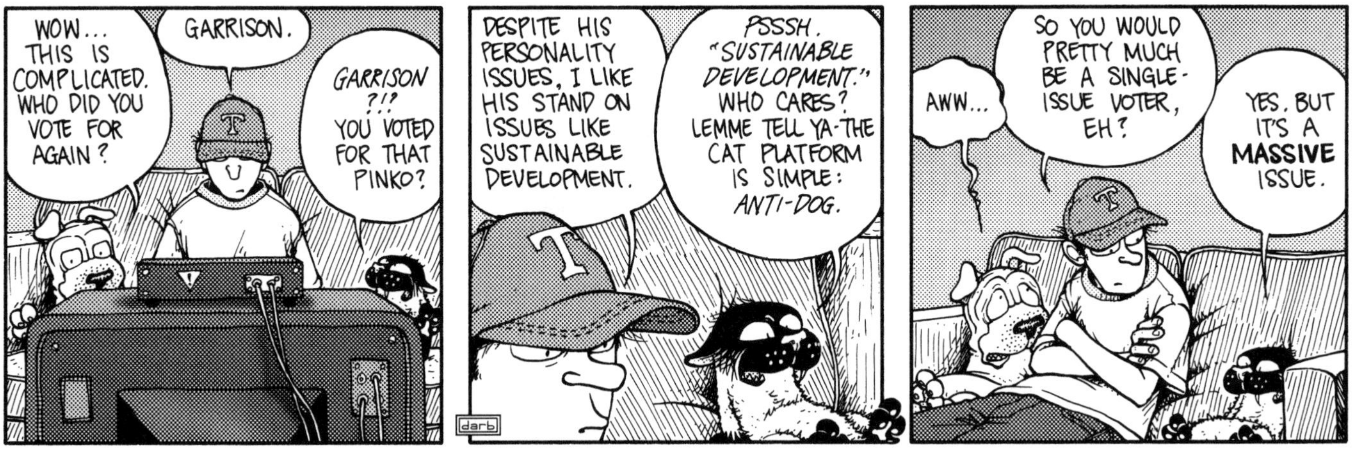
WOW... THIS IS COMPLICATED. WHO DID YOU VOTE FOR AGAIN?
GARRISON.
GARRISON?!? YOU VOTED FOR THAT PINKO?
DESPITE HIS PERSONALITY ISSUES, I LIKE HIS STAND ON ISSUES LIKE SUSTAINABLE DEVELOPMENT.
PSSSH. "SUSTAINABLE DEVELOPMENT." WHO CARES? LEMME TELL YA-THE CAT PLATFORM IS SIMPLE: ANTI-DOG.
AWW...
SO YOU WOULD PRETTY MUCH BE A SINGLE-ISSUE VOTER, EH?
YES. BUT IT'S A **MASSIVE** ISSUE.

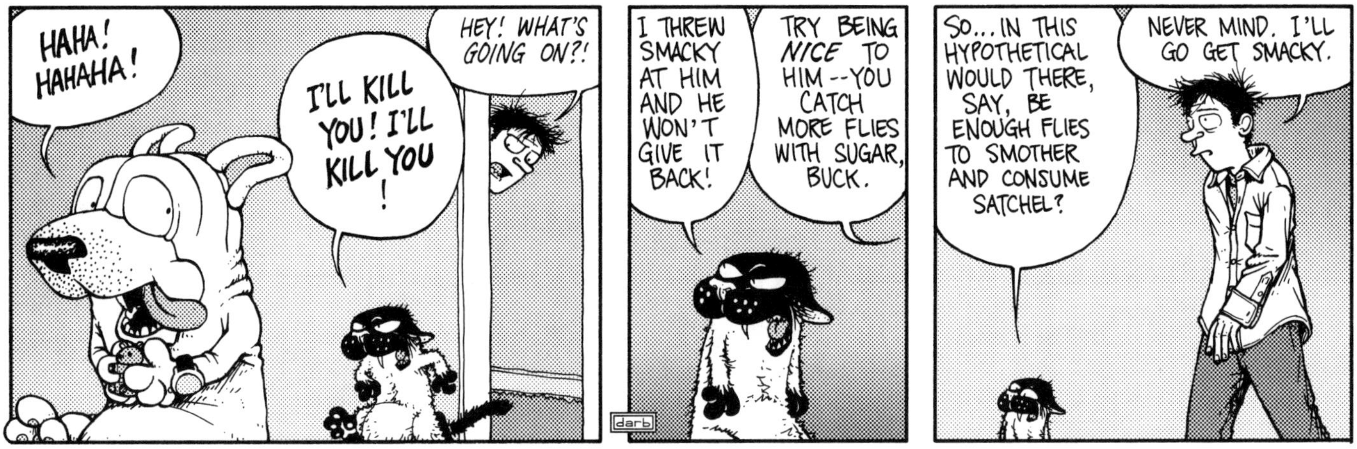
HAHA! HAHAHA!
I'LL KILL YOU! I'LL KILL YOU!
HEY! WHAT'S GOING ON?!
I THREW SMACKY AT HIM AND HE WON'T GIVE IT BACK!
TRY BEING *NICE* TO HIM--YOU CATCH MORE FLIES WITH SUGAR, BUCK.
SO... IN THIS HYPOTHETICAL WOULD THERE, SAY, BE ENOUGH FLIES TO SMOTHER AND CONSUME SATCHEL?
NEVER MIND. I'LL GO GET SMACKY.

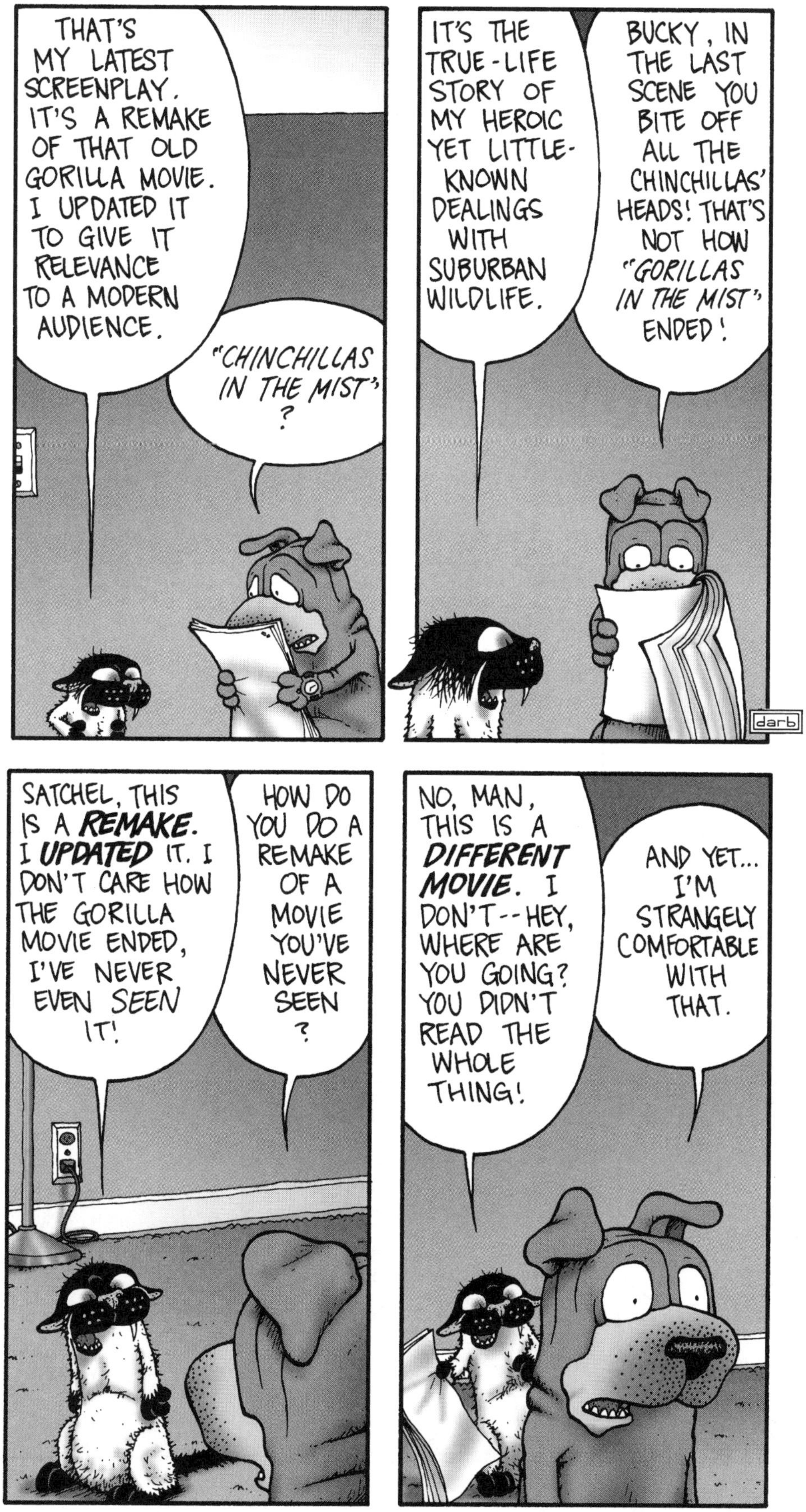
THAT'S MY LATEST SCREENPLAY. IT'S A REMAKE OF THAT OLD GORILLA MOVIE. I UPDATED IT TO GIVE IT RELEVANCE TO A MODERN AUDIENCE.
"CHINCHILLAS IN THE MIST"?
IT'S THE TRUE-LIFE STORY OF MY HEROIC YET LITTLE-KNOWN DEALINGS WITH SUBURBAN WILDLIFE.
BUCKY, IN THE LAST SCENE YOU BITE OFF ALL THE CHINCHILLAS' HEADS! THAT'S NOT HOW "GORILLAS IN THE MIST" ENDED!
darb
SATCHEL, THIS IS A **REMAKE**. I **UPDATED** IT. I DON'T CARE HOW THE GORILLA MOVIE ENDED, I'VE NEVER EVEN SEEN IT!
HOW DO YOU DO A REMAKE OF A MOVIE YOU'VE NEVER SEEN?
NO, MAN, THIS IS A **DIFFERENT MOVIE**. I DON'T--HEY, WHERE ARE YOU GOING? YOU DIDN'T READ THE WHOLE THING!
AND YET... I'M STRANGELY COMFORTABLE WITH THAT.

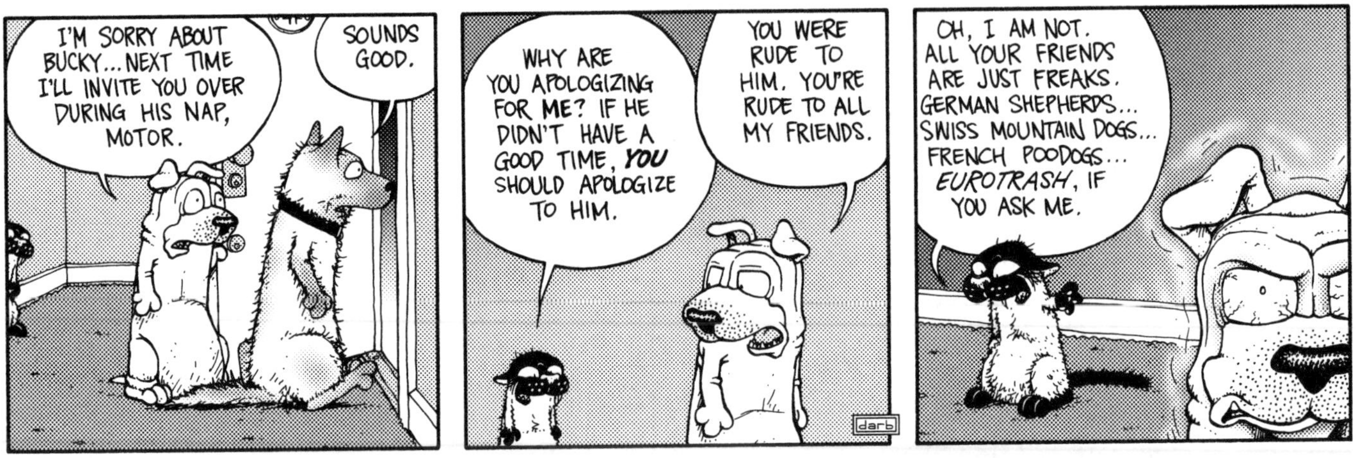
I'M SORRY ABOUT BUCKY...NEXT TIME I'LL INVITE YOU OVER DURING HIS NAP, MOTOR.
SOUNDS GOOD.
WHY ARE YOU APOLOGIZING FOR **ME**? IF HE DIDN'T HAVE A GOOD TIME, ***YOU*** SHOULD APOLOGIZE TO HIM.
YOU WERE RUDE TO HIM. YOU'RE RUDE TO ALL MY FRIENDS.
darb
OH, I AM NOT. ALL YOUR FRIENDS ARE JUST FREAKS. GERMAN SHEPHERDS... SWISS MOUNTAIN DOGS... FRENCH POODOGS... *EUROTRASH*, IF YOU ASK ME.

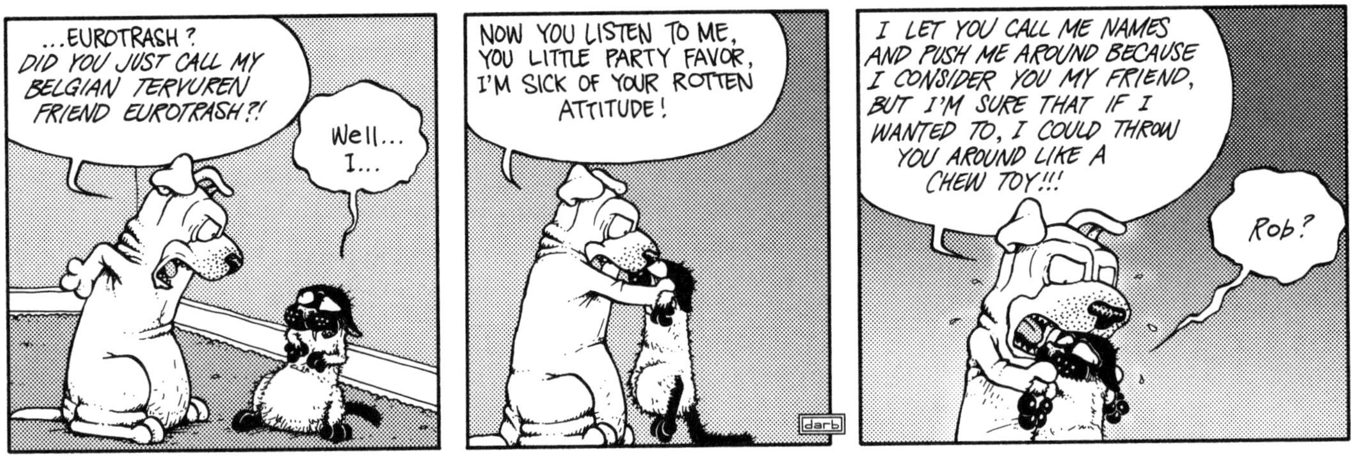
...EUROTRASH? *DID YOU JUST CALL MY BELGIAN TERVUREN FRIEND EUROTRASH?!*
Well... I...
NOW YOU LISTEN TO ME, YOU LITTLE PARTY FAVOR, I'M SICK OF YOUR ROTTEN ATTITUDE!
darb
I LET YOU CALL ME NAMES AND PUSH ME AROUND BECAUSE I CONSIDER YOU MY FRIEND, BUT I'M SURE THAT IF I WANTED TO, I COULD THROW YOU AROUND LIKE A CHEW TOY!!!
Rob?

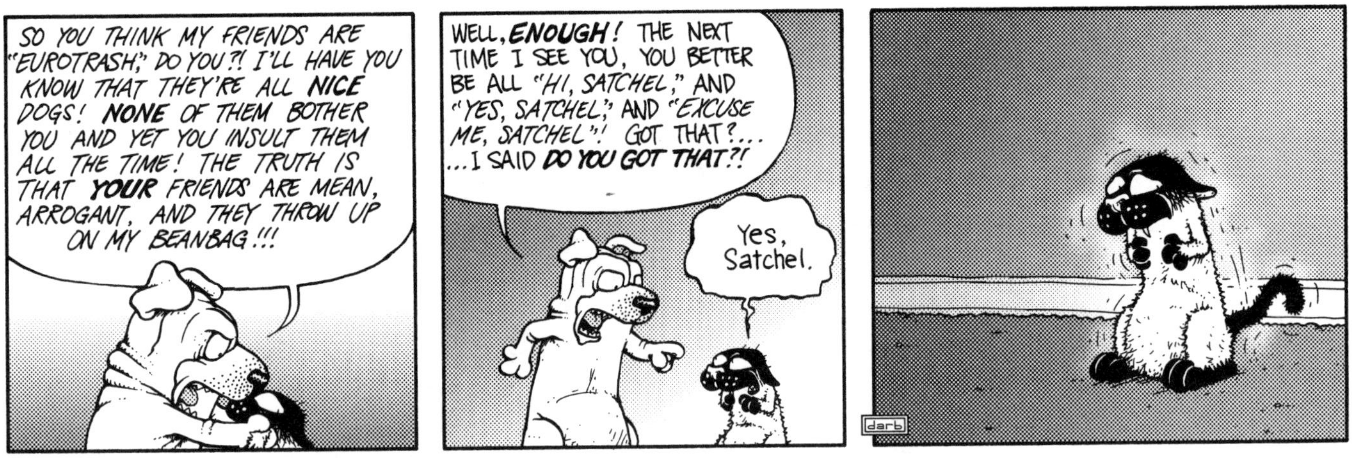
*SO YOU THINK MY FRIENDS ARE "EUROTRASH," DO YOU?! I'LL HAVE YOU KNOW THAT THEY'RE ALL **NICE** DOGS! **NONE** OF THEM BOTHER YOU AND YET YOU INSULT THEM ALL THE TIME! THE TRUTH IS THAT **YOUR** FRIENDS ARE MEAN, ARROGANT, AND THEY THROW UP ON MY BEANBAG!!!*
WELL, ***ENOUGH***! THE NEXT TIME I SEE YOU, YOU BETTER BE ALL *"HI, SATCHEL,"* AND *"YES, SATCHEL,"* AND *"EXCUSE ME, SATCHEL"*! GOT THAT?... ...I SAID ***DO YOU GOT THAT?!***
Yes, Satchel.
darb

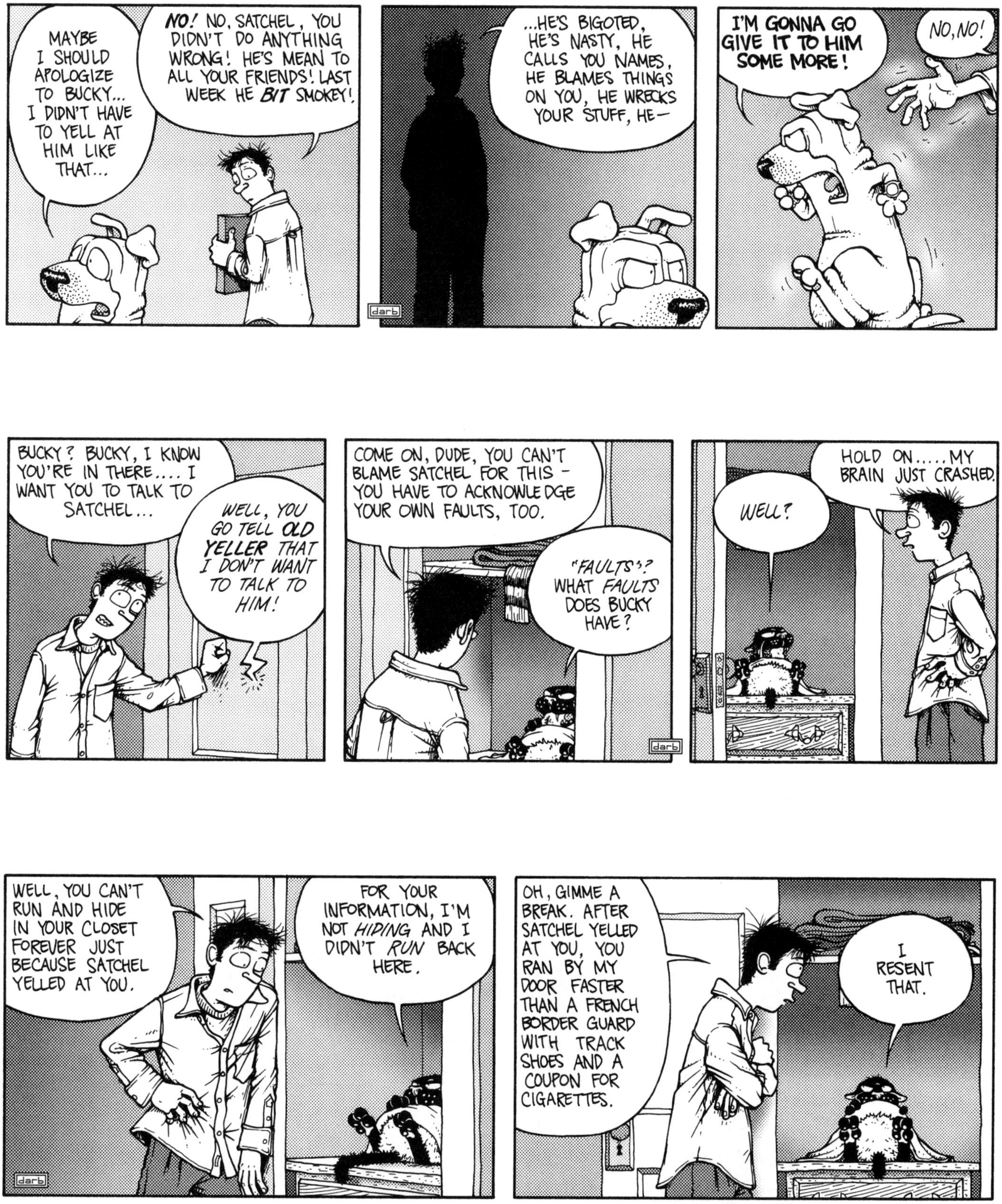

MAYBE I SHOULD APOLOGIZE TO BUCKY... I DIDN'T HAVE TO YELL AT HIM LIKE THAT...
NO! NO, SATCHEL, YOU DIDN'T DO ANYTHING WRONG! HE'S MEAN TO ALL YOUR FRIENDS! LAST WEEK HE BIT SMOKEY!
...HE'S BIGOTED, HE'S NASTY, HE CALLS YOU NAMES, HE BLAMES THINGS ON YOU, HE WRECKS YOUR STUFF, HE—
darb
I'M GONNA GO GIVE IT TO HIM SOME MORE!
NO, NO!
BUCKY? BUCKY, I KNOW YOU'RE IN THERE.... I WANT YOU TO TALK TO SATCHEL...
WELL, YOU GO TELL OLD YELLER THAT I DON'T WANT TO TALK TO HIM!
COME ON, DUDE, YOU CAN'T BLAME SATCHEL FOR THIS - YOU HAVE TO ACKNOWLEDGE YOUR OWN FAULTS, TOO.
"FAULTS"? WHAT FAULTS DOES BUCKY HAVE?
darb
WELL?
HOLD ON..... MY BRAIN JUST CRASHED.
WELL, YOU CAN'T RUN AND HIDE IN YOUR CLOSET FOREVER JUST BECAUSE SATCHEL YELLED AT YOU.
FOR YOUR INFORMATION, I'M NOT HIDING AND I DIDN'T RUN BACK HERE.
darb
OH, GIMME A BREAK. AFTER SATCHEL YELLED AT YOU, YOU RAN BY MY DOOR FASTER THAN A FRENCH BORDER GUARD WITH TRACK SHOES AND A COUPON FOR CIGARETTES.
I RESENT THAT.

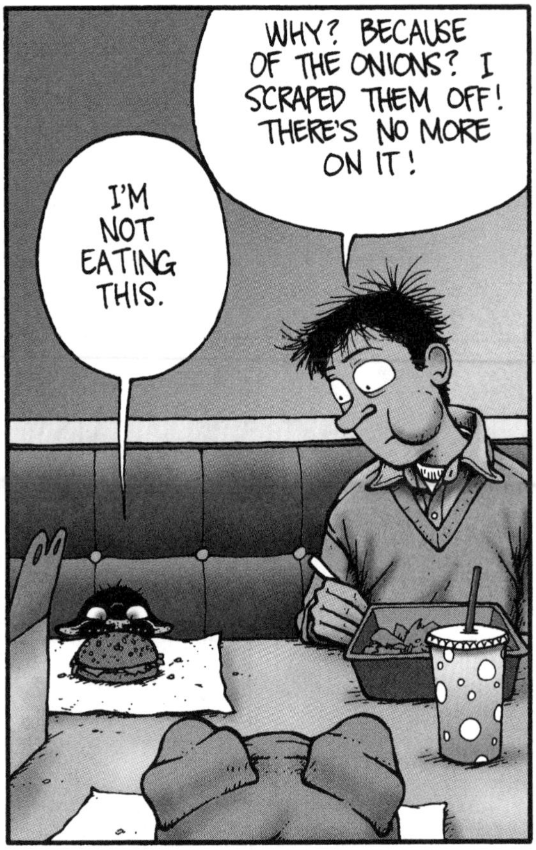
I'M NOT EATING THIS.
WHY? BECAUSE OF THE ONIONS? I SCRAPED THEM OFF! THERE'S NO MORE ON IT!

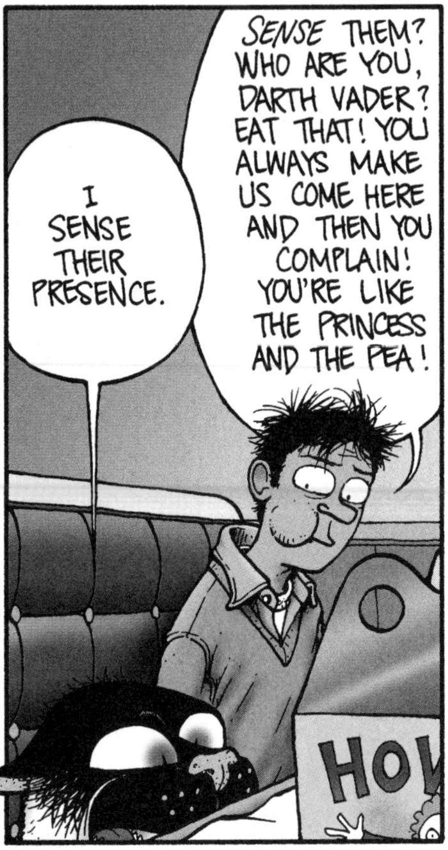
I SENSE THEIR PRESENCE.
SENSE THEM? WHO ARE YOU, DARTH VADER? EAT THAT! YOU ALWAYS MAKE US COME HERE AND THEN YOU COMPLAIN! YOU'RE LIKE THE PRINCESS AND THE PEA!
HOW

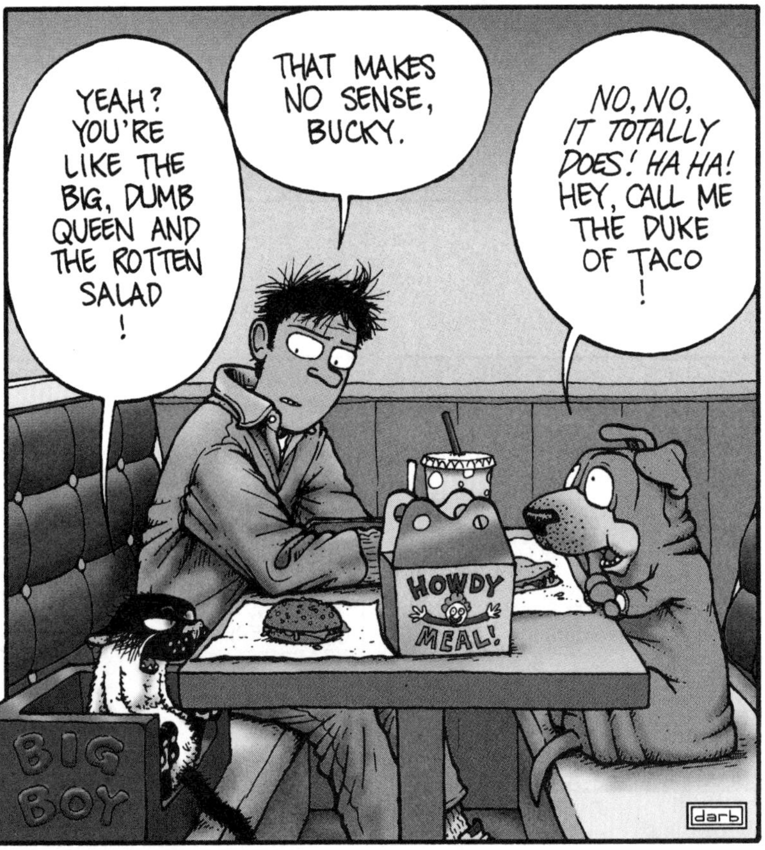
YEAH? YOU'RE LIKE THE BIG, DUMB QUEEN AND THE ROTTEN SALAD!
THAT MAKES NO SENSE, BUCKY.
NO, NO, IT TOTALLY DOES! HA HA! HEY, CALL ME THE DUKE OF TACO!
HOWDY MEAL!
BIG BOY
darb

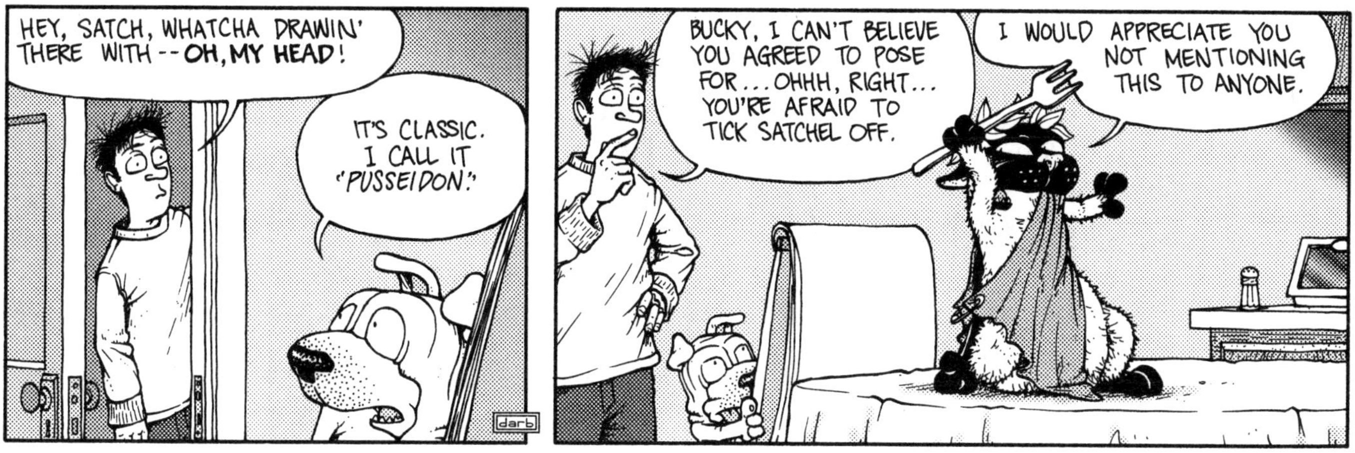
HEY, SATCH, WHATCHA DRAWIN' THERE WITH -- **OH, MY HEAD**!
IT'S CLASSIC. I CALL IT "*PUSSEIDON*."
BUCKY, I CAN'T BELIEVE YOU AGREED TO POSE FOR... OHHH, RIGHT... YOU'RE AFRAID TO TICK SATCHEL OFF.
I WOULD APPRECIATE YOU NOT MENTIONING THIS TO ANYONE.
darb

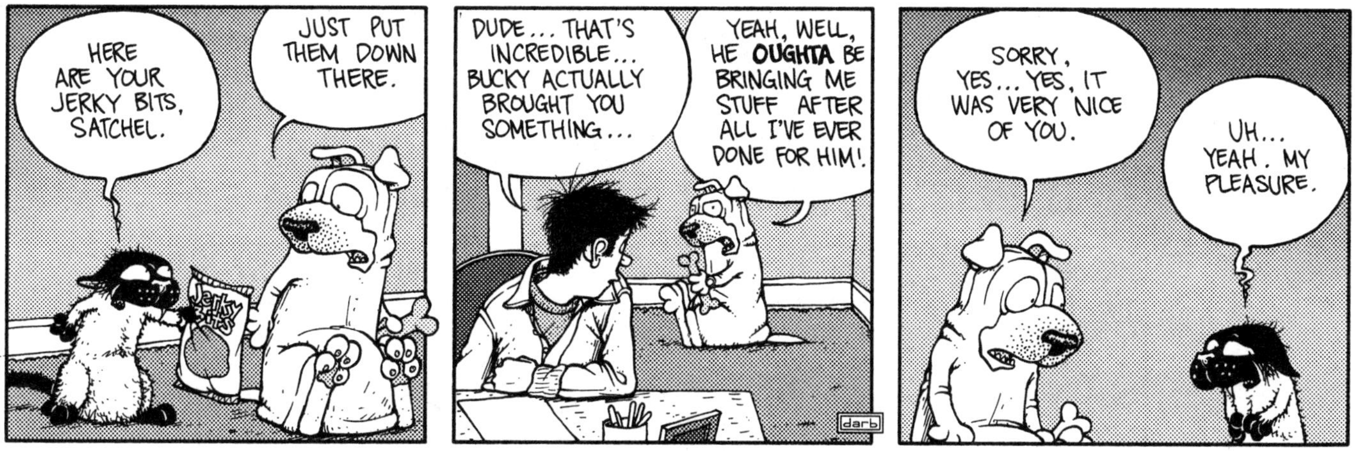
HERE ARE YOUR JERKY BITS, SATCHEL.
JUST PUT THEM DOWN THERE.
Jerky Bits
DUDE... THAT'S INCREDIBLE... BUCKY ACTUALLY BROUGHT YOU SOMETHING...
YEAH, WELL, HE **OUGHTA** BE BRINGING ME STUFF AFTER ALL I'VE EVER DONE FOR HIM!
darb
SORRY, YES... YES, IT WAS VERY NICE OF YOU.
UH... YEAH. MY PLEASURE.

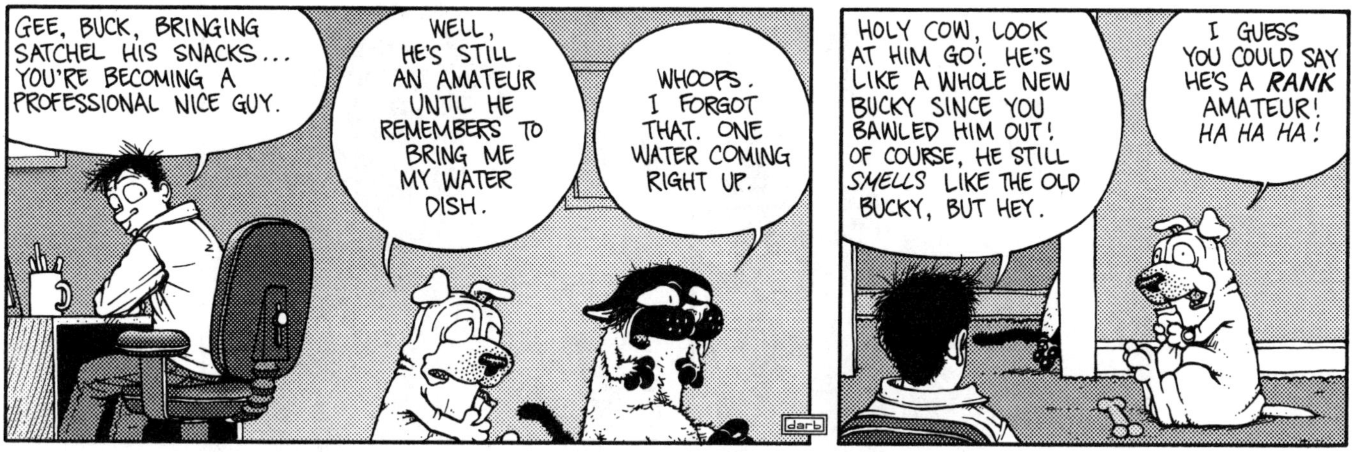
GEE, BUCK, BRINGING SATCHEL HIS SNACKS... YOU'RE BECOMING A PROFESSIONAL NICE GUY.
WELL, HE'S STILL AN AMATEUR UNTIL HE REMEMBERS TO BRING ME MY WATER DISH.
WHOOPS. I FORGOT THAT. ONE WATER COMING RIGHT UP.
darb
HOLY COW, LOOK AT HIM GO! HE'S LIKE A WHOLE NEW BUCKY SINCE YOU BAWLED HIM OUT! OF COURSE, HE STILL *SMELLS* LIKE THE OLD BUCKY, BUT HEY.
I GUESS YOU COULD SAY HE'S A ***RANK*** AMATEUR! *HA HA HA!*

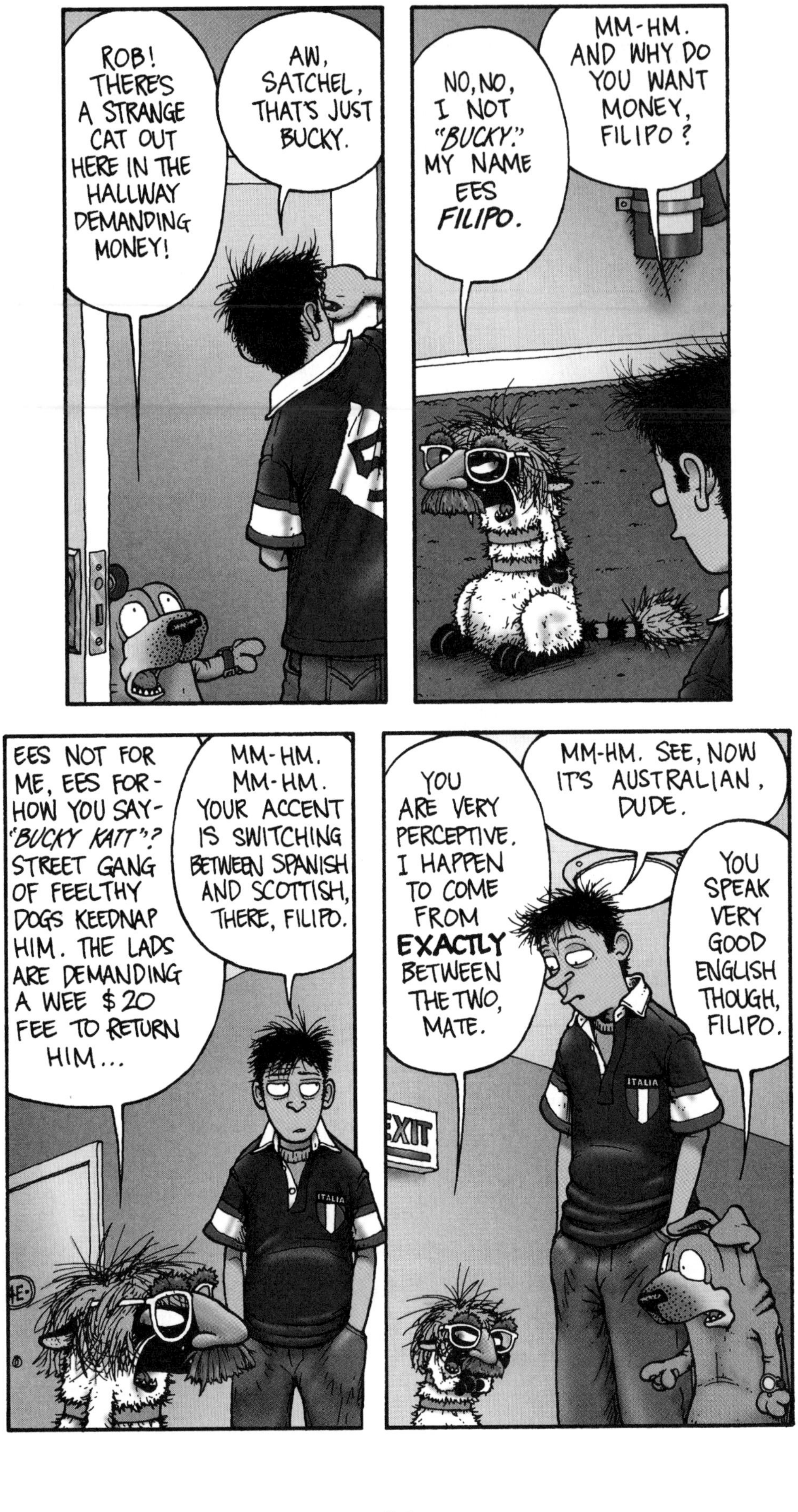
ROB! THERE'S A STRANGE CAT OUT HERE IN THE HALLWAY DEMANDING MONEY!
AW, SATCHEL, THAT'S JUST BUCKY.
NO, NO, I NOT "BUCKY." MY NAME EES FILIPO.
MM-HM. AND WHY DO YOU WANT MONEY, FILIPO?
EES NOT FOR ME, EES FOR- HOW YOU SAY- "BUCKY KATT"? STREET GANG OF FEELTHY DOGS KEEDNAP HIM. THE LADS ARE DEMANDING A WEE $20 FEE TO RETURN HIM...
MM-HM. MM-HM. YOUR ACCENT IS SWITCHING BETWEEN SPANISH AND SCOTTISH, THERE, FILIPO.
YOU ARE VERY PERCEPTIVE. I HAPPEN TO COME FROM EXACTLY BETWEEN THE TWO, MATE.
MM-HM. SEE, NOW IT'S AUSTRALIAN, DUDE.
YOU SPEAK VERY GOOD ENGLISH THOUGH, FILIPO.
EXIT
ITALIA

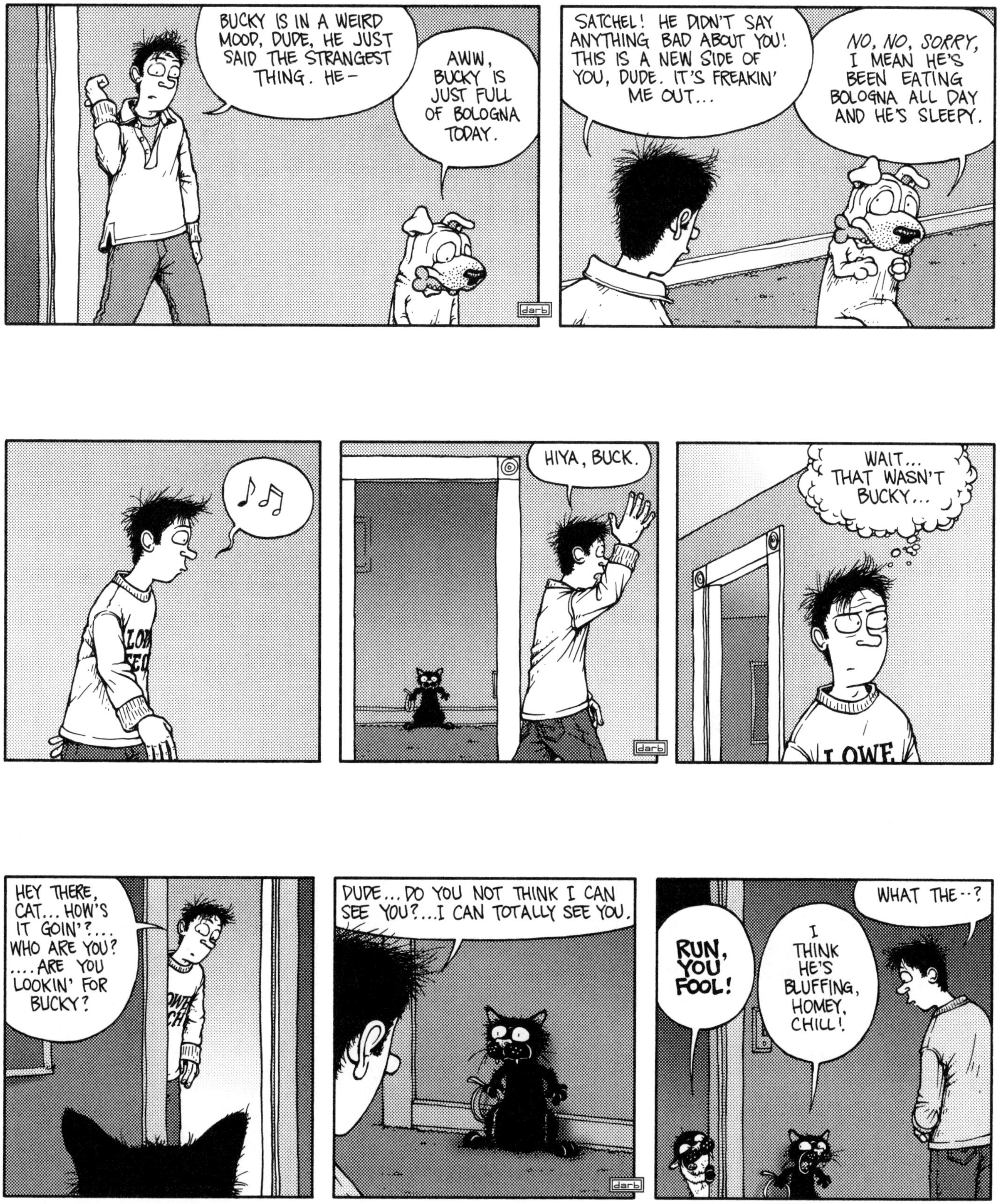
BUCKY IS IN A WEIRD MOOD, DUDE, HE JUST SAID THE STRANGEST THING. HE–
AWW, BUCKY IS JUST FULL OF BOLOGNA TODAY.
SATCHEL! HE DIDN'T SAY ANYTHING BAD ABOUT YOU! THIS IS A NEW SIDE OF YOU, DUDE. IT'S FREAKIN' ME OUT...
NO, NO, SORRY, I MEAN HE'S BEEN EATING BOLOGNA ALL DAY AND HE'S SLEEPY.
♪♫
HIYA, BUCK.
WAIT... THAT WASN'T BUCKY...
HEY THERE, CAT... HOW'S IT GOIN'?... WHO ARE YOU? ....ARE YOU LOOKIN' FOR BUCKY?
DUDE... DO YOU NOT THINK I CAN SEE YOU?...I CAN TOTALLY SEE YOU.
WHAT THE--?
RUN, YOU FOOL!
I THINK HE'S BLUFFING, HOMEY, CHILL!

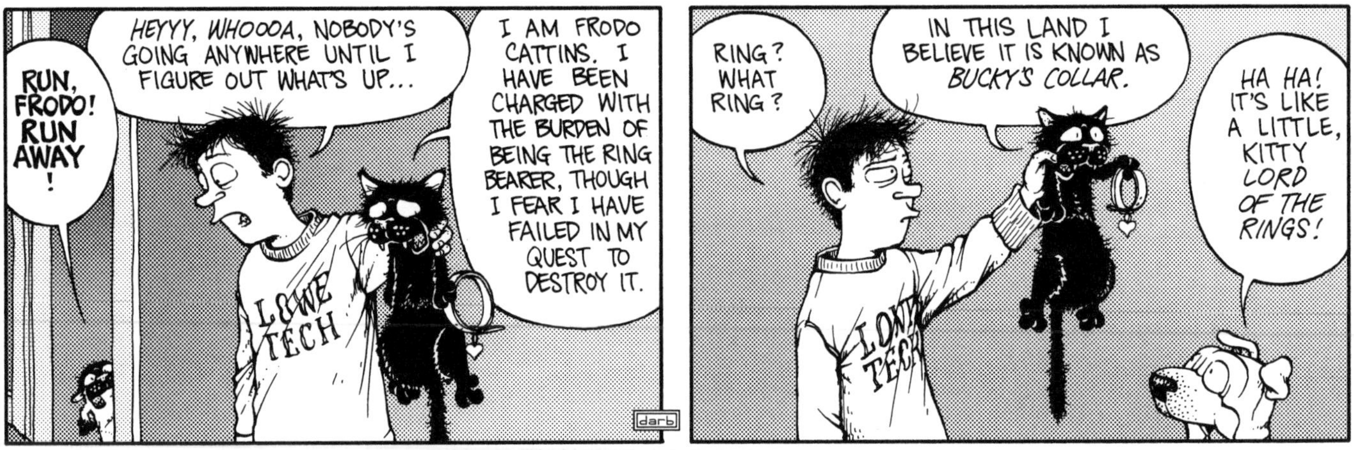
RUN, FRODO! RUN AWAY!
HEYYY, WHOOOA, NOBODY'S GOING ANYWHERE UNTIL I FIGURE OUT WHAT'S UP...
I AM FRODO CATTINS. I HAVE BEEN CHARGED WITH THE BURDEN OF BEING THE RING BEARER, THOUGH I FEAR I HAVE FAILED IN MY QUEST TO DESTROY IT.
RING? WHAT RING?
IN THIS LAND I BELIEVE IT IS KNOWN AS BUCKY'S COLLAR.
HA HA! IT'S LIKE A LITTLE, KITTY LORD OF THE RINGS!

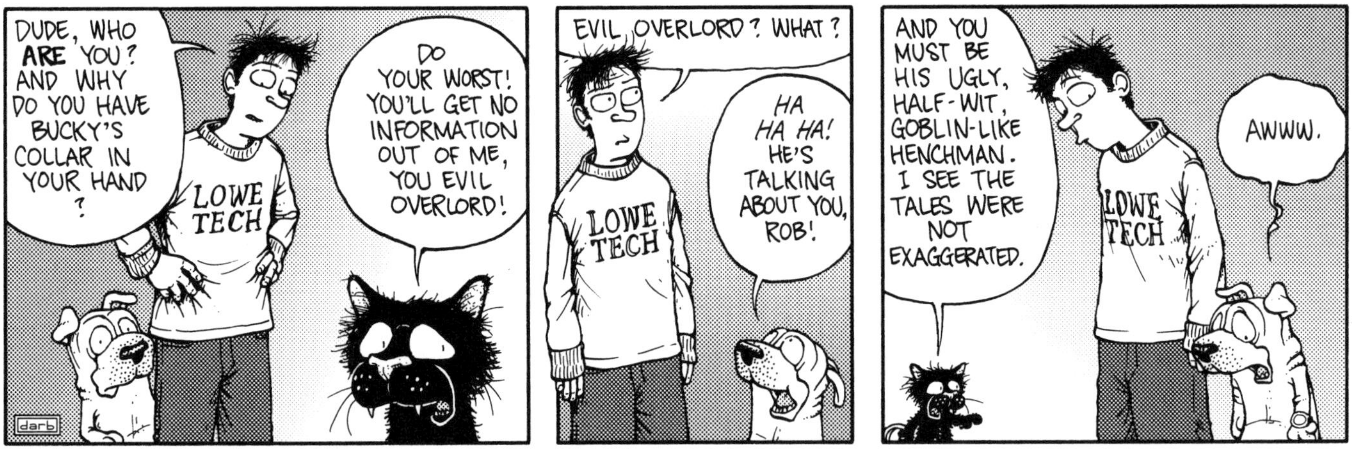
DUDE, WHO ARE YOU? AND WHY DO YOU HAVE BUCKY'S COLLAR IN YOUR HAND?
DO YOUR WORST! YOU'LL GET NO INFORMATION OUT OF ME, YOU EVIL OVERLORD!
EVIL OVERLORD? WHAT?
HA HA HA! HE'S TALKING ABOUT YOU, ROB!
AND YOU MUST BE HIS UGLY, HALF-WIT, GOBLIN-LIKE HENCHMAN. I SEE THE TALES WERE NOT EXAGGERATED.
AWWW.

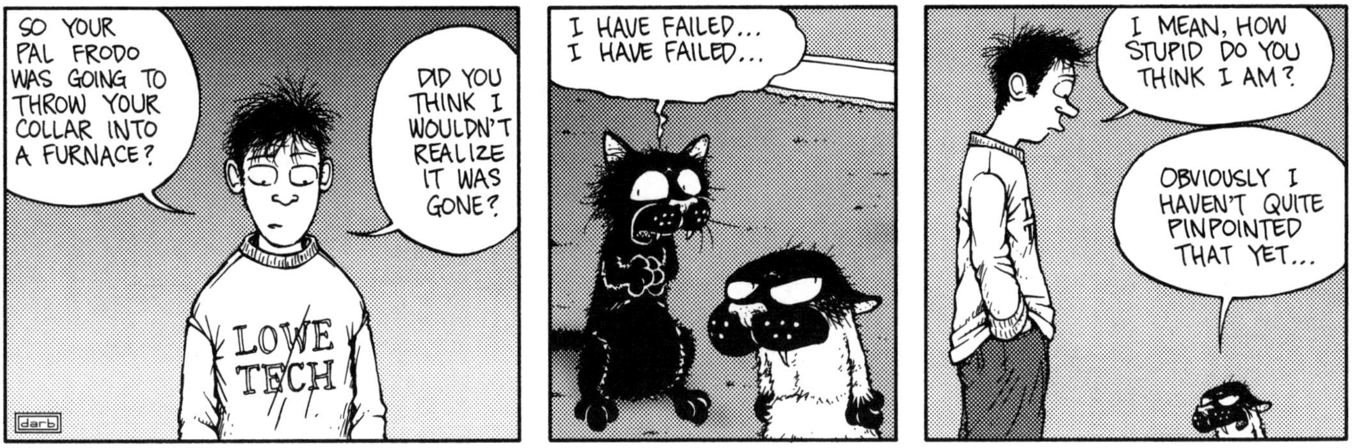
SO YOUR PAL FRODO WAS GOING TO THROW YOUR COLLAR INTO A FURNACE?
DID YOU THINK I WOULDN'T REALIZE IT WAS GONE?
I HAVE FAILED... I HAVE FAILED...
I MEAN, HOW STUPID DO YOU THINK I AM?
OBVIOUSLY I HAVEN'T QUITE PINPOINTED THAT YET...

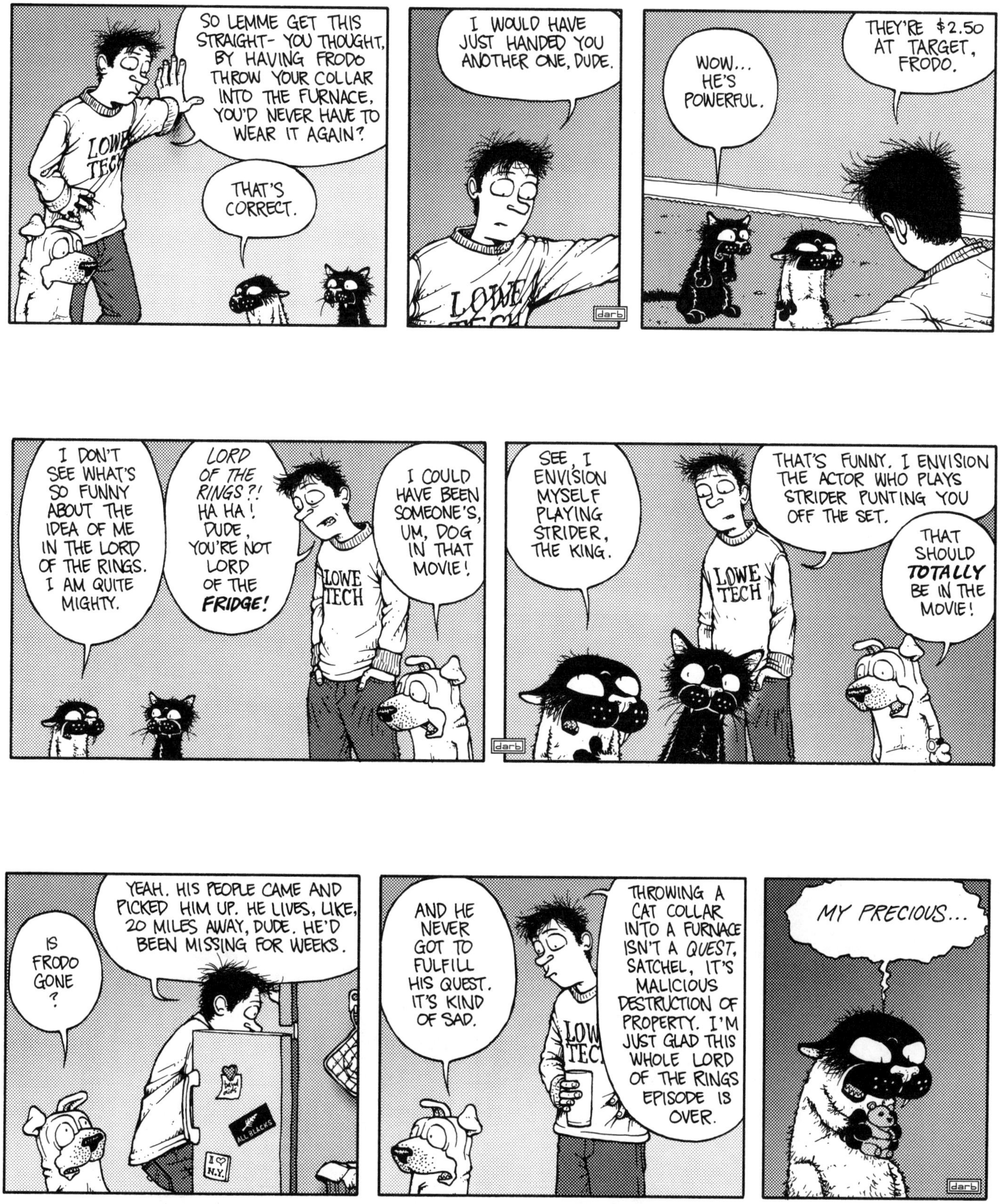
SO LEMME GET THIS STRAIGHT- YOU THOUGHT, BY HAVING FRODO THROW YOUR COLLAR INTO THE FURNACE, YOU'D NEVER HAVE TO WEAR IT AGAIN?
THAT'S CORRECT.
I WOULD HAVE JUST HANDED YOU ANOTHER ONE, DUDE.
WOW... HE'S POWERFUL.
THEY'RE $2.50 AT TARGET, FRODO.
I DON'T SEE WHAT'S SO FUNNY ABOUT THE IDEA OF ME IN THE LORD OF THE RINGS. I AM QUITE MIGHTY.
LORD OF THE RINGS?! HA HA! DUDE, YOU'RE NOT LORD OF THE FRIDGE!
I COULD HAVE BEEN SOMEONE'S, UM, DOG IN THAT MOVIE!
SEE, I ENVISION MYSELF PLAYING STRIDER, THE KING.
THAT'S FUNNY. I ENVISION THE ACTOR WHO PLAYS STRIDER PUNTING YOU OFF THE SET.
THAT SHOULD TOTALLY BE IN THE MOVIE!
IS FRODO GONE?
YEAH. HIS PEOPLE CAME AND PICKED HIM UP. HE LIVES, LIKE, 20 MILES AWAY, DUDE. HE'D BEEN MISSING FOR WEEKS.
AND HE NEVER GOT TO FULFILL HIS QUEST. IT'S KIND OF SAD.
THROWING A CAT COLLAR INTO A FURNACE ISN'T A QUEST, SATCHEL, IT'S MALICIOUS DESTRUCTION OF PROPERTY. I'M JUST GLAD THIS WHOLE LORD OF THE RINGS EPISODE IS OVER.
MY PRECIOUS...

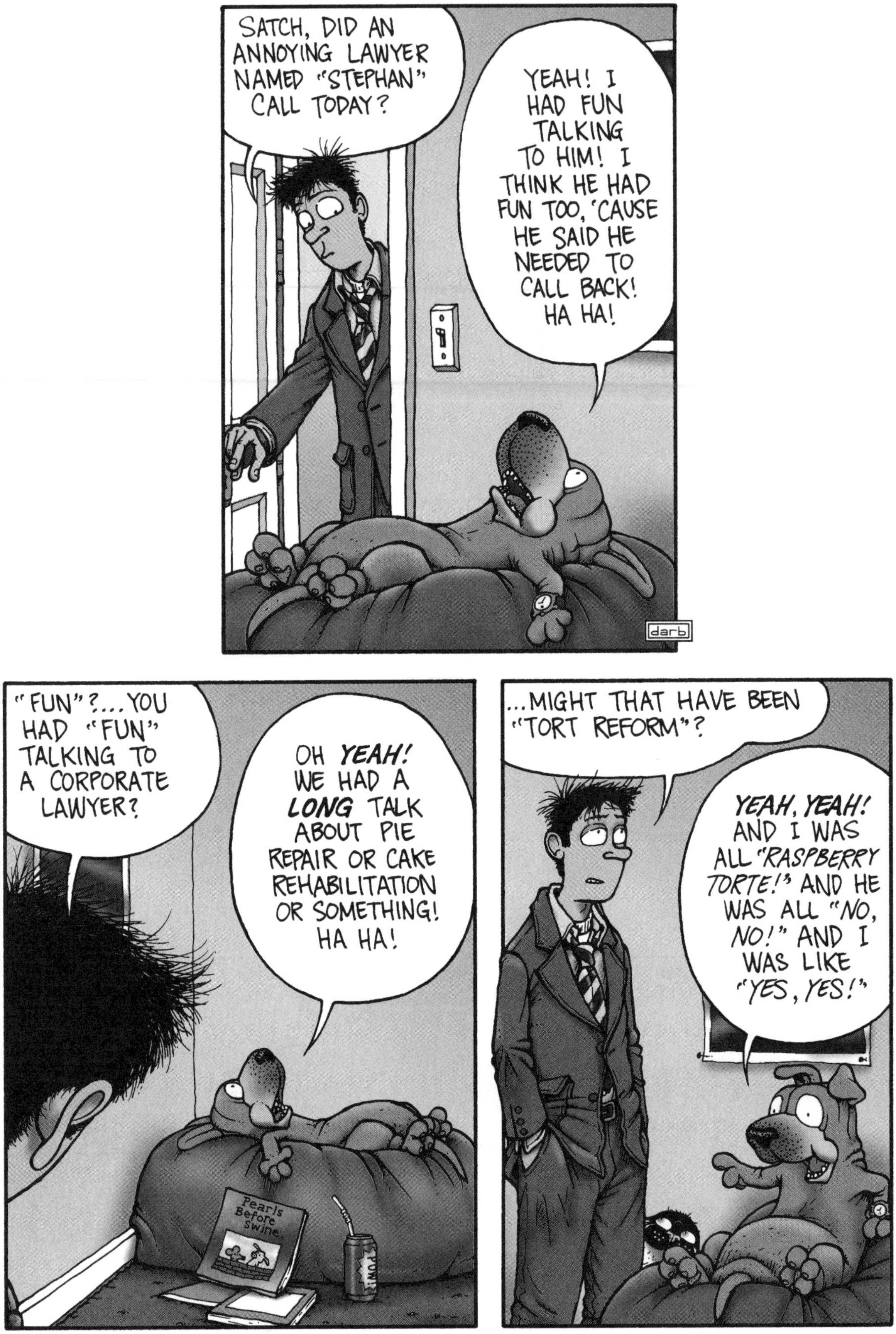
SATCH, DID AN ANNOYING LAWYER NAMED "STEPHAN" CALL TODAY?
YEAH! I HAD FUN TALKING TO HIM! I THINK HE HAD FUN TOO, 'CAUSE HE SAID HE NEEDED TO CALL BACK! HA HA!
darb
"FUN"?... YOU HAD "FUN" TALKING TO A CORPORATE LAWYER?
OH YEAH! WE HAD A LONG TALK ABOUT PIE REPAIR OR CAKE REHABILITATION OR SOMETHING! HA HA!
Pearls Before Swine
POW
...MIGHT THAT HAVE BEEN "TORT REFORM"?
YEAH, YEAH! AND I WAS ALL "RASPBERRY TORTE!" AND HE WAS ALL "NO, NO!" AND I WAS LIKE "YES, YES!"

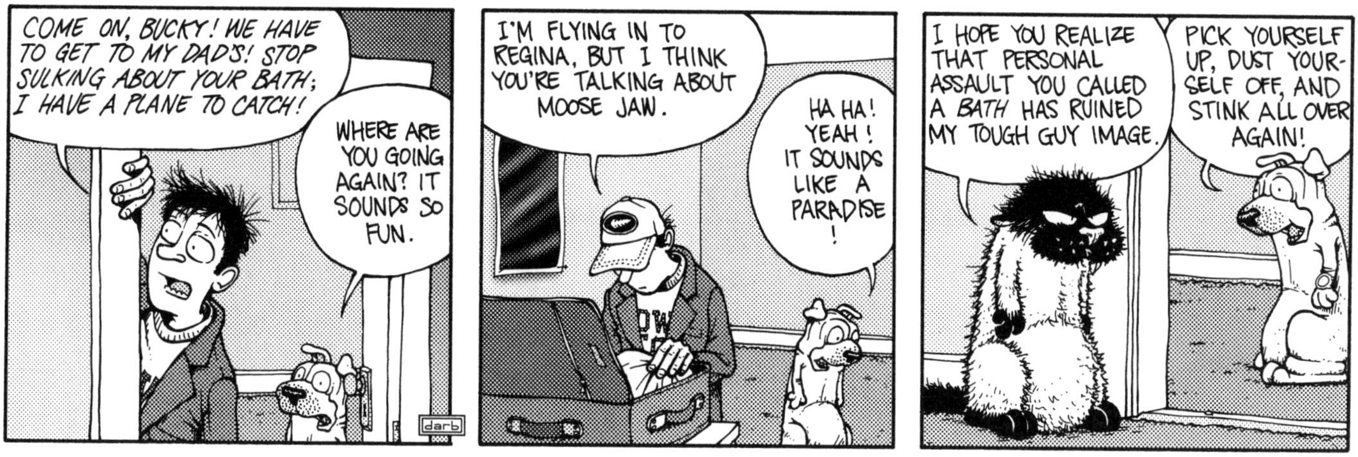
COME ON, BUCKY! WE HAVE TO GET TO MY DAD'S! STOP SULKING ABOUT YOUR BATH; I HAVE A PLANE TO CATCH!
WHERE ARE YOU GOING AGAIN? IT SOUNDS SO FUN.
darb
I'M FLYING IN TO REGINA, BUT I THINK YOU'RE TALKING ABOUT MOOSE JAW.
HA HA! YEAH! IT SOUNDS LIKE A PARADISE!
I HOPE YOU REALIZE THAT PERSONAL ASSAULT YOU CALLED A BATH HAS RUINED MY TOUGH GUY IMAGE.
PICK YOURSELF UP, DUST YOURSELF OFF, AND STINK ALL OVER AGAIN!

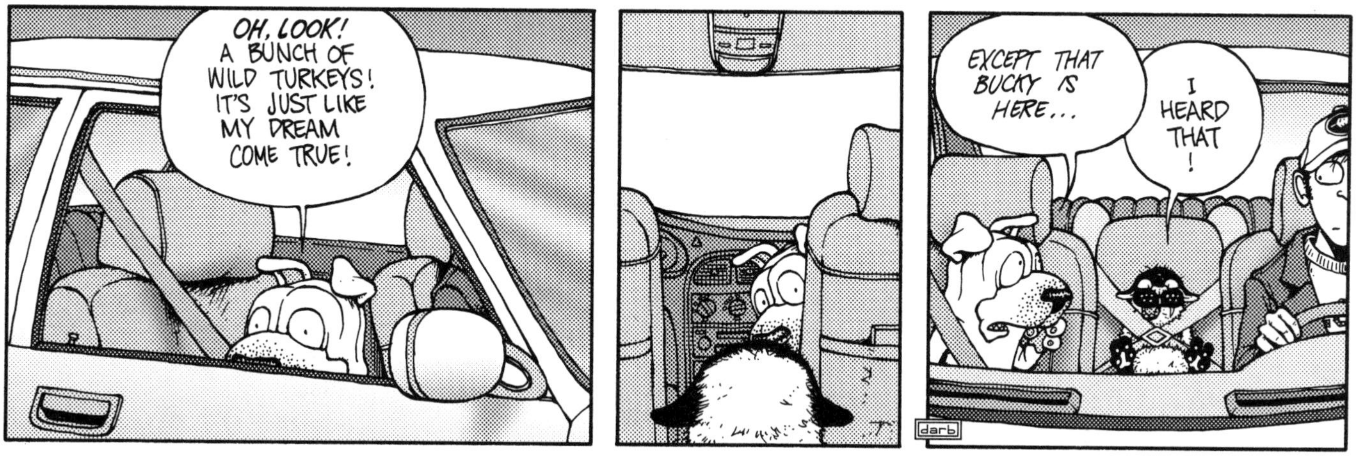
OH, LOOK! A BUNCH OF WILD TURKEYS! IT'S JUST LIKE MY DREAM COME TRUE!
EXCEPT THAT BUCKY IS HERE...
I HEARD THAT!
darb

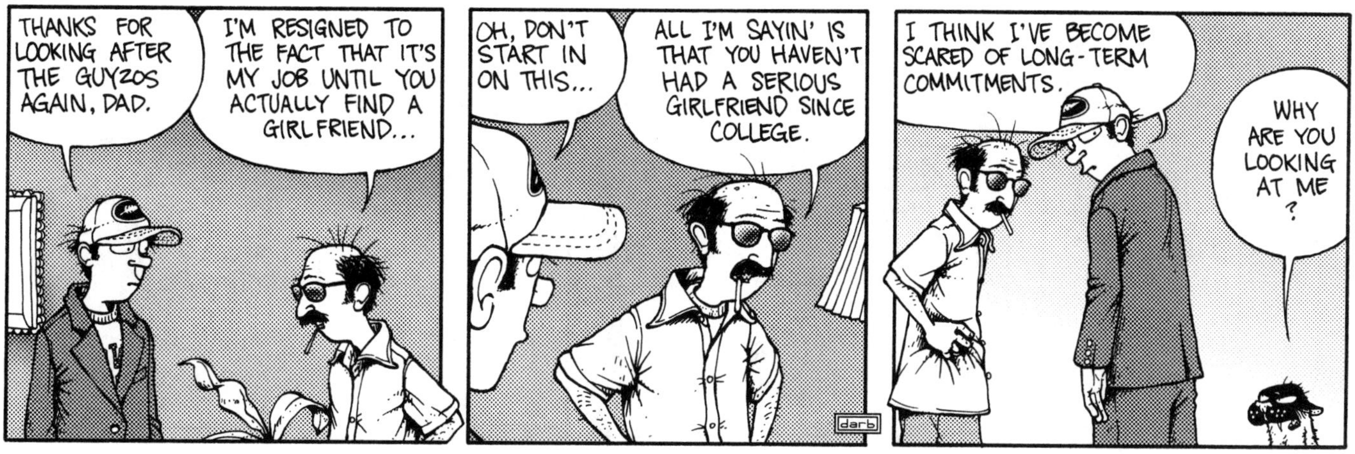
THANKS FOR LOOKING AFTER THE GUYZOS AGAIN, DAD.
I'M RESIGNED TO THE FACT THAT IT'S MY JOB UNTIL YOU ACTUALLY FIND A GIRLFRIEND...
OH, DON'T START IN ON THIS...
ALL I'M SAYIN' IS THAT YOU HAVEN'T HAD A SERIOUS GIRLFRIEND SINCE COLLEGE.
darb
I THINK I'VE BECOME SCARED OF LONG-TERM COMMITMENTS.
WHY ARE YOU LOOKING AT ME?

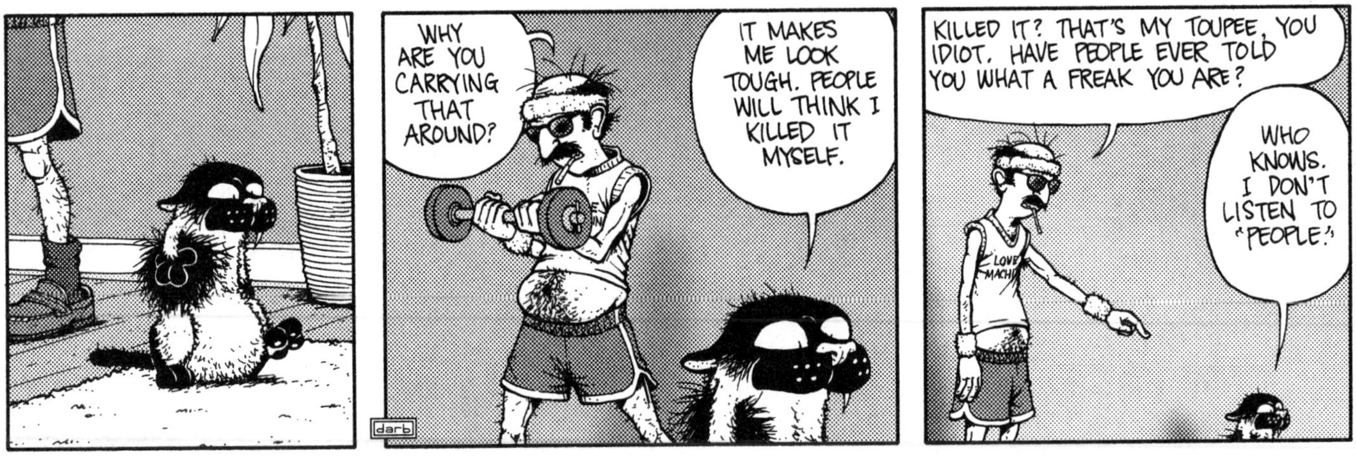

WHY ARE YOU CARRYING THAT AROUND?
IT MAKES ME LOOK TOUGH. PEOPLE WILL THINK I KILLED IT MYSELF.
darb
KILLED IT? THAT'S MY TOUPEE, YOU IDIOT. HAVE PEOPLE EVER TOLD YOU WHAT A FREAK YOU ARE?
WHO KNOWS. I DON'T LISTEN TO "PEOPLE."

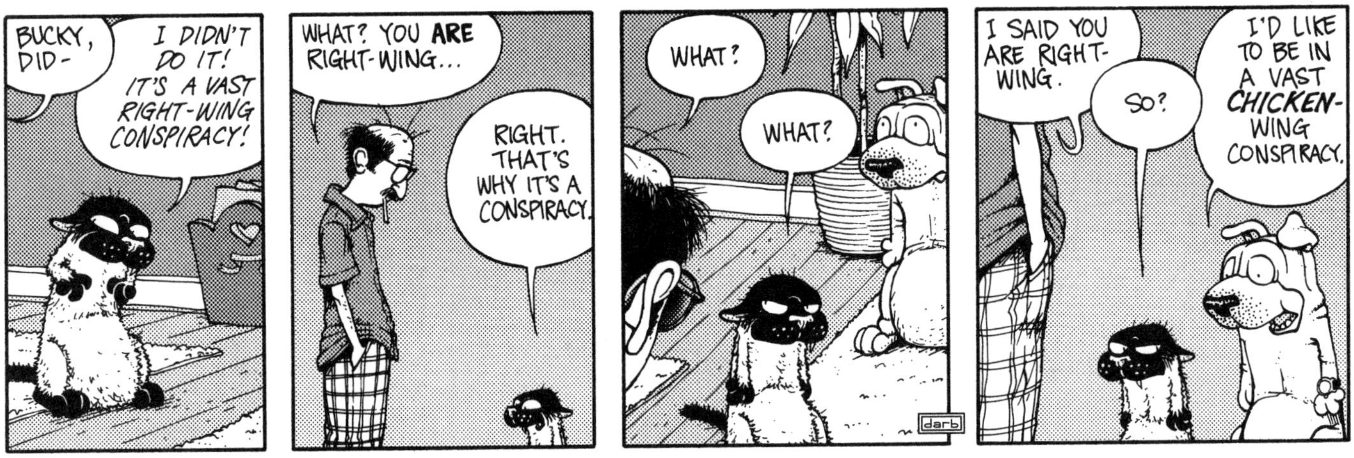

BUCKY, DID-
I DIDN'T DO IT! IT'S A VAST RIGHT-WING CONSPIRACY!
WHAT? YOU **ARE** RIGHT-WING...
RIGHT. THAT'S WHY IT'S A CONSPIRACY.
WHAT?
WHAT?
darb
I SAID YOU ARE RIGHT-WING.
SO?
I'D LIKE TO BE IN A VAST ***CHICKEN***-WING CONSPIRACY.

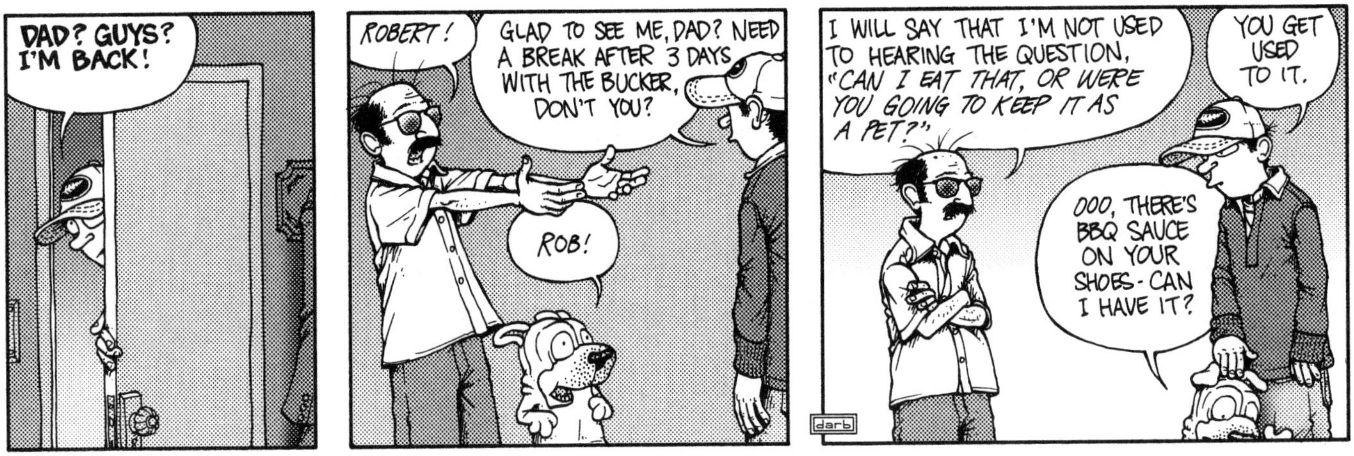

DAD? GUYS? I'M BACK!
ROBERT!
GLAD TO SEE ME, DAD? NEED A BREAK AFTER 3 DAYS WITH THE BUCKER, DON'T YOU?
ROB!
darb
I WILL SAY THAT I'M NOT USED TO HEARING THE QUESTION, "CAN I EAT THAT, OR WERE YOU GOING TO KEEP IT AS A PET?"
YOU GET USED TO IT.
OOO, THERE'S BBQ SAUCE ON YOUR SHOES- CAN I HAVE IT?

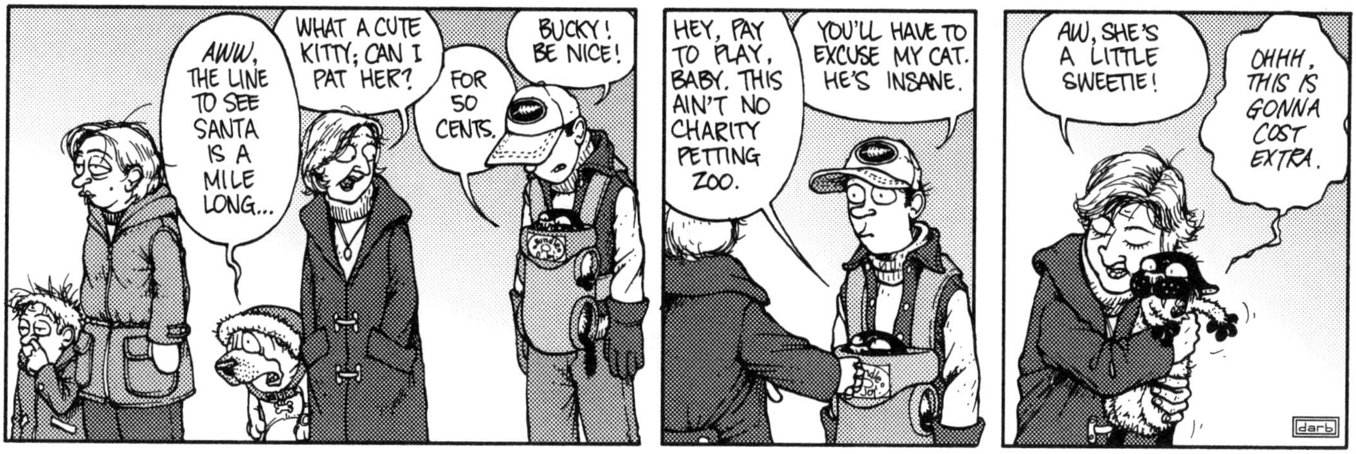
AWW, THE LINE TO SEE SANTA IS A MILE LONG...
WHAT A CUTE KITTY; CAN I PAT HER?
FOR 50 CENTS.
BUCKY! BE NICE!
HEY, PAY TO PLAY, BABY. THIS AIN'T NO CHARITY PETTING ZOO.
YOU'LL HAVE TO EXCUSE MY CAT. HE'S INSANE.
AW, SHE'S A LITTLE SWEETIE!
OHHH, THIS IS GONNA COST EXTRA.
darb

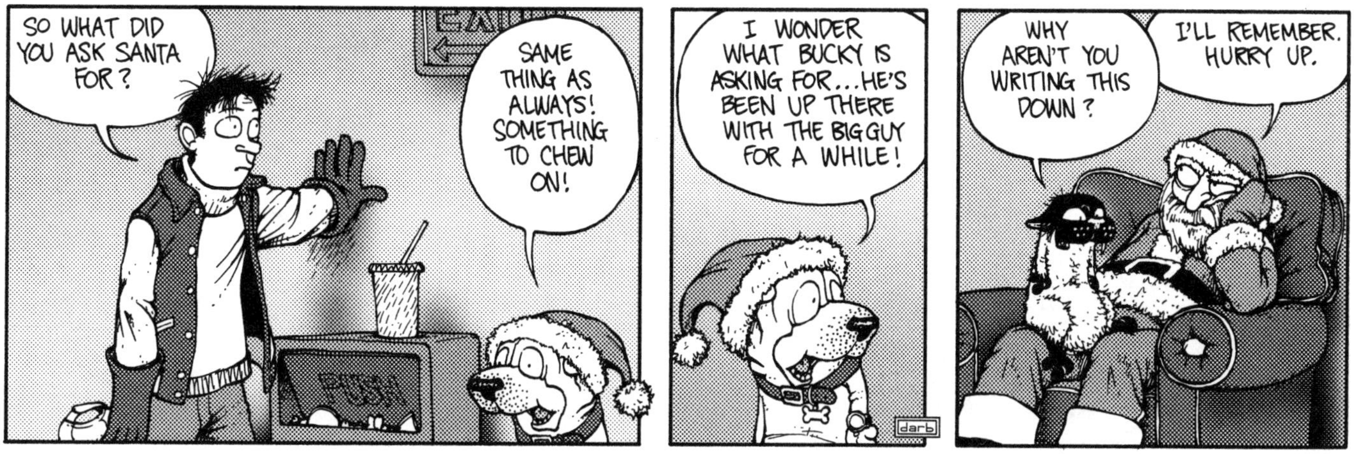
SO WHAT DID YOU ASK SANTA FOR?
SAME THING AS ALWAYS! SOMETHING TO CHEW ON!
I WONDER WHAT BUCKY IS ASKING FOR... HE'S BEEN UP THERE WITH THE BIG GUY FOR A WHILE!
darb
WHY AREN'T YOU WRITING THIS DOWN?
I'LL REMEMBER. HURRY UP.

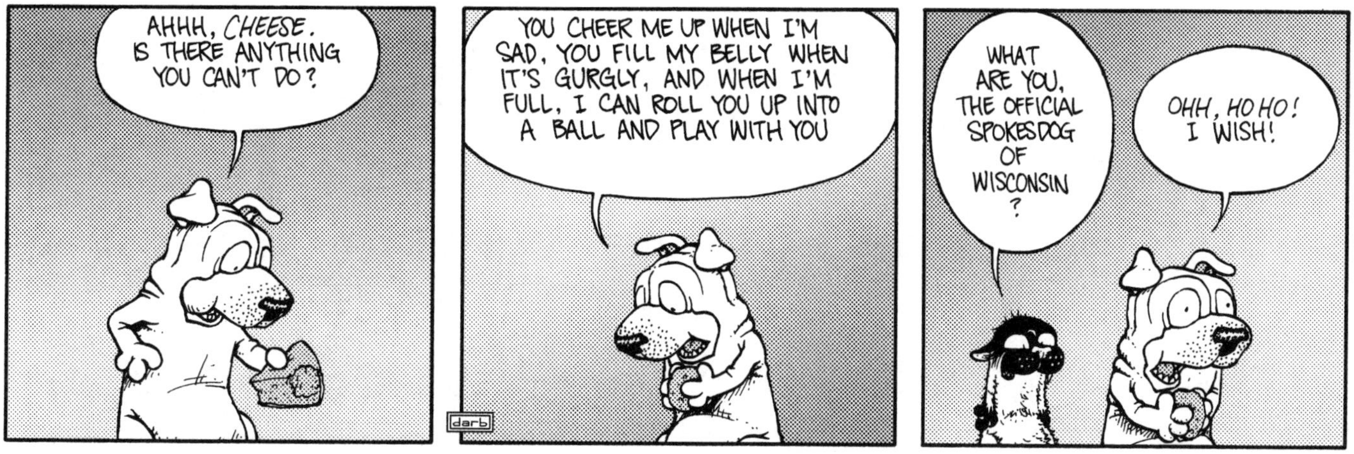
AHHH, *CHEESE*. IS THERE ANYTHING YOU CAN'T DO?
darb
YOU CHEER ME UP WHEN I'M SAD, YOU FILL MY BELLY WHEN IT'S GURGLY, AND WHEN I'M FULL, I CAN ROLL YOU UP INTO A BALL AND PLAY WITH YOU
WHAT ARE YOU, THE OFFICIAL SPOKESDOG OF WISCONSIN?
OHH, *HO HO!* I WISH!

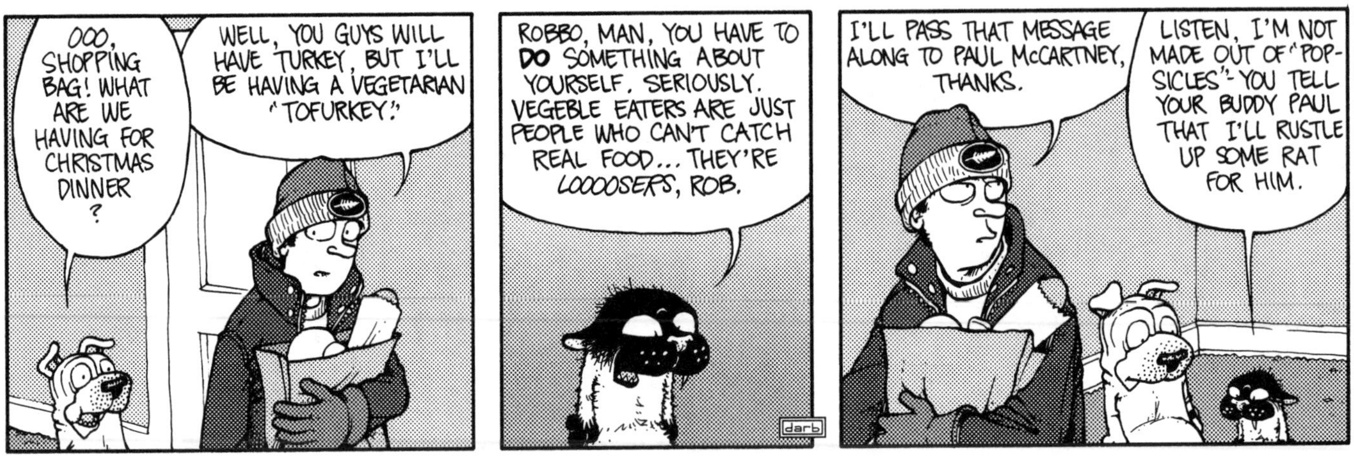
OOO, SHOPPING BAG! WHAT ARE WE HAVING FOR CHRISTMAS DINNER?
WELL, YOU GUYS WILL HAVE TURKEY, BUT I'LL BE HAVING A VEGETARIAN "TOFURKEY."
ROBBO, MAN, YOU HAVE TO **DO** SOMETHING ABOUT YOURSELF. SERIOUSLY. VEGEBLE EATERS ARE JUST PEOPLE WHO CAN'T CATCH REAL FOOD... THEY'RE *LOOOOSERS*, ROB.
I'LL PASS THAT MESSAGE ALONG TO PAUL McCARTNEY, THANKS.
LISTEN, I'M NOT MADE OUT OF "POP-SICLES"- YOU TELL YOUR BUDDY PAUL THAT I'LL RUSTLE UP SOME RAT FOR HIM.
darb

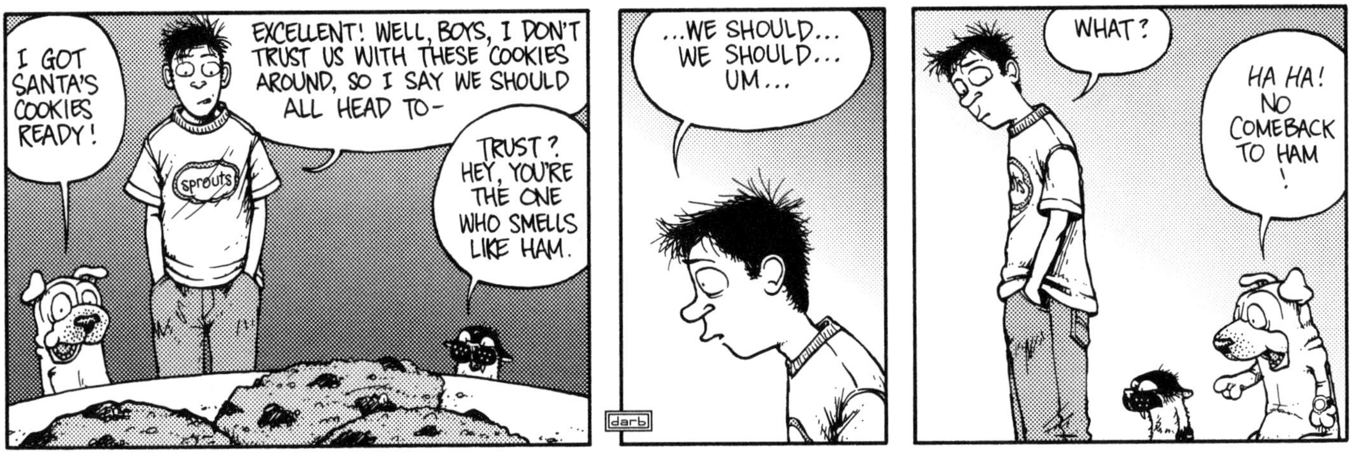
I GOT SANTA'S COOKIES READY!
EXCELLENT! WELL, BOYS, I DON'T TRUST US WITH THESE COOKIES AROUND, SO I SAY WE SHOULD ALL HEAD TO-
TRUST? HEY, YOU'RE THE ONE WHO SMELLS LIKE HAM.
sprouts
darb
...WE SHOULD... WE SHOULD... UM...
WHAT?
HA HA! NO COMEBACK TO HAM!

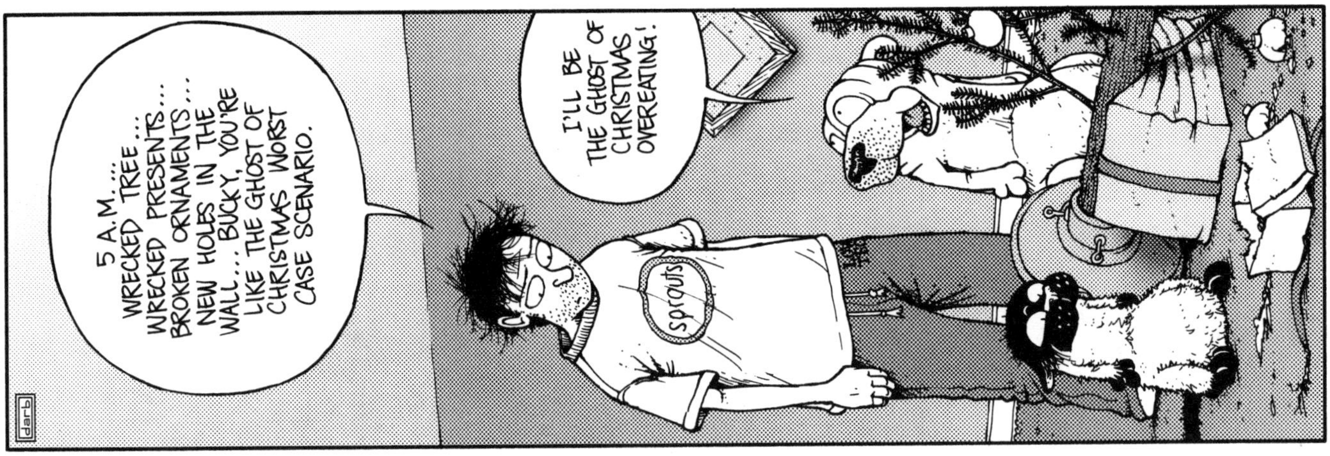
5 A.M.... WRECKED TREE... WRECKED PRESENTS... BROKEN ORNAMENTS... NEW HOLES IN THE WALL... BUCKY, YOU'RE LIKE THE GHOST OF CHRISTMAS WORST CASE SCENARIO.
I'LL BE THE GHOST OF CHRISTMAS OVEREATING!
sprouts
darb

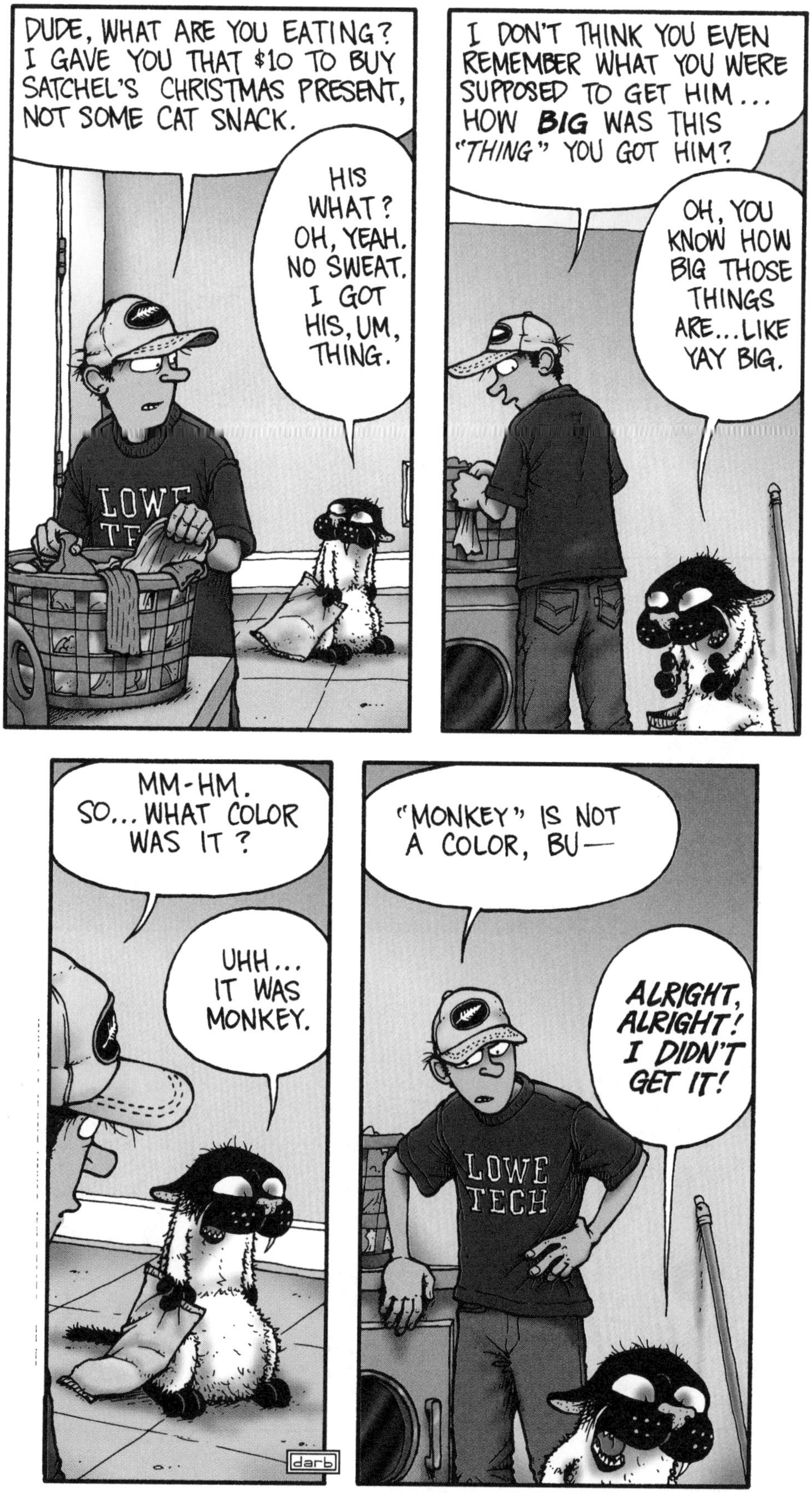
DUDE, WHAT ARE YOU EATING? I GAVE YOU THAT $10 TO BUY SATCHEL'S CHRISTMAS PRESENT, NOT SOME CAT SNACK.
HIS WHAT? OH, YEAH. NO SWEAT. I GOT HIS, UM, THING.
LOWE TECH
I DON'T THINK YOU EVEN REMEMBER WHAT YOU WERE SUPPOSED TO GET HIM... HOW **BIG** WAS THIS *"THING"* YOU GOT HIM?
OH, YOU KNOW HOW BIG THOSE THINGS ARE... LIKE YAY BIG.
MM-HM. SO... WHAT COLOR WAS IT?
UHH... IT WAS MONKEY.
darb
"MONKEY" IS NOT A COLOR, BU—
ALRIGHT, ALRIGHT! I DIDN'T GET IT!
LOWE TECH

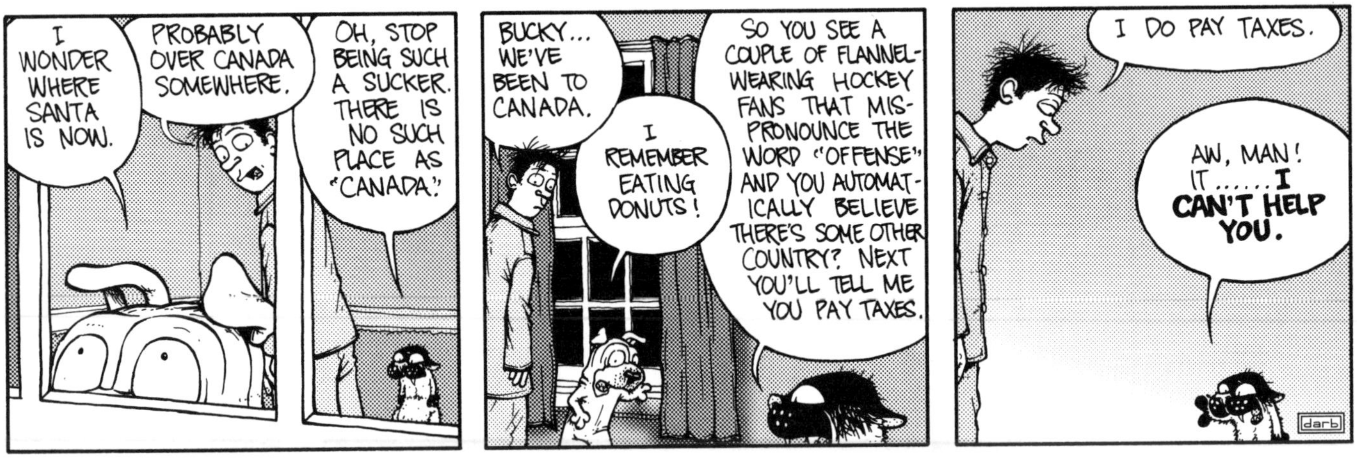
I WONDER WHERE SANTA IS NOW.
PROBABLY OVER CANADA SOMEWHERE.
OH, STOP BEING SUCH A SUCKER. THERE IS NO SUCH PLACE AS "CANADA."
BUCKY... WE'VE BEEN TO CANADA.
I REMEMBER EATING DONUTS!
SO YOU SEE A COUPLE OF FLANNEL-WEARING HOCKEY FANS THAT MISPRONOUNCE THE WORD "OFFENSE" AND YOU AUTOMATICALLY BELIEVE THERE'S SOME OTHER COUNTRY? NEXT YOU'LL TELL ME YOU PAY TAXES.
I DO PAY TAXES.
AW, MAN! IT...... I CAN'T HELP YOU.

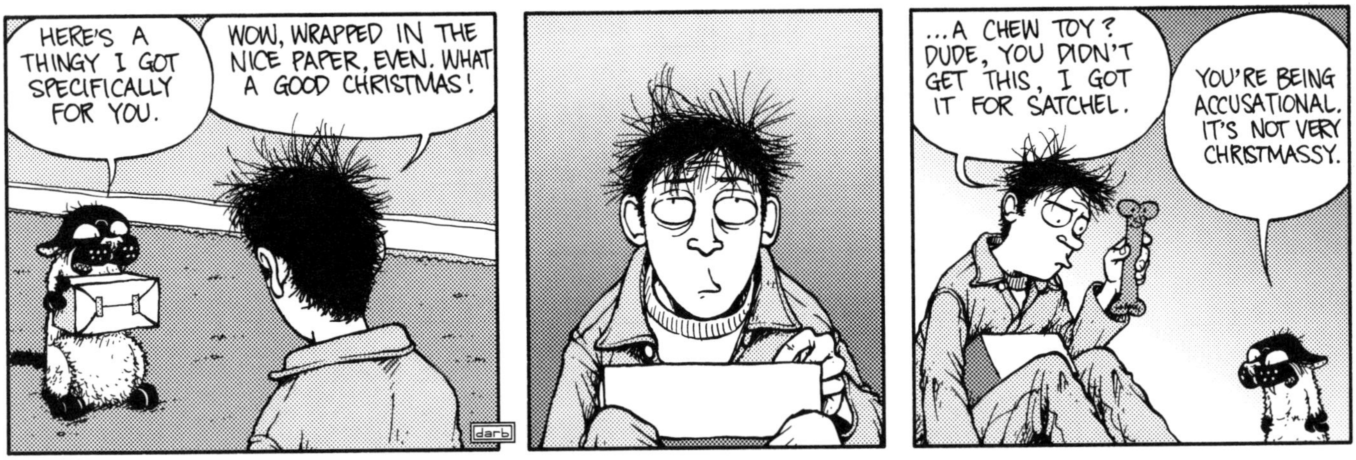
HERE'S A THINGY I GOT SPECIFICALLY FOR YOU.
WOW, WRAPPED IN THE NICE PAPER, EVEN. WHAT A GOOD CHRISTMAS!
...A CHEW TOY? DUDE, YOU DIDN'T GET THIS, I GOT IT FOR SATCHEL.
YOU'RE BEING ACCUSATIONAL. IT'S NOT VERY CHRISTMASSY.

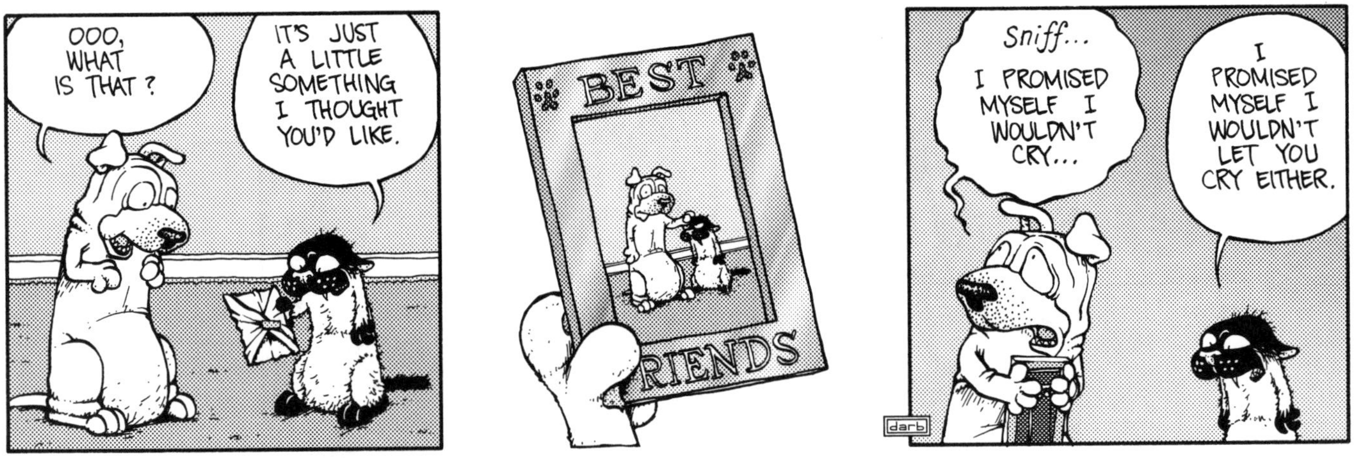
OOO, WHAT IS THAT?
IT'S JUST A LITTLE SOMETHING I THOUGHT YOU'D LIKE.
BEST FRIENDS
Sniff...
I PROMISED MYSELF I WOULDN'T CRY...
I PROMISED MYSELF I WOULDN'T LET YOU CRY EITHER.

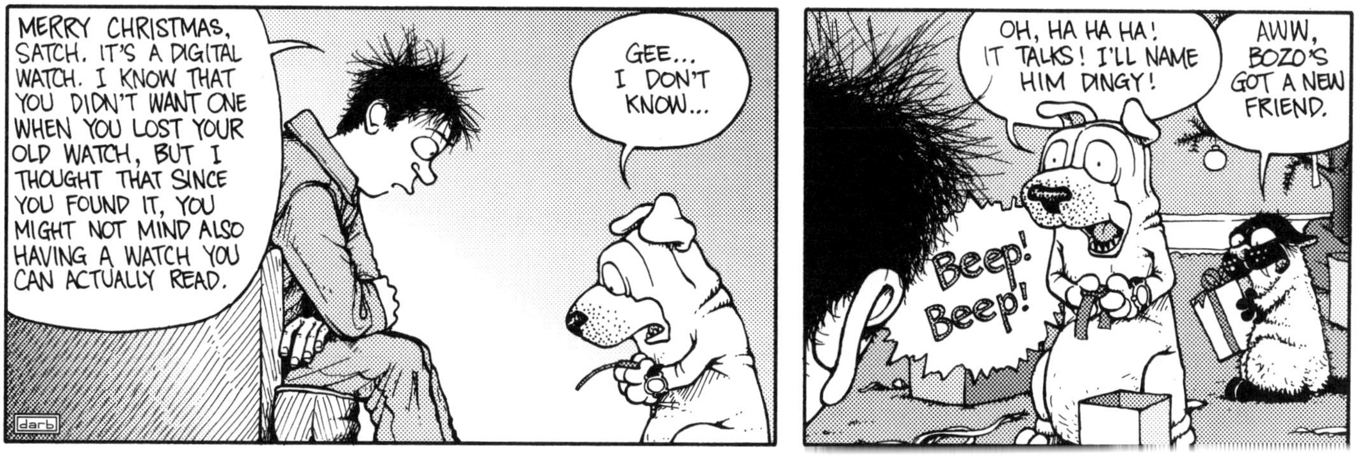
MERRY CHRISTMAS, SATCH. IT'S A DIGITAL WATCH. I KNOW THAT YOU DIDN'T WANT ONE WHEN YOU LOST YOUR OLD WATCH, BUT I THOUGHT THAT SINCE YOU FOUND IT, YOU MIGHT NOT MIND ALSO HAVING A WATCH YOU CAN ACTUALLY READ.
GEE... I DON'T KNOW...
darb
Beep! Beep!
OH, HA HA HA! IT TALKS! I'LL NAME HIM DINGY!
AWW, BOZO'S GOT A NEW FRIEND.

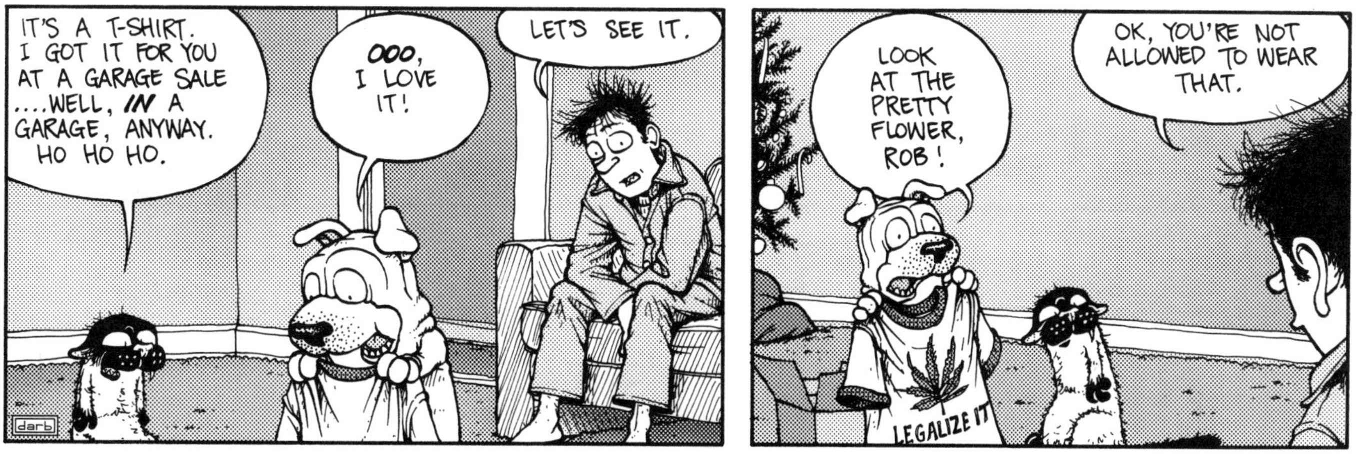
IT'S A T-SHIRT. I GOT IT FOR YOU AT A GARAGE SALE ....WELL, IN A GARAGE, ANYWAY. HO HO HO.
OOO, I LOVE IT!
LET'S SEE IT.
darb
LOOK AT THE PRETTY FLOWER, ROB!
OK, YOU'RE NOT ALLOWED TO WEAR THAT.
LEGALIZE IT

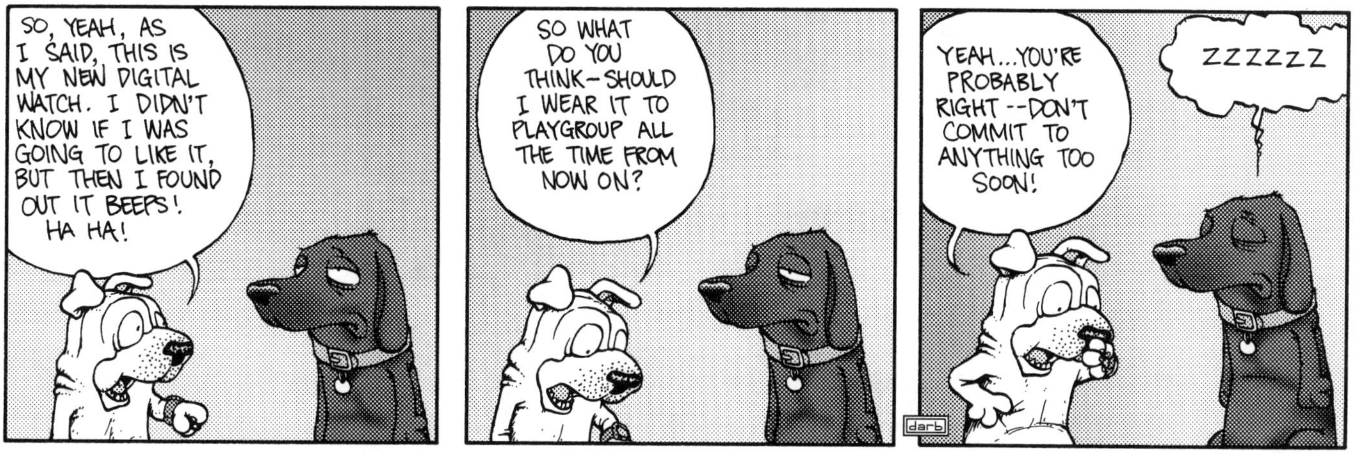
SO, YEAH, AS I SAID, THIS IS MY NEW DIGITAL WATCH. I DIDN'T KNOW IF I WAS GOING TO LIKE IT, BUT THEN I FOUND OUT IT BEEPS! HA HA!
SO WHAT DO YOU THINK—SHOULD I WEAR IT TO PLAYGROUP ALL THE TIME FROM NOW ON?
YEAH...YOU'RE PROBABLY RIGHT --DON'T COMMIT TO ANYTHING TOO SOON!
ZZZZZZ
darb

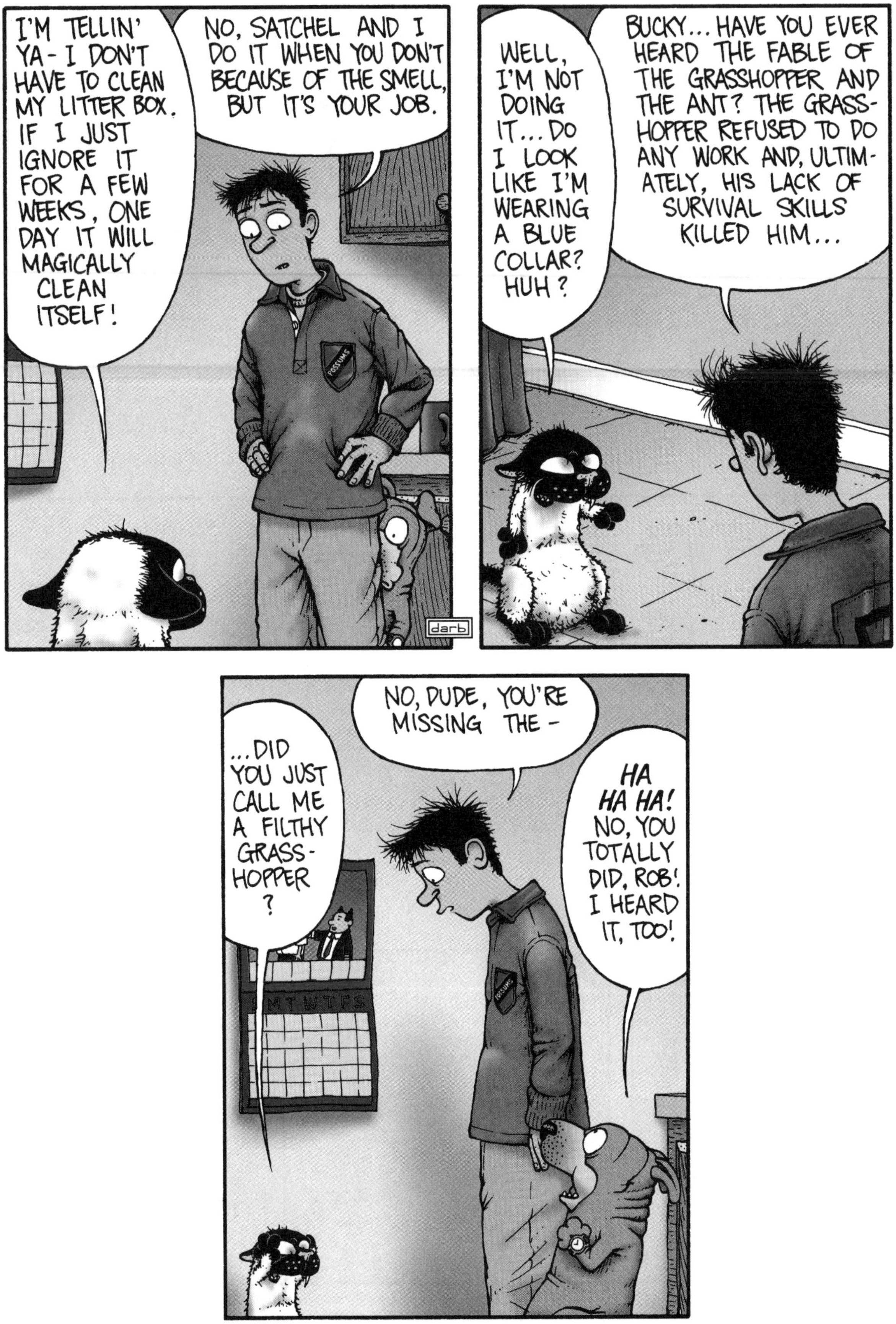
I'M TELLIN' YA- I DON'T HAVE TO CLEAN MY LITTER BOX. IF I JUST IGNORE IT FOR A FEW WEEKS, ONE DAY IT WILL MAGICALLY CLEAN ITSELF!
NO, SATCHEL AND I DO IT WHEN YOU DON'T BECAUSE OF THE SMELL, BUT IT'S YOUR JOB.
WELL, I'M NOT DOING IT... DO I LOOK LIKE I'M WEARING A BLUE COLLAR? HUH?
BUCKY... HAVE YOU EVER HEARD THE FABLE OF THE GRASSHOPPER AND THE ANT? THE GRASS-HOPPER REFUSED TO DO ANY WORK AND, ULTIM-ATELY, HIS LACK OF SURVIVAL SKILLS KILLED HIM...
...DID YOU JUST CALL ME A FILTHY GRASS-HOPPER?
NO, DUDE, YOU'RE MISSING THE-
HA HA HA! NO, YOU TOTALLY DID, ROB! I HEARD IT, TOO!

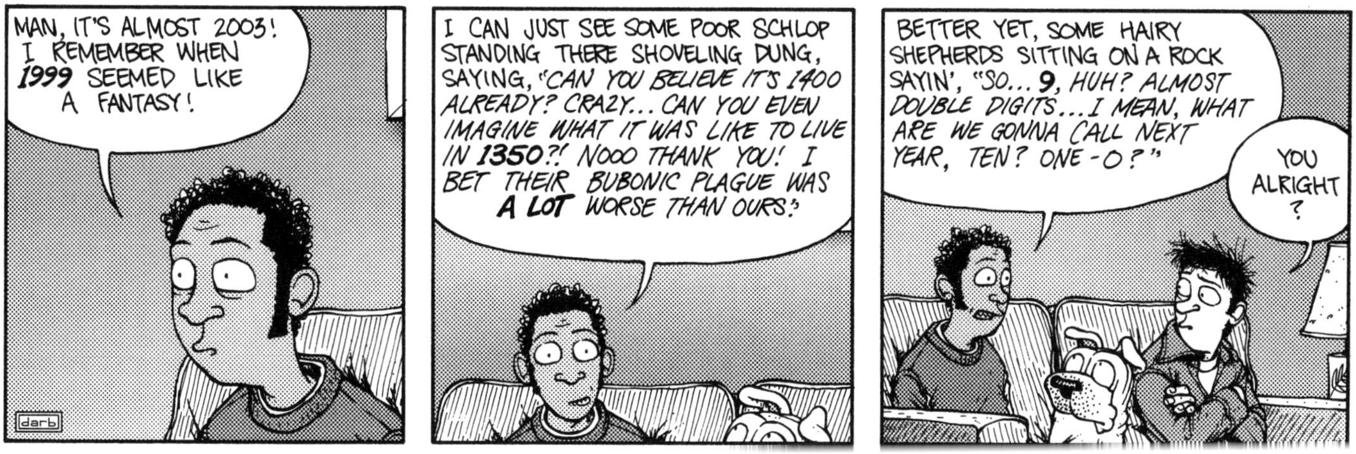
MAN, IT'S ALMOST 2003! I REMEMBER WHEN 1999 SEEMED LIKE A FANTASY!
I CAN JUST SEE SOME POOR SCHLOP STANDING THERE SHOVELING DUNG, SAYING, "CAN YOU BELIEVE IT'S 1400 ALREADY? CRAZY... CAN YOU EVEN IMAGINE WHAT IT WAS LIKE TO LIVE IN 1350?! NOOO THANK YOU! I BET THEIR BUBONIC PLAGUE WAS A LOT WORSE THAN OURS."
BETTER YET, SOME HAIRY SHEPHERDS SITTING ON A ROCK SAYIN', "SO... 9, HUH? ALMOST DOUBLE DIGITS... I MEAN, WHAT ARE WE GONNA CALL NEXT YEAR, TEN? ONE-O?"
YOU ALRIGHT?

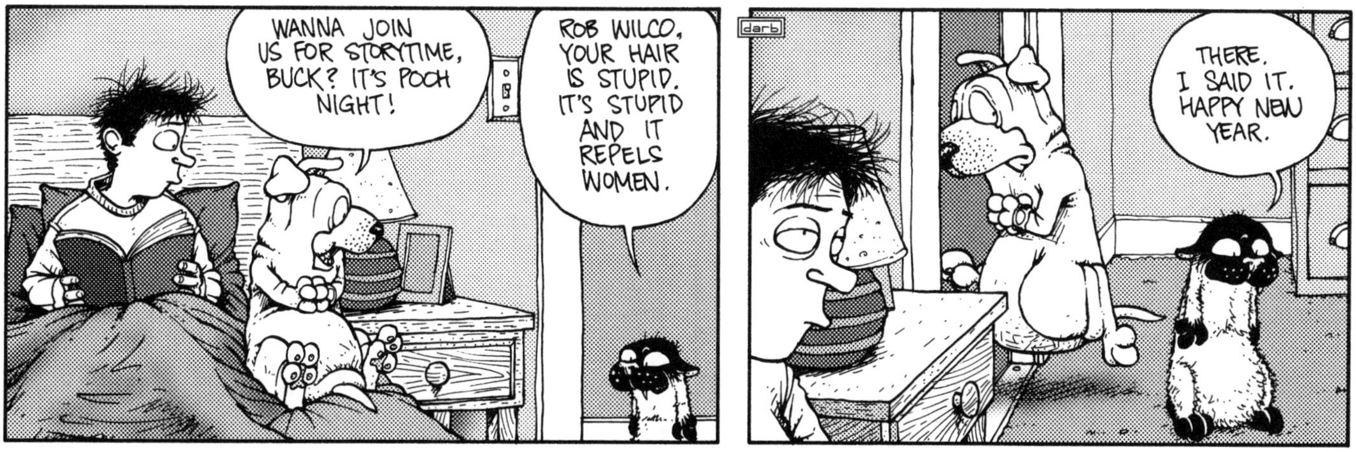
WANNA JOIN US FOR STORYTIME, BUCK? IT'S POOCH NIGHT!
ROB WILCO, YOUR HAIR IS STUPID. IT'S STUPID AND IT REPELS WOMEN.
THERE. I SAID IT. HAPPY NEW YEAR.

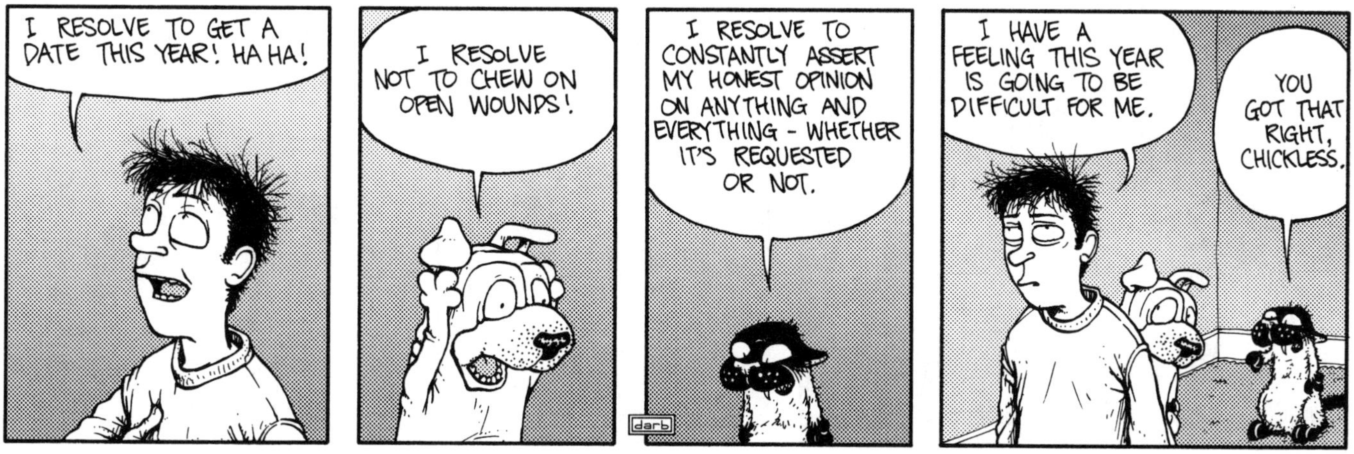
I RESOLVE TO GET A DATE THIS YEAR! HA HA!
I RESOLVE NOT TO CHEW ON OPEN WOUNDS!
I RESOLVE TO CONSTANTLY ASSERT MY HONEST OPINION ON ANYTHING AND EVERYTHING - WHETHER IT'S REQUESTED OR NOT.
I HAVE A FEELING THIS YEAR IS GOING TO BE DIFFICULT FOR ME.
YOU GOT THAT RIGHT, CHICKLESS.

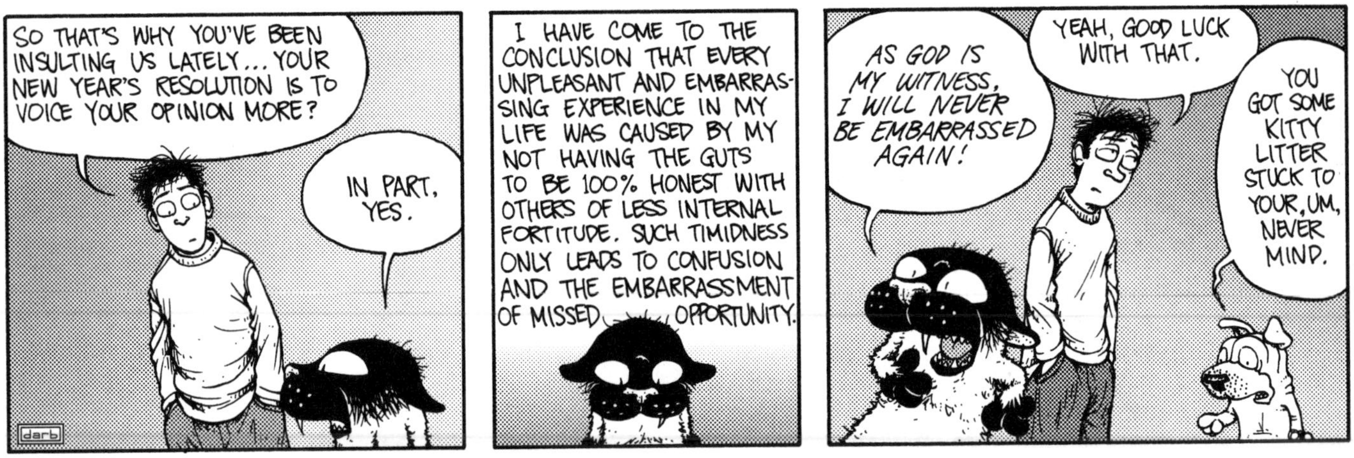
SO THAT'S WHY YOU'VE BEEN INSULTING US LATELY... YOUR NEW YEAR'S RESOLUTION IS TO VOICE YOUR OPINION MORE?
IN PART, YES.
darb
I HAVE COME TO THE CONCLUSION THAT EVERY UNPLEASANT AND EMBARRASSING EXPERIENCE IN MY LIFE WAS CAUSED BY MY NOT HAVING THE GUTS TO BE 100% HONEST WITH OTHERS OF LESS INTERNAL FORTITUDE. SUCH TIMIDNESS ONLY LEADS TO CONFUSION AND THE EMBARRASSMENT OF MISSED OPPORTUNITY.
AS GOD IS MY WITNESS, I WILL NEVER BE EMBARRASSED AGAIN!
YEAH, GOOD LUCK WITH THAT.
YOU GOT SOME KITTY LITTER STUCK TO YOUR, UM, NEVER MIND.

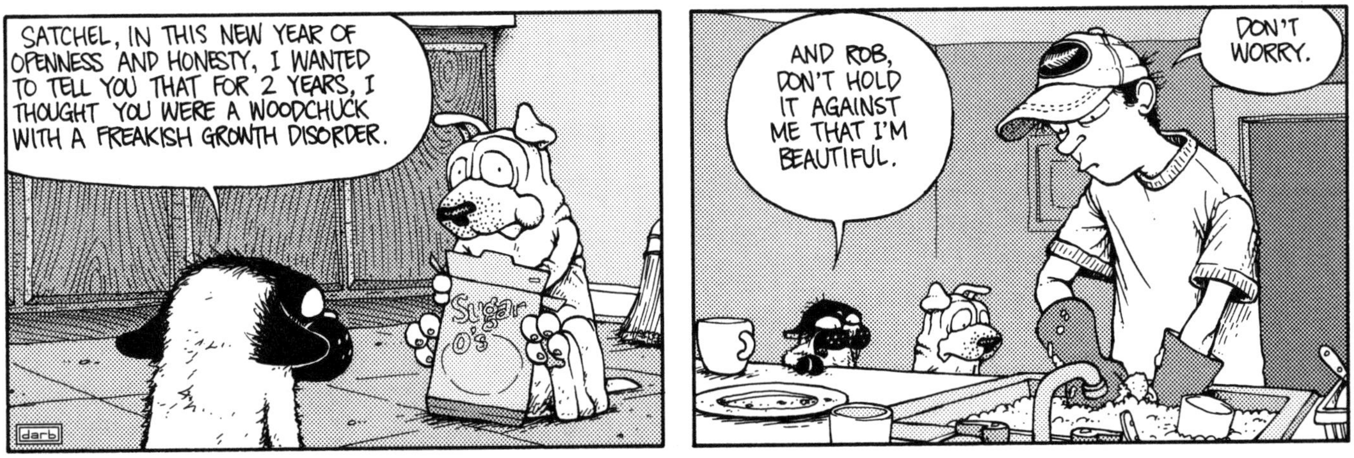
SATCHEL, IN THIS NEW YEAR OF OPENNESS AND HONESTY, I WANTED TO TELL YOU THAT FOR 2 YEARS, I THOUGHT YOU WERE A WOODCHUCK WITH A FREAKISH GROWTH DISORDER.
Sugar O's
darb
AND ROB, DON'T HOLD IT AGAINST ME THAT I'M BEAUTIFUL.
DON'T WORRY.

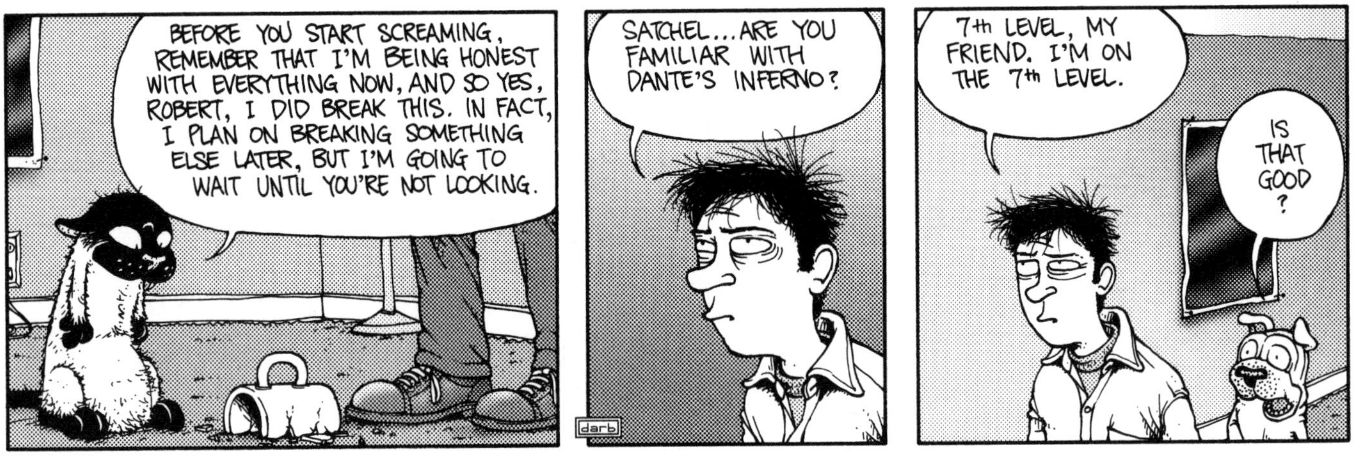
BEFORE YOU START SCREAMING, REMEMBER THAT I'M BEING HONEST WITH EVERYTHING NOW, AND SO YES, ROBERT, I DID BREAK THIS. IN FACT, I PLAN ON BREAKING SOMETHING ELSE LATER, BUT I'M GOING TO WAIT UNTIL YOU'RE NOT LOOKING.
SATCHEL... ARE YOU FAMILIAR WITH DANTE'S INFERNO?
darb
7th LEVEL, MY FRIEND. I'M ON THE 7th LEVEL.
IS THAT GOOD?

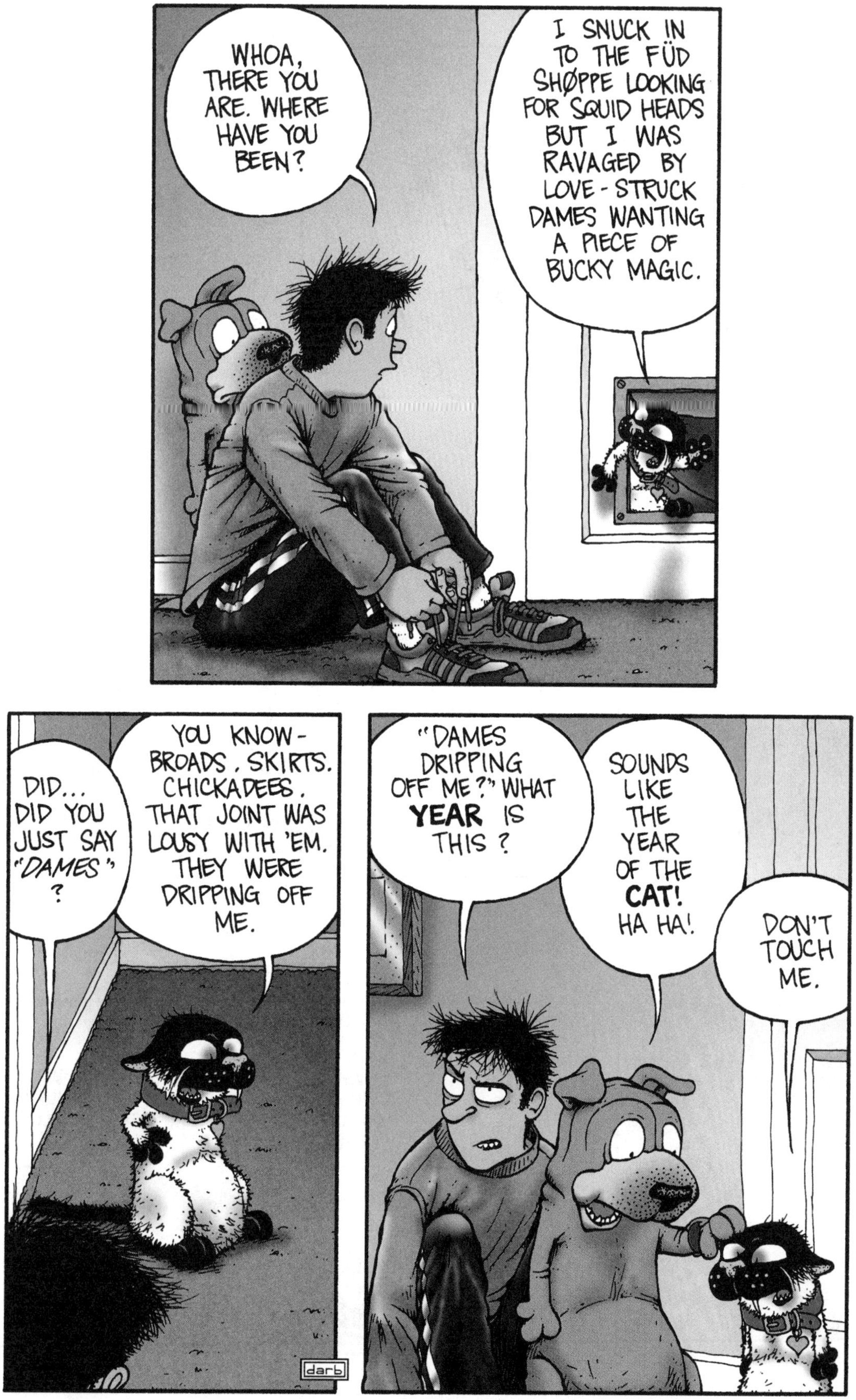
WHOA, THERE YOU ARE. WHERE HAVE YOU BEEN?
I SNUCK IN TO THE FÜD SHØPPE LOOKING FOR SQUID HEADS BUT I WAS RAVAGED BY LOVE-STRUCK DAMES WANTING A PIECE OF BUCKY MAGIC.
DID... DID YOU JUST SAY "DAMES"?
YOU KNOW- BROADS, SKIRTS. CHICKADEES. THAT JOINT WAS LOUSY WITH 'EM. THEY WERE DRIPPING OFF ME.
darb
"DAMES DRIPPING OFF ME?" WHAT **YEAR** IS THIS?
SOUNDS LIKE THE YEAR OF THE **CAT!** HA HA!
DON'T TOUCH ME.

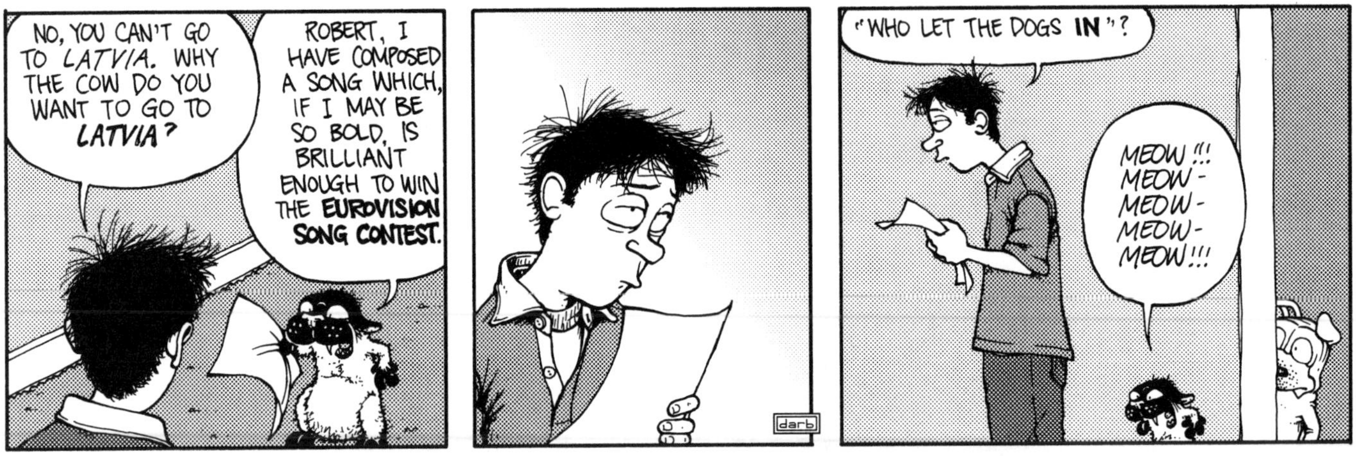
NO, YOU CAN'T GO TO *LATVIA*. WHY THE COW DO YOU WANT TO GO TO **LATVIA**?
ROBERT, I HAVE COMPOSED A SONG WHICH, IF I MAY BE SO BOLD, IS BRILLIANT ENOUGH TO WIN THE **EUROVISION SONG CONTEST**.
darb
"WHO LET THE DOGS **IN**"?
MEOW!!! MEOW-MEOW-MEOW-MEOW!!!

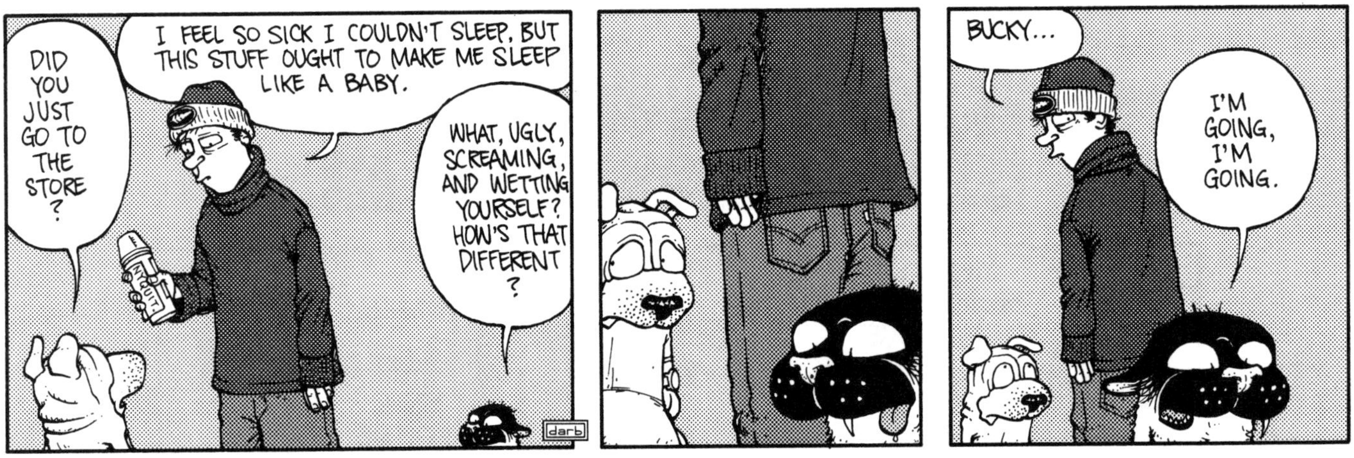
DID YOU JUST GO TO THE STORE?
I FEEL SO SICK I COULDN'T SLEEP, BUT THIS STUFF OUGHT TO MAKE ME SLEEP LIKE A BABY.
WHAT, UGLY, SCREAMING, AND WETTING YOURSELF? HOW'S THAT DIFFERENT?
darb
BUCKY...
I'M GOING, I'M GOING.

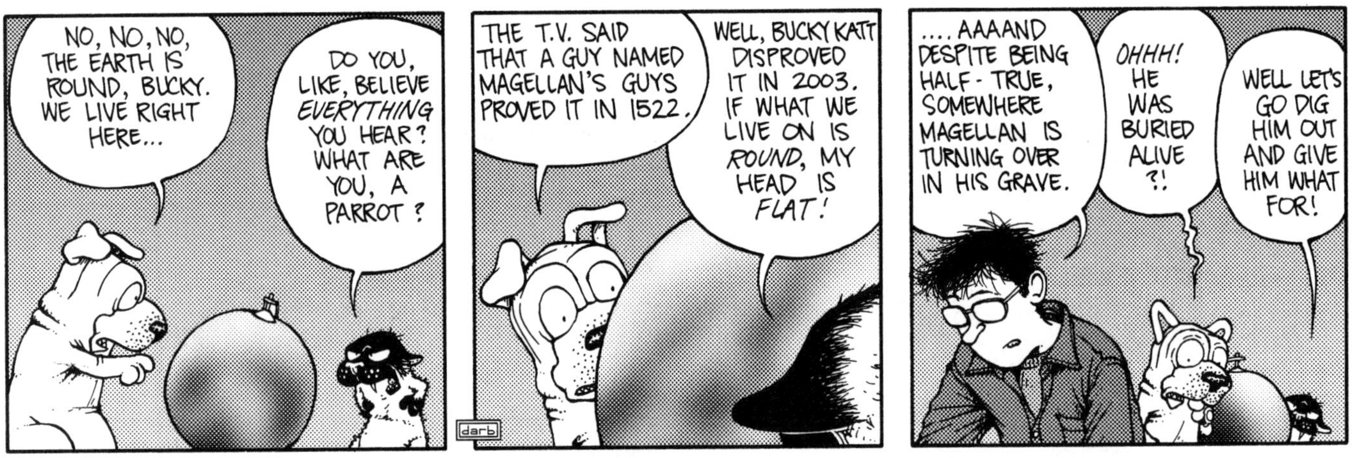
NO, NO, NO, THE EARTH IS ROUND, BUCKY. WE LIVE RIGHT HERE...
DO YOU, LIKE, BELIEVE *EVERYTHING* YOU HEAR? WHAT ARE YOU, A PARROT?
darb
THE T.V. SAID THAT A GUY NAMED MAGELLAN'S GUYS PROVED IT IN 1522.
WELL, BUCKY KATT DISPROVED IT IN 2003. IF WHAT WE LIVE ON IS *ROUND*, MY HEAD IS *FLAT*!
....AAAAND DESPITE BEING HALF-TRUE, SOMEWHERE MAGELLAN IS TURNING OVER IN HIS GRAVE.
OHHH! HE WAS BURIED ALIVE?!
WELL LET'S GO DIG HIM OUT AND GIVE HIM WHAT FOR!

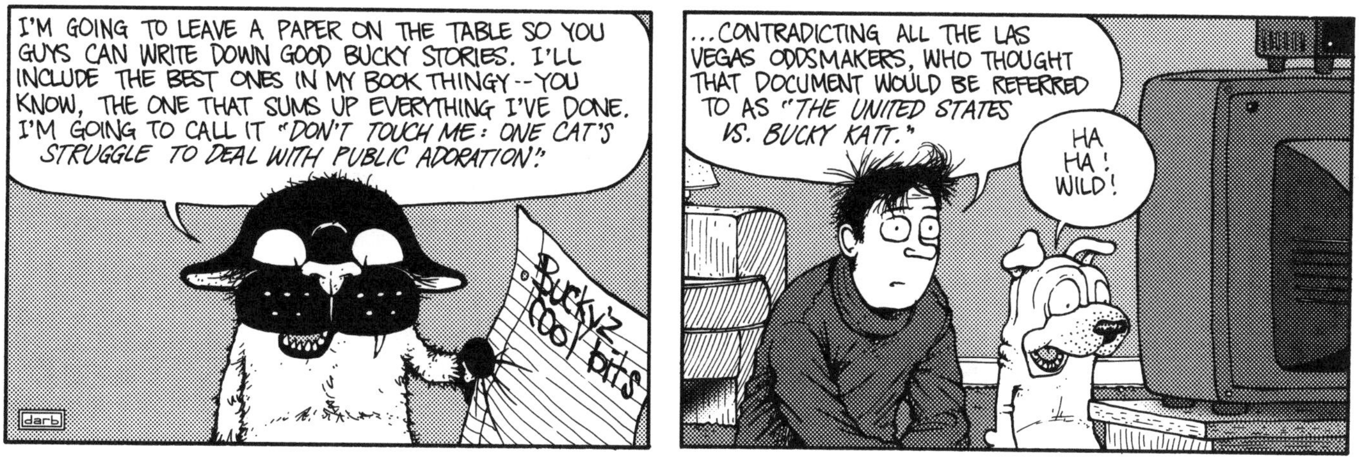
I'M GOING TO LEAVE A PAPER ON THE TABLE SO YOU GUYS CAN WRITE DOWN GOOD BUCKY STORIES. I'LL INCLUDE THE BEST ONES IN MY BOOK THINGY--YOU KNOW, THE ONE THAT SUMS UP EVERYTHING I'VE DONE. I'M GOING TO CALL IT "DON'T TOUCH ME: ONE CAT'S STRUGGLE TO DEAL WITH PUBLIC ADORATION."
Bucky'z cool bits
...CONTRADICTING ALL THE LAS VEGAS ODDSMAKERS, WHO THOUGHT THAT DOCUMENT WOULD BE REFERRED TO AS "THE UNITED STATES VS. BUCKY KATT."
HA HA! WILD!

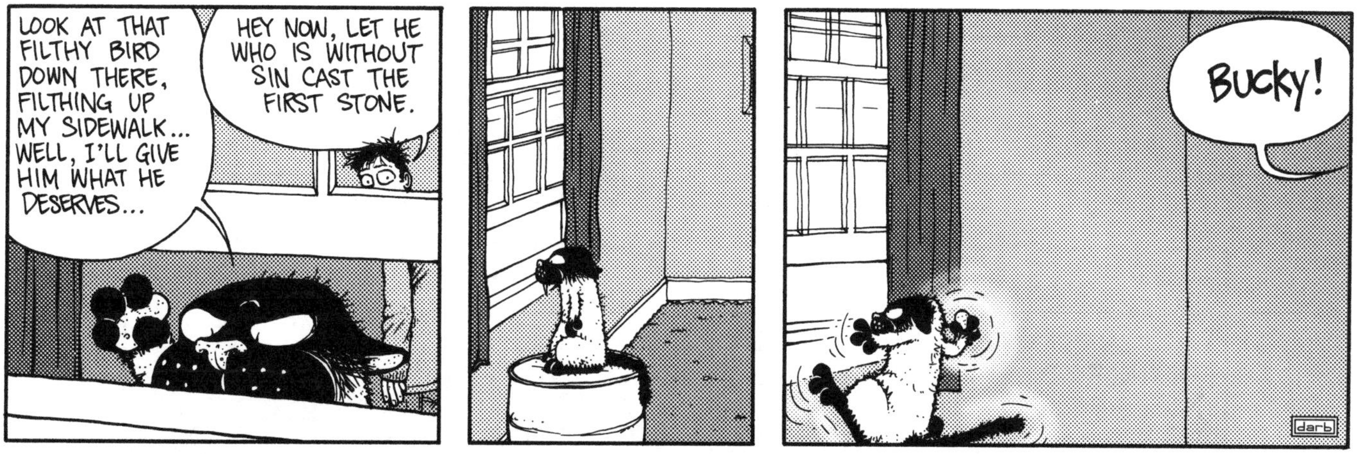
LOOK AT THAT FILTHY BIRD DOWN THERE, FILTHING UP MY SIDEWALK... WELL, I'LL GIVE HIM WHAT HE DESERVES...
HEY NOW, LET HE WHO IS WITHOUT SIN CAST THE FIRST STONE.
BUCKY!

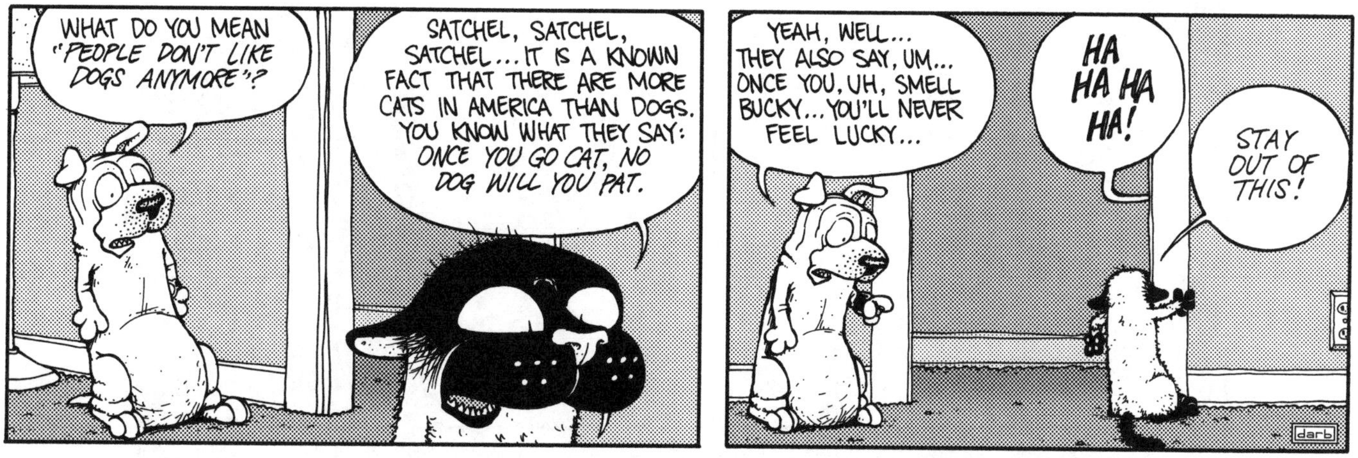
WHAT DO YOU MEAN "PEOPLE DON'T LIKE DOGS ANYMORE"?
SATCHEL, SATCHEL, SATCHEL... IT IS A KNOWN FACT THAT THERE ARE MORE CATS IN AMERICA THAN DOGS. YOU KNOW WHAT THEY SAY: ONCE YOU GO CAT, NO DOG WILL YOU PAT.
YEAH, WELL... THEY ALSO SAY, UM... ONCE YOU, UH, SMELL BUCKY... YOU'LL NEVER FEEL LUCKY...
HA HA HA HA!
STAY OUT OF THIS!

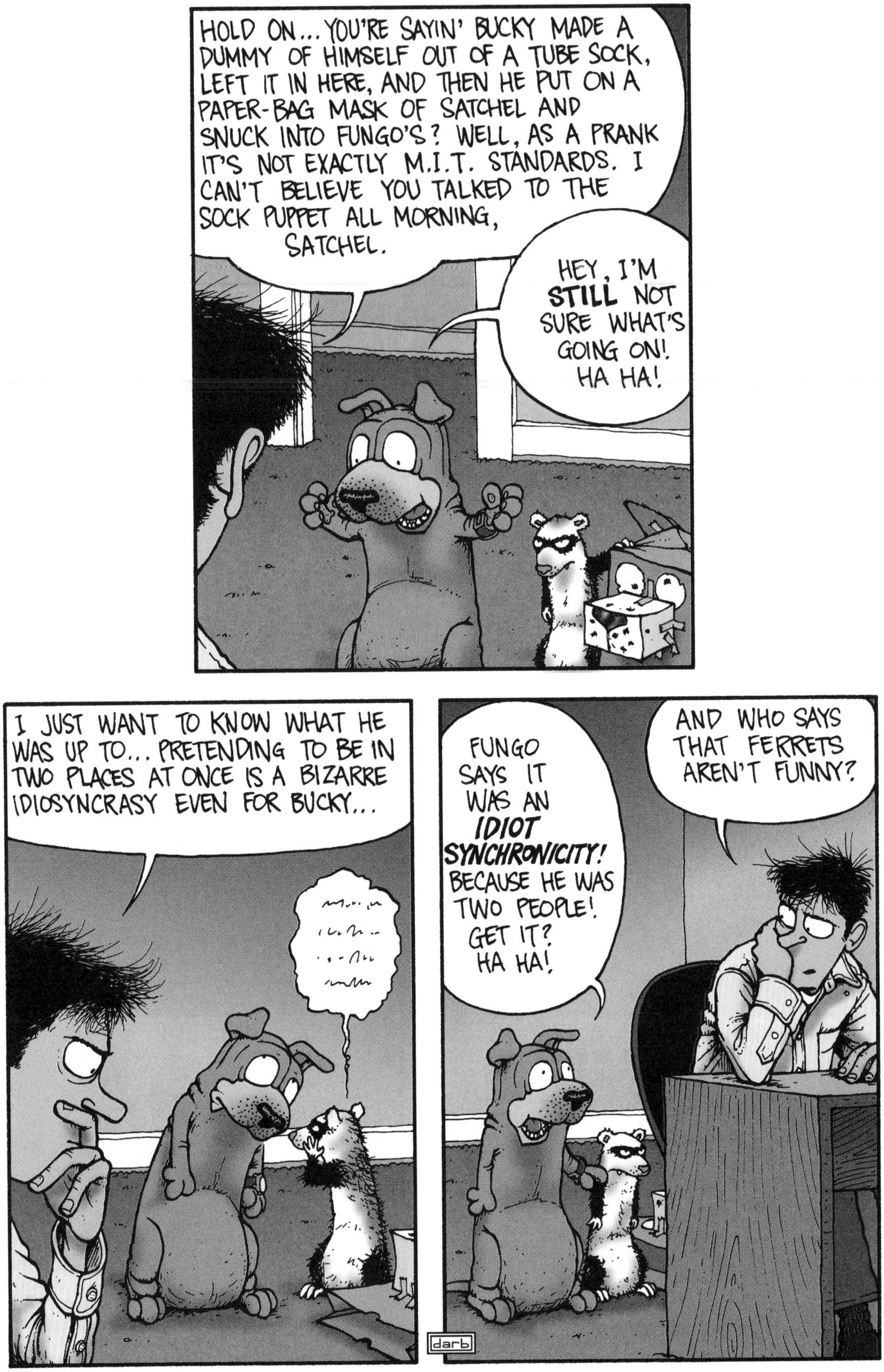
HOLD ON... YOU'RE SAYIN' BUCKY MADE A DUMMY OF HIMSELF OUT OF A TUBE SOCK, LEFT IT IN HERE, AND THEN HE PUT ON A PAPER-BAG MASK OF SATCHEL AND SNUCK INTO FUNGO'S? WELL, AS A PRANK IT'S NOT EXACTLY M.I.T. STANDARDS. I CAN'T BELIEVE YOU TALKED TO THE SOCK PUPPET ALL MORNING, SATCHEL.
HEY, I'M **STILL** NOT SURE WHAT'S GOING ON! HA HA!
I JUST WANT TO KNOW WHAT HE WAS UP TO... PRETENDING TO BE IN TWO PLACES AT ONCE IS A BIZARRE IDIOSYNCRASY EVEN FOR BUCKY...
FUNGO SAYS IT WAS AN ***IDIOT SYNCHRONICITY!*** BECAUSE HE WAS TWO PEOPLE! GET IT? HA HA!
AND WHO SAYS THAT FERRETS AREN'T FUNNY?
darb

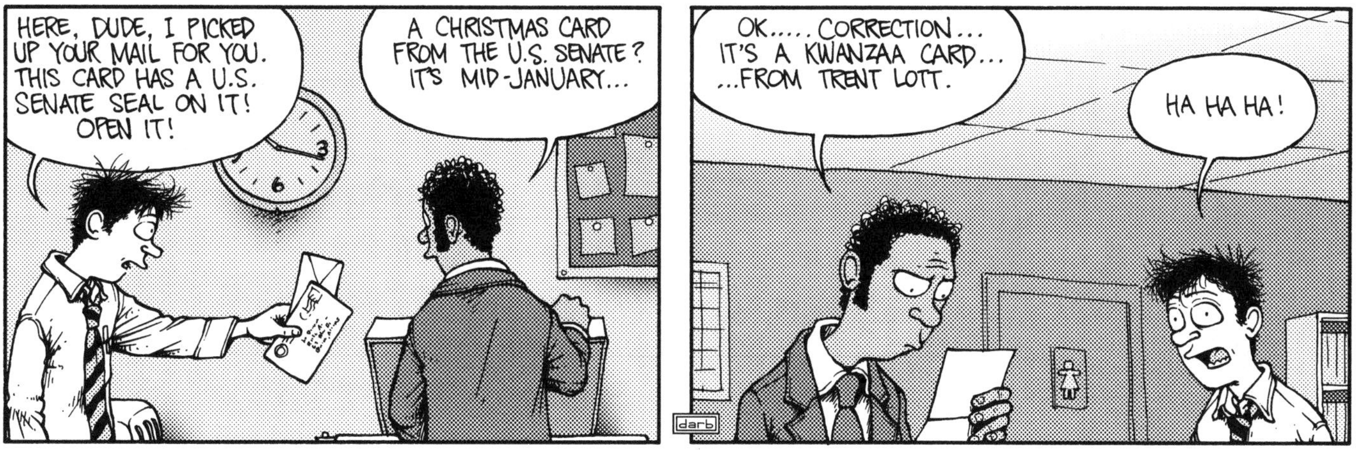
HERE, DUDE, I PICKED UP YOUR MAIL FOR YOU. THIS CARD HAS A U.S. SENATE SEAL ON IT! OPEN IT!
A CHRISTMAS CARD FROM THE U.S. SENATE? IT'S MID-JANUARY...
OK..... CORRECTION... IT'S A KWANZAA CARD... ...FROM TRENT LOTT.
HA HA HA!

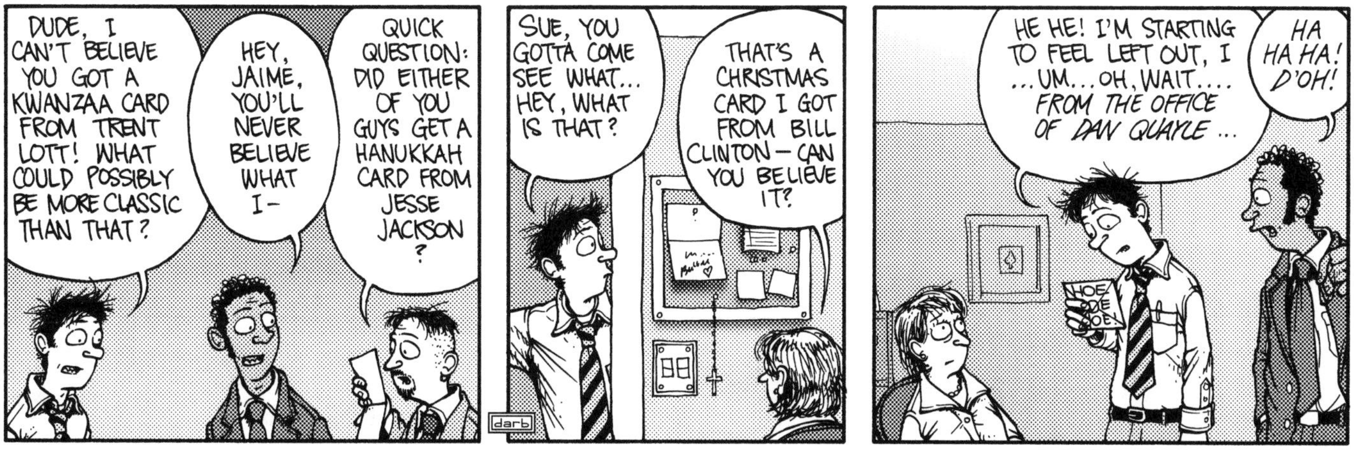
DUDE, I CAN'T BELIEVE YOU GOT A KWANZAA CARD FROM TRENT LOTT! WHAT COULD POSSIBLY BE MORE CLASSIC THAN THAT?
HEY, JAIME, YOU'LL NEVER BELIEVE WHAT I–
QUICK QUESTION: DID EITHER OF YOU GUYS GET A HANUKKAH CARD FROM JESSE JACKSON?
SUE, YOU GOTTA COME SEE WHAT... HEY, WHAT IS THAT?
THAT'S A CHRISTMAS CARD I GOT FROM BILL CLINTON – CAN YOU BELIEVE IT?
HE HE! I'M STARTING TO FEEL LEFT OUT, I ...UM...OH, WAIT.... *FROM THE OFFICE OF DAN QUAYLE...*
HA HA HA! D'OH!

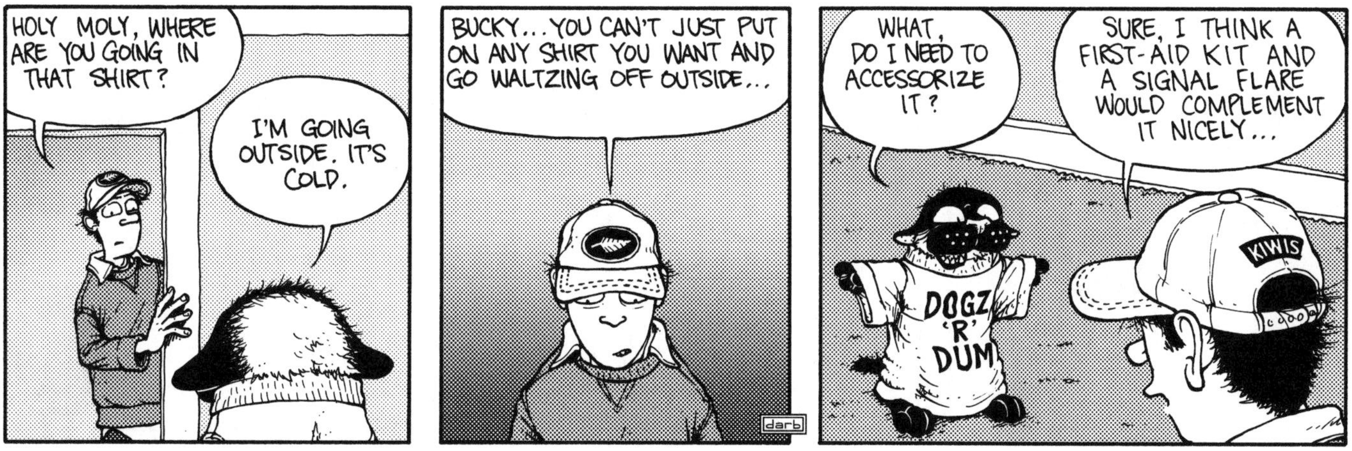
HOLY MOLY, WHERE ARE YOU GOING IN THAT SHIRT?
I'M GOING OUTSIDE. IT'S COLD.
BUCKY... YOU CAN'T JUST PUT ON ANY SHIRT YOU WANT AND GO WALTZING OFF OUTSIDE...
WHAT, DO I NEED TO ACCESSORIZE IT?
SURE, I THINK A FIRST-AID KIT AND A SIGNAL FLARE WOULD COMPLEMENT IT NICELY...
DOGZ 'R' DUM
KIWIS

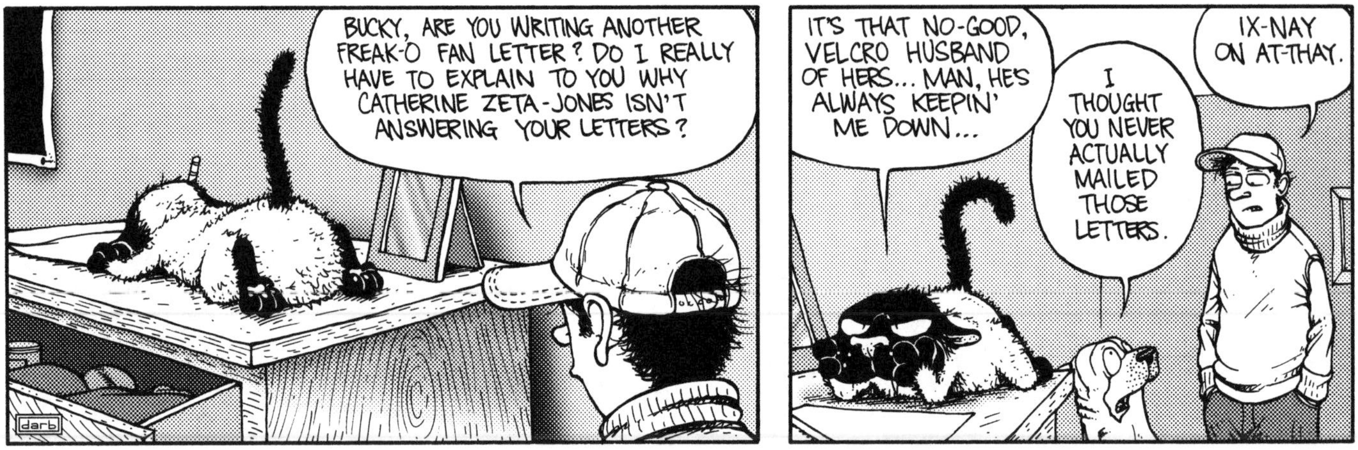
BUCKY, ARE YOU WRITING ANOTHER FREAK-O FAN LETTER? DO I REALLY HAVE TO EXPLAIN TO YOU WHY CATHERINE ZETA-JONES ISN'T ANSWERING YOUR LETTERS?
darb
IT'S THAT NO-GOOD, VELCRO HUSBAND OF HERS... MAN, HE'S ALWAYS KEEPIN' ME DOWN...
I THOUGHT YOU NEVER ACTUALLY MAILED THOSE LETTERS.
IX-NAY ON AT-THAY.

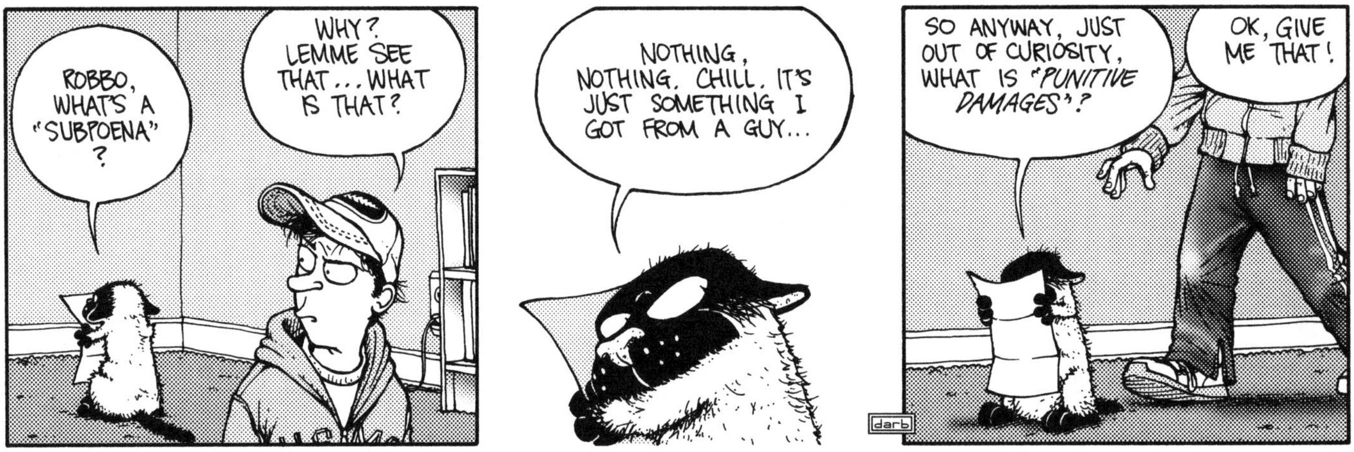
ROBBO, WHAT'S A "SUBPOENA"?
WHY? LEMME SEE THAT... WHAT IS THAT?
NOTHING, NOTHING. CHILL. IT'S JUST SOMETHING I GOT FROM A GUY...
darb
SO ANYWAY, JUST OUT OF CURIOSITY, WHAT IS "PUNITIVE DAMAGES"?
OK, GIVE ME THAT!

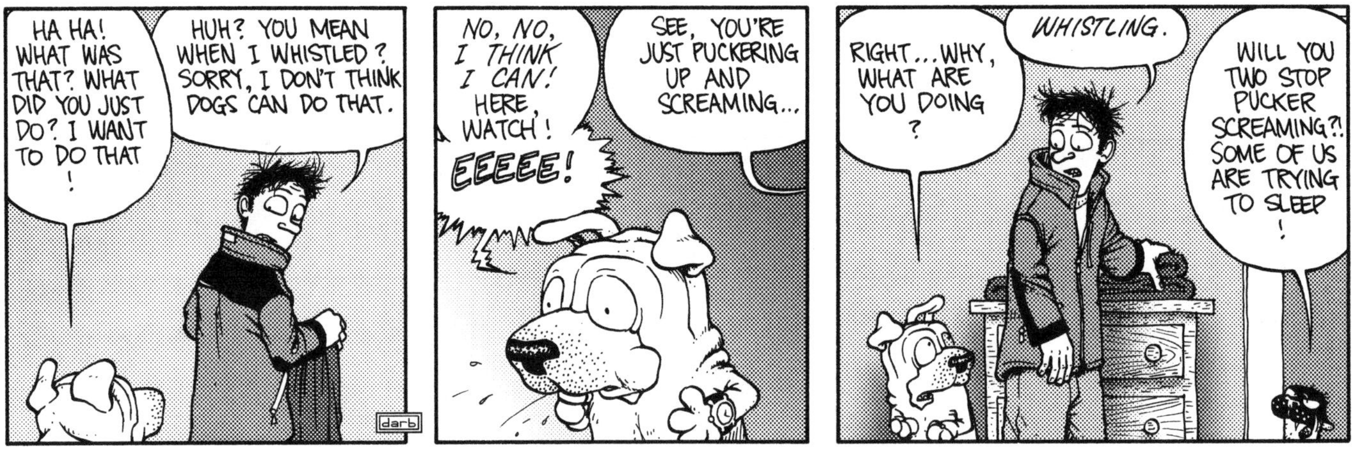
HA HA! WHAT WAS THAT? WHAT DID YOU JUST DO? I WANT TO DO THAT!
HUH? YOU MEAN WHEN I WHISTLED? SORRY, I DON'T THINK DOGS CAN DO THAT.
darb
NO, NO, I THINK I CAN! HERE, WATCH!
EEEEE!
SEE, YOU'RE JUST PUCKERING UP AND SCREAMING...
RIGHT... WHY, WHAT ARE YOU DOING?
WHISTLING.
WILL YOU TWO STOP PUCKER SCREAMING?! SOME OF US ARE TRYING TO SLEEP!

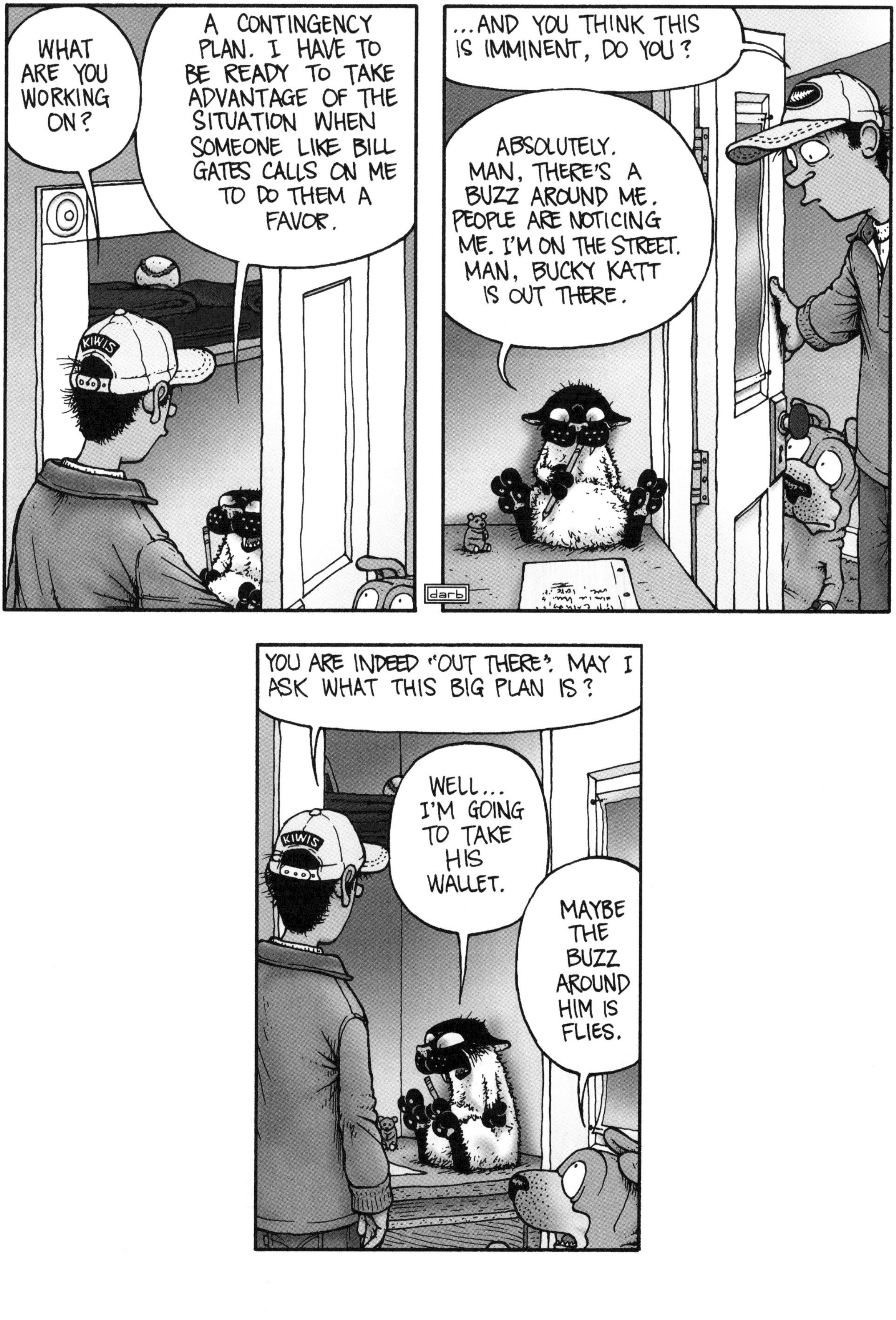
WHAT ARE YOU WORKING ON?
A CONTINGENCY PLAN. I HAVE TO BE READY TO TAKE ADVANTAGE OF THE SITUATION WHEN SOMEONE LIKE BILL GATES CALLS ON ME TO DO THEM A FAVOR.
KIWIS
...AND YOU THINK THIS IS IMMINENT, DO YOU?
ABSOLUTELY. MAN, THERE'S A BUZZ AROUND ME. PEOPLE ARE NOTICING ME. I'M ON THE STREET. MAN, BUCKY KATT IS OUT THERE.
darb
YOU ARE INDEED "OUT THERE". MAY I ASK WHAT THIS BIG PLAN IS?
WELL... I'M GOING TO TAKE HIS WALLET.
MAYBE THE BUZZ AROUND HIM IS FLIES.
KIWIS

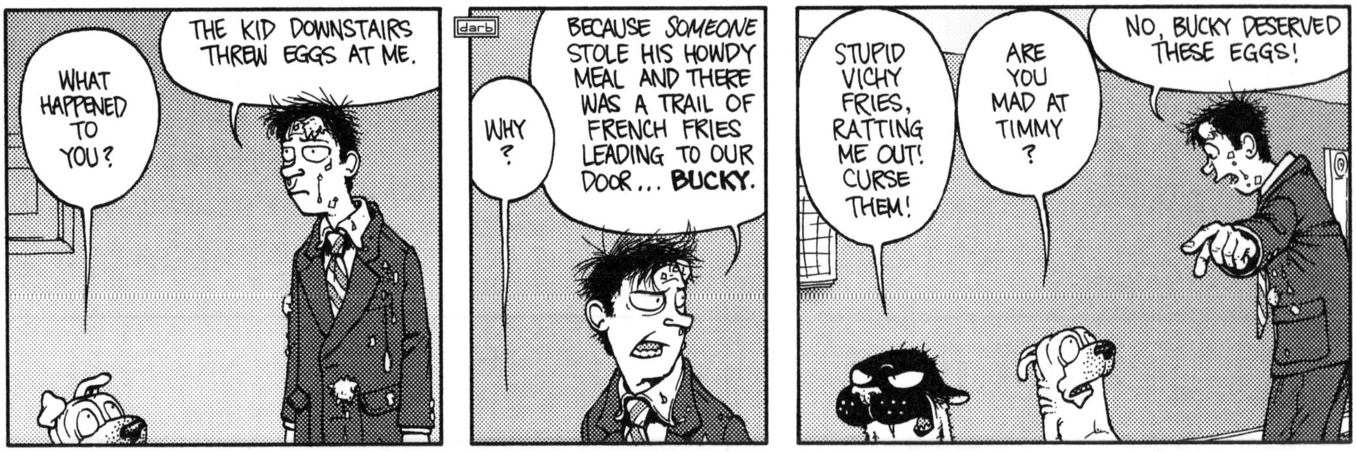
WHAT HAPPENED TO YOU?
THE KID DOWNSTAIRS THREW EGGS AT ME.
WHY?
BECAUSE *SOMEONE* STOLE HIS HOWDY MEAL AND THERE WAS A TRAIL OF FRENCH FRIES LEADING TO OUR DOOR... **BUCKY.**
NO, BUCKY DESERVED THESE EGGS!
ARE YOU MAD AT TIMMY?
STUPID VICHY FRIES, RATTING ME OUT! CURSE THEM!

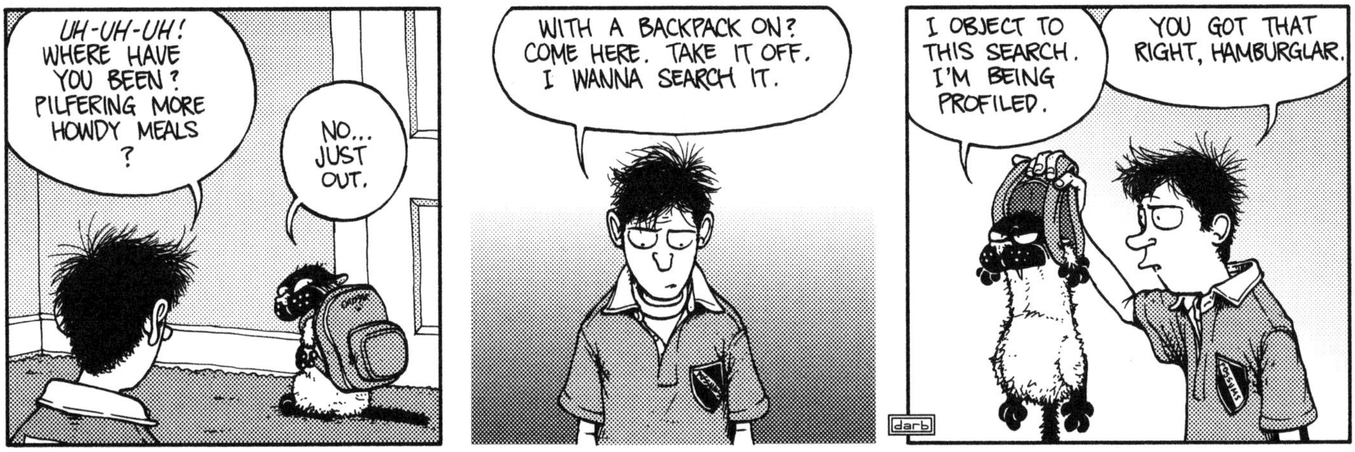
UH-UH-UH! WHERE HAVE YOU BEEN? PILFERING MORE HOWDY MEALS?
NO... JUST OUT.
WITH A BACKPACK ON? COME HERE. TAKE IT OFF. I WANNA SEARCH IT.
I OBJECT TO THIS SEARCH. I'M BEING PROFILED.
YOU GOT THAT RIGHT, HAMBURGLAR.

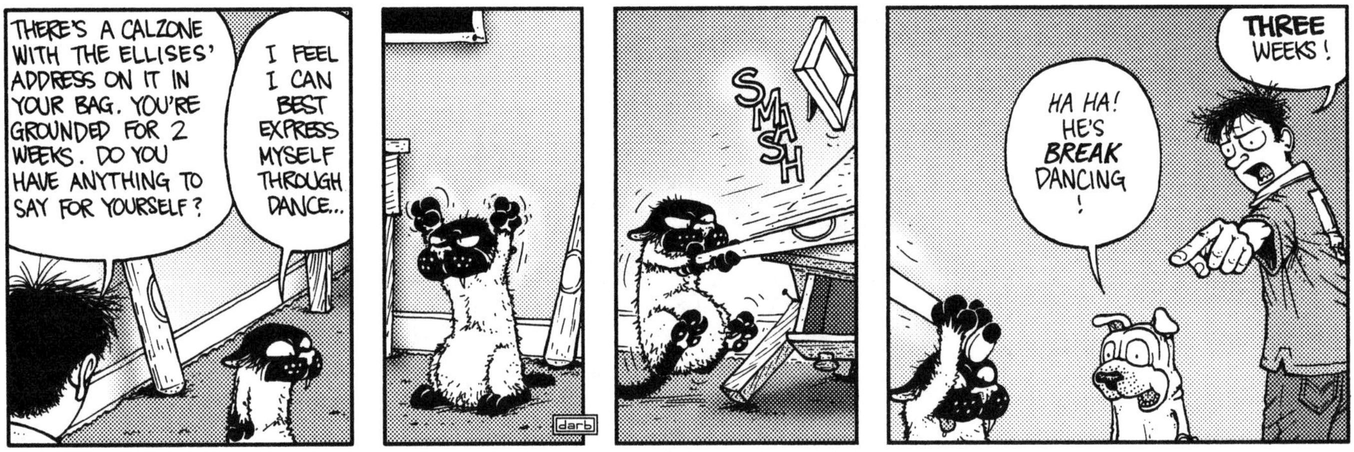
THERE'S A CALZONE WITH THE ELLISES' ADDRESS ON IT IN YOUR BAG. YOU'RE GROUNDED FOR 2 WEEKS. DO YOU HAVE ANYTHING TO SAY FOR YOURSELF?
I FEEL I CAN BEST EXPRESS MYSELF THROUGH DANCE...
SMASH
THREE WEEKS!
HA HA! HE'S ***BREAK*** DANCING!

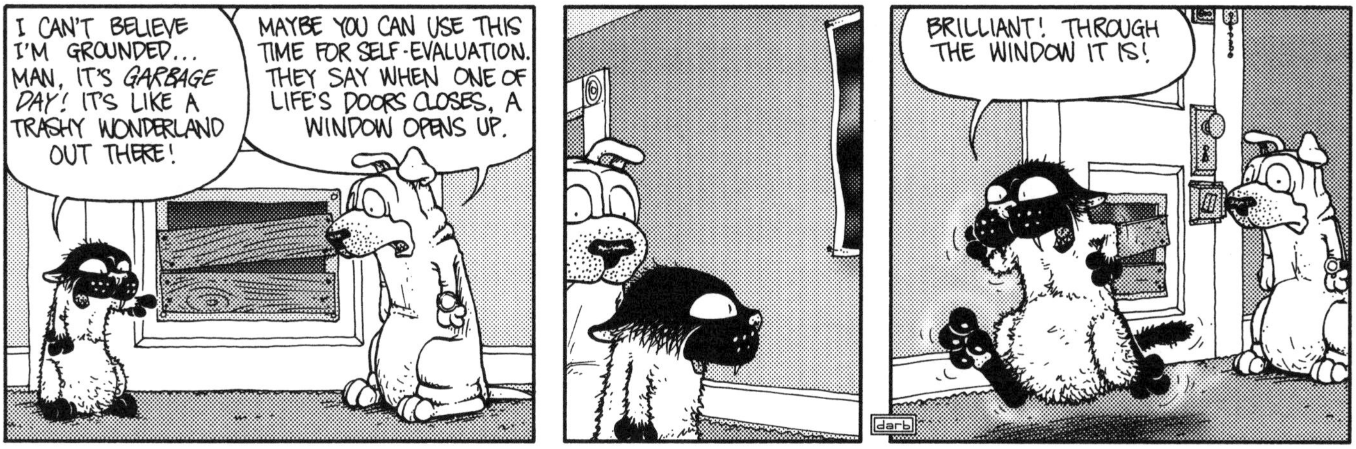
I CAN'T BELIEVE I'M GROUNDED... MAN, IT'S GARBAGE DAY! IT'S LIKE A TRASHY WONDERLAND OUT THERE!
MAYBE YOU CAN USE THIS TIME FOR SELF-EVALUATION. THEY SAY WHEN ONE OF LIFE'S DOORS CLOSES, A WINDOW OPENS UP.
BRILLIANT! THROUGH THE WINDOW IT IS!
darb

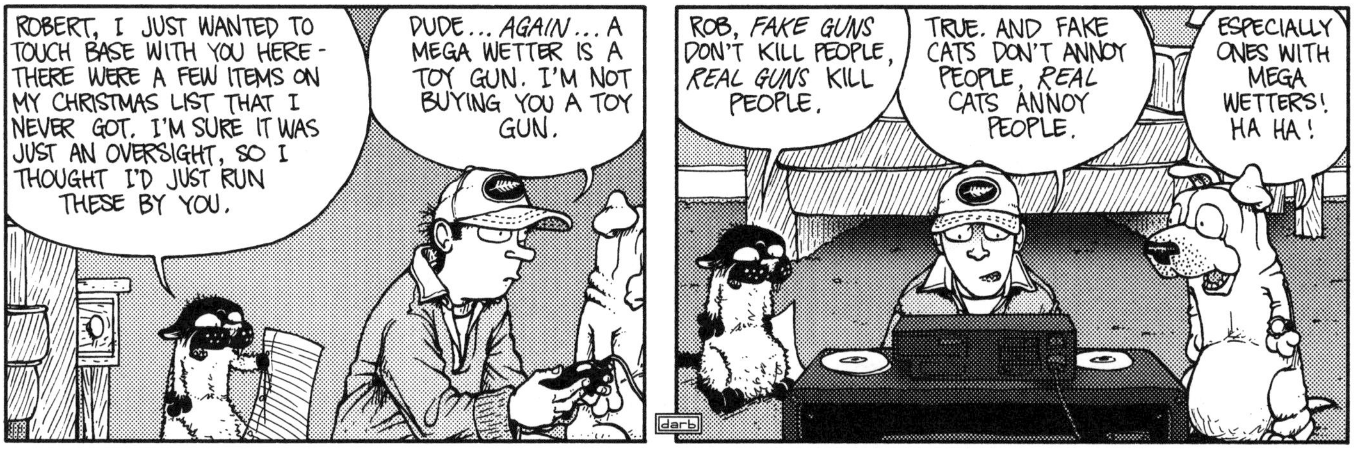
ROBERT, I JUST WANTED TO TOUCH BASE WITH YOU HERE - THERE WERE A FEW ITEMS ON MY CHRISTMAS LIST THAT I NEVER GOT. I'M SURE IT WAS JUST AN OVERSIGHT, SO I THOUGHT I'D JUST RUN THESE BY YOU.
DUDE... AGAIN... A MEGA WETTER IS A TOY GUN. I'M NOT BUYING YOU A TOY GUN.
darb
ROB, FAKE GUNS DON'T KILL PEOPLE, REAL GUNS KILL PEOPLE.
TRUE. AND FAKE CATS DON'T ANNOY PEOPLE, REAL CATS ANNOY PEOPLE.
ESPECIALLY ONES WITH MEGA WETTERS! HA HA!

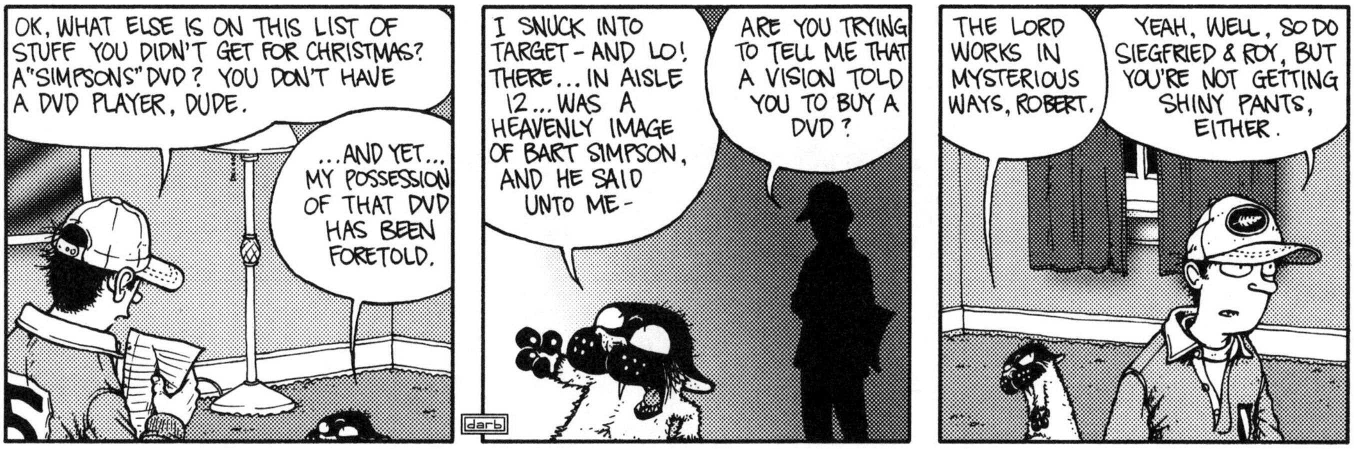
OK, WHAT ELSE IS ON THIS LIST OF STUFF YOU DIDN'T GET FOR CHRISTMAS? A "SIMPSONS" DVD? YOU DON'T HAVE A DVD PLAYER, DUDE.
...AND YET... MY POSSESSION OF THAT DVD HAS BEEN FORETOLD.
darb
I SNUCK INTO TARGET - AND LO! THERE... IN AISLE 12... WAS A HEAVENLY IMAGE OF BART SIMPSON, AND HE SAID UNTO ME-
ARE YOU TRYING TO TELL ME THAT A VISION TOLD YOU TO BUY A DVD?
THE LORD WORKS IN MYSTERIOUS WAYS, ROBERT.
YEAH, WELL, SO DO SIEGFRIED & ROY, BUT YOU'RE NOT GETTING SHINY PANTS, EITHER.

MEAT FROM THE SALAD BAR? NO WAY.
OHHH... THAT COUNTER HAS TUNA. CAN WE GET SOME?
Nut Crunch
LOWE
TECHNICAL
AWW. WHY NOT? I'M REALLY HUNGRY...
BECAUSE IF YOU GET THAT TUNA, YOU'LL ALSO GET SALMONELLA.
darb
SALMONELLA IS NOT LITTLE SALMONS, DUDE.
HEY, IF SATCHEL GETS SALMONELLA, *I* GET SALMONELLA TOO!
BUCKY CAN HAVE MY SALMO-NELLAS; I DON'T MIND.

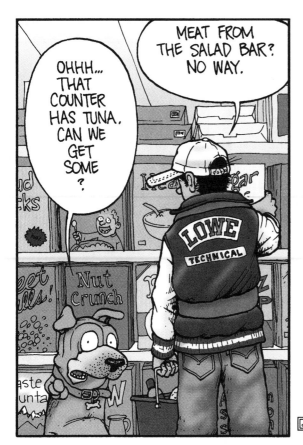

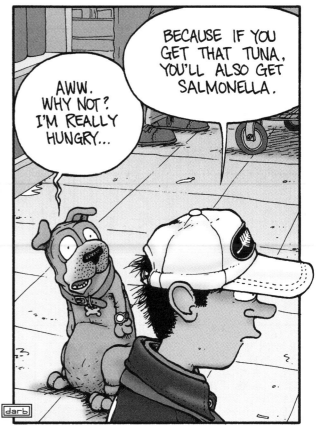

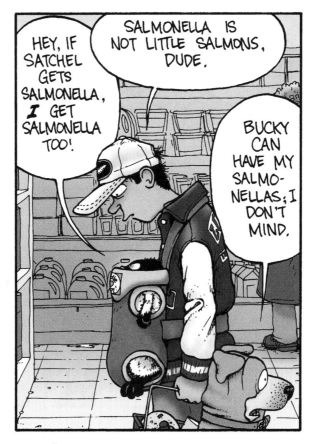

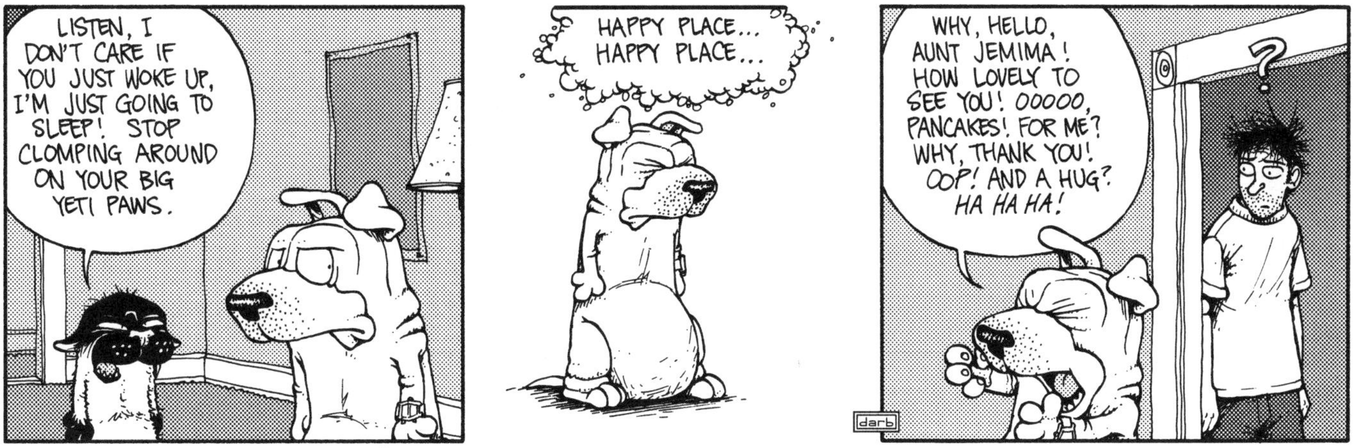
LISTEN, I DON'T CARE IF YOU JUST WOKE UP, I'M JUST GOING TO SLEEP! STOP CLOMPING AROUND ON YOUR BIG YETI PAWS.
HAPPY PLACE... HAPPY PLACE...
WHY, HELLO, AUNT JEMIMA! HOW LOVELY TO SEE YOU! OOOOO, PANCAKES! FOR ME? WHY, THANK YOU! OOP! AND A HUG? HA HA HA!
?
darb

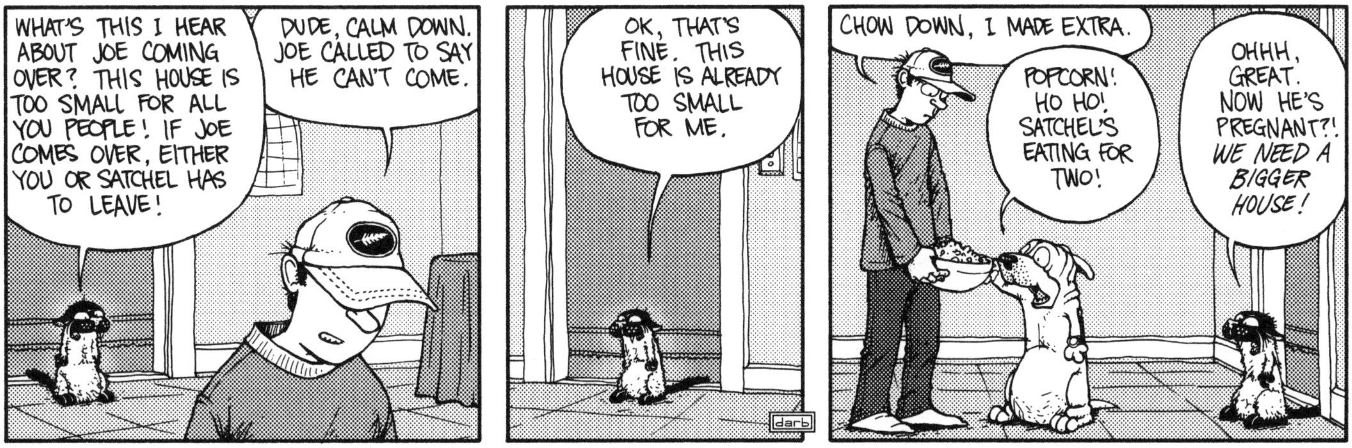
WHAT'S THIS I HEAR ABOUT JOE COMING OVER? THIS HOUSE IS TOO SMALL FOR ALL YOU PEOPLE! IF JOE COMES OVER, EITHER YOU OR SATCHEL HAS TO LEAVE!
DUDE, CALM DOWN. JOE CALLED TO SAY HE CAN'T COME.
OK, THAT'S FINE. THIS HOUSE IS ALREADY TOO SMALL FOR ME.
darb
CHOW DOWN, I MADE EXTRA.
POPCORN! HO HO! SATCHEL'S EATING FOR TWO!
OHHH, GREAT. NOW HE'S PREGNANT?! WE NEED A BIGGER HOUSE!

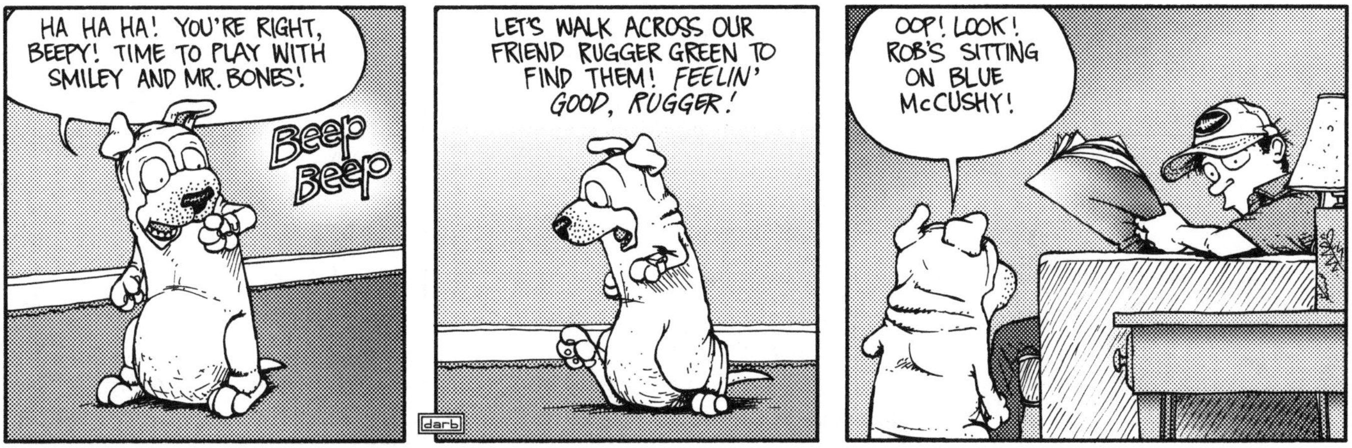
HA HA HA! YOU'RE RIGHT, BEEPY! TIME TO PLAY WITH SMILEY AND MR. BONES!
Beep Beep
darb
LET'S WALK ACROSS OUR FRIEND RUGGER GREEN TO FIND THEM! FEELIN' GOOD, RUGGER!
OOP! LOOK! ROB'S SITTING ON BLUE McCUSHY!

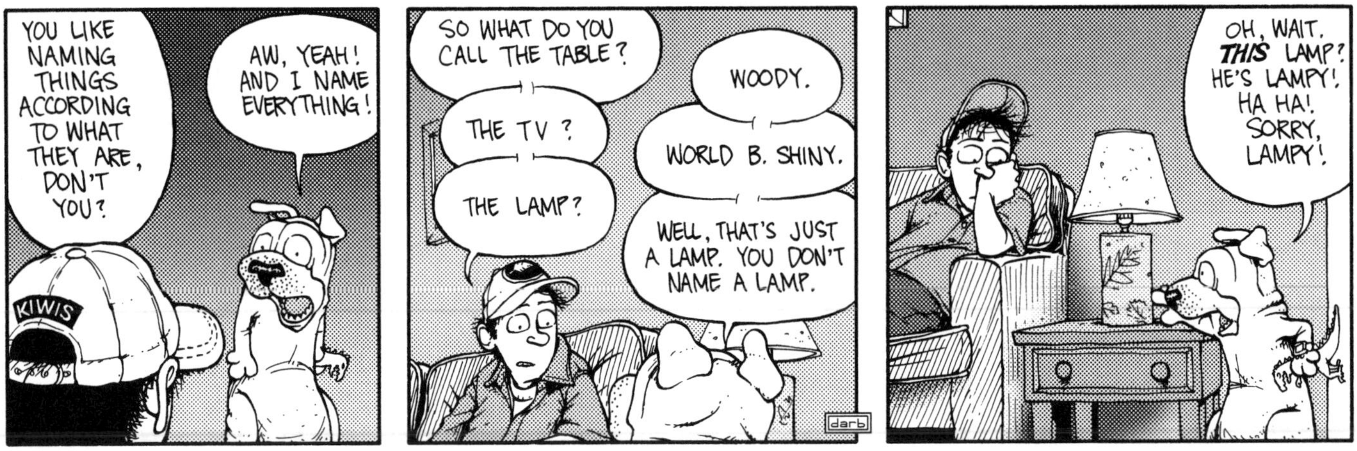
YOU LIKE NAMING THINGS ACCORDING TO WHAT THEY ARE, DON'T YOU?
AW, YEAH! AND I NAME EVERYTHING!
SO WHAT DO YOU CALL THE TABLE?
WOODY.
THE TV?
WORLD B. SHINY.
THE LAMP?
WELL, THAT'S JUST A LAMP. YOU DON'T NAME A LAMP.
OH, WAIT. ***THIS*** LAMP? HE'S LAMPY! HA HA! SORRY, LAMPY!
KIWIS
darb

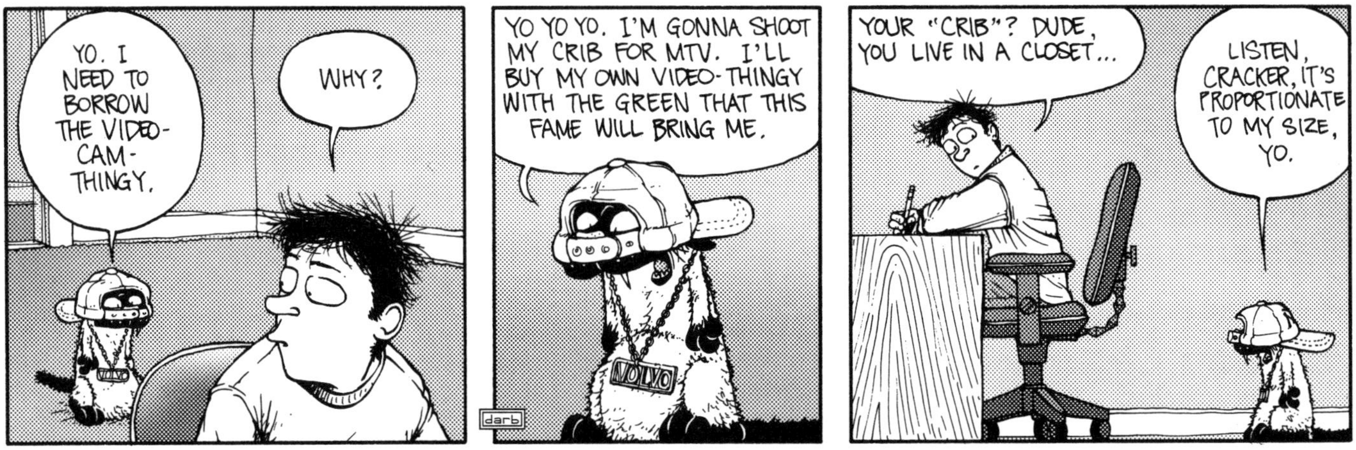
YO. I NEED TO BORROW THE VIDEO-CAM-THINGY.
WHY?
YO YO YO. I'M GONNA SHOOT MY CRIB FOR MTV. I'LL BUY MY OWN VIDEO-THINGY WITH THE GREEN THAT THIS FAME WILL BRING ME.
YOUR "CRIB"? DUDE, YOU LIVE IN A CLOSET...
LISTEN, CRACKER, IT'S PROPORTIONATE TO MY SIZE, YO.
VOLVO
darb

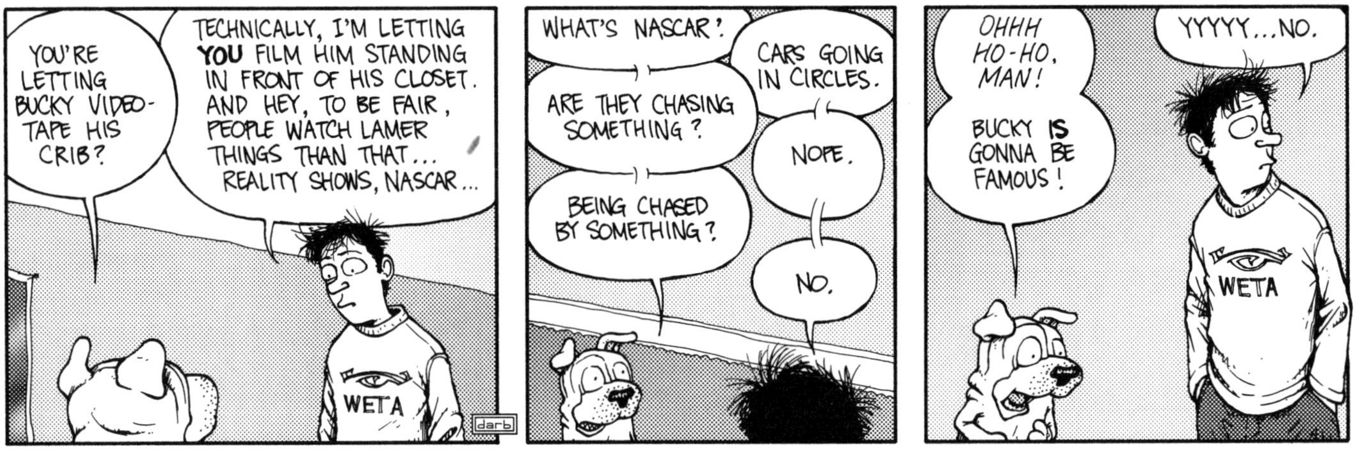
YOU'RE LETTING BUCKY VIDEO-TAPE HIS CRIB?
TECHNICALLY, I'M LETTING **YOU** FILM HIM STANDING IN FRONT OF HIS CLOSET. AND HEY, TO BE FAIR, PEOPLE WATCH LAMER THINGS THAN THAT... REALITY SHOWS, NASCAR...
WHAT'S NASCAR?
CARS GOING IN CIRCLES.
ARE THEY CHASING SOMETHING?
NOPE.
BEING CHASED BY SOMETHING?
NO.
OHHH HO-HO, MAN!
BUCKY **IS** GONNA BE FAMOUS!
YYYYY...NO.
WETA
darb

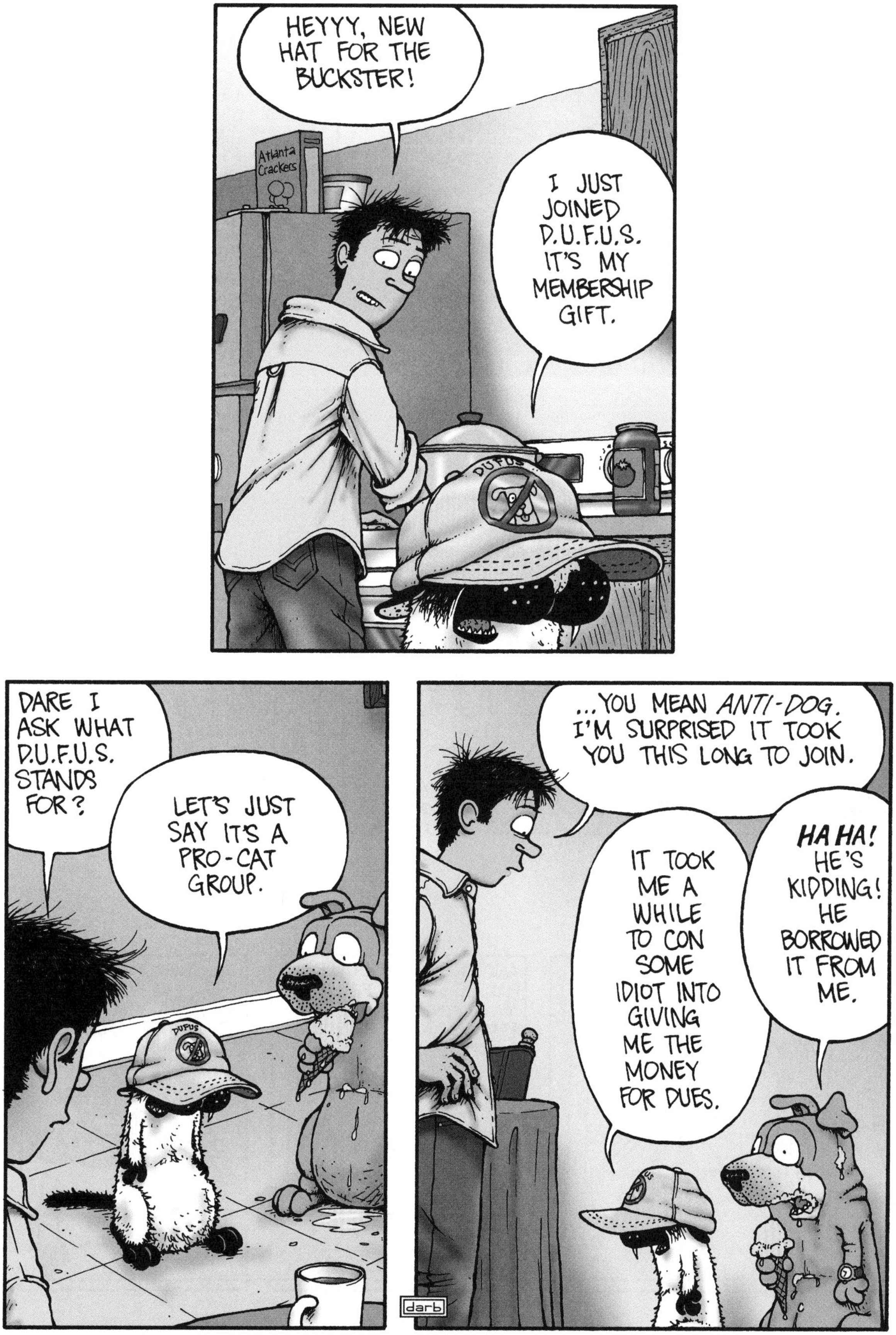
HEYYY, NEW HAT FOR THE BUCKSTER!
Atlanta Crackers
I JUST JOINED D.U.F.U.S. IT'S MY MEMBERSHIP GIFT.
DUFUS
DARE I ASK WHAT D.U.F.U.S. STANDS FOR?
LET'S JUST SAY IT'S A PRO-CAT GROUP.
DUFUS
...YOU MEAN *ANTI-DOG*. I'M SURPRISED IT TOOK YOU THIS LONG TO JOIN.
IT TOOK ME A WHILE TO CON SOME IDIOT INTO GIVING ME THE MONEY FOR DUES.
HA HA! HE'S KIDDING! HE BORROWED IT FROM ME.
darb

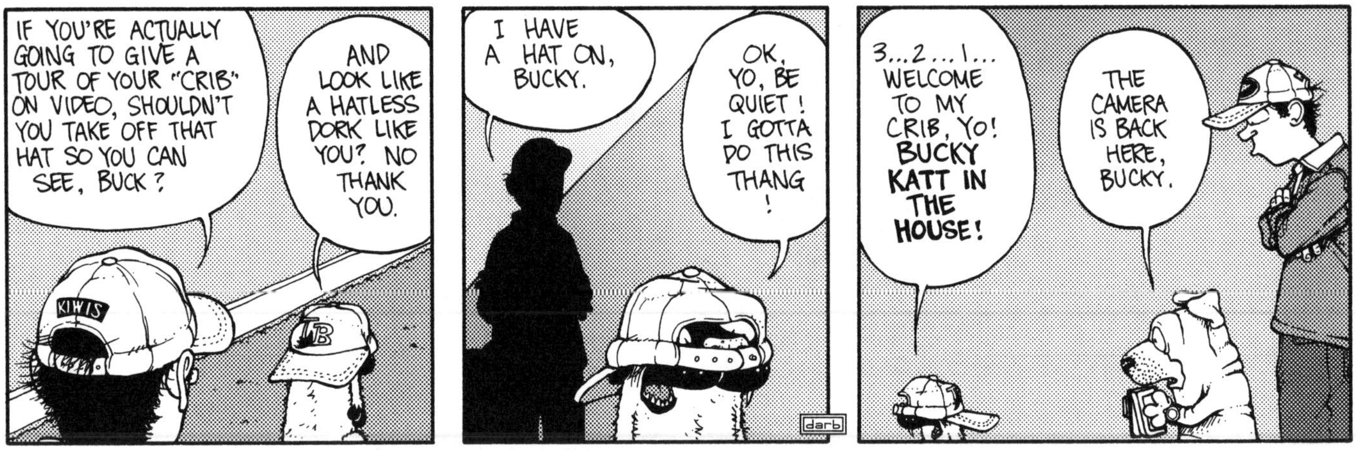
IF YOU'RE ACTUALLY GOING TO GIVE A TOUR OF YOUR "CRIB" ON VIDEO, SHOULDN'T YOU TAKE OFF THAT HAT SO YOU CAN SEE, BUCK?
AND LOOK LIKE A HATLESS DORK LIKE YOU? NO THANK YOU.
KIWIS
I HAVE A HAT ON, BUCKY.
OK, YO, BE QUIET! I GOTTA DO THIS THANG!
3...2...1... WELCOME TO MY CRIB, YO! BUCKY KATT IN THE HOUSE!
THE CAMERA IS BACK HERE, BUCKY.
darb

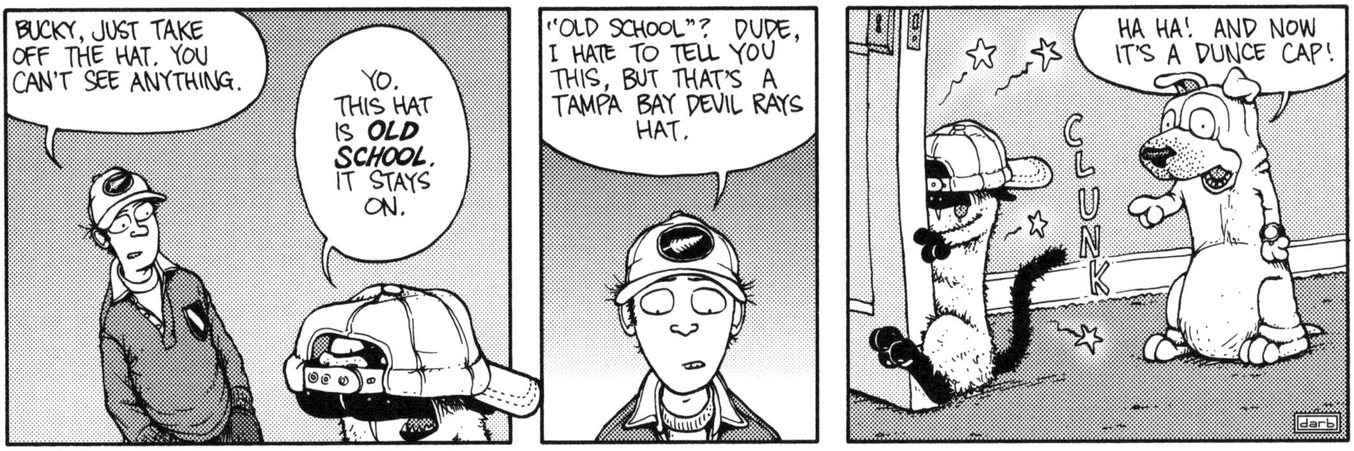
BUCKY, JUST TAKE OFF THE HAT. YOU CAN'T SEE ANYTHING.
YO. THIS HAT IS OLD SCHOOL. IT STAYS ON.
"OLD SCHOOL"? DUDE, I HATE TO TELL YOU THIS, BUT THAT'S A TAMPA BAY DEVIL RAYS HAT.
HA HA! AND NOW IT'S A DUNCE CAP!
CLUNK
darb

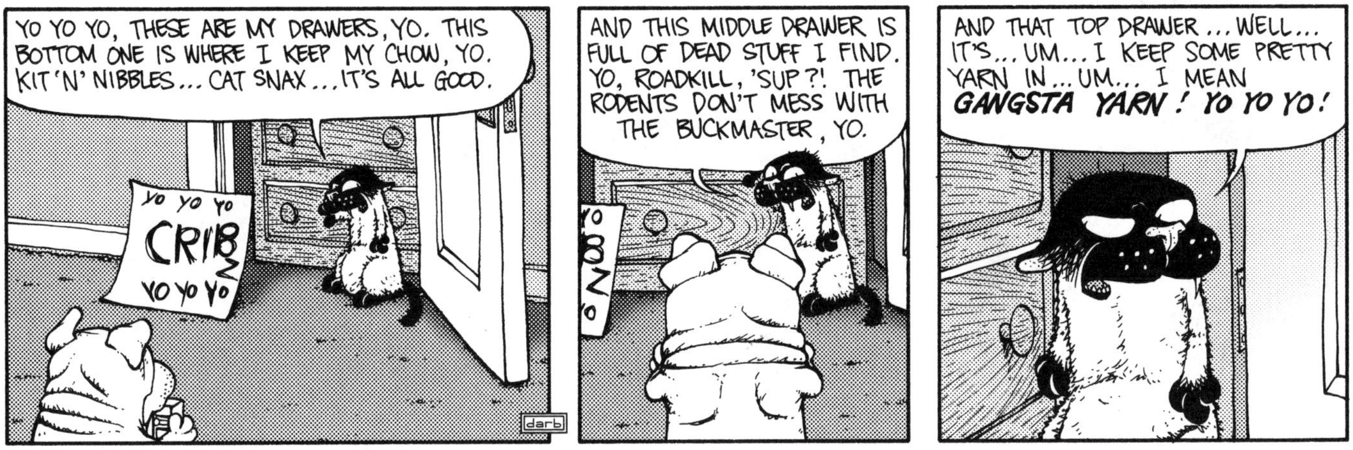
YO YO YO, THESE ARE MY DRAWERS, YO. THIS BOTTOM ONE IS WHERE I KEEP MY CHOW, YO. KIT 'N' NIBBLES... CAT SNAX... IT'S ALL GOOD.
YO YO YO
CRIBZ
YO YO YO
AND THIS MIDDLE DRAWER IS FULL OF DEAD STUFF I FIND. YO, ROADKILL, 'SUP?! THE RODENTS DON'T MESS WITH THE BUCKMASTER, YO.
AND THAT TOP DRAWER... WELL... IT'S... UM... I KEEP SOME PRETTY YARN IN... UM... I MEAN GANGSTA YARN! YO YO YO!
darb

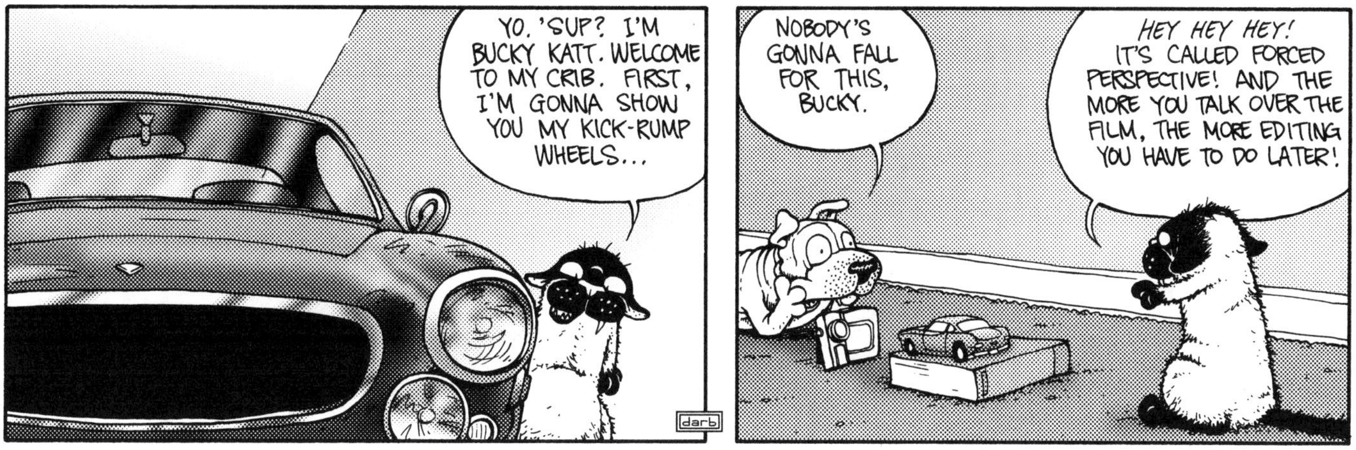
YO. 'SUP? I'M BUCKY KATT. WELCOME TO MY CRIB. FIRST, I'M GONNA SHOW YOU MY KICK-RUMP WHEELS...
NOBODY'S GONNA FALL FOR THIS, BUCKY.
HEY HEY HEY! IT'S CALLED FORCED PERSPECTIVE! AND THE MORE YOU TALK OVER THE FILM, THE MORE EDITING YOU HAVE TO DO LATER!
darb

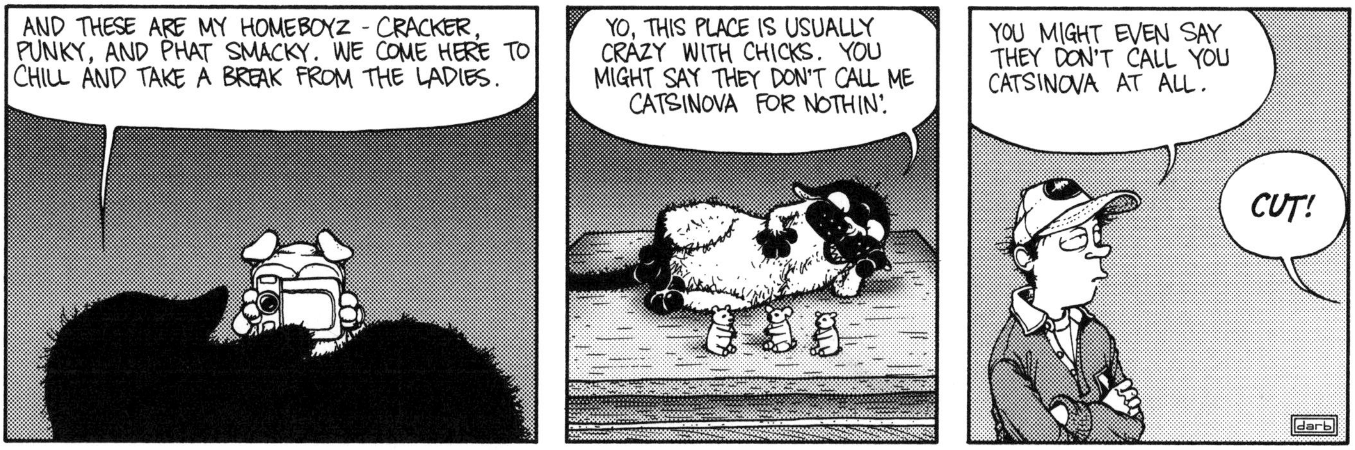
AND THESE ARE MY HOMEBOYZ - CRACKER, PUNKY, AND PHAT SMACKY. WE COME HERE TO CHILL AND TAKE A BREAK FROM THE LADIES.
YO, THIS PLACE IS USUALLY CRAZY WITH CHICKS. YOU MIGHT SAY THEY DON'T CALL ME CATSINOVA FOR NOTHIN'.
YOU MIGHT EVEN SAY THEY DON'T CALL YOU CATSINOVA AT ALL.
CUT!
darb

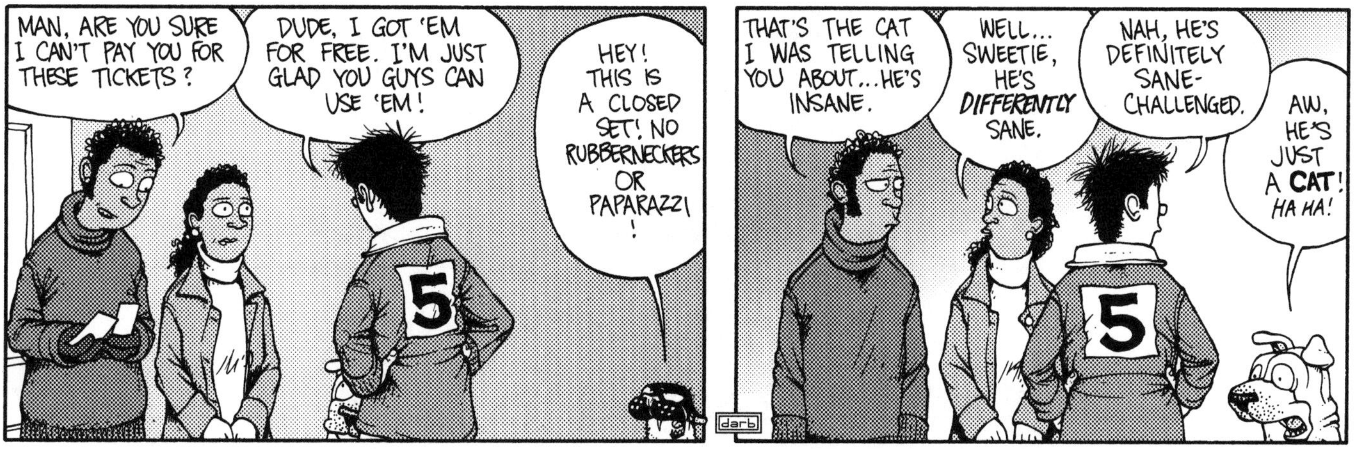
MAN, ARE YOU SURE I CAN'T PAY YOU FOR THESE TICKETS?
DUDE, I GOT 'EM FOR FREE. I'M JUST GLAD YOU GUYS CAN USE 'EM!
HEY! THIS IS A CLOSED SET! NO RUBBERNECKERS OR PAPARAZZI!
5
darb
THAT'S THE CAT I WAS TELLING YOU ABOUT...HE'S INSANE.
WELL... SWEETIE, HE'S DIFFERENTLY SANE.
NAH, HE'S DEFINITELY SANE-CHALLENGED.
AW, HE'S JUST A CAT! HA HA!
5

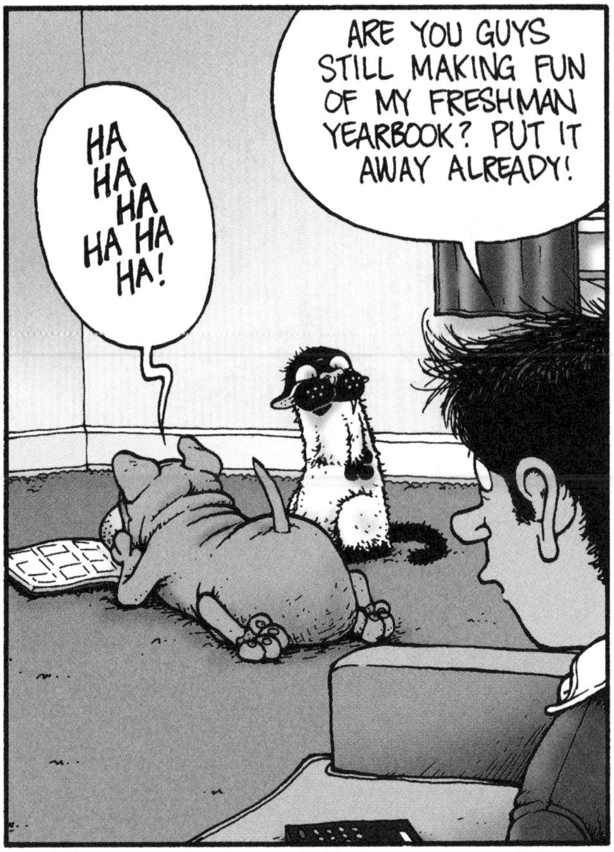
ARE YOU GUYS STILL MAKING FUN OF MY FRESHMAN YEARBOOK? PUT IT AWAY ALREADY!
HA HA HA HA HA HA!

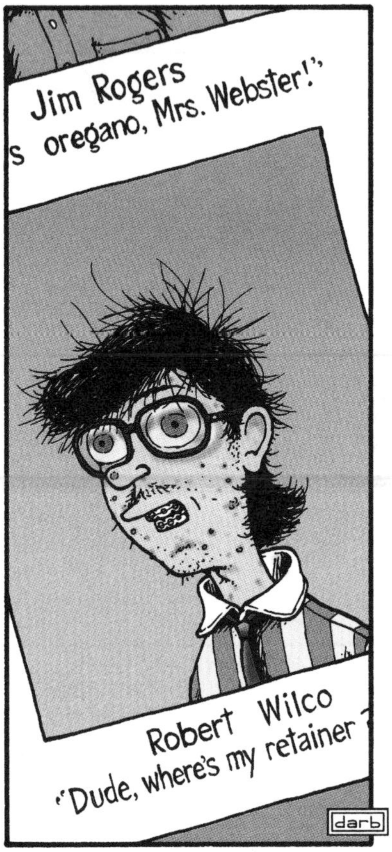
Jim Rogers
s oregano, Mrs. Webster!"
Robert Wilco
"Dude, where's my retainer
darb

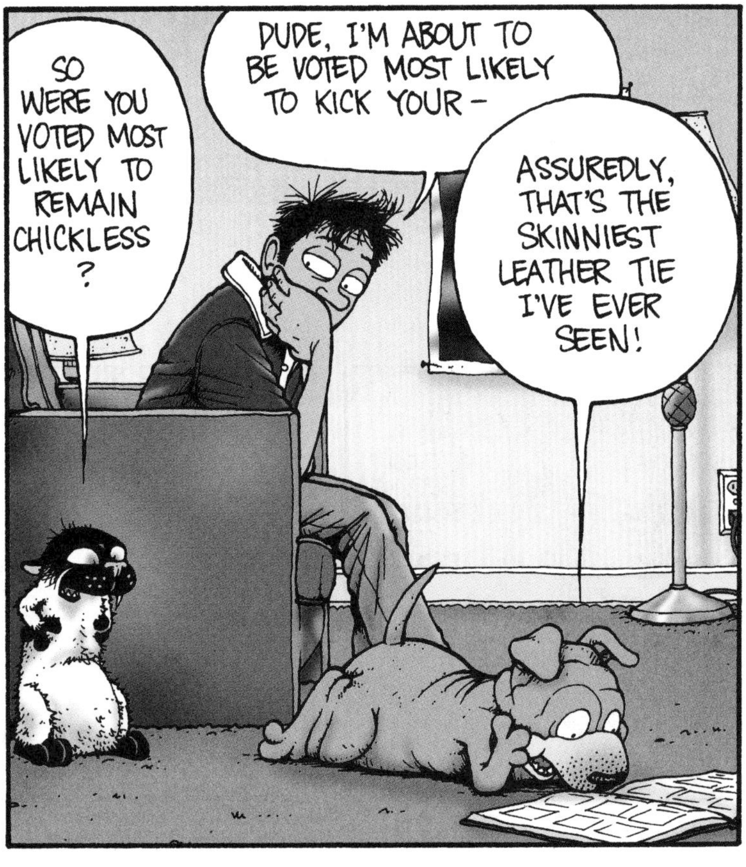
SO WERE YOU VOTED MOST LIKELY TO REMAIN CHICKLESS?
DUDE, I'M ABOUT TO BE VOTED MOST LIKELY TO KICK YOUR–
ASSUREDLY, THAT'S THE SKINNIEST LEATHER TIE I'VE EVER SEEN!

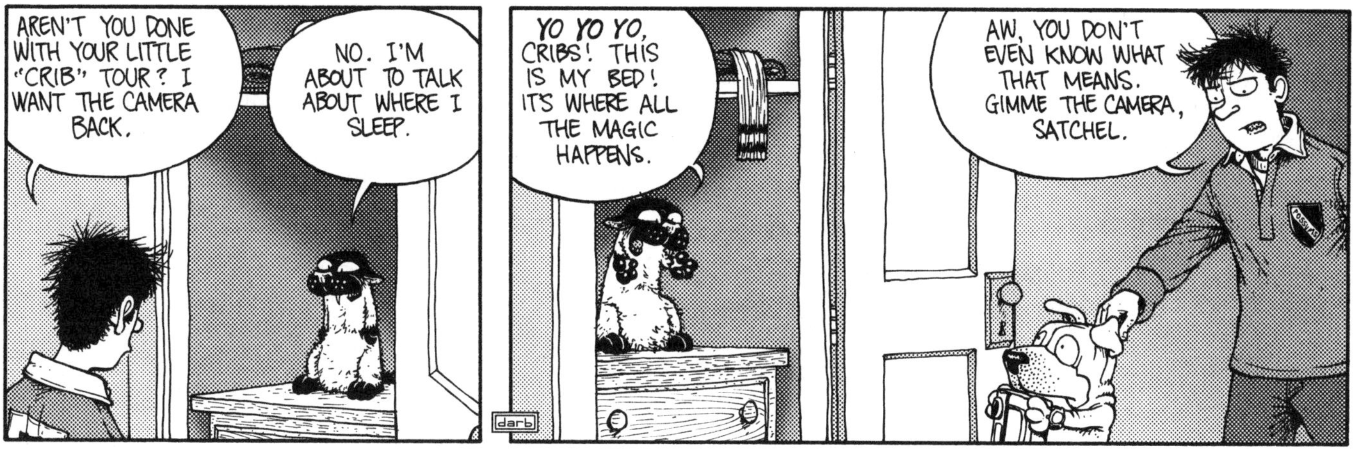
AREN'T YOU DONE WITH YOUR LITTLE "CRIB" TOUR? I WANT THE CAMERA BACK.
NO. I'M ABOUT TO TALK ABOUT WHERE I SLEEP.
YO YO YO, CRIBS! THIS IS MY BED! IT'S WHERE ALL THE MAGIC HAPPENS.
AW, YOU DON'T EVEN KNOW WHAT THAT MEANS. GIMME THE CAMERA, SATCHEL.
darb

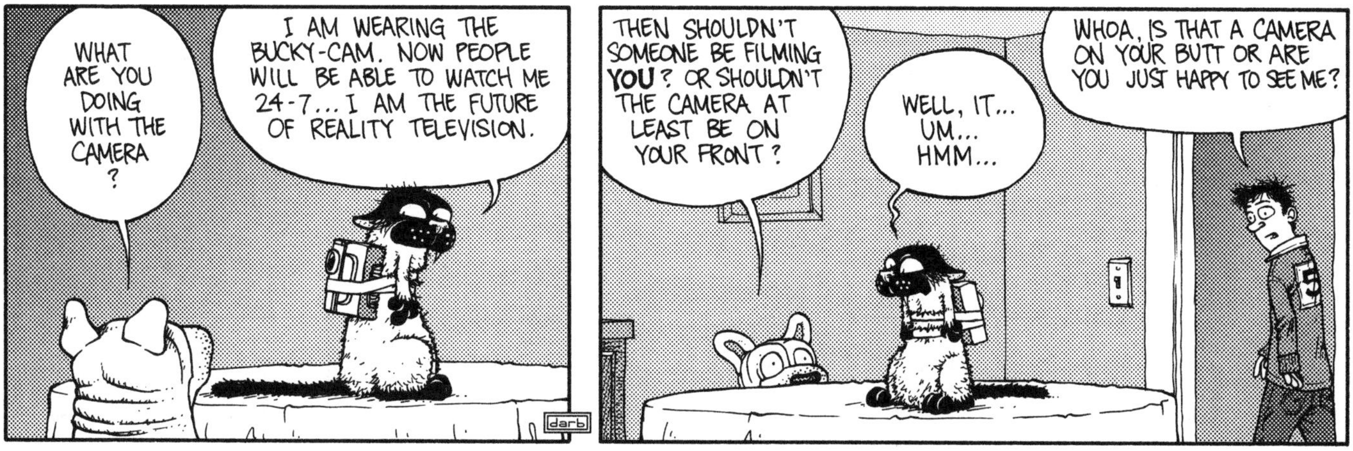
WHAT ARE YOU DOING WITH THE CAMERA?
I AM WEARING THE BUCKY-CAM. NOW PEOPLE WILL BE ABLE TO WATCH ME 24-7... I AM THE FUTURE OF REALITY TELEVISION.
darb
THEN SHOULDN'T SOMEONE BE FILMING **YOU**? OR SHOULDN'T THE CAMERA AT LEAST BE ON YOUR FRONT?
WELL, IT... UM... HMM...
WHOA, IS THAT A CAMERA ON YOUR BUTT OR ARE YOU JUST HAPPY TO SEE ME?

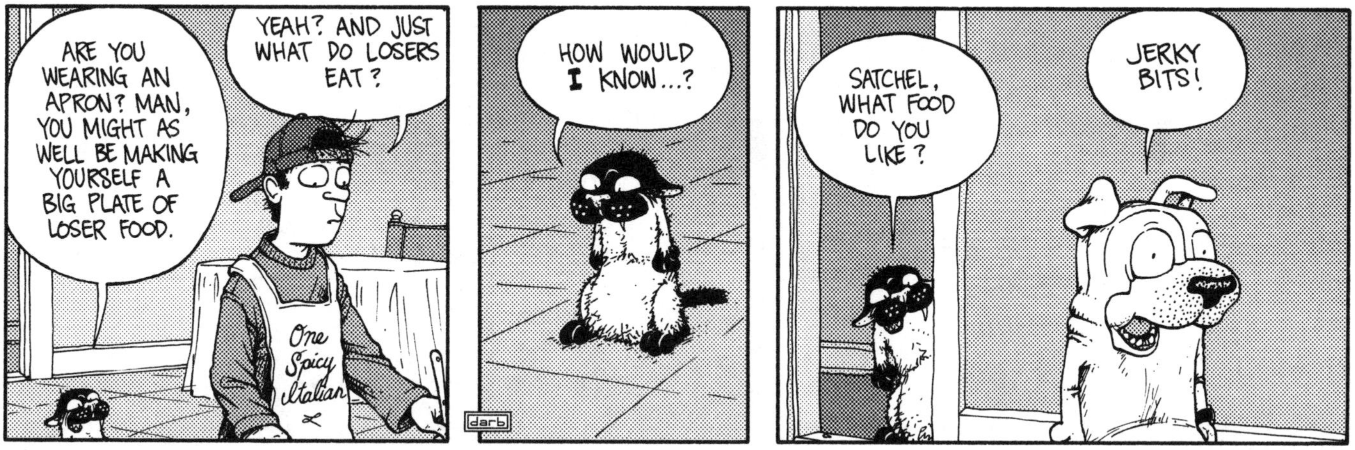
ARE YOU WEARING AN APRON? MAN, YOU MIGHT AS WELL BE MAKING YOURSELF A BIG PLATE OF LOSER FOOD.
YEAH? AND JUST WHAT DO LOSERS EAT?
One Spicy Italian
HOW WOULD **I** KNOW...?
darb
SATCHEL, WHAT FOOD DO YOU LIKE?
JERKY BITS!

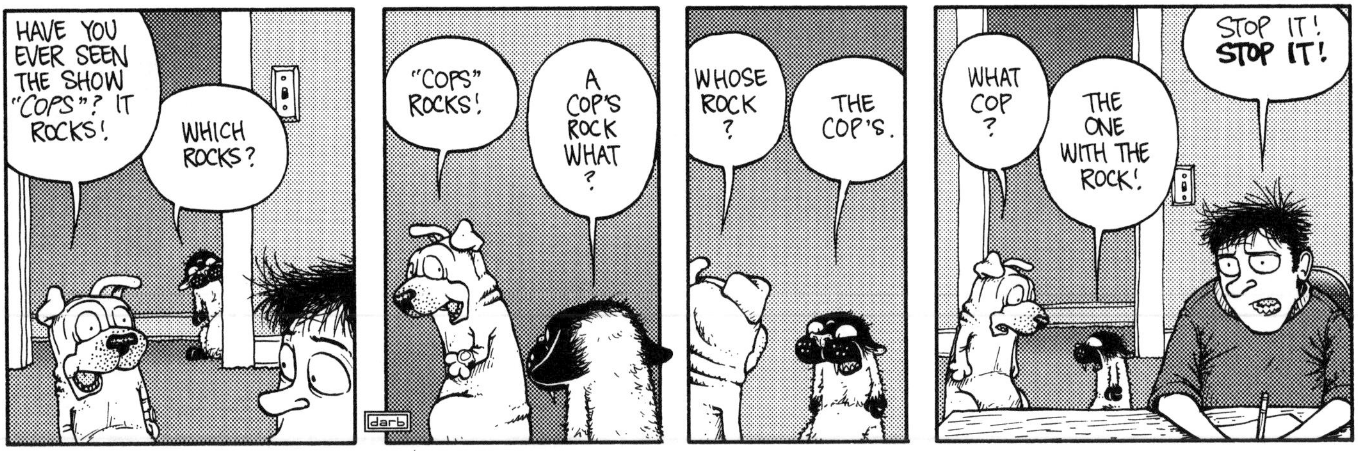
HAVE YOU EVER SEEN THE SHOW "COPS"? IT ROCKS!
WHICH ROCKS?
darb
"COPS" ROCKS!
A COP'S ROCK WHAT?
WHOSE ROCK?
THE COP'S.
WHAT COP?
THE ONE WITH THE ROCK!
STOP IT! **STOP IT!**

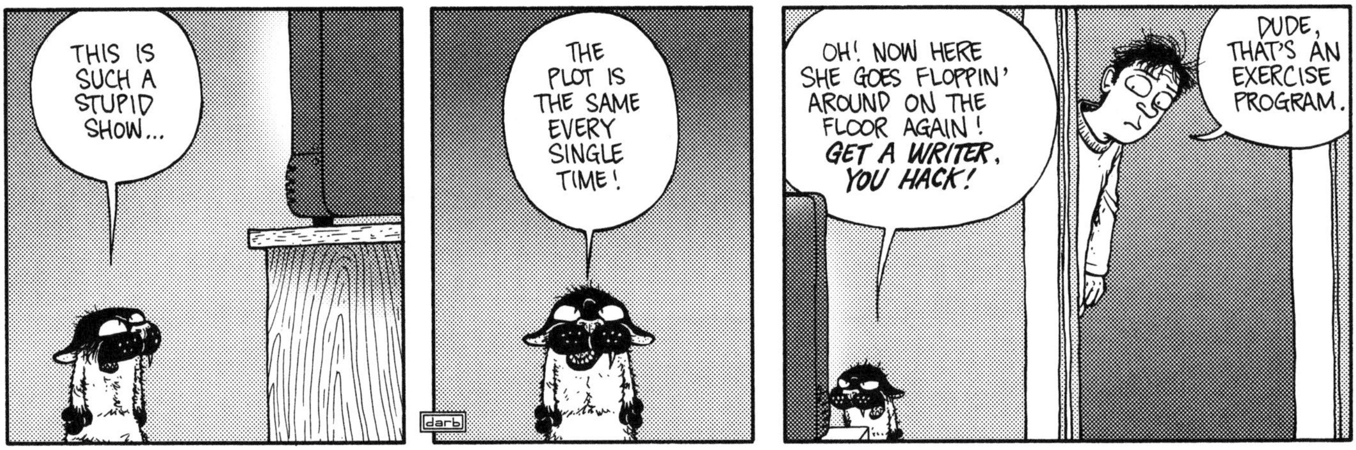
THIS IS SUCH A STUPID SHOW...
darb
THE PLOT IS THE SAME EVERY SINGLE TIME!
OH! NOW HERE SHE GOES FLOPPIN' AROUND ON THE FLOOR AGAIN! ***GET A WRITER, YOU HACK!***
DUDE, THAT'S AN EXERCISE PROGRAM.

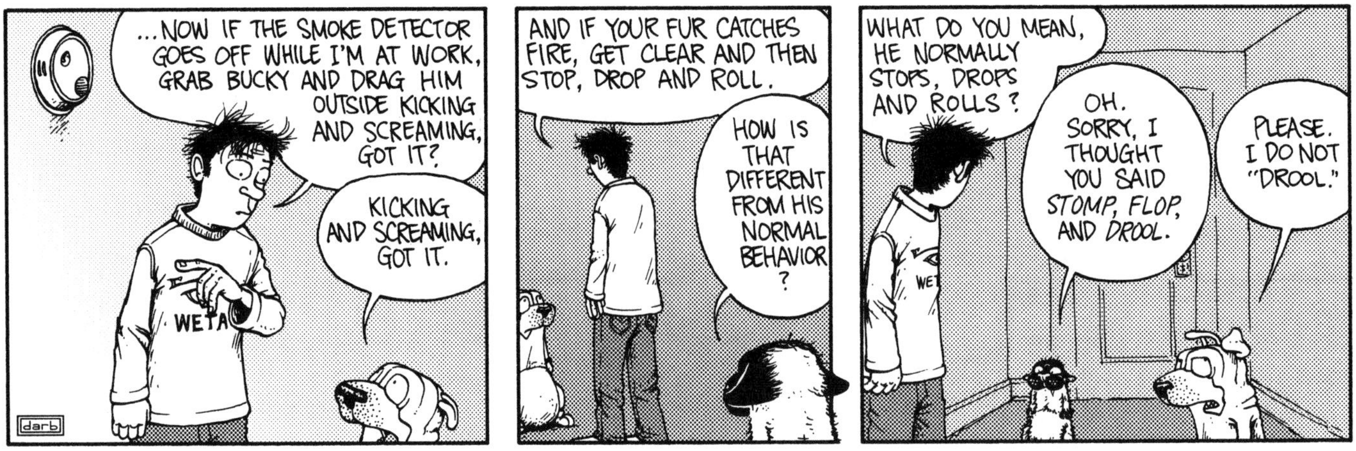
...NOW IF THE SMOKE DETECTOR GOES OFF WHILE I'M AT WORK, GRAB BUCKY AND DRAG HIM OUTSIDE KICKING AND SCREAMING, GOT IT?
KICKING AND SCREAMING, GOT IT.
WETA
darb
AND IF YOUR FUR CATCHES FIRE, GET CLEAR AND THEN STOP, DROP AND ROLL.
HOW IS THAT DIFFERENT FROM HIS NORMAL BEHAVIOR?
WHAT DO YOU MEAN, HE NORMALLY STOPS, DROPS AND ROLLS?
OH. SORRY, I THOUGHT YOU SAID *STOMP, FLOP,* AND *DROOL.*
PLEASE. I DO NOT "DROOL."

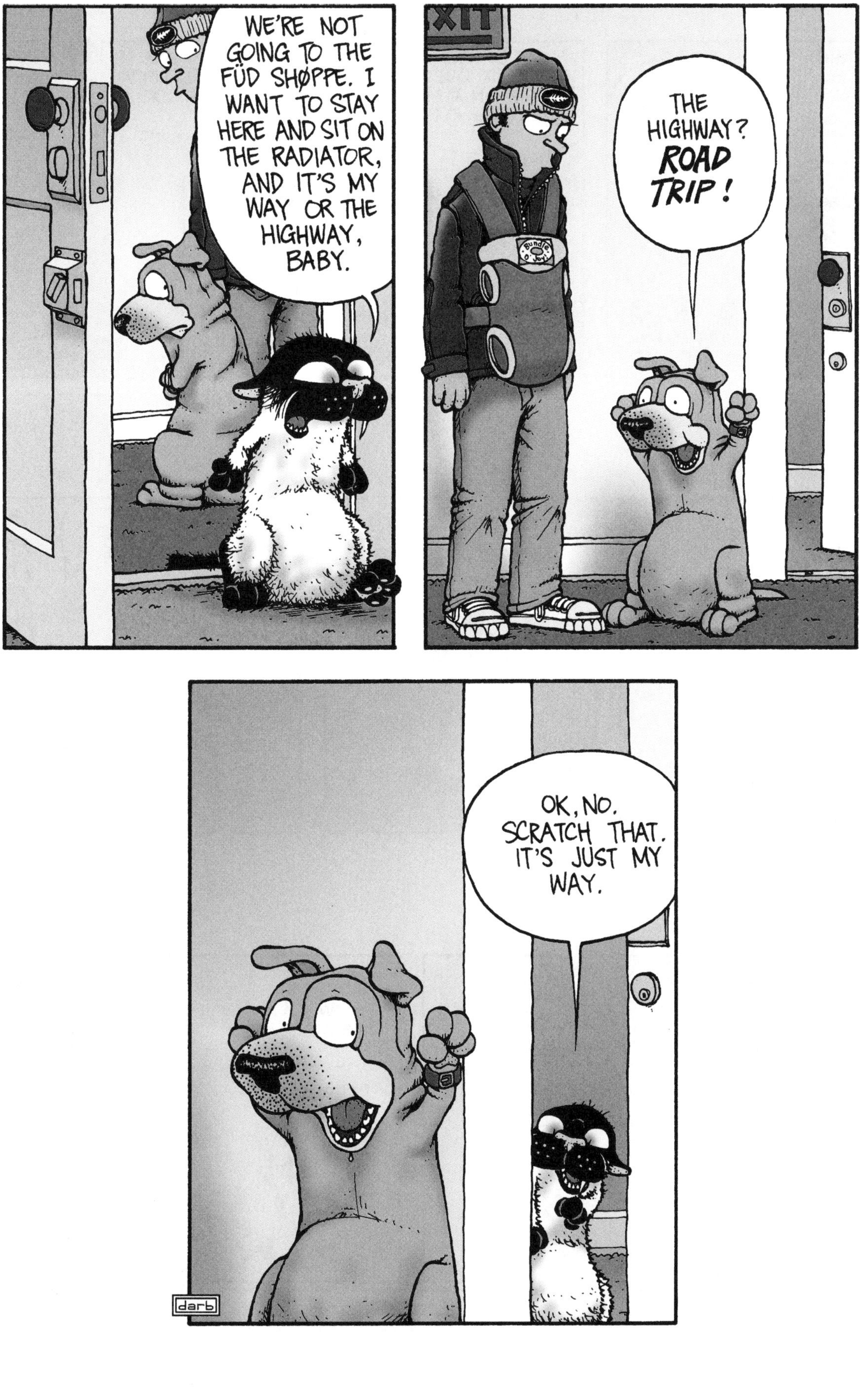
WE'RE NOT GOING TO THE FÜD SHØPPE. I WANT TO STAY HERE AND SIT ON THE RADIATOR, AND IT'S MY WAY OR THE HIGHWAY, BABY.
THE HIGHWAY? ROAD TRIP!
OK, NO. SCRATCH THAT. IT'S JUST MY WAY.

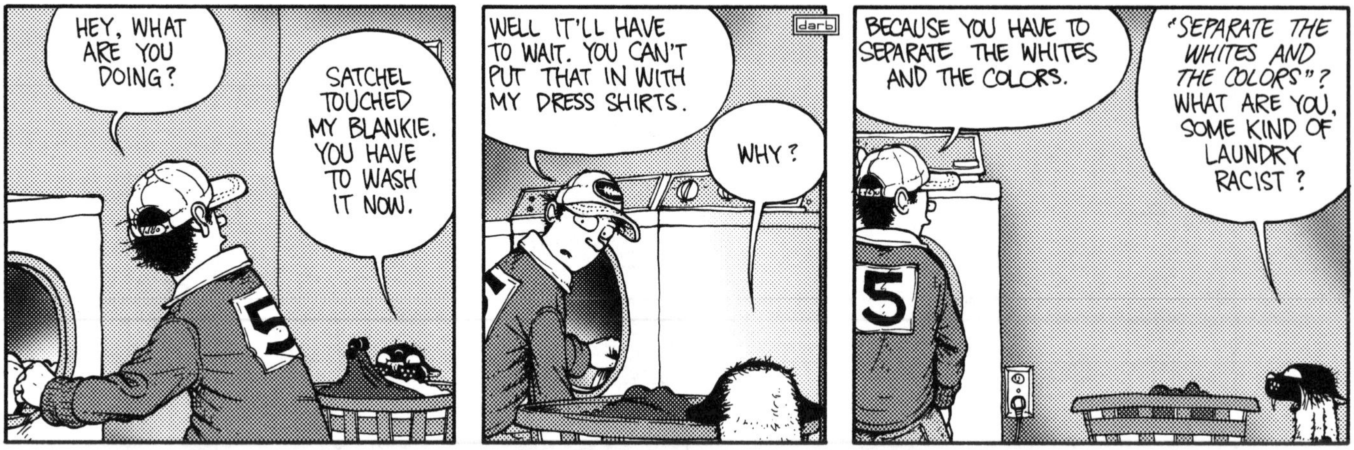
HEY, WHAT ARE YOU DOING?
SATCHEL TOUCHED MY BLANKIE. YOU HAVE TO WASH IT NOW.
WELL IT'LL HAVE TO WAIT. YOU CAN'T PUT THAT IN WITH MY DRESS SHIRTS.
WHY?
BECAUSE YOU HAVE TO SEPARATE THE WHITES AND THE COLORS.
"SEPARATE THE WHITES AND THE COLORS"? WHAT ARE YOU, SOME KIND OF LAUNDRY RACIST?
darb

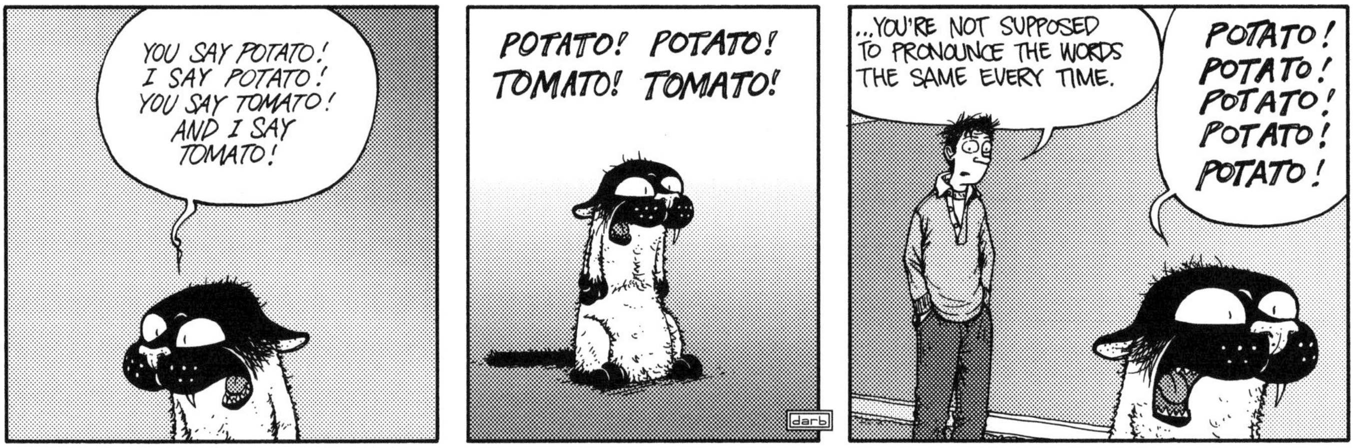
YOU SAY POTATO! I SAY POTATO! YOU SAY TOMATO! AND I SAY TOMATO!
POTATO! POTATO! TOMATO! TOMATO!
darb
...YOU'RE NOT SUPPOSED TO PRONOUNCE THE WORDS THE SAME EVERY TIME.
POTATO! POTATO! POTATO! POTATO! POTATO!

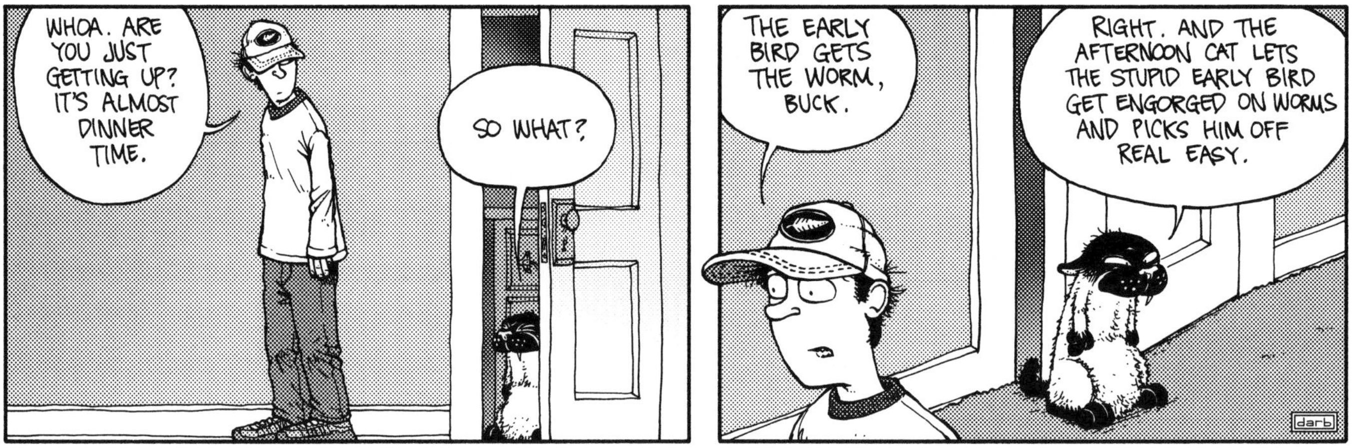
WHOA. ARE YOU JUST GETTING UP? IT'S ALMOST DINNER TIME.
SO WHAT?
THE EARLY BIRD GETS THE WORM, BUCK.
RIGHT. AND THE AFTERNOON CAT LETS THE STUPID EARLY BIRD GET ENGORGED ON WORMS AND PICKS HIM OFF REAL EASY.
darb

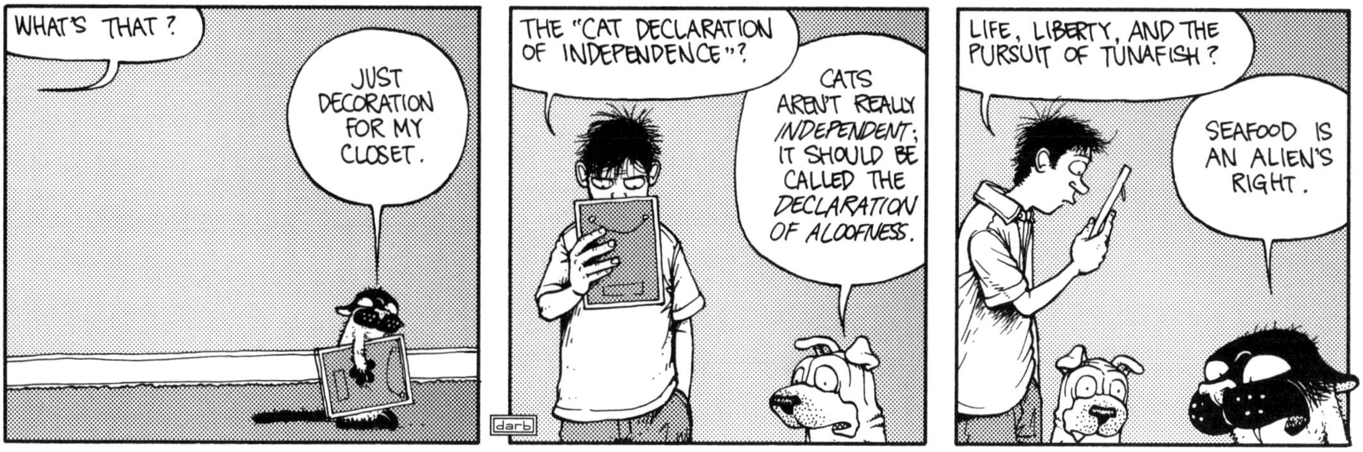
WHAT'S THAT?
JUST DECORATION FOR MY CLOSET.
THE "CAT DECLARATION OF INDEPENDENCE"?
CATS AREN'T REALLY *INDEPENDENT*; IT SHOULD BE CALLED THE *DECLARATION OF ALOOFNESS*.
LIFE, LIBERTY, AND THE PURSUIT OF TUNAFISH?
SEAFOOD IS AN ALIEN'S RIGHT.
darb

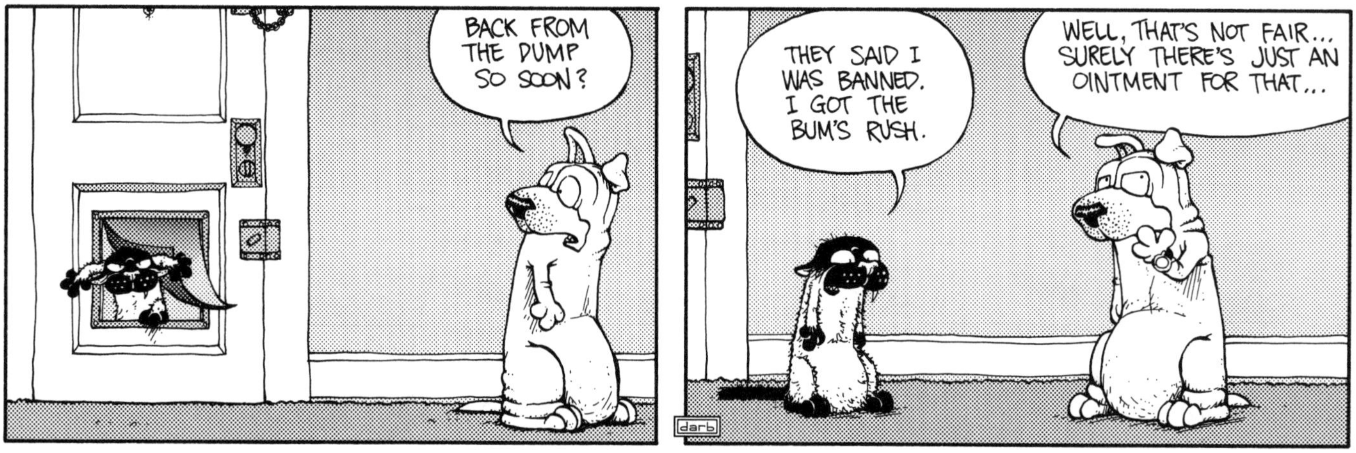
BACK FROM THE DUMP SO SOON?
THEY SAID I WAS BANNED. I GOT THE BUM'S RUSH.
WELL, THAT'S NOT FAIR... SURELY THERE'S JUST AN OINTMENT FOR THAT...
darb

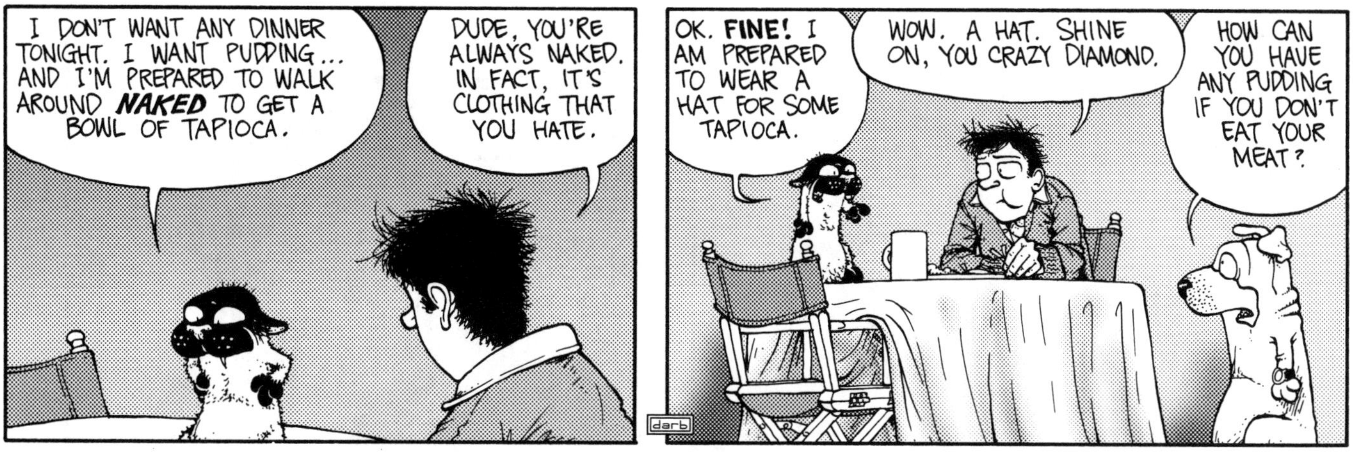
I DON'T WANT ANY DINNER TONIGHT. I WANT PUDDING... AND I'M PREPARED TO WALK AROUND ***NAKED*** TO GET A BOWL OF TAPIOCA.
DUDE, YOU'RE ALWAYS NAKED. IN FACT, IT'S CLOTHING THAT YOU HATE.
OK. **FINE!** I AM PREPARED TO WEAR A HAT FOR SOME TAPIOCA.
WOW. A HAT. SHINE ON, YOU CRAZY DIAMOND.
HOW CAN YOU HAVE ANY PUDDING IF YOU DON'T EAT YOUR MEAT?
darb

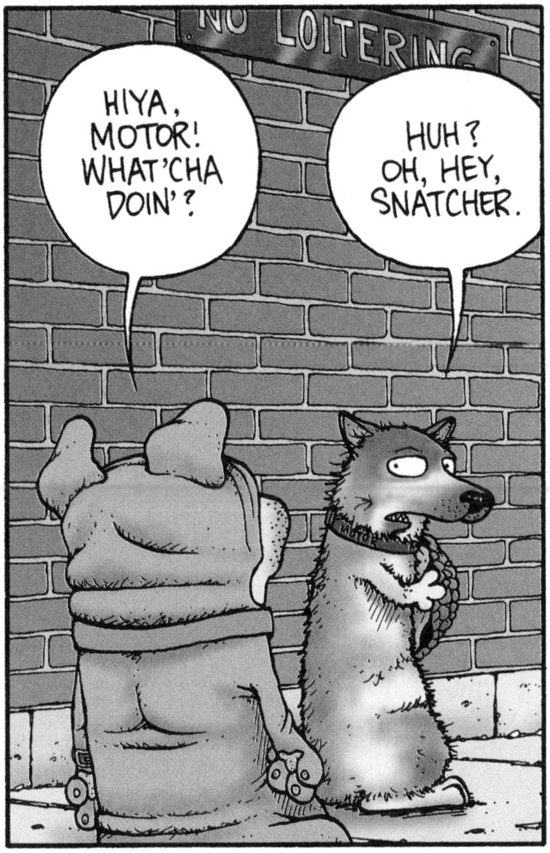
NO LOITERING
HIYA, MOTOR! WHAT'CHA DOIN'?
HUH? OH, HEY, SNATCHER.

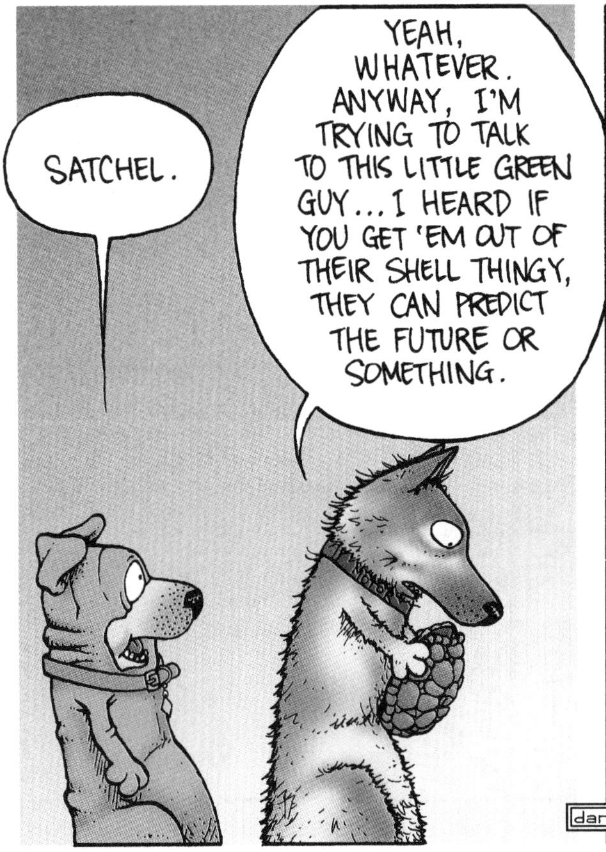
SATCHEL.
YEAH, WHATEVER. ANYWAY, I'M TRYING TO TALK TO THIS LITTLE GREEN GUY... I HEARD IF YOU GET 'EM OUT OF THEIR SHELL THINGY, THEY CAN PREDICT THE FUTURE OR SOMETHING.
darb

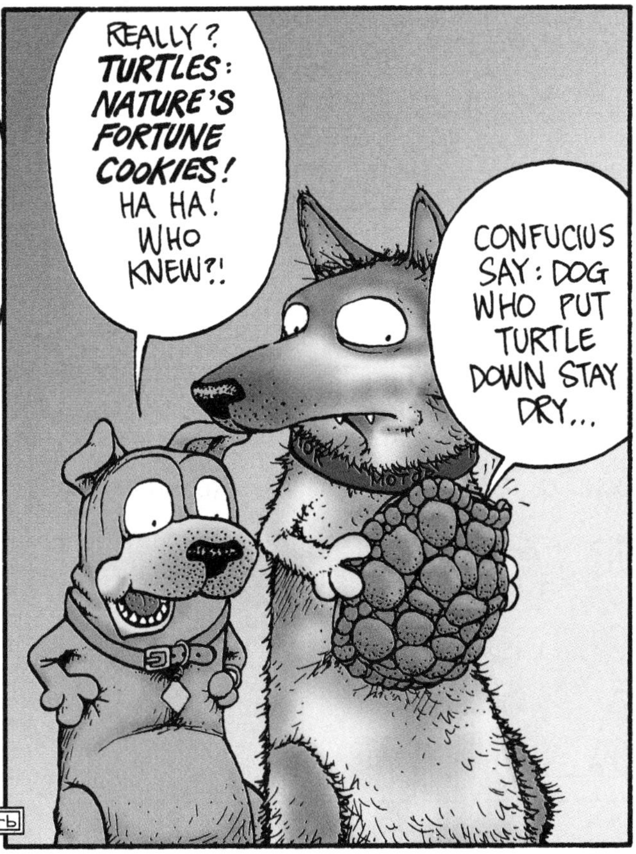
REALLY? **TURTLES: NATURE'S FORTUNE COOKIES!** HA HA! WHO KNEW?!
CONFUCIUS SAY: DOG WHO PUT TURTLE DOWN STAY DRY...

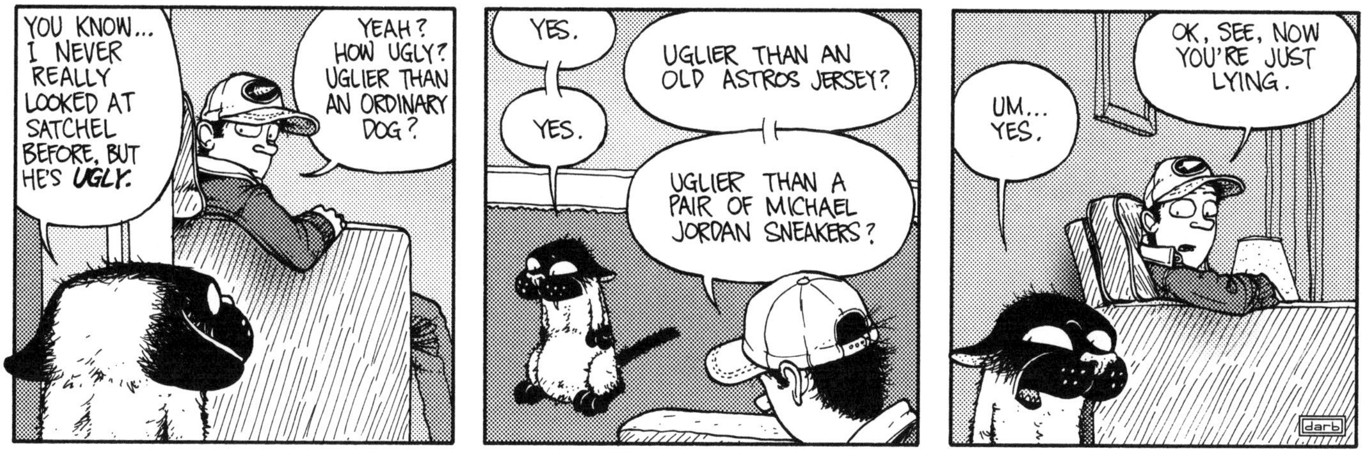
YOU KNOW... I NEVER REALLY LOOKED AT SATCHEL BEFORE, BUT HE'S **UGLY.**
YEAH? HOW UGLY? UGLIER THAN AN ORDINARY DOG?
YES.
UGLIER THAN AN OLD ASTROS JERSEY?
YES.
UGLIER THAN A PAIR OF MICHAEL JORDAN SNEAKERS?
UM... YES.
OK, SEE, NOW YOU'RE JUST LYING.
darb

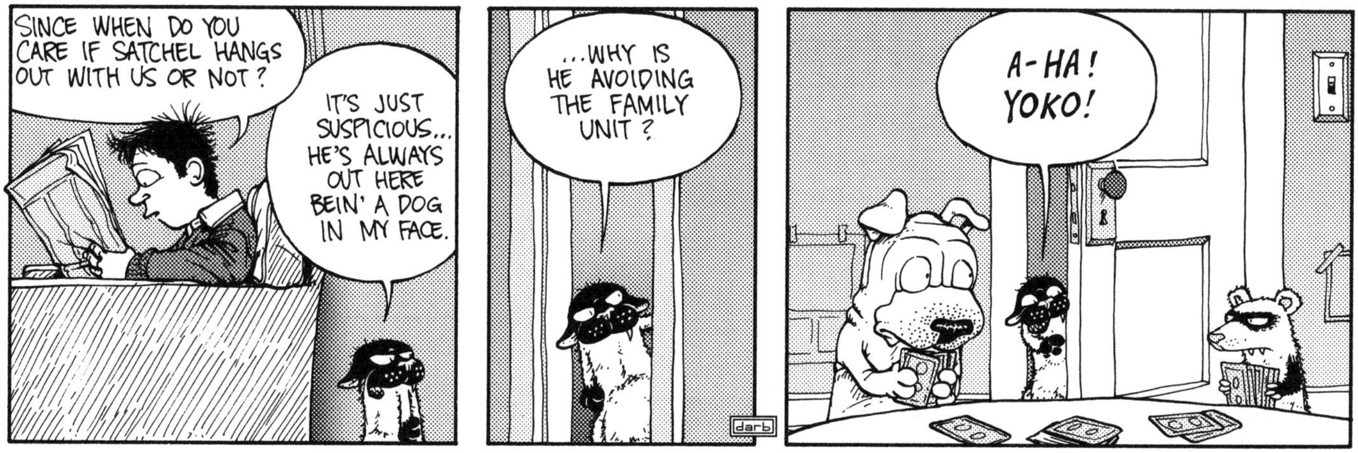
SINCE WHEN DO YOU CARE IF SATCHEL HANGS OUT WITH US OR NOT?
IT'S JUST SUSPICIOUS... HE'S ALWAYS OUT HERE BEIN' A DOG IN MY FACE.
...WHY IS HE AVOIDING THE FAMILY UNIT?
darb
A-HA! YOKO!

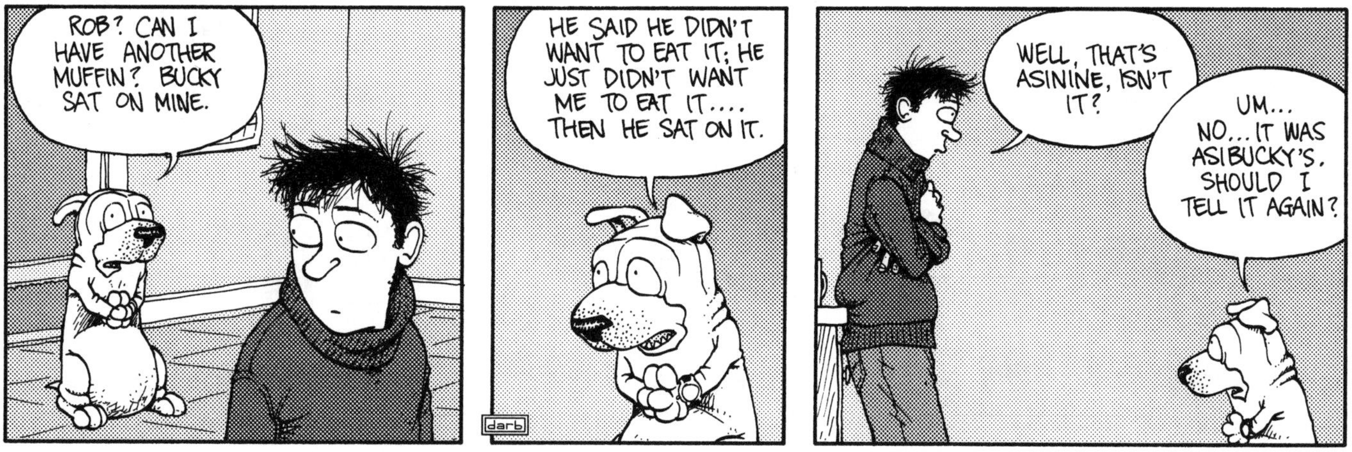
ROB? CAN I HAVE ANOTHER MUFFIN? BUCKY SAT ON MINE.
HE SAID HE DIDN'T WANT TO EAT IT; HE JUST DIDN'T WANT ME TO EAT IT.... THEN HE SAT ON IT.
darb
WELL, THAT'S ASININE, ISN'T IT?
UM... NO... IT WAS ASIBUCKY'S. SHOULD I TELL IT AGAIN?

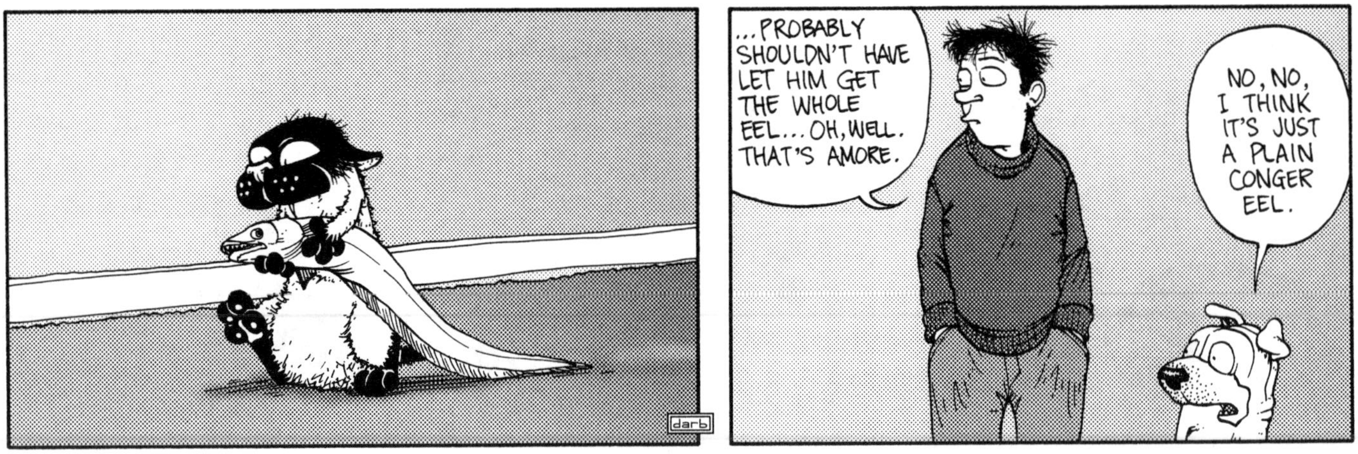
...PROBABLY SHOULDN'T HAVE LET HIM GET THE WHOLE EEL...OH, WELL. THAT'S AMORE.
NO, NO, I THINK IT'S JUST A PLAIN CONGER EEL.
darb

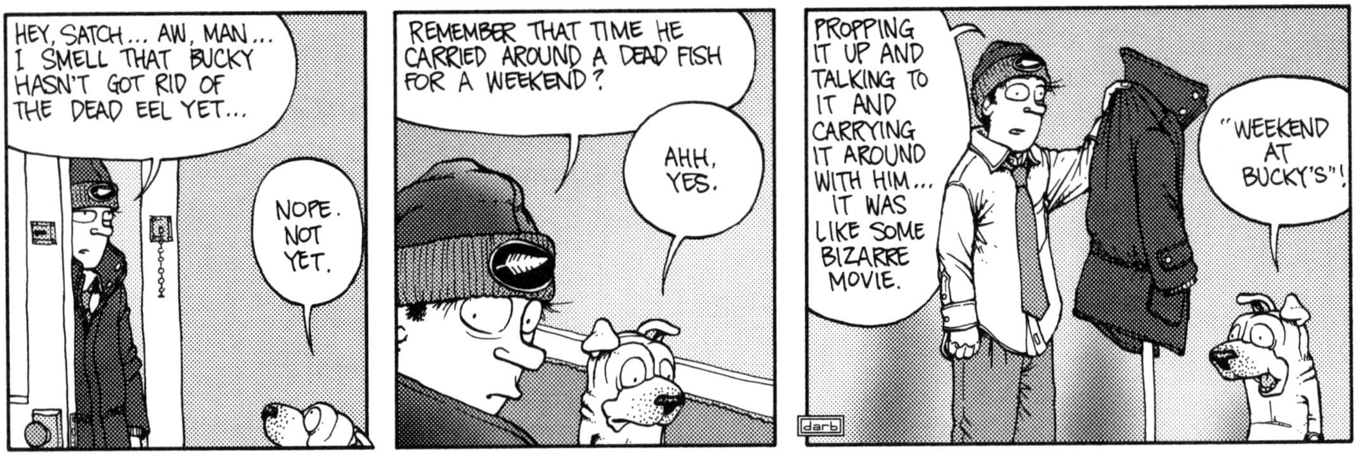
HEY, SATCH... AW, MAN... I SMELL THAT BUCKY HASN'T GOT RID OF THE DEAD EEL YET...
NOPE. NOT YET.
REMEMBER THAT TIME HE CARRIED AROUND A DEAD FISH FOR A WEEKEND?
AHH, YES.
PROPPING IT UP AND TALKING TO IT AND CARRYING IT AROUND WITH HIM... IT WAS LIKE SOME BIZARRE MOVIE.
"WEEKEND AT BUCKY'S"!
darb

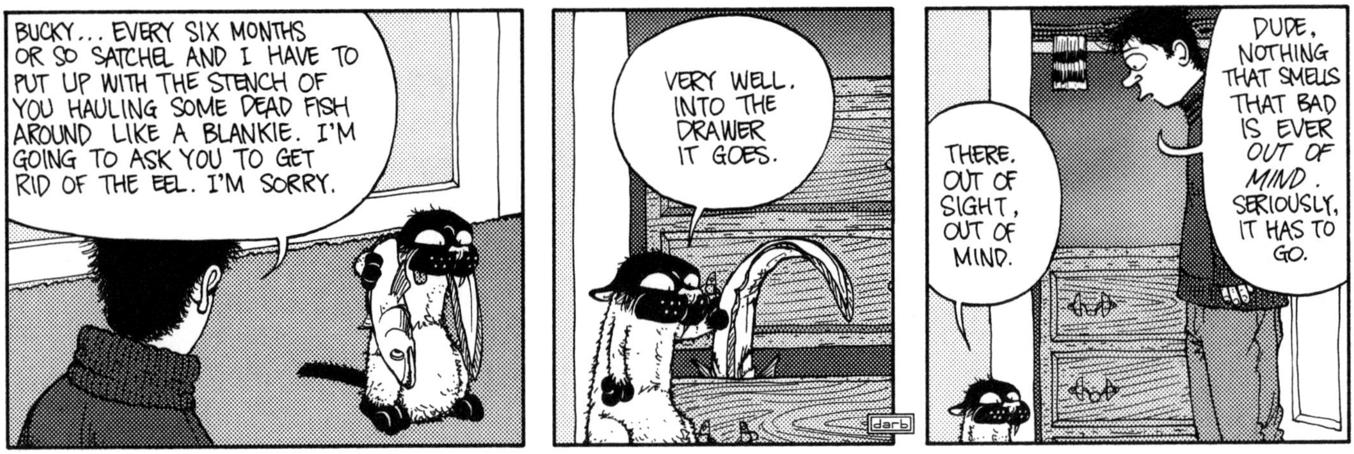
BUCKY... EVERY SIX MONTHS OR SO SATCHEL AND I HAVE TO PUT UP WITH THE STENCH OF YOU HAULING SOME DEAD FISH AROUND LIKE A BLANKIE. I'M GOING TO ASK YOU TO GET RID OF THE EEL. I'M SORRY.
VERY WELL. INTO THE DRAWER IT GOES.
THERE. OUT OF SIGHT, OUT OF MIND.
DUDE, NOTHING THAT SMELLS THAT BAD IS EVER *OUT OF MIND*. SERIOUSLY, IT HAS TO GO.
darb

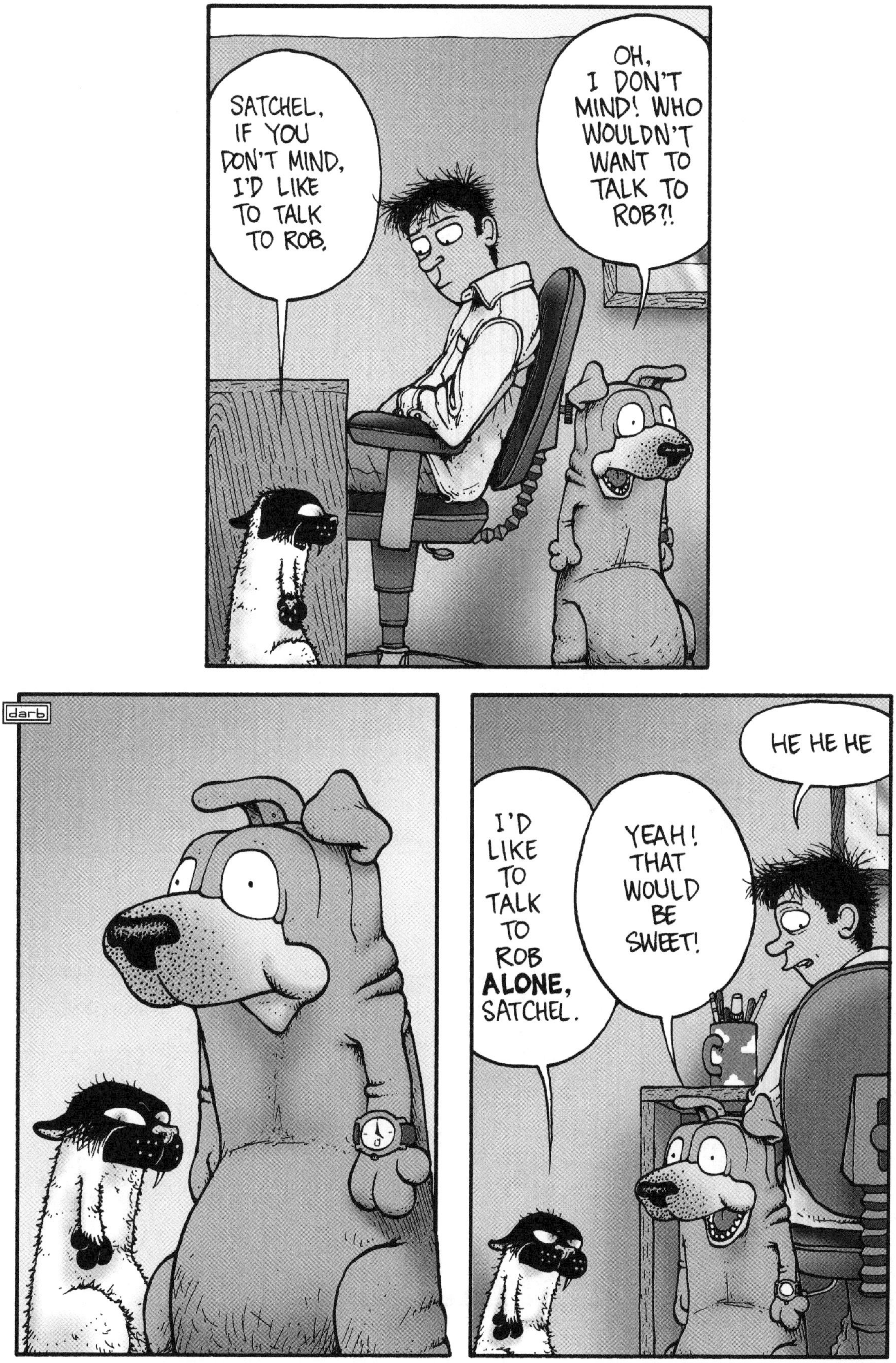
SATCHEL, IF YOU DON'T MIND, I'D LIKE TO TALK TO ROB.
OH, I DON'T MIND! WHO WOULDN'T WANT TO TALK TO ROB?!
darb
I'D LIKE TO TALK TO ROB **ALONE,** SATCHEL.
YEAH! THAT WOULD BE SWEET!
HE HE HE

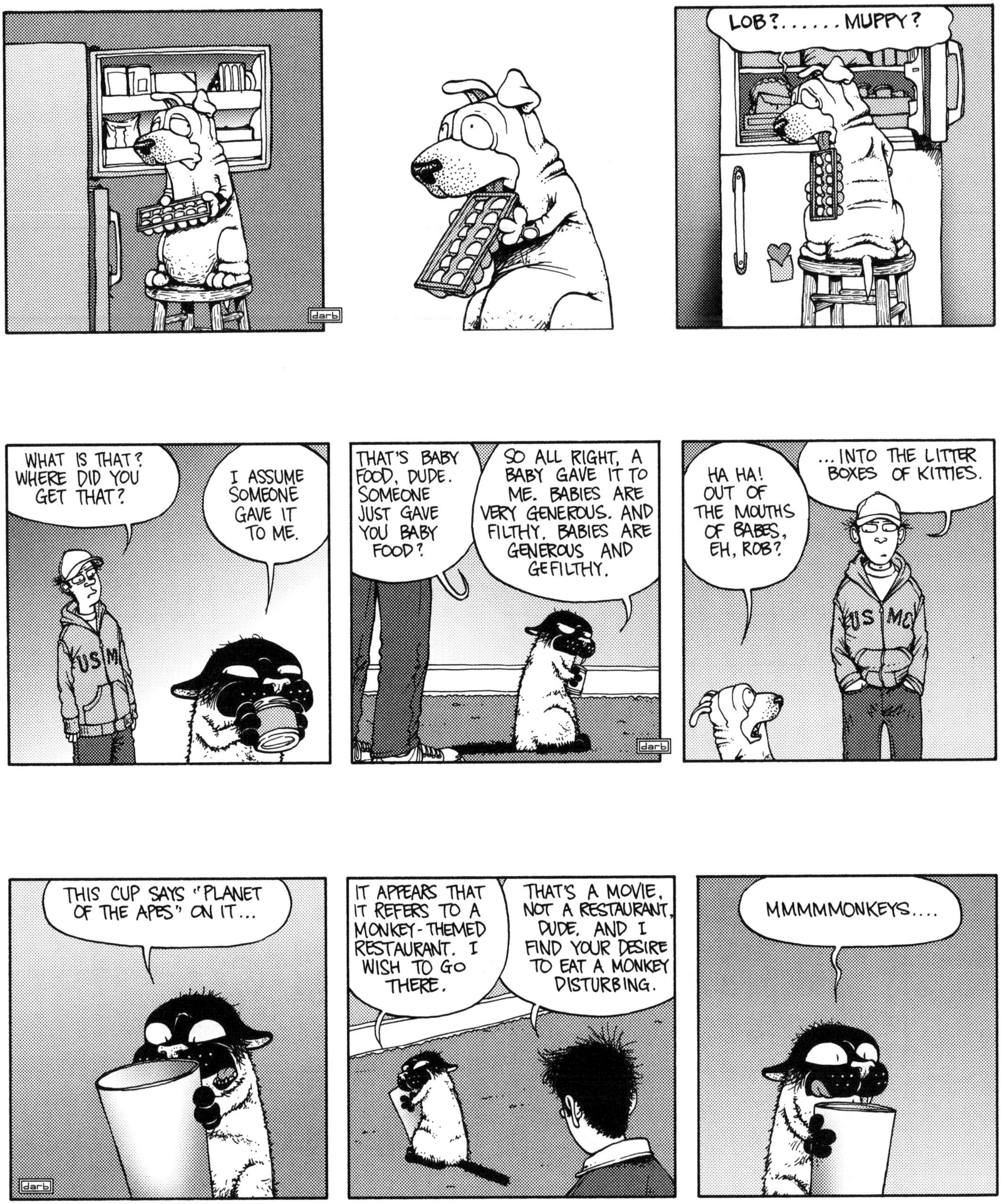
darb
LOB?......MUPPY?
WHAT IS THAT? WHERE DID YOU GET THAT?
I ASSUME SOMEONE GAVE IT TO ME.
THAT'S BABY FOOD, DUDE. SOMEONE JUST GAVE YOU BABY FOOD?
SO ALL RIGHT, A BABY GAVE IT TO ME. BABIES ARE VERY GENEROUS. AND FILTHY. BABIES ARE GENEROUS AND GEFILTHY.
darb
HA HA! OUT OF THE MOUTHS OF BABES, EH, ROB?
...INTO THE LITTER BOXES OF KITTIES.
THIS CUP SAYS "PLANET OF THE APES" ON IT...
darb
IT APPEARS THAT IT REFERS TO A MONKEY-THEMED RESTAURANT. I WISH TO GO THERE.
THAT'S A MOVIE, NOT A RESTAURANT, DUDE. AND I FIND YOUR DESIRE TO EAT A MONKEY DISTURBING.
MMMMMONKEYS....

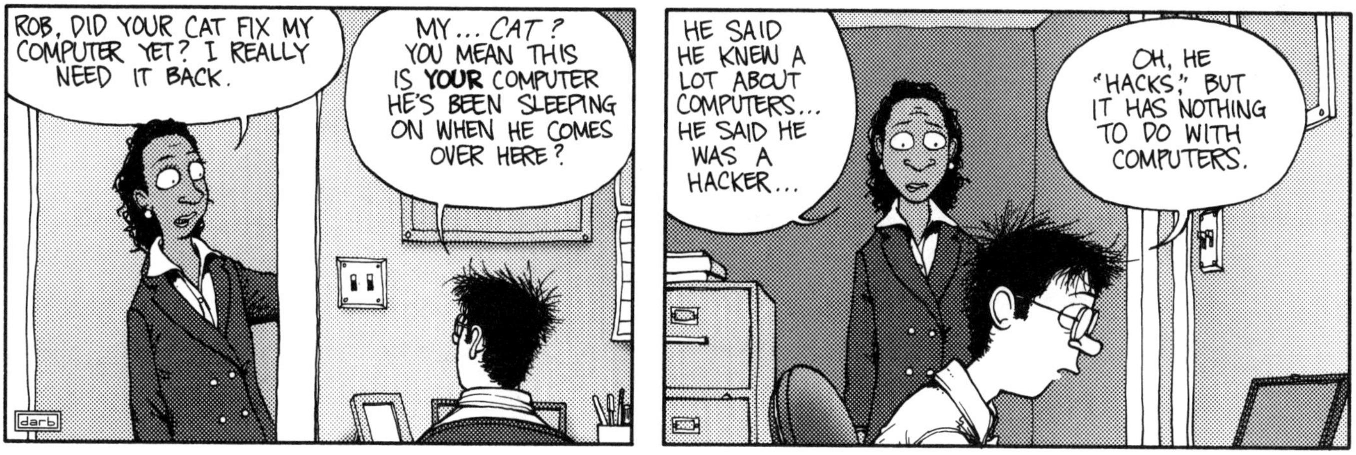
ROB, DID YOUR CAT FIX MY COMPUTER YET? I REALLY NEED IT BACK.
MY... *CAT*? YOU MEAN THIS IS **YOUR** COMPUTER HE'S BEEN SLEEPING ON WHEN HE COMES OVER HERE?
darb
HE SAID HE KNEW A LOT ABOUT COMPUTERS... HE SAID HE WAS A HACKER...
OH, HE "HACKS," BUT IT HAS NOTHING TO DO WITH COMPUTERS.

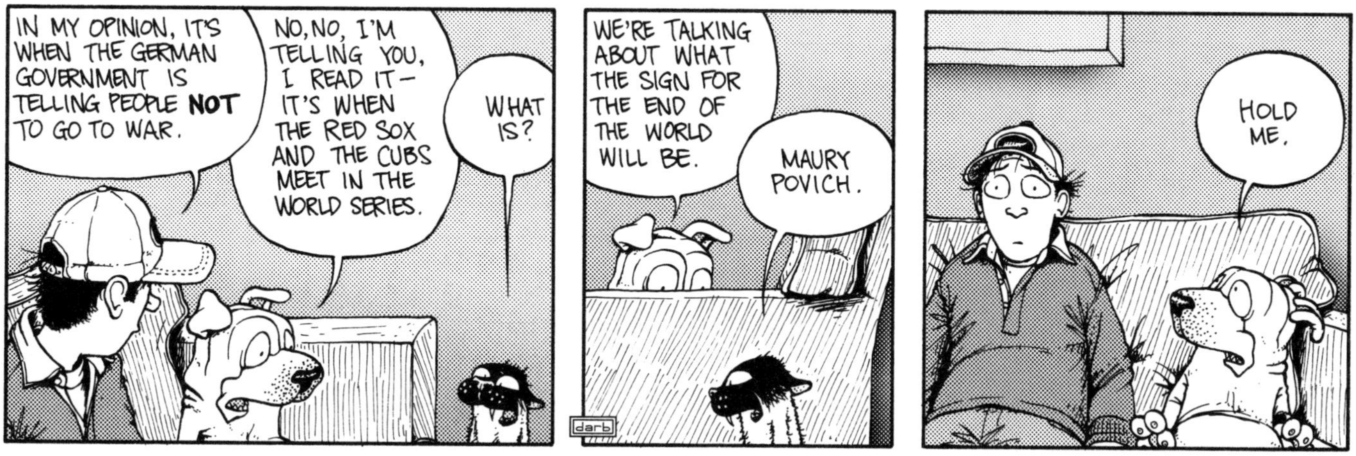
IN MY OPINION, IT'S WHEN THE GERMAN GOVERNMENT IS TELLING PEOPLE **NOT** TO GO TO WAR.
NO, NO, I'M TELLING YOU, I READ IT— IT'S WHEN THE RED SOX AND THE CUBS MEET IN THE WORLD SERIES.
WHAT IS?
darb
WE'RE TALKING ABOUT WHAT THE SIGN FOR THE END OF THE WORLD WILL BE.
MAURY POVICH.
HOLD ME.

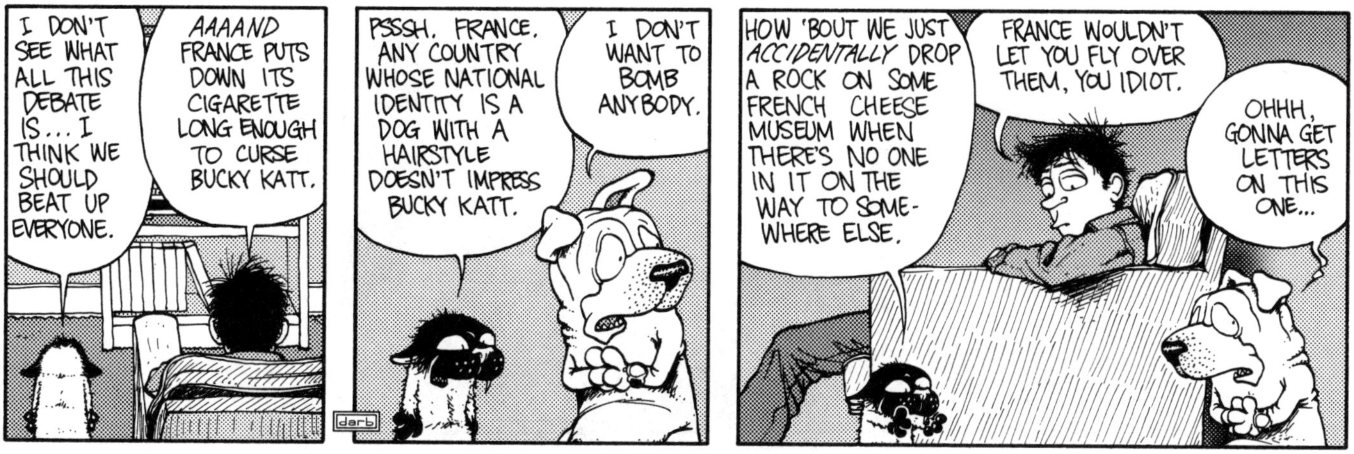
I DON'T SEE WHAT ALL THIS DEBATE IS... I THINK WE SHOULD BEAT UP EVERYONE.
AAAAND FRANCE PUTS DOWN ITS CIGARETTE LONG ENOUGH TO CURSE BUCKY KATT.
darb
PSSSH. FRANCE. ANY COUNTRY WHOSE NATIONAL IDENTITY IS A DOG WITH A HAIRSTYLE DOESN'T IMPRESS BUCKY KATT.
I DON'T WANT TO BOMB ANYBODY.
HOW 'BOUT WE JUST *ACCIDENTALLY* DROP A ROCK ON SOME FRENCH CHEESE MUSEUM WHEN THERE'S NO ONE IN IT ON THE WAY TO SOME-WHERE ELSE.
FRANCE WOULDN'T LET YOU FLY OVER THEM, YOU IDIOT.
OHHH, GONNA GET LETTERS ON THIS ONE...

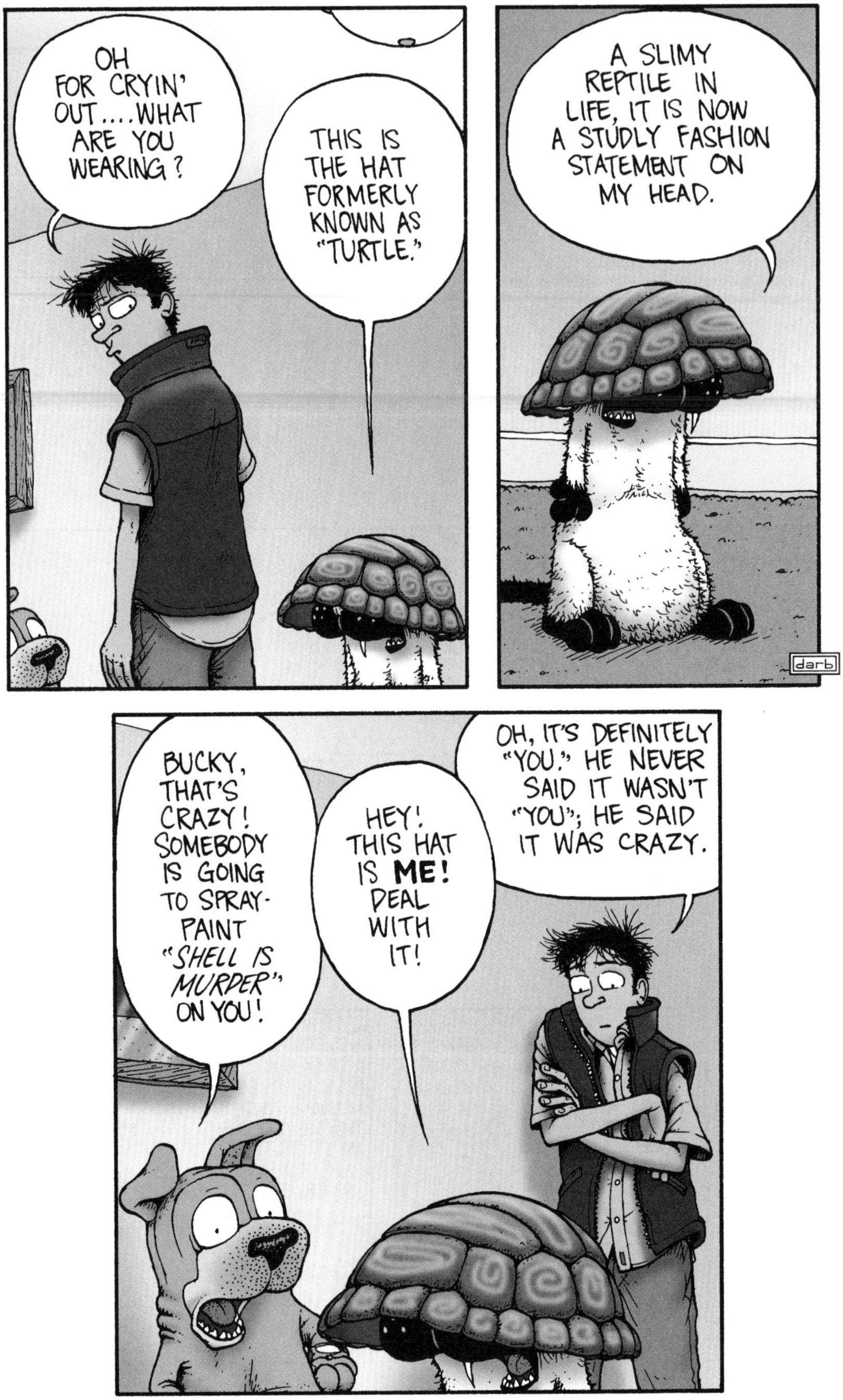
OH FOR CRYIN' OUT....WHAT ARE YOU WEARING?
THIS IS THE HAT FORMERLY KNOWN AS "TURTLE."
A SLIMY REPTILE IN LIFE, IT IS NOW A STUDLY FASHION STATEMENT ON MY HEAD.
darb
BUCKY, THAT'S CRAZY! SOMEBODY IS GOING TO SPRAY-PAINT "SHELL IS MURDER" ON YOU!
HEY! THIS HAT IS ME! DEAL WITH IT!
OH, IT'S DEFINITELY "YOU." HE NEVER SAID IT WASN'T "YOU"; HE SAID IT WAS CRAZY.

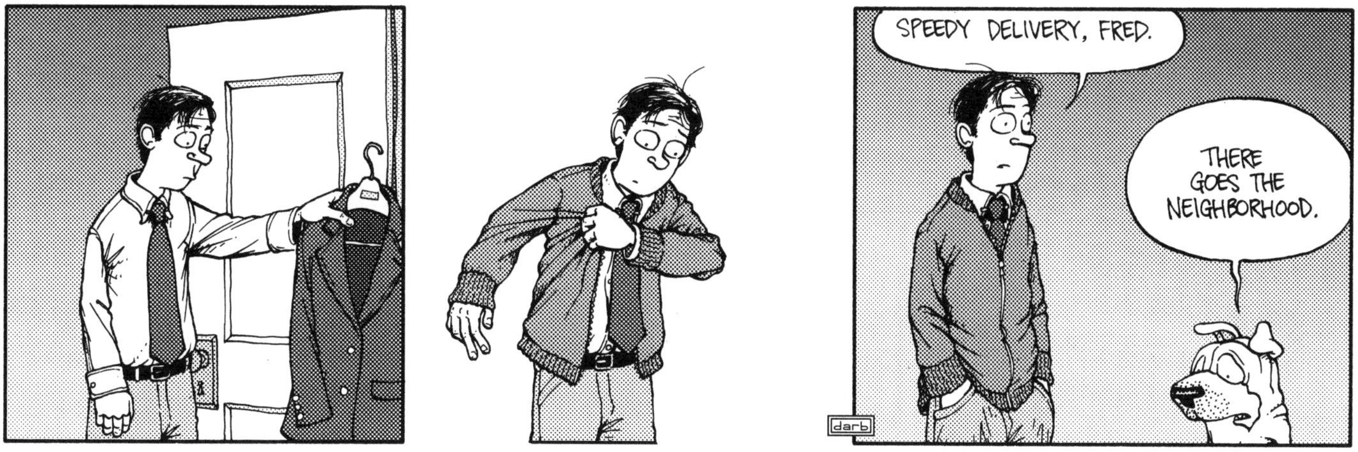
SPEEDY DELIVERY, FRED.
THERE GOES THE NEIGHBORHOOD.

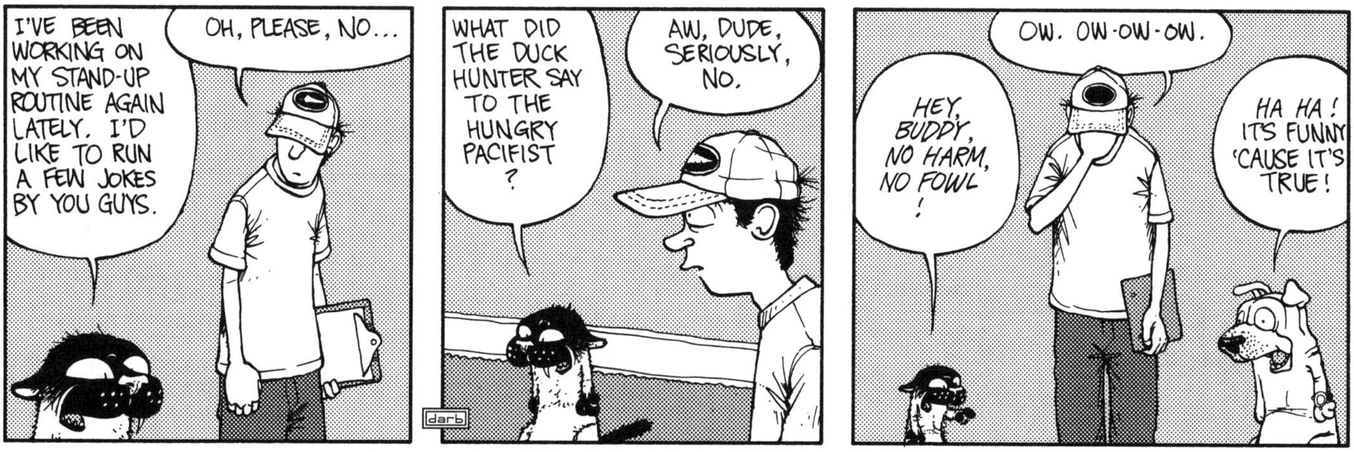
I'VE BEEN WORKING ON MY STAND-UP ROUTINE AGAIN LATELY. I'D LIKE TO RUN A FEW JOKES BY YOU GUYS.
OH, PLEASE, NO...
WHAT DID THE DUCK HUNTER SAY TO THE HUNGRY PACIFIST?
AW, DUDE, SERIOUSLY, NO.
OW. OW-OW-OW.
HEY, BUDDY, NO HARM, NO FOWL!
HA HA! IT'S FUNNY 'CAUSE IT'S TRUE!

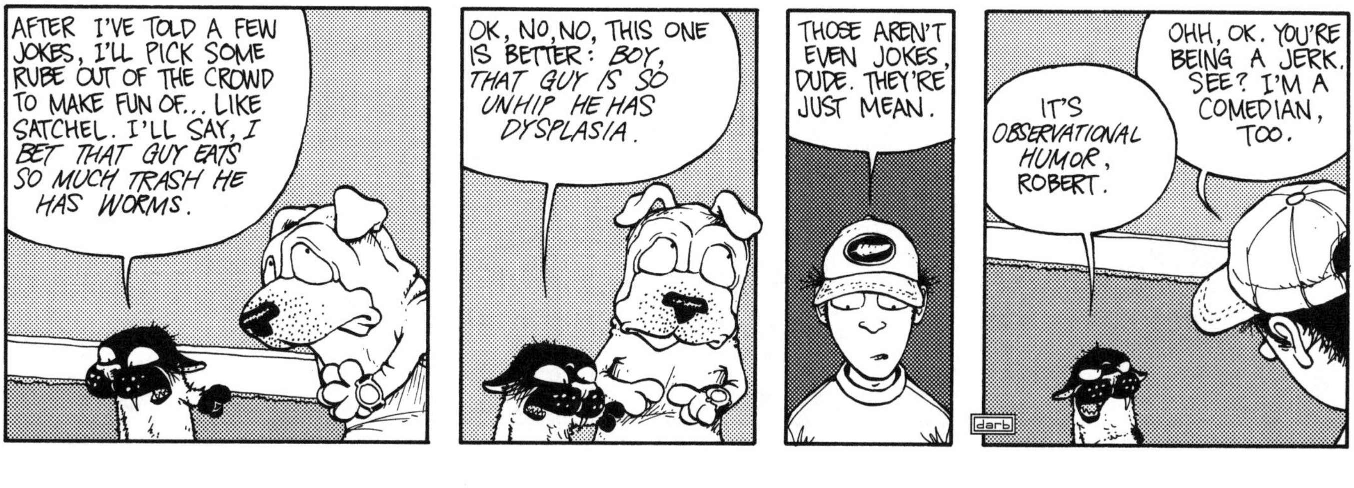
AFTER I'VE TOLD A FEW JOKES, I'LL PICK SOME RUBE OUT OF THE CROWD TO MAKE FUN OF... LIKE SATCHEL. I'LL SAY, *I BET THAT GUY EATS SO MUCH TRASH HE HAS WORMS*.
OK, NO, NO, THIS ONE IS BETTER: *BOY, THAT GUY IS SO UNHIP HE HAS DYSPLASIA*.
THOSE AREN'T EVEN JOKES, DUDE. THEY'RE JUST MEAN.
IT'S *OBSERVATIONAL HUMOR*, ROBERT.
OHH, OK. YOU'RE BEING A JERK. SEE? I'M A COMEDIAN, TOO.

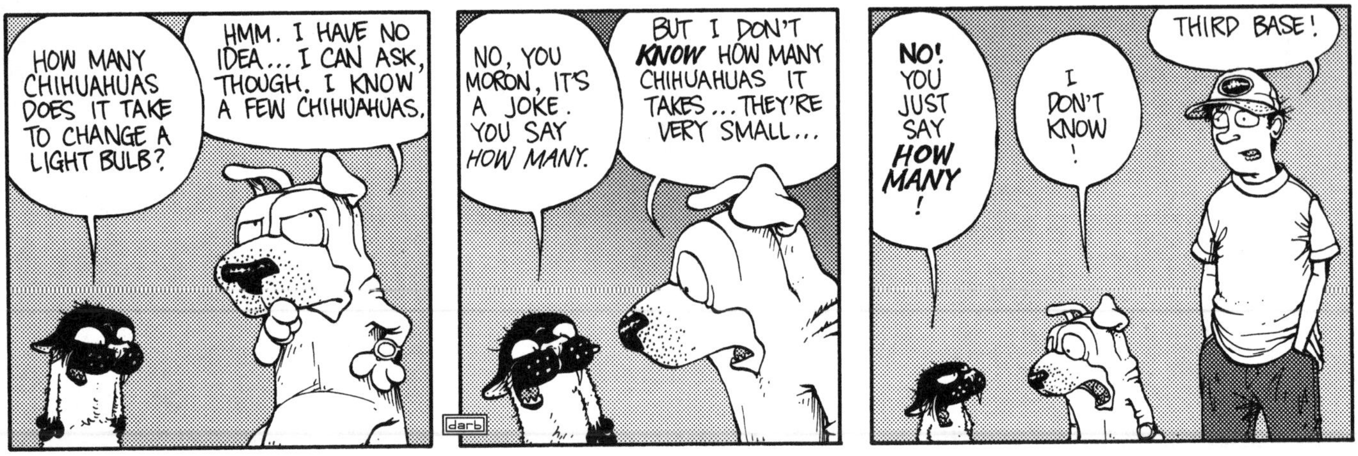
HOW MANY CHIHUAHUAS DOES IT TAKE TO CHANGE A LIGHT BULB?
HMM. I HAVE NO IDEA... I CAN ASK, THOUGH. I KNOW A FEW CHIHUAHUAS.
NO, YOU MORON, IT'S A JOKE. YOU SAY *HOW MANY.*
BUT I DON'T ***KNOW*** HOW MANY CHIHUAHUAS IT TAKES... THEY'RE VERY SMALL...
darb
NO! YOU JUST SAY ***HOW MANY!***
I DON'T KNOW!
THIRD BASE!

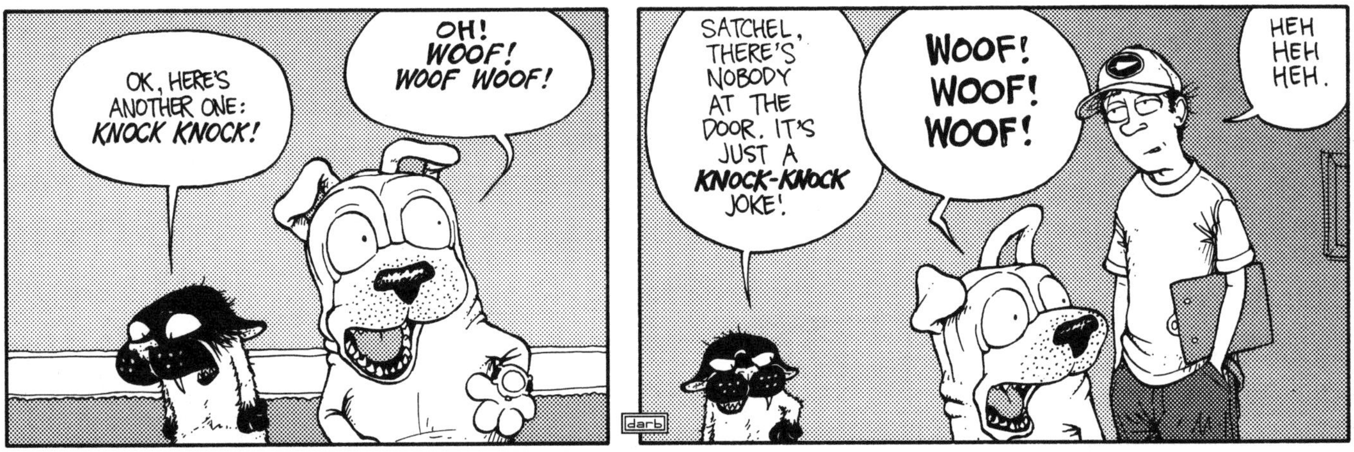
OK, HERE'S ANOTHER ONE: ***KNOCK KNOCK!***
OH! WOOF! WOOF WOOF!
SATCHEL, THERE'S NOBODY AT THE DOOR. IT'S JUST A ***KNOCK-KNOCK*** JOKE!
darb
WOOF! WOOF! WOOF!
HEH HEH HEH.

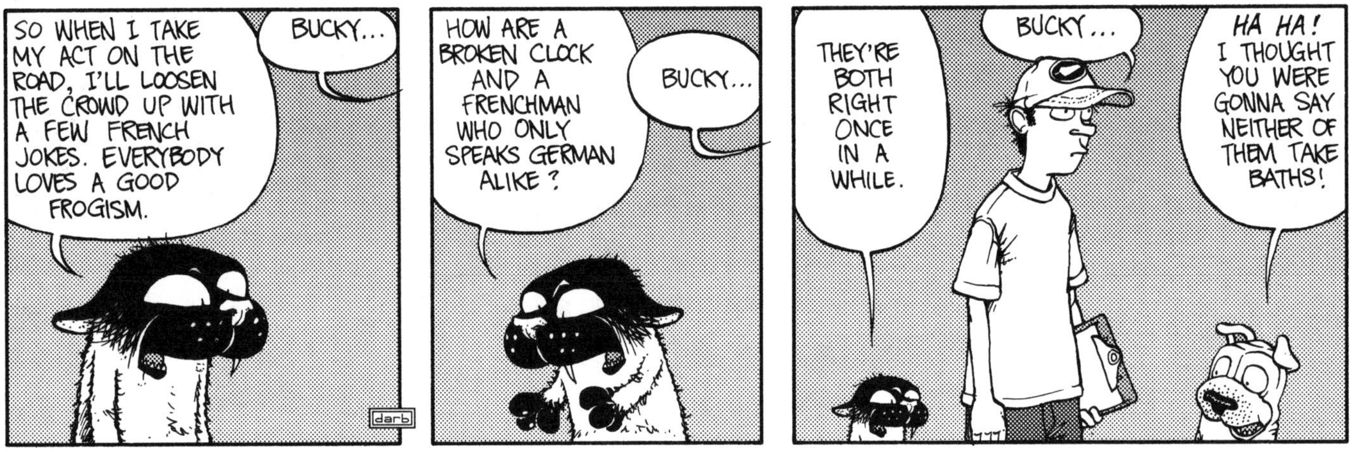
SO WHEN I TAKE MY ACT ON THE ROAD, I'LL LOOSEN THE CROWD UP WITH A FEW FRENCH JOKES. EVERYBODY LOVES A GOOD FROGISM.
BUCKY...
darb
HOW ARE A BROKEN CLOCK AND A FRENCHMAN WHO ONLY SPEAKS GERMAN ALIKE?
BUCKY...
THEY'RE BOTH RIGHT ONCE IN A WHILE.
BUCKY...
HA HA! I THOUGHT YOU WERE GONNA SAY NEITHER OF THEM TAKE BATHS!

AAAAAAEEEE!
darb

CRASH
TAKE YOUR STRING OUTSIDE!
HE'S GONNA SLEEP WELL TONIGHT! HA HA! AGAIN!

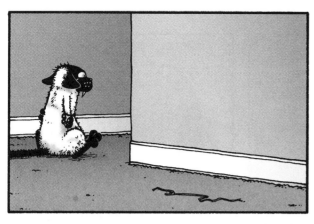

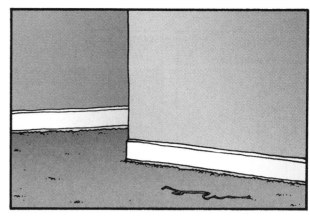

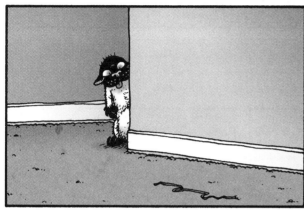

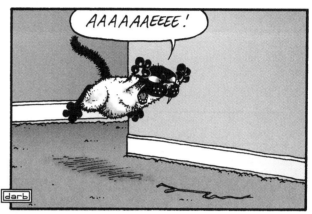

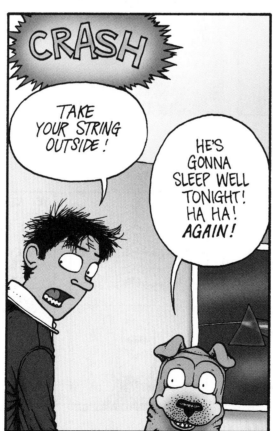

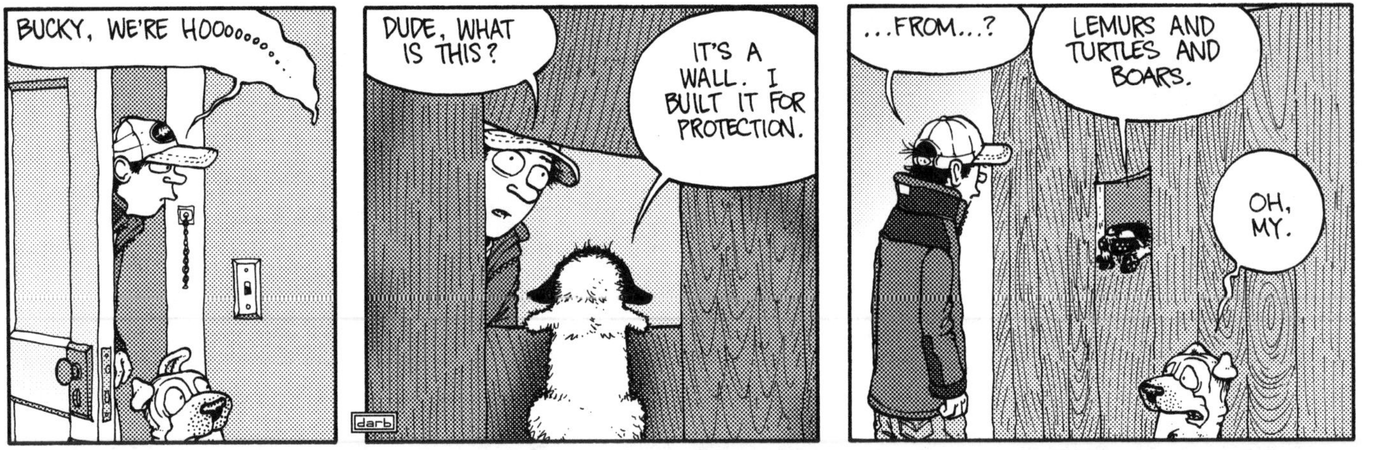
BUCKY, WE'RE HOOoooooo...
DUDE, WHAT IS THIS?
IT'S A WALL. I BUILT IT FOR PROTECTION.
...FROM...?
LEMURS AND TURTLES AND BOARS.
OH, MY.

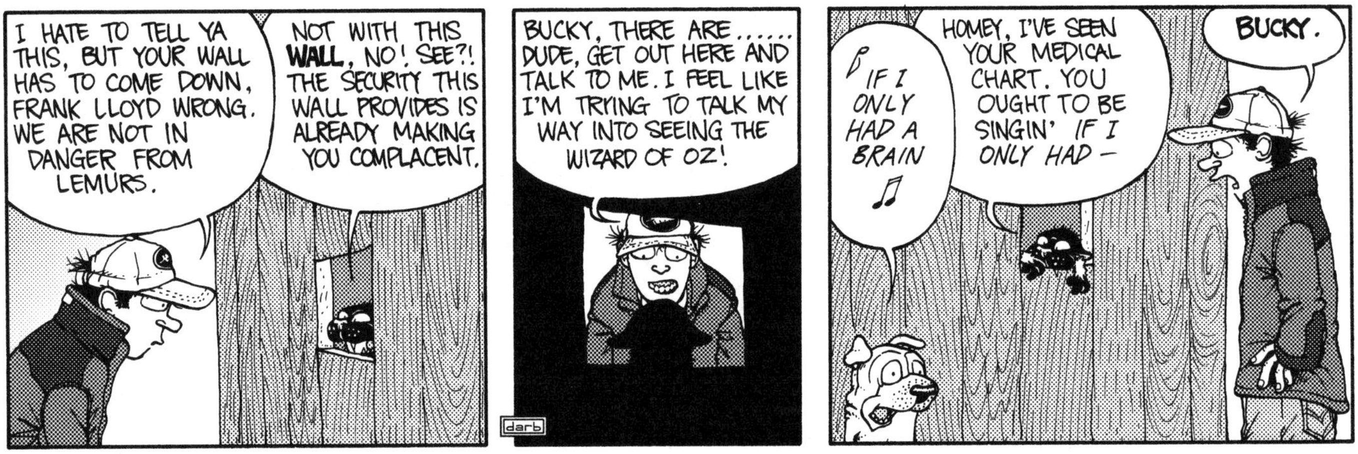
I HATE TO TELL YA THIS, BUT YOUR WALL HAS TO COME DOWN, FRANK LLOYD WRONG. WE ARE NOT IN DANGER FROM LEMURS.
NOT WITH THIS **WALL**, NO! SEE?! THE SECURITY THIS WALL PROVIDES IS ALREADY MAKING YOU COMPLACENT.
BUCKY, THERE ARE...... DUDE, GET OUT HERE AND TALK TO ME. I FEEL LIKE I'M TRYING TO TALK MY WAY INTO SEEING THE WIZARD OF OZ!
IF I ONLY HAD A BRAIN
HOMEY, I'VE SEEN YOUR MEDICAL CHART. YOU OUGHT TO BE SINGIN' *IF I ONLY HAD—*
BUCKY.

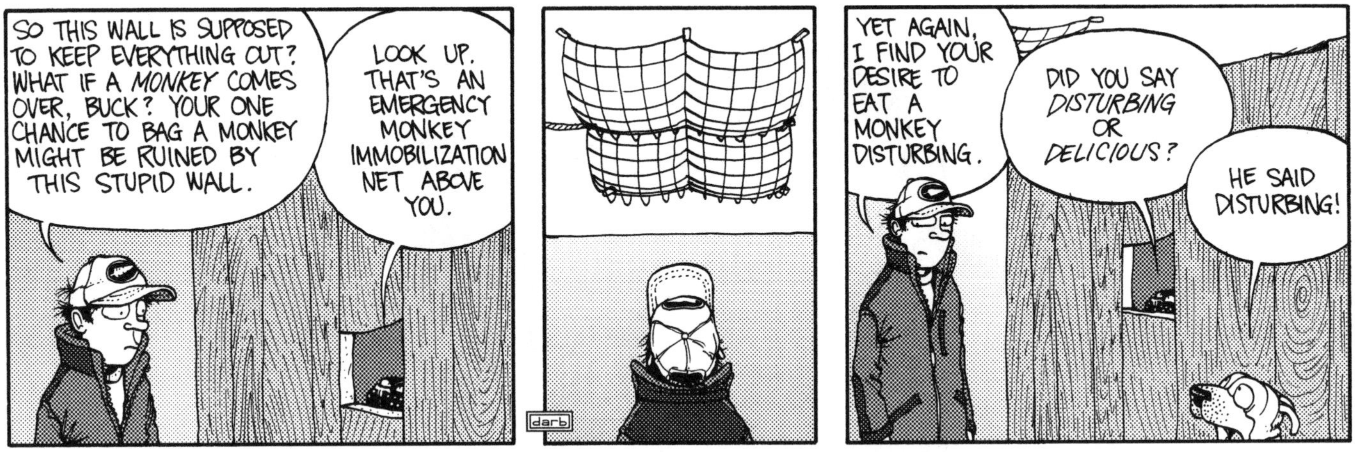
SO THIS WALL IS SUPPOSED TO KEEP EVERYTHING OUT? WHAT IF A *MONKEY* COMES OVER, BUCK? YOUR ONE CHANCE TO BAG A MONKEY MIGHT BE RUINED BY THIS STUPID WALL.
LOOK UP. THAT'S AN EMERGENCY MONKEY IMMOBILIZATION NET ABOVE YOU.
YET AGAIN, I FIND YOUR DESIRE TO EAT A MONKEY DISTURBING.
DID YOU SAY *DISTURBING* OR *DELICIOUS*?
HE SAID DISTURBING!

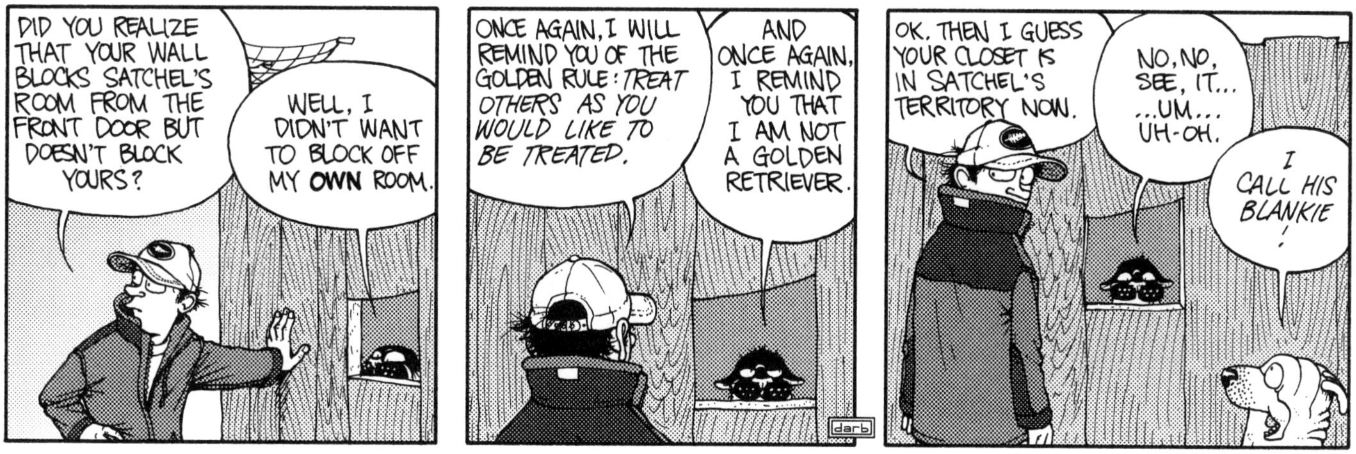

DID YOU REALIZE THAT YOUR WALL BLOCKS SATCHEL'S ROOM FROM THE FRONT DOOR BUT DOESN'T BLOCK YOURS?
WELL, I DIDN'T WANT TO BLOCK OFF MY **OWN** ROOM.
ONCE AGAIN, I WILL REMIND YOU OF THE GOLDEN RULE: *TREAT OTHERS AS YOU WOULD LIKE TO BE TREATED.*
AND ONCE AGAIN, I REMIND YOU THAT I AM NOT A GOLDEN RETRIEVER.
darb
OK. THEN I GUESS YOUR CLOSET IS IN SATCHEL'S TERRITORY NOW.
NO, NO, SEE, IT... ...UM... UH-OH.
I CALL HIS BLANKIE!

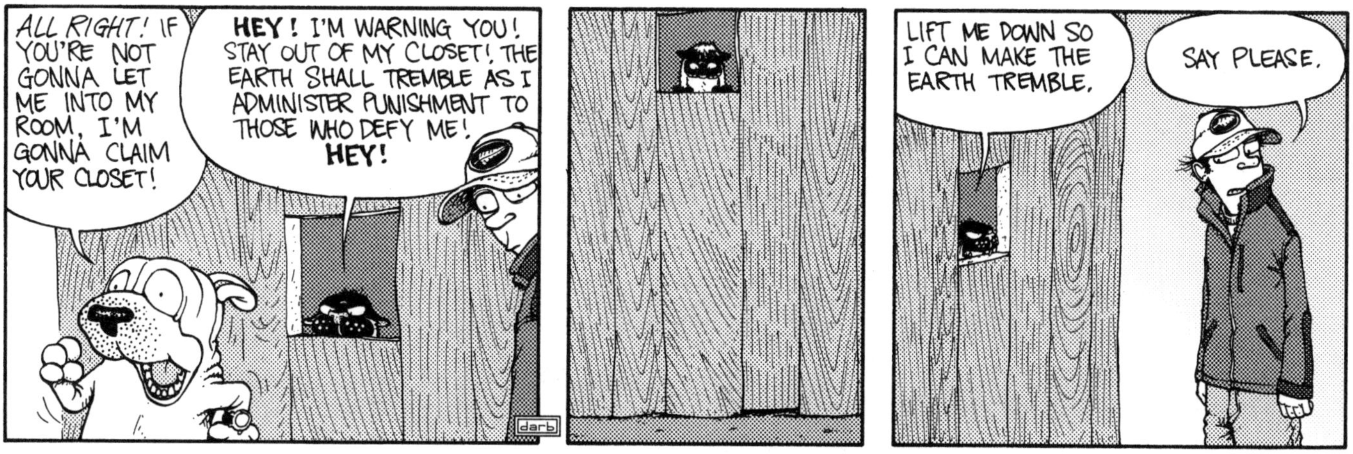

ALL RIGHT! IF YOU'RE NOT GONNA LET ME INTO MY ROOM, I'M GONNA CLAIM YOUR CLOSET!
HEY! I'M WARNING YOU! STAY OUT OF MY CLOSET! THE EARTH SHALL TREMBLE AS I ADMINISTER PUNISHMENT TO THOSE WHO DEFY ME! **HEY!**
darb
LIFT ME DOWN SO I CAN MAKE THE EARTH TREMBLE.
SAY PLEASE.

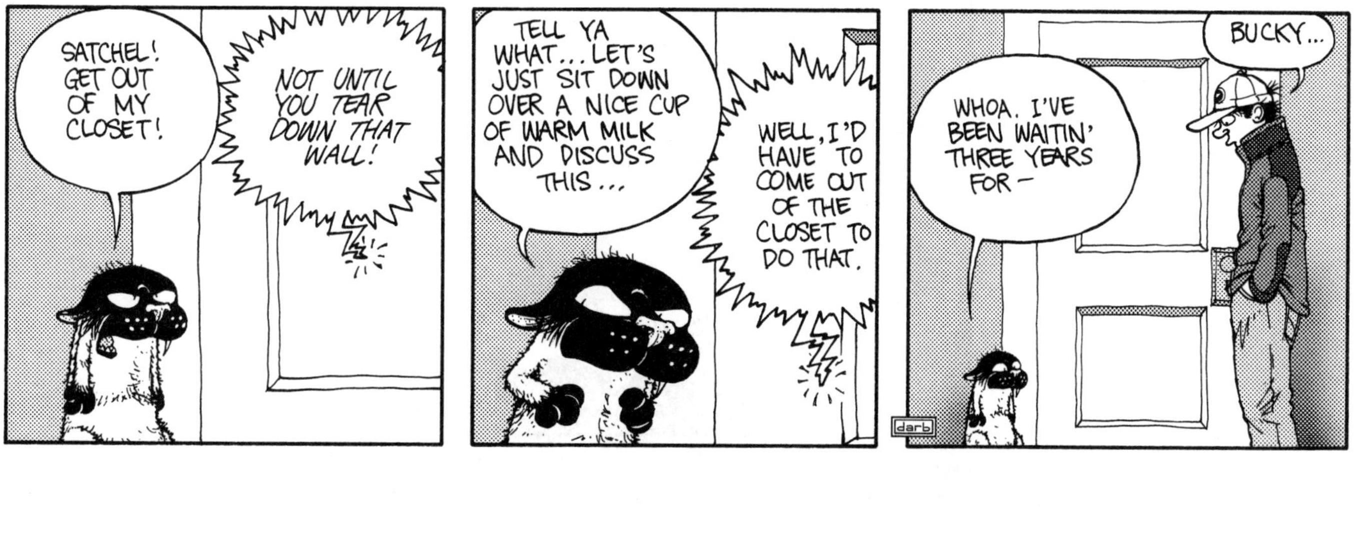

SATCHEL! GET OUT OF MY CLOSET!
NOT UNTIL YOU TEAR DOWN THAT WALL!
TELL YA WHAT... LET'S JUST SIT DOWN OVER A NICE CUP OF WARM MILK AND DISCUSS THIS...
WELL, I'D HAVE TO COME OUT OF THE CLOSET TO DO THAT.
darb
BUCKY...
WHOA. I'VE BEEN WAITIN' THREE YEARS FOR—

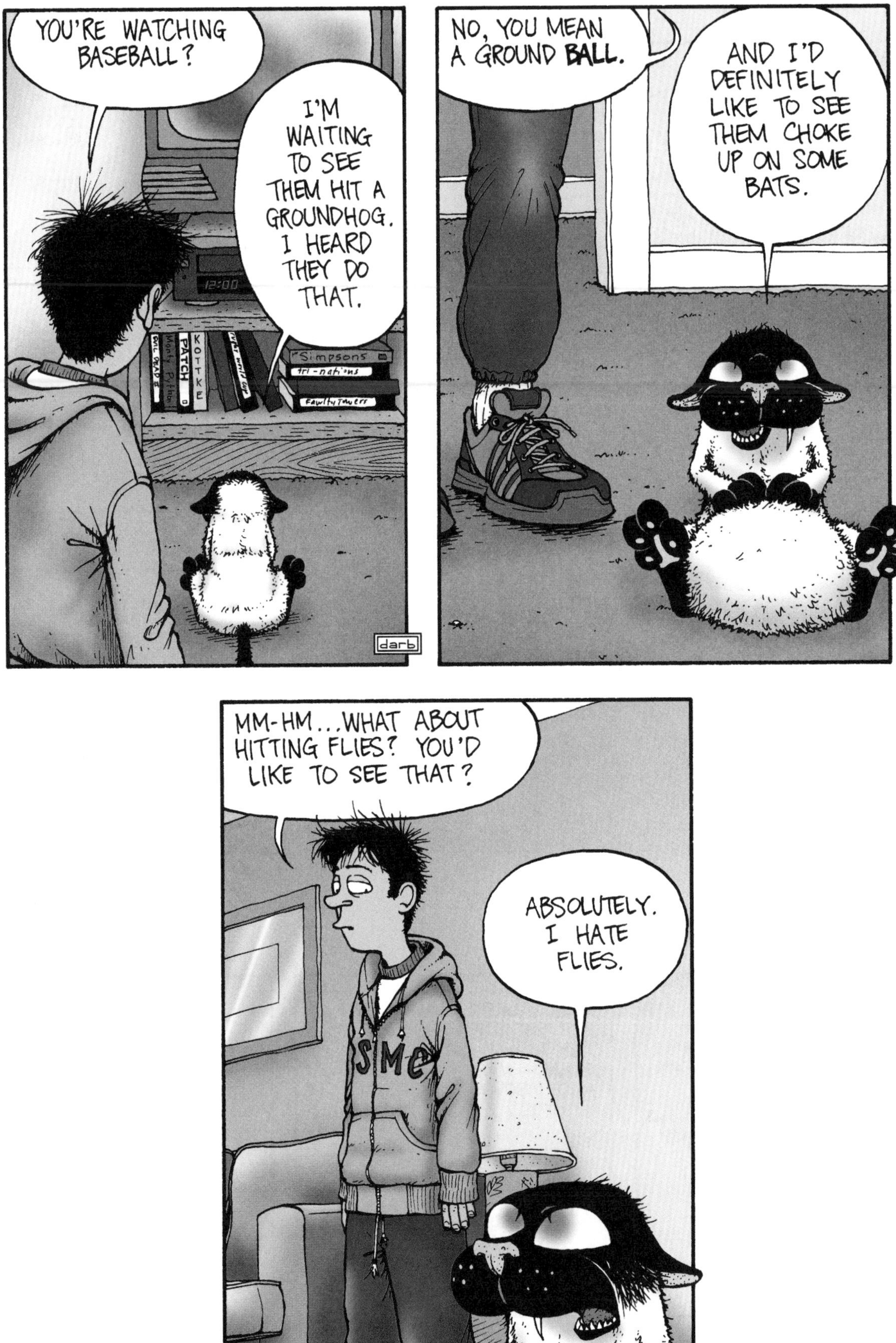
YOU'RE WATCHING BASEBALL?
I'M WAITING TO SEE THEM HIT A GROUNDHOG. I HEARD THEY DO THAT.
NO, YOU MEAN A GROUND **BALL.**
AND I'D DEFINITELY LIKE TO SEE THEM CHOKE UP ON SOME BATS.
MM-HM...WHAT ABOUT HITTING FLIES? YOU'D LIKE TO SEE THAT?
ABSOLUTELY. I HATE FLIES.

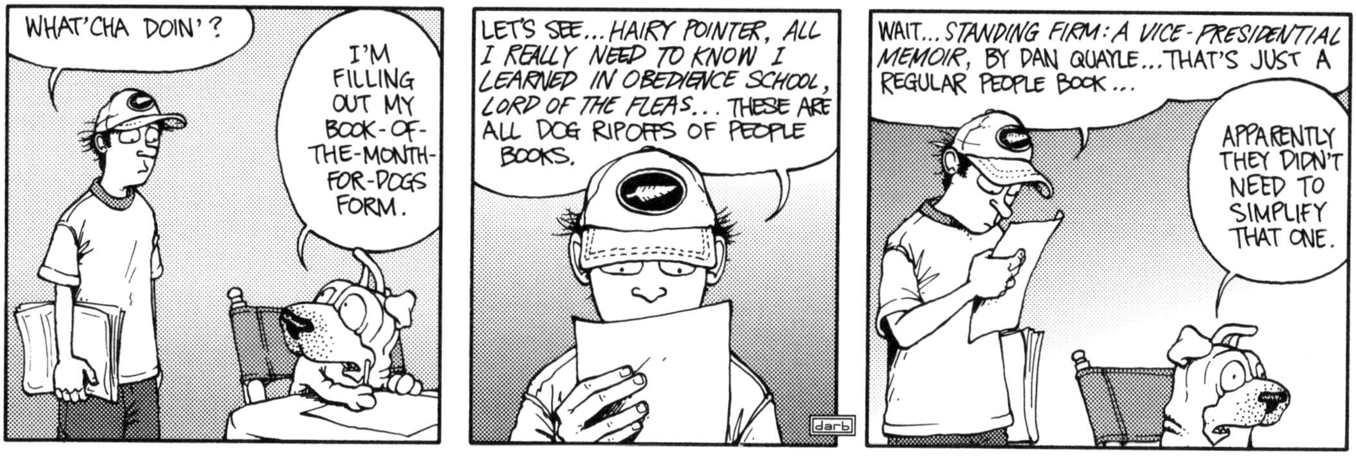
WHAT'CHA DOIN'?
I'M FILLING OUT MY BOOK-OF-THE-MONTH-FOR-DOGS FORM.
LET'S SEE... *HAIRY POINTER, ALL I REALLY NEED TO KNOW I LEARNED IN OBEDIENCE SCHOOL, LORD OF THE FLEAS*... THESE ARE ALL DOG RIPOFFS OF PEOPLE BOOKS.
WAIT... *STANDING FIRM: A VICE-PRESIDENTIAL MEMOIR*, BY DAN QUAYLE... THAT'S JUST A REGULAR PEOPLE BOOK...
APPARENTLY THEY DIDN'T NEED TO SIMPLIFY THAT ONE.

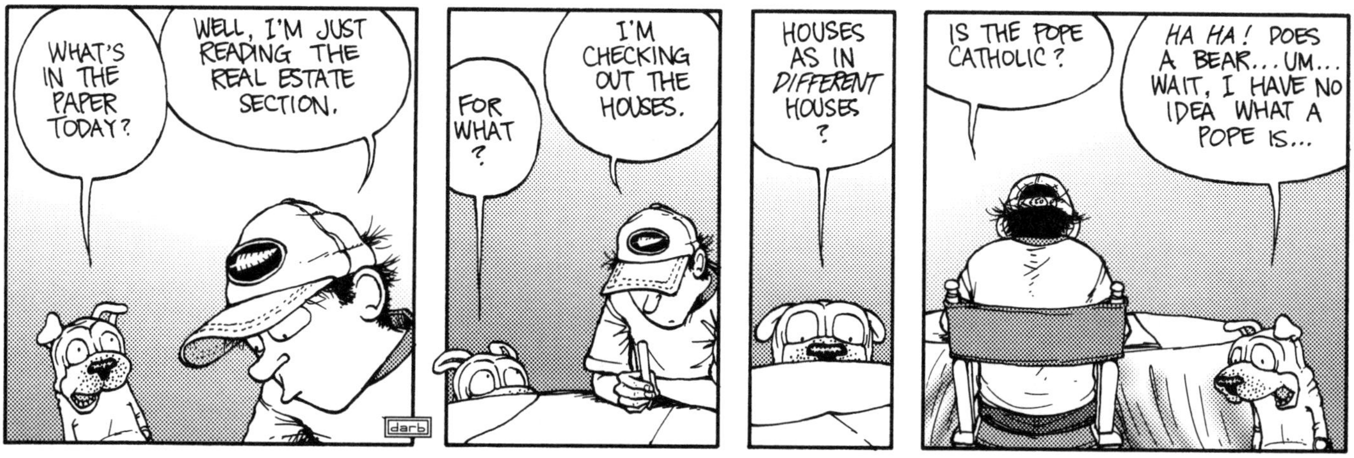
WHAT'S IN THE PAPER TODAY?
WELL, I'M JUST READING THE REAL ESTATE SECTION.
FOR WHAT?
I'M CHECKING OUT THE HOUSES.
HOUSES AS IN *DIFFERENT* HOUSES?
IS THE POPE CATHOLIC?
HA HA! DOES A BEAR... UM... WAIT, I HAVE NO IDEA WHAT A POPE IS...

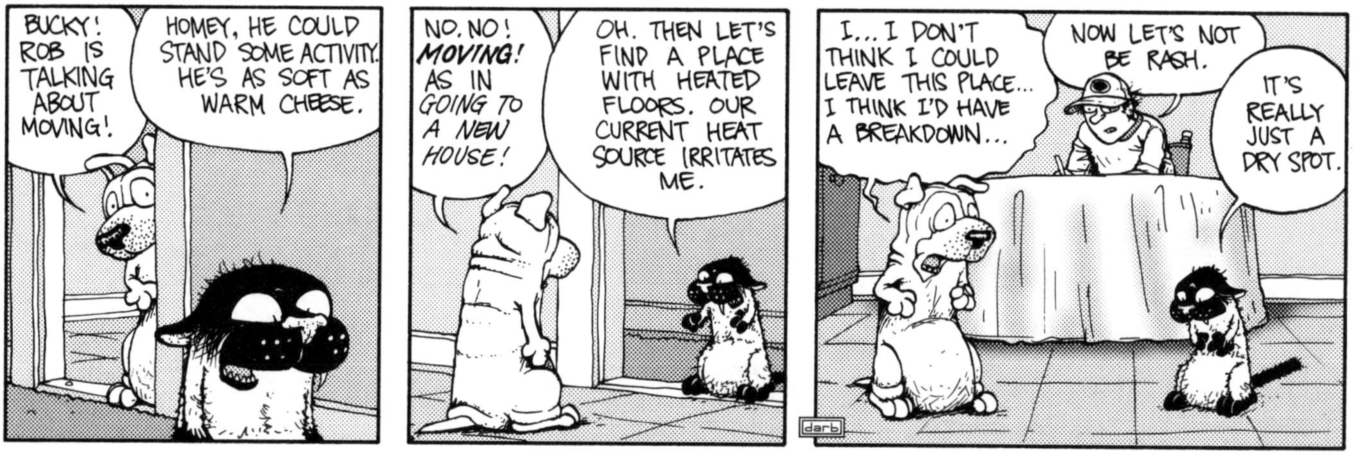
BUCKY! ROB IS TALKING ABOUT MOVING!
HOMEY, HE COULD STAND SOME ACTIVITY. HE'S AS SOFT AS WARM CHEESE.
NO, NO! ***MOVING!*** AS IN *GOING TO A NEW HOUSE!*
OH. THEN LET'S FIND A PLACE WITH HEATED FLOORS. OUR CURRENT HEAT SOURCE IRRITATES ME.
I... I DON'T THINK I COULD LEAVE THIS PLACE... I THINK I'D HAVE A BREAKDOWN...
NOW LET'S NOT BE RASH.
IT'S REALLY JUST A DRY SPOT.

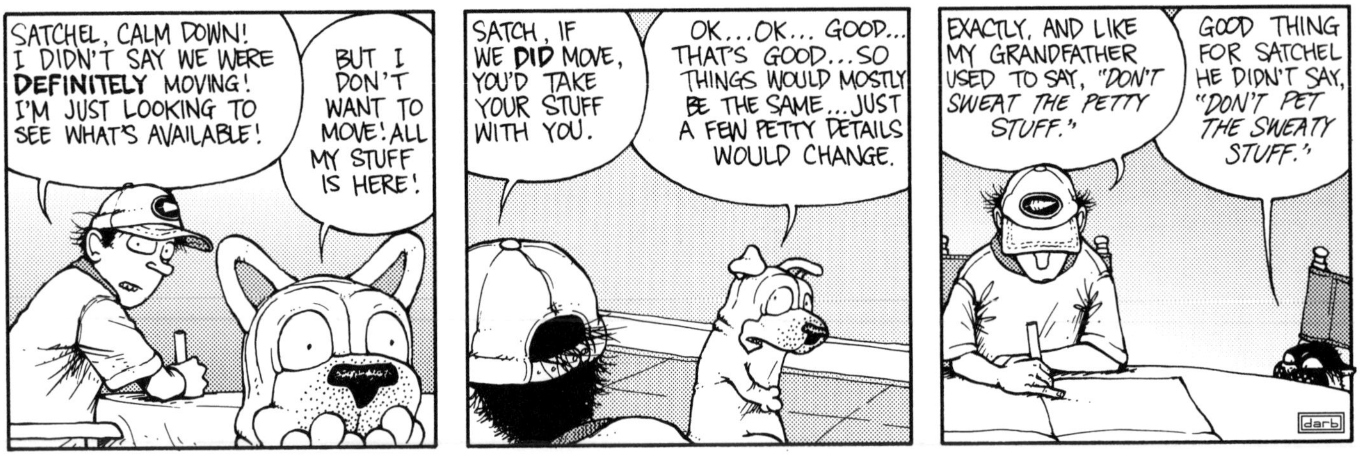
SATCHEL, CALM DOWN! I DIDN'T SAY WE WERE **DEFINITELY** MOVING! I'M JUST LOOKING TO SEE WHAT'S AVAILABLE!
BUT I DON'T WANT TO MOVE! ALL MY STUFF IS HERE!
SATCH, IF WE **DID** MOVE, YOU'D TAKE YOUR STUFF WITH YOU.
OK...OK... GOOD... THAT'S GOOD...SO THINGS WOULD MOSTLY BE THE SAME...JUST A FEW PETTY DETAILS WOULD CHANGE.
EXACTLY, AND LIKE MY GRANDFATHER USED TO SAY, *"DON'T SWEAT THE PETTY STUFF."*
GOOD THING FOR SATCHEL HE DIDN'T SAY, *"DON'T PET THE SWEATY STUFF."*
darb

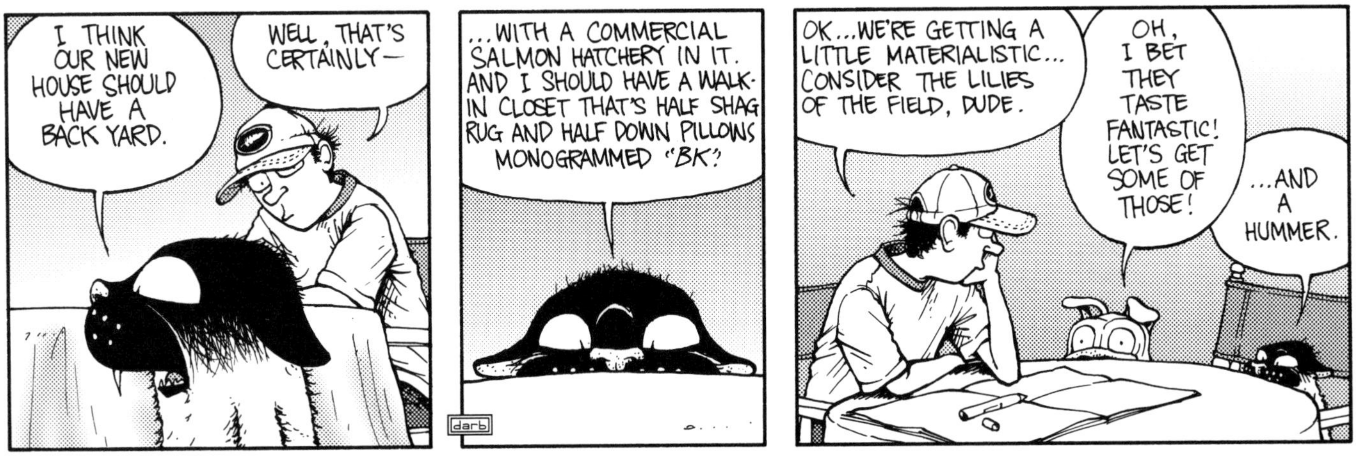
I THINK OUR NEW HOUSE SHOULD HAVE A BACK YARD.
WELL, THAT'S CERTAINLY—
darb
...WITH A COMMERCIAL SALMON HATCHERY IN IT. AND I SHOULD HAVE A WALK-IN CLOSET THAT'S HALF SHAG RUG AND HALF DOWN PILLOWS MONOGRAMMED *"BK"*.
OK...WE'RE GETTING A LITTLE MATERIALISTIC... CONSIDER THE LILIES OF THE FIELD, DUDE.
OH, I BET THEY TASTE FANTASTIC! LET'S GET SOME OF THOSE!
...AND A HUMMER.

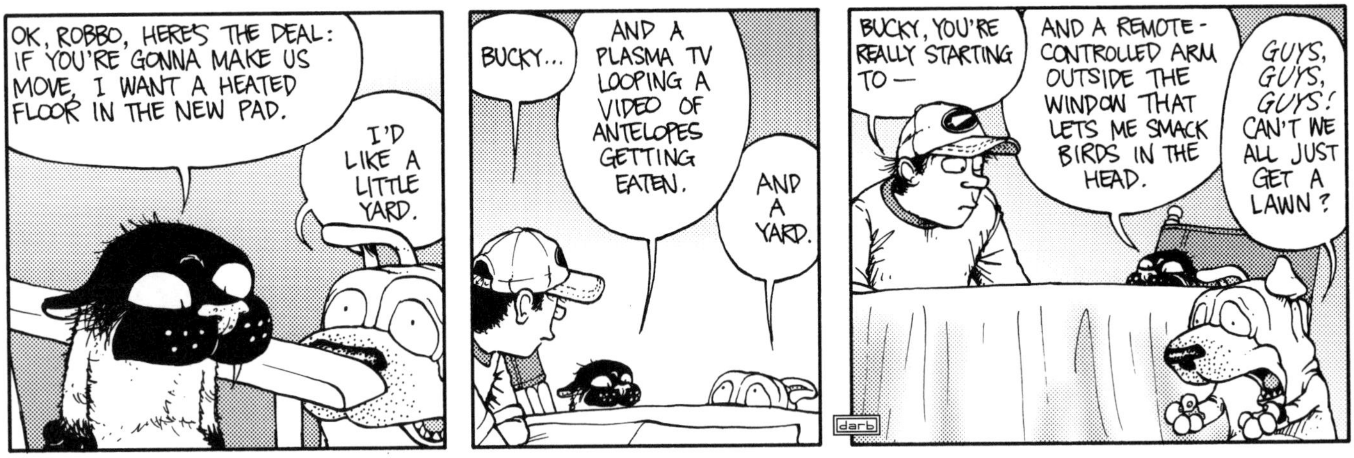
OK, ROBBO, HERE'S THE DEAL: IF YOU'RE GONNA MAKE US MOVE, I WANT A HEATED FLOOR IN THE NEW PAD.
I'D LIKE A LITTLE YARD.
BUCKY...
AND A PLASMA TV LOOPING A VIDEO OF ANTELOPES GETTING EATEN.
AND A YARD.
darb
BUCKY, YOU'RE REALLY STARTING TO—
AND A REMOTE-CONTROLLED ARM OUTSIDE THE WINDOW THAT LETS ME SMACK BIRDS IN THE HEAD.
GUYS, GUYS, GUYS! CAN'T WE ALL JUST GET A LAWN?

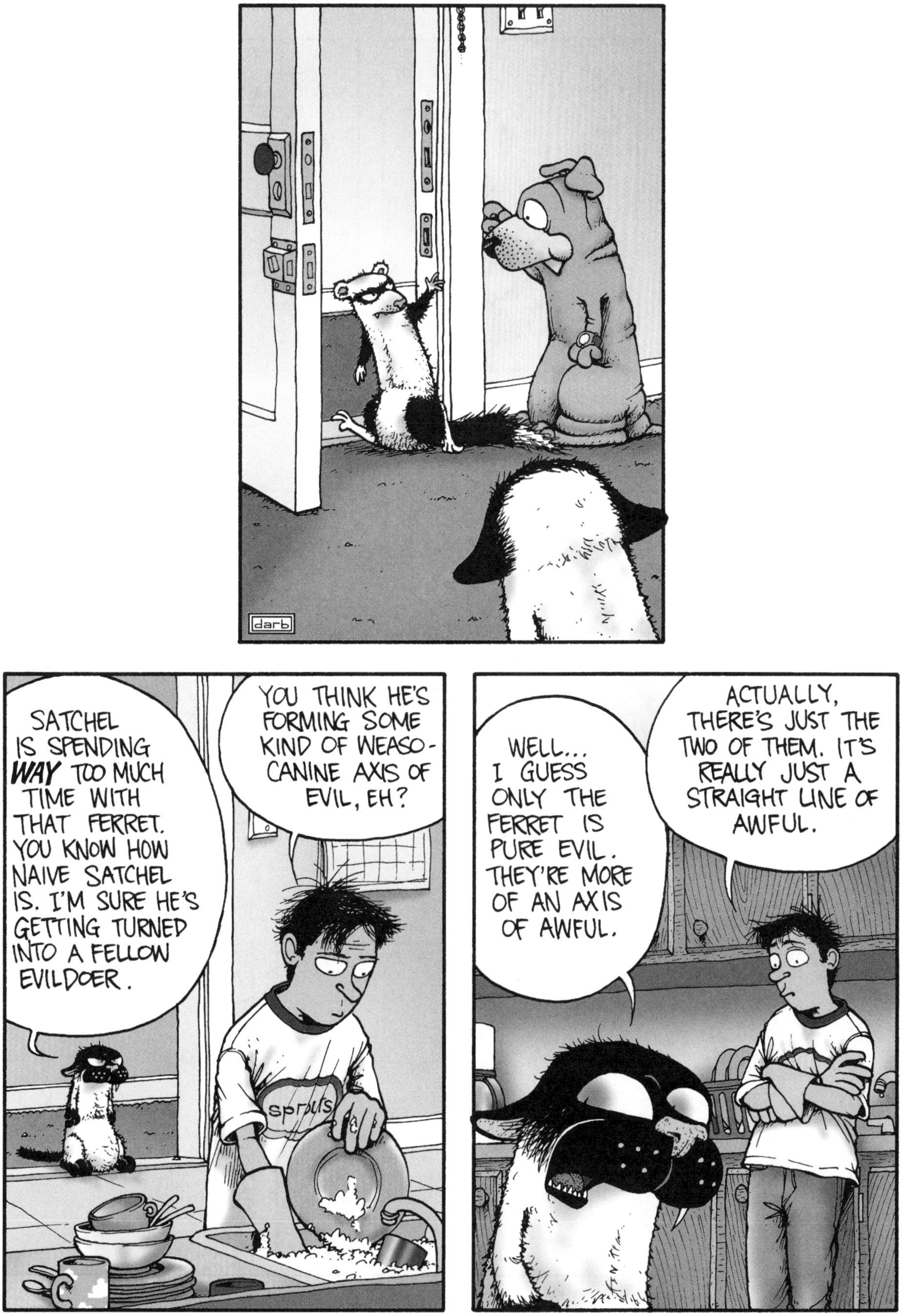
darb
SATCHEL IS SPENDING **WAY** TOO MUCH TIME WITH THAT FERRET. YOU KNOW HOW NAIVE SATCHEL IS. I'M SURE HE'S GETTING TURNED INTO A FELLOW EVILDOER.
YOU THINK HE'S FORMING SOME KIND OF WEASO-CANINE AXIS OF EVIL, EH?
sprouts
WELL... I GUESS ONLY THE FERRET IS PURE EVIL. THEY'RE MORE OF AN AXIS OF AWFUL.
ACTUALLY, THERE'S JUST THE TWO OF THEM. IT'S REALLY JUST A STRAIGHT LINE OF AWFUL.

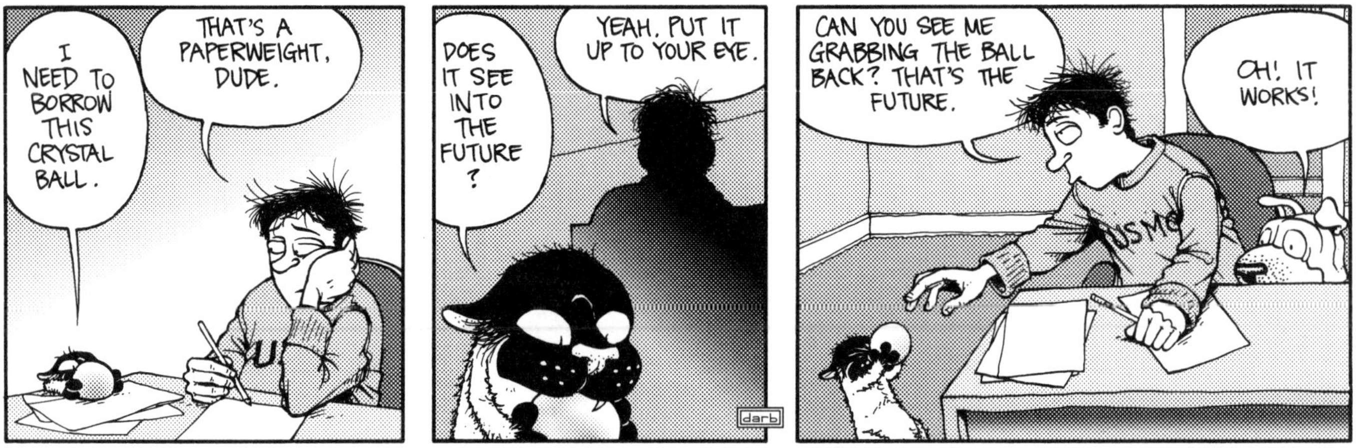
I NEED TO BORROW THIS CRYSTAL BALL.
THAT'S A PAPERWEIGHT, DUDE.
DOES IT SEE INTO THE FUTURE?
YEAH, PUT IT UP TO YOUR EYE.
CAN YOU SEE ME GRABBING THE BALL BACK? THAT'S THE FUTURE.
OH! IT WORKS!
darb

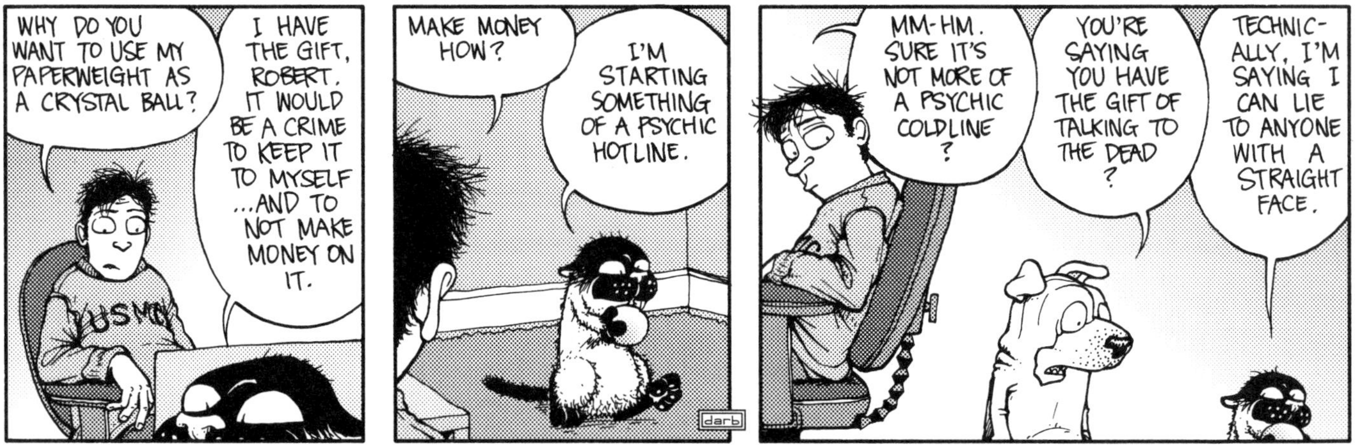
WHY DO YOU WANT TO USE MY PAPERWEIGHT AS A CRYSTAL BALL?
I HAVE THE GIFT, ROBERT. IT WOULD BE A CRIME TO KEEP IT TO MYSELF ...AND TO NOT MAKE MONEY ON IT.
MAKE MONEY HOW?
I'M STARTING SOMETHING OF A PSYCHIC HOTLINE.
MM-HM. SURE IT'S NOT MORE OF A PSYCHIC COLDLINE?
YOU'RE SAYING YOU HAVE THE GIFT OF TALKING TO THE DEAD?
TECHNICALLY, I'M SAYING I CAN LIE TO ANYONE WITH A STRAIGHT FACE.
darb

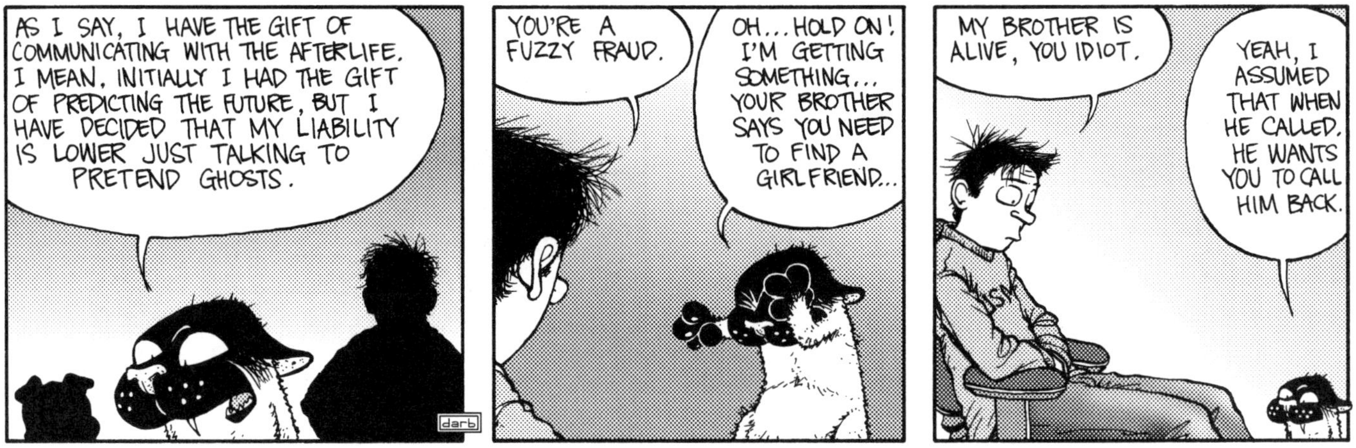
AS I SAY, I HAVE THE GIFT OF COMMUNICATING WITH THE AFTERLIFE. I MEAN, INITIALLY I HAD THE GIFT OF PREDICTING THE FUTURE, BUT I HAVE DECIDED THAT MY LIABILITY IS LOWER JUST TALKING TO PRETEND GHOSTS.
YOU'RE A FUZZY FRAUD.
OH... HOLD ON! I'M GETTING SOMETHING... YOUR BROTHER SAYS YOU NEED TO FIND A GIRLFRIEND...
MY BROTHER IS ALIVE, YOU IDIOT.
YEAH, I ASSUMED THAT WHEN HE CALLED. HE WANTS YOU TO CALL HIM BACK.
darb

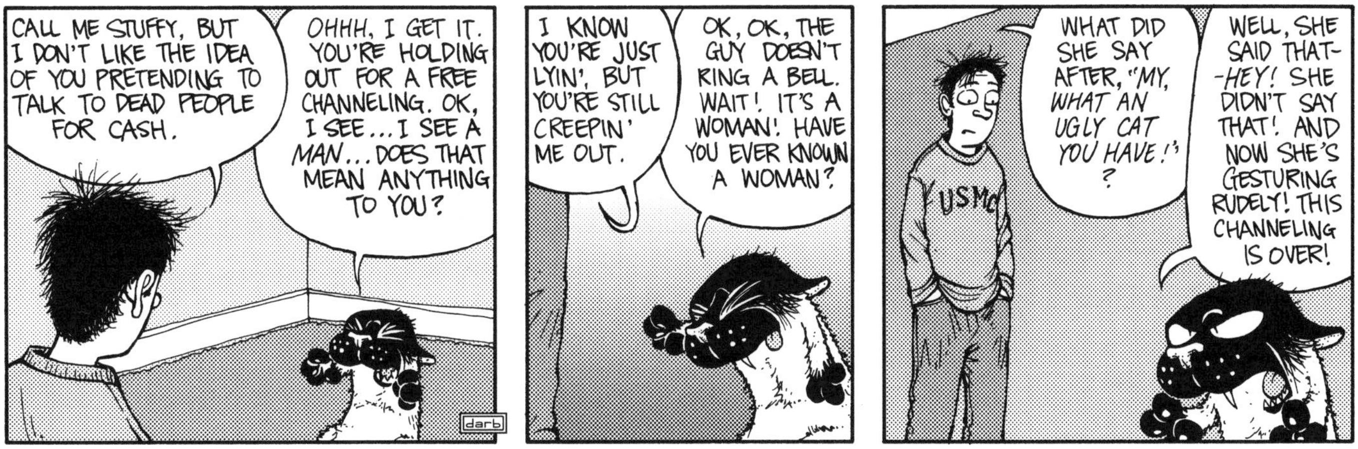
CALL ME STUFFY, BUT I DON'T LIKE THE IDEA OF YOU PRETENDING TO TALK TO DEAD PEOPLE FOR CASH.
OHHH, I GET IT. YOU'RE HOLDING OUT FOR A FREE CHANNELING. OK, I SEE... I SEE A MAN... DOES THAT MEAN ANYTHING TO YOU?
darb
I KNOW YOU'RE JUST LYIN', BUT YOU'RE STILL CREEPIN' ME OUT.
OK, OK, THE GUY DOESN'T RING A BELL. WAIT! IT'S A WOMAN! HAVE YOU EVER KNOWN A WOMAN?
WHAT DID SHE SAY AFTER, "MY, WHAT AN UGLY CAT YOU HAVE!"?
USMC
WELL, SHE SAID THAT- -HEY! SHE DIDN'T SAY THAT! AND NOW SHE'S GESTURING RUDELY! THIS CHANNELING IS OVER!

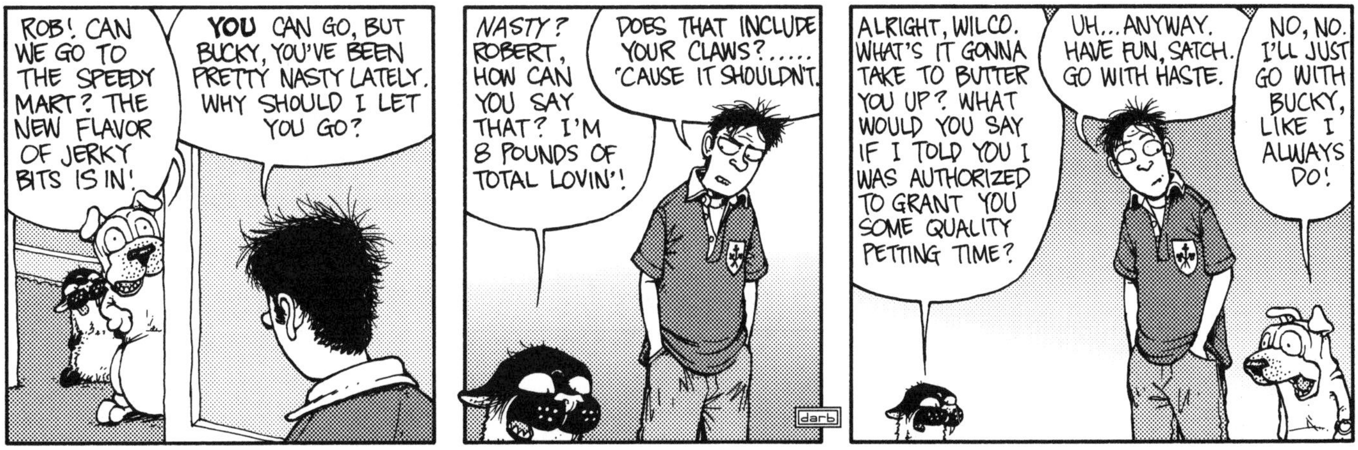
ROB! CAN WE GO TO THE SPEEDY MART? THE NEW FLAVOR OF JERKY BITS IS IN!
YOU CAN GO, BUT BUCKY, YOU'VE BEEN PRETTY NASTY LATELY. WHY SHOULD I LET YOU GO?
NASTY? ROBERT, HOW CAN YOU SAY THAT? I'M 8 POUNDS OF TOTAL LOVIN'!
DOES THAT INCLUDE YOUR CLAWS?..... 'CAUSE IT SHOULDN'T.
darb
ALRIGHT, WILCO. WHAT'S IT GONNA TAKE TO BUTTER YOU UP? WHAT WOULD YOU SAY IF I TOLD YOU I WAS AUTHORIZED TO GRANT YOU SOME QUALITY PETTING TIME?
UH... ANYWAY. HAVE FUN, SATCH. GO WITH HASTE.
NO, NO. I'LL JUST GO WITH BUCKY, LIKE I ALWAYS DO!

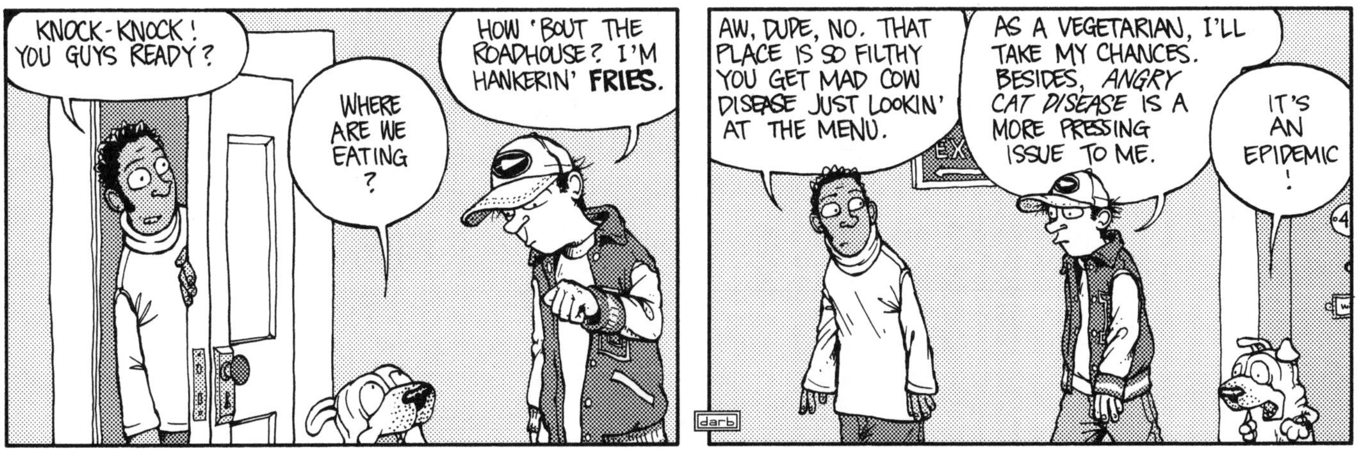
KNOCK-KNOCK! YOU GUYS READY?
WHERE ARE WE EATING?
HOW 'BOUT THE ROADHOUSE? I'M HANKERIN' FRIES.
darb
AW, DUDE, NO. THAT PLACE IS SO FILTHY YOU GET MAD COW DISEASE JUST LOOKIN' AT THE MENU.
AS A VEGETARIAN, I'LL TAKE MY CHANCES. BESIDES, ANGRY CAT DISEASE IS A MORE PRESSING ISSUE TO ME.
IT'S AN EPIDEMIC!

WHY DO WE ALWAYS HAVE TO GET VIOLENT? WHY CAN'T WE ALL SETTLE DIFFERENCES THROUGH SPORTS OR SOMETHING?
THAT'S A GOOD QUESTION, SATCH. CARE TO ANSWER THAT, BUCK?
BECAUSE THEN NEW ZEALAND WOULD RULE THE WORLD, THAT'S WHY.
BUCKY, I HOPE YOU DIDN'T LASH OUT TODAY BECAUSE I'M A BIT MORE POPULAR THAN YOU WITH SOME PEOPLE...
MORE POPULAR THAN ME? WHOA, THERE, GARFUNKEL, I'M BIGGER THAN YOU'LL EVER BE! I'M BIGGER THAN YOU WOULD BE WITH A ROOM SERVICE MENU AND A CREDIT CARD! YOU'RE JUST JEALOUS.
darb
LUNGE AT A BABY, GET THE HARNESS. THAT'S THE RULE.

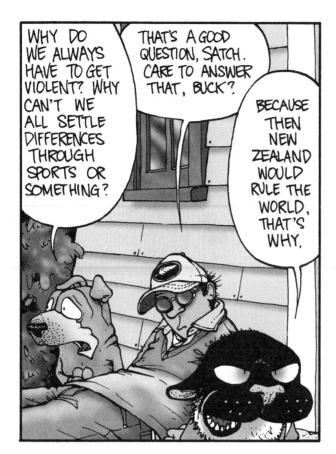

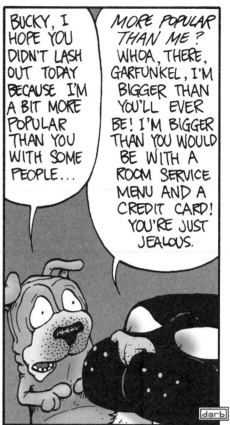

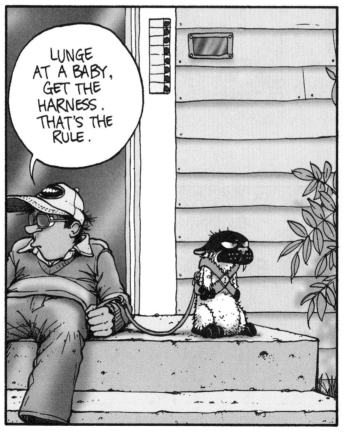

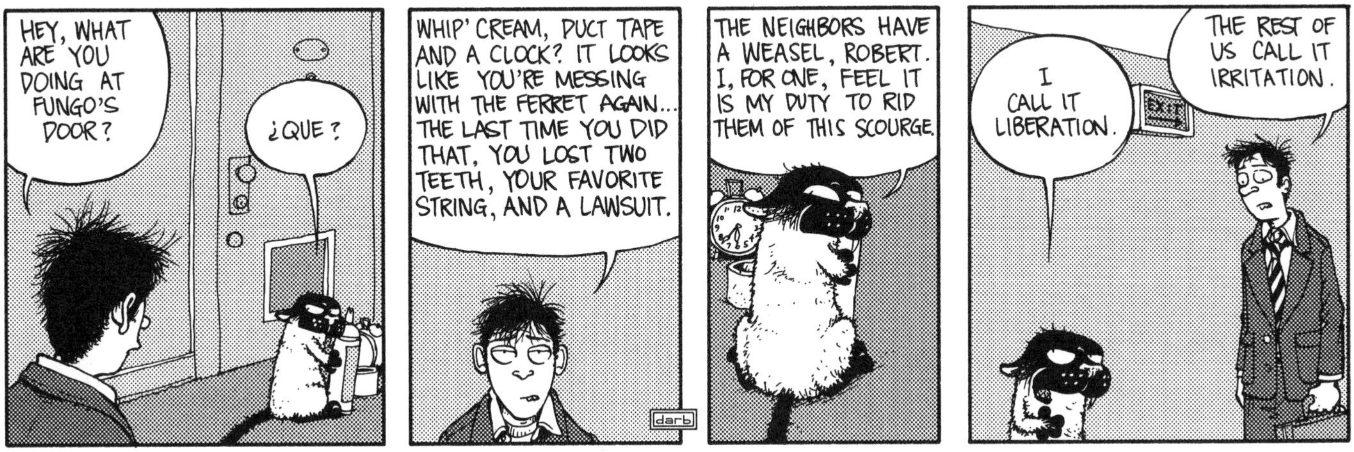
HEY, WHAT ARE YOU DOING AT FUNGO'S DOOR?
¿QUE?
WHIP' CREAM, DUCT TAPE AND A CLOCK? IT LOOKS LIKE YOU'RE MESSING WITH THE FERRET AGAIN... THE LAST TIME YOU DID THAT, YOU LOST TWO TEETH, YOUR FAVORITE STRING, AND A LAWSUIT.
darb
THE NEIGHBORS HAVE A WEASEL, ROBERT. I, FOR ONE, FEEL IT IS MY DUTY TO RID THEM OF THIS SCOURGE.
I CALL IT LIBERATION.
EXIT
THE REST OF US CALL IT IRRITATION.

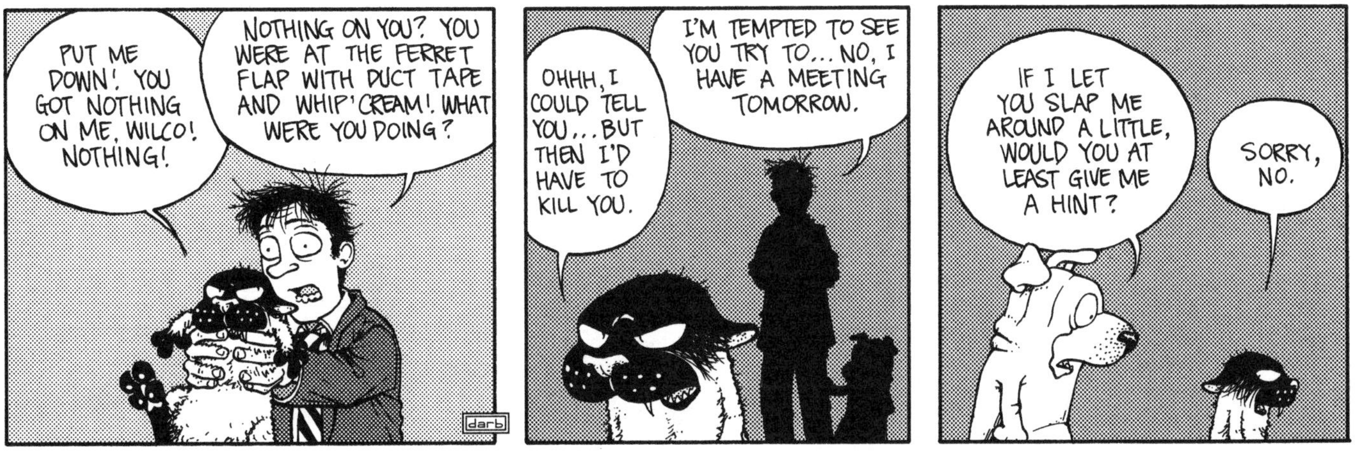
PUT ME DOWN! YOU GOT NOTHING ON ME, WILCO! NOTHING!
NOTHING ON YOU? YOU WERE AT THE FERRET FLAP WITH DUCT TAPE AND WHIP' CREAM! WHAT WERE YOU DOING?
darb
OHHH, I COULD TELL YOU... BUT THEN I'D HAVE TO KILL YOU.
I'M TEMPTED TO SEE YOU TRY TO... NO, I HAVE A MEETING TOMORROW.
IF I LET YOU SLAP ME AROUND A LITTLE, WOULD YOU AT LEAST GIVE ME A HINT?
SORRY, NO.

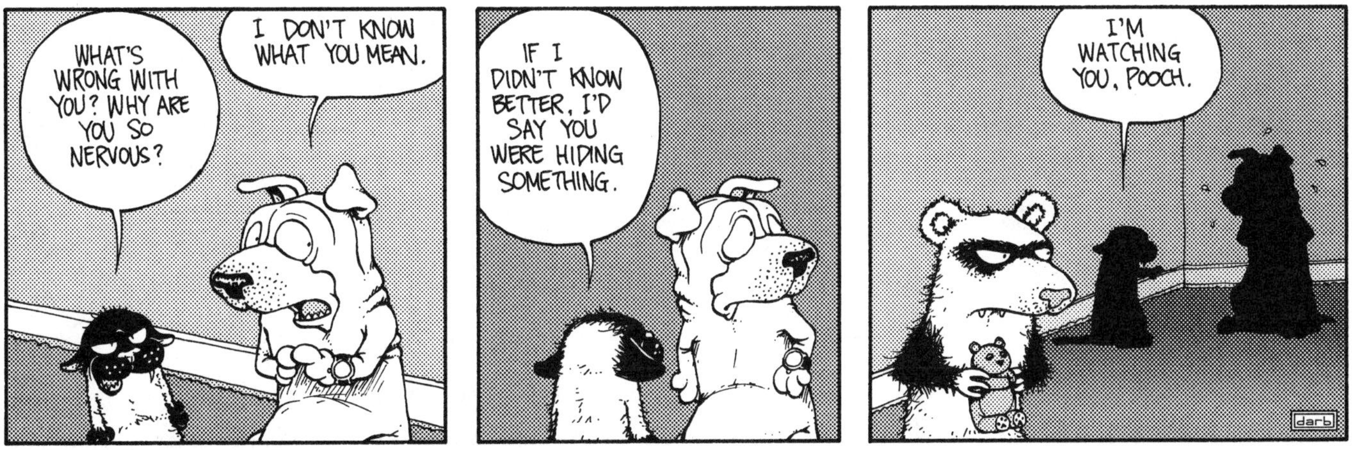
WHAT'S WRONG WITH YOU? WHY ARE YOU SO NERVOUS?
I DON'T KNOW WHAT YOU MEAN.
IF I DIDN'T KNOW BETTER, I'D SAY YOU WERE HIDING SOMETHING.
I'M WATCHING YOU, POOCH.
darb

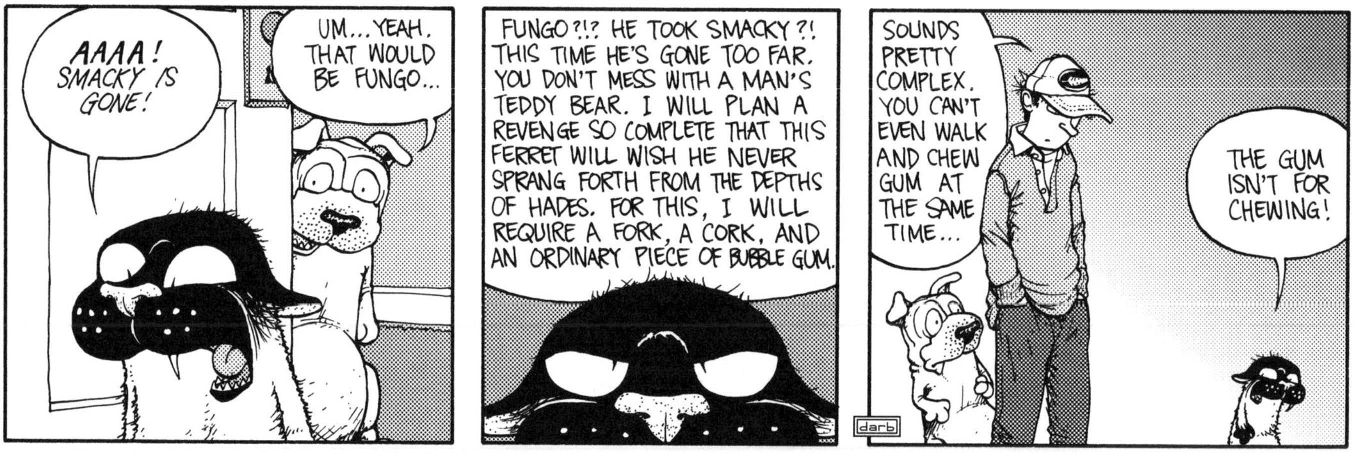
AAAA! SMACKY IS GONE!
UM... YEAH. THAT WOULD BE FUNGO...
FUNGO?!? HE TOOK SMACKY?! THIS TIME HE'S GONE TOO FAR. YOU DON'T MESS WITH A MAN'S TEDDY BEAR. I WILL PLAN A REVENGE SO COMPLETE THAT THIS FERRET WILL WISH HE NEVER SPRANG FORTH FROM THE DEPTHS OF HADES. FOR THIS, I WILL REQUIRE A FORK, A CORK, AND AN ORDINARY PIECE OF BUBBLE GUM.
darb
SOUNDS PRETTY COMPLEX. YOU CAN'T EVEN WALK AND CHEW GUM AT THE SAME TIME...
THE GUM ISN'T FOR CHEWING!

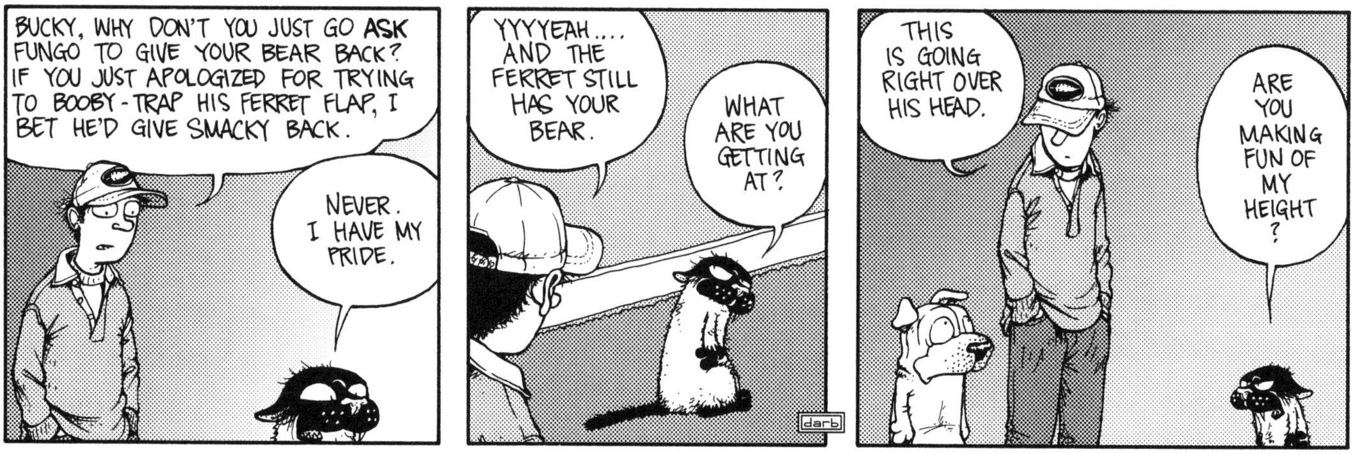
BUCKY, WHY DON'T YOU JUST GO ASK FUNGO TO GIVE YOUR BEAR BACK? IF YOU JUST APOLOGIZED FOR TRYING TO BOOBY-TRAP HIS FERRET FLAP, I BET HE'D GIVE SMACKY BACK.
NEVER. I HAVE MY PRIDE.
YYYYEAH.... AND THE FERRET STILL HAS YOUR BEAR.
WHAT ARE YOU GETTING AT?
darb
THIS IS GOING RIGHT OVER HIS HEAD.
ARE YOU MAKING FUN OF MY HEIGHT?

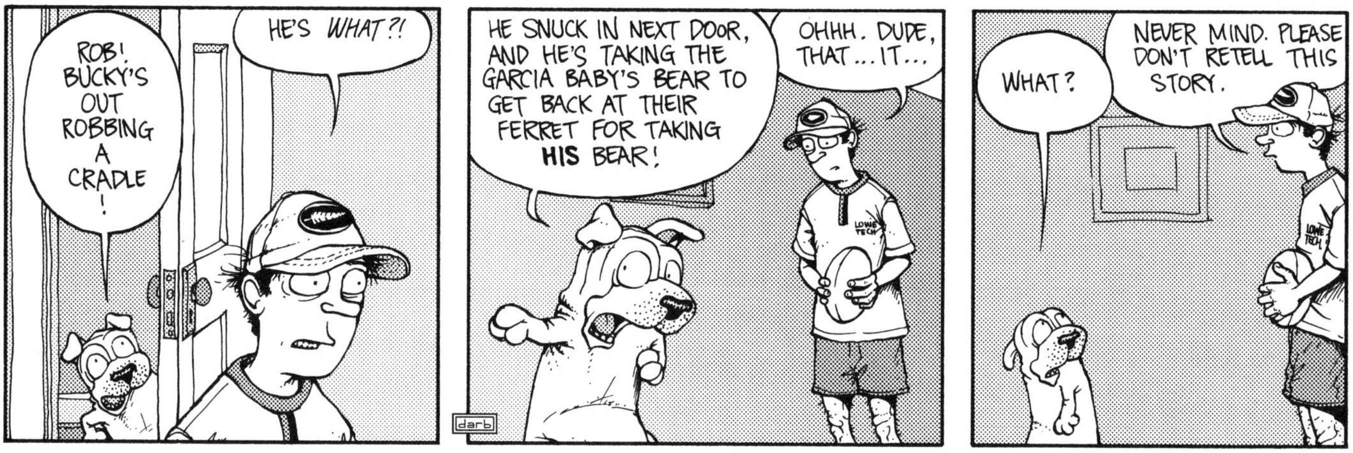
ROB! BUCKY'S OUT ROBBING A CRADLE!
HE'S WHAT?!
darb
HE SNUCK IN NEXT DOOR, AND HE'S TAKING THE GARCIA BABY'S BEAR TO GET BACK AT THEIR FERRET FOR TAKING HIS BEAR!
OHHH. DUDE, THAT... IT...
WHAT?
NEVER MIND. PLEASE DON'T RETELL THIS STORY.

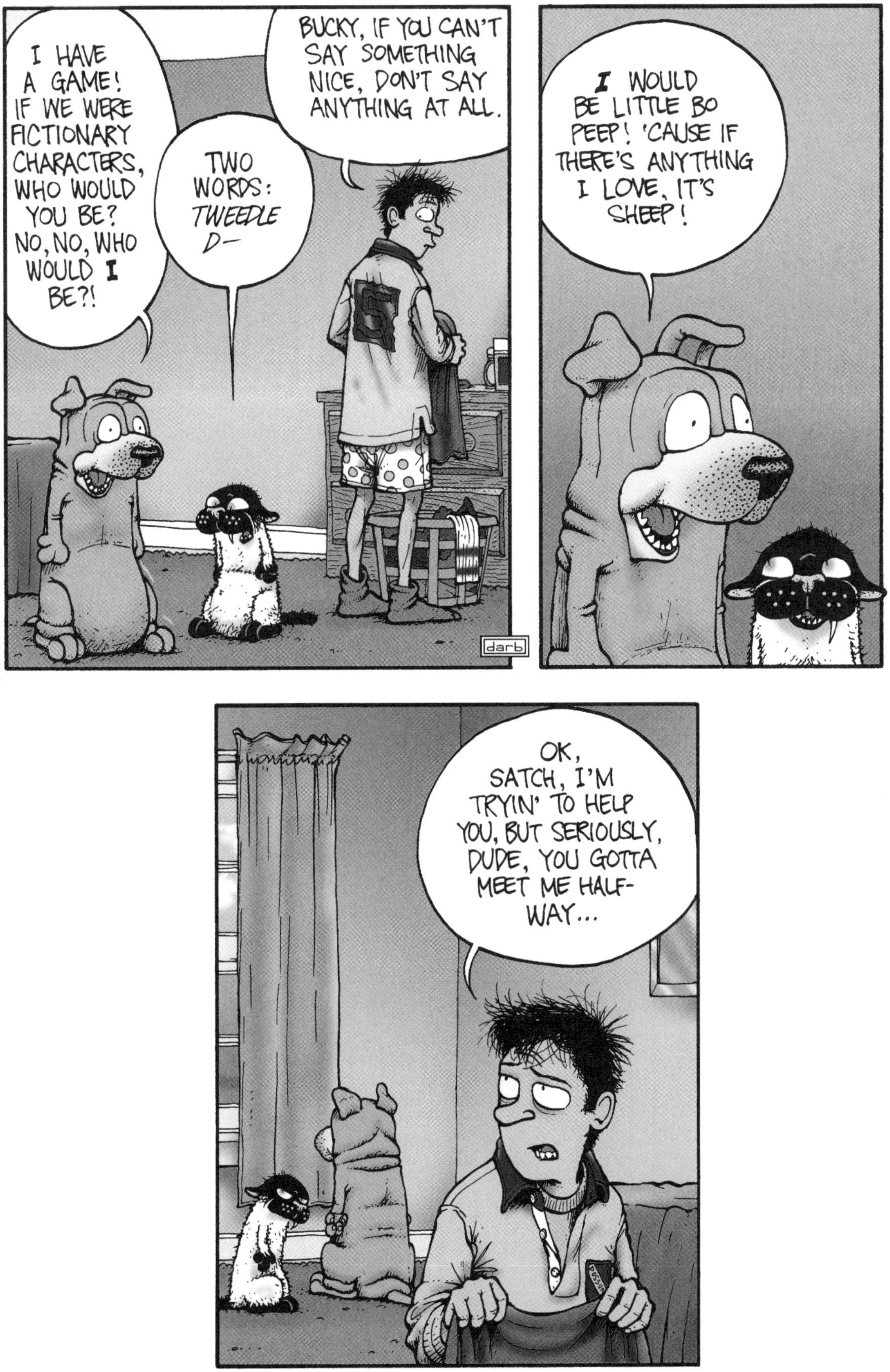
I HAVE A GAME! IF WE WERE FICTIONARY CHARACTERS, WHO WOULD YOU BE? NO, NO, WHO WOULD I BE?!
TWO WORDS: TWEEDLE D—
BUCKY, IF YOU CAN'T SAY SOMETHING NICE, DON'T SAY ANYTHING AT ALL.
darb
I WOULD BE LITTLE BO PEEP! 'CAUSE IF THERE'S ANYTHING I LOVE, IT'S SHEEP!
OK, SATCH, I'M TRYIN' TO HELP YOU, BUT SERIOUSLY, DUDE, YOU GOTTA MEET ME HALF-WAY...

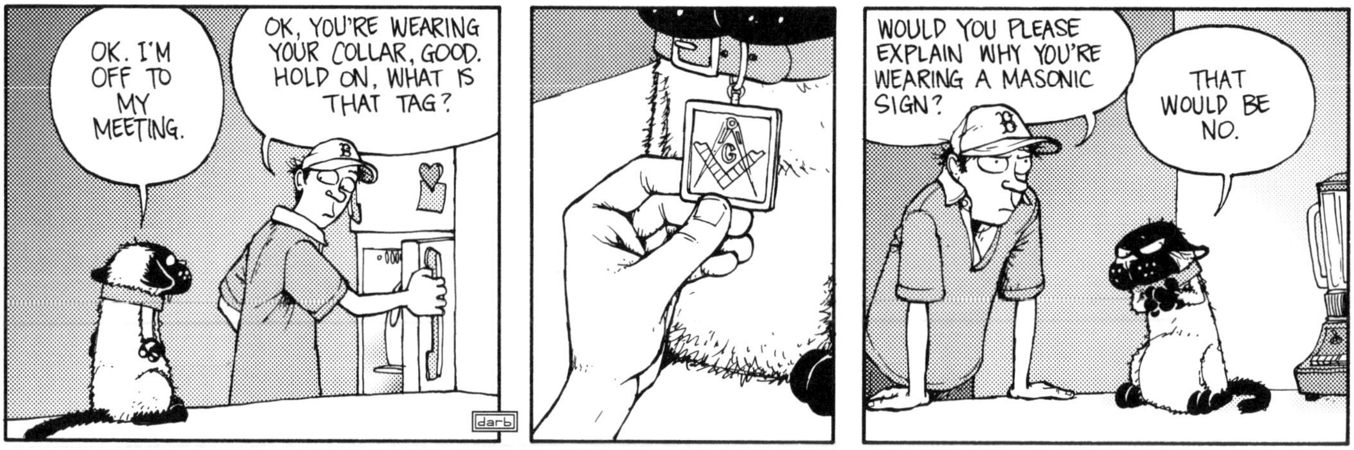
OK. I'M OFF TO MY MEETING.
OK, YOU'RE WEARING YOUR COLLAR, GOOD. HOLD ON, WHAT IS THAT TAG?
darb
WOULD YOU PLEASE EXPLAIN WHY YOU'RE WEARING A MASONIC SIGN?
THAT WOULD BE NO.

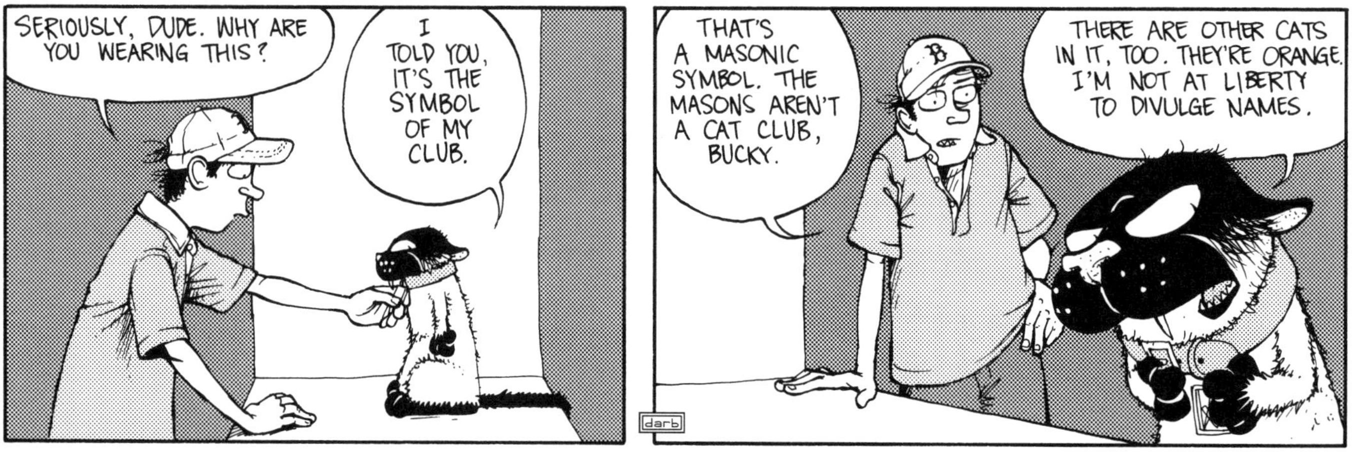
SERIOUSLY, DUDE. WHY ARE YOU WEARING THIS?
I TOLD YOU, IT'S THE SYMBOL OF MY CLUB.
darb
THAT'S A MASONIC SYMBOL. THE MASONS AREN'T A CAT CLUB, BUCKY.
THERE ARE OTHER CATS IN IT, TOO. THEY'RE ORANGE. I'M NOT AT LIBERTY TO DIVULGE NAMES.

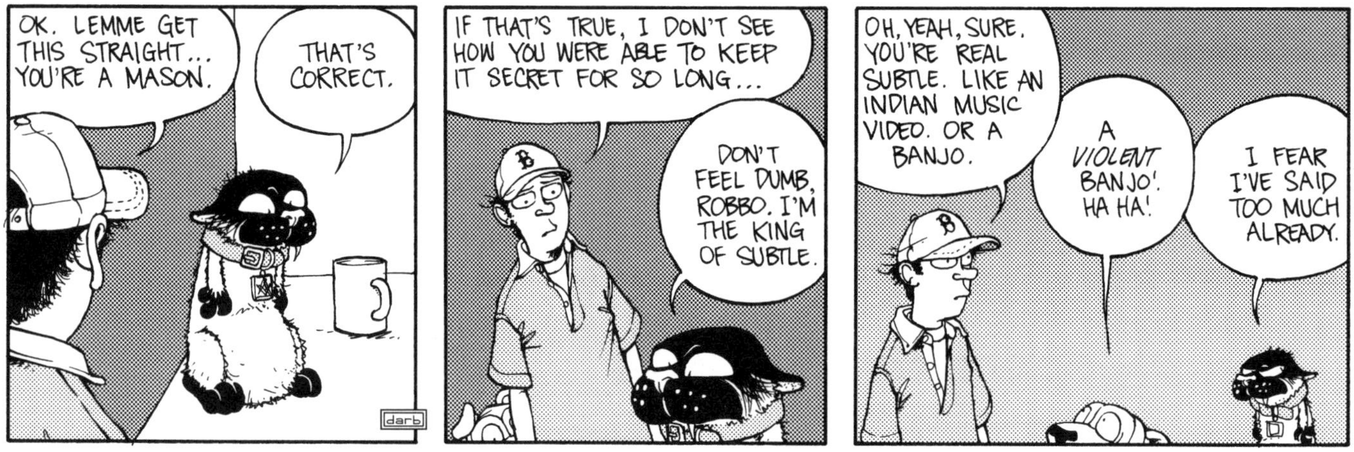
OK. LEMME GET THIS STRAIGHT... YOU'RE A MASON.
THAT'S CORRECT.
darb
IF THAT'S TRUE, I DON'T SEE HOW YOU WERE ABLE TO KEEP IT SECRET FOR SO LONG...
DON'T FEEL DUMB, ROBBO. I'M THE KING OF SUBTLE.
OH, YEAH, SURE. YOU'RE REAL SUBTLE. LIKE AN INDIAN MUSIC VIDEO. OR A BANJO.
A *VIOLENT* BANJO! HA HA!
I FEAR I'VE SAID TOO MUCH ALREADY.

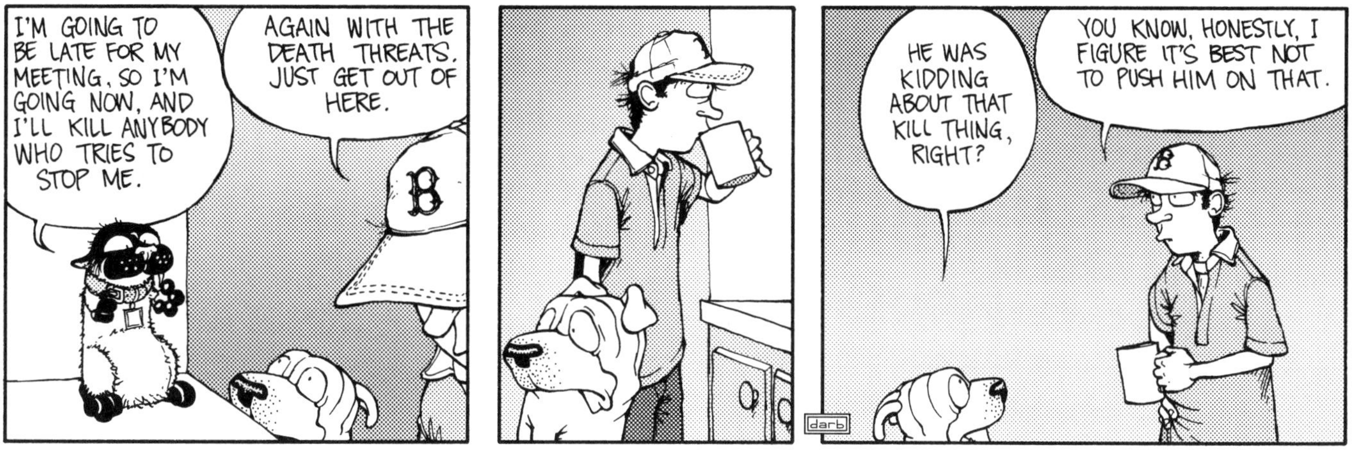
I'M GOING TO BE LATE FOR MY MEETING. SO I'M GOING NOW, AND I'LL KILL ANYBODY WHO TRIES TO STOP ME.
AGAIN WITH THE DEATH THREATS. JUST GET OUT OF HERE.
HE WAS KIDDING ABOUT THAT KILL THING, RIGHT?
YOU KNOW, HONESTLY, I FIGURE IT'S BEST NOT TO PUSH HIM ON THAT.
darb

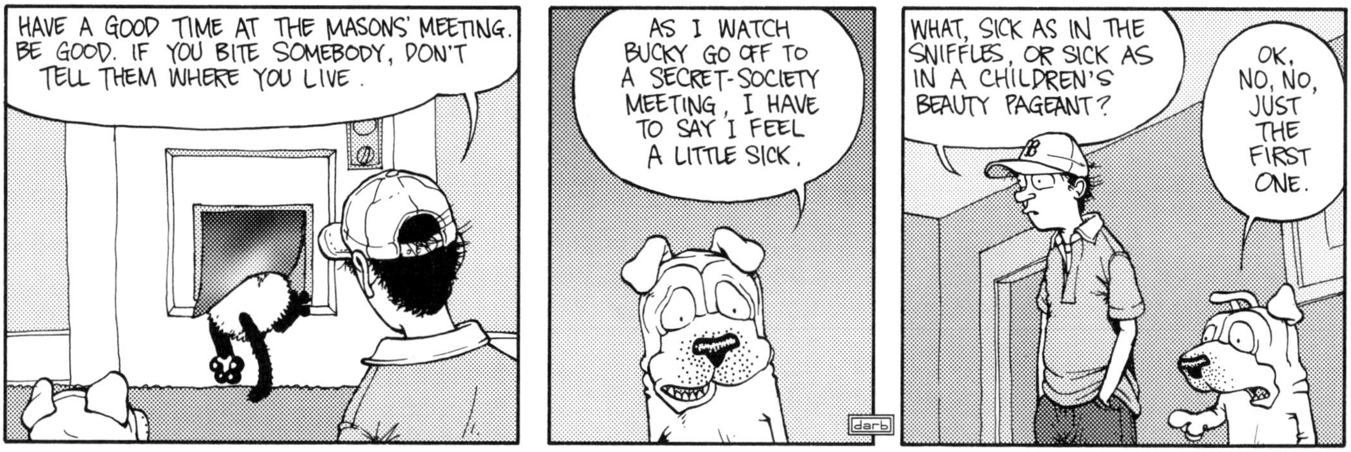
HAVE A GOOD TIME AT THE MASONS' MEETING. BE GOOD. IF YOU BITE SOMEBODY, DON'T TELL THEM WHERE YOU LIVE.
AS I WATCH BUCKY GO OFF TO A SECRET-SOCIETY MEETING, I HAVE TO SAY I FEEL A LITTLE SICK.
WHAT, SICK AS IN THE SNIFFLES, OR SICK AS IN A CHILDREN'S BEAUTY PAGEANT?
OK, NO, NO, JUST THE FIRST ONE.
darb

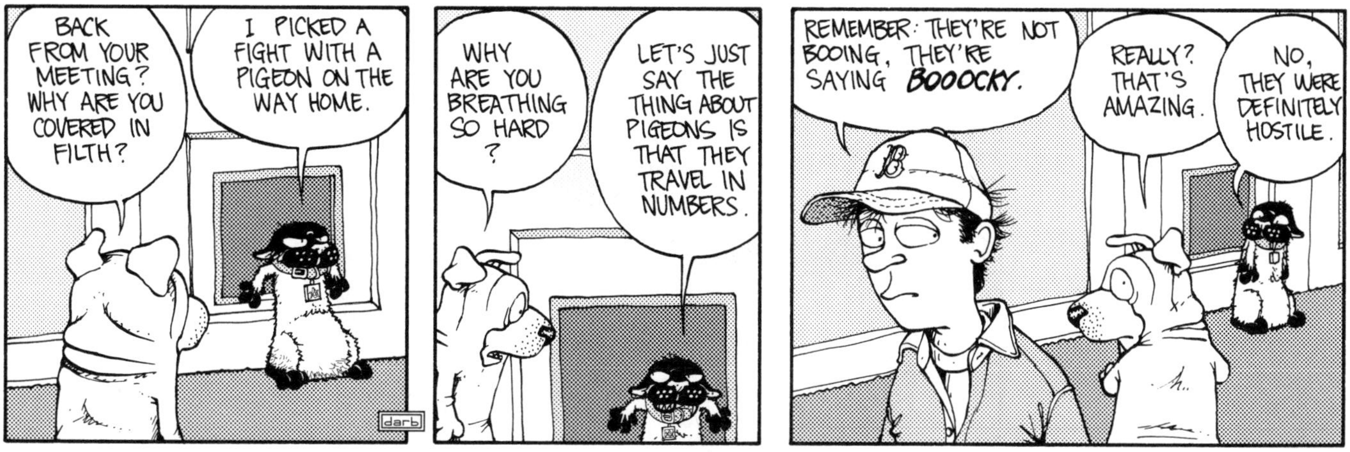
BACK FROM YOUR MEETING? WHY ARE YOU COVERED IN FILTH?
I PICKED A FIGHT WITH A PIGEON ON THE WAY HOME.
WHY ARE YOU BREATHING SO HARD?
LET'S JUST SAY THE THING ABOUT PIGEONS IS THAT THEY TRAVEL IN NUMBERS.
REMEMBER: THEY'RE NOT BOOING, THEY'RE SAYING BOOOCKY.
REALLY? THAT'S AMAZING.
NO, THEY WERE DEFINITELY HOSTILE.
darb

ARE YOU ALRIGHT? I HEARD A HUGE CRASH!

THERE I WAS...ON TOP OF THE FRIDGE... TRYING TO EAT ROB'S LAST PLANT...

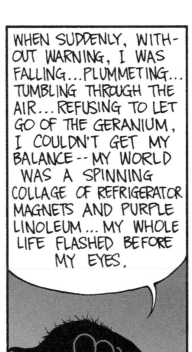

WHEN SUDDENLY, WITH-OUT WARNING, I WAS FALLING...PLUMMETING... TUMBLING THROUGH THE AIR...REFUSING TO LET GO OF THE GERANIUM, I COULDN'T GET MY BALANCE -- MY WORLD WAS A SPINNING COLLAGE OF REFRIGERATOR MAGNETS AND PURPLE LINOLEUM... MY WHOLE LIFE FLASHED BEFORE MY EYES.

darb

MAN, I SLEPT A **LOT**, DIDN'T I?

DID YOU HAPPEN TO SEE WHERE YOU LOST MY BLANKIE LAST YEAR?

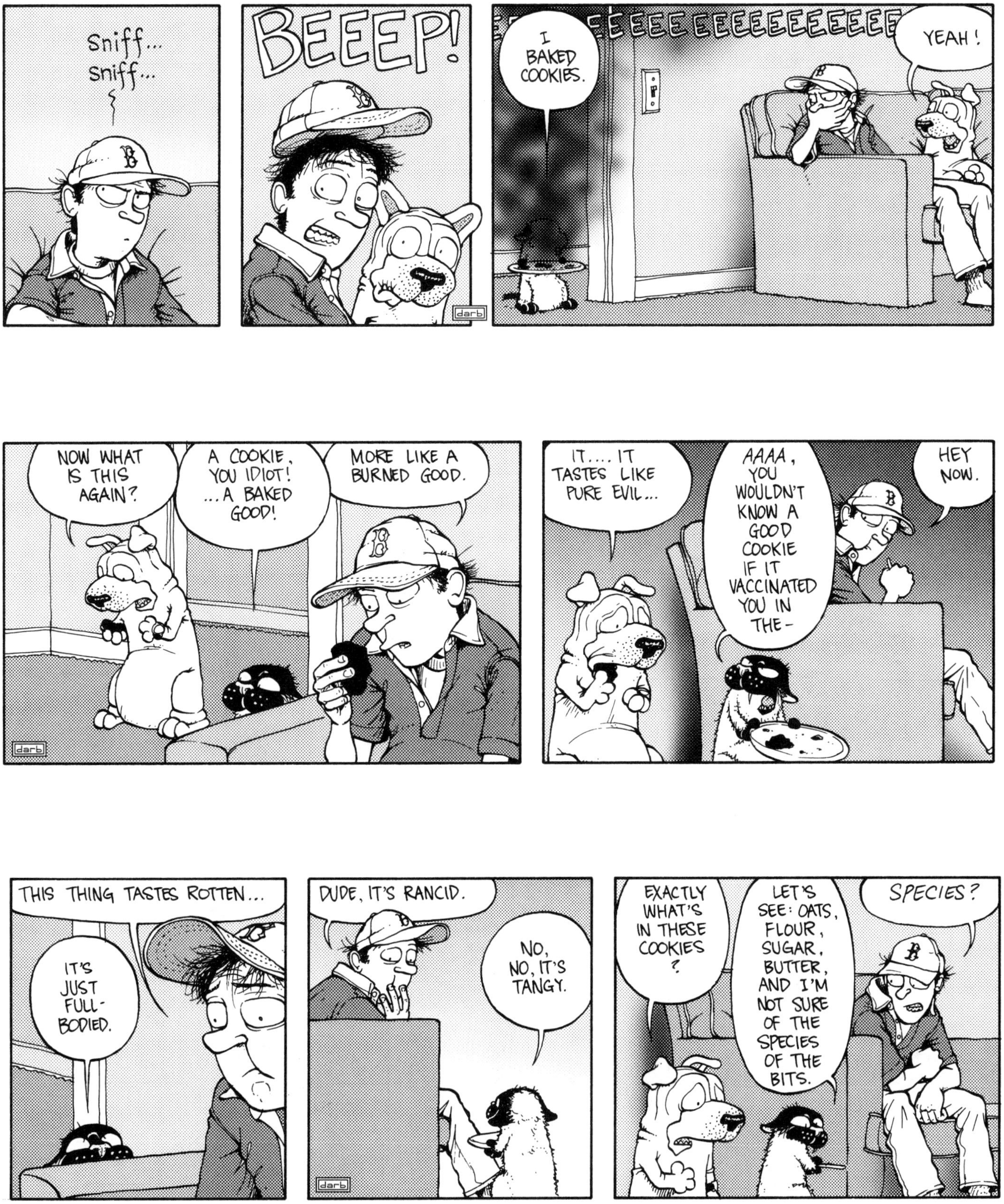
Sniff... sniff...
BEEEP!
darb
EEEEEEEEEEEEEEEEE
I BAKED COOKIES.
YEAH!
NOW WHAT IS THIS AGAIN?
A COOKIE, YOU IDIOT! ...A BAKED GOOD!
MORE LIKE A BURNED GOOD.
darb
IT.... IT TASTES LIKE PURE EVIL...
AAAA, YOU WOULDN'T KNOW A GOOD COOKIE IF IT VACCINATED YOU IN THE-
HEY NOW.
THIS THING TASTES ROTTEN...
IT'S JUST FULL-BODIED.
DUDE, IT'S RANCID.
NO, NO, IT'S TANGY.
darb
EXACTLY WHAT'S IN THESE COOKIES?
LET'S SEE: OATS, FLOUR, SUGAR, BUTTER, AND I'M NOT SURE OF THE SPECIES OF THE BITS.
SPECIES?

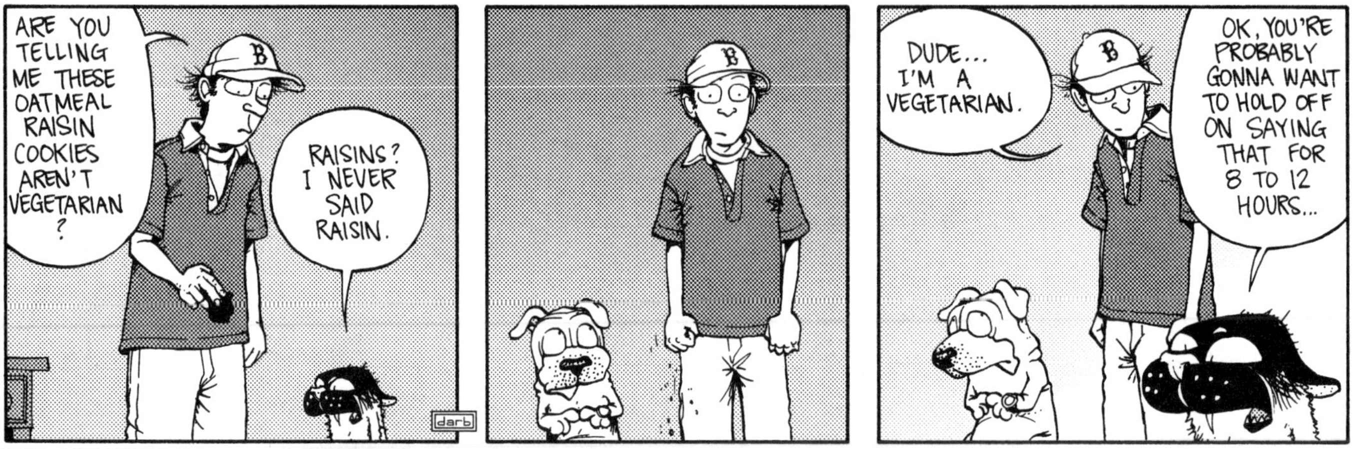
ARE YOU TELLING ME THESE OATMEAL RAISIN COOKIES AREN'T VEGETARIAN ?
RAISINS? I NEVER SAID RAISIN.
darb
DUDE... I'M A VEGETARIAN.
OK, YOU'RE PROBABLY GONNA WANT TO HOLD OFF ON SAYING THAT FOR 8 TO 12 HOURS...

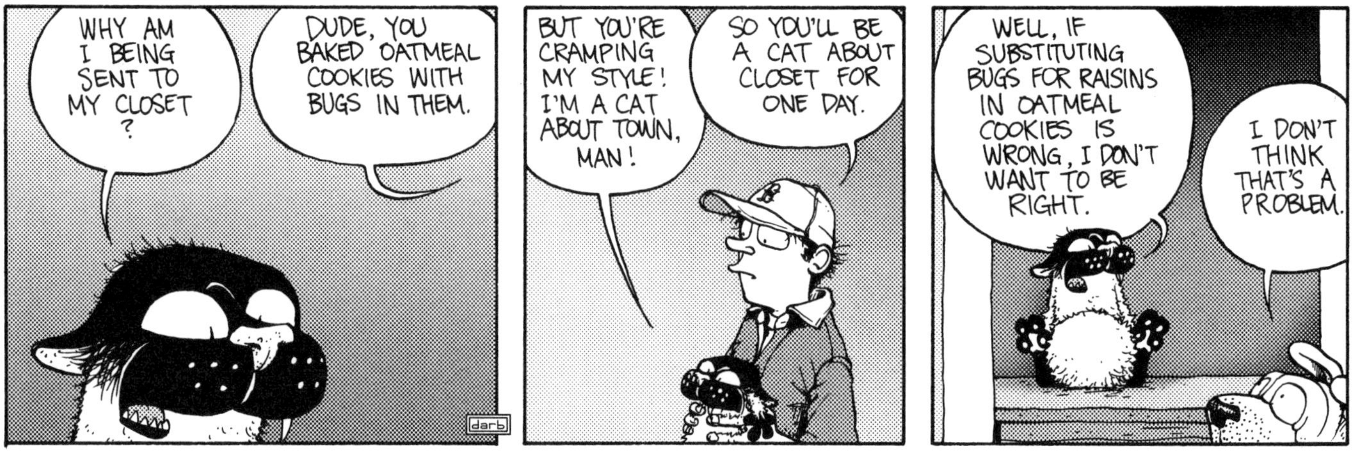
WHY AM I BEING SENT TO MY CLOSET ?
DUDE, YOU BAKED OATMEAL COOKIES WITH BUGS IN THEM.
darb
BUT YOU'RE CRAMPING MY STYLE! I'M A CAT ABOUT TOWN, MAN!
SO YOU'LL BE A CAT ABOUT CLOSET FOR ONE DAY.
WELL, IF SUBSTITUTING BUGS FOR RAISINS IN OATMEAL COOKIES IS WRONG, I DON'T WANT TO BE RIGHT.
I DON'T THINK THAT'S A PROBLEM.

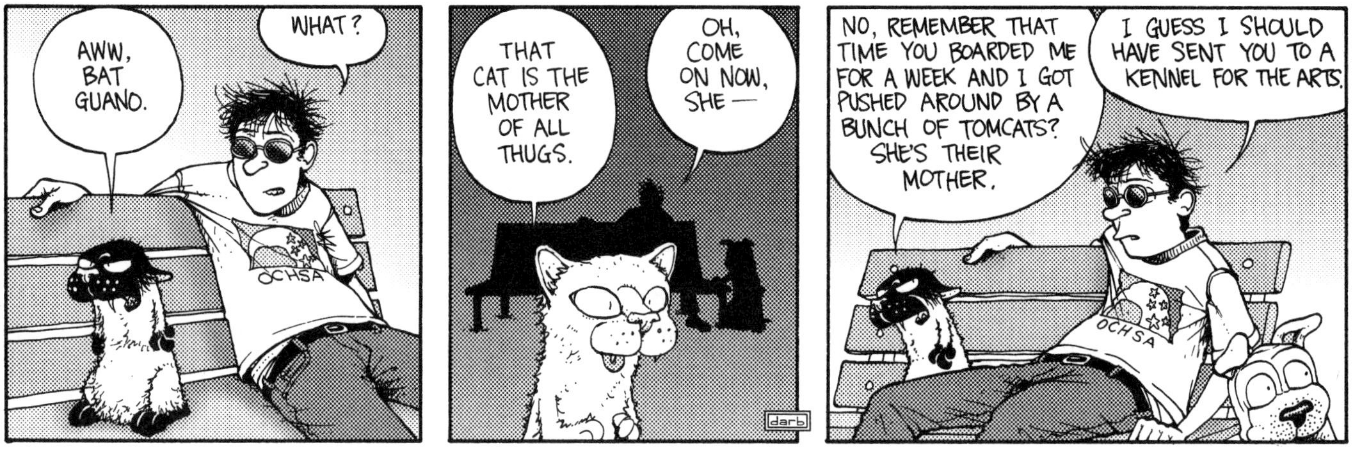
AWW, BAT GUANO.
WHAT?
OCHSA
THAT CAT IS THE MOTHER OF ALL THUGS.
OH, COME ON NOW, SHE—
darb
NO, REMEMBER THAT TIME YOU BOARDED ME FOR A WEEK AND I GOT PUSHED AROUND BY A BUNCH OF TOMCATS? SHE'S THEIR MOTHER.
I GUESS I SHOULD HAVE SENT YOU TO A KENNEL FOR THE ARTS.
OCHSA

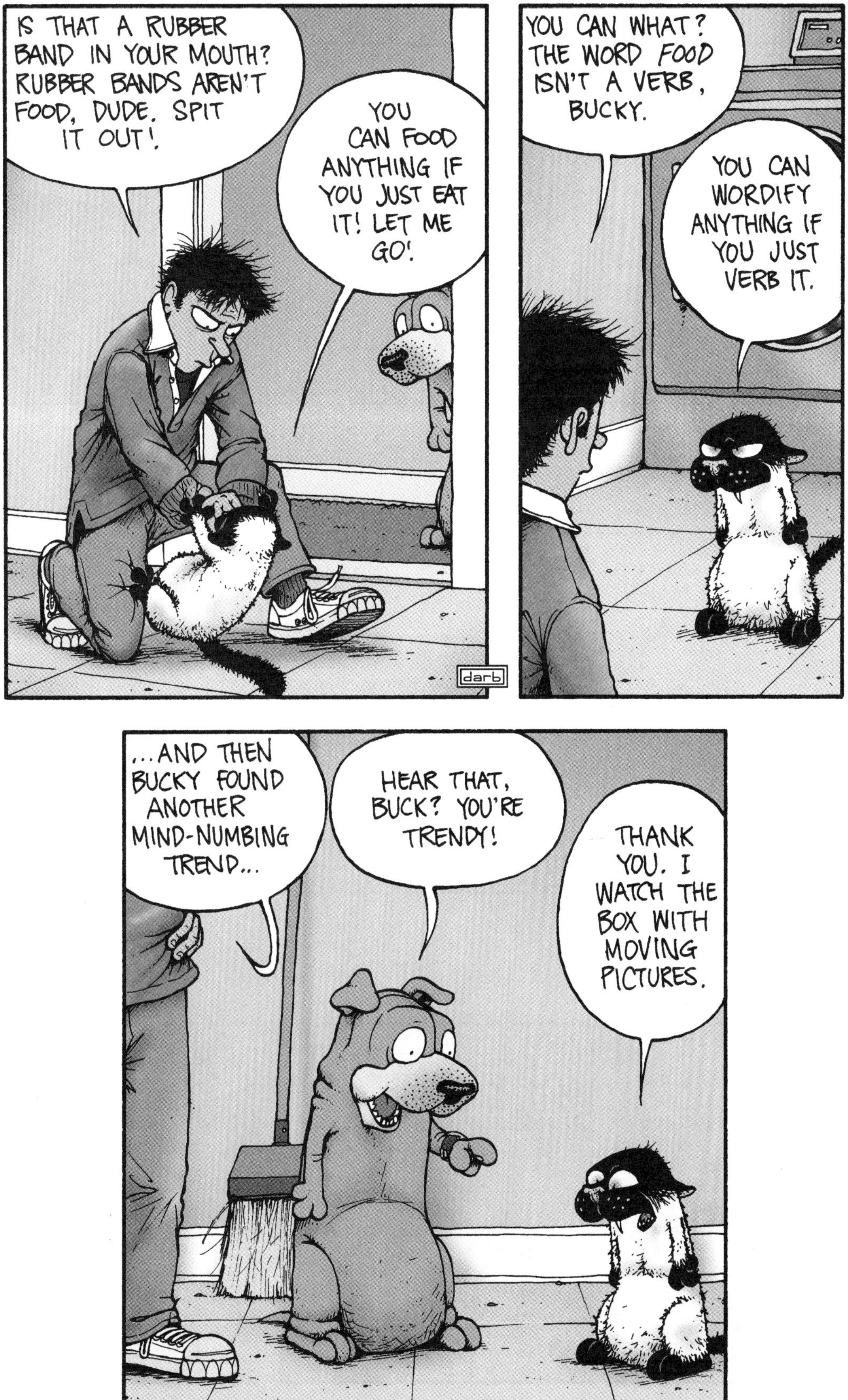
IS THAT A RUBBER BAND IN YOUR MOUTH? RUBBER BANDS AREN'T FOOD, DUDE. SPIT IT OUT!
YOU CAN FOOD ANYTHING IF YOU JUST EAT IT! LET ME GO!
darb
YOU CAN WHAT? THE WORD *FOOD* ISN'T A VERB, BUCKY.
YOU CAN WORDIFY ANYTHING IF YOU JUST VERB IT.
...AND THEN BUCKY FOUND ANOTHER MIND-NUMBING TREND...
HEAR THAT, BUCK? YOU'RE TRENDY!
THANK YOU. I WATCH THE BOX WITH MOVING PICTURES.

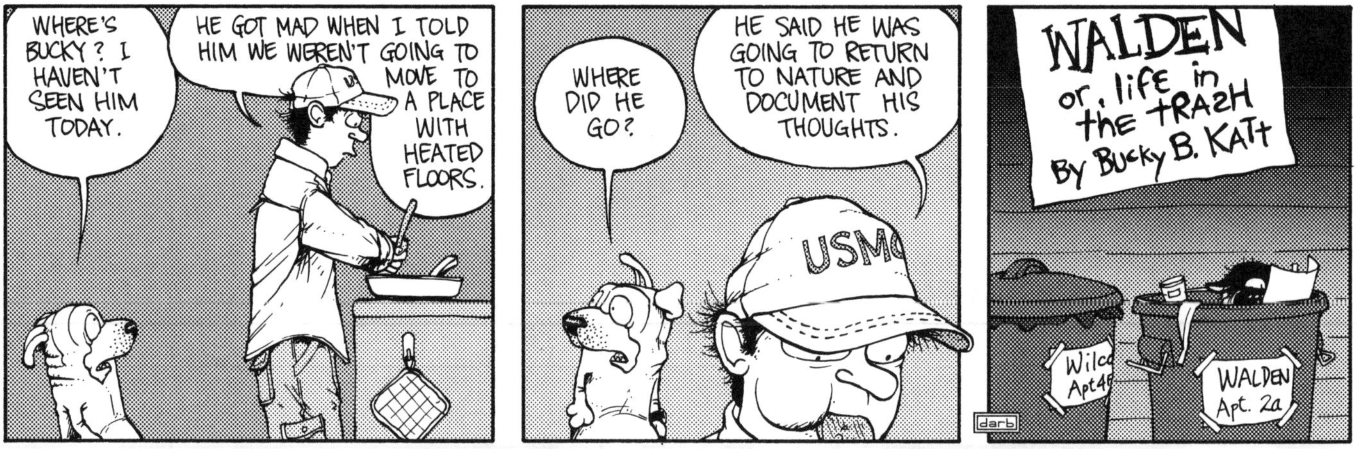
WHERE'S BUCKY? I HAVEN'T SEEN HIM TODAY.
HE GOT MAD WHEN I TOLD HIM WE WEREN'T GOING TO MOVE TO A PLACE WITH HEATED FLOORS.
WHERE DID HE GO?
HE SAID HE WAS GOING TO RETURN TO NATURE AND DOCUMENT HIS THOUGHTS.
USMC
WALDEN or, life in the TRAZH By Bucky B. KAtt
Wilco Apt4B
WALDEN Apt. 2a
darb

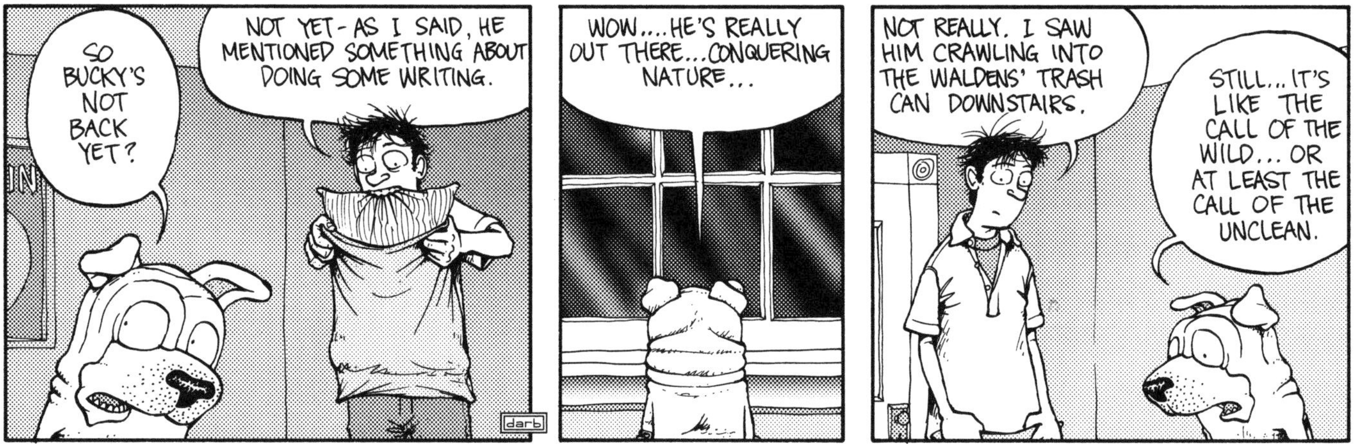
SO BUCKY'S NOT BACK YET?
NOT YET- AS I SAID, HE MENTIONED SOMETHING ABOUT DOING SOME WRITING.
darb
WOW....HE'S REALLY OUT THERE...CONQUERING NATURE...
NOT REALLY. I SAW HIM CRAWLING INTO THE WALDENS' TRASH CAN DOWNSTAIRS.
STILL... IT'S LIKE THE CALL OF THE WILD... OR AT LEAST THE CALL OF THE UNCLEAN.

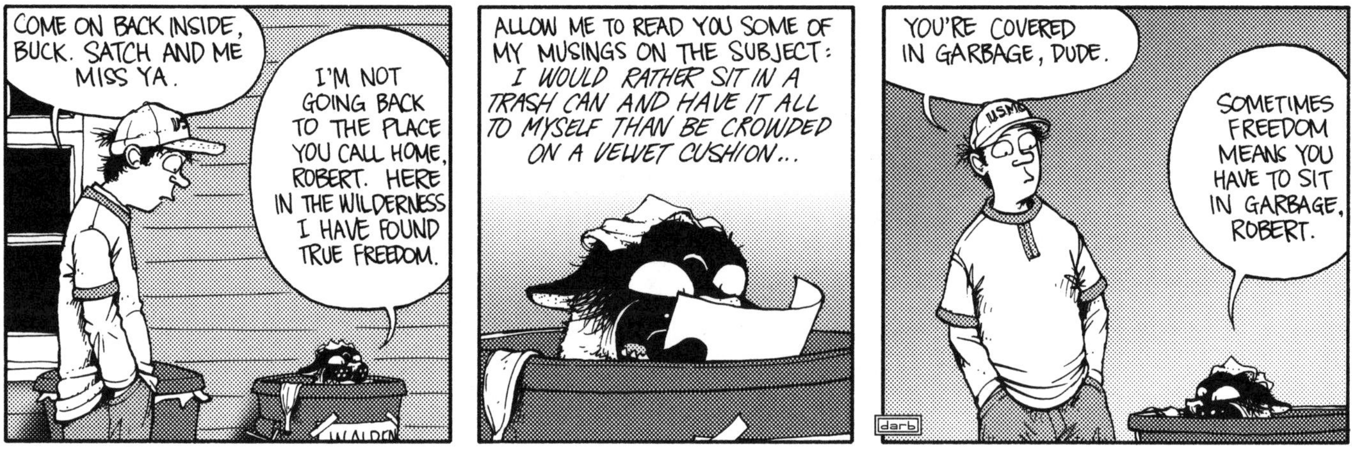
COME ON BACK INSIDE, BUCK. SATCH AND ME MISS YA.
I'M NOT GOING BACK TO THE PLACE YOU CALL HOME, ROBERT. HERE IN THE WILDERNESS I HAVE FOUND TRUE FREEDOM.
ALLOW ME TO READ YOU SOME OF MY MUSINGS ON THE SUBJECT: *I WOULD RATHER SIT IN A TRASH CAN AND HAVE IT ALL TO MYSELF THAN BE CROWDED ON A VELVET CUSHION...*
YOU'RE COVERED IN GARBAGE, DUDE.
USMC
SOMETIMES FREEDOM MEANS YOU HAVE TO SIT IN GARBAGE, ROBERT.
darb

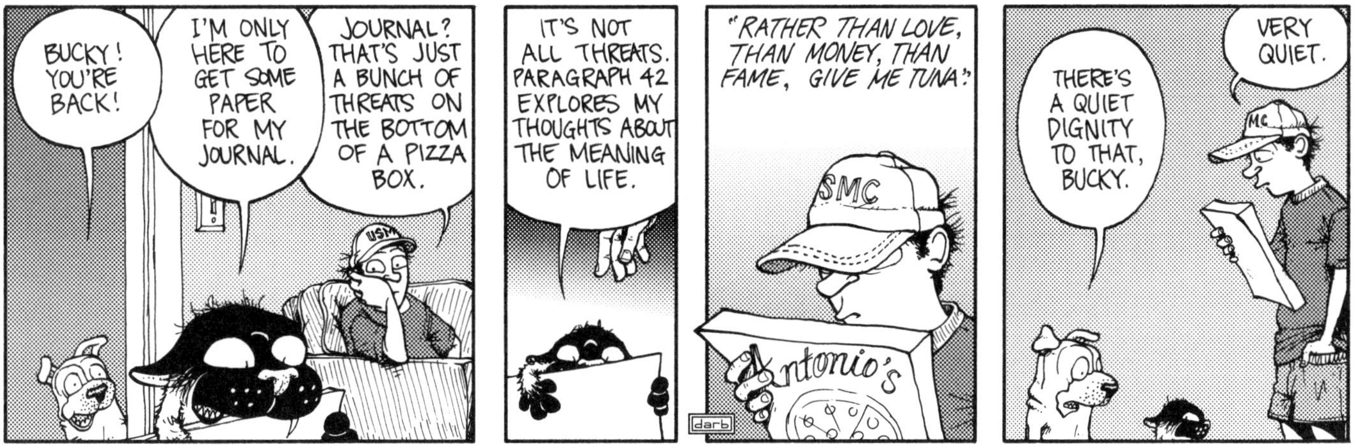
BUCKY! YOU'RE BACK!
I'M ONLY HERE TO GET SOME PAPER FOR MY JOURNAL.
JOURNAL? THAT'S JUST A BUNCH OF THREATS ON THE BOTTOM OF A PIZZA BOX.
IT'S NOT ALL THREATS. PARAGRAPH 42 EXPLORES MY THOUGHTS ABOUT THE MEANING OF LIFE.
"RATHER THAN LOVE, THAN MONEY, THAN FAME, GIVE ME TUNA."
Antonio's
THERE'S A QUIET DIGNITY TO THAT, BUCKY.
VERY QUIET.

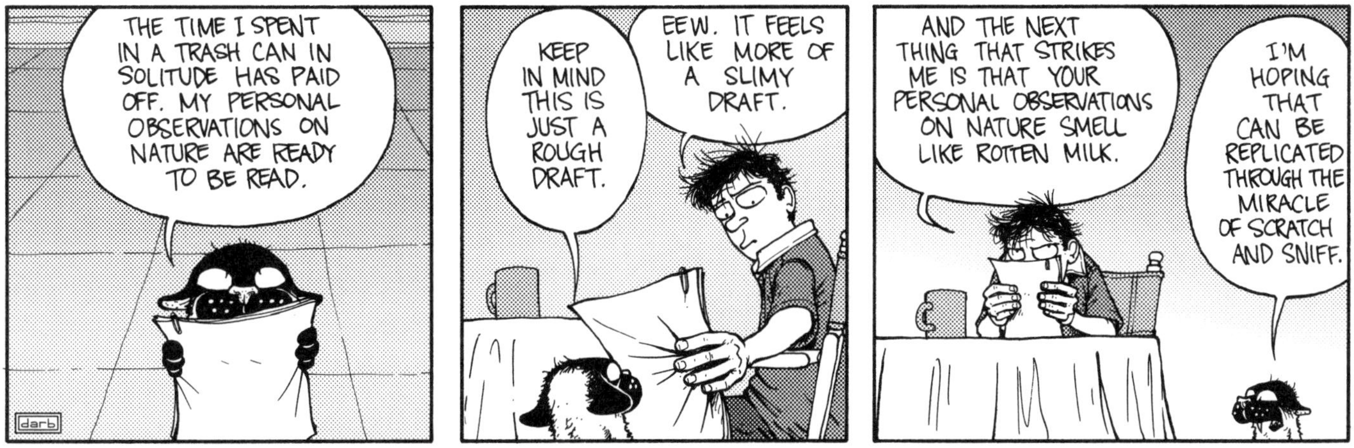
THE TIME I SPENT IN A TRASH CAN IN SOLITUDE HAS PAID OFF. MY PERSONAL OBSERVATIONS ON NATURE ARE READY TO BE READ.
KEEP IN MIND THIS IS JUST A ROUGH DRAFT.
EEW. IT FEELS LIKE MORE OF A SLIMY DRAFT.
AND THE NEXT THING THAT STRIKES ME IS THAT YOUR PERSONAL OBSERVATIONS ON NATURE SMELL LIKE ROTTEN MILK.
I'M HOPING THAT CAN BE REPLICATED THROUGH THE MIRACLE OF SCRATCH AND SNIFF.

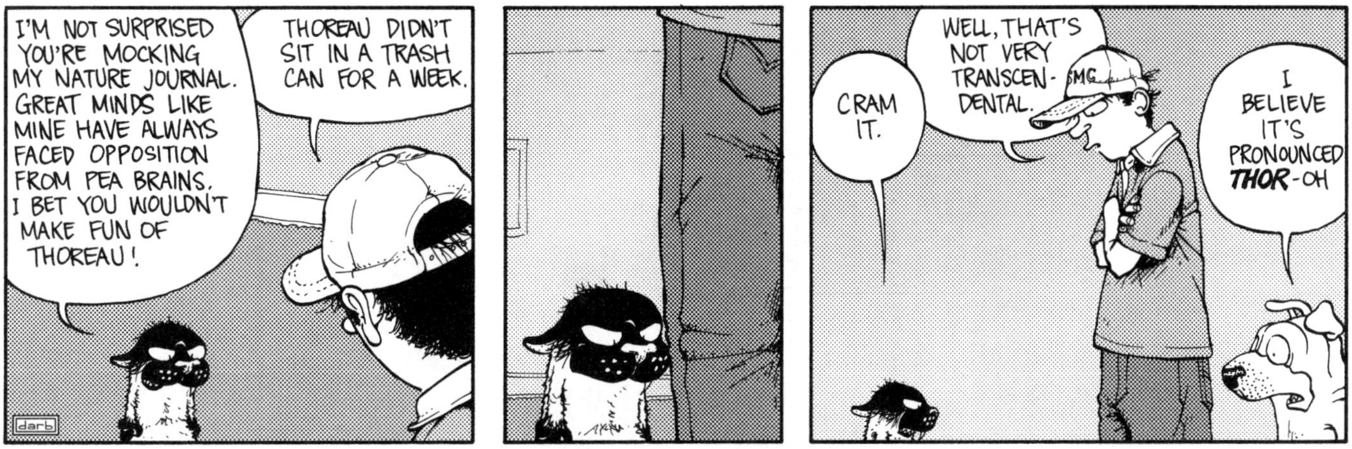
I'M NOT SURPRISED YOU'RE MOCKING MY NATURE JOURNAL. GREAT MINDS LIKE MINE HAVE ALWAYS FACED OPPOSITION FROM PEA BRAINS. I BET YOU WOULDN'T MAKE FUN OF THOREAU!
THOREAU DIDN'T SIT IN A TRASH CAN FOR A WEEK.
CRAM IT.
WELL, THAT'S NOT VERY TRANSCEN-DENTAL.
I BELIEVE IT'S PRONOUNCED THOR-OH

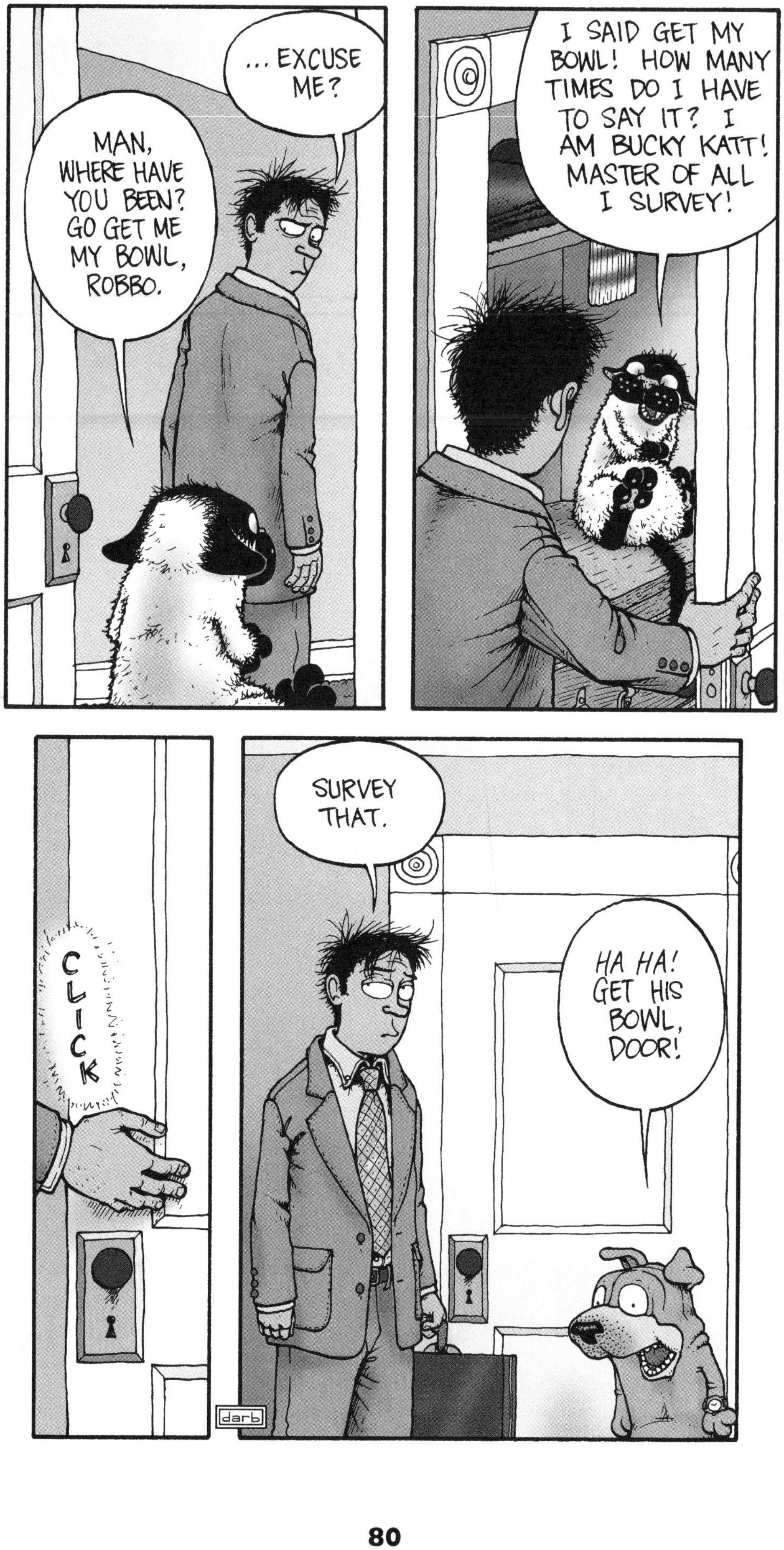
MAN, WHERE HAVE YOU BEEN? GO GET ME MY BOWL, ROBBO.
... EXCUSE ME?
I SAID GET MY BOWL! HOW MANY TIMES DO I HAVE TO SAY IT? I AM BUCKY KATT! MASTER OF ALL I SURVEY!
CLICK
SURVEY THAT.
HA HA! GET HIS BOWL, DOOR!
darb

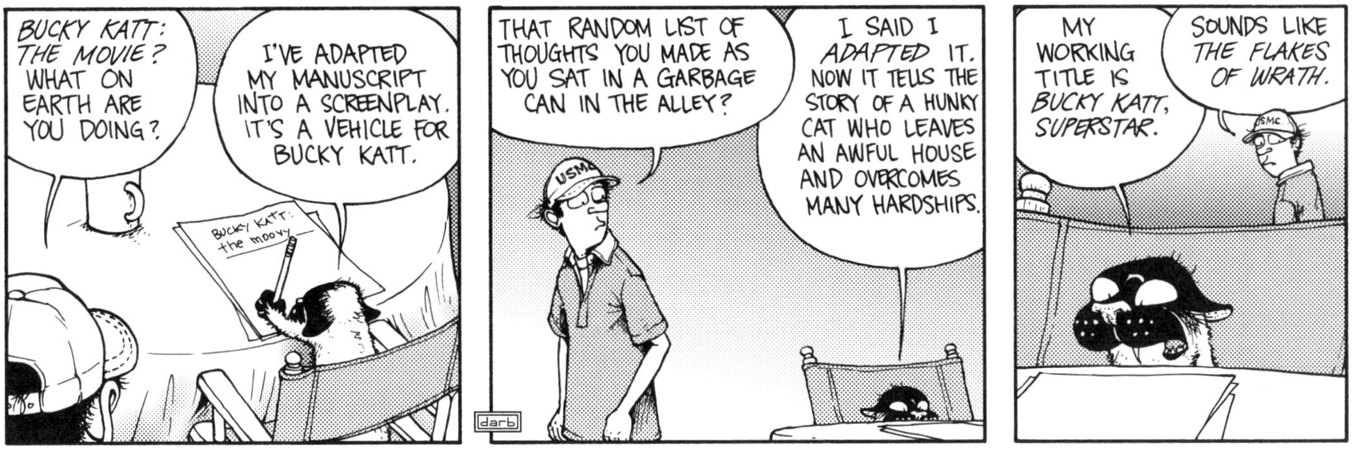
BUCKY KATT: THE MOVIE? WHAT ON EARTH ARE YOU DOING?
I'VE ADAPTED MY MANUSCRIPT INTO A SCREENPLAY. IT'S A VEHICLE FOR BUCKY KATT.
BUCKY KATT: the moovy
THAT RANDOM LIST OF THOUGHTS YOU MADE AS YOU SAT IN A GARBAGE CAN IN THE ALLEY?
I SAID I ADAPTED IT. NOW IT TELLS THE STORY OF A HUNKY CAT WHO LEAVES AN AWFUL HOUSE AND OVERCOMES MANY HARDSHIPS.
MY WORKING TITLE IS BUCKY KATT, SUPERSTAR.
SOUNDS LIKE THE FLAKES OF WRATH.

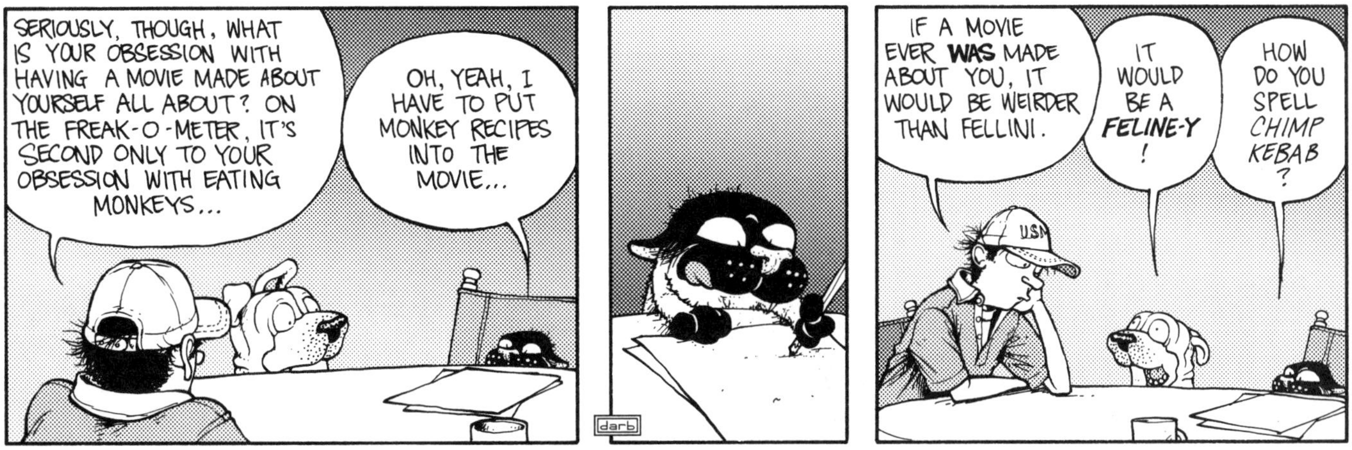
SERIOUSLY, THOUGH, WHAT IS YOUR OBSESSION WITH HAVING A MOVIE MADE ABOUT YOURSELF ALL ABOUT? ON THE FREAK-O-METER, IT'S SECOND ONLY TO YOUR OBSESSION WITH EATING MONKEYS...
OH, YEAH, I HAVE TO PUT MONKEY RECIPES INTO THE MOVIE...
IF A MOVIE EVER WAS MADE ABOUT YOU, IT WOULD BE WEIRDER THAN FELLINI.
IT WOULD BE A FELINE-Y!
HOW DO YOU SPELL CHIMP KEBAB?

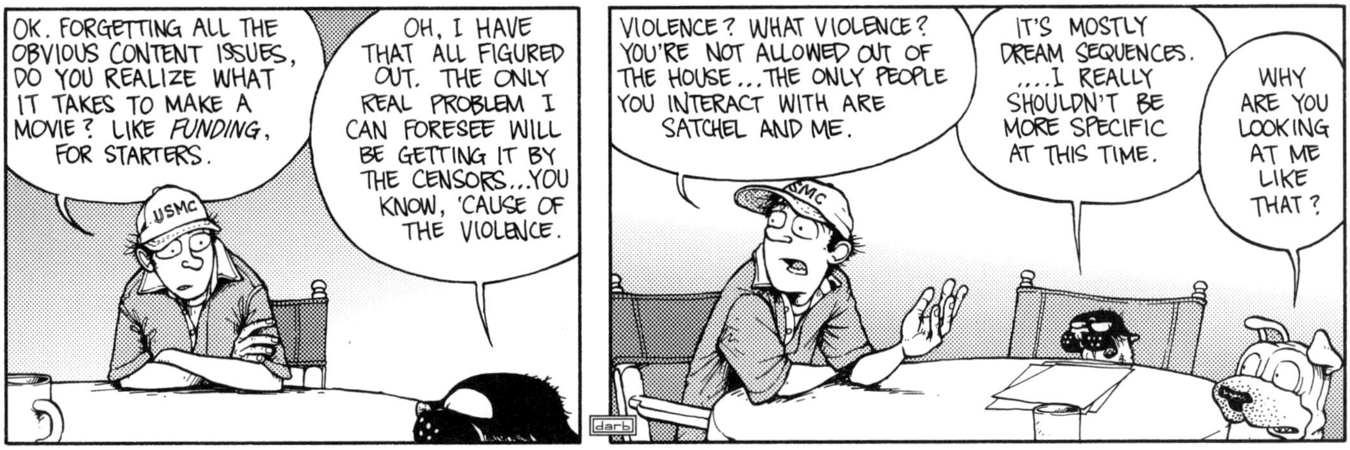
OK. FORGETTING ALL THE OBVIOUS CONTENT ISSUES, DO YOU REALIZE WHAT IT TAKES TO MAKE A MOVIE? LIKE FUNDING, FOR STARTERS.
OH, I HAVE THAT ALL FIGURED OUT. THE ONLY REAL PROBLEM I CAN FORESEE WILL BE GETTING IT BY THE CENSORS...YOU KNOW, 'CAUSE OF THE VIOLENCE.
VIOLENCE? WHAT VIOLENCE? YOU'RE NOT ALLOWED OUT OF THE HOUSE...THE ONLY PEOPLE YOU INTERACT WITH ARE SATCHEL AND ME.
IT'S MOSTLY DREAM SEQUENCES. ....I REALLY SHOULDN'T BE MORE SPECIFIC AT THIS TIME.
WHY ARE YOU LOOKING AT ME LIKE THAT?

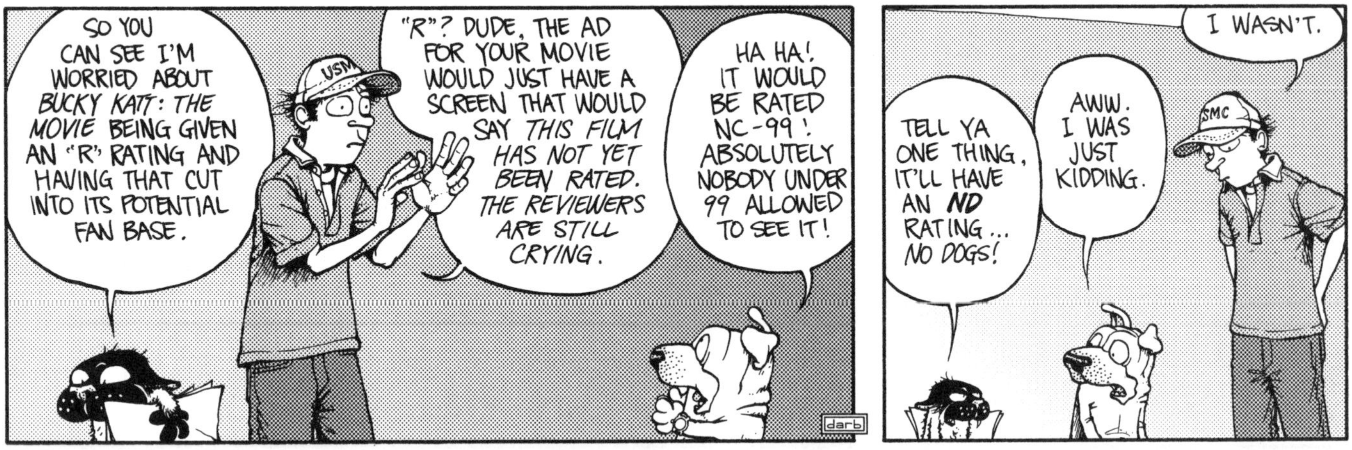
SO YOU CAN SEE I'M WORRIED ABOUT *BUCKY KATT: THE MOVIE* BEING GIVEN AN "R" RATING AND HAVING THAT CUT INTO ITS POTENTIAL FAN BASE.
"R"? DUDE, THE AD FOR YOUR MOVIE WOULD JUST HAVE A SCREEN THAT WOULD SAY *THIS FILM HAS NOT YET BEEN RATED. THE REVIEWERS ARE STILL CRYING.*
HA HA! IT WOULD BE RATED NC-99! ABSOLUTELY NOBODY UNDER 99 ALLOWED TO SEE IT!
darb
TELL YA ONE THING, IT'LL HAVE AN ***ND*** RATING... *NO DOGS!*
AWW. I WAS JUST KIDDING.
I WASN'T.

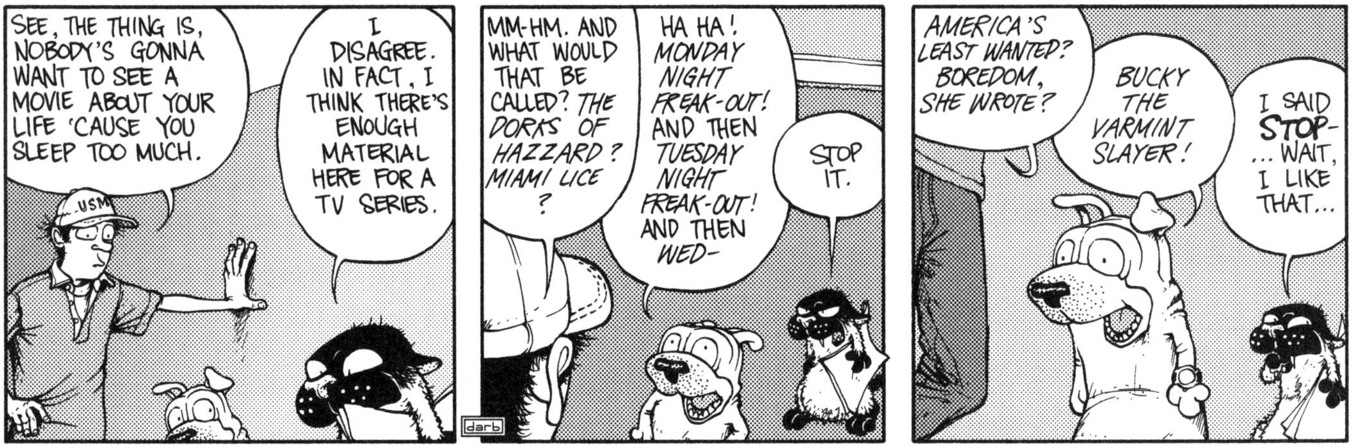
SEE, THE THING IS, NOBODY'S GONNA WANT TO SEE A MOVIE ABOUT YOUR LIFE 'CAUSE YOU SLEEP TOO MUCH.
I DISAGREE. IN FACT, I THINK THERE'S ENOUGH MATERIAL HERE FOR A TV SERIES.
darb
MM-HM. AND WHAT WOULD THAT BE CALLED? *THE DORKS OF HAZZARD? MIAMI LICE?*
HA HA! *MONDAY NIGHT FREAK-OUT!* AND THEN *TUESDAY NIGHT FREAK-OUT!* AND THEN *WED-*
STOP IT.
AMERICA'S LEAST WANTED? BOREDOM, SHE WROTE?
BUCKY THE VARMINT SLAYER!
I SAID **STOP**-... WAIT, I LIKE THAT...

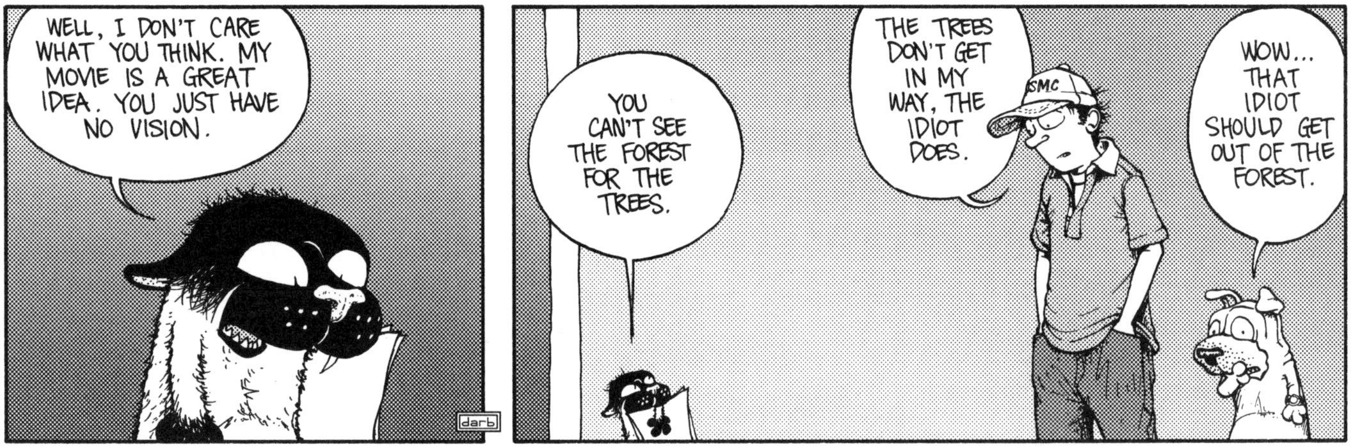
WELL, I DON'T CARE WHAT YOU THINK. MY MOVIE IS A GREAT IDEA. YOU JUST HAVE NO VISION.
darb
YOU CAN'T SEE THE FOREST FOR THE TREES.
THE TREES DON'T GET IN MY WAY, THE IDIOT DOES.
WOW... THAT IDIOT SHOULD GET OUT OF THE FOREST.

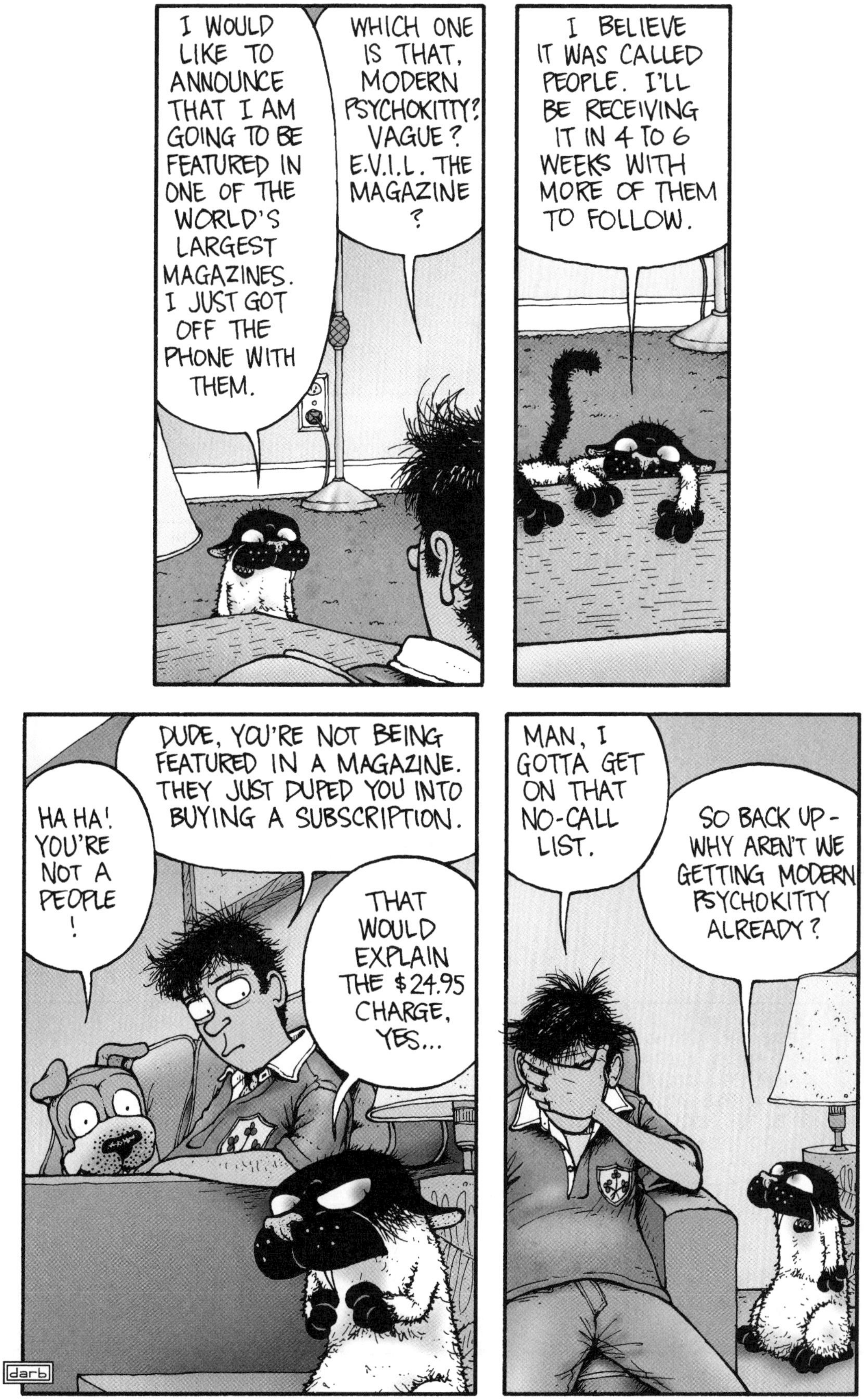
I WOULD LIKE TO ANNOUNCE THAT I AM GOING TO BE FEATURED IN ONE OF THE WORLD'S LARGEST MAGAZINES. I JUST GOT OFF THE PHONE WITH THEM.
WHICH ONE IS THAT, MODERN PSYCHOKITTY? VAGUE? E.V.I.L. THE MAGAZINE?
I BELIEVE IT WAS CALLED PEOPLE. I'LL BE RECEIVING IT IN 4 TO 6 WEEKS WITH MORE OF THEM TO FOLLOW.
HA HA! YOU'RE NOT A PEOPLE!
DUDE, YOU'RE NOT BEING FEATURED IN A MAGAZINE. THEY JUST DUPED YOU INTO BUYING A SUBSCRIPTION.
THAT WOULD EXPLAIN THE $24.95 CHARGE, YES...
MAN, I GOTTA GET ON THAT NO-CALL LIST.
SO BACK UP - WHY AREN'T WE GETTING MODERN PSYCHOKITTY ALREADY?
darb

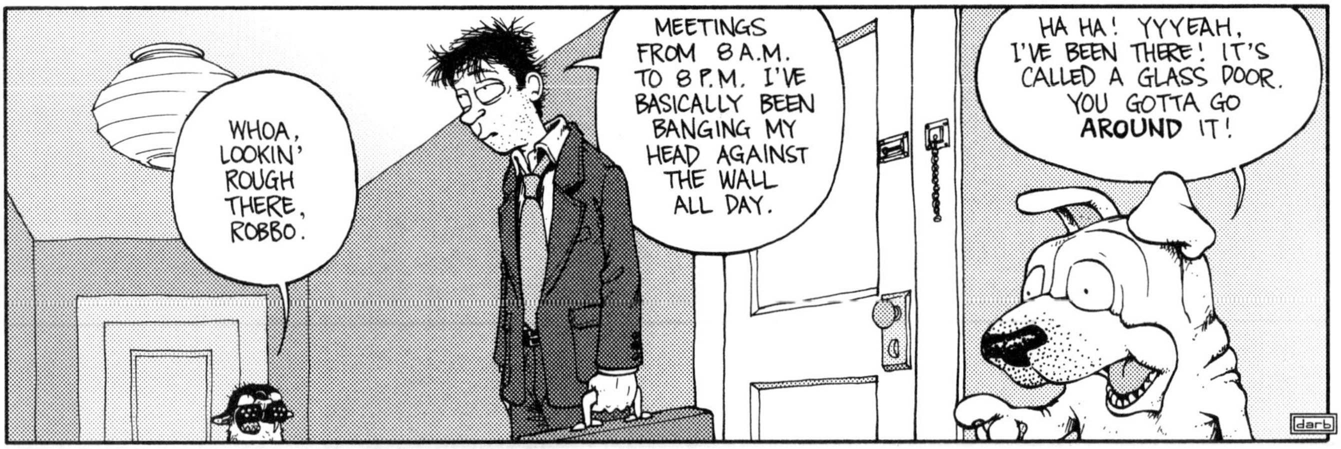
WHOA, LOOKIN' ROUGH THERE, ROBBO.
MEETINGS FROM 8 A.M. TO 8 P.M. I'VE BASICALLY BEEN BANGING MY HEAD AGAINST THE WALL ALL DAY.
HA HA! YYYEAH, I'VE BEEN THERE! IT'S CALLED A GLASS DOOR. YOU GOTTA GO **AROUND** IT!
darb

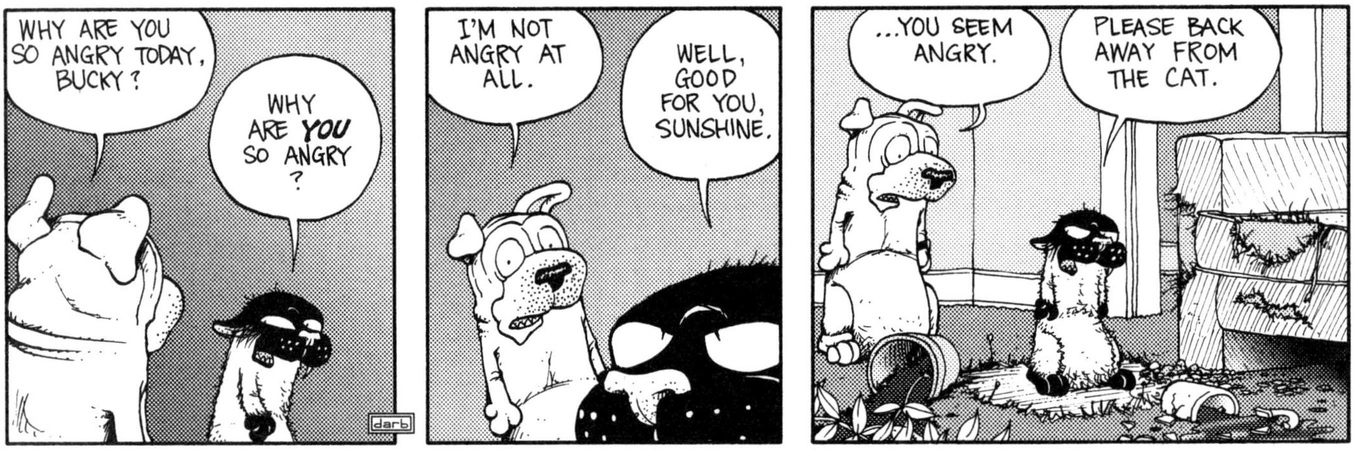
WHY ARE YOU SO ANGRY TODAY, BUCKY?
WHY ARE *YOU* SO ANGRY?
darb
I'M NOT ANGRY AT ALL.
WELL, GOOD FOR YOU, SUNSHINE.
...YOU SEEM ANGRY.
PLEASE BACK AWAY FROM THE CAT.

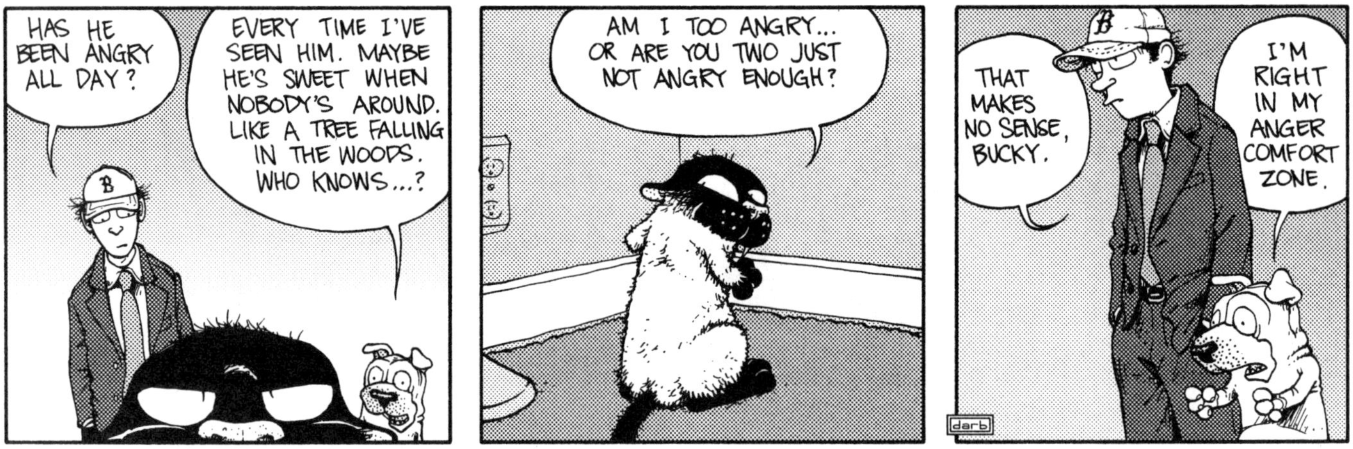
HAS HE BEEN ANGRY ALL DAY?
EVERY TIME I'VE SEEN HIM. MAYBE HE'S SWEET WHEN NOBODY'S AROUND. LIKE A TREE FALLING IN THE WOODS. WHO KNOWS...?
AM I TOO ANGRY... OR ARE YOU TWO JUST NOT ANGRY ENOUGH?
darb
THAT MAKES NO SENSE, BUCKY.
I'M RIGHT IN MY ANGER COMFORT ZONE.

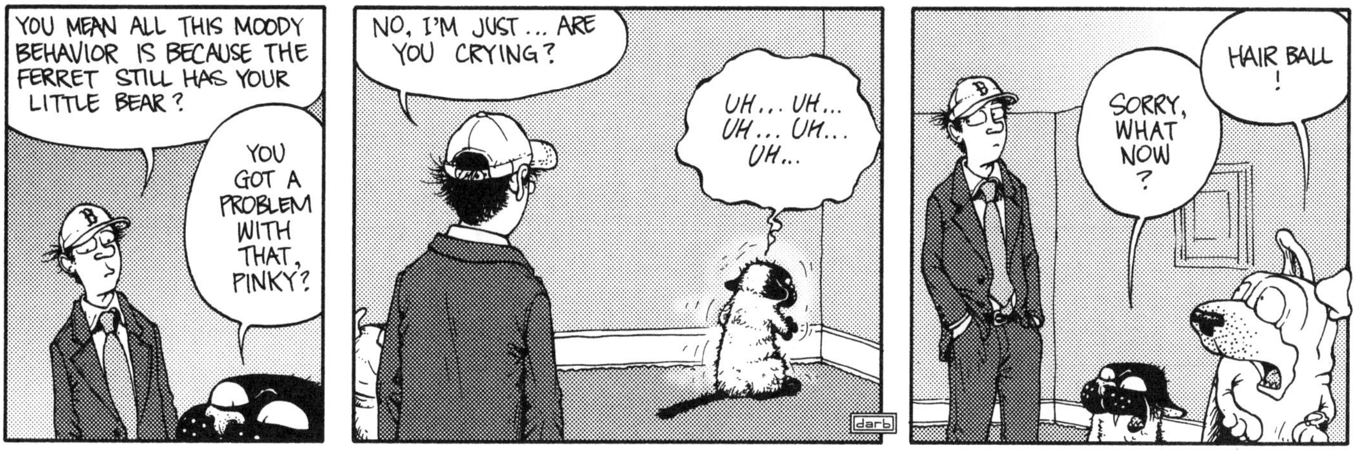
YOU MEAN ALL THIS MOODY BEHAVIOR IS BECAUSE THE FERRET STILL HAS YOUR LITTLE BEAR?
YOU GOT A PROBLEM WITH THAT, PINKY?
NO, I'M JUST... ARE YOU CRYING?
UH... UH... UH... UH... UH...
SORRY, WHAT NOW?
HAIR BALL!

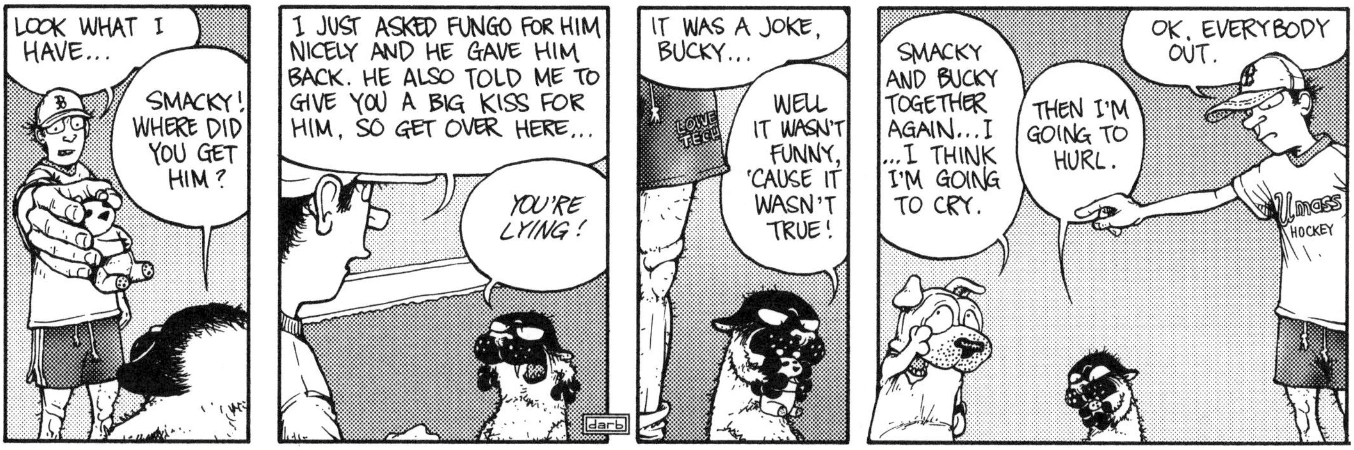
LOOK WHAT I HAVE...
SMACKY! WHERE DID YOU GET HIM?
I JUST ASKED FUNGO FOR HIM NICELY AND HE GAVE HIM BACK. HE ALSO TOLD ME TO GIVE YOU A BIG KISS FOR HIM, SO GET OVER HERE...
YOU'RE LYING!
IT WAS A JOKE, BUCKY...
WELL IT WASN'T FUNNY, 'CAUSE IT WASN'T TRUE!
SMACKY AND BUCKY TOGETHER AGAIN... I ...I THINK I'M GOING TO CRY.
THEN I'M GOING TO HURL.
OK, EVERYBODY OUT.

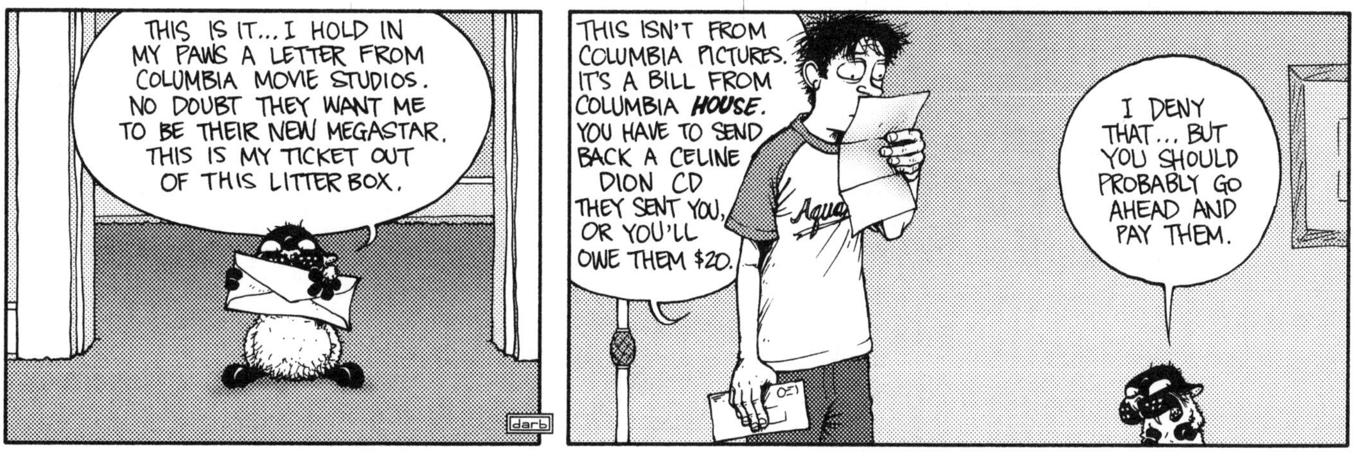
THIS IS IT... I HOLD IN MY PAWS A LETTER FROM COLUMBIA MOVIE STUDIOS. NO DOUBT THEY WANT ME TO BE THEIR NEW MEGASTAR. THIS IS MY TICKET OUT OF THIS LITTER BOX.
THIS ISN'T FROM COLUMBIA PICTURES. IT'S A BILL FROM COLUMBIA HOUSE. YOU HAVE TO SEND BACK A CELINE DION CD THEY SENT YOU, OR YOU'LL OWE THEM $20.
I DENY THAT... BUT YOU SHOULD PROBABLY GO AHEAD AND PAY THEM.

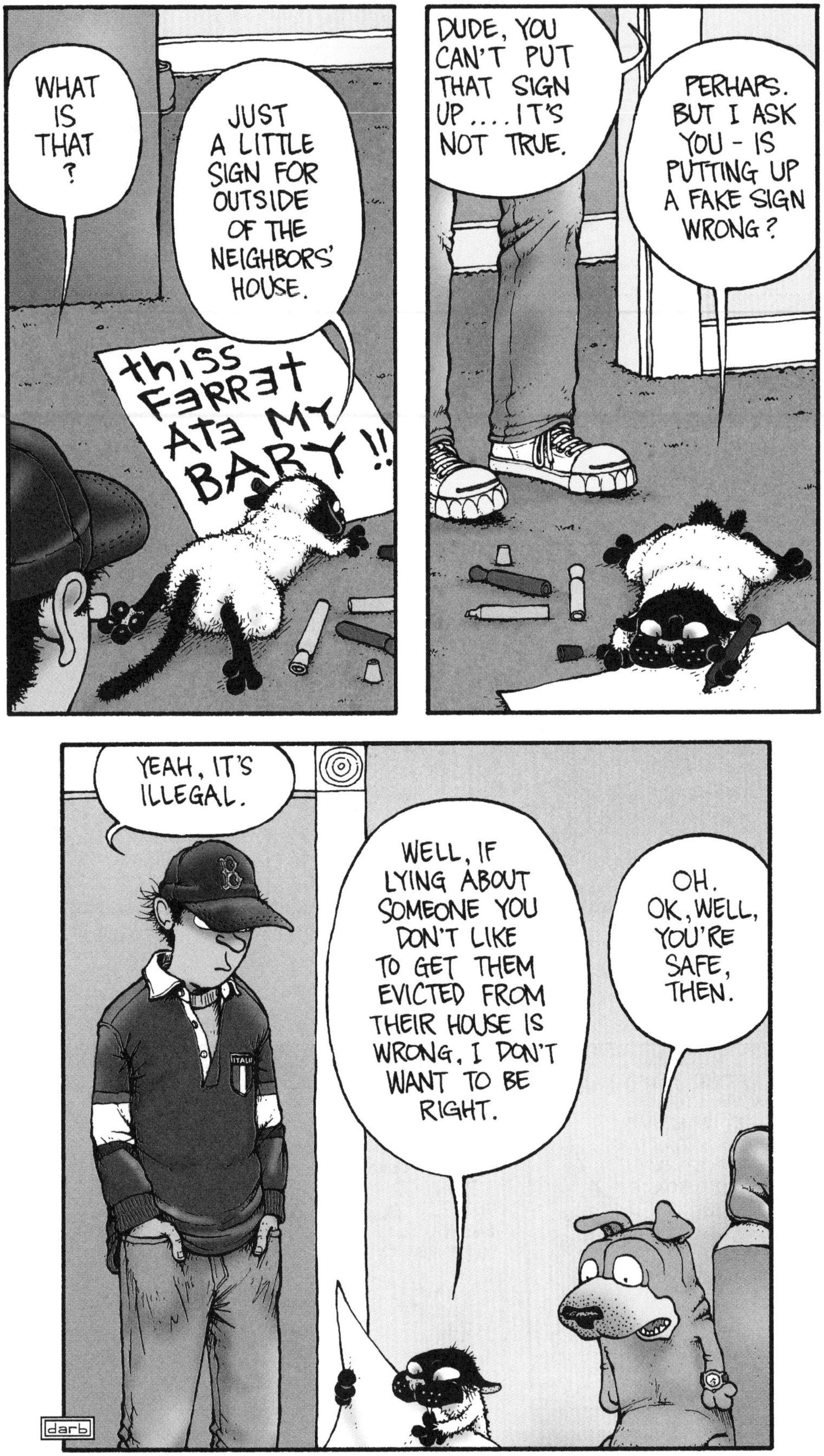
WHAT IS THAT ?
JUST A LITTLE SIGN FOR OUTSIDE OF THE NEIGHBORS' HOUSE.
thiss FƎRRƎt AtƎ MY BABY !!
DUDE, YOU CAN'T PUT THAT SIGN UP.... IT'S NOT TRUE.
PERHAPS. BUT I ASK YOU - IS PUTTING UP A FAKE SIGN WRONG ?
YEAH, IT'S ILLEGAL.
WELL, IF LYING ABOUT SOMEONE YOU DON'T LIKE TO GET THEM EVICTED FROM THEIR HOUSE IS WRONG, I DON'T WANT TO BE RIGHT.
OH. OK, WELL, YOU'RE SAFE, THEN.
darb

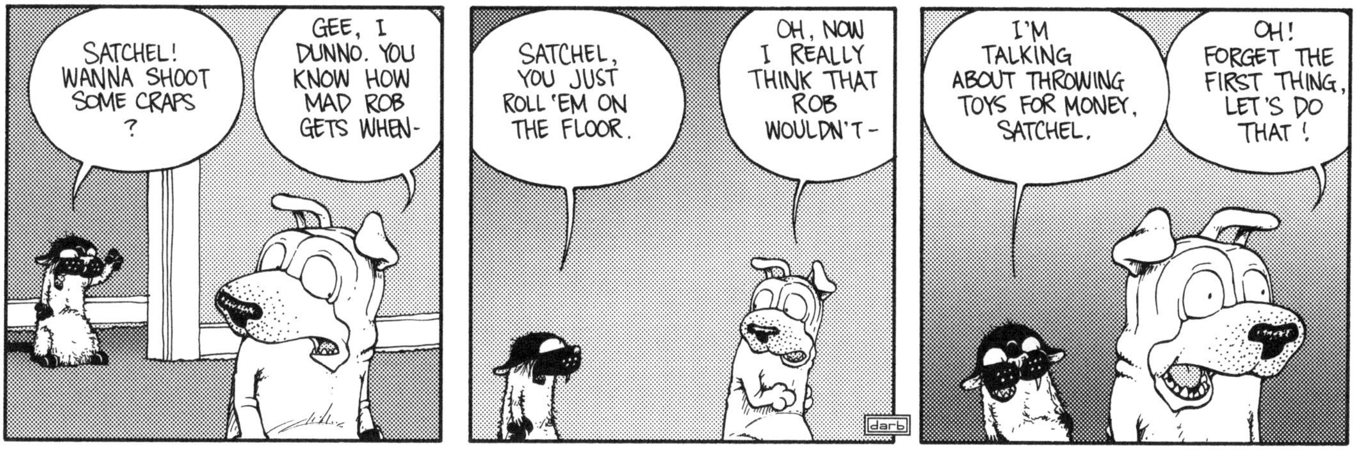
SATCHEL! WANNA SHOOT SOME CRAPS ?
GEE, I DUNNO. YOU KNOW HOW MAD ROB GETS WHEN-
SATCHEL, YOU JUST ROLL 'EM ON THE FLOOR.
OH, NOW I REALLY THINK THAT ROB WOULDN'T -
I'M TALKING ABOUT THROWING TOYS FOR MONEY, SATCHEL.
OH! FORGET THE FIRST THING, LET'S DO THAT !
darb

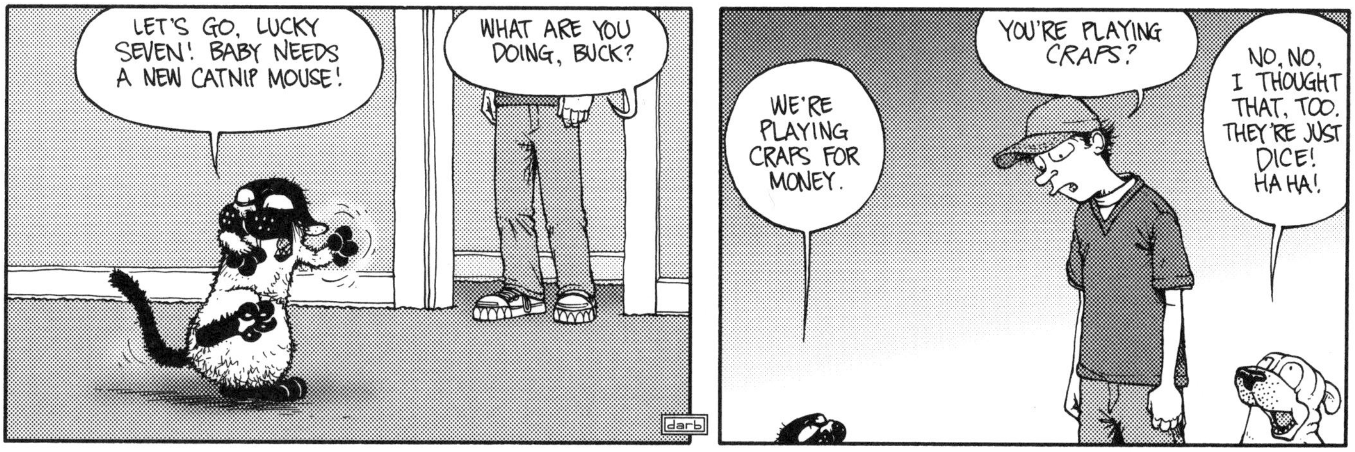
LET'S GO, LUCKY SEVEN! BABY NEEDS A NEW CATNIP MOUSE!
WHAT ARE YOU DOING, BUCK?
WE'RE PLAYING CRAPS FOR MONEY.
YOU'RE PLAYING *CRAPS?*
NO, NO, I THOUGHT THAT, TOO. THEY'RE JUST DICE! HA HA!
darb

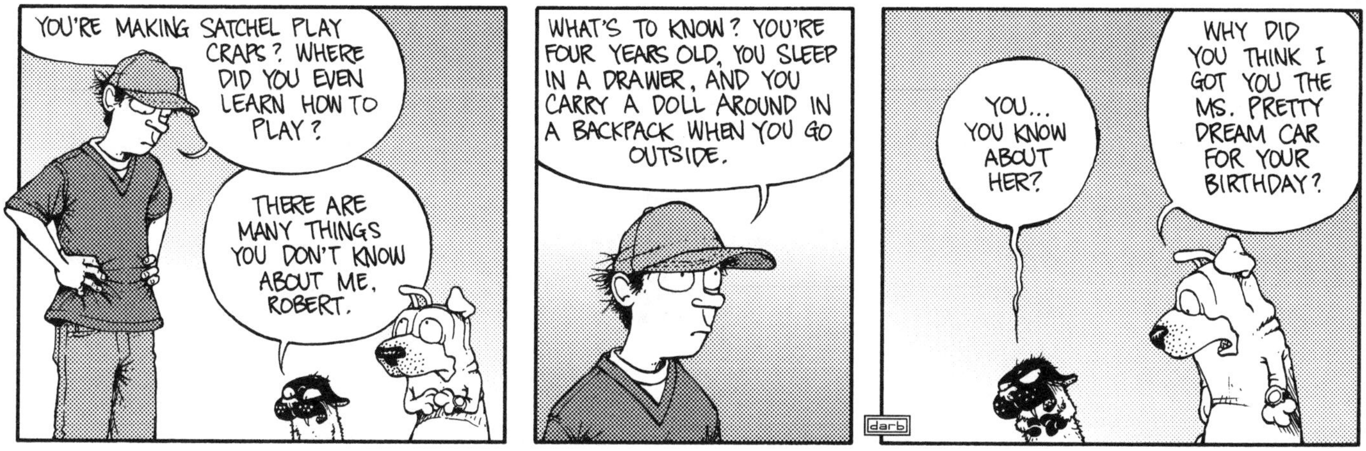
YOU'RE MAKING SATCHEL PLAY CRAPS? WHERE DID YOU EVEN LEARN HOW TO PLAY?
THERE ARE MANY THINGS YOU DON'T KNOW ABOUT ME, ROBERT.
WHAT'S TO KNOW? YOU'RE FOUR YEARS OLD, YOU SLEEP IN A DRAWER, AND YOU CARRY A DOLL AROUND IN A BACKPACK WHEN YOU GO OUTSIDE.
YOU... YOU KNOW ABOUT HER?
WHY DID YOU THINK I GOT YOU THE MS. PRETTY DREAM CAR FOR YOUR BIRTHDAY?
darb

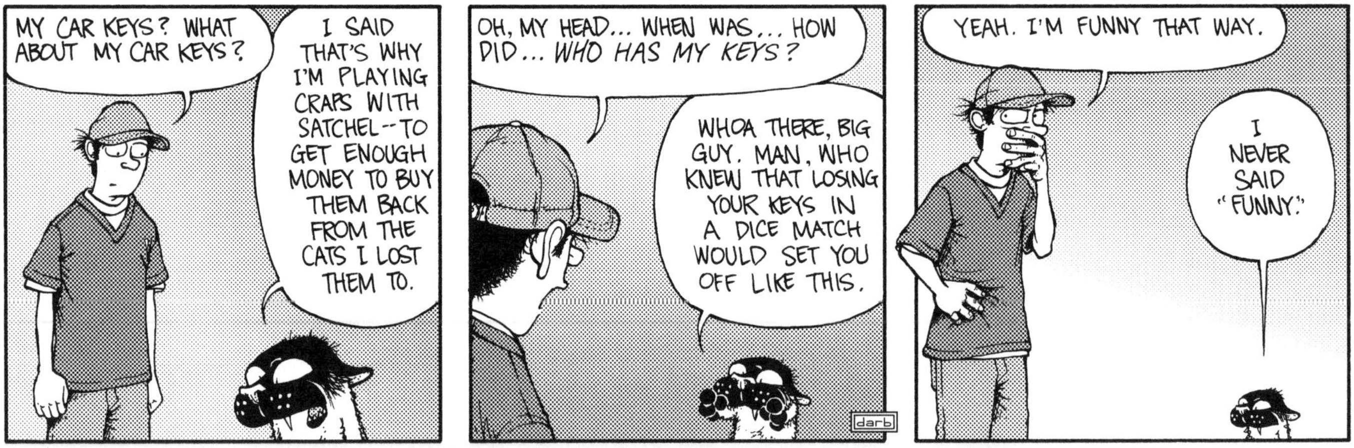
MY CAR KEYS? WHAT ABOUT MY CAR KEYS?
I SAID THAT'S WHY I'M PLAYING CRAPS WITH SATCHEL--TO GET ENOUGH MONEY TO BUY THEM BACK FROM THE CATS I LOST THEM TO.
OH, MY HEAD... WHEN WAS... HOW DID... *WHO HAS MY KEYS?*
WHOA THERE, BIG GUY. MAN, WHO KNEW THAT LOSING YOUR KEYS IN A DICE MATCH WOULD SET YOU OFF LIKE THIS.
YEAH. I'M FUNNY THAT WAY.
I NEVER SAID "FUNNY."
darb

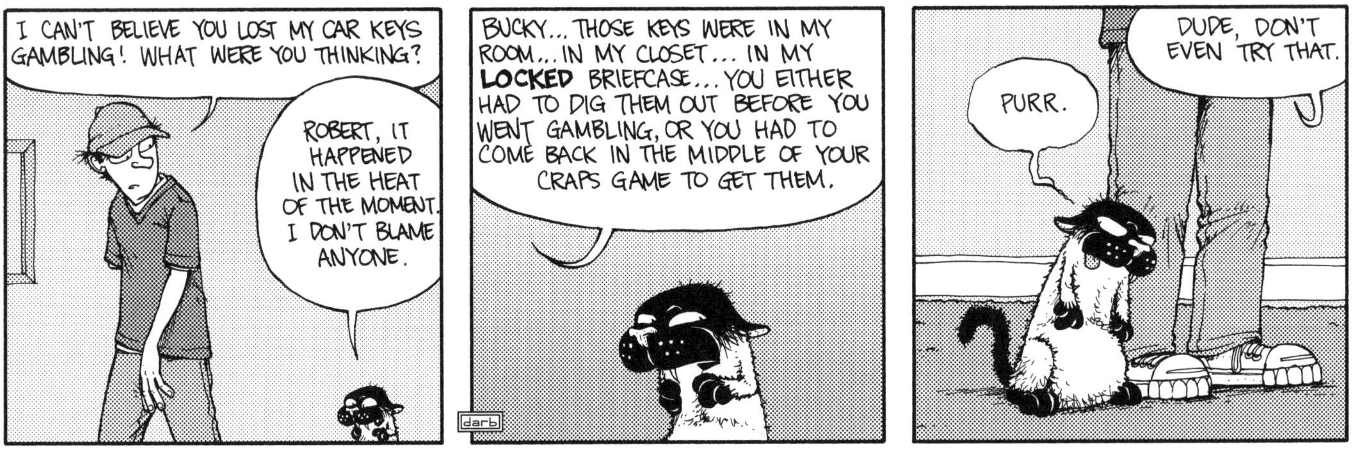
I CAN'T BELIEVE YOU LOST MY CAR KEYS GAMBLING! WHAT WERE YOU THINKING?
ROBERT, IT HAPPENED IN THE HEAT OF THE MOMENT. I DON'T BLAME ANYONE.
darb
BUCKY... THOSE KEYS WERE IN MY ROOM... IN MY CLOSET... IN MY **LOCKED** BRIEFCASE... YOU EITHER HAD TO DIG THEM OUT BEFORE YOU WENT GAMBLING, OR YOU HAD TO COME BACK IN THE MIDDLE OF YOUR CRAPS GAME TO GET THEM.
PURR.
DUDE, DON'T EVEN TRY THAT.

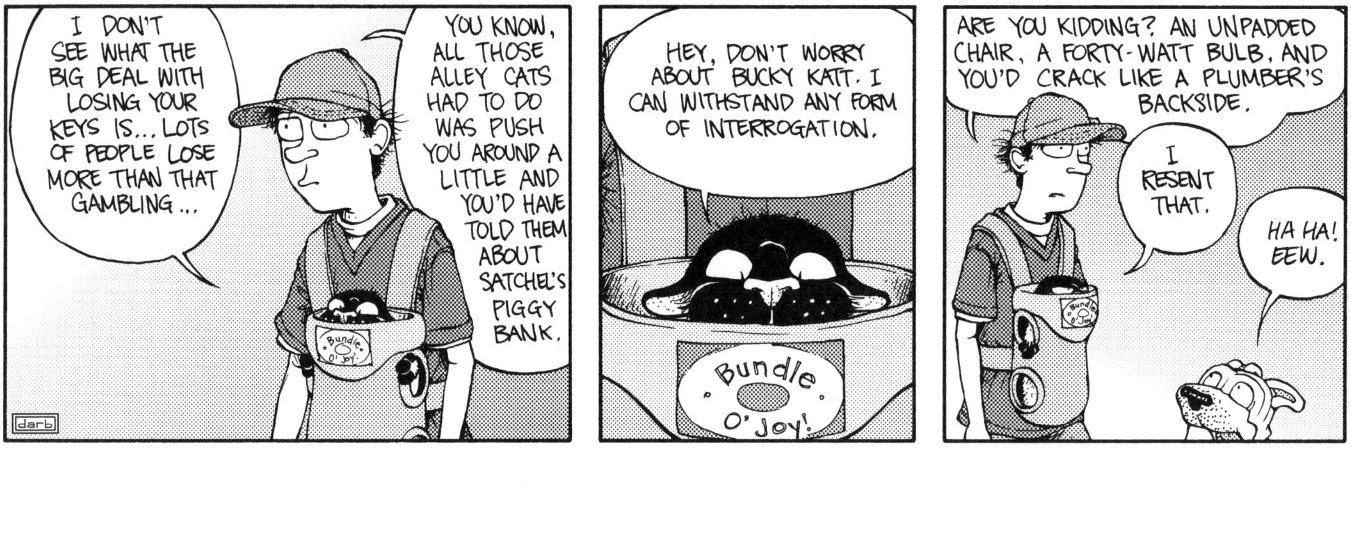
I DON'T SEE WHAT THE BIG DEAL WITH LOSING YOUR KEYS IS... LOTS OF PEOPLE LOSE MORE THAN THAT GAMBLING...
YOU KNOW, ALL THOSE ALLEY CATS HAD TO DO WAS PUSH YOU AROUND A LITTLE AND YOU'D HAVE TOLD THEM ABOUT SATCHEL'S PIGGY BANK.
Bundle O' Joy
darb
HEY, DON'T WORRY ABOUT BUCKY KATT. I CAN WITHSTAND ANY FORM OF INTERROGATION.
Bundle O' Joy!
ARE YOU KIDDING? AN UNPADDED CHAIR, A FORTY-WATT BULB, AND YOU'D CRACK LIKE A PLUMBER'S BACKSIDE.
I RESENT THAT.
HA HA! EEW.

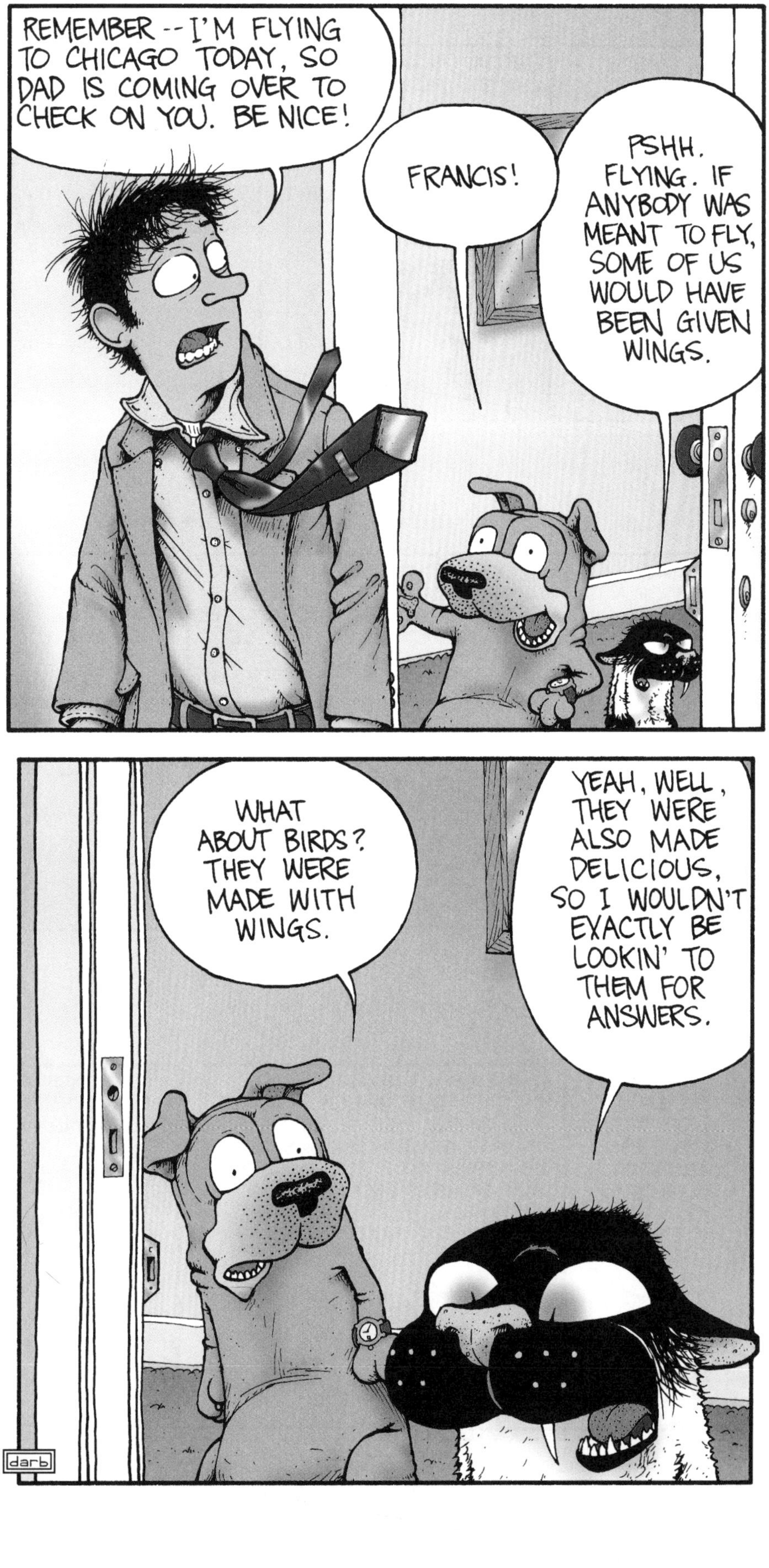
REMEMBER -- I'M FLYING TO CHICAGO TODAY, SO DAD IS COMING OVER TO CHECK ON YOU. BE NICE!
FRANCIS!
PSHH. FLYING. IF ANYBODY WAS MEANT TO FLY, SOME OF US WOULD HAVE BEEN GIVEN WINGS.
WHAT ABOUT BIRDS? THEY WERE MADE WITH WINGS.
YEAH, WELL, THEY WERE ALSO MADE DELICIOUS, SO I WOULDN'T EXACTLY BE LOOKIN' TO THEM FOR ANSWERS.
darb

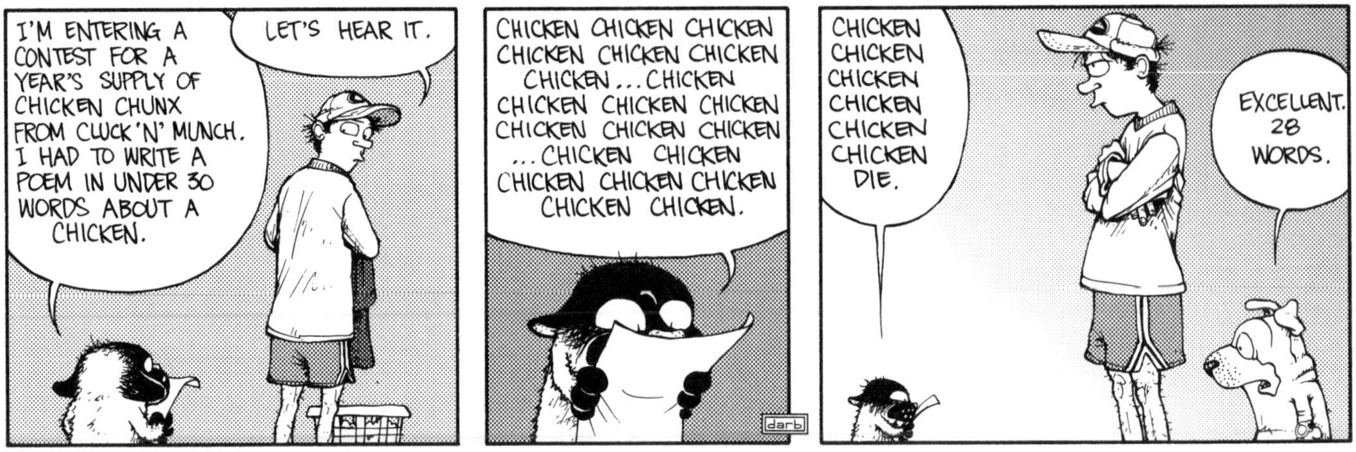
I'M ENTERING A CONTEST FOR A YEAR'S SUPPLY OF CHICKEN CHUNX FROM CLUCK 'N' MUNCH. I HAD TO WRITE A POEM IN UNDER 30 WORDS ABOUT A CHICKEN.
LET'S HEAR IT.
CHICKEN CHICKEN CHICKEN CHICKEN CHICKEN CHICKEN CHICKEN... CHICKEN CHICKEN CHICKEN CHICKEN CHICKEN CHICKEN CHICKEN ...CHICKEN CHICKEN CHICKEN CHICKEN CHICKEN CHICKEN CHICKEN.
darb
CHICKEN CHICKEN CHICKEN CHICKEN CHICKEN CHICKEN DIE.
EXCELLENT. 28 WORDS.

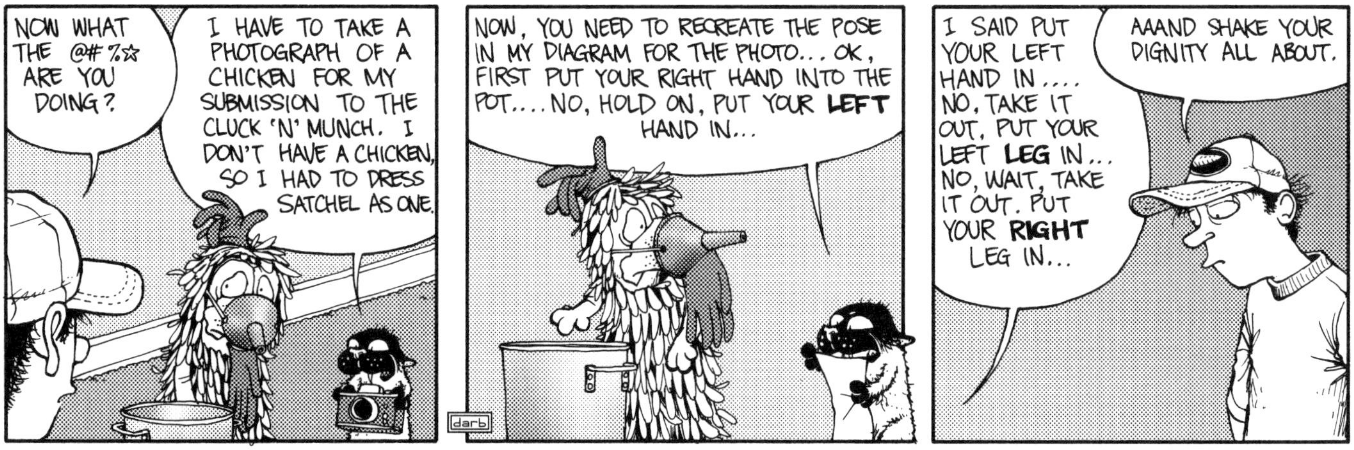
NOW WHAT THE @#%☆ ARE YOU DOING?
I HAVE TO TAKE A PHOTOGRAPH OF A CHICKEN FOR MY SUBMISSION TO THE CLUCK 'N' MUNCH. I DON'T HAVE A CHICKEN, SO I HAD TO DRESS SATCHEL AS ONE.
darb
NOW, YOU NEED TO RECREATE THE POSE IN MY DIAGRAM FOR THE PHOTO... OK, FIRST PUT YOUR RIGHT HAND INTO THE POT.... NO, HOLD ON, PUT YOUR **LEFT** HAND IN...
I SAID PUT YOUR LEFT HAND IN.... NO, TAKE IT OUT, PUT YOUR LEFT **LEG** IN... NO, WAIT, TAKE IT OUT. PUT YOUR **RIGHT** LEG IN...
AAAND SHAKE YOUR DIGNITY ALL ABOUT.

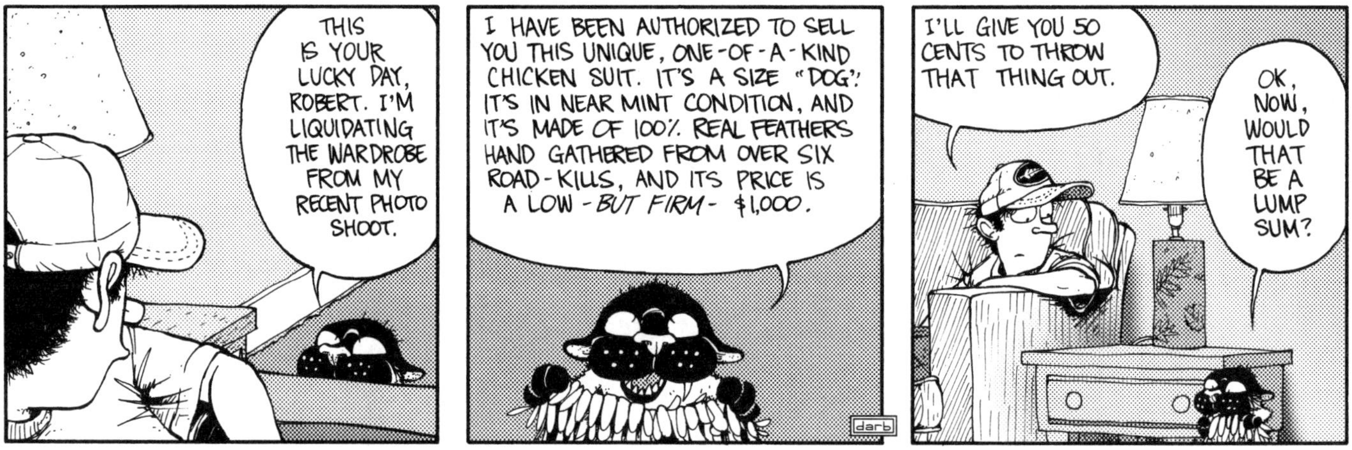
THIS IS YOUR LUCKY DAY, ROBERT. I'M LIQUIDATING THE WARDROBE FROM MY RECENT PHOTO SHOOT.
I HAVE BEEN AUTHORIZED TO SELL YOU THIS UNIQUE, ONE-OF-A-KIND CHICKEN SUIT. IT'S A SIZE "DOG." IT'S IN NEAR MINT CONDITION, AND IT'S MADE OF 100% REAL FEATHERS HAND GATHERED FROM OVER SIX ROAD-KILLS, AND ITS PRICE IS A LOW *-BUT FIRM-* $1,000.
darb
I'LL GIVE YOU 50 CENTS TO THROW THAT THING OUT.
OK, NOW, WOULD THAT BE A LUMP SUM?

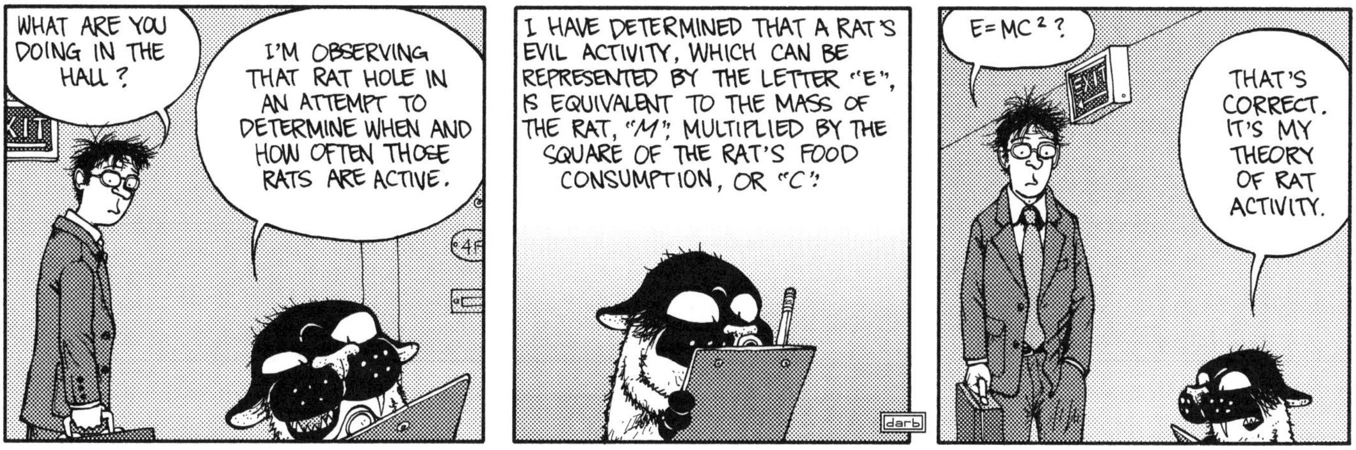
WHAT ARE YOU DOING IN THE HALL?
I'M OBSERVING THAT RAT HOLE IN AN ATTEMPT TO DETERMINE WHEN AND HOW OFTEN THOSE RATS ARE ACTIVE.
I HAVE DETERMINED THAT A RAT'S EVIL ACTIVITY, WHICH CAN BE REPRESENTED BY THE LETTER "E", IS EQUIVALENT TO THE MASS OF THE RAT, "M", MULTIPLIED BY THE SQUARE OF THE RAT'S FOOD CONSUMPTION, OR "C".
E=MC²?
THAT'S CORRECT. IT'S MY THEORY OF RAT ACTIVITY.

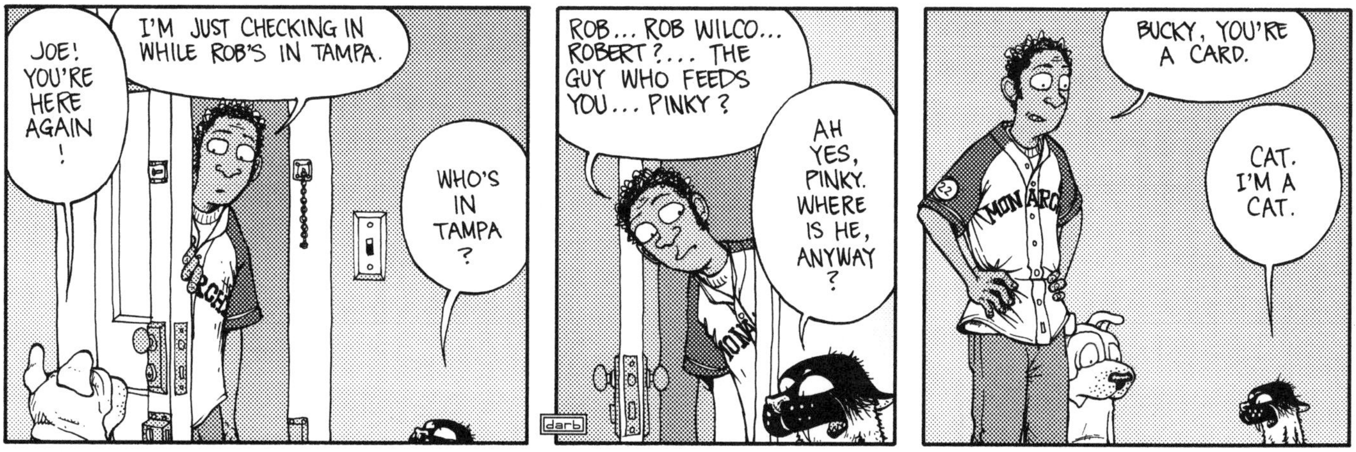
JOE! YOU'RE HERE AGAIN!
I'M JUST CHECKING IN WHILE ROB'S IN TAMPA.
WHO'S IN TAMPA?
ROB... ROB WILCO... ROBERT?... THE GUY WHO FEEDS YOU... PINKY?
AH YES, PINKY. WHERE IS HE, ANYWAY?
BUCKY, YOU'RE A CARD.
CAT. I'M A CAT.

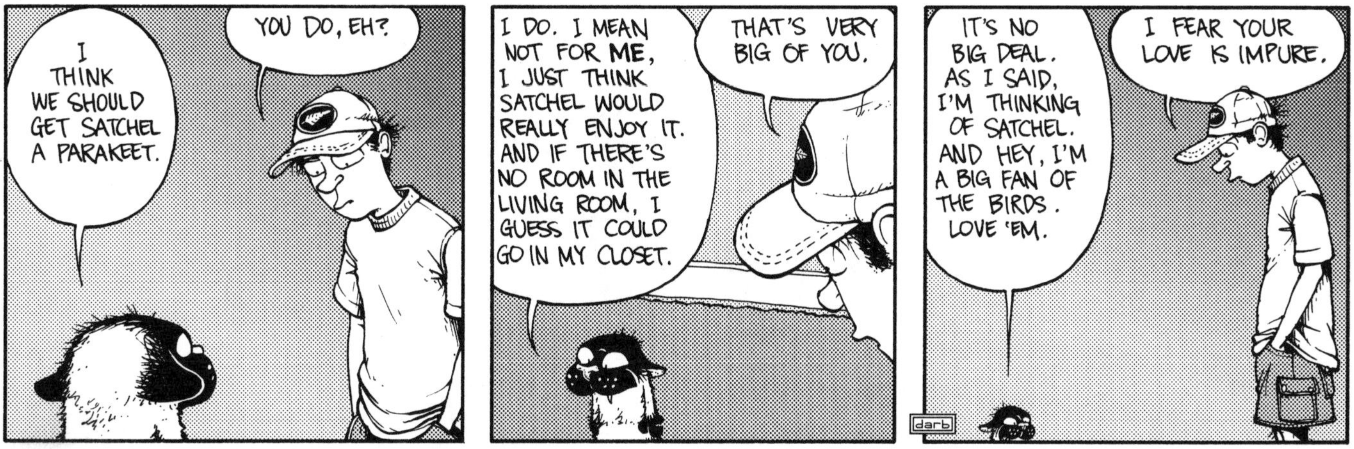
I THINK WE SHOULD GET SATCHEL A PARAKEET.
YOU DO, EH?
I DO. I MEAN NOT FOR **ME**, I JUST THINK SATCHEL WOULD REALLY ENJOY IT. AND IF THERE'S NO ROOM IN THE LIVING ROOM, I GUESS IT COULD GO IN MY CLOSET.
THAT'S VERY BIG OF YOU.
IT'S NO BIG DEAL. AS I SAID, I'M THINKING OF SATCHEL. AND HEY, I'M A BIG FAN OF THE BIRDS. LOVE 'EM.
I FEAR YOUR LOVE IS IMPURE.

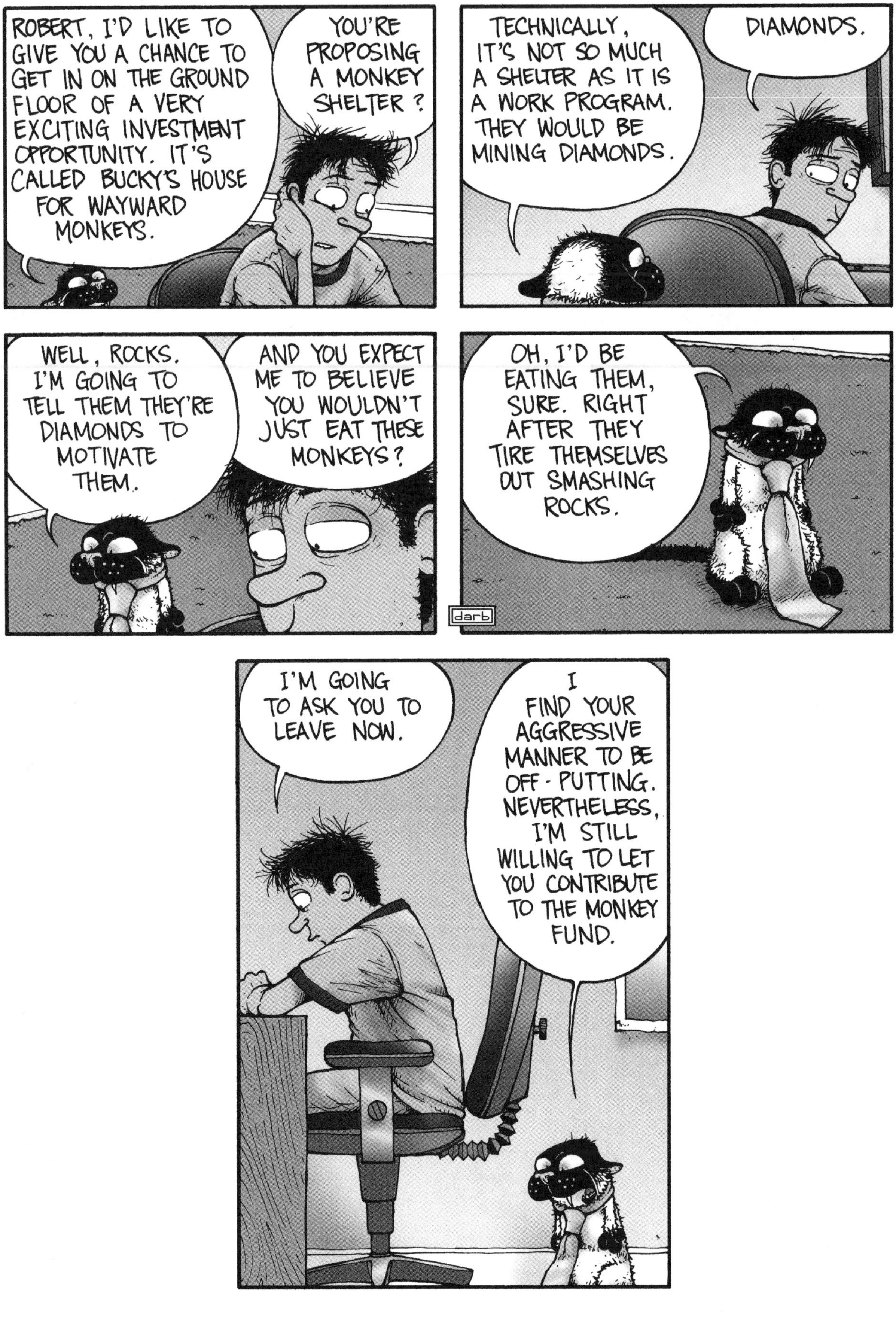
ROBERT, I'D LIKE TO GIVE YOU A CHANCE TO GET IN ON THE GROUND FLOOR OF A VERY EXCITING INVESTMENT OPPORTUNITY. IT'S CALLED BUCKY'S HOUSE FOR WAYWARD MONKEYS.
YOU'RE PROPOSING A MONKEY SHELTER?
TECHNICALLY, IT'S NOT SO MUCH A SHELTER AS IT IS A WORK PROGRAM. THEY WOULD BE MINING DIAMONDS.
DIAMONDS.
WELL, ROCKS. I'M GOING TO TELL THEM THEY'RE DIAMONDS TO MOTIVATE THEM.
AND YOU EXPECT ME TO BELIEVE YOU WOULDN'T JUST EAT THESE MONKEYS?
OH, I'D BE EATING THEM, SURE. RIGHT AFTER THEY TIRE THEMSELVES OUT SMASHING ROCKS.
darb
I'M GOING TO ASK YOU TO LEAVE NOW.
I FIND YOUR AGGRESSIVE MANNER TO BE OFF-PUTTING. NEVERTHELESS, I'M STILL WILLING TO LET YOU CONTRIBUTE TO THE MONKEY FUND.

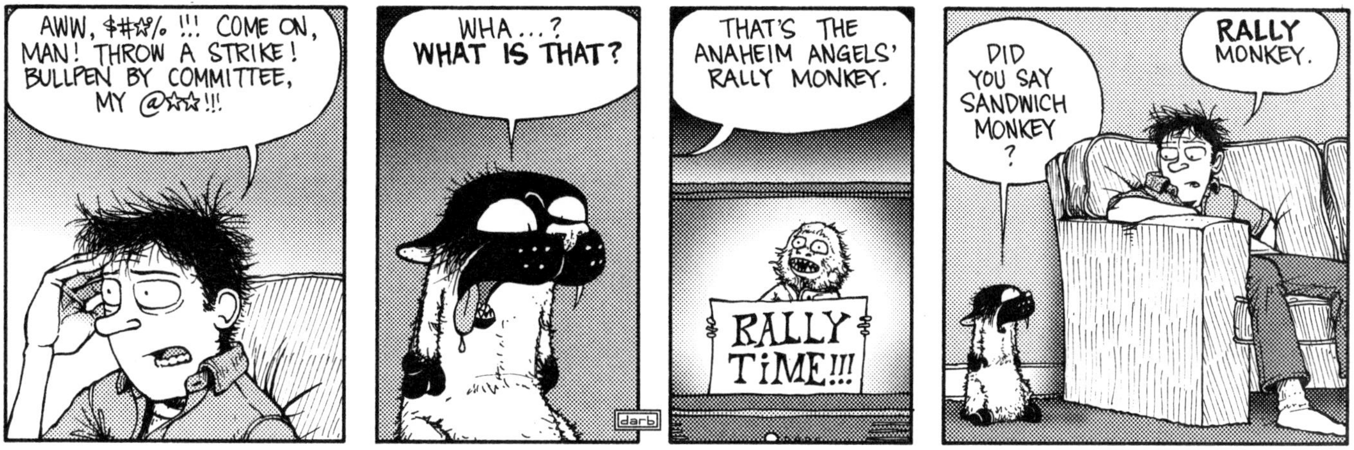
AWW, $#☆% !!! COME ON, MAN! THROW A STRIKE! BULLPEN BY COMMITTEE, MY @☆☆!!!
WHA...? **WHAT IS THAT?**
THAT'S THE ANAHEIM ANGELS' RALLY MONKEY.
RALLY TiME!!!
DID YOU SAY SANDWICH MONKEY?
RALLY MONKEY.
darb

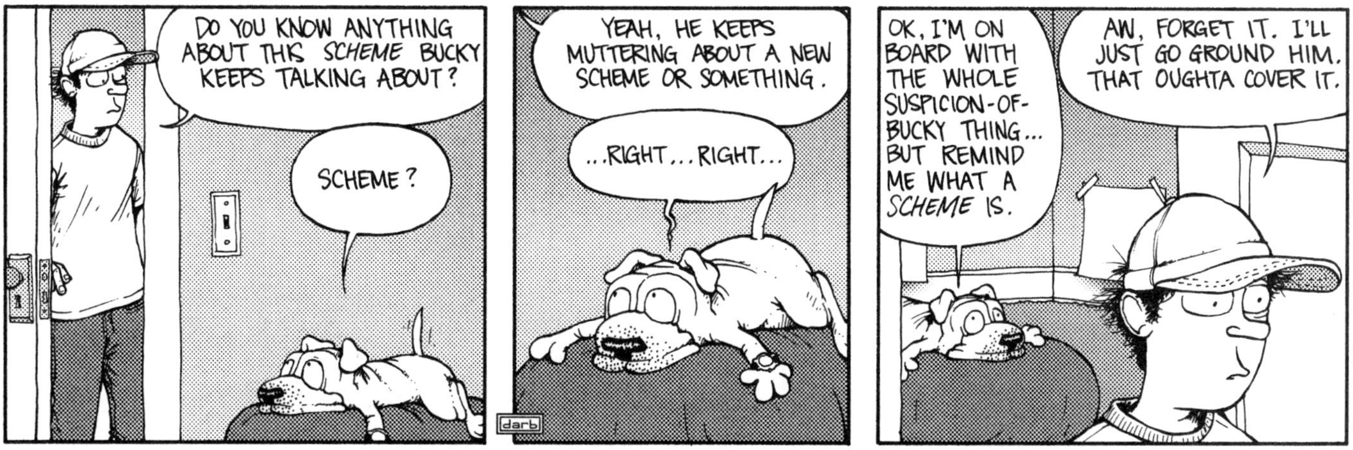
DO YOU KNOW ANYTHING ABOUT THIS *SCHEME* BUCKY KEEPS TALKING ABOUT?
SCHEME?
YEAH, HE KEEPS MUTTERING ABOUT A NEW SCHEME OR SOMETHING.
...RIGHT...RIGHT...
darb
OK, I'M ON BOARD WITH THE WHOLE SUSPICION-OF-BUCKY THING... BUT REMIND ME WHAT A *SCHEME* IS.
AW, FORGET IT. I'LL JUST GO GROUND HIM. THAT OUGHTA COVER IT.

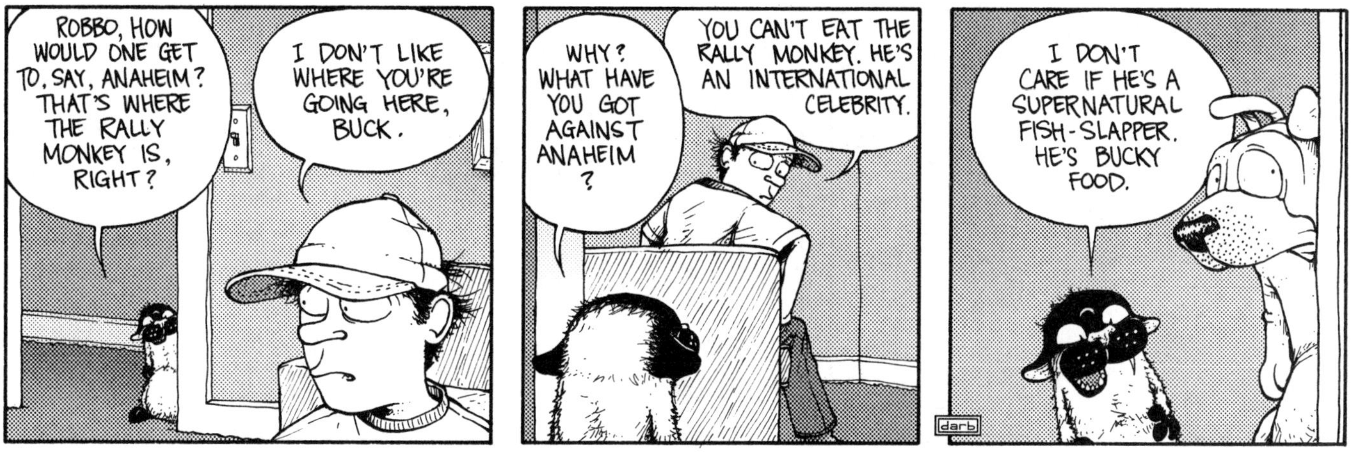
ROBBO, HOW WOULD ONE GET TO, SAY, ANAHEIM? THAT'S WHERE THE RALLY MONKEY IS, RIGHT?
I DON'T LIKE WHERE YOU'RE GOING HERE, BUCK.
WHY? WHAT HAVE YOU GOT AGAINST ANAHEIM?
YOU CAN'T EAT THE RALLY MONKEY. HE'S AN INTERNATIONAL CELEBRITY.
I DON'T CARE IF HE'S A SUPERNATURAL FISH-SLAPPER. HE'S BUCKY FOOD.
darb

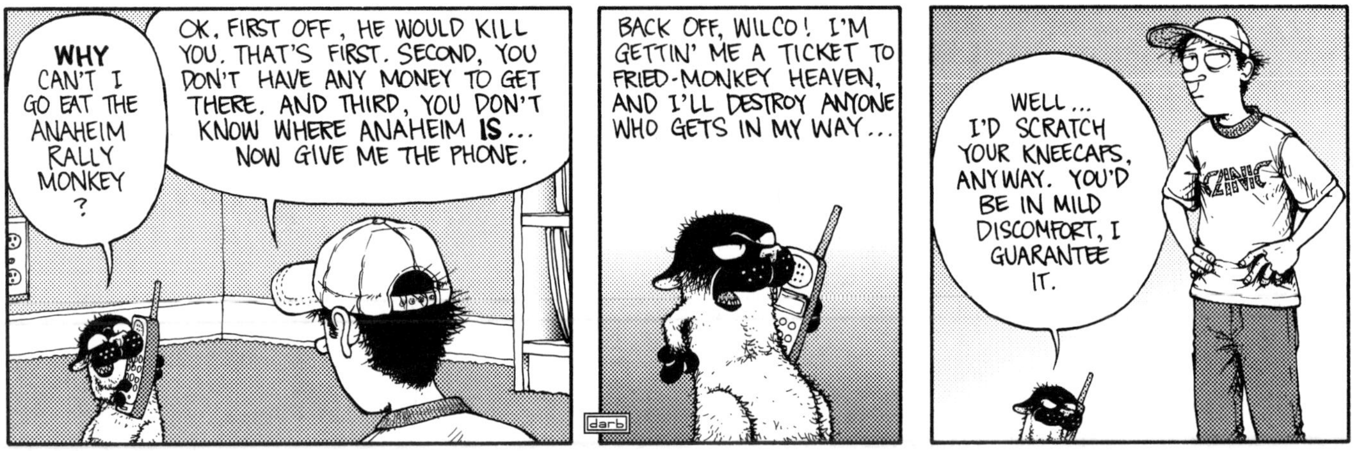
WHY CAN'T I GO EAT THE ANAHEIM RALLY MONKEY ?
OK, FIRST OFF, HE WOULD KILL YOU. THAT'S FIRST. SECOND, YOU DON'T HAVE ANY MONEY TO GET THERE. AND THIRD, YOU DON'T KNOW WHERE ANAHEIM **IS**... NOW GIVE ME THE PHONE.
BACK OFF, WILCO! I'M GETTIN' ME A TICKET TO FRIED-MONKEY HEAVEN, AND I'LL DESTROY ANYONE WHO GETS IN MY WAY...
darb
WELL... I'D SCRATCH YOUR KNEECAPS, ANYWAY. YOU'D BE IN MILD DISCOMFORT, I GUARANTEE IT.

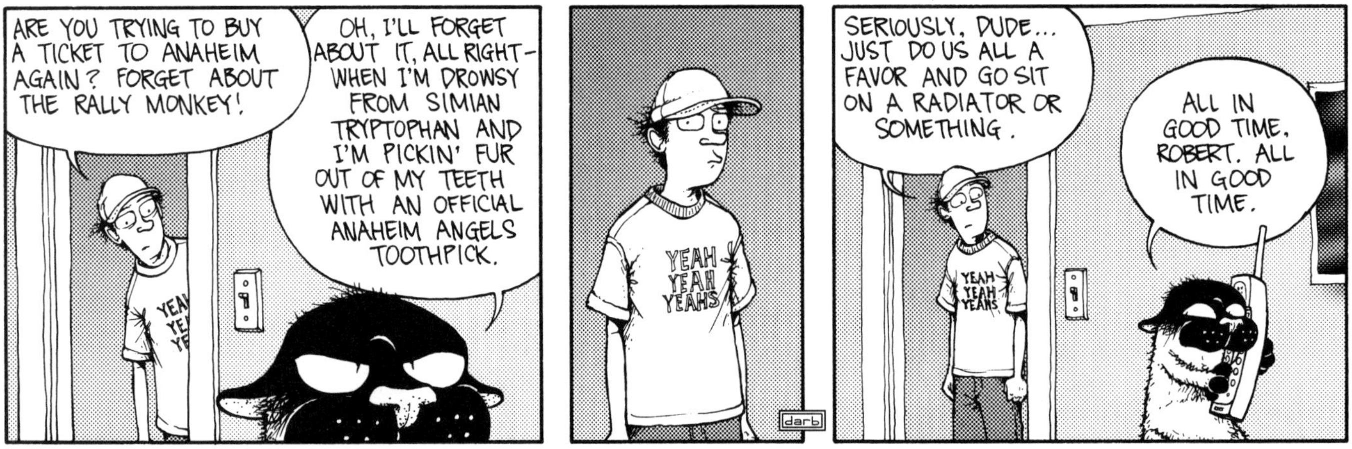
ARE YOU TRYING TO BUY A TICKET TO ANAHEIM AGAIN? FORGET ABOUT THE RALLY MONKEY!
OH, I'LL FORGET ABOUT IT, ALL RIGHT- WHEN I'M DROWSY FROM SIMIAN TRYPTOPHAN AND I'M PICKIN' FUR OUT OF MY TEETH WITH AN OFFICIAL ANAHEIM ANGELS TOOTHPICK.
YEAH YEAH YEAHS
darb
SERIOUSLY, DUDE... JUST DO US ALL A FAVOR AND GO SIT ON A RADIATOR OR SOMETHING.
ALL IN GOOD TIME, ROBERT. ALL IN GOOD TIME.

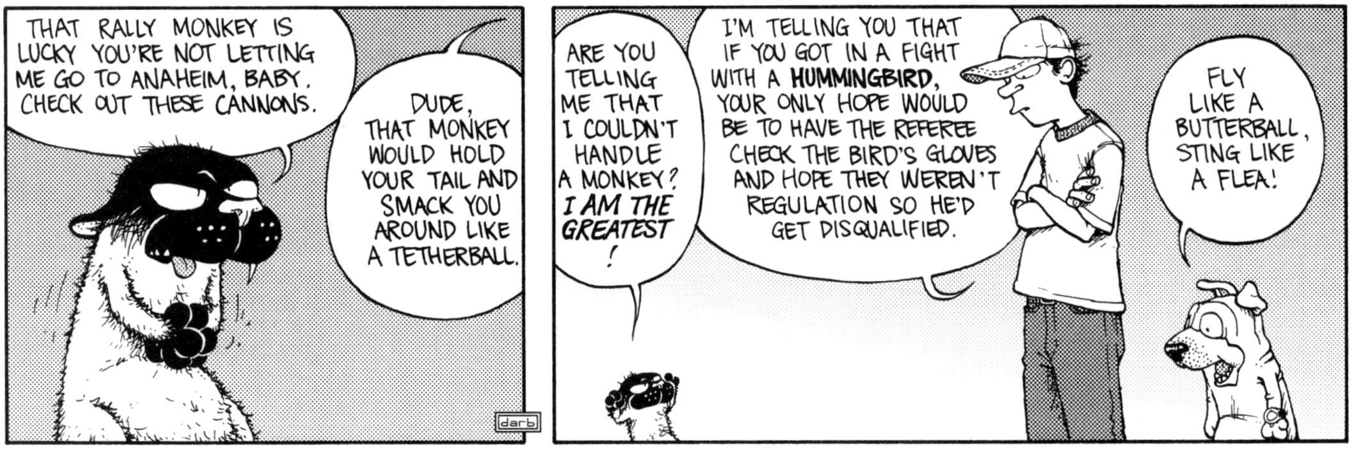
THAT RALLY MONKEY IS LUCKY YOU'RE NOT LETTING ME GO TO ANAHEIM, BABY. CHECK OUT THESE CANNONS.
DUDE, THAT MONKEY WOULD HOLD YOUR TAIL AND SMACK YOU AROUND LIKE A TETHERBALL.
darb
ARE YOU TELLING ME THAT I COULDN'T HANDLE A MONKEY? ***I AM THE GREATEST*** !
I'M TELLING YOU THAT IF YOU GOT IN A FIGHT WITH A **HUMMINGBIRD**, YOUR ONLY HOPE WOULD BE TO HAVE THE REFEREE CHECK THE BIRD'S GLOVES AND HOPE THEY WEREN'T REGULATION SO HE'D GET DISQUALIFIED.
FLY LIKE A BUTTERBALL, STING LIKE A FLEA!

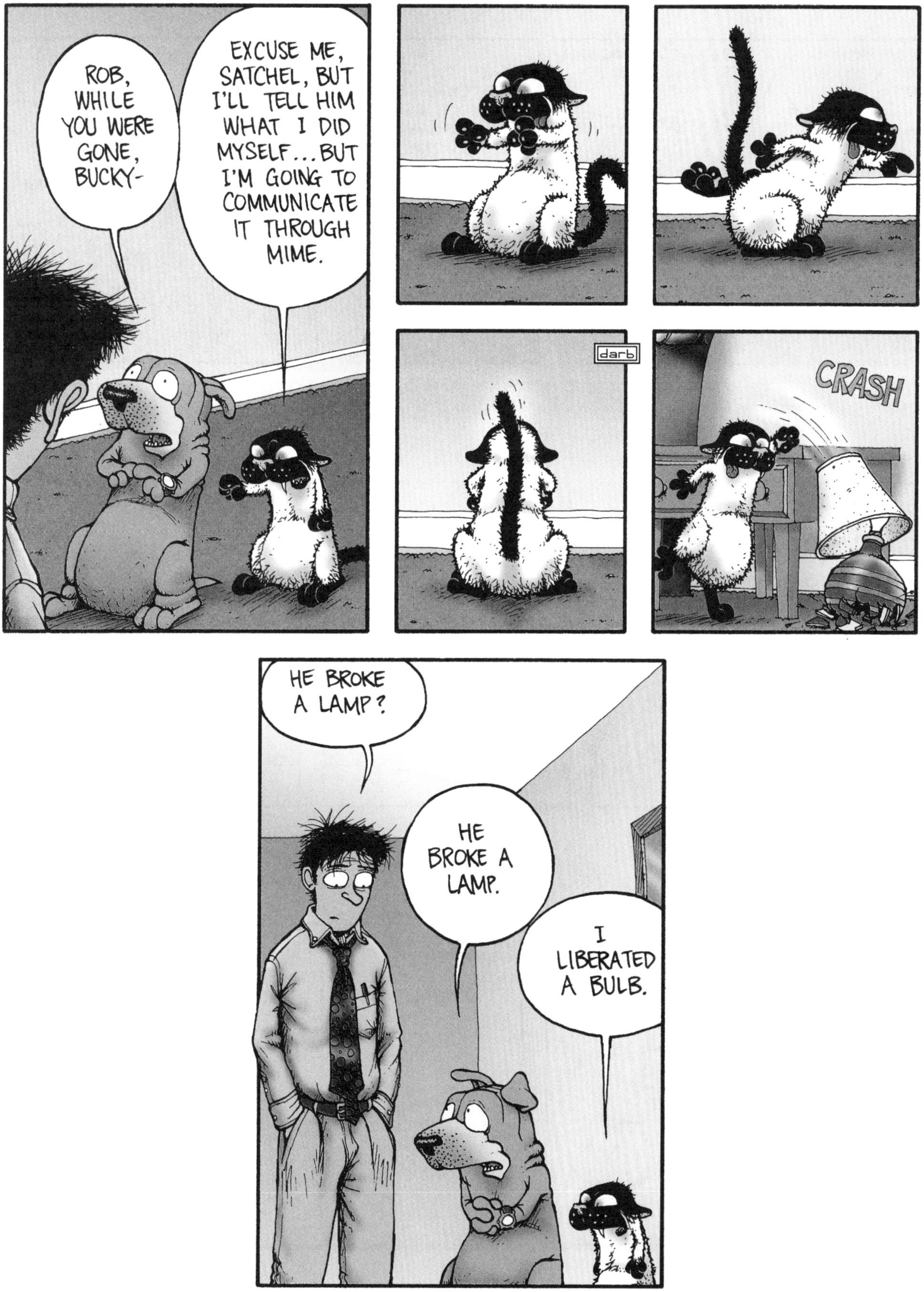
ROB, WHILE YOU WERE GONE, BUCKY-
EXCUSE ME, SATCHEL, BUT I'LL TELL HIM WHAT I DID MYSELF...BUT I'M GOING TO COMMUNICATE IT THROUGH MIME.
darb
CRASH
HE BROKE A LAMP?
HE BROKE A LAMP.
I LIBERATED A BULB.

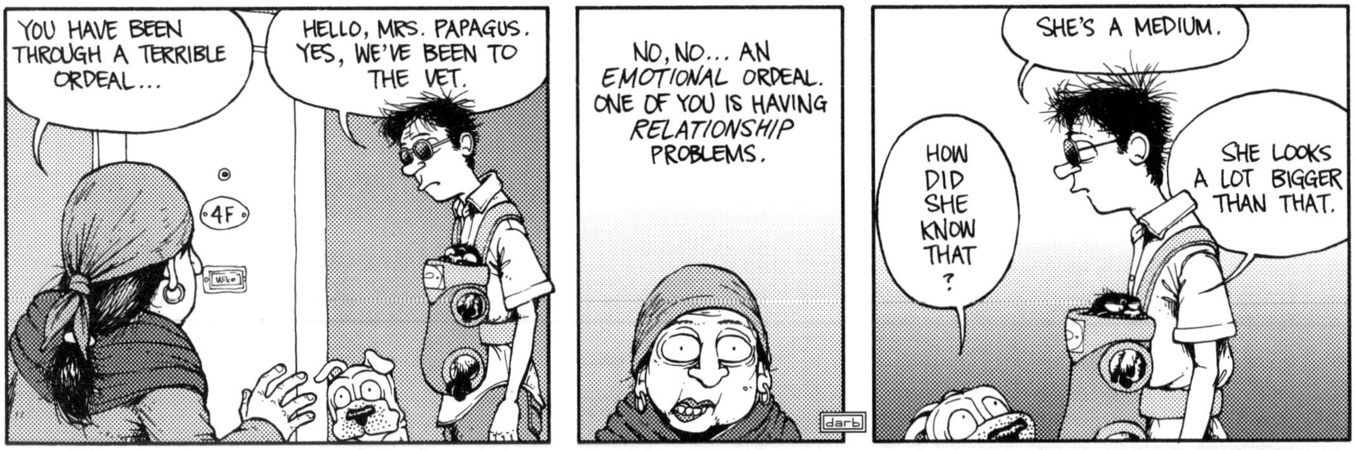
YOU HAVE BEEN THROUGH A TERRIBLE ORDEAL...
HELLO, MRS. PAPAGUS. YES, WE'VE BEEN TO THE VET.
NO, NO... AN *EMOTIONAL* ORDEAL. ONE OF YOU IS HAVING *RELATIONSHIP* PROBLEMS.
SHE'S A MEDIUM.
HOW DID SHE KNOW THAT?
SHE LOOKS A LOT BIGGER THAN THAT.
darb

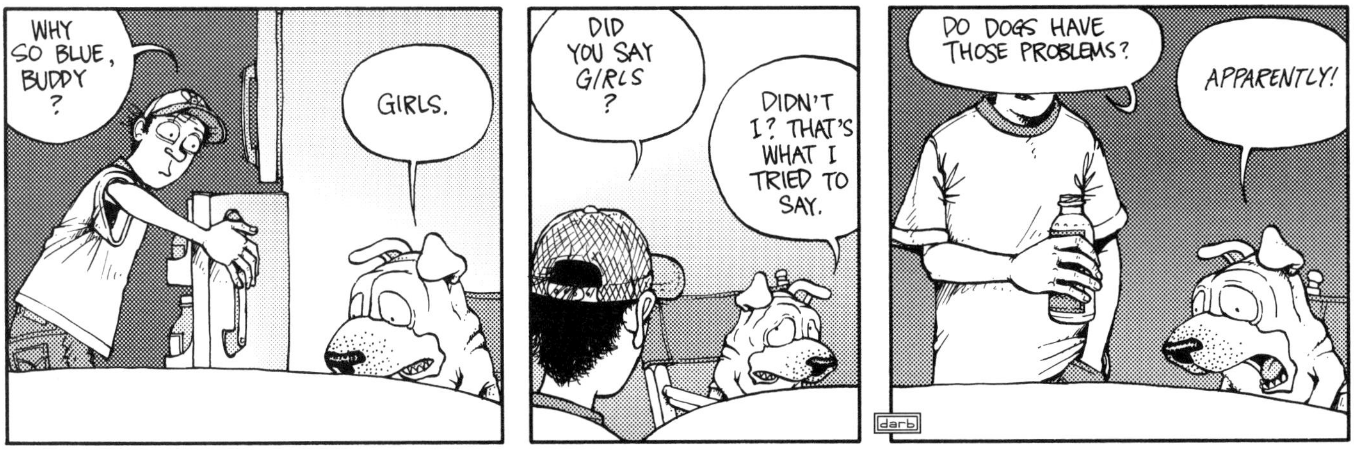
WHY SO BLUE, BUDDY?
GIRLS.
DID YOU SAY *GIRLS*?
DIDN'T I? THAT'S WHAT I TRIED TO SAY.
DO DOGS HAVE THOSE PROBLEMS?
APPARENTLY!
darb

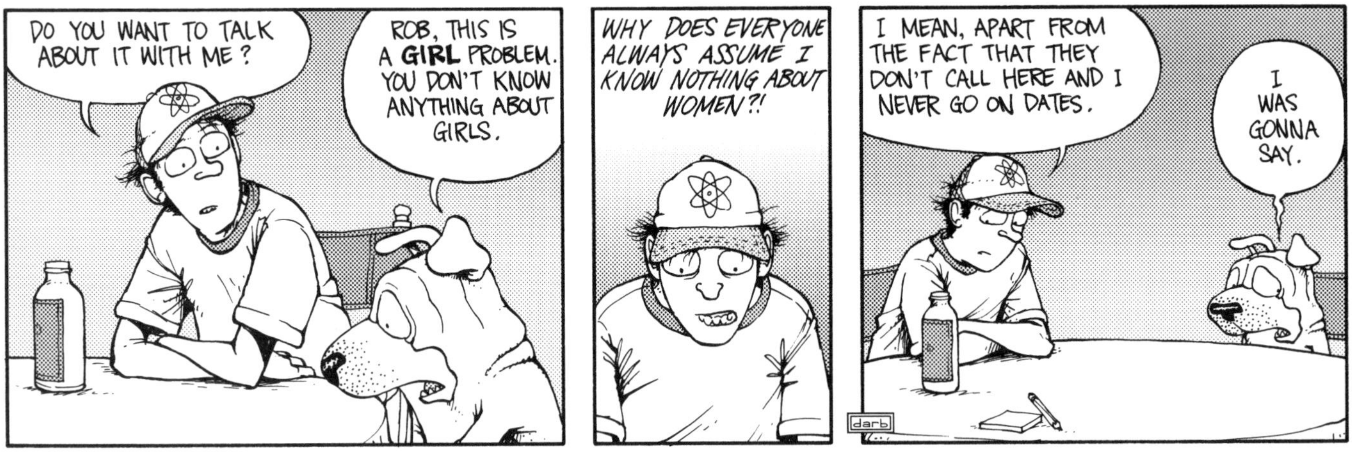
DO YOU WANT TO TALK ABOUT IT WITH ME?
ROB, THIS IS A **GIRL** PROBLEM. YOU DON'T KNOW ANYTHING ABOUT GIRLS.
WHY DOES EVERYONE ALWAYS ASSUME I KNOW NOTHING ABOUT WOMEN?!
I MEAN, APART FROM THE FACT THAT THEY DON'T CALL HERE AND I NEVER GO ON DATES.
I WAS GONNA SAY.
darb

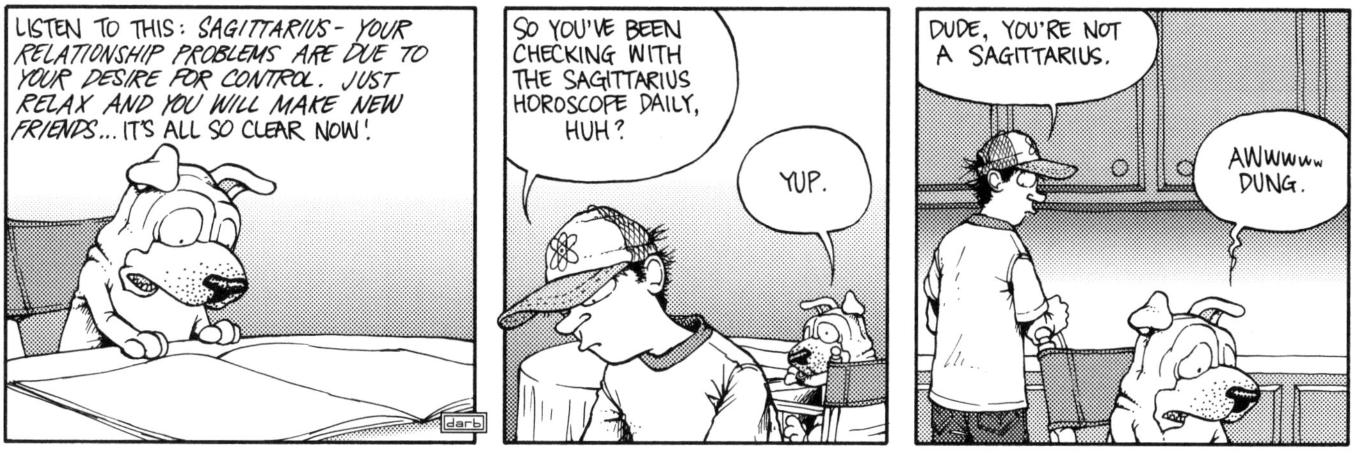

LISTEN TO THIS: SAGITTARIUS - YOUR RELATIONSHIP PROBLEMS ARE DUE TO YOUR DESIRE FOR CONTROL. JUST RELAX AND YOU WILL MAKE NEW FRIENDS... IT'S ALL SO CLEAR NOW!
darb
SO YOU'VE BEEN CHECKING WITH THE SAGITTARIUS HOROSCOPE DAILY, HUH?
YUP.
DUDE, YOU'RE NOT A SAGITTARIUS.
AWWWWW DUNG.

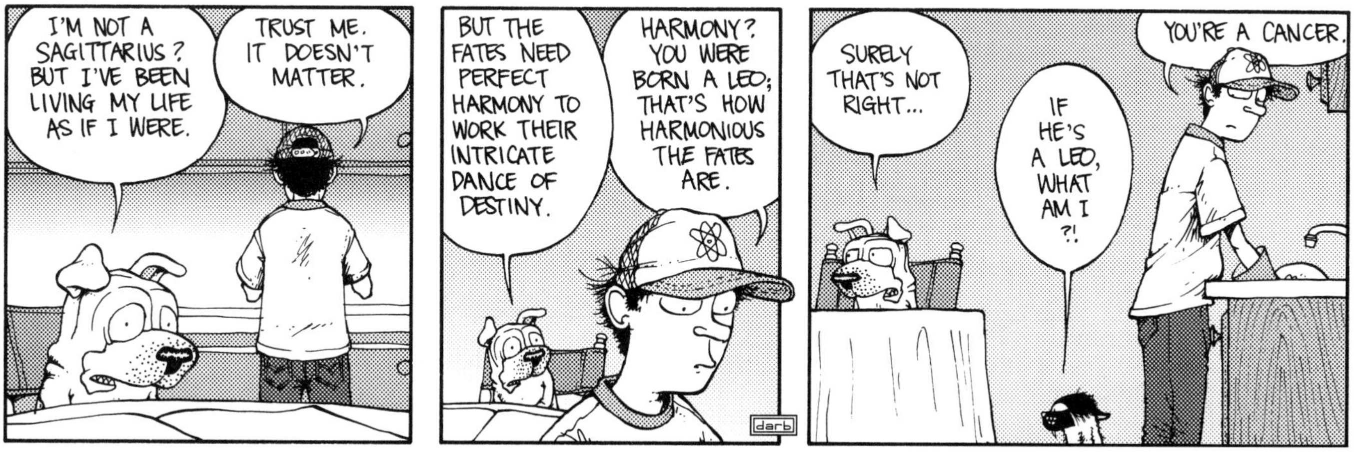

I'M NOT A SAGITTARIUS? BUT I'VE BEEN LIVING MY LIFE AS IF I WERE.
TRUST ME. IT DOESN'T MATTER.
BUT THE FATES NEED PERFECT HARMONY TO WORK THEIR INTRICATE DANCE OF DESTINY.
HARMONY? YOU WERE BORN A LEO; THAT'S HOW HARMONIOUS THE FATES ARE.
darb
SURELY THAT'S NOT RIGHT...
YOU'RE A CANCER.
IF HE'S A LEO, WHAT AM I ?!

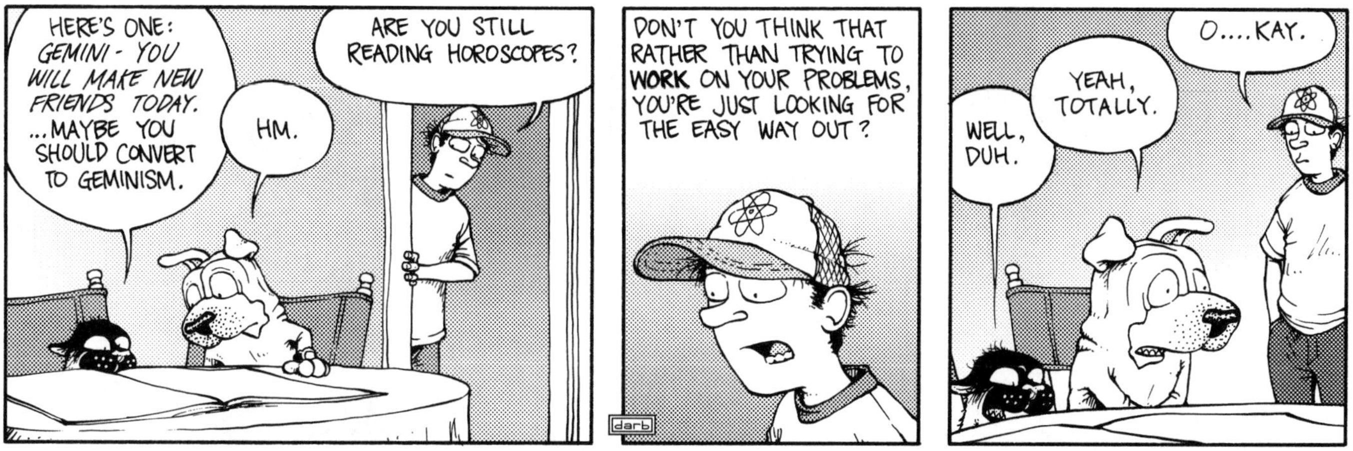

HERE'S ONE: GEMINI - YOU WILL MAKE NEW FRIENDS TODAY. ...MAYBE YOU SHOULD CONVERT TO GEMINISM.
HM.
ARE YOU STILL READING HOROSCOPES?
darb
DON'T YOU THINK THAT RATHER THAN TRYING TO WORK ON YOUR PROBLEMS, YOU'RE JUST LOOKING FOR THE EASY WAY OUT?
WELL, DUH.
YEAH, TOTALLY.
O....KAY.

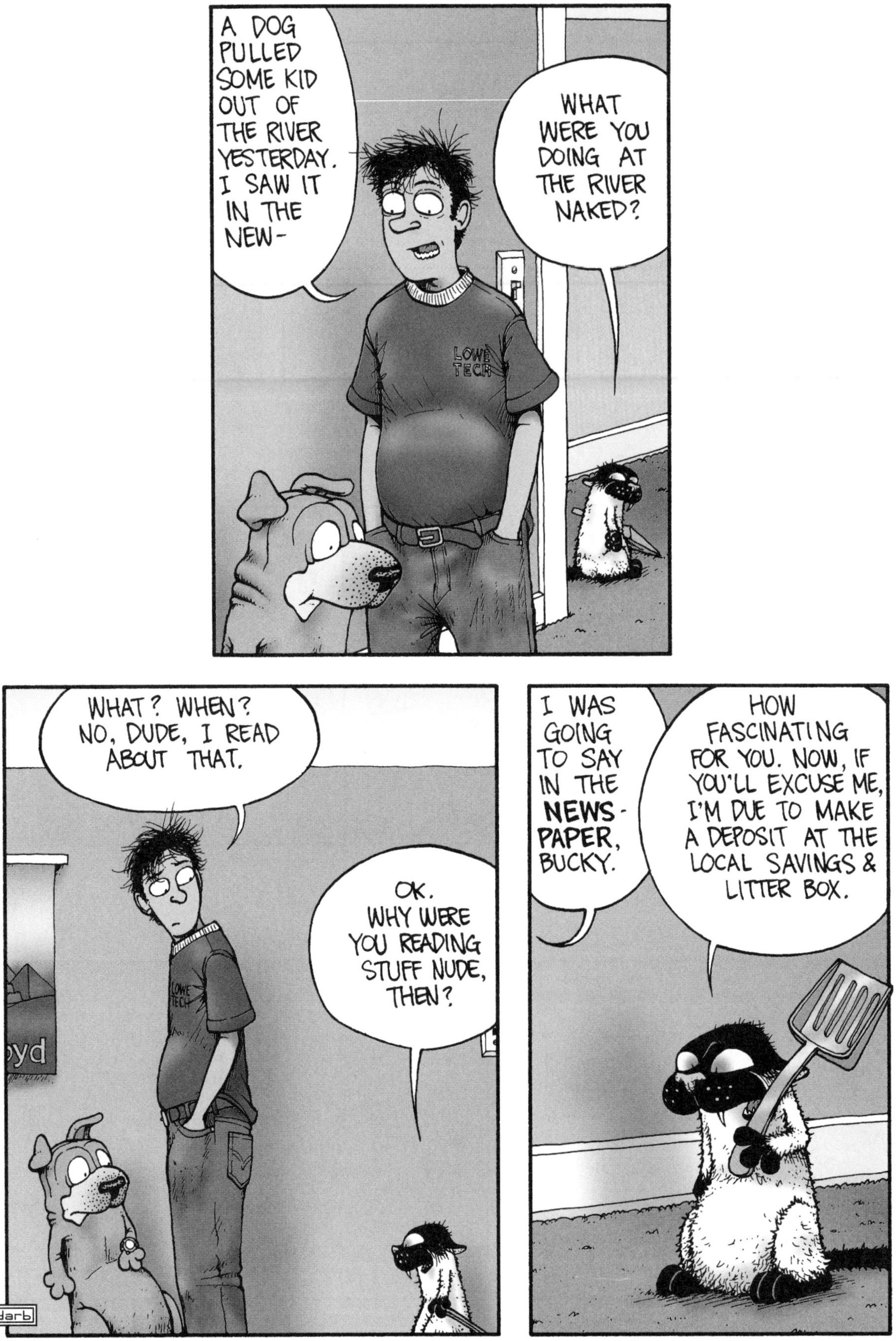
A DOG PULLED SOME KID OUT OF THE RIVER YESTERDAY. I SAW IT IN THE NEW-
WHAT WERE YOU DOING AT THE RIVER NAKED?
LOWE TECH
WHAT? WHEN? NO, DUDE, I READ ABOUT THAT.
OK. WHY WERE YOU READING STUFF NUDE, THEN?
darb
I WAS GOING TO SAY IN THE **NEWS-PAPER**, BUCKY.
HOW FASCINATING FOR YOU. NOW, IF YOU'LL EXCUSE ME, I'M DUE TO MAKE A DEPOSIT AT THE LOCAL SAVINGS & LITTER BOX.

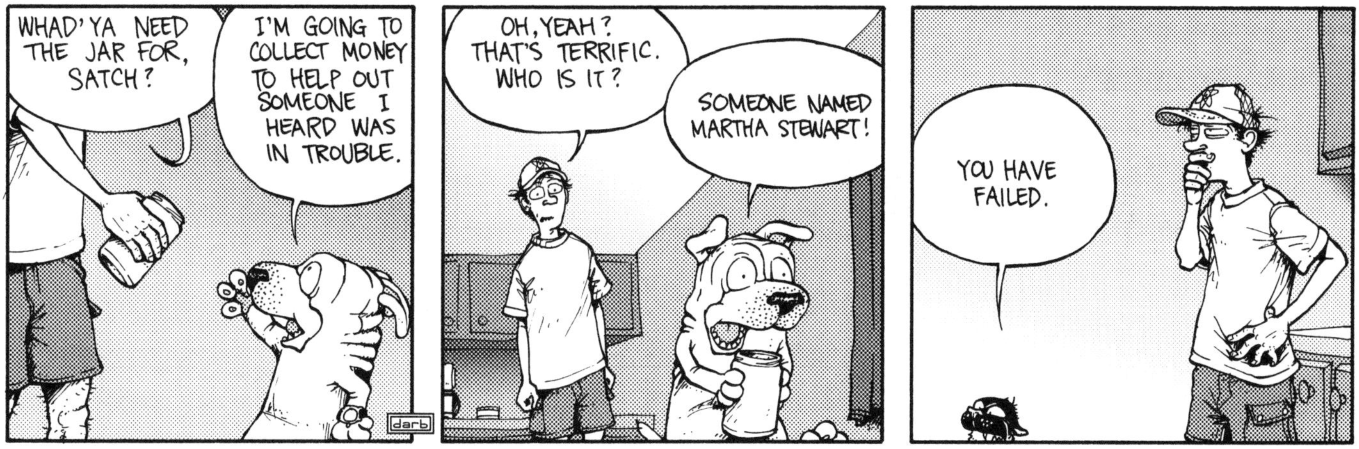
WHAD'YA NEED THE JAR FOR, SATCH?
I'M GOING TO COLLECT MONEY TO HELP OUT SOMEONE I HEARD WAS IN TROUBLE.
darb
OH, YEAH? THAT'S TERRIFIC. WHO IS IT?
SOMEONE NAMED MARTHA STEWART!
YOU HAVE FAILED.

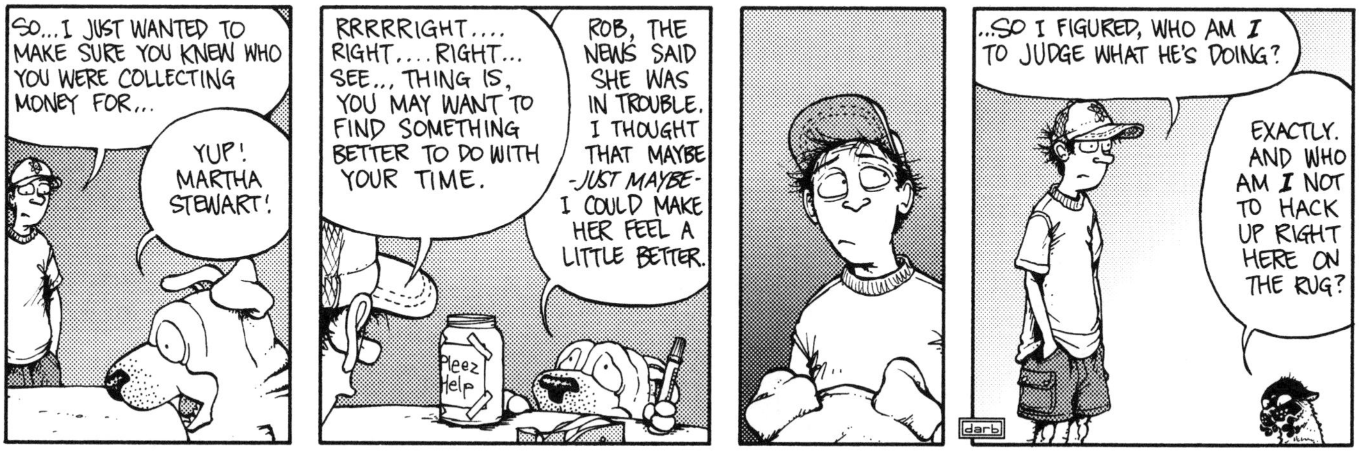
SO... I JUST WANTED TO MAKE SURE YOU KNEW WHO YOU WERE COLLECTING MONEY FOR...
YUP! MARTHA STEWART!
RRRRRIGHT.... RIGHT.... RIGHT... SEE.., THING IS, YOU MAY WANT TO FIND SOMETHING BETTER TO DO WITH YOUR TIME.
ROB, THE NEWS SAID SHE WAS IN TROUBLE. I THOUGHT THAT MAYBE -JUST MAYBE- I COULD MAKE HER FEEL A LITTLE BETTER.
Pleez Help
...SO I FIGURED, WHO AM I TO JUDGE WHAT HE'S DOING?
EXACTLY. AND WHO AM I NOT TO HACK UP RIGHT HERE ON THE RUG?
darb

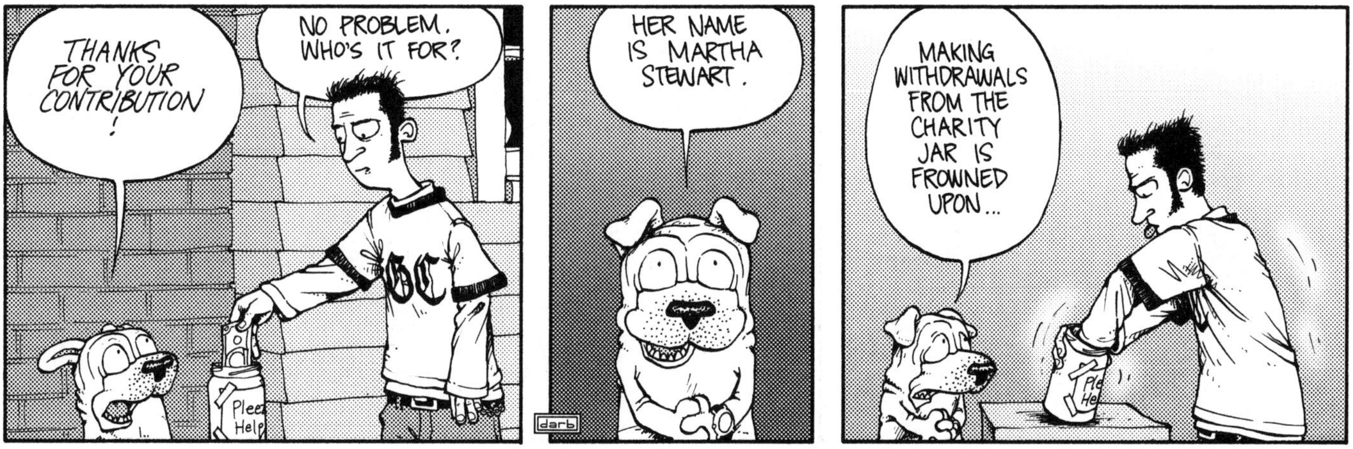
THANKS FOR YOUR CONTRIBUTION!
NO PROBLEM. WHO'S IT FOR?
Pleez Help
darb
HER NAME IS MARTHA STEWART.
MAKING WITHDRAWALS FROM THE CHARITY JAR IS FROWNED UPON...

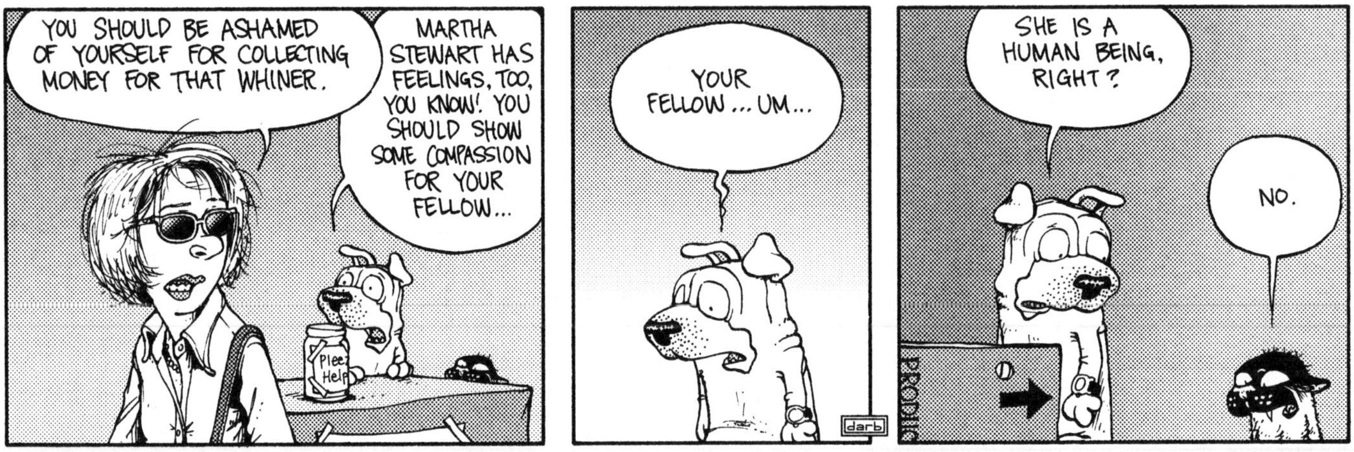
YOU SHOULD BE ASHAMED OF YOURSELF FOR COLLECTING MONEY FOR THAT WHINER.
MARTHA STEWART HAS FEELINGS, TOO, YOU KNOW! YOU SHOULD SHOW SOME COMPASSION FOR YOUR FELLOW...
YOUR FELLOW... UM...
SHE IS A HUMAN BEING, RIGHT?
NO.

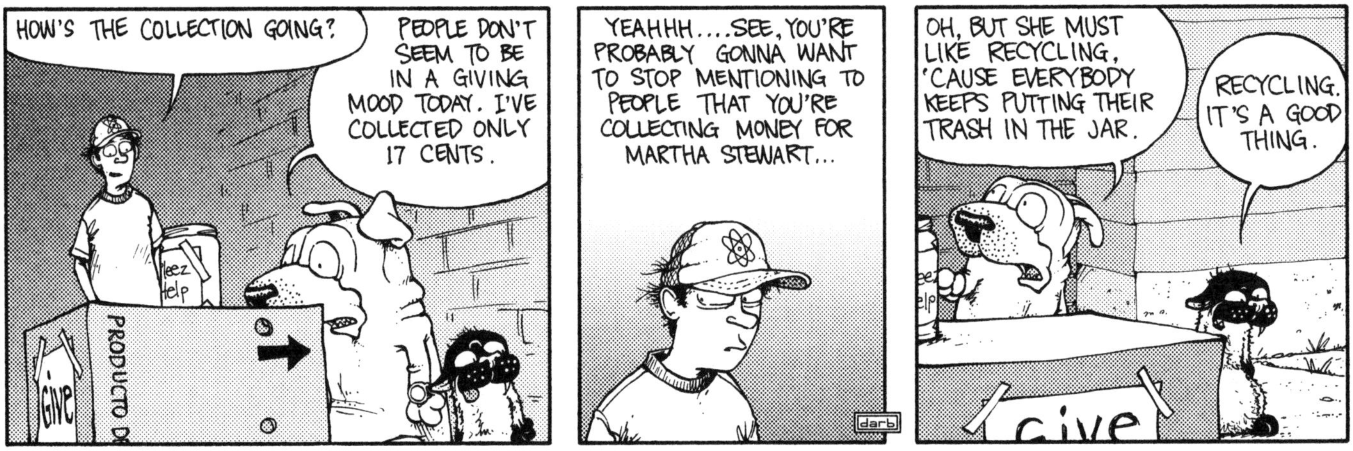
HOW'S THE COLLECTION GOING?
PEOPLE DON'T SEEM TO BE IN A GIVING MOOD TODAY. I'VE COLLECTED ONLY 17 CENTS.
YEAHHH.... SEE, YOU'RE PROBABLY GONNA WANT TO STOP MENTIONING TO PEOPLE THAT YOU'RE COLLECTING MONEY FOR MARTHA STEWART...
OH, BUT SHE MUST LIKE RECYCLING, 'CAUSE EVERYBODY KEEPS PUTTING THEIR TRASH IN THE JAR.
RECYCLING. IT'S A GOOD THING.

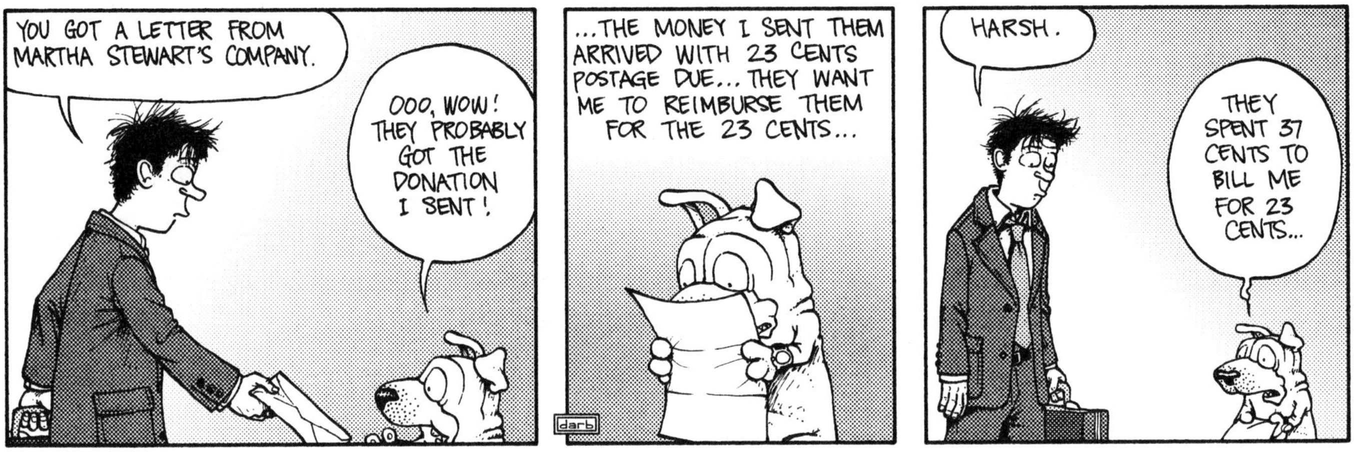
YOU GOT A LETTER FROM MARTHA STEWART'S COMPANY.
OOO, WOW! THEY PROBABLY GOT THE DONATION I SENT!
...THE MONEY I SENT THEM ARRIVED WITH 23 CENTS POSTAGE DUE... THEY WANT ME TO REIMBURSE THEM FOR THE 23 CENTS...
HARSH.
THEY SPENT 37 CENTS TO BILL ME FOR 23 CENTS...

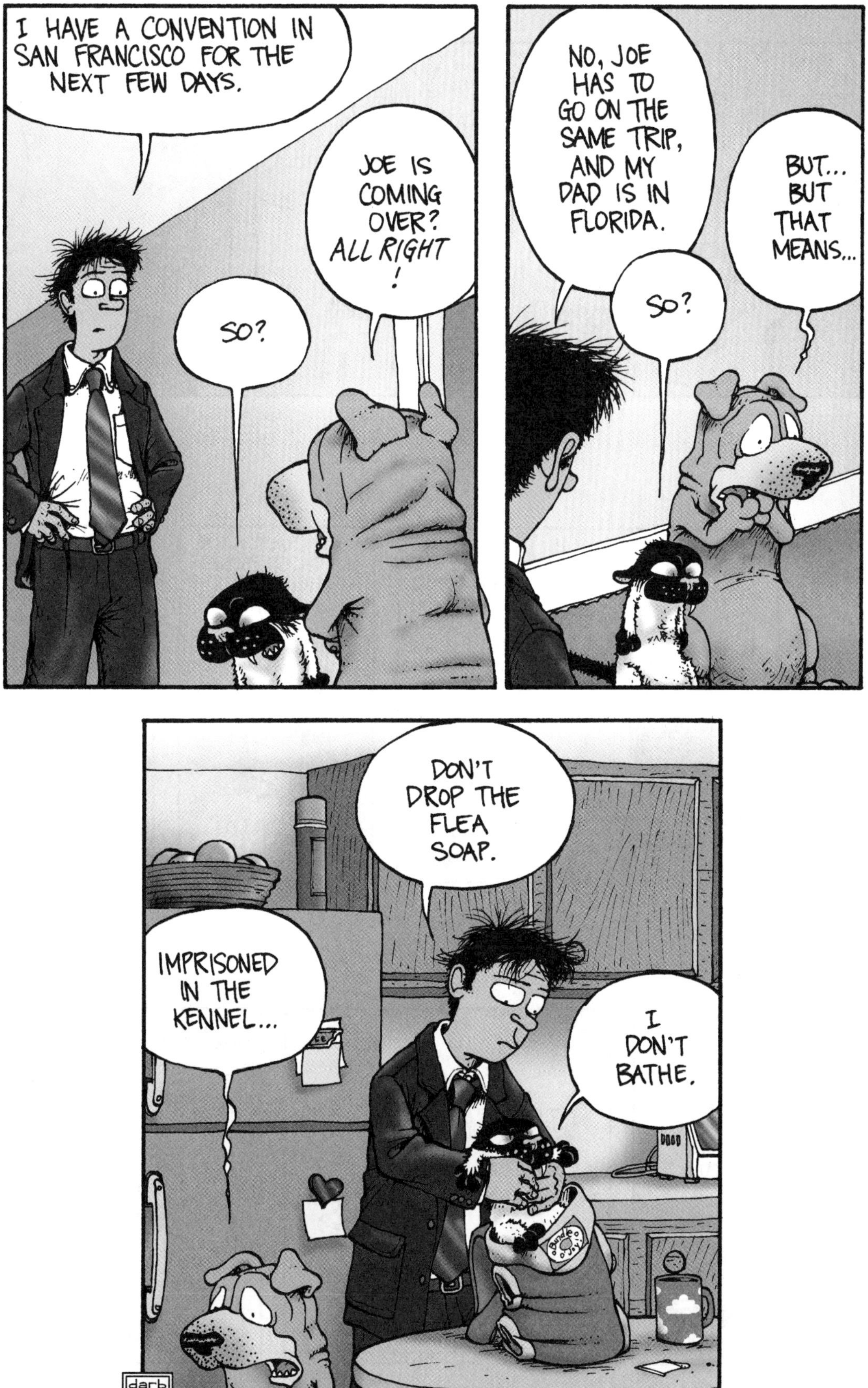
I HAVE A CONVENTION IN SAN FRANCISCO FOR THE NEXT FEW DAYS.
SO?
JOE IS COMING OVER? ALL RIGHT!
NO, JOE HAS TO GO ON THE SAME TRIP, AND MY DAD IS IN FLORIDA.
SO?
BUT... BUT THAT MEANS...
DON'T DROP THE FLEA SOAP.
IMPRISONED IN THE KENNEL...
I DON'T BATHE.
darb

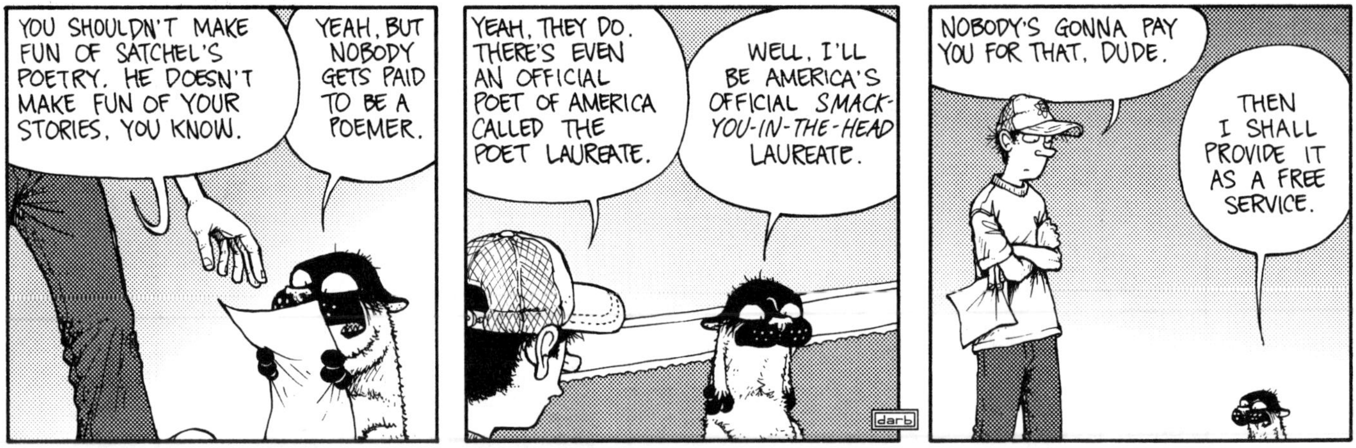
YOU SHOULDN'T MAKE FUN OF SATCHEL'S POETRY. HE DOESN'T MAKE FUN OF YOUR STORIES, YOU KNOW.
YEAH, BUT NOBODY GETS PAID TO BE A POEMER.
YEAH, THEY DO. THERE'S EVEN AN OFFICIAL POET OF AMERICA CALLED THE POET LAUREATE.
WELL, I'LL BE AMERICA'S OFFICIAL *SMACK-YOU-IN-THE-HEAD* LAUREATE.
NOBODY'S GONNA PAY YOU FOR THAT, DUDE.
THEN I SHALL PROVIDE IT AS A FREE SERVICE.
darb

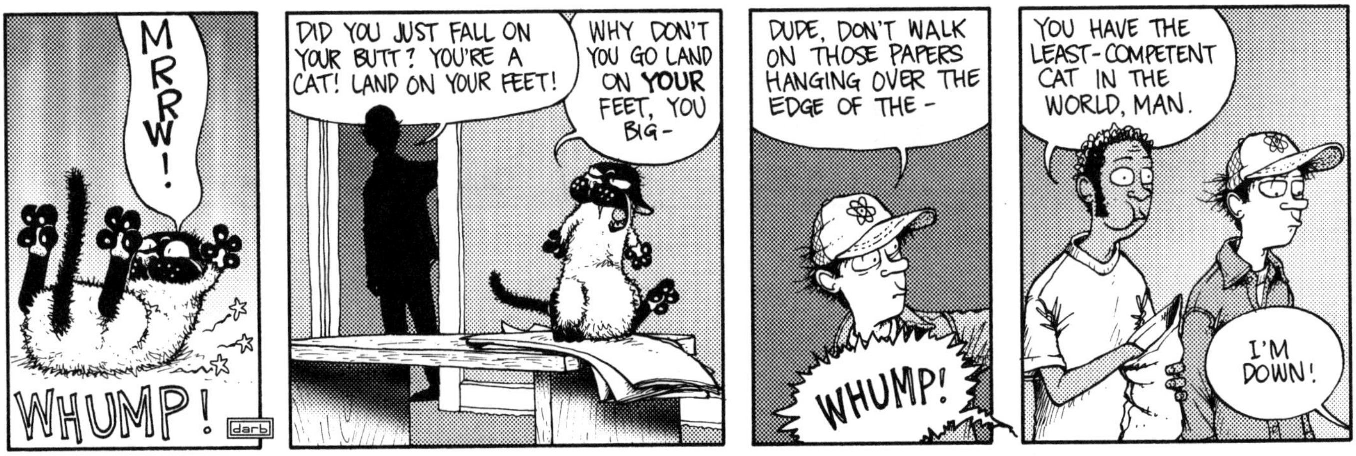
MRRW!
WHUMP!
darb
DID YOU JUST FALL ON YOUR BUTT? YOU'RE A CAT! LAND ON YOUR FEET!
WHY DON'T YOU GO LAND ON **YOUR** FEET, YOU BIG-
DUDE, DON'T WALK ON THOSE PAPERS HANGING OVER THE EDGE OF THE-
WHUMP!
YOU HAVE THE LEAST-COMPETENT CAT IN THE WORLD, MAN.
I'M DOWN!

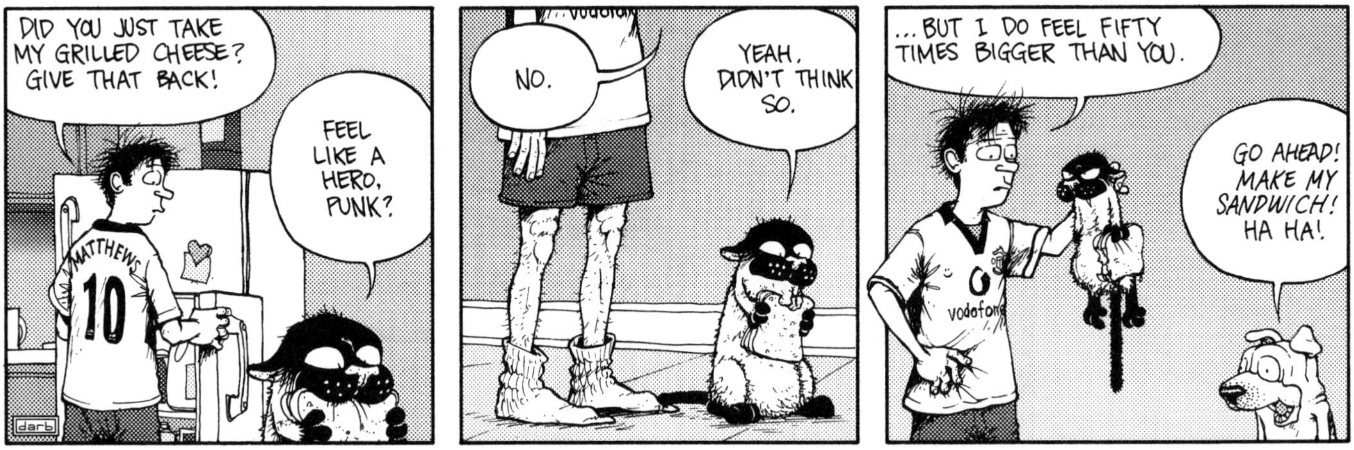
DID YOU JUST TAKE MY GRILLED CHEESE? GIVE THAT BACK!
FEEL LIKE A HERO, PUNK?
MATTHEWS
10
darb
NO.
YEAH, DIDN'T THINK SO.
...BUT I DO FEEL FIFTY TIMES BIGGER THAN YOU.
GO AHEAD! MAKE MY SANDWICH! HA HA!

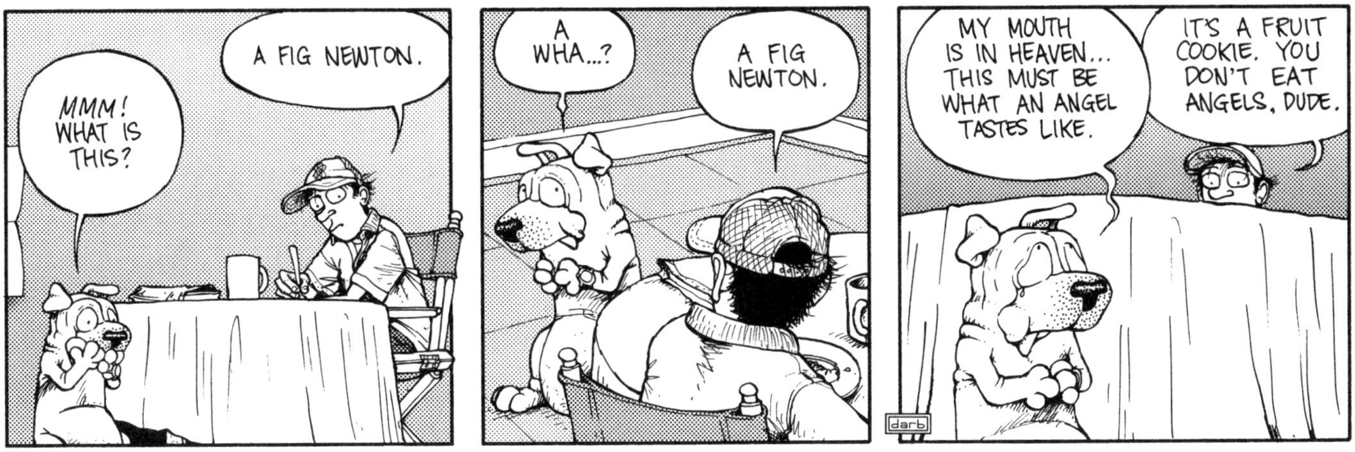
MMM! WHAT IS THIS?
A FIG NEWTON.
A WHA...?
A FIG NEWTON.
MY MOUTH IS IN HEAVEN... THIS MUST BE WHAT AN ANGEL TASTES LIKE.
IT'S A FRUIT COOKIE. YOU DON'T EAT ANGELS, DUDE.
darb

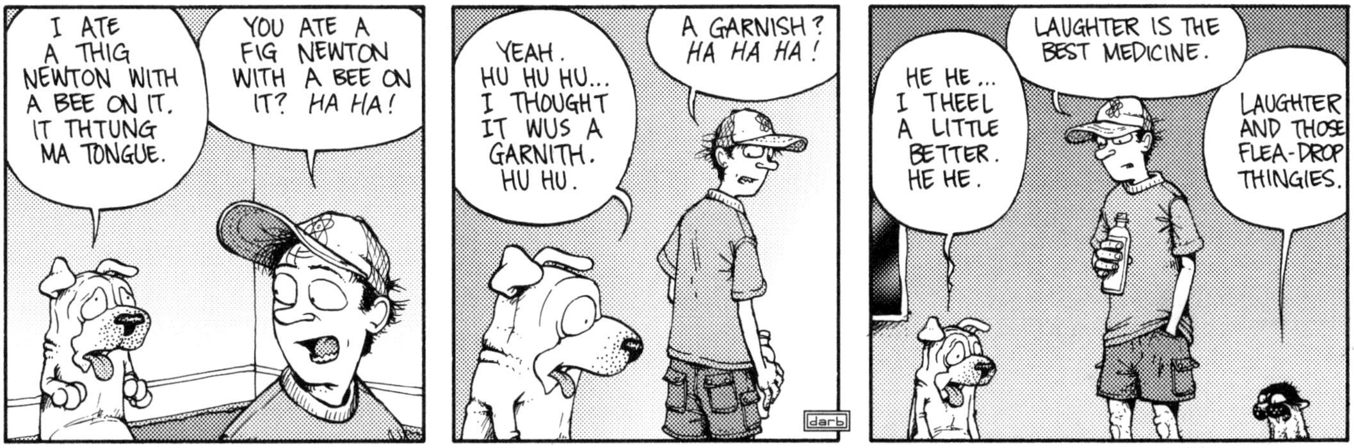
I ATE A THIG NEWTON WITH A BEE ON IT. IT THTUNG MA TONGUE.
YOU ATE A FIG NEWTON WITH A BEE ON IT? HA HA!
YEAH. HU HU HU... I THOUGHT IT WUS A GARNITH. HU HU.
A GARNISH? HA HA HA!
darb
HE HE... I THEEL A LITTLE BETTER. HE HE.
LAUGHTER IS THE BEST MEDICINE.
LAUGHTER AND THOSE FLEA-DROP THINGIES.

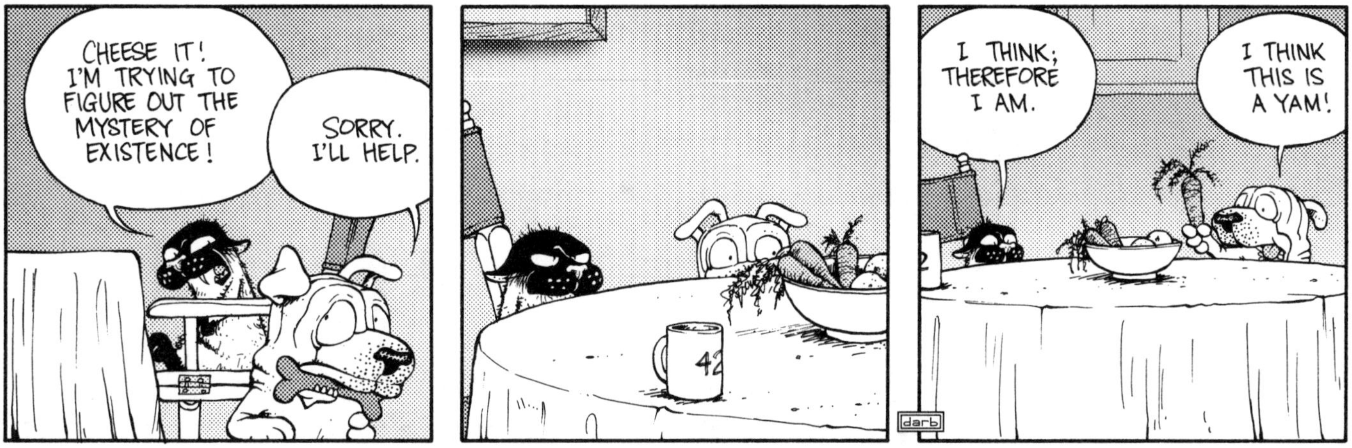
CHEESE IT! I'M TRYING TO FIGURE OUT THE MYSTERY OF EXISTENCE!
SORRY. I'LL HELP.
42
darb
I THINK; THEREFORE I AM.
I THINK THIS IS A YAM!

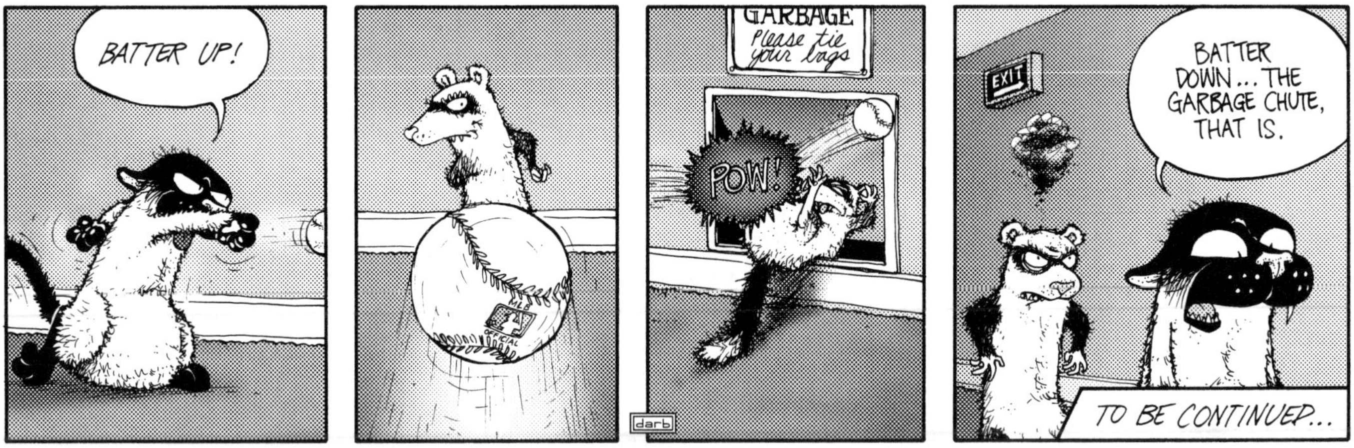
BATTER UP!
GARBAGE
Please tie your bags
POW!
EXIT
BATTER DOWN... THE GARBAGE CHUTE, THAT IS.
TO BE CONTINUED...
darb

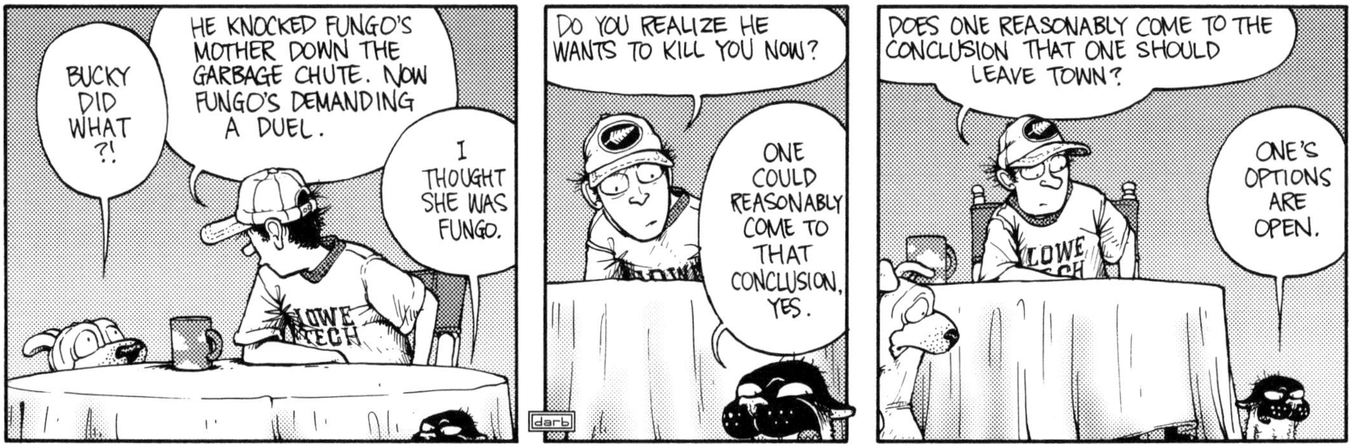
BUCKY DID WHAT ?!
HE KNOCKED FUNGO'S MOTHER DOWN THE GARBAGE CHUTE. NOW FUNGO'S DEMANDING A DUEL.
I THOUGHT SHE WAS FUNGO.
darb
DO YOU REALIZE HE WANTS TO KILL YOU NOW?
ONE COULD REASONABLY COME TO THAT CONCLUSION, YES.
DOES ONE REASONABLY COME TO THE CONCLUSION THAT ONE SHOULD LEAVE TOWN?
ONE'S OPTIONS ARE OPEN.

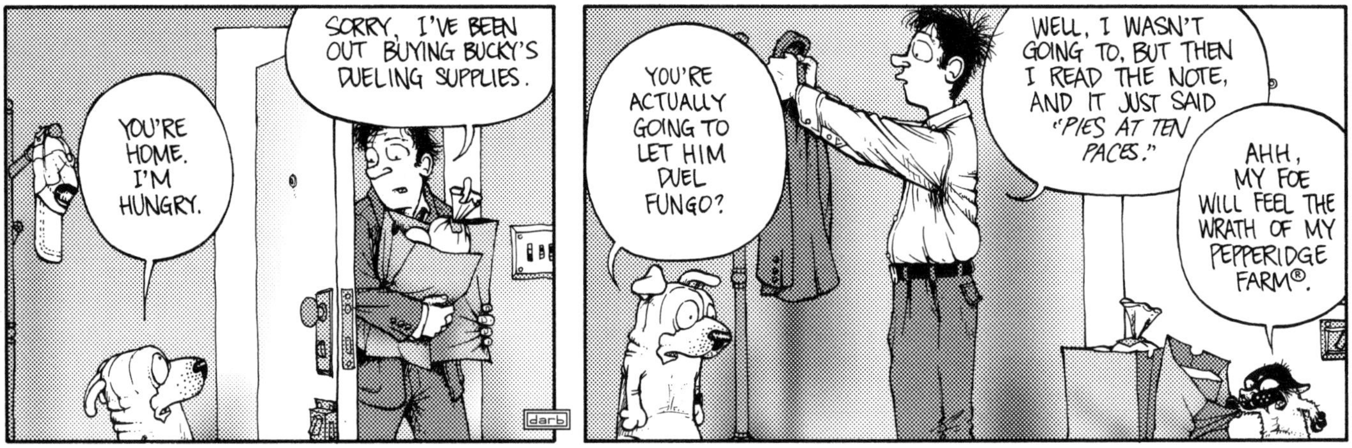
YOU'RE HOME. I'M HUNGRY.
SORRY, I'VE BEEN OUT BUYING BUCKY'S DUELING SUPPLIES.
darb
YOU'RE ACTUALLY GOING TO LET HIM DUEL FUNGO?
WELL, I WASN'T GOING TO, BUT THEN I READ THE NOTE, AND IT JUST SAID "PIES AT TEN PACES."
AHH, MY FOE WILL FEEL THE WRATH OF MY PEPPERIDGE FARM®.

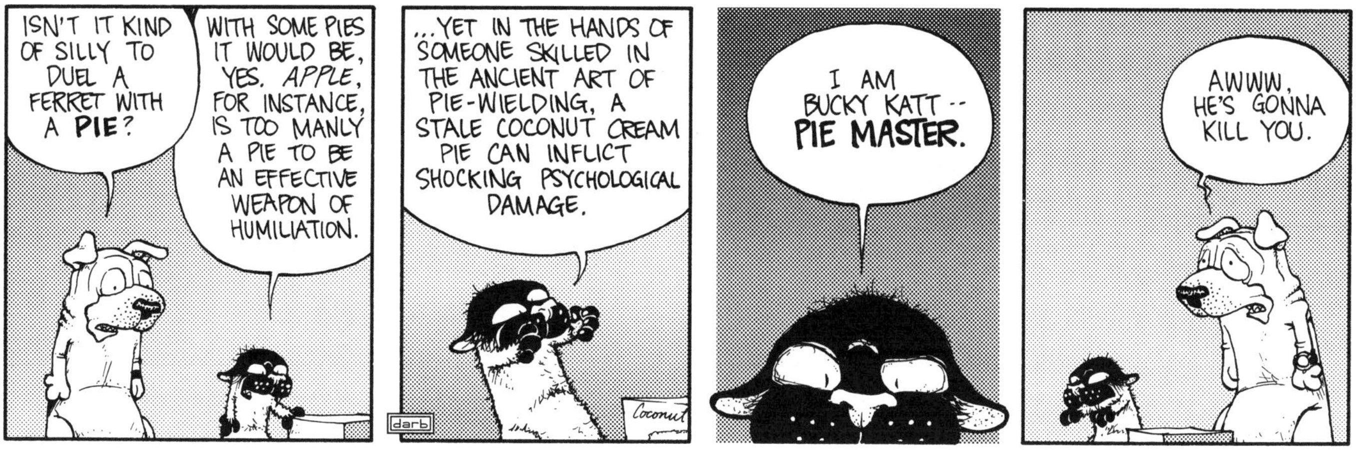
ISN'T IT KIND OF SILLY TO DUEL A FERRET WITH A **PIE**?
WITH SOME PIES IT WOULD BE, YES. *APPLE*, FOR INSTANCE, IS TOO MANLY A PIE TO BE AN EFFECTIVE WEAPON OF HUMILIATION.
darb
...YET IN THE HANDS OF SOMEONE SKILLED IN THE ANCIENT ART OF PIE-WIELDING, A STALE COCONUT CREAM PIE CAN INFLICT SHOCKING PSYCHOLOGICAL DAMAGE.
Coconut
I AM BUCKY KATT -- **PIE MASTER**.
AWWW. HE'S GONNA KILL YOU.

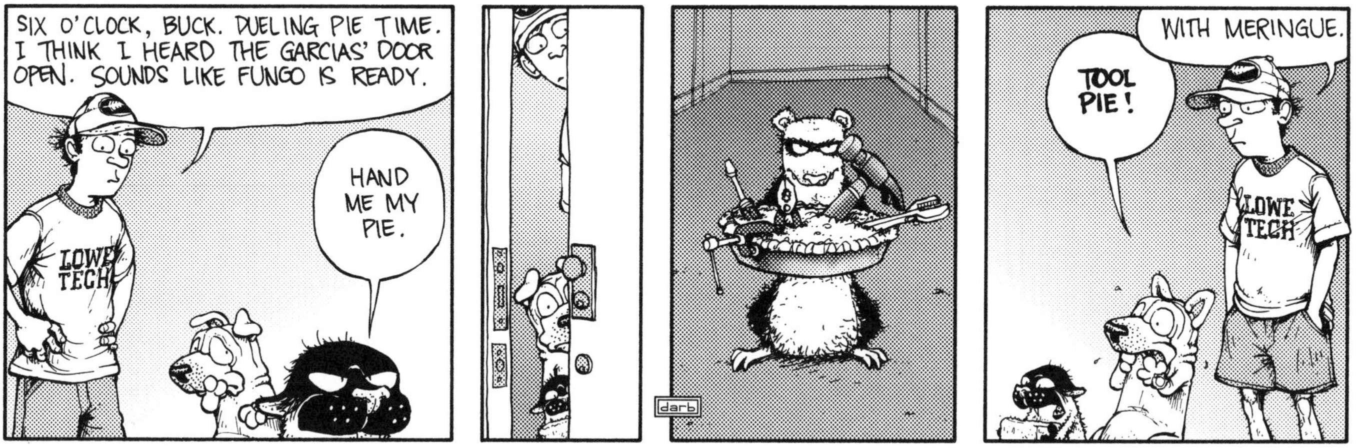
SIX O'CLOCK, BUCK. DUELING PIE TIME. I THINK I HEARD THE GARCIAS' DOOR OPEN. SOUNDS LIKE FUNGO IS READY.
LOWE TECH
HAND ME MY PIE.
darb
TOOL PIE!
WITH MERINGUE.
LOWE TECH

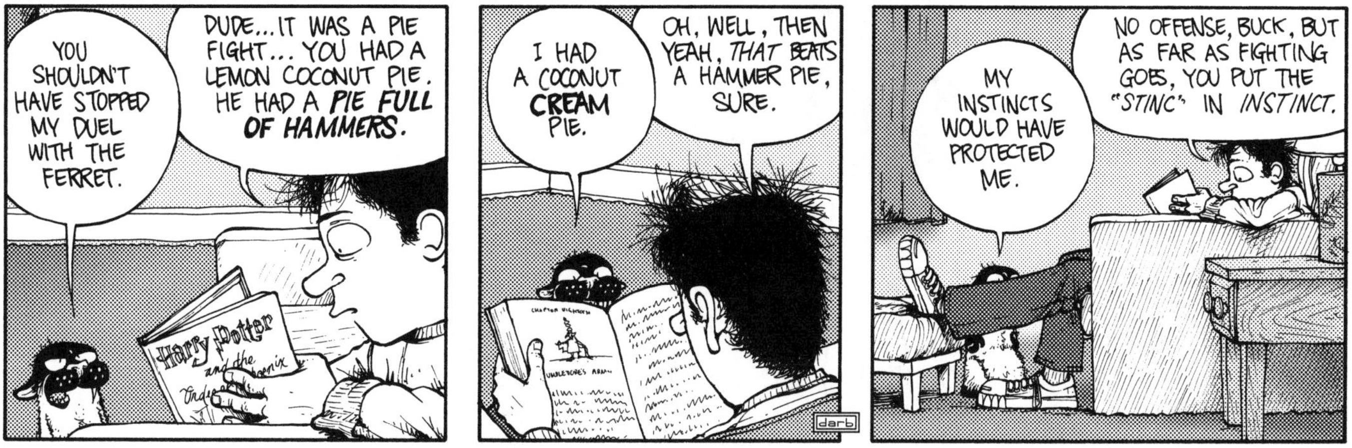
YOU SHOULDN'T HAVE STOPPED MY DUEL WITH THE FERRET.
DUDE...IT WAS A PIE FIGHT... YOU HAD A LEMON COCONUT PIE. HE HAD A ***PIE FULL OF HAMMERS***.
Harry Potter
I HAD A COCONUT **CREAM** PIE.
OH, WELL, THEN YEAH, *THAT* BEATS A HAMMER PIE, SURE.
darb
MY INSTINCTS WOULD HAVE PROTECTED ME.
NO OFFENSE, BUCK, BUT AS FAR AS FIGHTING GOES, YOU PUT THE "*STINC*" IN *INSTINCT*.

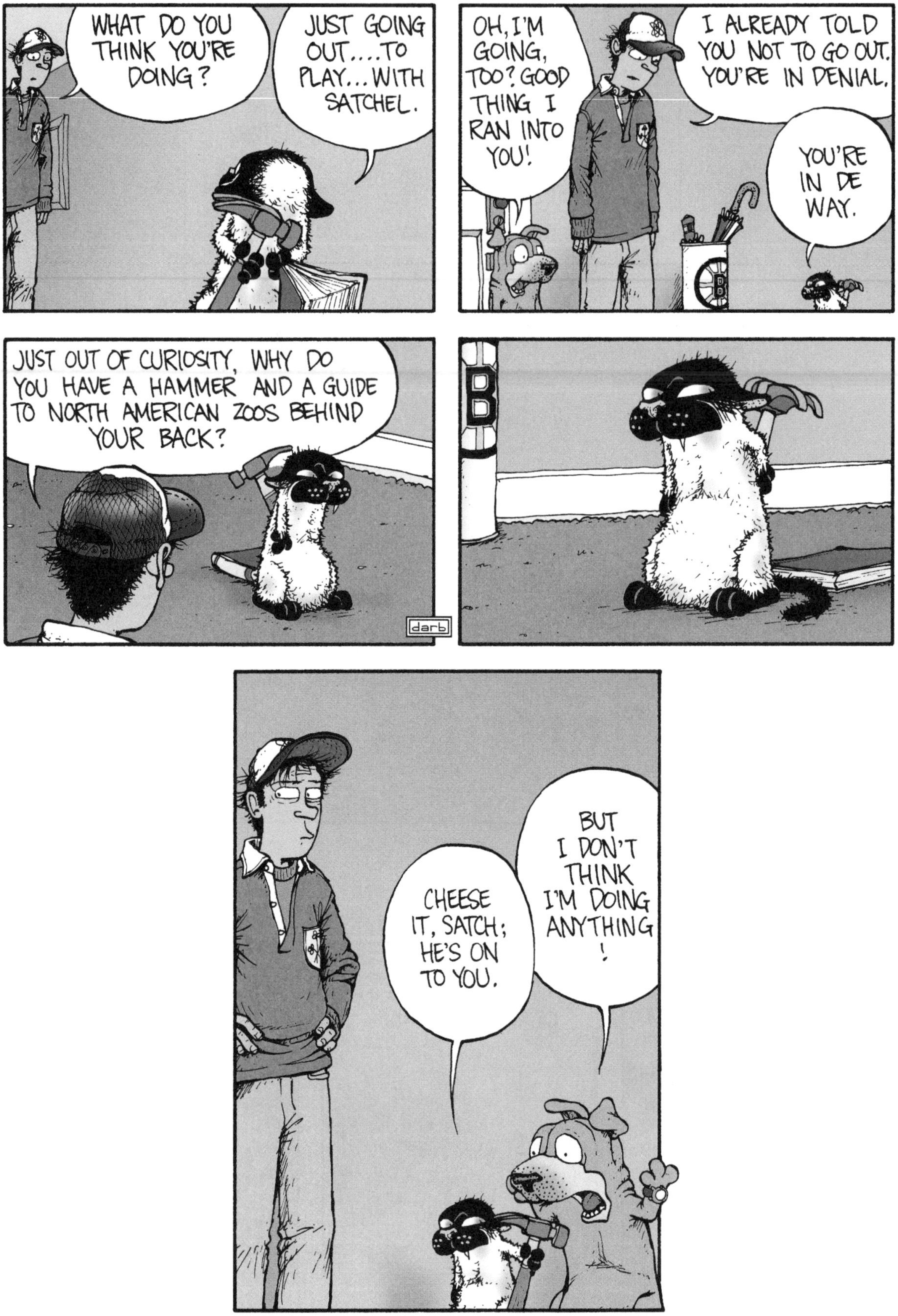

WHAT DO YOU THINK YOU'RE DOING?
JUST GOING OUT....TO PLAY...WITH SATCHEL.
OH, I'M GOING, TOO? GOOD THING I RAN INTO YOU!
I ALREADY TOLD YOU NOT TO GO OUT. YOU'RE IN DENIAL.
YOU'RE IN DE WAY.
JUST OUT OF CURIOSITY, WHY DO YOU HAVE A HAMMER AND A GUIDE TO NORTH AMERICAN ZOOS BEHIND YOUR BACK?
darb
CHEESE IT, SATCH; HE'S ON TO YOU.
BUT I DON'T THINK I'M DOING ANYTHING!

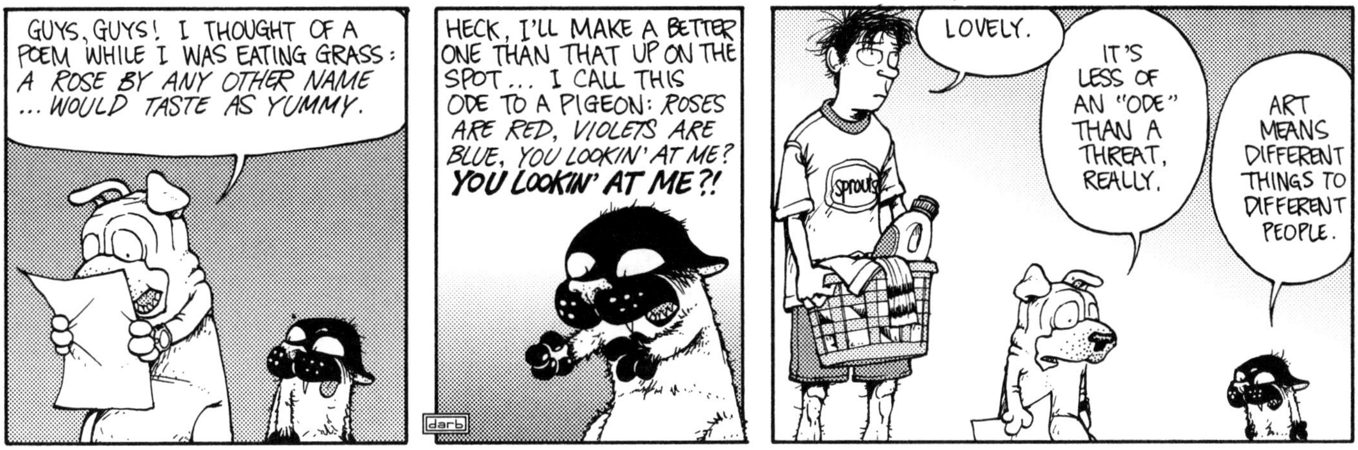
GUYS, GUYS! I THOUGHT OF A POEM WHILE I WAS EATING GRASS: *A ROSE BY ANY OTHER NAME ... WOULD TASTE AS YUMMY.*
HECK, I'LL MAKE A BETTER ONE THAN THAT UP ON THE SPOT... I CALL THIS ODE TO A PIGEON: *ROSES ARE RED, VIOLETS ARE BLUE, YOU LOOKIN' AT ME?* **YOU LOOKIN' AT ME?!**
darb
LOVELY.
SPROUTS
IT'S LESS OF AN "ODE" THAN A THREAT, REALLY.
ART MEANS DIFFERENT THINGS TO DIFFERENT PEOPLE.

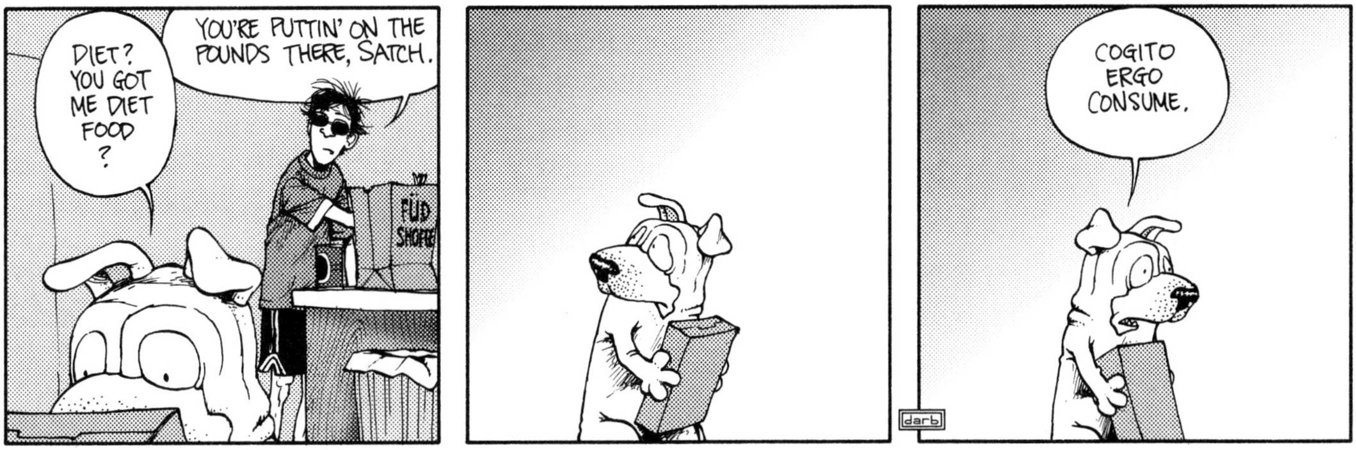
YOU'RE PUTTIN' ON THE POUNDS THERE, SATCH.
DIET? YOU GOT ME DIET FOOD ?
FUD SHOPPE
COGITO ERGO CONSUME.
darb

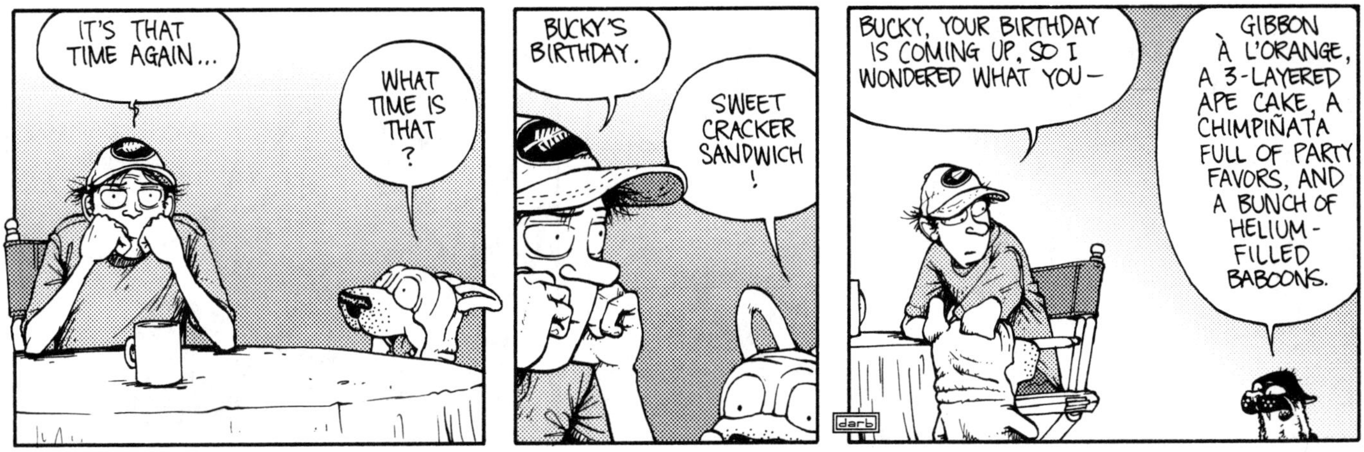
IT'S THAT TIME AGAIN...
WHAT TIME IS THAT ?
BUCKY'S BIRTHDAY.
SWEET CRACKER SANDWICH !
BUCKY, YOUR BIRTHDAY IS COMING UP, SO I WONDERED WHAT YOU—
GIBBON À L'ORANGE, A 3-LAYERED APE CAKE, A CHIMPIÑATA FULL OF PARTY FAVORS, AND A BUNCH OF HELIUM-FILLED BABOONS.
darb

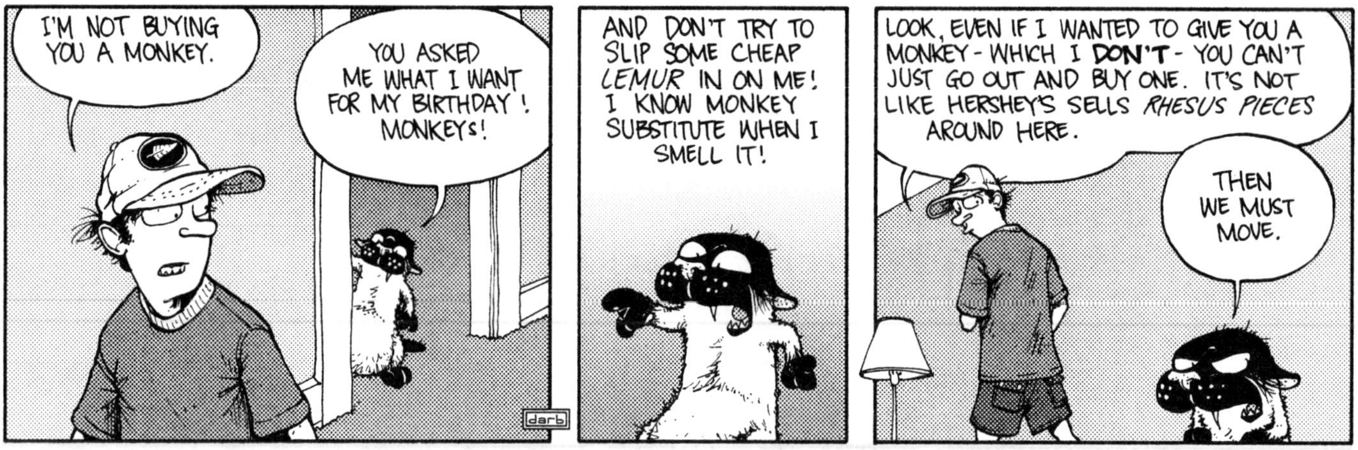
I'M NOT BUYING YOU A MONKEY.
YOU ASKED ME WHAT I WANT FOR MY BIRTHDAY! MONKEYS!
AND DON'T TRY TO SLIP SOME CHEAP *LEMUR* IN ON ME! I KNOW MONKEY SUBSTITUTE WHEN I SMELL IT!
LOOK, EVEN IF I WANTED TO GIVE YOU A MONKEY - WHICH I **DON'T** - YOU CAN'T JUST GO OUT AND BUY ONE. IT'S NOT LIKE HERSHEY'S SELLS *RHESUS PIECES* AROUND HERE.
THEN WE MUST MOVE.

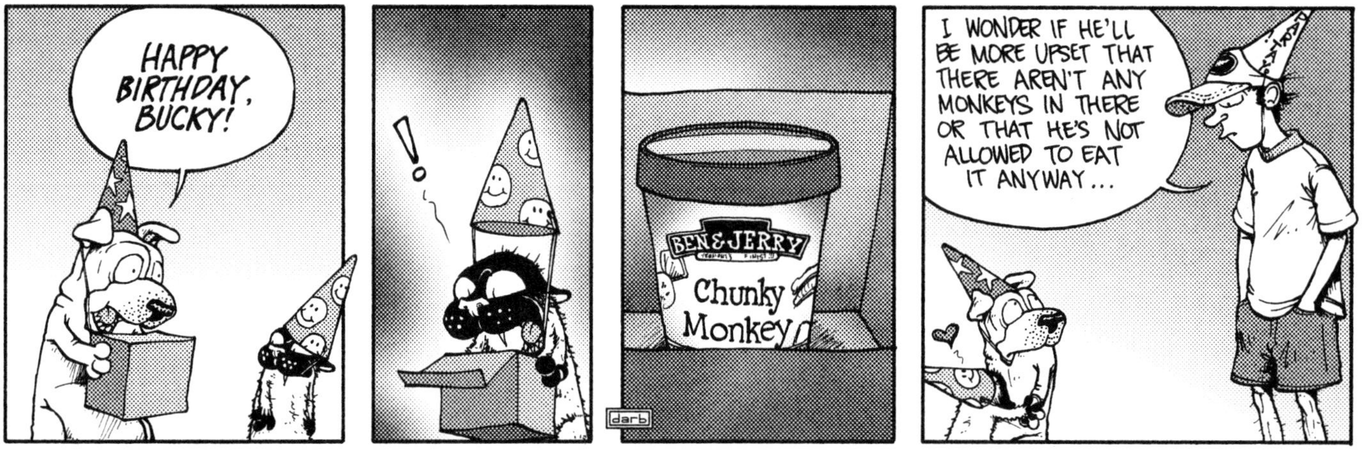
HAPPY BIRTHDAY, BUCKY!
!
BEN & JERRY
Chunky Monkey
I WONDER IF HE'LL BE MORE UPSET THAT THERE AREN'T ANY MONKEYS IN THERE OR THAT HE'S NOT ALLOWED TO EAT IT ANYWAY...

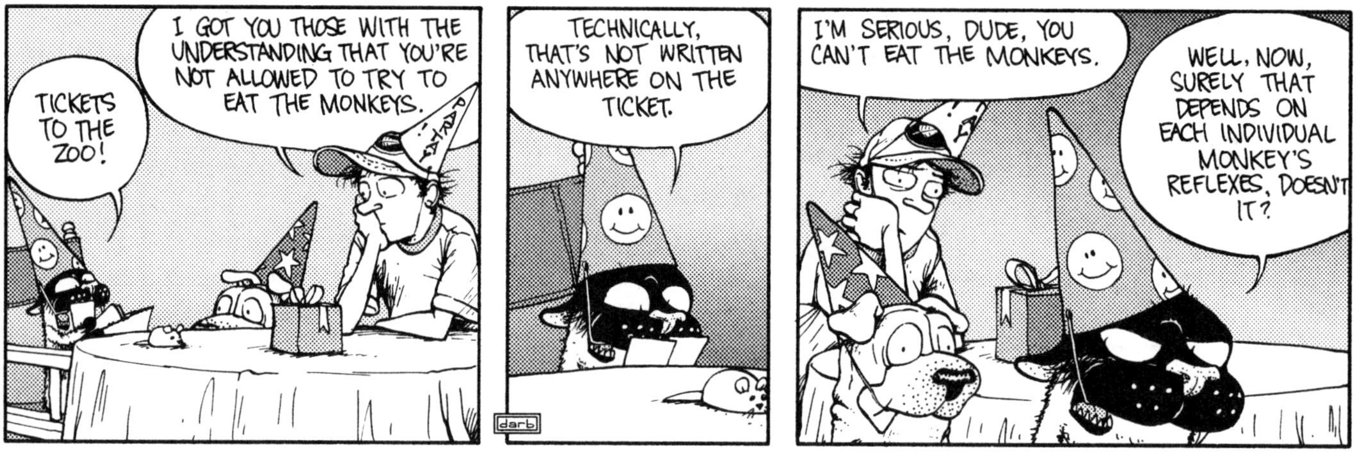
TICKETS TO THE ZOO!
I GOT YOU THOSE WITH THE UNDERSTANDING THAT YOU'RE NOT ALLOWED TO TRY TO EAT THE MONKEYS.
TECHNICALLY, THAT'S NOT WRITTEN ANYWHERE ON THE TICKET.
I'M SERIOUS, DUDE, YOU CAN'T EAT THE MONKEYS.
WELL, NOW, SURELY THAT DEPENDS ON EACH INDIVIDUAL MONKEY'S REFLEXES, DOESN'T IT?

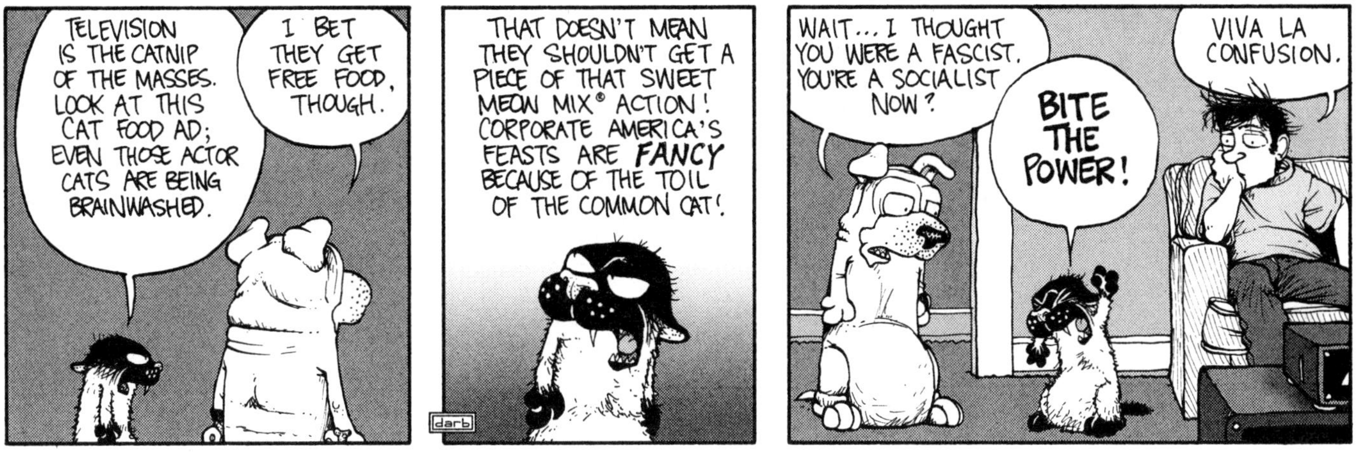
TELEVISION IS THE CATNIP OF THE MASSES. LOOK AT THIS CAT FOOD AD; EVEN THOSE ACTOR CATS ARE BEING BRAINWASHED.
I BET THEY GET FREE FOOD, THOUGH.
THAT DOESN'T MEAN THEY SHOULDN'T GET A PIECE OF THAT SWEET MEOW MIX® ACTION! CORPORATE AMERICA'S FEASTS ARE FANCY BECAUSE OF THE TOIL OF THE COMMON CAT!
darb
WAIT... I THOUGHT YOU WERE A FASCIST. YOU'RE A SOCIALIST NOW?
BITE THE POWER!
VIVA LA CONFUSION.

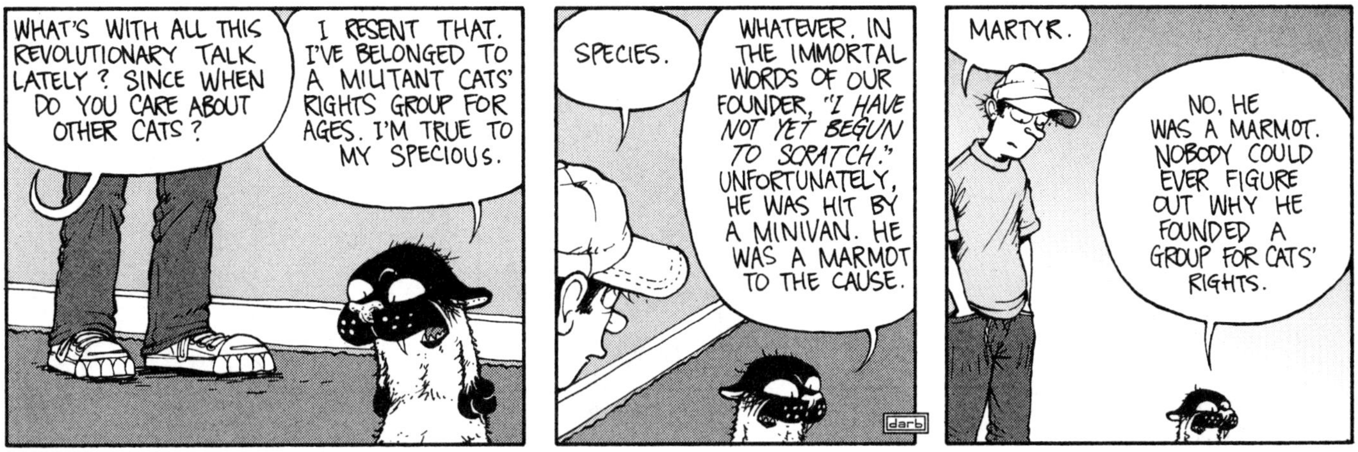
WHAT'S WITH ALL THIS REVOLUTIONARY TALK LATELY? SINCE WHEN DO YOU CARE ABOUT OTHER CATS?
I RESENT THAT. I'VE BELONGED TO A MILITANT CATS' RIGHTS GROUP FOR AGES. I'M TRUE TO MY SPECIOUS.
SPECIES.
WHATEVER. IN THE IMMORTAL WORDS OF OUR FOUNDER, "I HAVE NOT YET BEGUN TO SCRATCH." UNFORTUNATELY, HE WAS HIT BY A MINIVAN. HE WAS A MARMOT TO THE CAUSE.
darb
MARTYR.
NO, HE WAS A MARMOT. NOBODY COULD EVER FIGURE OUT WHY HE FOUNDED A GROUP FOR CATS' RIGHTS.

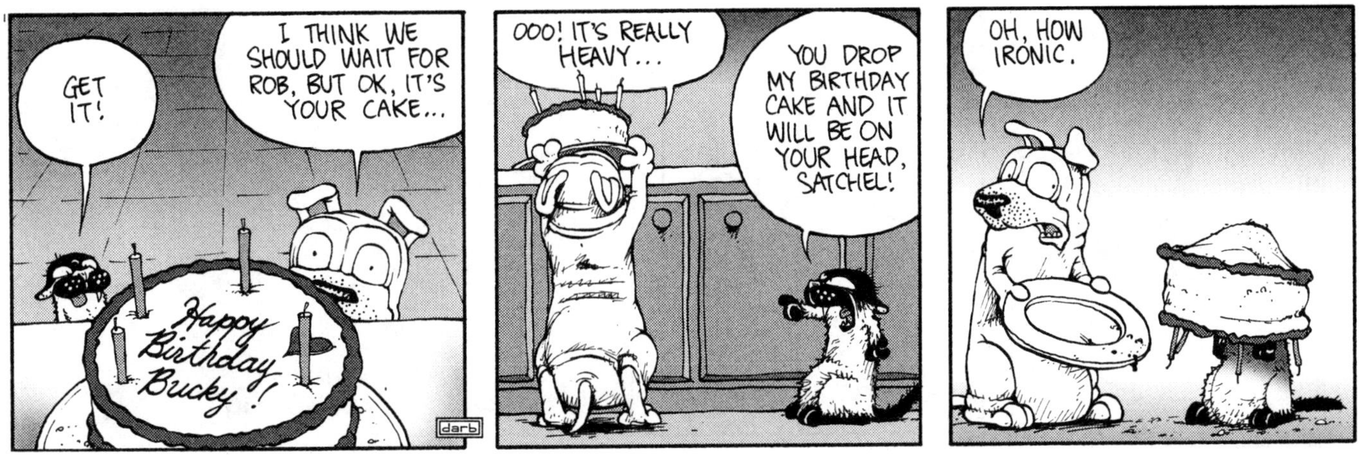
GET IT!
I THINK WE SHOULD WAIT FOR ROB, BUT OK, IT'S YOUR CAKE...
Happy Birthday Bucky!
darb
OOO! IT'S REALLY HEAVY...
YOU DROP MY BIRTHDAY CAKE AND IT WILL BE ON YOUR HEAD, SATCHEL!
OH, HOW IRONIC.

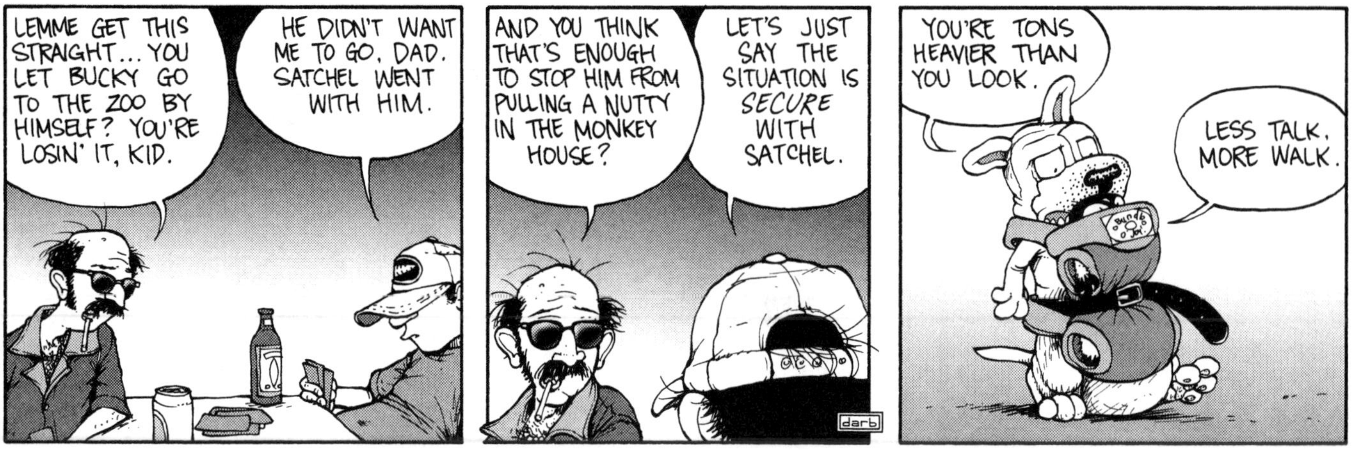
LEMME GET THIS STRAIGHT... YOU LET BUCKY GO TO THE ZOO BY HIMSELF? YOU'RE LOSIN' IT, KID.
HE DIDN'T WANT ME TO GO, DAD. SATCHEL WENT WITH HIM.
AND YOU THINK THAT'S ENOUGH TO STOP HIM FROM PULLING A NUTTY IN THE MONKEY HOUSE?
LET'S JUST SAY THE SITUATION IS *SECURE* WITH SATCHEL.
darb
YOU'RE TONS HEAVIER THAN YOU LOOK.
LESS TALK. MORE WALK.

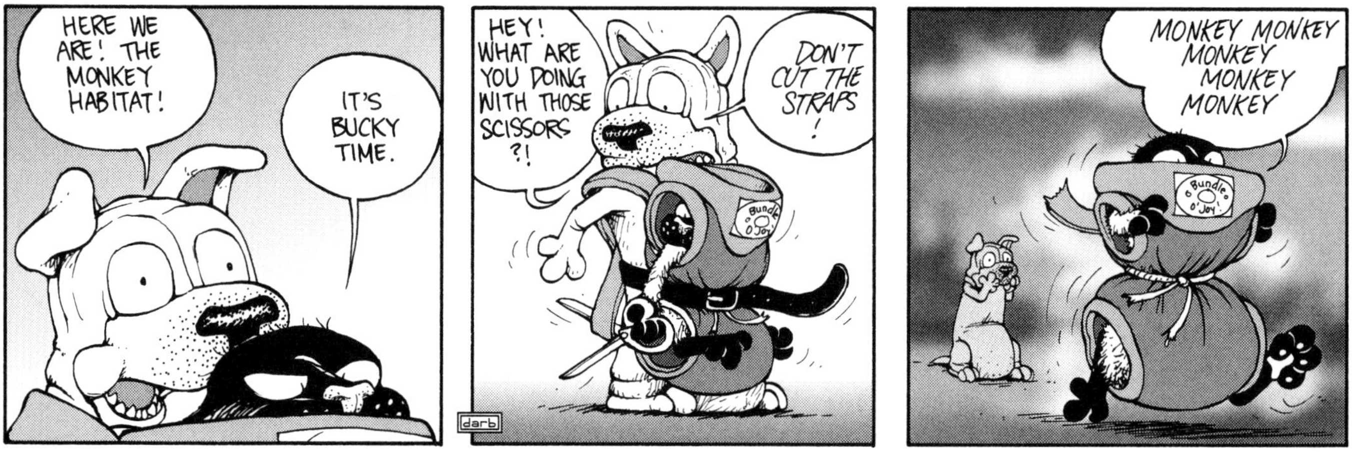
HERE WE ARE! THE MONKEY HABITAT!
IT'S BUCKY TIME.
darb
HEY! WHAT ARE YOU DOING WITH THOSE SCISSORS ?!
DON'T CUT THE STRAPS !
MONKEY MONKEY MONKEY MONKEY MONKEY

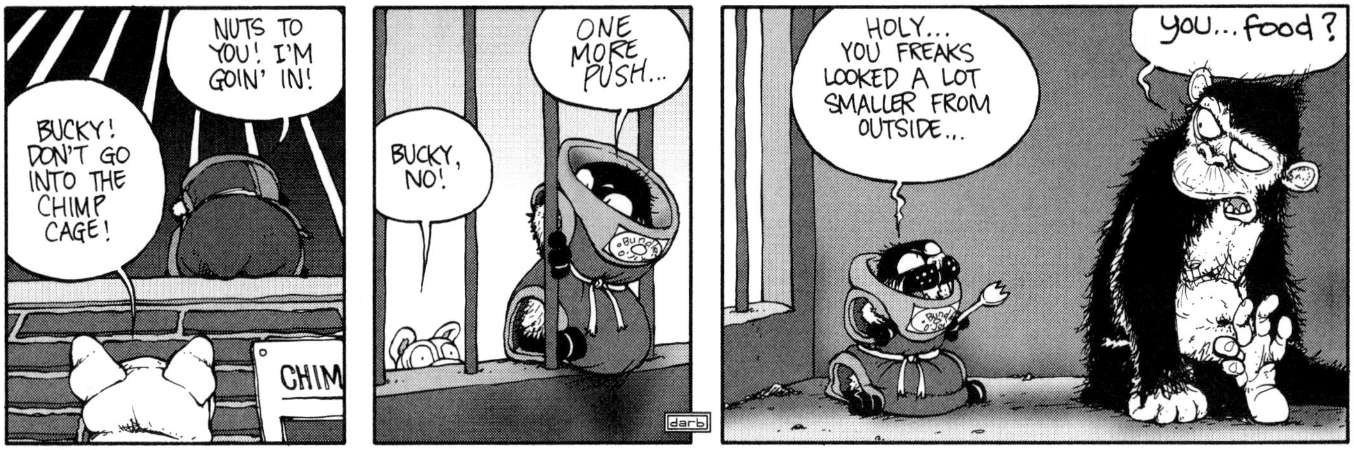
NUTS TO YOU! I'M GOIN' IN!
BUCKY! DON'T GO INTO THE CHIMP CAGE!
CHIM
ONE MORE PUSH...
BUCKY, NO!
darb
HOLY... YOU FREAKS LOOKED A LOT SMALLER FROM OUTSIDE...
you... food ?

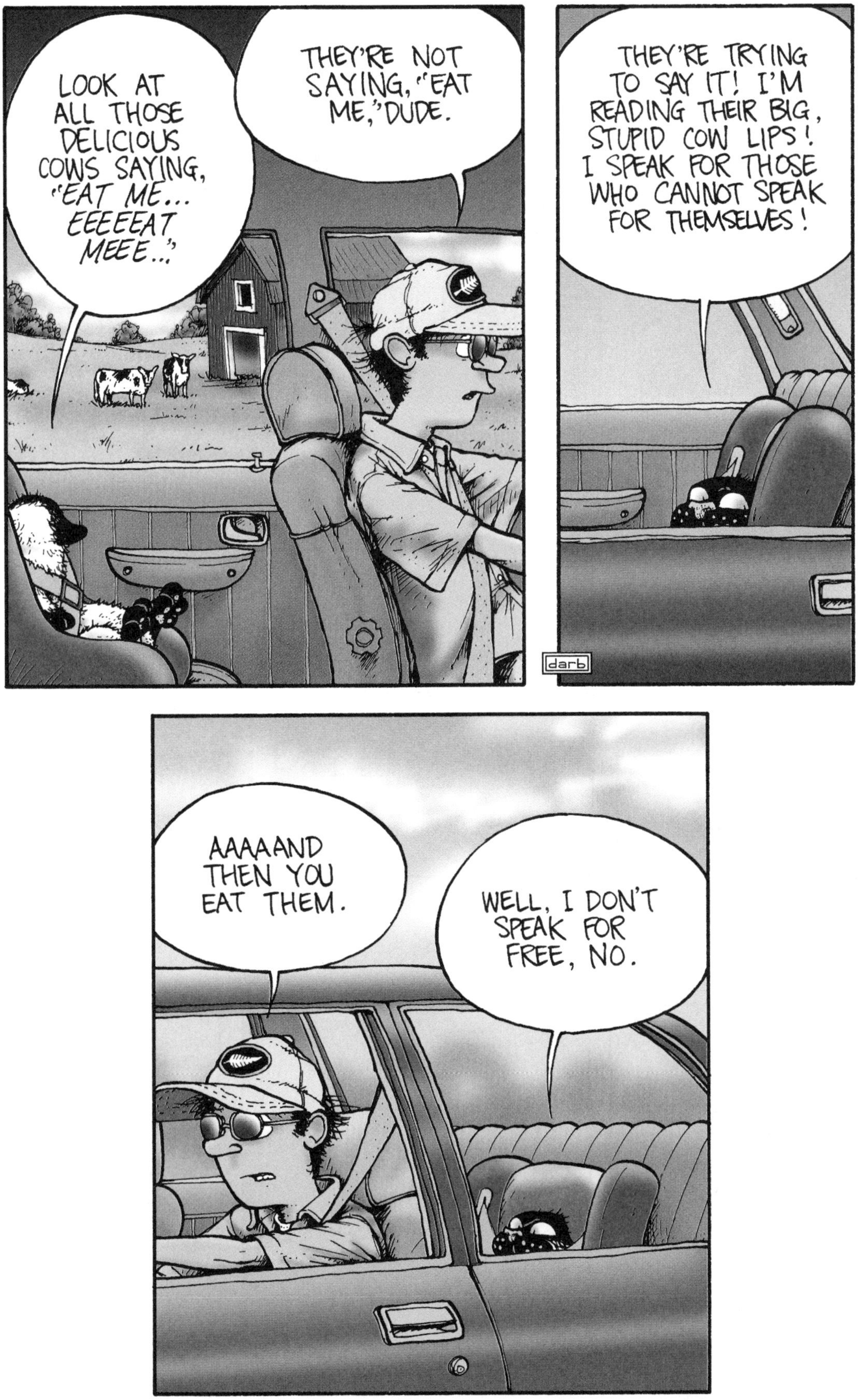
LOOK AT ALL THOSE DELICIOUS COWS SAYING, "EAT ME... EEEEEAT MEEE..."
THEY'RE NOT SAYING, "EAT ME," DUDE.
THEY'RE TRYING TO SAY IT! I'M READING THEIR BIG, STUPID COW LIPS! I SPEAK FOR THOSE WHO CANNOT SPEAK FOR THEMSELVES!
darb
AAAAAND THEN YOU EAT THEM.
WELL, I DON'T SPEAK FOR FREE, NO.

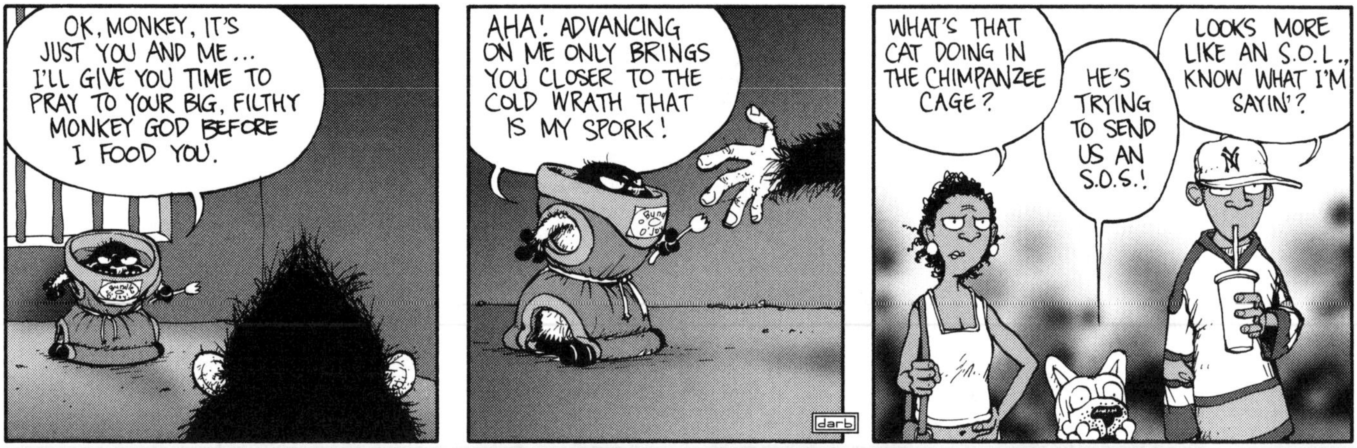
OK, MONKEY, IT'S JUST YOU AND ME... I'LL GIVE YOU TIME TO PRAY TO YOUR BIG, FILTHY MONKEY GOD BEFORE I FOOD YOU.
AHA! ADVANCING ON ME ONLY BRINGS YOU CLOSER TO THE COLD WRATH THAT IS MY SPORK!
WHAT'S THAT CAT DOING IN THE CHIMPANZEE CAGE?
HE'S TRYING TO SEND US AN S.O.S.!
LOOKS MORE LIKE AN S.O.L., KNOW WHAT I'M SAYIN'?
darb

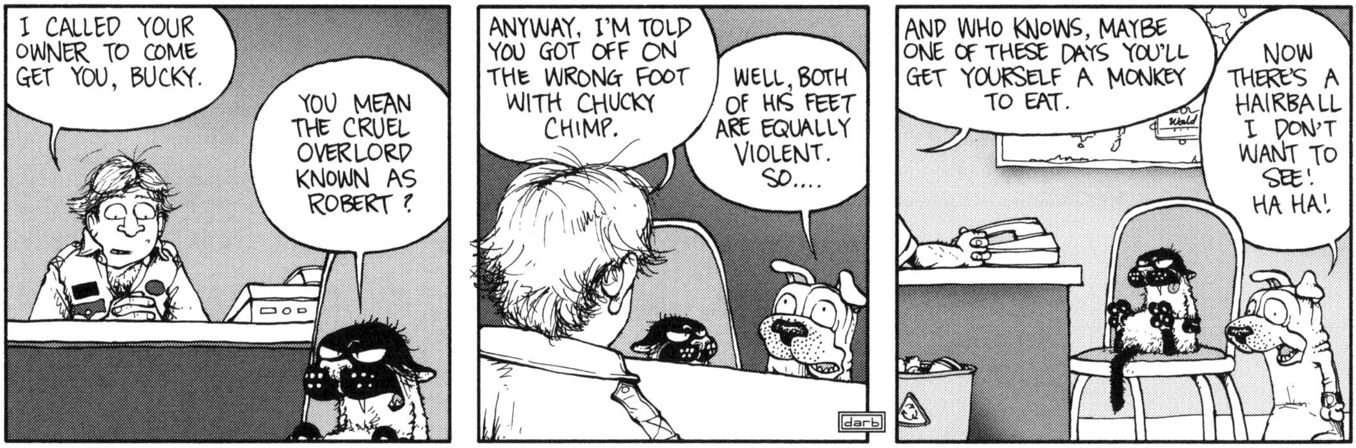
I CALLED YOUR OWNER TO COME GET YOU, BUCKY.
YOU MEAN THE CRUEL OVERLORD KNOWN AS ROBERT?
ANYWAY, I'M TOLD YOU GOT OFF ON THE WRONG FOOT WITH CHUCKY CHIMP.
WELL, BOTH OF HIS FEET ARE EQUALLY VIOLENT. SO....
AND WHO KNOWS, MAYBE ONE OF THESE DAYS YOU'LL GET YOURSELF A MONKEY TO EAT.
NOW THERE'S A HAIRBALL I DON'T WANT TO SEE! HA HA!
darb

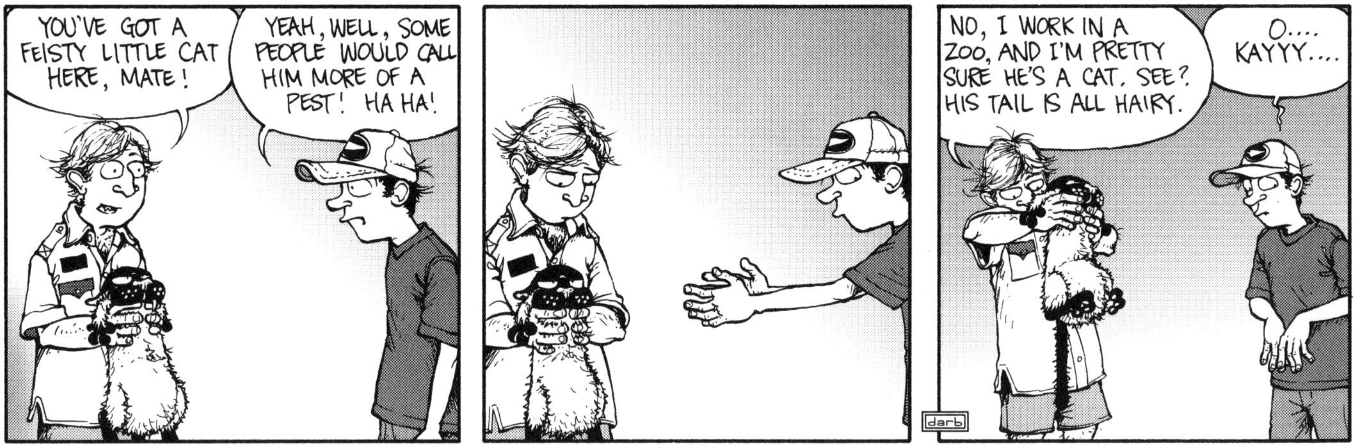
YOU'VE GOT A FEISTY LITTLE CAT HERE, MATE!
YEAH, WELL, SOME PEOPLE WOULD CALL HIM MORE OF A PEST! HA HA!
NO, I WORK IN A ZOO, AND I'M PRETTY SURE HE'S A CAT. SEE? HIS TAIL IS ALL HAIRY.
O.... KAYYY....
darb

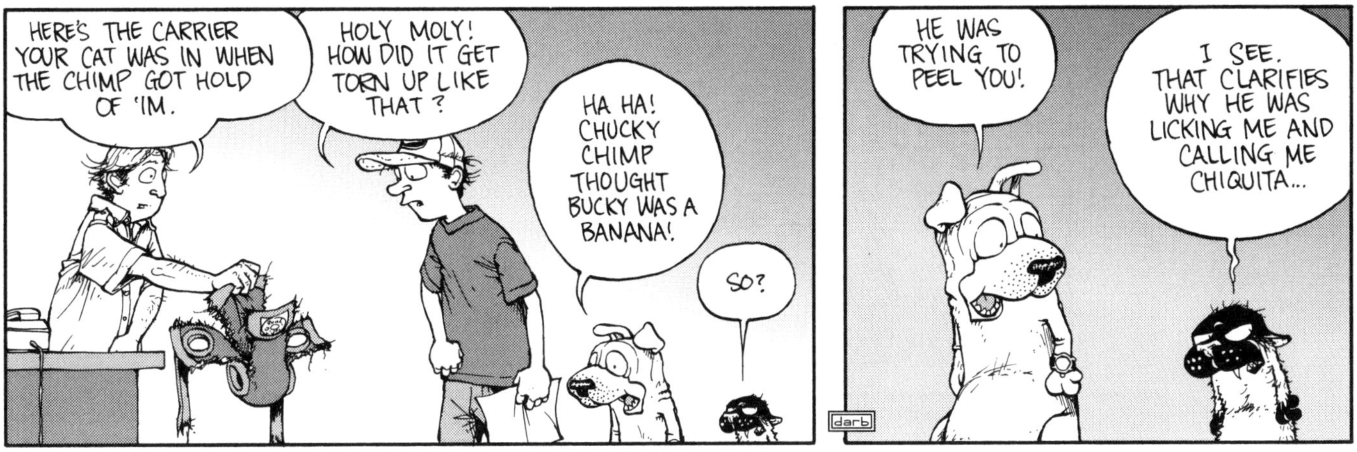
HERE'S THE CARRIER YOUR CAT WAS IN WHEN THE CHIMP GOT HOLD OF 'IM.
HOLY MOLY! HOW DID IT GET TORN UP LIKE THAT?
HA HA! CHUCKY CHIMP THOUGHT BUCKY WAS A BANANA!
SO?
HE WAS TRYING TO PEEL YOU!
I SEE. THAT CLARIFIES WHY HE WAS LICKING ME AND CALLING ME CHIQUITA...
darb

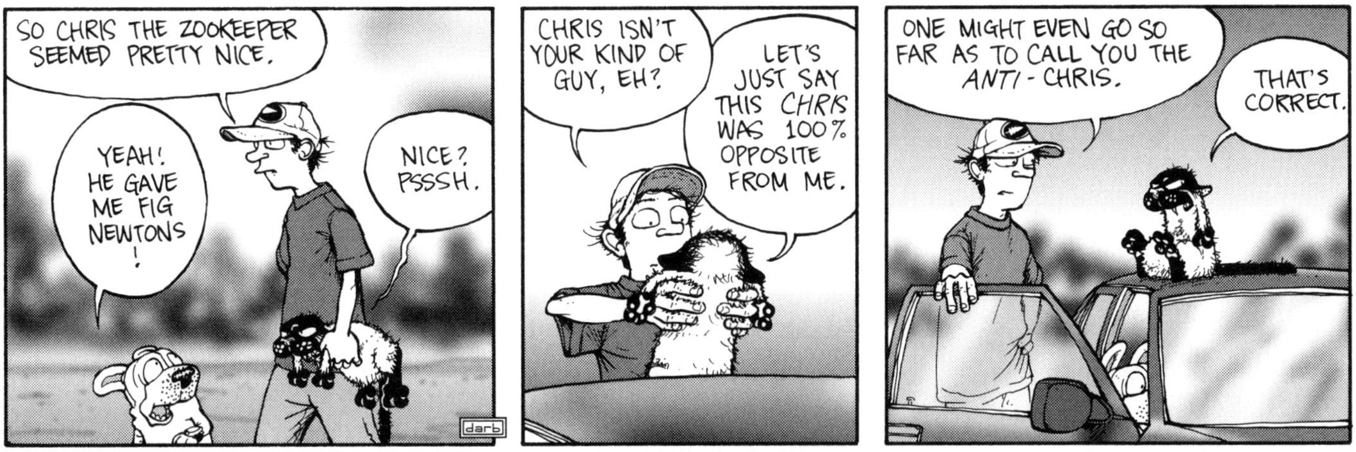
SO CHRIS THE ZOOKEEPER SEEMED PRETTY NICE.
YEAH! HE GAVE ME FIG NEWTONS!
NICE? PSSSH.
darb
CHRIS ISN'T YOUR KIND OF GUY, EH?
LET'S JUST SAY THIS *CHRIS* WAS 100% OPPOSITE FROM ME.
ONE MIGHT EVEN GO SO FAR AS TO CALL YOU THE *ANTI*-CHRIS.
THAT'S CORRECT.

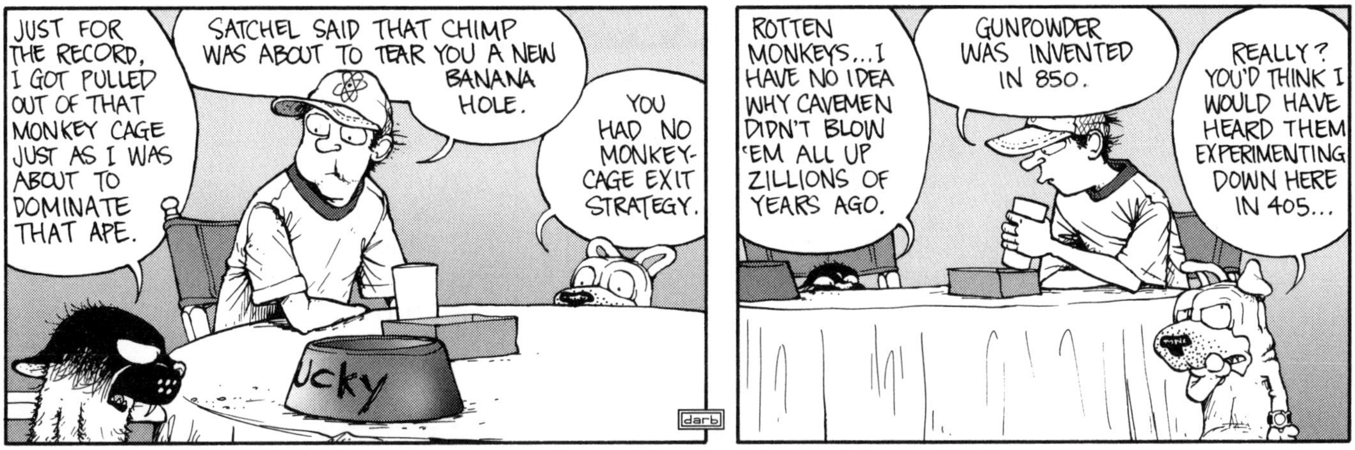
JUST FOR THE RECORD, I GOT PULLED OUT OF THAT MONKEY CAGE JUST AS I WAS ABOUT TO DOMINATE THAT APE.
SATCHEL SAID THAT CHIMP WAS ABOUT TO TEAR YOU A NEW BANANA HOLE.
YOU HAD NO MONKEY-CAGE EXIT STRATEGY.
ucky
darb
ROTTEN MONKEYS... I HAVE NO IDEA WHY CAVEMEN DIDN'T BLOW 'EM ALL UP ZILLIONS OF YEARS AGO.
GUNPOWDER WAS INVENTED IN 850.
REALLY? YOU'D THINK I WOULD HAVE HEARD THEM EXPERIMENTING DOWN HERE IN 405...

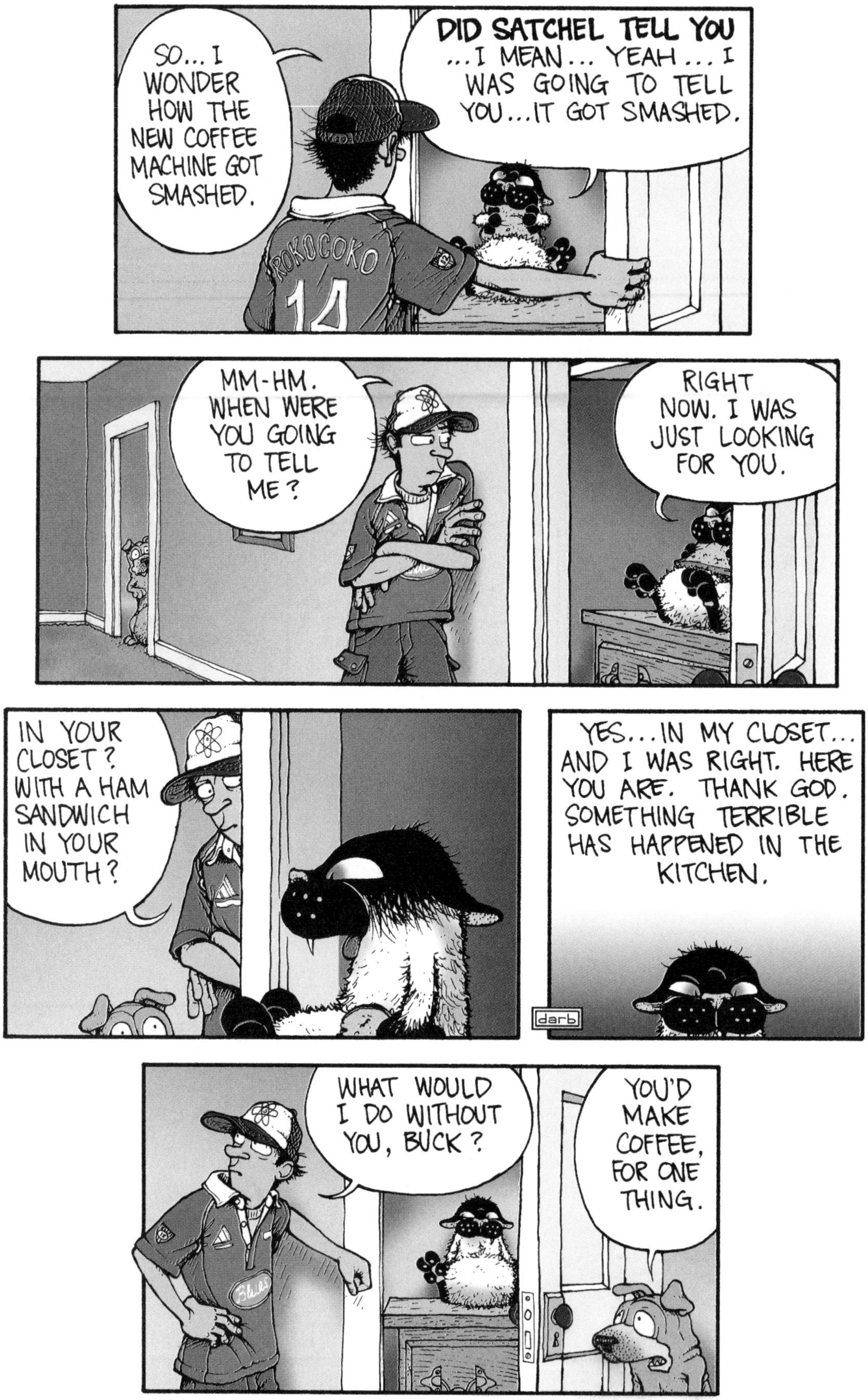
SO... I WONDER HOW THE NEW COFFEE MACHINE GOT SMASHED.
DID SATCHEL TELL YOU ...I MEAN... YEAH... I WAS GOING TO TELL YOU...IT GOT SMASHED.
ROKOCOKO
14
MM-HM. WHEN WERE YOU GOING TO TELL ME?
RIGHT NOW. I WAS JUST LOOKING FOR YOU.
IN YOUR CLOSET? WITH A HAM SANDWICH IN YOUR MOUTH?
YES...IN MY CLOSET... AND I WAS RIGHT. HERE YOU ARE. THANK GOD. SOMETHING TERRIBLE HAS HAPPENED IN THE KITCHEN.
darb
WHAT WOULD I DO WITHOUT YOU, BUCK?
YOU'D MAKE COFFEE, FOR ONE THING.

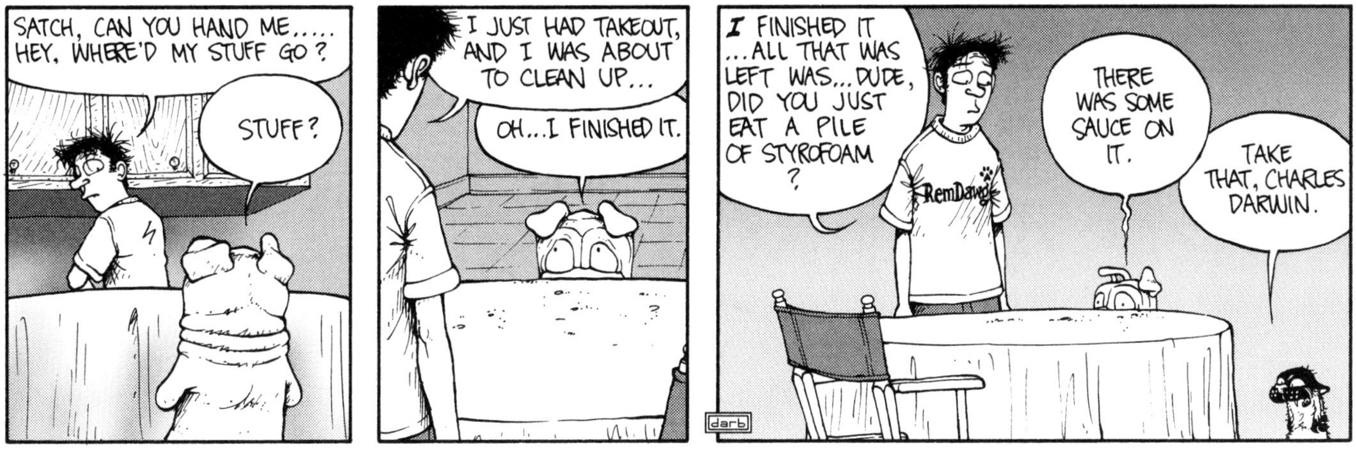
SATCH, CAN YOU HAND ME..... HEY, WHERE'D MY STUFF GO?
STUFF?
I JUST HAD TAKEOUT, AND I WAS ABOUT TO CLEAN UP...
OH...I FINISHED IT.
I FINISHED IT ...ALL THAT WAS LEFT WAS...DUDE, DID YOU JUST EAT A PILE OF STYROFOAM?
RemDawg
THERE WAS SOME SAUCE ON IT.
TAKE THAT, CHARLES DARWIN.
darb

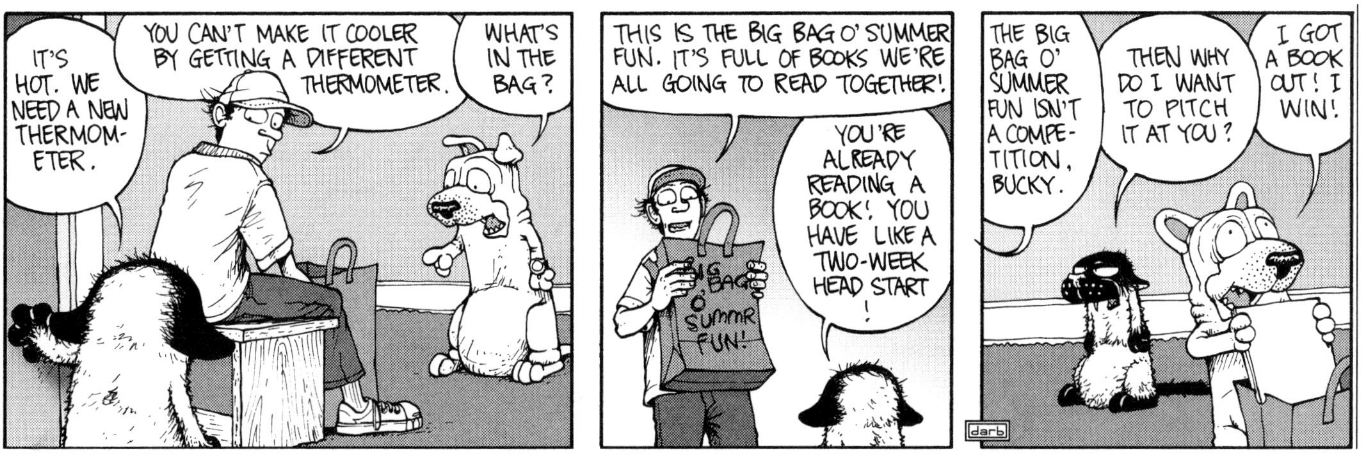
IT'S HOT. WE NEED A NEW THERMOMETER.
YOU CAN'T MAKE IT COOLER BY GETTING A DIFFERENT THERMOMETER.
WHAT'S IN THE BAG?
THIS IS THE BIG BAG O' SUMMER FUN. IT'S FULL OF BOOKS WE'RE ALL GOING TO READ TOGETHER!
BAG O' SUMMR FUN!
YOU'RE ALREADY READING A BOOK! YOU HAVE LIKE A TWO-WEEK HEAD START!
THE BIG BAG O' SUMMER FUN ISN'T A COMPETITION, BUCKY.
THEN WHY DO I WANT TO PITCH IT AT YOU?
I GOT A BOOK OUT! I WIN!
darb

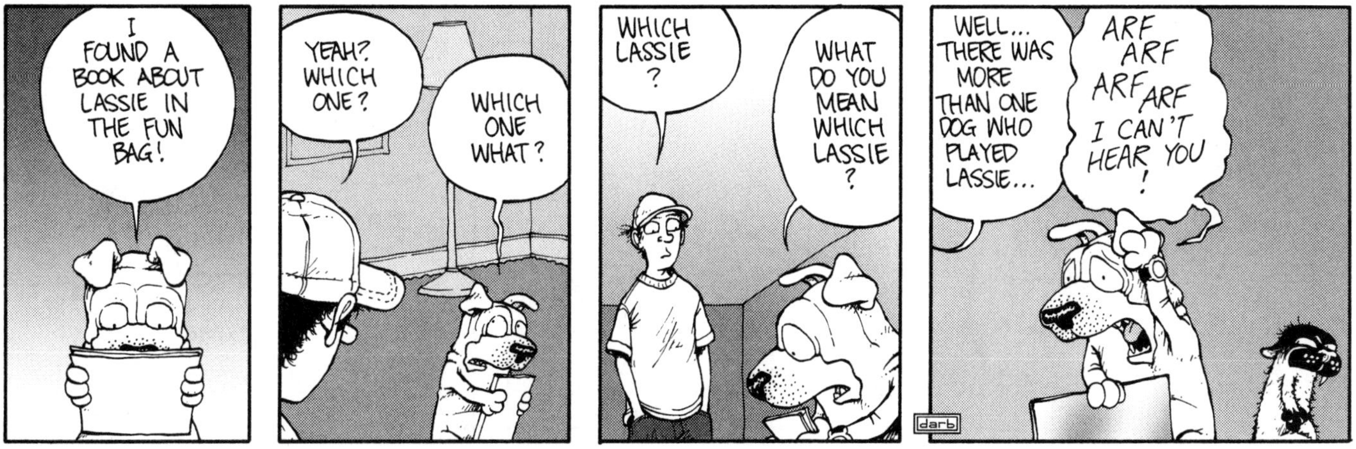
I FOUND A BOOK ABOUT LASSIE IN THE FUN BAG!
YEAH? WHICH ONE?
WHICH ONE WHAT?
WHICH LASSIE?
WHAT DO YOU MEAN WHICH LASSIE?
WELL... THERE WAS MORE THAN ONE DOG WHO PLAYED LASSIE...
ARF ARF ARF ARF I CAN'T HEAR YOU!
darb

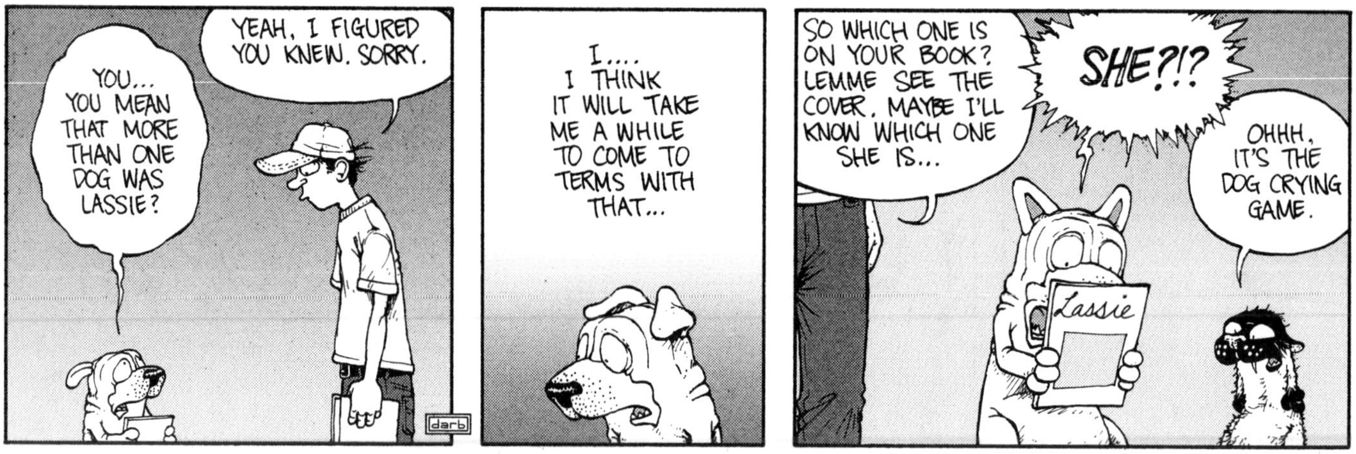
YOU... YOU MEAN THAT MORE THAN ONE DOG WAS LASSIE?
YEAH, I FIGURED YOU KNEW. SORRY.
I.... I THINK IT WILL TAKE ME A WHILE TO COME TO TERMS WITH THAT...
SO WHICH ONE IS ON YOUR BOOK? LEMME SEE THE COVER. MAYBE I'LL KNOW WHICH ONE SHE IS...
SHE?!?
OHHH, IT'S THE DOG CRYING GAME.
Lassie

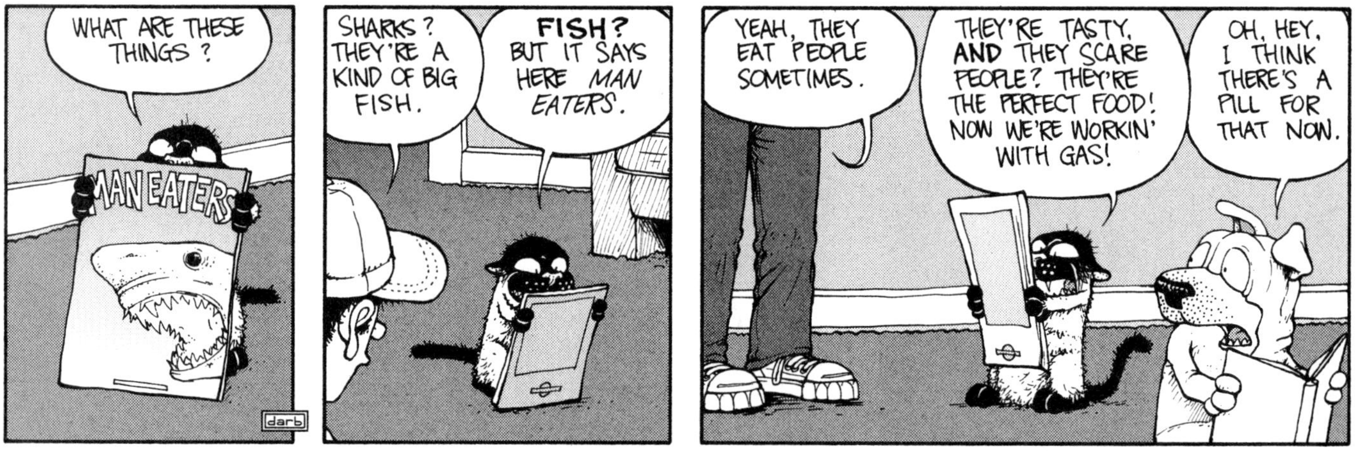
WHAT ARE THESE THINGS?
MAN EATERS
SHARKS? THEY'RE A KIND OF BIG FISH.
FISH? BUT IT SAYS HERE MAN EATERS.
YEAH, THEY EAT PEOPLE SOMETIMES.
THEY'RE TASTY, AND THEY SCARE PEOPLE? THEY'RE THE PERFECT FOOD! NOW WE'RE WORKIN' WITH GAS!
OH, HEY, I THINK THERE'S A PILL FOR THAT NOW.

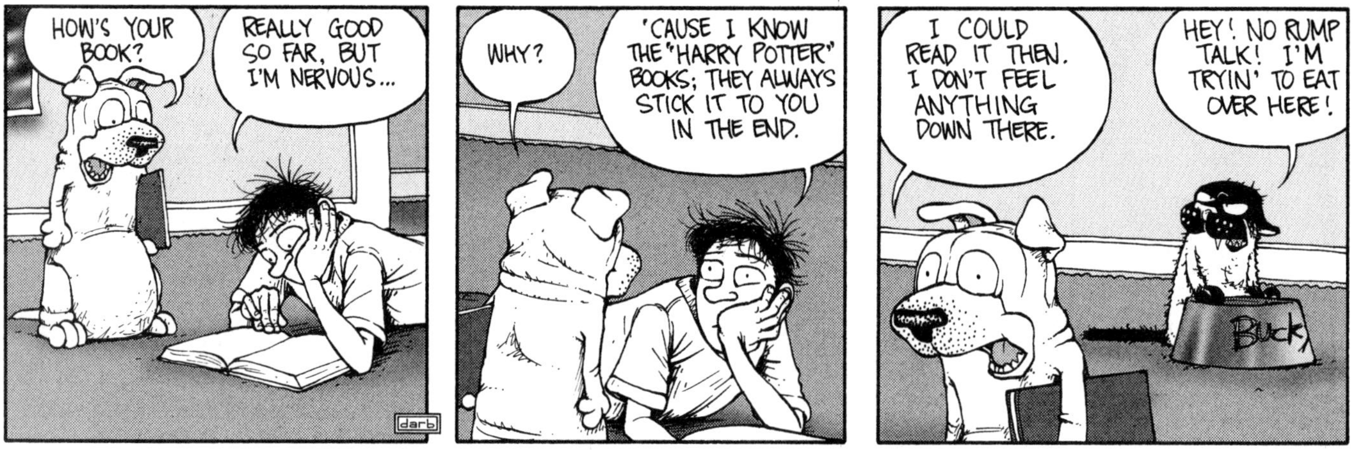
HOW'S YOUR BOOK?
REALLY GOOD SO FAR, BUT I'M NERVOUS...
WHY?
'CAUSE I KNOW THE "HARRY POTTER" BOOKS; THEY ALWAYS STICK IT TO YOU IN THE END.
I COULD READ IT THEN. I DON'T FEEL ANYTHING DOWN THERE.
HEY! NO RUMP TALK! I'M TRYIN' TO EAT OVER HERE!
BUCK

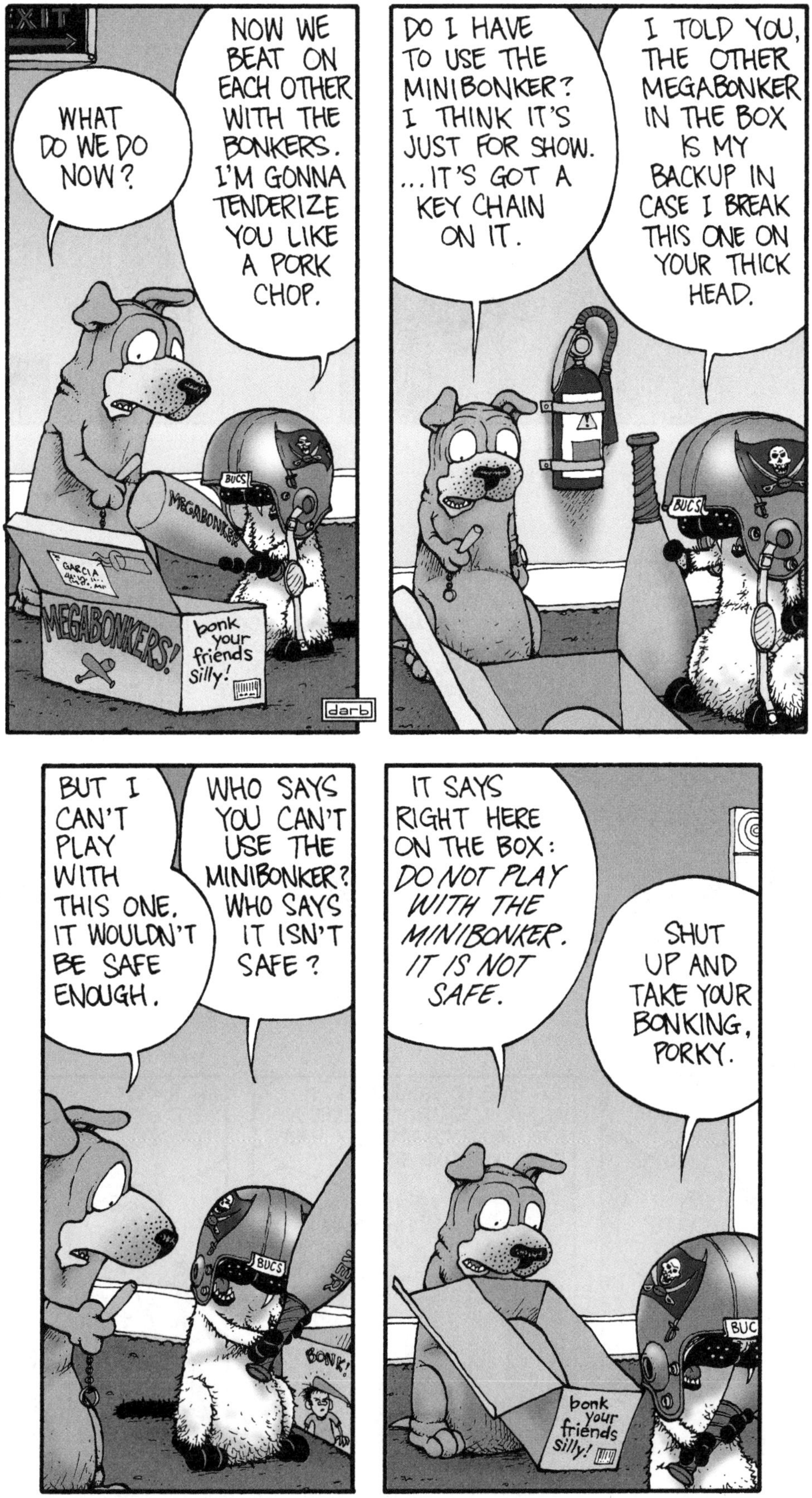
EXIT
WHAT DO WE DO NOW?
NOW WE BEAT ON EACH OTHER WITH THE BONKERS. I'M GONNA TENDERIZE YOU LIKE A PORK CHOP.
MEGABONKERS!
bonk your friends silly!
BUCS
DO I HAVE TO USE THE MINIBONKER? I THINK IT'S JUST FOR SHOW. ...IT'S GOT A KEY CHAIN ON IT.
I TOLD YOU, THE OTHER MEGABONKER IN THE BOX IS MY BACKUP IN CASE I BREAK THIS ONE ON YOUR THICK HEAD.
BUCS
BUT I CAN'T PLAY WITH THIS ONE. IT WOULDN'T BE SAFE ENOUGH.
WHO SAYS YOU CAN'T USE THE MINIBONKER? WHO SAYS IT ISN'T SAFE?
BUCS
BONK!
IT SAYS RIGHT HERE ON THE BOX: *DO NOT PLAY WITH THE MINIBONKER. IT IS NOT SAFE.*
SHUT UP AND TAKE YOUR BONKING, PORKY.
bonk your friends silly!
BUC

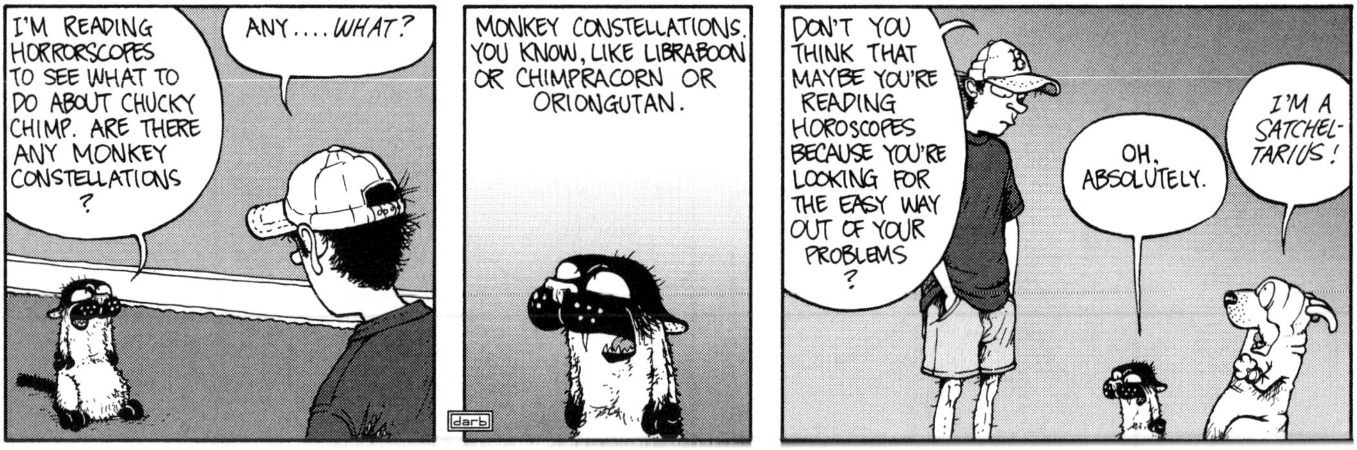
I'M READING HORRORSCOPES TO SEE WHAT TO DO ABOUT CHUCKY CHIMP. ARE THERE ANY MONKEY CONSTELLATIONS ?
ANY.... *WHAT?*
MONKEY CONSTELLATIONS. YOU KNOW, LIKE LIBRABOON OR CHIMPRACORN OR ORIONGUTAN.
darb
DON'T YOU THINK THAT MAYBE YOU'RE READING HOROSCOPES BECAUSE YOU'RE LOOKING FOR THE EASY WAY OUT OF YOUR PROBLEMS ?
OH, ABSOLUTELY.
I'M A SATCHEL-TARIUS!

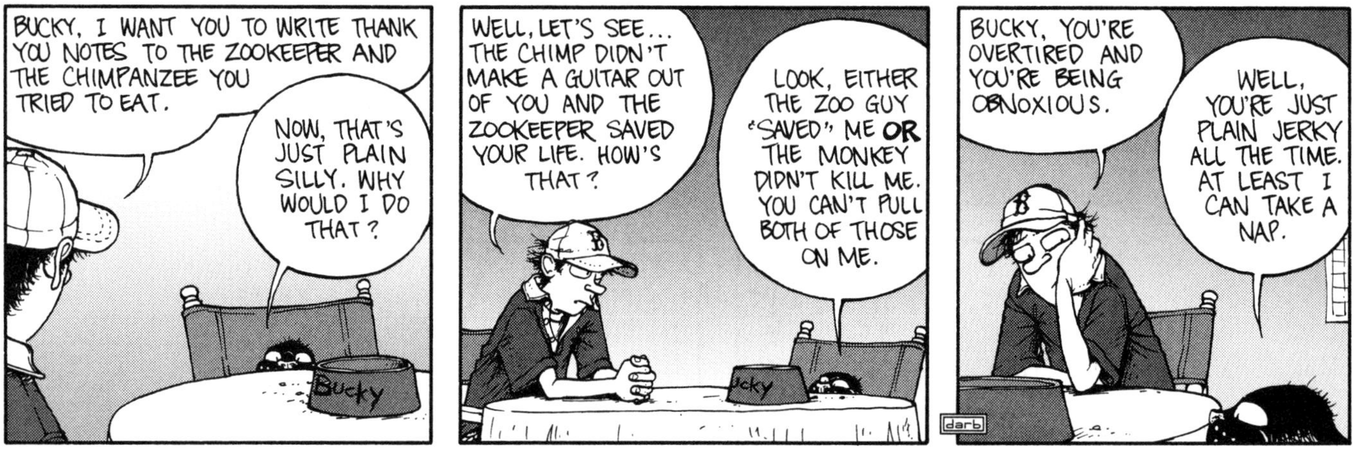
BUCKY, I WANT YOU TO WRITE THANK YOU NOTES TO THE ZOOKEEPER AND THE CHIMPANZEE YOU TRIED TO EAT.
NOW, THAT'S JUST PLAIN SILLY. WHY WOULD I DO THAT ?
Bucky
WELL, LET'S SEE... THE CHIMP DIDN'T MAKE A GUITAR OUT OF YOU AND THE ZOOKEEPER SAVED YOUR LIFE. HOW'S THAT ?
LOOK, EITHER THE ZOO GUY "SAVED" ME **OR** THE MONKEY DIDN'T KILL ME. YOU CAN'T PULL BOTH OF THOSE ON ME.
BUCKY, YOU'RE OVERTIRED AND YOU'RE BEING OBNOXIOUS.
WELL, YOU'RE JUST PLAIN JERKY ALL THE TIME. AT LEAST I CAN TAKE A NAP.
darb

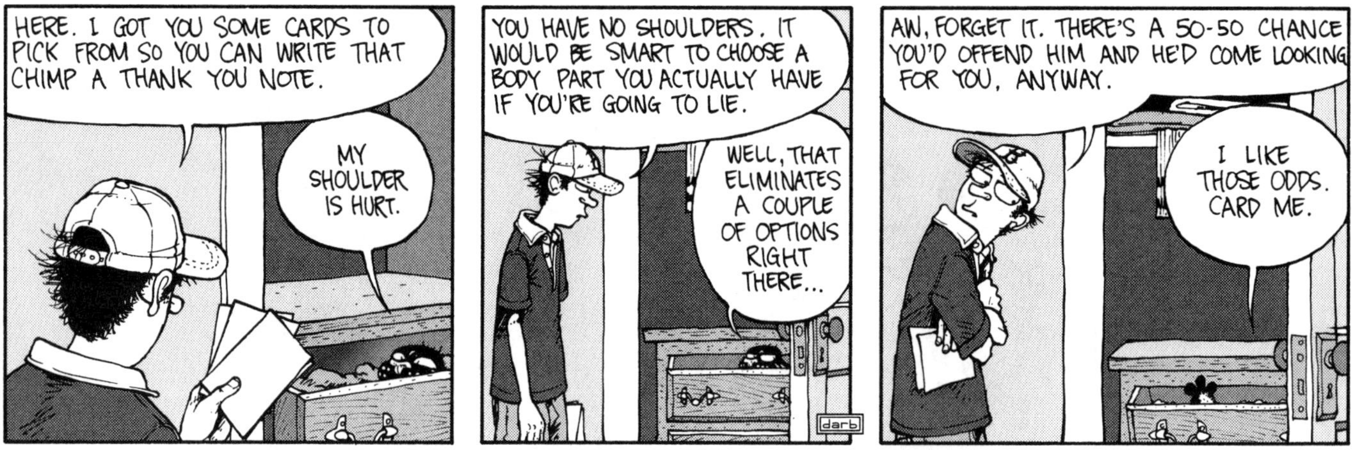
HERE. I GOT YOU SOME CARDS TO PICK FROM SO YOU CAN WRITE THAT CHIMP A THANK YOU NOTE.
MY SHOULDER IS HURT.
YOU HAVE NO SHOULDERS. IT WOULD BE SMART TO CHOOSE A BODY PART YOU ACTUALLY HAVE IF YOU'RE GOING TO LIE.
WELL, THAT ELIMINATES A COUPLE OF OPTIONS RIGHT THERE...
darb
AW, FORGET IT. THERE'S A 50-50 CHANCE YOU'D OFFEND HIM AND HE'D COME LOOKING FOR YOU, ANYWAY.
I LIKE THOSE ODDS. CARD ME.

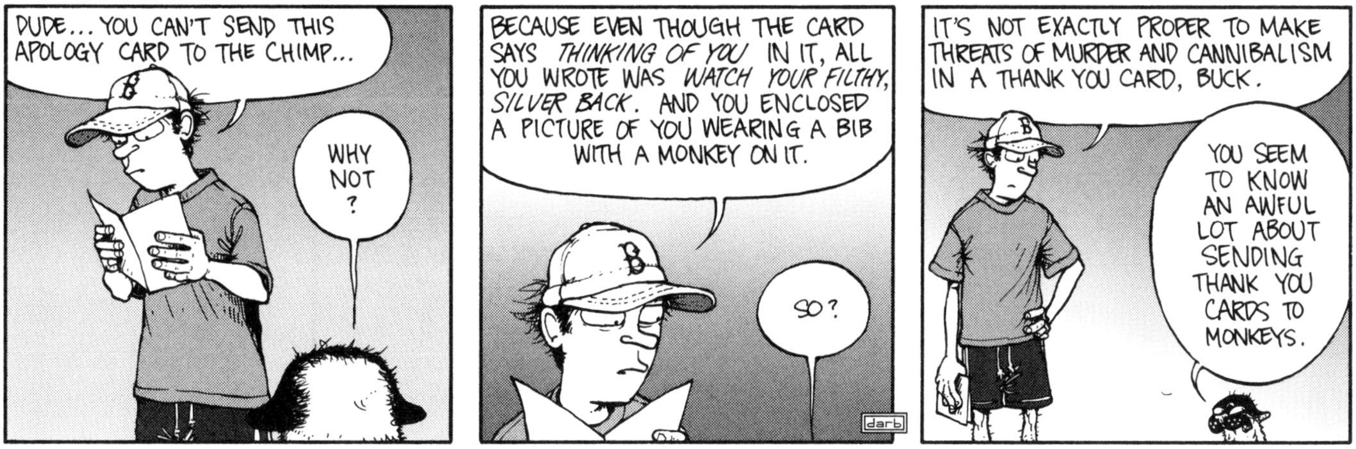
DUDE... YOU CAN'T SEND THIS APOLOGY CARD TO THE CHIMP...
WHY NOT ?
BECAUSE EVEN THOUGH THE CARD SAYS *THINKING OF YOU* IN IT, ALL YOU WROTE WAS *WATCH YOUR FILTHY, SILVER BACK*. AND YOU ENCLOSED A PICTURE OF YOU WEARING A BIB WITH A MONKEY ON IT.
SO?
IT'S NOT EXACTLY PROPER TO MAKE THREATS OF MURDER AND CANNIBALISM IN A THANK YOU CARD, BUCK.
YOU SEEM TO KNOW AN AWFUL LOT ABOUT SENDING THANK YOU CARDS TO MONKEYS.
darb

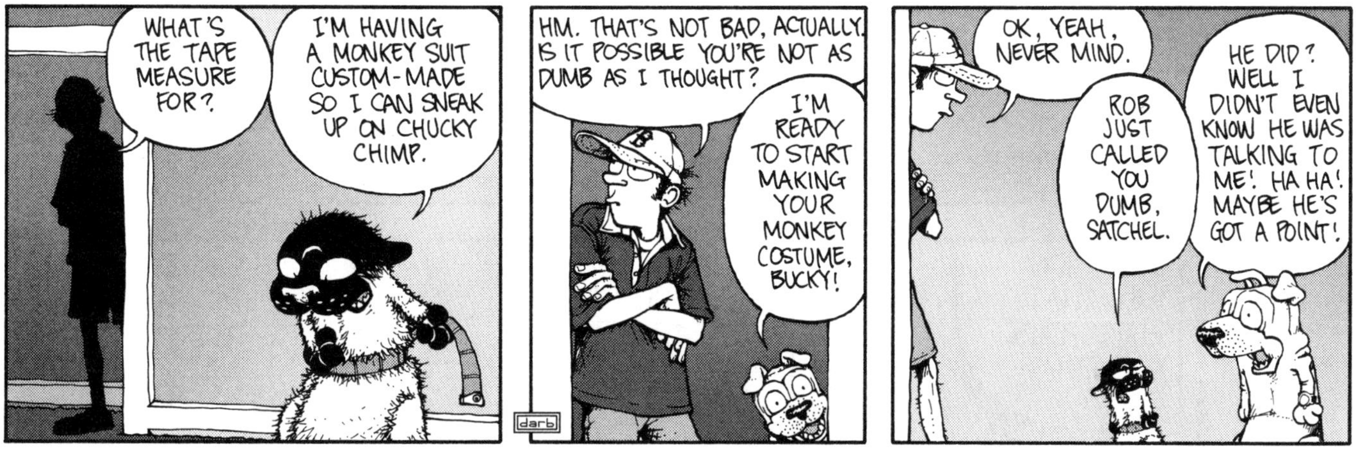
WHAT'S THE TAPE MEASURE FOR?
I'M HAVING A MONKEY SUIT CUSTOM-MADE SO I CAN SNEAK UP ON CHUCKY CHIMP.
darb
HM. THAT'S NOT BAD, ACTUALLY. IS IT POSSIBLE YOU'RE NOT AS DUMB AS I THOUGHT?
I'M READY TO START MAKING YOUR MONKEY COSTUME, BUCKY!
OK, YEAH, NEVER MIND.
ROB JUST CALLED YOU DUMB, SATCHEL.
HE DID? WELL I DIDN'T EVEN KNOW HE WAS TALKING TO ME! HA HA! MAYBE HE'S GOT A POINT!

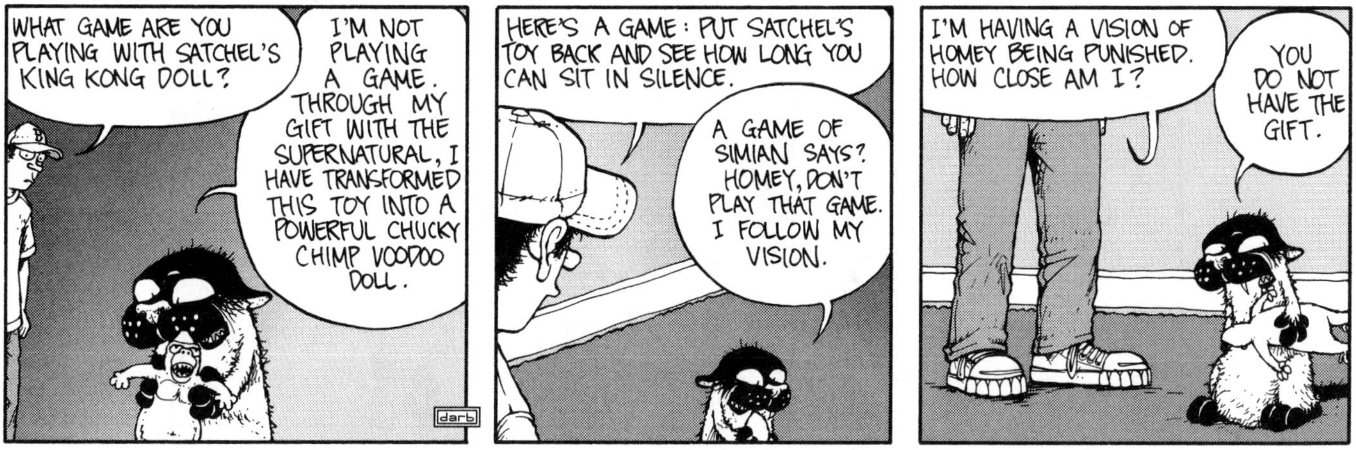
WHAT GAME ARE YOU PLAYING WITH SATCHEL'S KING KONG DOLL?
I'M NOT PLAYING A GAME. THROUGH MY GIFT WITH THE SUPERNATURAL, I HAVE TRANSFORMED THIS TOY INTO A POWERFUL CHUCKY CHIMP VOODOO DOLL.
darb
HERE'S A GAME: PUT SATCHEL'S TOY BACK AND SEE HOW LONG YOU CAN SIT IN SILENCE.
A GAME OF SIMIAN SAYS? HOMEY, DON'T PLAY THAT GAME. I FOLLOW MY VISION.
I'M HAVING A VISION OF HOMEY BEING PUNISHED. HOW CLOSE AM I?
YOU DO NOT HAVE THE GIFT.

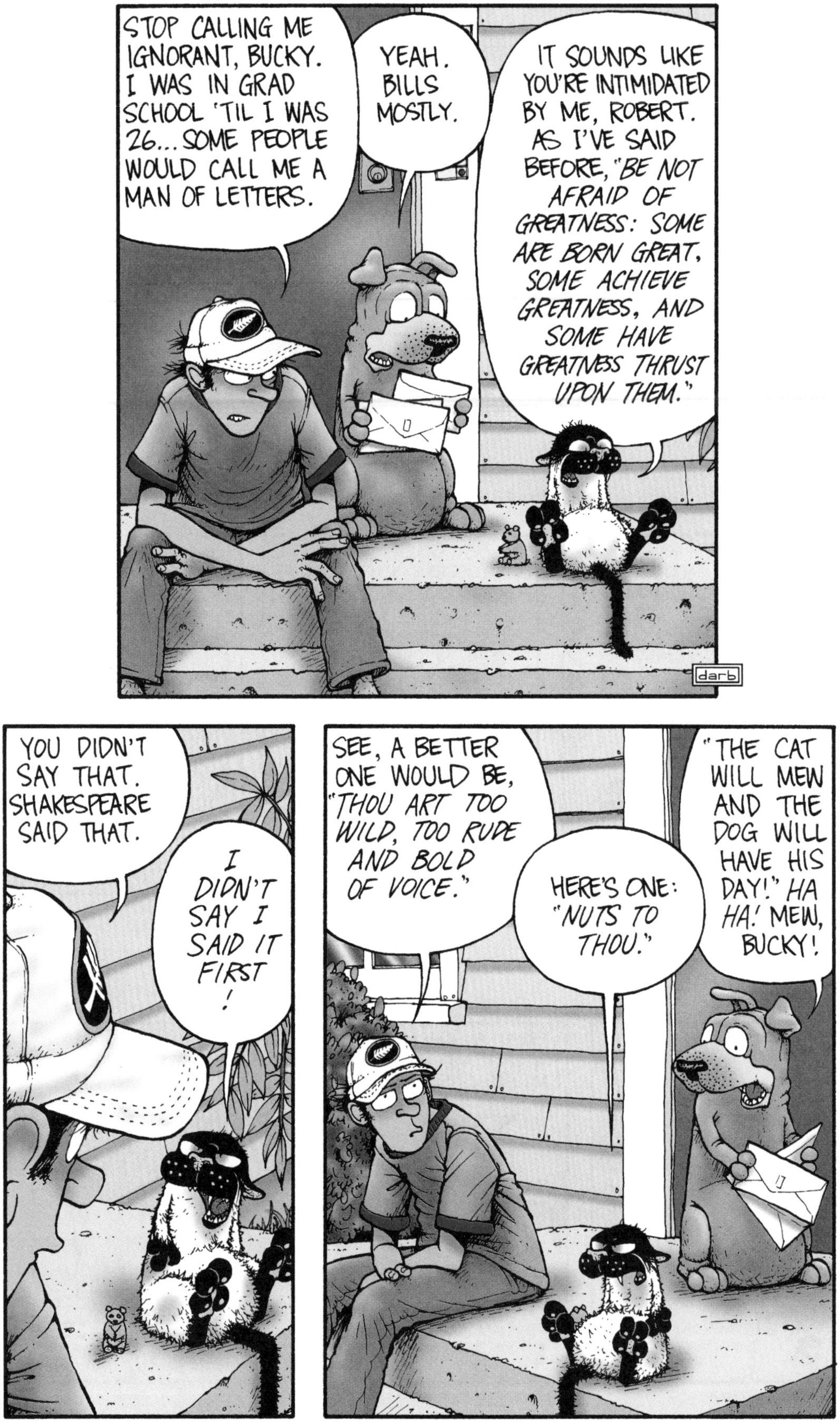
STOP CALLING ME IGNORANT, BUCKY. I WAS IN GRAD SCHOOL 'TIL I WAS 26... SOME PEOPLE WOULD CALL ME A MAN OF LETTERS.
YEAH. BILLS MOSTLY.
IT SOUNDS LIKE YOU'RE INTIMIDATED BY ME, ROBERT. AS I'VE SAID BEFORE, "BE NOT AFRAID OF GREATNESS: SOME ARE BORN GREAT, SOME ACHIEVE GREATNESS, AND SOME HAVE GREATNESS THRUST UPON THEM."
darb
YOU DIDN'T SAY THAT. SHAKESPEARE SAID THAT.
I DIDN'T SAY I SAID IT FIRST!
SEE, A BETTER ONE WOULD BE, "THOU ART TOO WILD, TOO RUDE AND BOLD OF VOICE."
HERE'S ONE: "NUTS TO THOU."
"THE CAT WILL MEW AND THE DOG WILL HAVE HIS DAY!" HA HA! MEW, BUCKY!

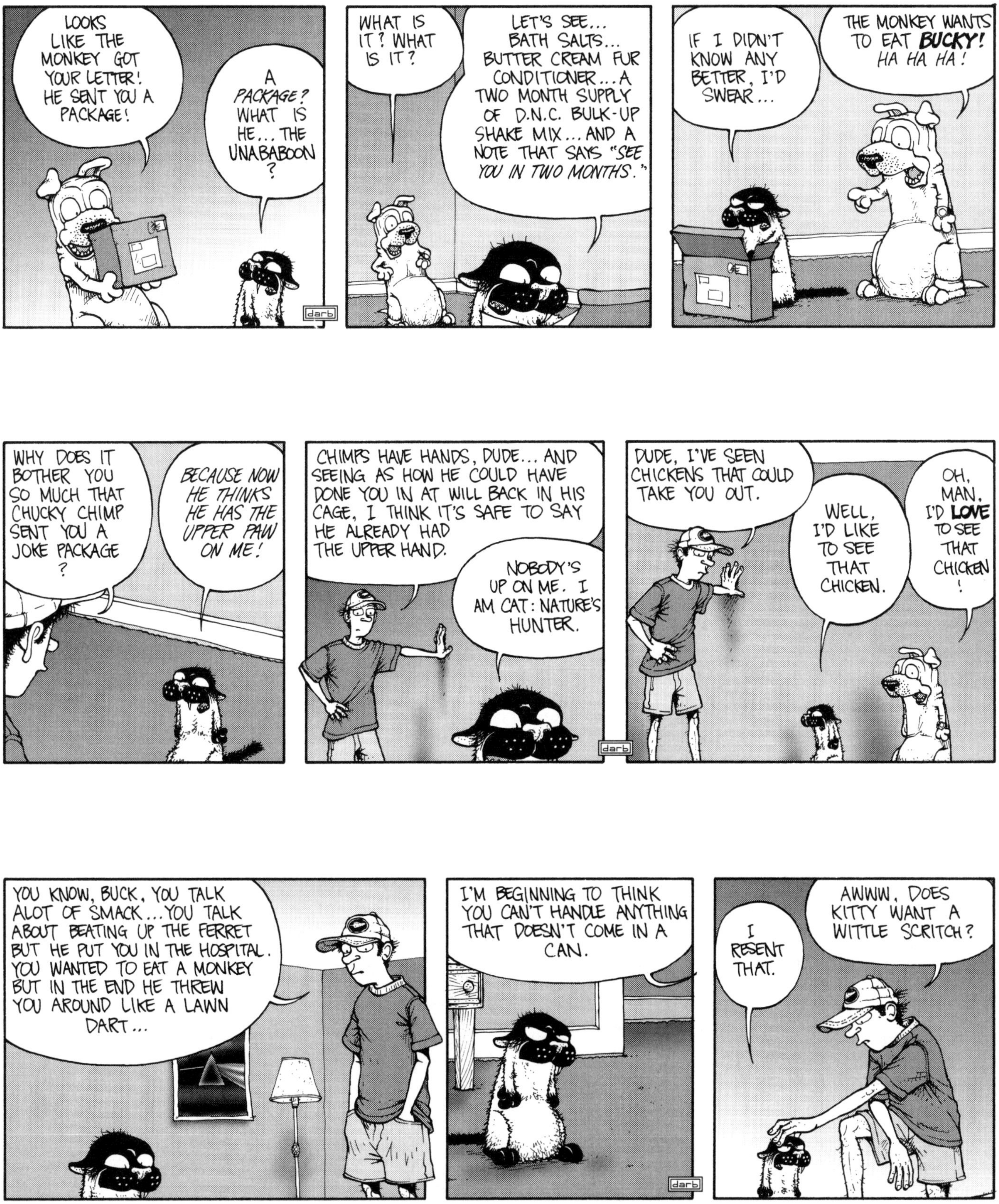
LOOKS LIKE THE MONKEY GOT YOUR LETTER! HE SENT YOU A PACKAGE!
A *PACKAGE?* WHAT IS HE... THE UNABABOON?
darb
WHAT IS IT? WHAT IS IT?
LET'S SEE... BATH SALTS... BUTTER CREAM FUR CONDITIONER... A TWO MONTH SUPPLY OF D.N.C. BULK-UP SHAKE MIX... AND A NOTE THAT SAYS "*SEE YOU IN TWO MONTHS.*"
IF I DIDN'T KNOW ANY BETTER, I'D SWEAR...
THE MONKEY WANTS TO EAT **BUCKY!** *HA HA HA!*
WHY DOES IT BOTHER YOU SO MUCH THAT CHUCKY CHIMP SENT YOU A JOKE PACKAGE?
BECAUSE NOW HE THINKS HE HAS THE UPPER PAW ON ME!
CHIMPS HAVE HANDS, DUDE... AND SEEING AS HOW HE COULD HAVE DONE YOU IN AT WILL BACK IN HIS CAGE, I THINK IT'S SAFE TO SAY HE ALREADY HAD THE UPPER HAND.
NOBODY'S UP ON ME. I AM CAT: NATURE'S HUNTER.
darb
DUDE, I'VE SEEN CHICKENS THAT COULD TAKE YOU OUT.
WELL, I'D LIKE TO SEE THAT CHICKEN.
OH, MAN. I'D **LOVE** TO SEE THAT CHICKEN!
YOU KNOW, BUCK, YOU TALK ALOT OF SMACK... YOU TALK ABOUT BEATING UP THE FERRET BUT HE PUT YOU IN THE HOSPITAL. YOU WANTED TO EAT A MONKEY BUT IN THE END HE THREW YOU AROUND LIKE A LAWN DART...
I'M BEGINNING TO THINK YOU CAN'T HANDLE ANYTHING THAT DOESN'T COME IN A CAN.
darb
I RESENT THAT.
AWWW. DOES KITTY WANT A WITTLE SCRITCH?

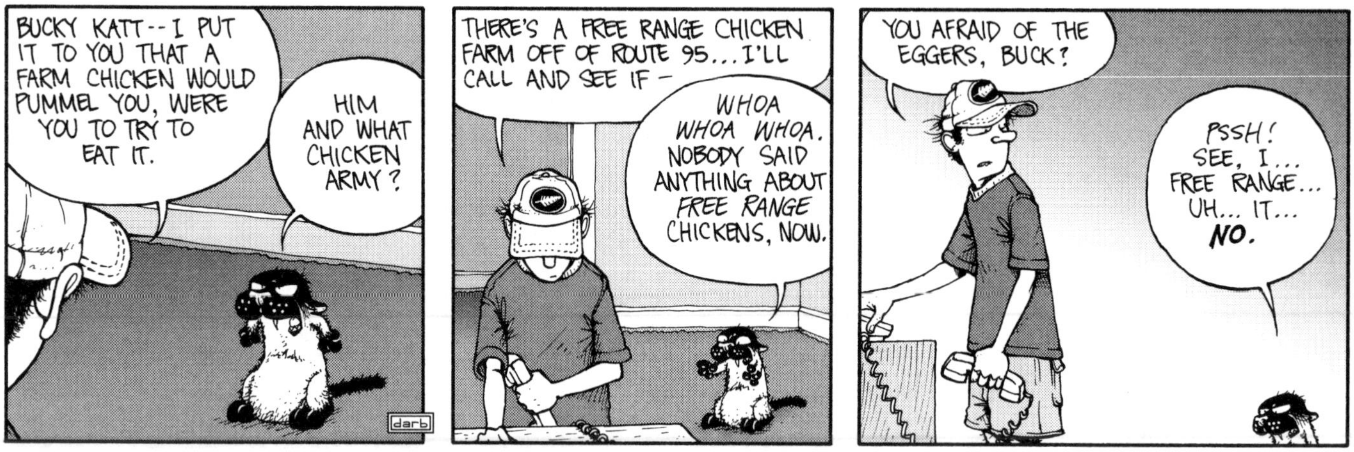
BUCKY KATT--I PUT IT TO YOU THAT A FARM CHICKEN WOULD PUMMEL YOU, WERE YOU TO TRY TO EAT IT.
HIM AND WHAT CHICKEN ARMY?
THERE'S A FREE RANGE CHICKEN FARM OFF OF ROUTE 95...I'LL CALL AND SEE IF–
WHOA WHOA WHOA. NOBODY SAID ANYTHING ABOUT FREE RANGE CHICKENS, NOW.
YOU AFRAID OF THE EGGERS, BUCK?
PSSH! SEE, I... FREE RANGE... UH... IT... NO.
darb

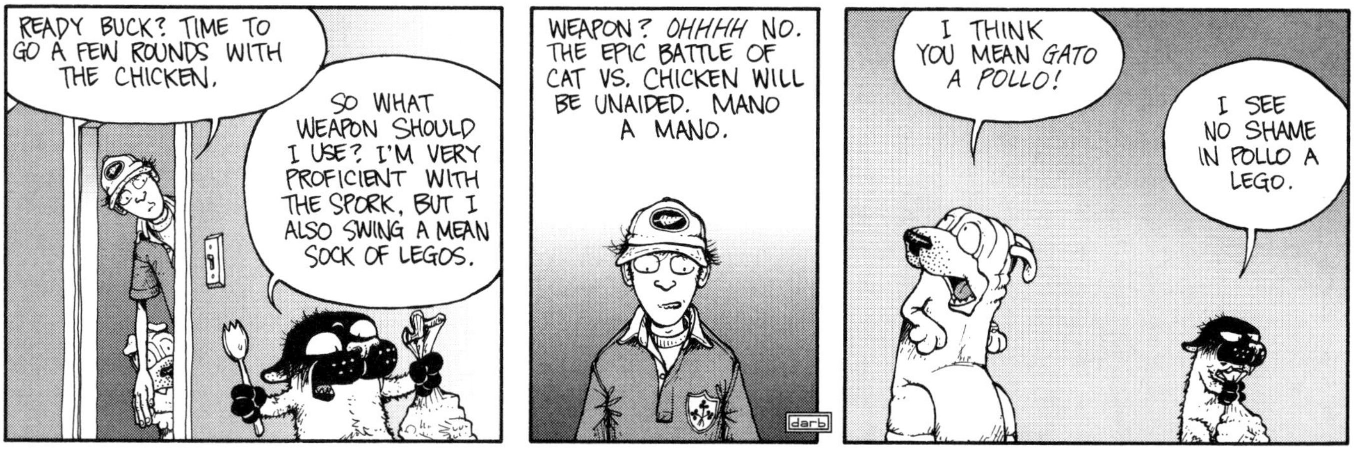
READY BUCK? TIME TO GO A FEW ROUNDS WITH THE CHICKEN.
SO WHAT WEAPON SHOULD I USE? I'M VERY PROFICIENT WITH THE SPORK, BUT I ALSO SWING A MEAN SOCK OF LEGOS.
WEAPON? OHHHH NO. THE EPIC BATTLE OF CAT VS. CHICKEN WILL BE UNAIDED. MANO A MANO.
darb
I THINK YOU MEAN GATO A POLLO!
I SEE NO SHAME IN POLLO A LEGO.

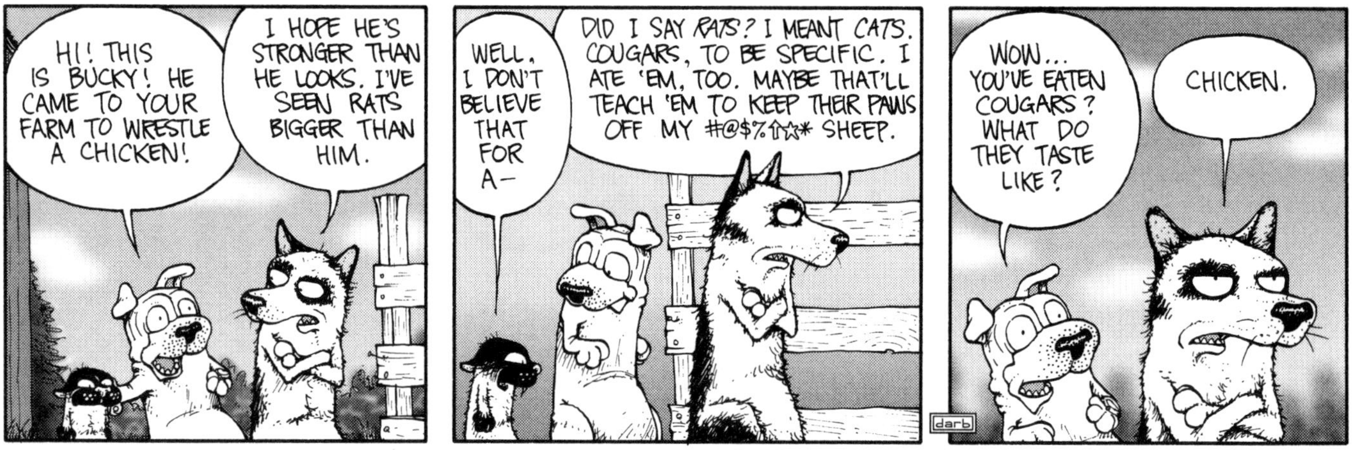
HI! THIS IS BUCKY! HE CAME TO YOUR FARM TO WRESTLE A CHICKEN!
I HOPE HE'S STRONGER THAN HE LOOKS. I'VE SEEN RATS BIGGER THAN HIM.
WELL, I DON'T BELIEVE THAT FOR A–
DID I SAY RATS? I MEANT CATS. COUGARS, TO BE SPECIFIC. I ATE 'EM, TOO. MAYBE THAT'LL TEACH 'EM TO KEEP THEIR PAWS OFF MY #@$%⇧☆* SHEEP.
darb
WOW... YOU'VE EATEN COUGARS? WHAT DO THEY TASTE LIKE?
CHICKEN.

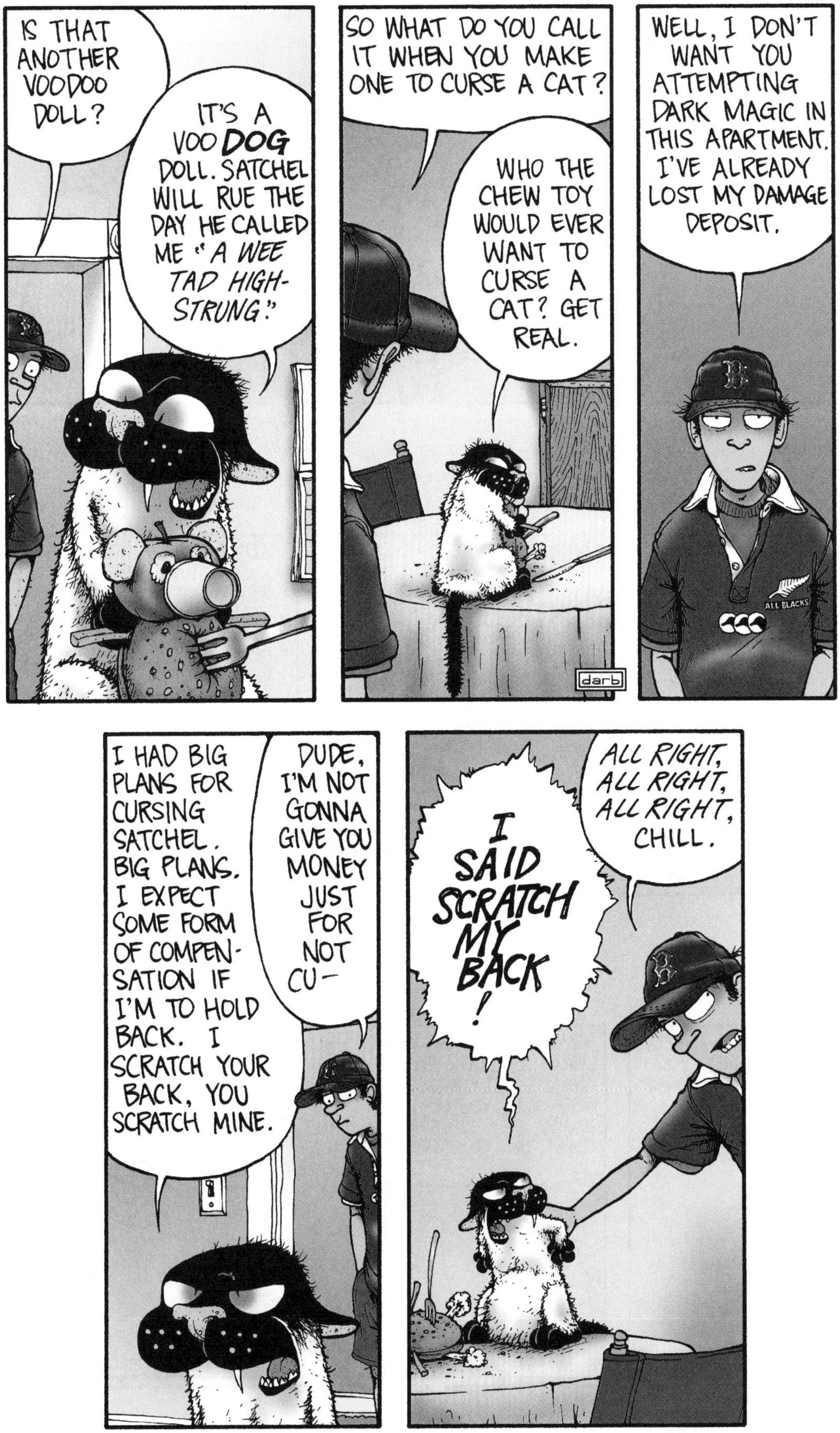
IS THAT ANOTHER VOODOO DOLL?
IT'S A VOO**DOG** DOLL. SATCHEL WILL RUE THE DAY HE CALLED ME "*A WEE TAD HIGH-STRUNG.*"
SO WHAT DO YOU CALL IT WHEN YOU MAKE ONE TO CURSE A CAT?
WHO THE CHEW TOY WOULD EVER WANT TO CURSE A CAT? GET REAL.
darb
WELL, I DON'T WANT YOU ATTEMPTING DARK MAGIC IN THIS APARTMENT. I'VE ALREADY LOST MY DAMAGE DEPOSIT.
ALL BLACKS
I HAD BIG PLANS FOR CURSING SATCHEL. BIG PLANS. I EXPECT SOME FORM OF COMPENSATION IF I'M TO HOLD BACK. I SCRATCH YOUR BACK, YOU SCRATCH MINE.
DUDE, I'M NOT GONNA GIVE YOU MONEY JUST FOR NOT CU–
I SAID SCRATCH MY BACK!
ALL RIGHT, ALL RIGHT, ALL RIGHT, CHILL.

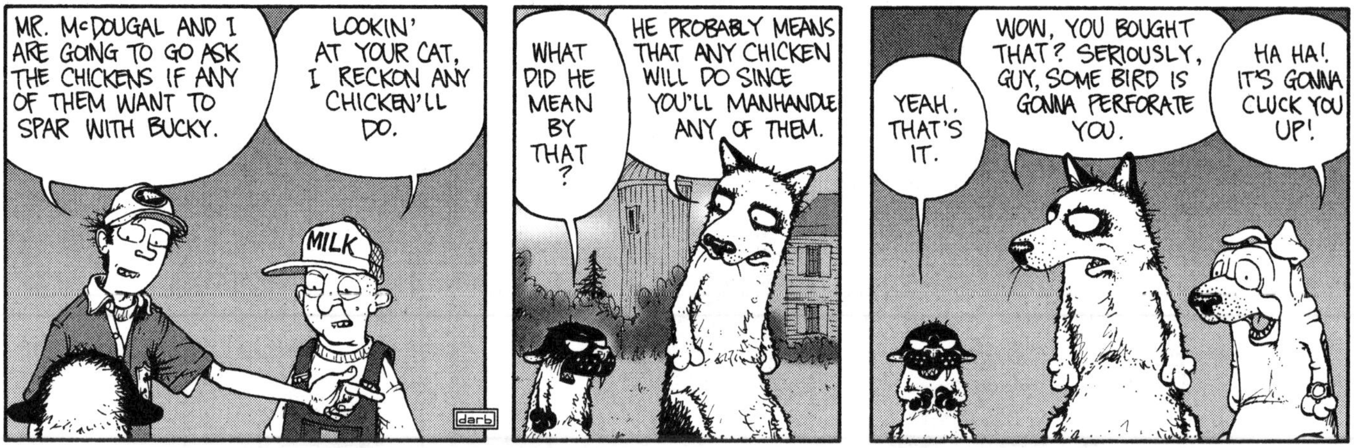
MR. McDOUGAL AND I ARE GOING TO GO ASK THE CHICKENS IF ANY OF THEM WANT TO SPAR WITH BUCKY.
LOOKIN' AT YOUR CAT, I RECKON ANY CHICKEN'LL DO.
MILK
darb
WHAT DID HE MEAN BY THAT?
HE PROBABLY MEANS THAT ANY CHICKEN WILL DO SINCE YOU'LL MANHANDLE ANY OF THEM.
YEAH. THAT'S IT.
WOW, YOU BOUGHT THAT? SERIOUSLY, GUY, SOME BIRD IS GONNA PERFORATE YOU.
HA HA!. IT'S GONNA CLUCK YOU UP!

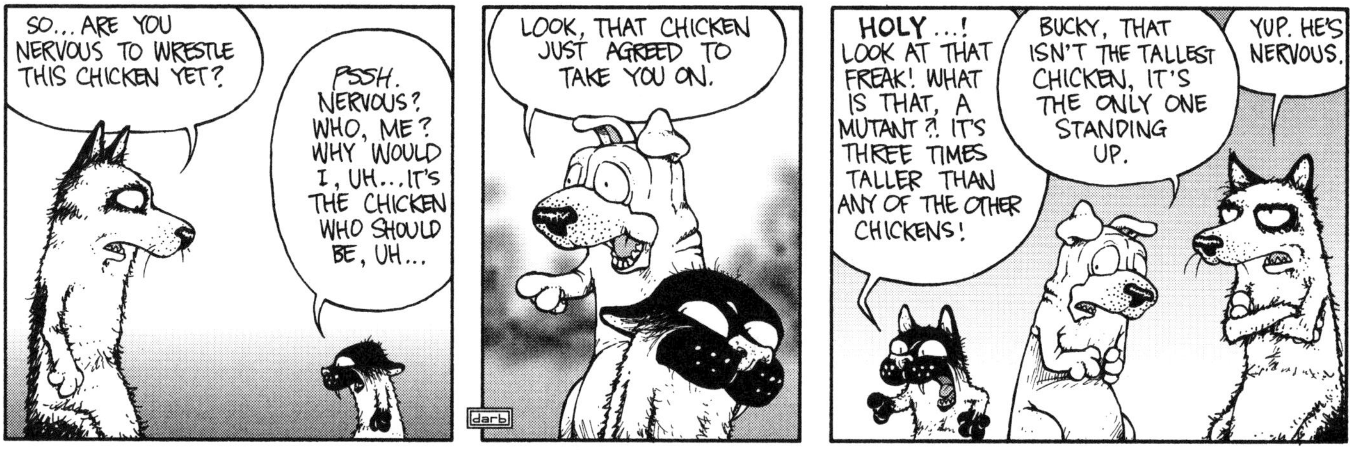
SO... ARE YOU NERVOUS TO WRESTLE THIS CHICKEN YET?
PSSH. NERVOUS? WHO, ME? WHY WOULD I, UH... IT'S THE CHICKEN WHO SHOULD BE, UH...
darb
LOOK, THAT CHICKEN JUST AGREED TO TAKE YOU ON.
HOLY...! LOOK AT THAT FREAK! WHAT IS THAT, A MUTANT?! IT'S THREE TIMES TALLER THAN ANY OF THE OTHER CHICKENS!
BUCKY, THAT ISN'T THE TALLEST CHICKEN, IT'S THE ONLY ONE STANDING UP.
YUP. HE'S NERVOUS.

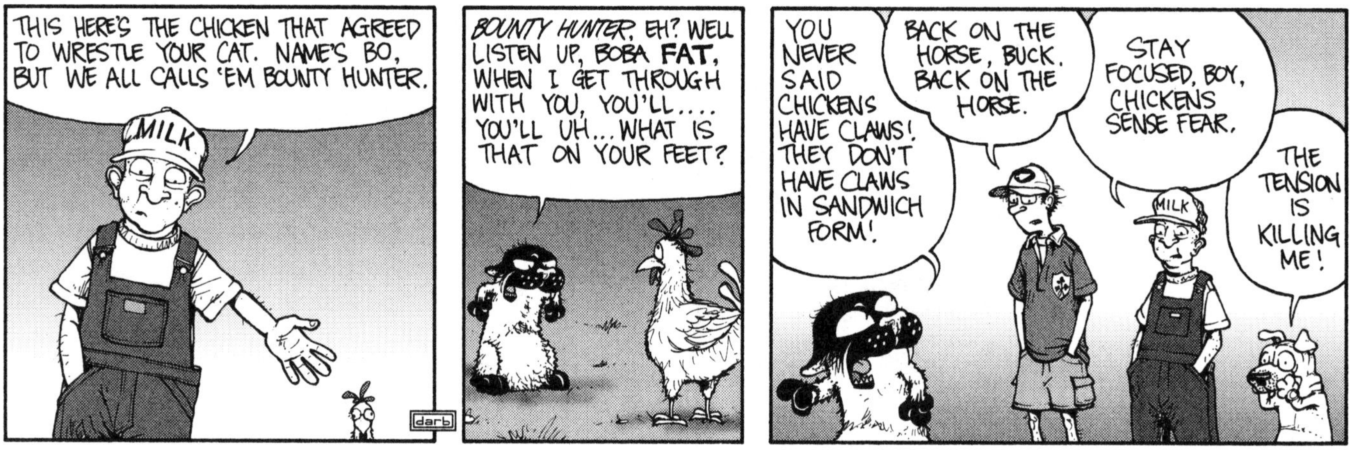
THIS HERE'S THE CHICKEN THAT AGREED TO WRESTLE YOUR CAT. NAME'S BO, BUT WE ALL CALLS 'EM BOUNTY HUNTER.
MILK
darb
BOUNTY HUNTER, EH? WELL LISTEN UP, BOBA FAT, WHEN I GET THROUGH WITH YOU, YOU'LL.... YOU'LL UH... WHAT IS THAT ON YOUR FEET?
YOU NEVER SAID CHICKENS HAVE CLAWS! THEY DON'T HAVE CLAWS IN SANDWICH FORM!
BACK ON THE HORSE, BUCK. BACK ON THE HORSE.
STAY FOCUSED, BOY, CHICKENS SENSE FEAR.
MILK
THE TENSION IS KILLING ME!

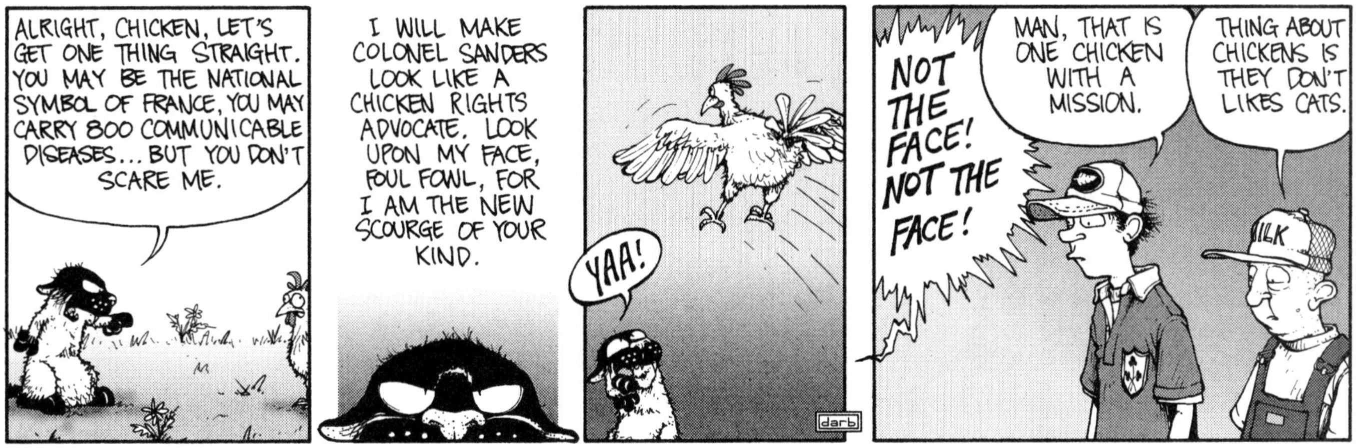
ALRIGHT, CHICKEN, LET'S GET ONE THING STRAIGHT. YOU MAY BE THE NATIONAL SYMBOL OF FRANCE, YOU MAY CARRY 800 COMMUNICABLE DISEASES... BUT YOU DON'T SCARE ME.
I WILL MAKE COLONEL SANDERS LOOK LIKE A CHICKEN RIGHTS ADVOCATE. LOOK UPON MY FACE, FOUL FOWL, FOR I AM THE NEW SCOURGE OF YOUR KIND.
YAA!
darb
NOT THE FACE! NOT THE FACE!
MAN, THAT IS ONE CHICKEN WITH A MISSION.
THING ABOUT CHICKENS IS THEY DON'T LIKES CATS.
MILK

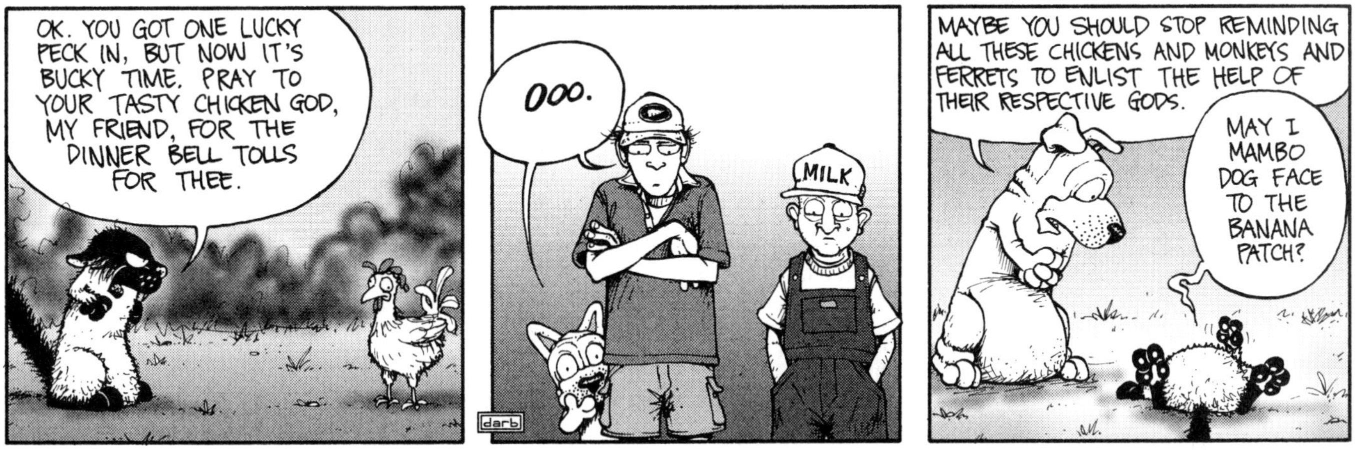
OK. YOU GOT ONE LUCKY PECK IN, BUT NOW IT'S BUCKY TIME. PRAY TO YOUR TASTY CHICKEN GOD, MY FRIEND, FOR THE DINNER BELL TOLLS FOR THEE.
darb
OOO.
MILK
MAYBE YOU SHOULD STOP REMINDING ALL THESE CHICKENS AND MONKEYS AND FERRETS TO ENLIST THE HELP OF THEIR RESPECTIVE GODS.
MAY I MAMBO DOG FACE TO THE BANANA PATCH?

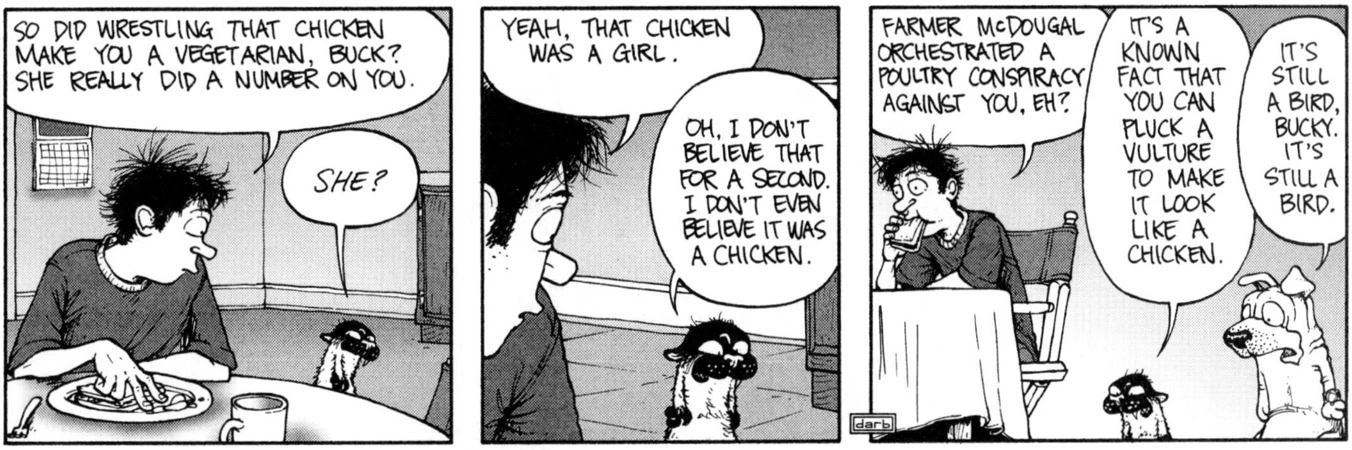
SO DID WRESTLING THAT CHICKEN MAKE YOU A VEGETARIAN, BUCK? SHE REALLY DID A NUMBER ON YOU.
SHE?
YEAH, THAT CHICKEN WAS A GIRL.
OH, I DON'T BELIEVE THAT FOR A SECOND. I DON'T EVEN BELIEVE IT WAS A CHICKEN.
darb
FARMER McDOUGAL ORCHESTRATED A POULTRY CONSPIRACY AGAINST YOU, EH?
IT'S A KNOWN FACT THAT YOU CAN PLUCK A VULTURE TO MAKE IT LOOK LIKE A CHICKEN.
IT'S STILL A BIRD, BUCKY. IT'S STILL A BIRD.

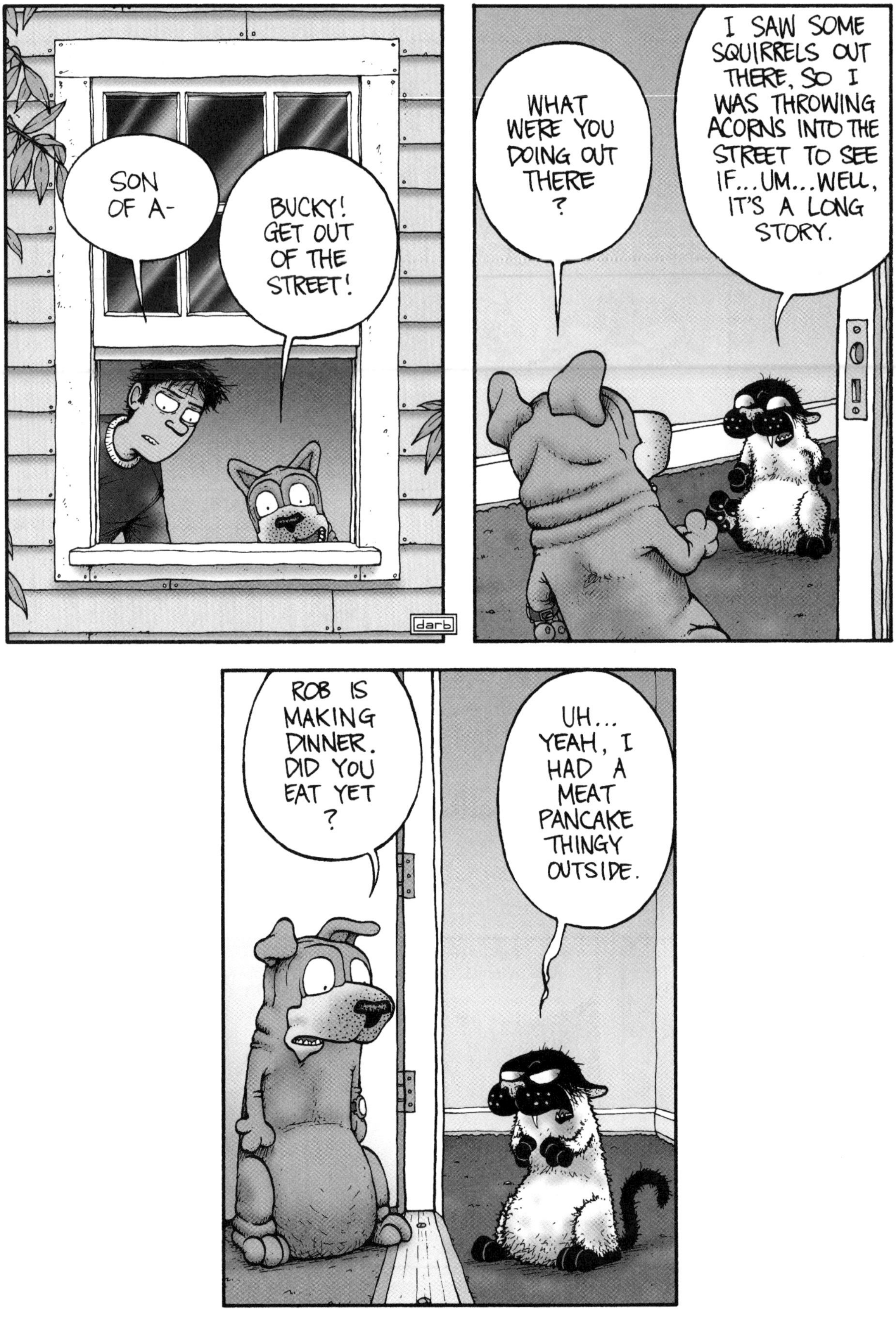
SON OF A-
BUCKY! GET OUT OF THE STREET!
darb
WHAT WERE YOU DOING OUT THERE?
I SAW SOME SQUIRRELS OUT THERE, SO I WAS THROWING ACORNS INTO THE STREET TO SEE IF...UM...WELL, IT'S A LONG STORY.
ROB IS MAKING DINNER. DID YOU EAT YET?
UH... YEAH, I HAD A MEAT PANCAKE THINGY OUTSIDE.

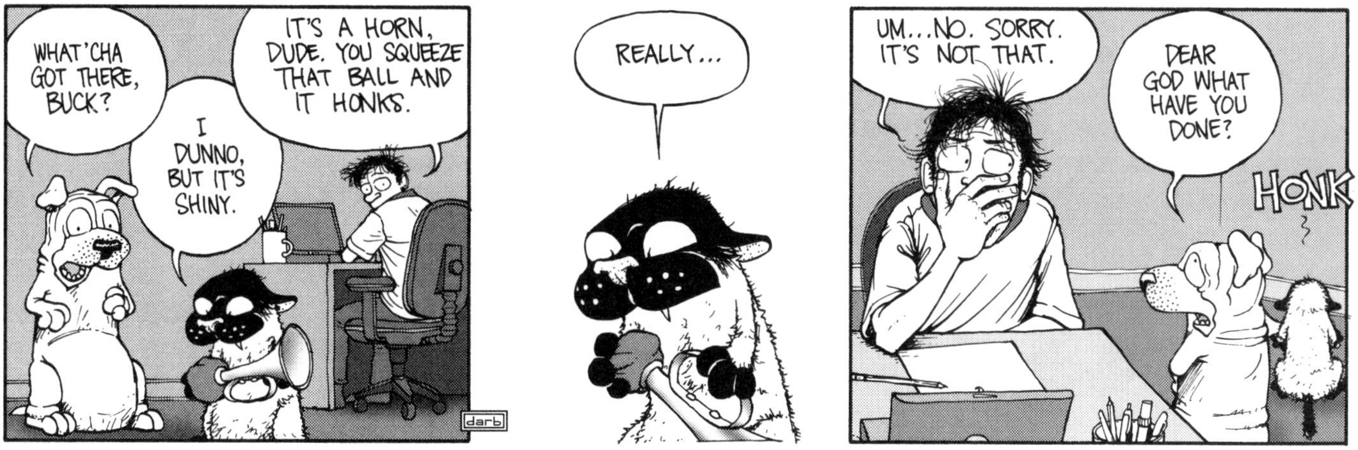
WHAT'CHA GOT THERE, BUCK?
I DUNNO, BUT IT'S SHINY.
IT'S A HORN, DUDE. YOU SQUEEZE THAT BALL AND IT HONKS.
REALLY...
UM...NO. SORRY. IT'S NOT THAT.
DEAR GOD WHAT HAVE YOU DONE?
HONK

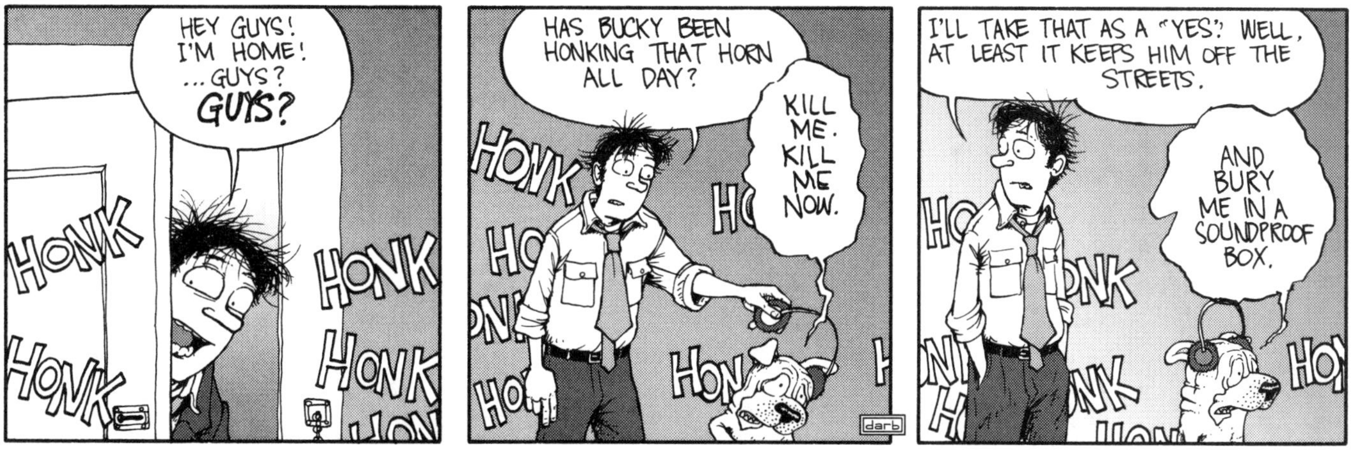
HEY GUYS! I'M HOME! ...GUYS? GUYS?
HONK
HONK
HONK
HONK
HAS BUCKY BEEN HONKING THAT HORN ALL DAY?
KILL ME. KILL ME NOW.
HONK
I'LL TAKE THAT AS A "YES." WELL, AT LEAST IT KEEPS HIM OFF THE STREETS.
AND BURY ME IN A SOUNDPROOF BOX.

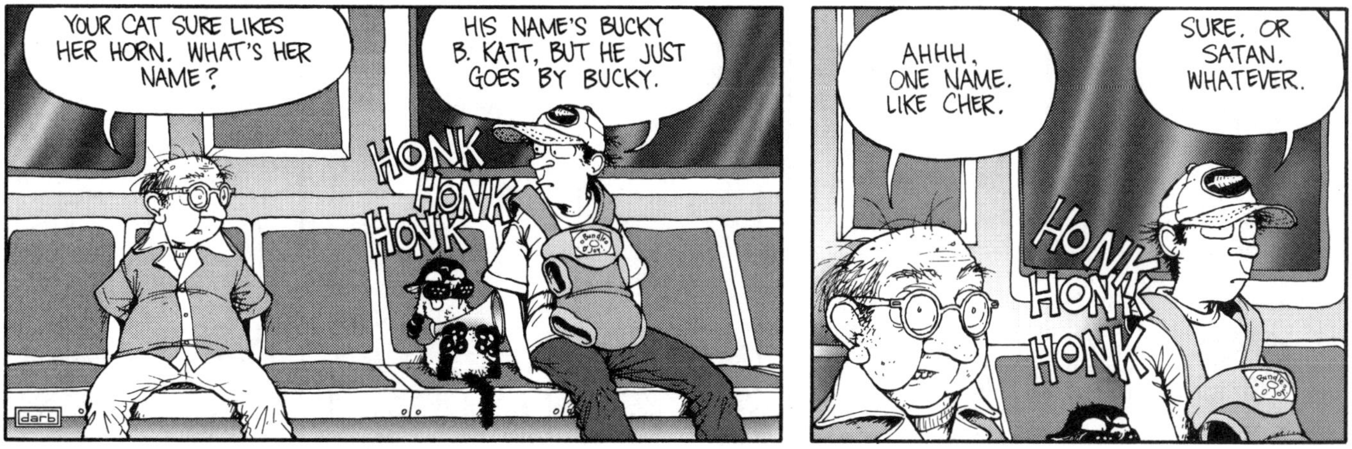
YOUR CAT SURE LIKES HER HORN. WHAT'S HER NAME?
HIS NAME'S BUCKY B. KATT, BUT HE JUST GOES BY BUCKY.
HONK
HONK
HONK
AHHH. ONE NAME. LIKE CHER.
SURE. OR SATAN. WHATEVER.
HONK
HONK
HONK

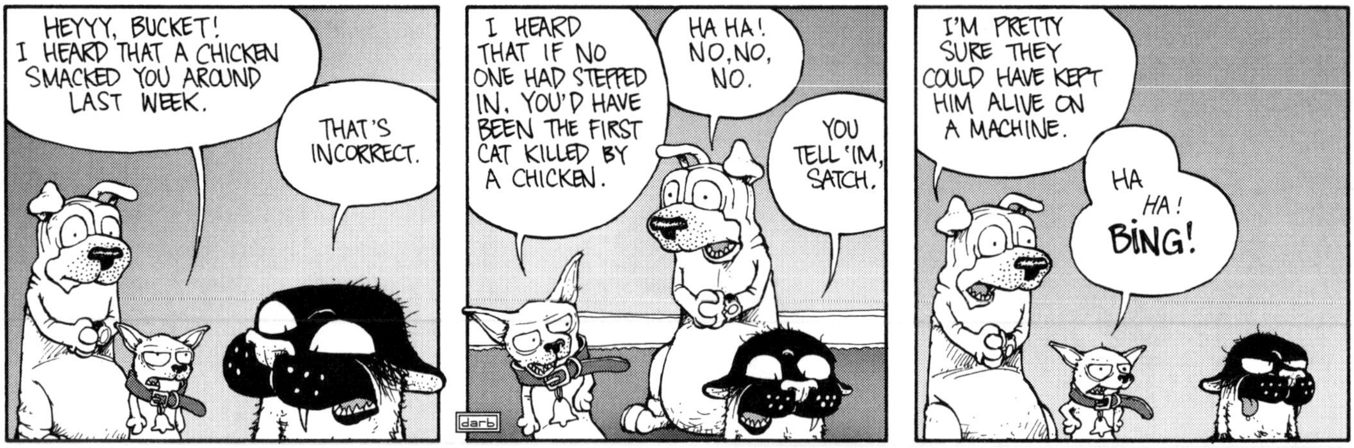
HEYYY, BUCKET! I HEARD THAT A CHICKEN SMACKED YOU AROUND LAST WEEK.
THAT'S INCORRECT.
I HEARD THAT IF NO ONE HAD STEPPED IN, YOU'D HAVE BEEN THE FIRST CAT KILLED BY A CHICKEN.
HA HA! NO, NO, NO.
YOU TELL 'IM, SATCH.
I'M PRETTY SURE THEY COULD HAVE KEPT HIM ALIVE ON A MACHINE.
HA HA! BING!
darb

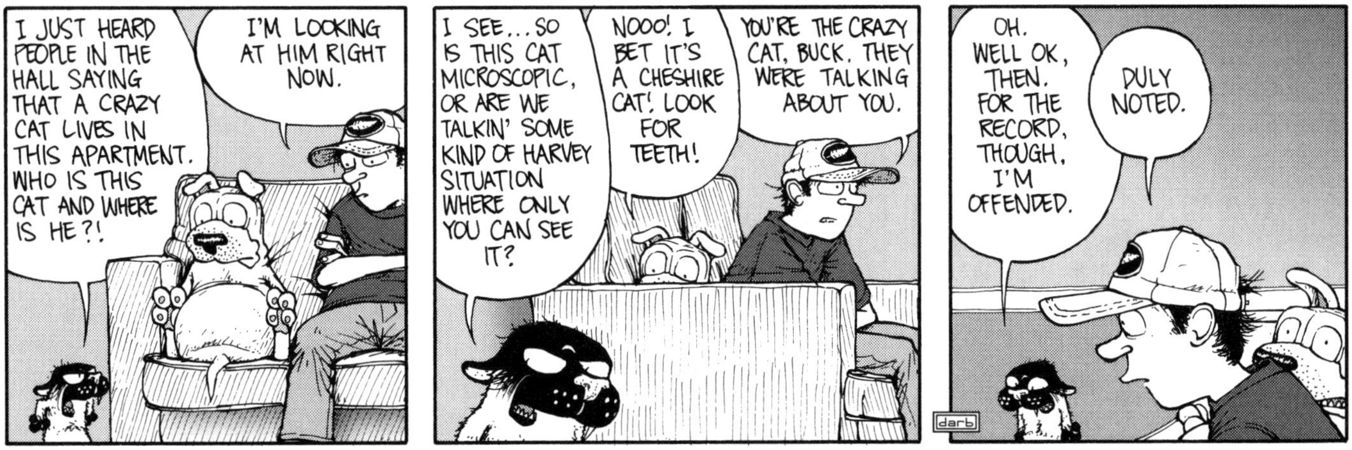
I JUST HEARD PEOPLE IN THE HALL SAYING THAT A CRAZY CAT LIVES IN THIS APARTMENT. WHO IS THIS CAT AND WHERE IS HE?!
I'M LOOKING AT HIM RIGHT NOW.
I SEE... SO IS THIS CAT MICROSCOPIC, OR ARE WE TALKIN' SOME KIND OF HARVEY SITUATION WHERE ONLY YOU CAN SEE IT?
NOOO! I BET IT'S A CHESHIRE CAT! LOOK FOR TEETH!
YOU'RE THE CRAZY CAT, BUCK. THEY WERE TALKING ABOUT YOU.
OH. WELL OK, THEN. FOR THE RECORD, THOUGH, I'M OFFENDED.
DULY NOTED.
darb

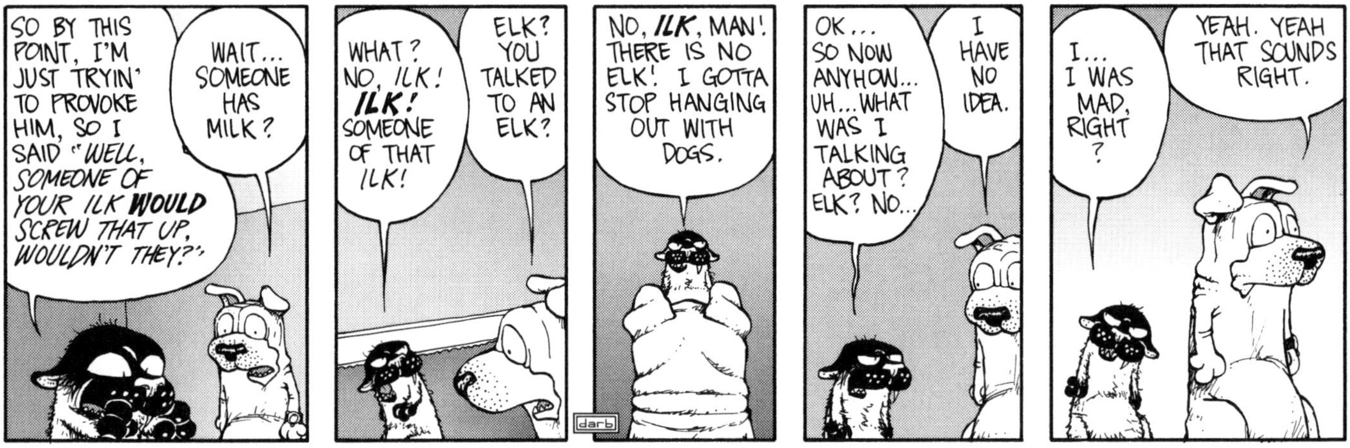
SO BY THIS POINT, I'M JUST TRYIN' TO PROVOKE HIM, SO I SAID "WELL, SOMEONE OF YOUR ILK WOULD SCREW THAT UP, WOULDN'T THEY?"
WAIT... SOMEONE HAS MILK?
WHAT? NO, ILK! ILK! SOMEONE OF THAT ILK!
ELK? YOU TALKED TO AN ELK?
NO, ILK, MAN! THERE IS NO ELK! I GOTTA STOP HANGING OUT WITH DOGS.
OK... SO NOW ANYHOW... UH... WHAT WAS I TALKING ABOUT? ELK? NO...
I HAVE NO IDEA.
I... I WAS MAD, RIGHT?
YEAH. YEAH THAT SOUNDS RIGHT.
darb

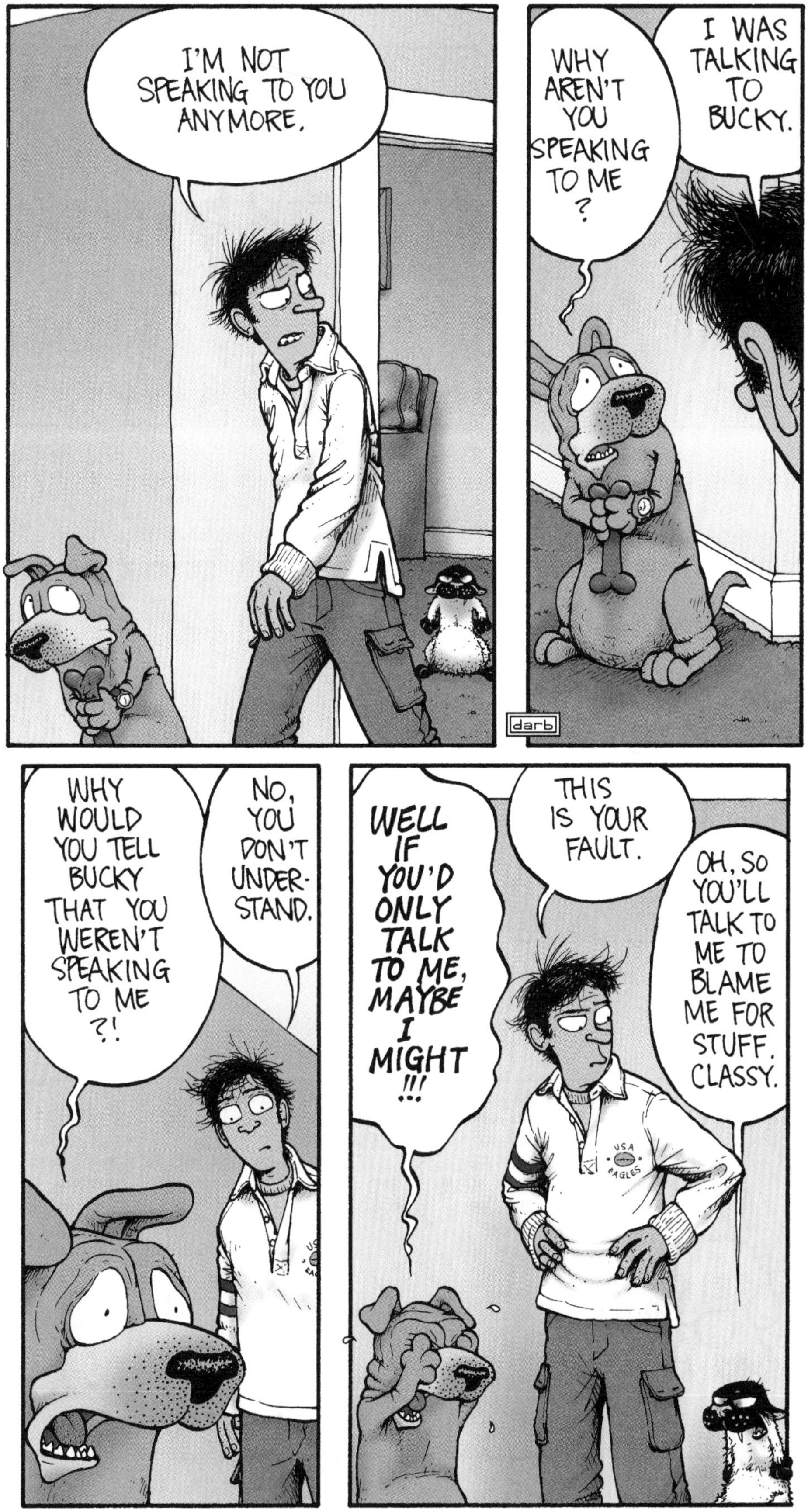
I'M NOT SPEAKING TO YOU ANYMORE.
WHY AREN'T YOU SPEAKING TO ME ?
I WAS TALKING TO BUCKY.
darb
WHY WOULD YOU TELL BUCKY THAT YOU WEREN'T SPEAKING TO ME ?!
NO, YOU DON'T UNDER-STAND.
WELL IF YOU'D ONLY TALK TO ME, MAYBE I MIGHT !!!
THIS IS YOUR FAULT.
OH, SO YOU'LL TALK TO ME TO BLAME ME FOR STUFF. CLASSY.
USA EAGLES

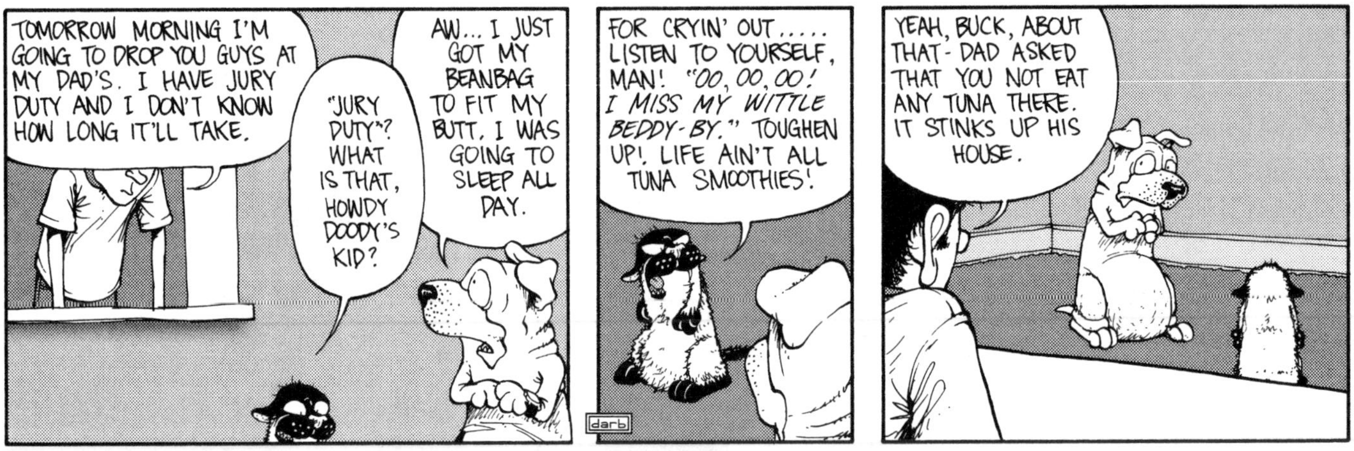
TOMORROW MORNING I'M GOING TO DROP YOU GUYS AT MY DAD'S. I HAVE JURY DUTY AND I DON'T KNOW HOW LONG IT'LL TAKE.
"JURY DUTY"? WHAT IS THAT, HOWDY DOODY'S KID?
AW... I JUST GOT MY BEANBAG TO FIT MY BUTT. I WAS GOING TO SLEEP ALL DAY.
darb
FOR CRYIN' OUT..... LISTEN TO YOURSELF, MAN! *"OO, OO, OO! I MISS MY WITTLE BEDDY-BY."* TOUGHEN UP!. LIFE AIN'T ALL TUNA SMOOTHIES!
YEAH, BUCK, ABOUT THAT- DAD ASKED THAT YOU NOT EAT ANY TUNA THERE. IT STINKS UP HIS HOUSE.

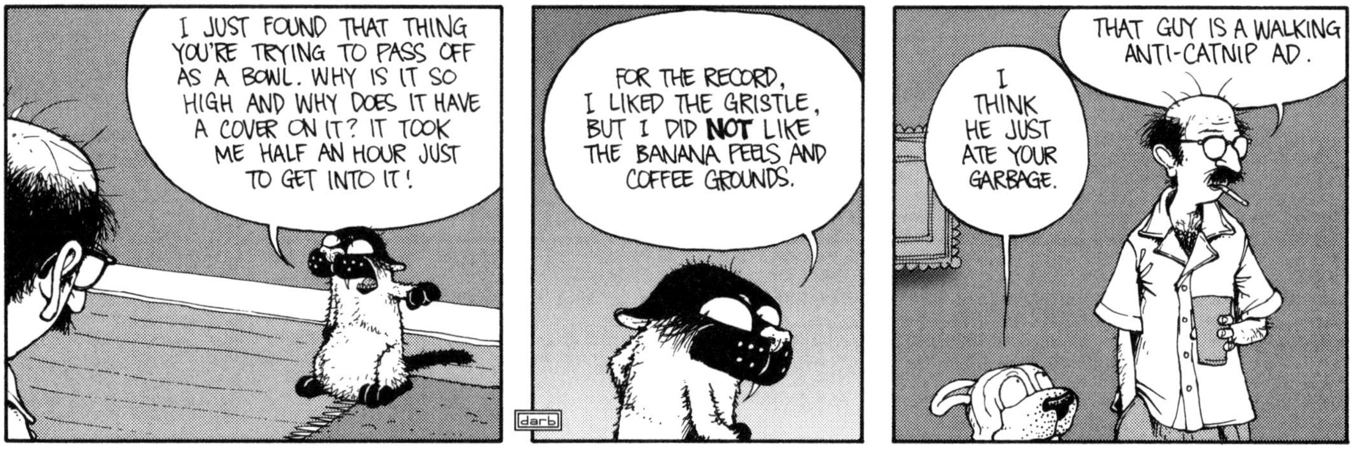
I JUST FOUND THAT THING YOU'RE TRYING TO PASS OFF AS A BOWL. WHY IS IT SO HIGH AND WHY DOES IT HAVE A COVER ON IT? IT TOOK ME HALF AN HOUR JUST TO GET INTO IT!
darb
FOR THE RECORD, I LIKED THE GRISTLE, BUT I DID **NOT** LIKE THE BANANA PEELS AND COFFEE GROUNDS.
I THINK HE JUST ATE YOUR GARBAGE.
THAT GUY IS A WALKING ANTI-CATNIP AD.

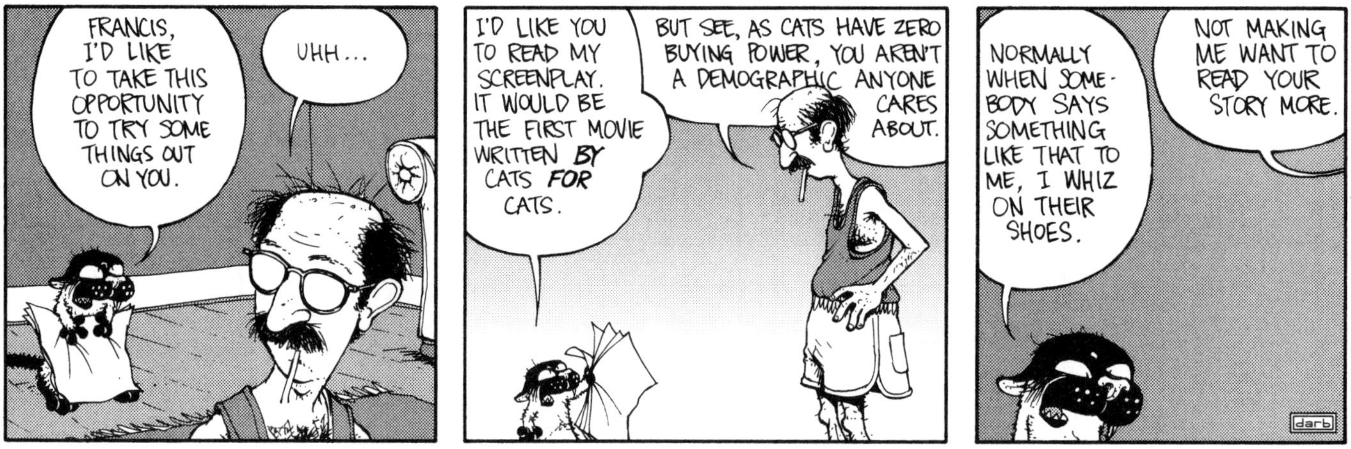
FRANCIS, I'D LIKE TO TAKE THIS OPPORTUNITY TO TRY SOME THINGS OUT ON YOU.
UHH...
I'D LIKE YOU TO READ MY SCREENPLAY. IT WOULD BE THE FIRST MOVIE WRITTEN ***BY*** CATS ***FOR*** CATS.
BUT SEE, AS CATS HAVE ZERO BUYING POWER, YOU AREN'T A DEMOGRAPHIC ANYONE CARES ABOUT.
NORMALLY WHEN SOME-BODY SAYS SOMETHING LIKE THAT TO ME, I WHIZ ON THEIR SHOES.
NOT MAKING ME WANT TO READ YOUR STORY MORE.
darb

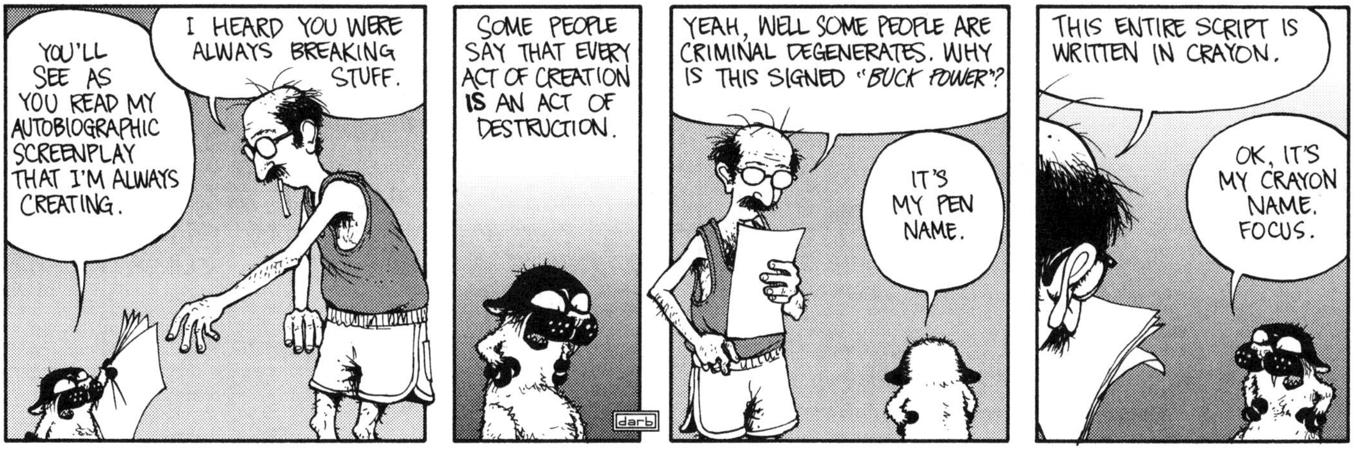
I HEARD YOU WERE ALWAYS BREAKING STUFF.
YOU'LL SEE AS YOU READ MY AUTOBIOGRAPHIC SCREENPLAY THAT I'M ALWAYS CREATING.
SOME PEOPLE SAY THAT EVERY ACT OF CREATION **IS** AN ACT OF DESTRUCTION.
darb
YEAH, WELL SOME PEOPLE ARE CRIMINAL DEGENERATES. WHY IS THIS SIGNED "*BUCK POWER*"?
IT'S MY PEN NAME.
THIS ENTIRE SCRIPT IS WRITTEN IN CRAYON.
OK, IT'S MY CRAYON NAME. FOCUS.

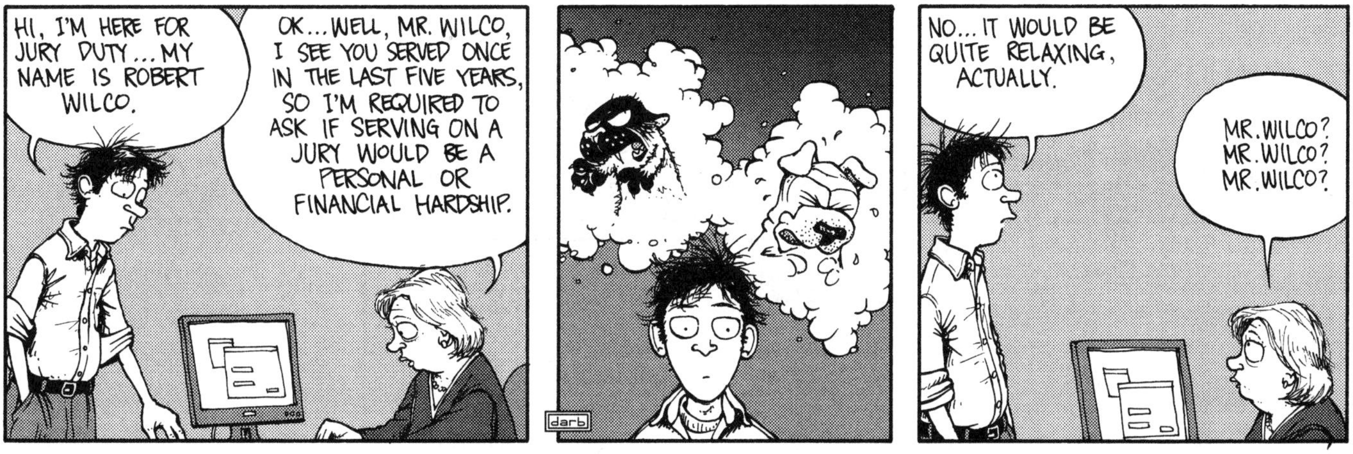
HI, I'M HERE FOR JURY DUTY... MY NAME IS ROBERT WILCO.
OK... WELL, MR. WILCO, I SEE YOU SERVED ONCE IN THE LAST FIVE YEARS, SO I'M REQUIRED TO ASK IF SERVING ON A JURY WOULD BE A PERSONAL OR FINANCIAL HARDSHIP.
darb
NO... IT WOULD BE QUITE RELAXING, ACTUALLY.
MR.WILCO? MR.WILCO? MR.WILCO?

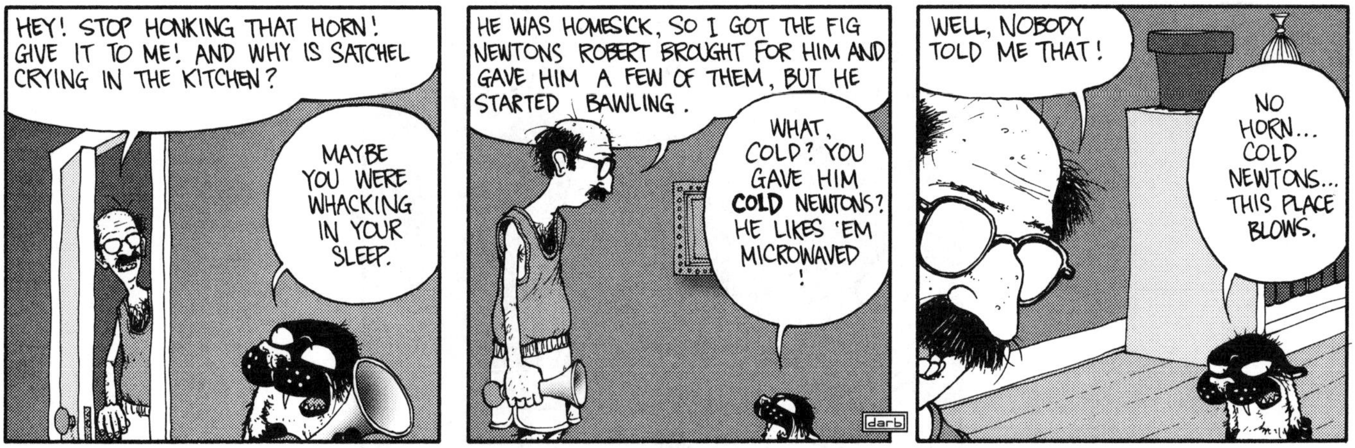
HEY! STOP HONKING THAT HORN! GIVE IT TO ME! AND WHY IS SATCHEL CRYING IN THE KITCHEN?
MAYBE YOU WERE WHACKING IN YOUR SLEEP.
HE WAS HOMESICK, SO I GOT THE FIG NEWTONS ROBERT BROUGHT FOR HIM AND GAVE HIM A FEW OF THEM, BUT HE STARTED BAWLING.
WHAT, COLD? YOU GAVE HIM **COLD** NEWTONS? HE LIKES 'EM MICROWAVED!
darb
WELL, NOBODY TOLD ME THAT!
NO HORN... COLD NEWTONS... THIS PLACE BLOWS.

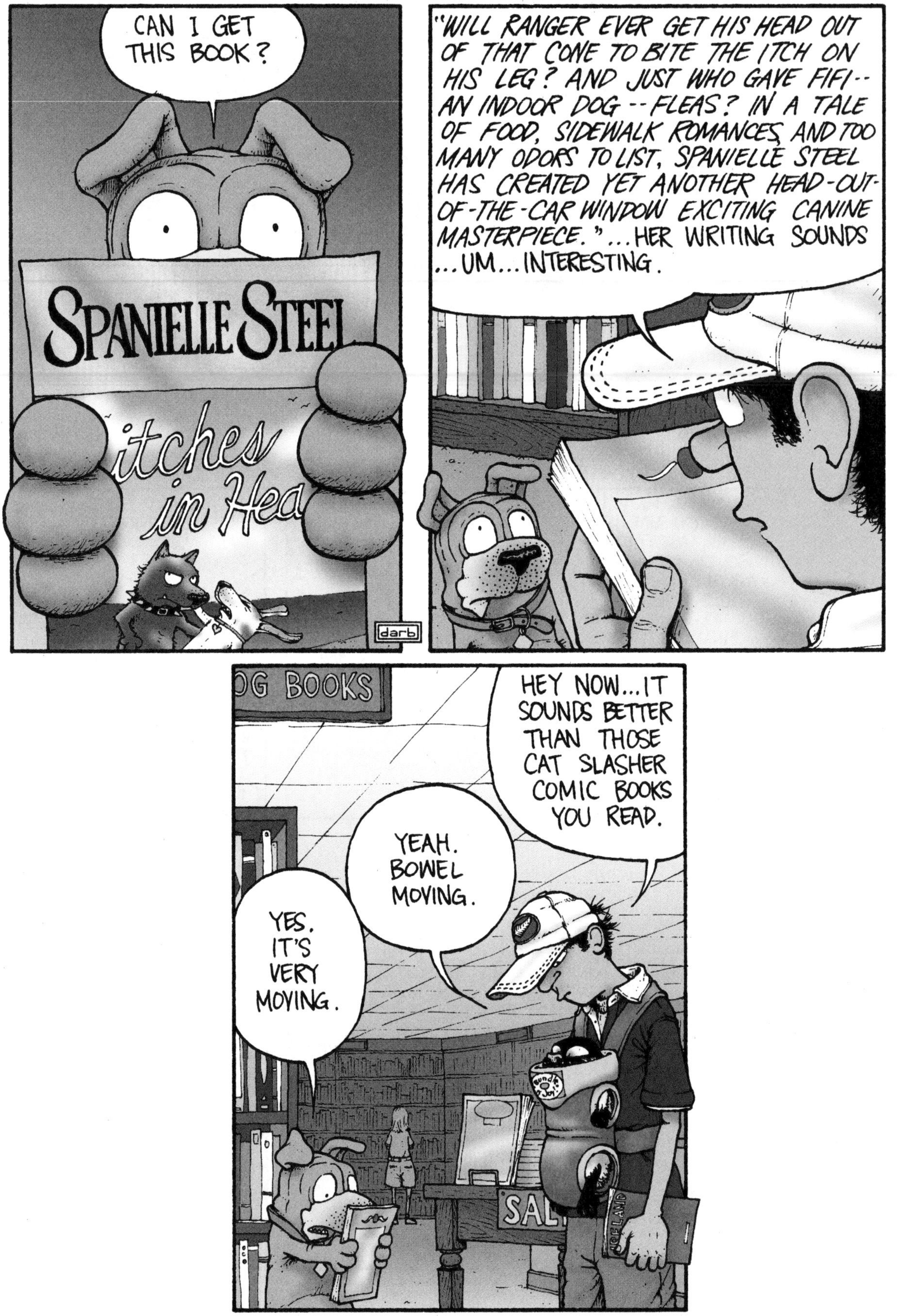
CAN I GET THIS BOOK?
SPANIELLE STEEL
itches in Hea
darb
"WILL RANGER EVER GET HIS HEAD OUT OF THAT CONE TO BITE THE ITCH ON HIS LEG? AND JUST WHO GAVE FIFI-- AN INDOOR DOG --FLEAS? IN A TALE OF FOOD, SIDEWALK ROMANCES, AND TOO MANY ODORS TO LIST, SPANIELLE STEEL HAS CREATED YET ANOTHER HEAD-OUT-OF-THE-CAR WINDOW EXCITING CANINE MASTERPIECE." ...HER WRITING SOUNDS ...UM... INTERESTING.
OG BOOKS
HEY NOW... IT SOUNDS BETTER THAN THOSE CAT SLASHER COMIC BOOKS YOU READ.
YEAH. BOWEL MOVING.
YES. IT'S VERY MOVING.
SAL

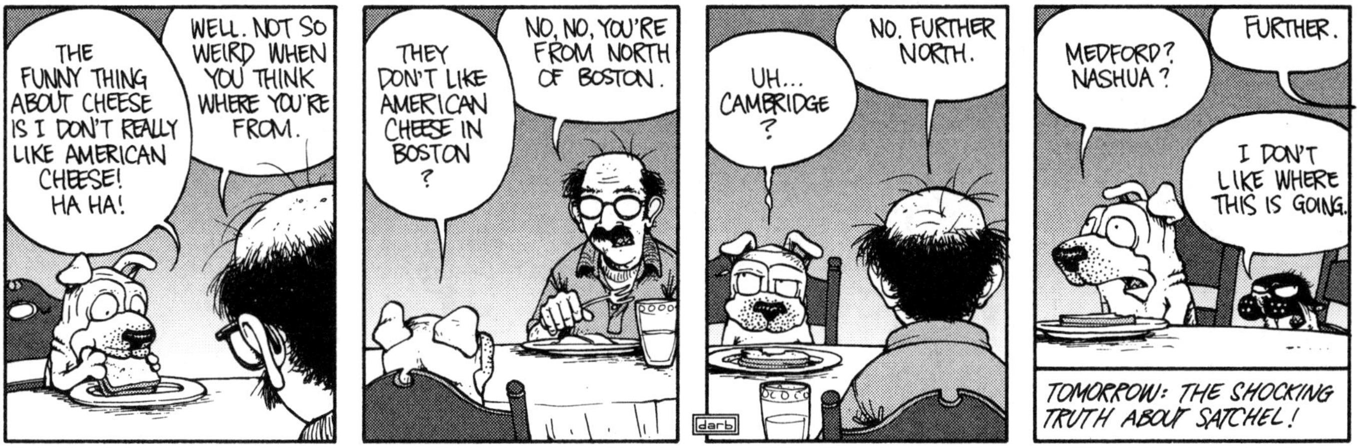
THE FUNNY THING ABOUT CHEESE IS I DON'T REALLY LIKE AMERICAN CHEESE! HA HA!
WELL. NOT SO WEIRD WHEN YOU THINK WHERE YOU'RE FROM.
THEY DON'T LIKE AMERICAN CHEESE IN BOSTON?
NO, NO, YOU'RE FROM NORTH OF BOSTON.
UH... CAMBRIDGE?
NO. FURTHER NORTH.
MEDFORD? NASHUA?
FURTHER.
I DON'T LIKE WHERE THIS IS GOING.
TOMORROW: THE SHOCKING TRUTH ABOUT SATCHEL!

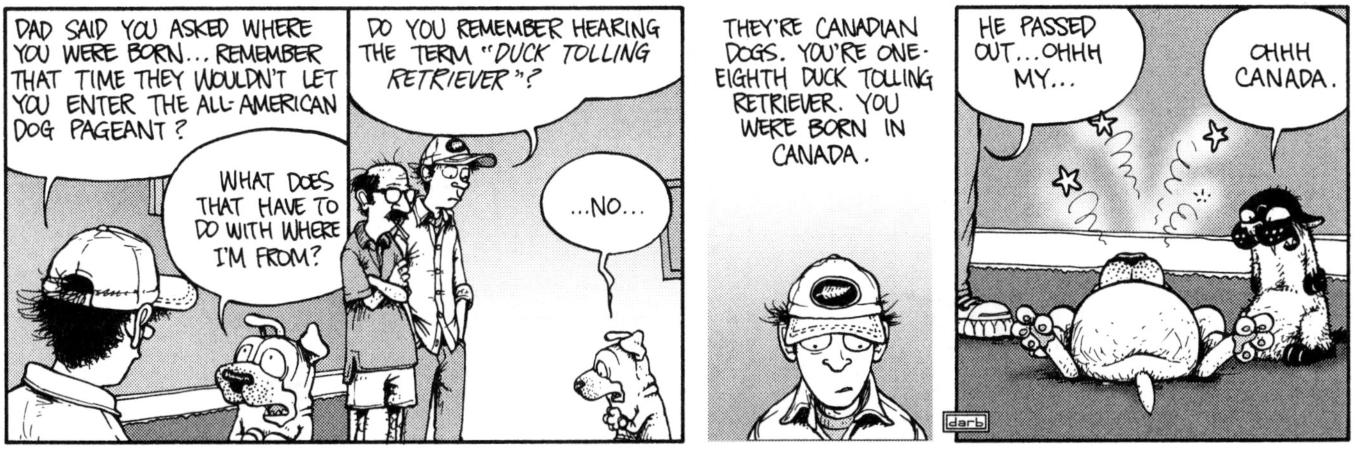
DAD SAID YOU ASKED WHERE YOU WERE BORN... REMEMBER THAT TIME THEY WOULDN'T LET YOU ENTER THE ALL-AMERICAN DOG PAGEANT?
WHAT DOES THAT HAVE TO DO WITH WHERE I'M FROM?
DO YOU REMEMBER HEARING THE TERM "DUCK TOLLING RETRIEVER"?
...NO...
THEY'RE CANADIAN DOGS. YOU'RE ONE-EIGHTH DUCK TOLLING RETRIEVER. YOU WERE BORN IN CANADA.
HE PASSED OUT... OHHH MY...
OHHH CANADA.

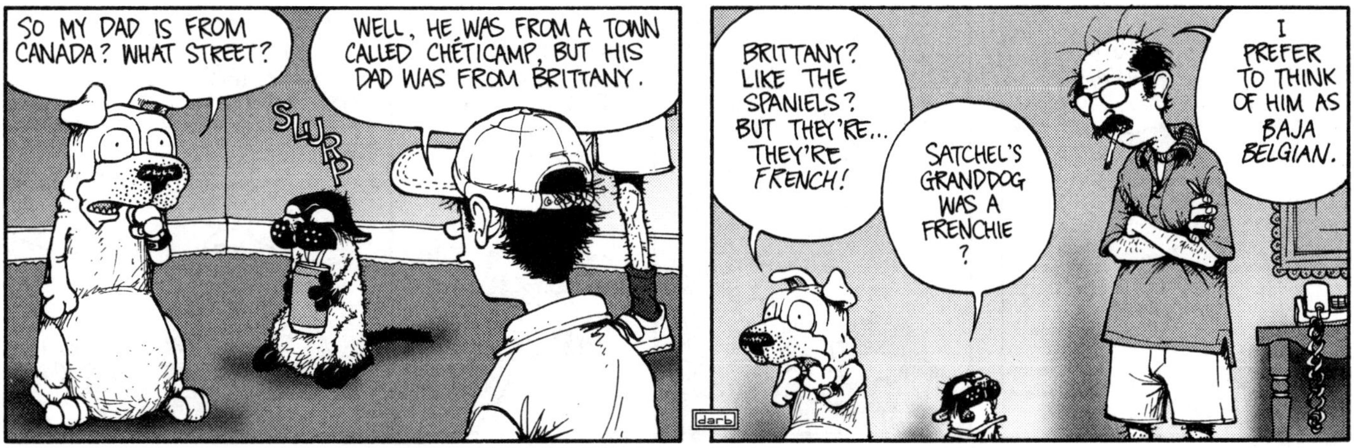
SO MY DAD IS FROM CANADA? WHAT STREET?
WELL, HE WAS FROM A TOWN CALLED CHÉTICAMP, BUT HIS DAD WAS FROM BRITTANY.
SLURP
BRITTANY? LIKE THE SPANIELS? BUT THEY'RE... THEY'RE FRENCH!
SATCHEL'S GRANDDOG WAS A FRENCHIE?
I PREFER TO THINK OF HIM AS BAJA BELGIAN.

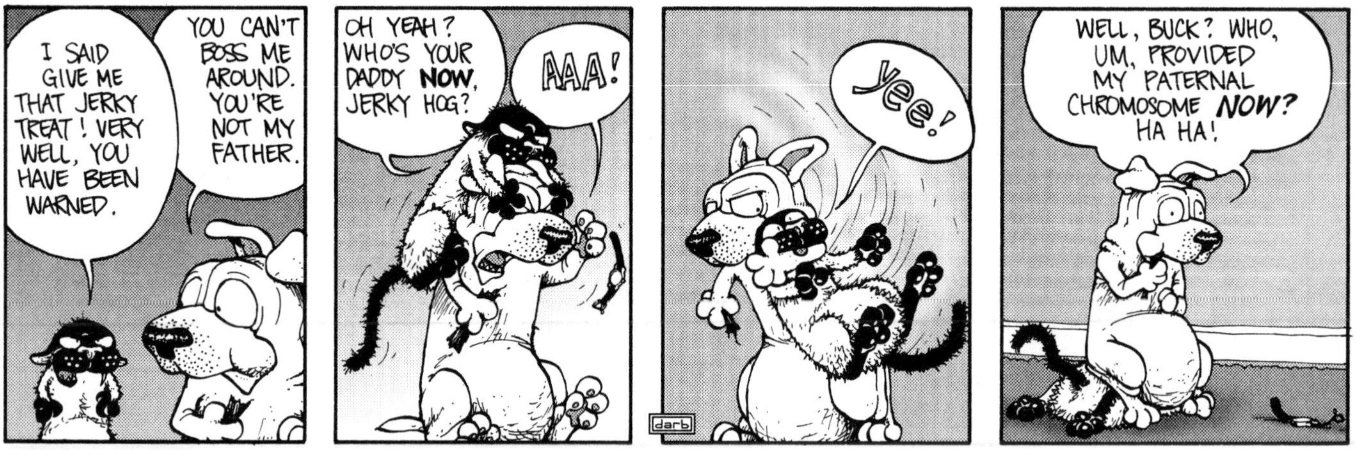
I SAID GIVE ME THAT JERKY TREAT! VERY WELL, YOU HAVE BEEN WARNED.
YOU CAN'T BOSS ME AROUND. YOU'RE NOT MY FATHER.
OH YEAH? WHO'S YOUR DADDY **NOW**, JERKY HOG?
AAA!
YEE!
WELL, BUCK? WHO, UM, PROVIDED MY PATERNAL CHROMOSOME ***NOW?*** HA HA!

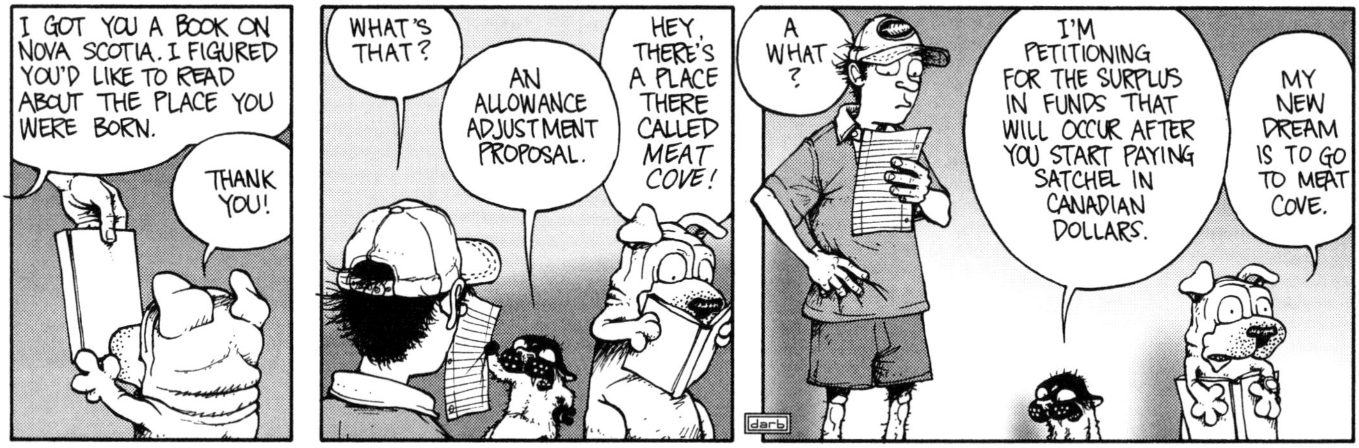
I GOT YOU A BOOK ON NOVA SCOTIA. I FIGURED YOU'D LIKE TO READ ABOUT THE PLACE YOU WERE BORN.
THANK YOU!
WHAT'S THAT?
AN ALLOWANCE ADJUSTMENT PROPOSAL.
HEY, THERE'S A PLACE THERE CALLED *MEAT COVE!*
A WHAT?
I'M PETITIONING FOR THE SURPLUS IN FUNDS THAT WILL OCCUR AFTER YOU START PAYING SATCHEL IN CANADIAN DOLLARS.
MY NEW DREAM IS TO GO TO MEAT COVE.

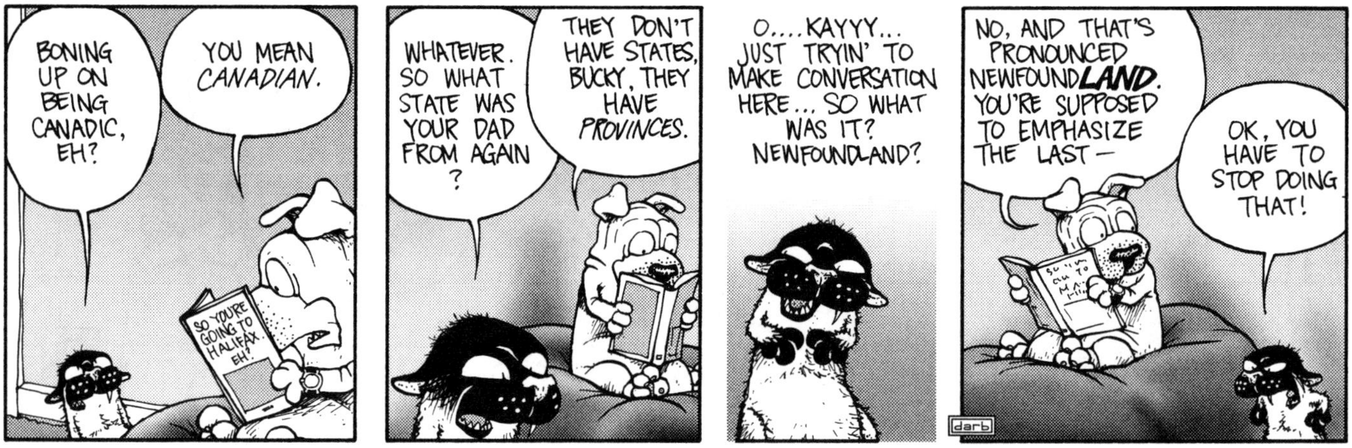
BONING UP ON BEING CANADIC, EH?
YOU MEAN *CANADIAN.*
SO YOU'RE GOING TO HALIFAX, EH?
WHATEVER. SO WHAT STATE WAS YOUR DAD FROM AGAIN?
THEY DON'T HAVE STATES, BUCKY, THEY HAVE *PROVINCES.*
O....KAYYY... JUST TRYIN' TO MAKE CONVERSATION HERE... SO WHAT WAS IT? NEWFOUNDLAND?
NO, AND THAT'S PRONOUNCED NEWFOUND***LAND***. YOU'RE SUPPOSED TO EMPHASIZE THE LAST—
OK, YOU HAVE TO STOP DOING THAT!

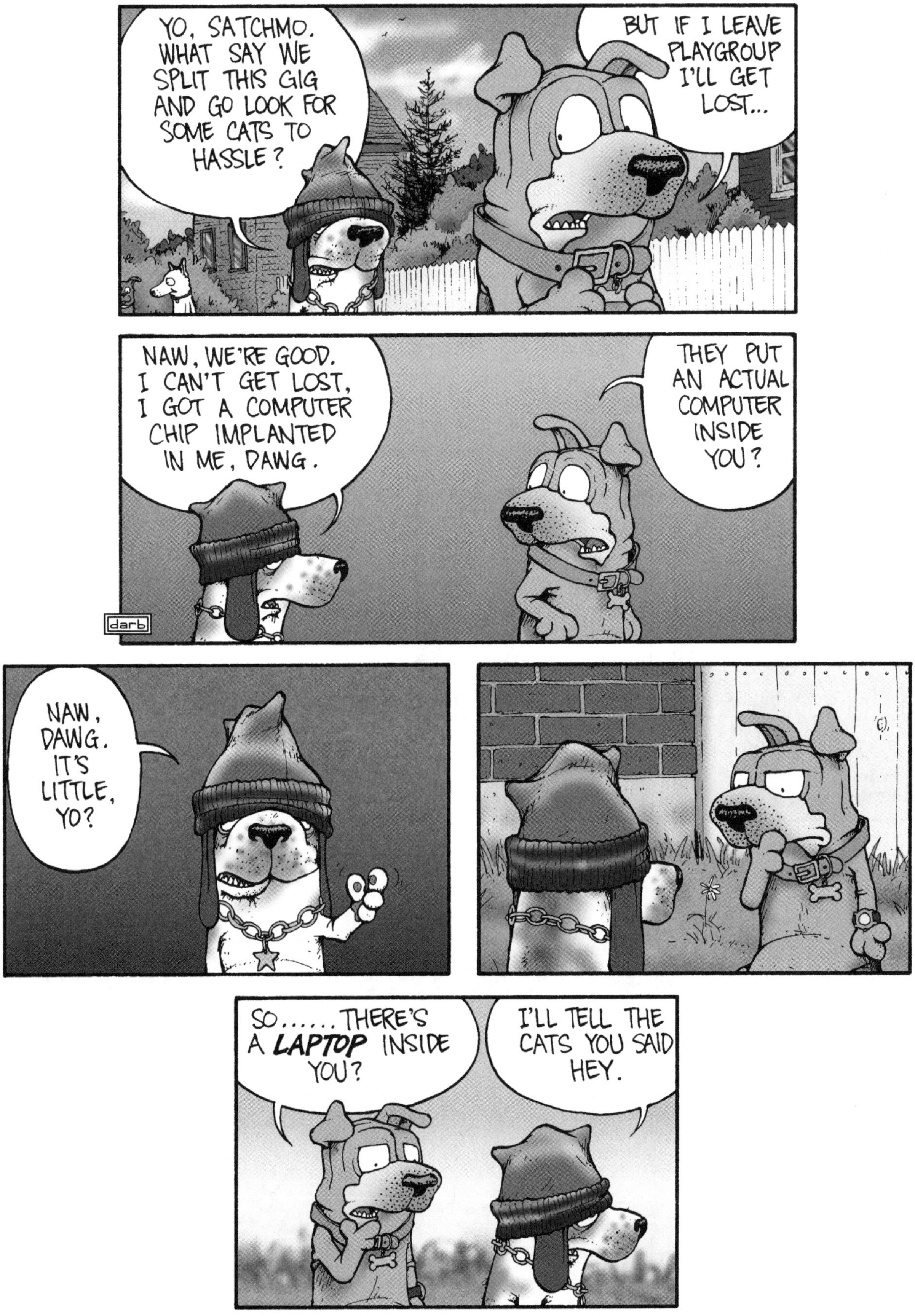
YO, SATCHMO. WHAT SAY WE SPLIT THIS GIG AND GO LOOK FOR SOME CATS TO HASSLE?
BUT IF I LEAVE PLAYGROUP I'LL GET LOST...
NAW, WE'RE GOOD. I CAN'T GET LOST, I GOT A COMPUTER CHIP IMPLANTED IN ME, DAWG.
THEY PUT AN ACTUAL COMPUTER INSIDE YOU?
darb
NAW, DAWG. IT'S LITTLE, YO?
SO......THERE'S A **LAPTOP** INSIDE YOU?
I'LL TELL THE CATS YOU SAID HEY.

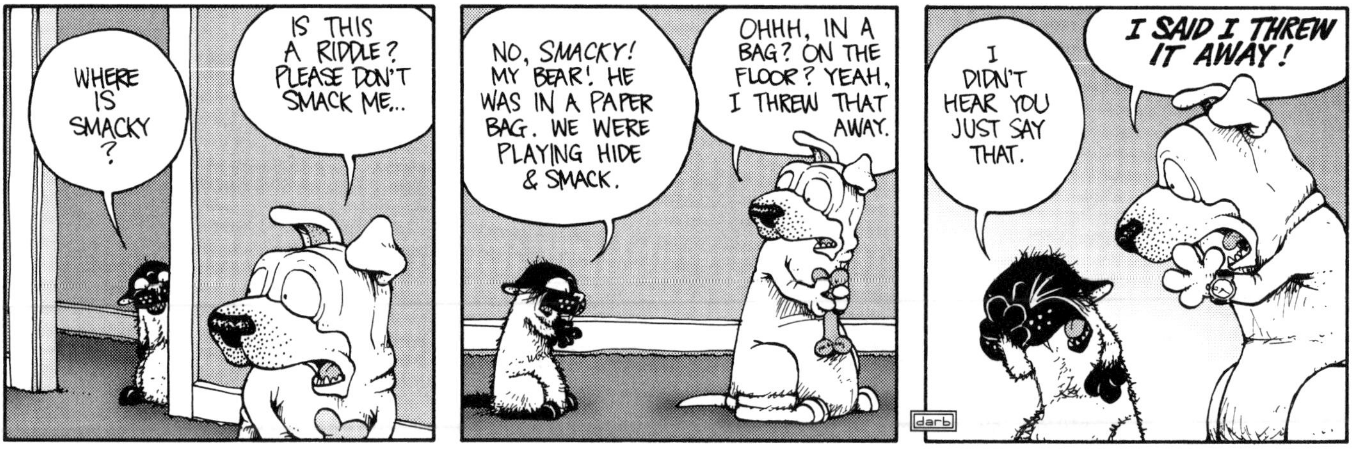
WHERE IS SMACKY ?
IS THIS A RIDDLE ? PLEASE DON'T SMACK ME...
NO, SMACKY! MY BEAR! HE WAS IN A PAPER BAG. WE WERE PLAYING HIDE & SMACK.
OHHH, IN A BAG? ON THE FLOOR? YEAH, I THREW THAT AWAY.
I DIDN'T HEAR YOU JUST SAY THAT.
I SAID I THREW IT AWAY!
darb

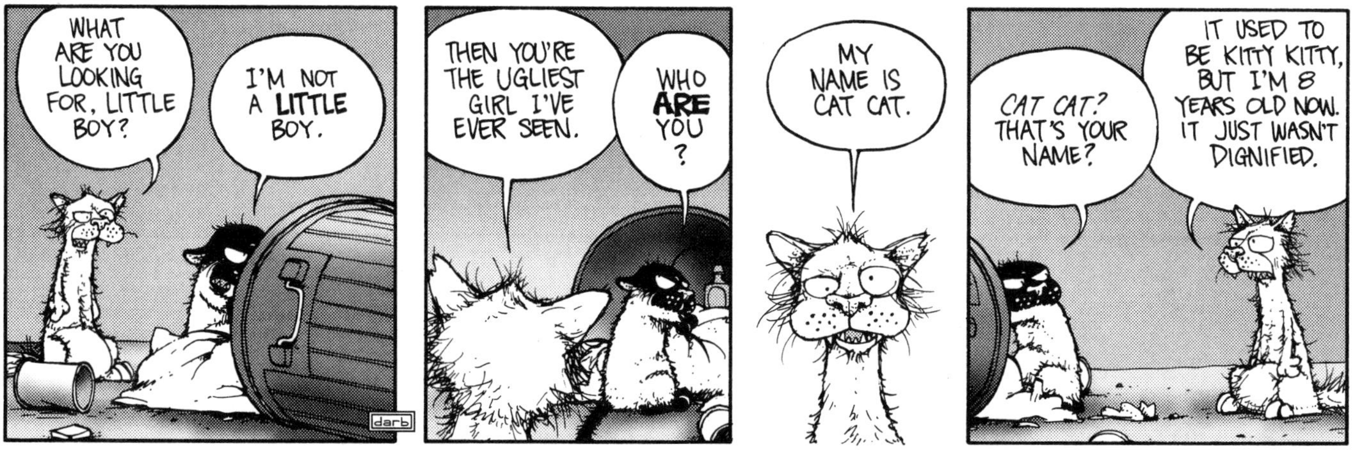
WHAT ARE YOU LOOKING FOR, LITTLE BOY?
I'M NOT A LITTLE BOY.
darb
THEN YOU'RE THE UGLIEST GIRL I'VE EVER SEEN.
WHO ARE YOU ?
MY NAME IS CAT CAT.
CAT CAT? THAT'S YOUR NAME?
IT USED TO BE KITTY KITTY, BUT I'M 8 YEARS OLD NOW. IT JUST WASN'T DIGNIFIED.

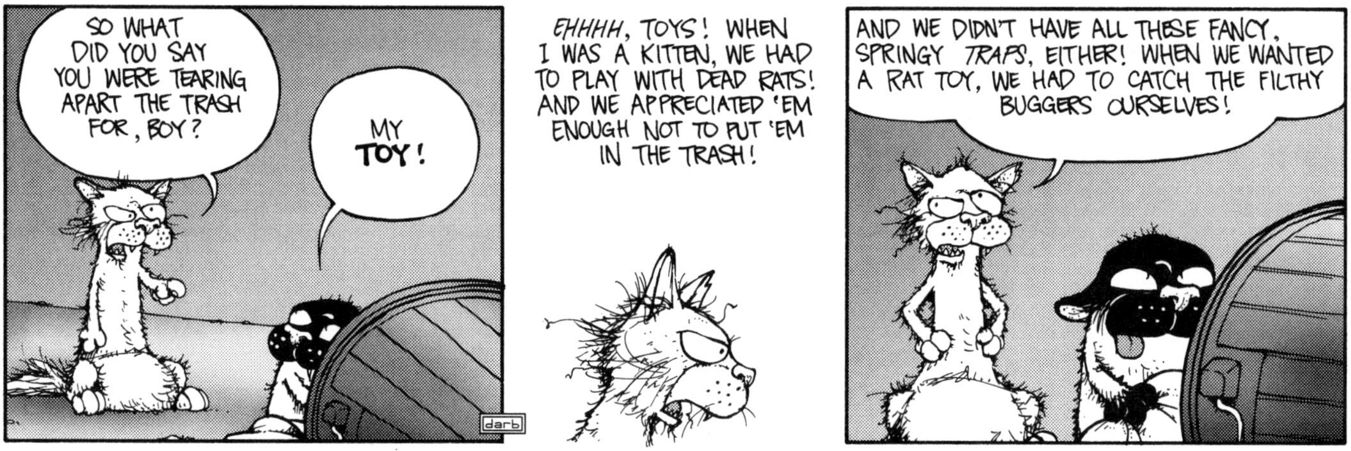
SO WHAT DID YOU SAY YOU WERE TEARING APART THE TRASH FOR, BOY?
MY TOY!
darb
EHHHH, TOYS! WHEN I WAS A KITTEN, WE HAD TO PLAY WITH DEAD RATS! AND WE APPRECIATED 'EM ENOUGH NOT TO PUT 'EM IN THE TRASH!
AND WE DIDN'T HAVE ALL THESE FANCY, SPRINGY TRAPS, EITHER! WHEN WE WANTED A RAT TOY, WE HAD TO CATCH THE FILTHY BUGGERS OURSELVES!

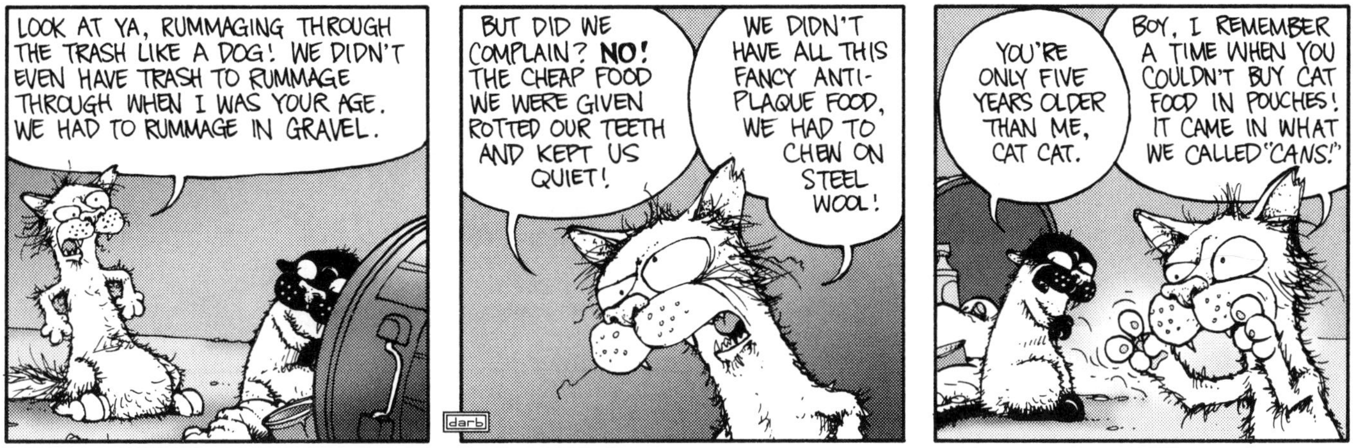
LOOK AT YA, RUMMAGING THROUGH THE TRASH LIKE A DOG! WE DIDN'T EVEN HAVE TRASH TO RUMMAGE THROUGH WHEN I WAS YOUR AGE. WE HAD TO RUMMAGE IN GRAVEL.
BUT DID WE COMPLAIN? NO! THE CHEAP FOOD WE WERE GIVEN ROTTED OUR TEETH AND KEPT US QUIET!
WE DIDN'T HAVE ALL THIS FANCY ANTI-PLAQUE FOOD, WE HAD TO CHEW ON STEEL WOOL!
darb
YOU'RE ONLY FIVE YEARS OLDER THAN ME, CAT CAT.
BOY, I REMEMBER A TIME WHEN YOU COULDN'T BUY CAT FOOD IN POUCHES! IT CAME IN WHAT WE CALLED "CANS!"

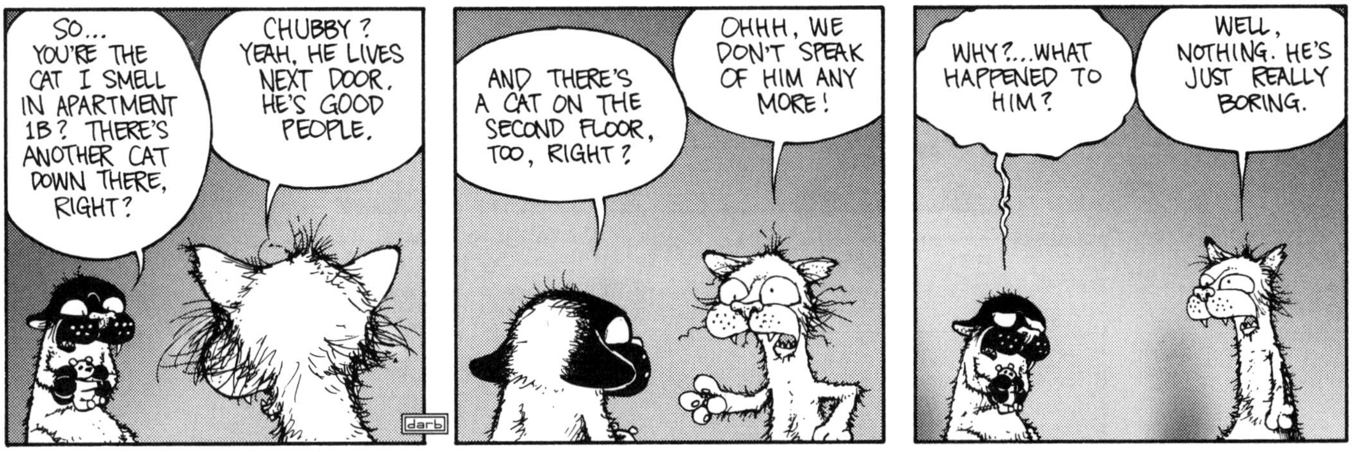
SO... YOU'RE THE CAT I SMELL IN APARTMENT 1B? THERE'S ANOTHER CAT DOWN THERE, RIGHT?
CHUBBY? YEAH, HE LIVES NEXT DOOR. HE'S GOOD PEOPLE.
darb
AND THERE'S A CAT ON THE SECOND FLOOR, TOO, RIGHT?
OHHH, WE DON'T SPEAK OF HIM ANY MORE!
WHY?...WHAT HAPPENED TO HIM?
WELL, NOTHING. HE'S JUST REALLY BORING.

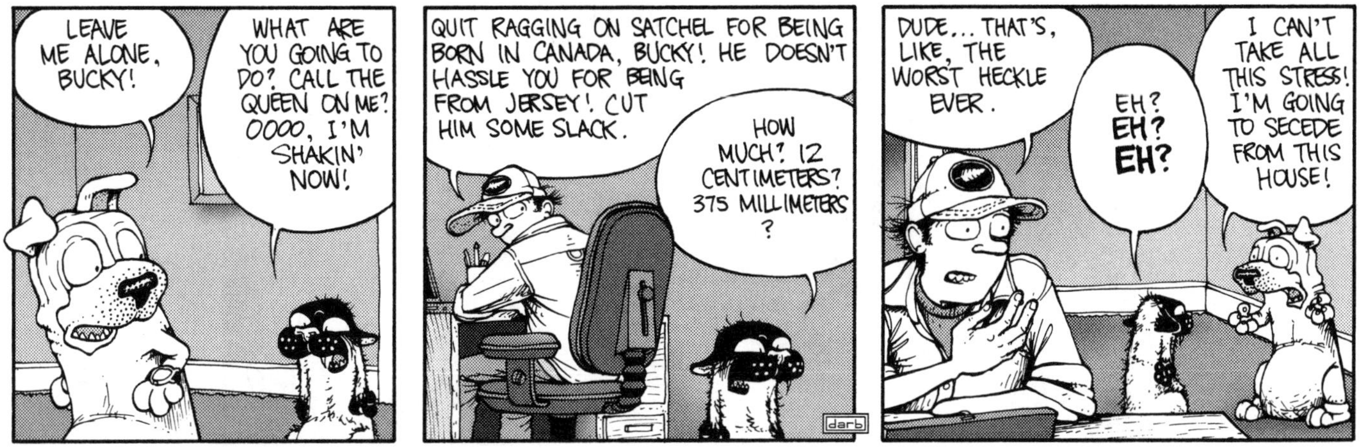
LEAVE ME ALONE, BUCKY!
WHAT ARE YOU GOING TO DO? CALL THE QUEEN ON ME? OOOO, I'M SHAKIN' NOW!
QUIT RAGGING ON SATCHEL FOR BEING BORN IN CANADA, BUCKY! HE DOESN'T HASSLE YOU FOR BEING FROM JERSEY! CUT HIM SOME SLACK.
HOW MUCH? 12 CENTIMETERS? 375 MILLIMETERS?
darb
DUDE... THAT'S, LIKE, THE WORST HECKLE EVER.
EH? EH? EH?
I CAN'T TAKE ALL THIS STRESS! I'M GOING TO SECEDE FROM THIS HOUSE!

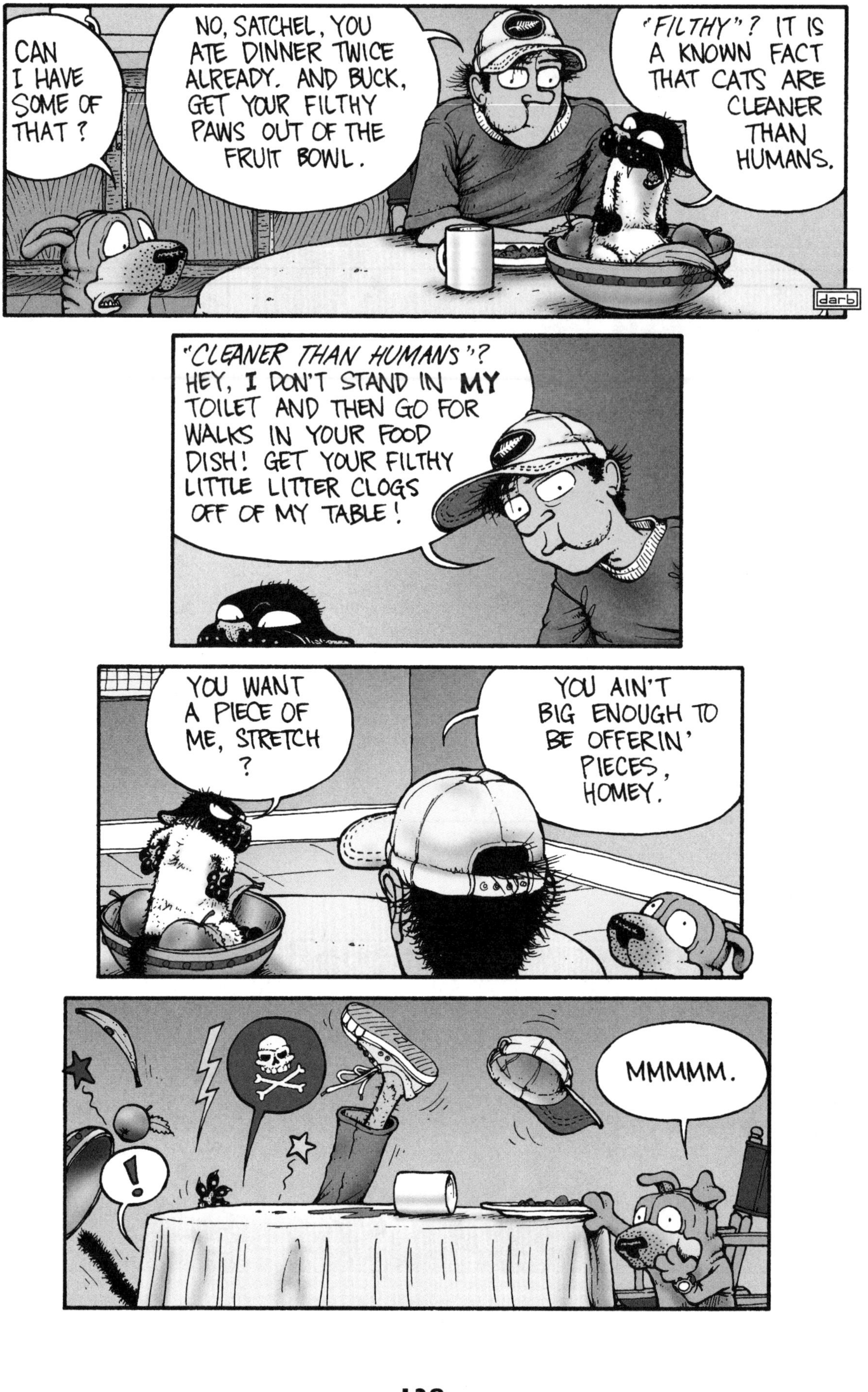
CAN I HAVE SOME OF THAT?
NO, SATCHEL, YOU ATE DINNER TWICE ALREADY. AND BUCK, GET YOUR FILTHY PAWS OUT OF THE FRUIT BOWL.
"FILTHY"? IT IS A KNOWN FACT THAT CATS ARE CLEANER THAN HUMANS.
darb
"CLEANER THAN HUMANS"? HEY, I DON'T STAND IN MY TOILET AND THEN GO FOR WALKS IN YOUR FOOD DISH! GET YOUR FILTHY LITTLE LITTER CLOGS OFF OF MY TABLE!
YOU WANT A PIECE OF ME, STRETCH?
YOU AIN'T BIG ENOUGH TO BE OFFERIN' PIECES, HOMEY.
!
MMMMM.

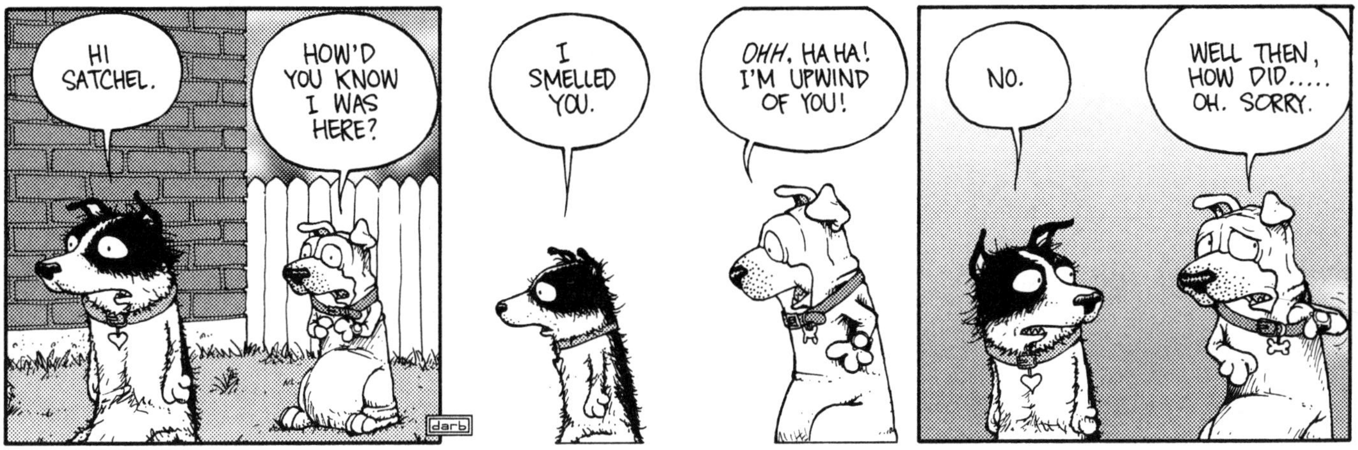
HI SATCHEL.
HOW'D YOU KNOW I WAS HERE?
I SMELLED YOU.
OHH. HA HA! I'M UPWIND OF YOU!
NO.
WELL THEN, HOW DID..... OH. SORRY.
darb

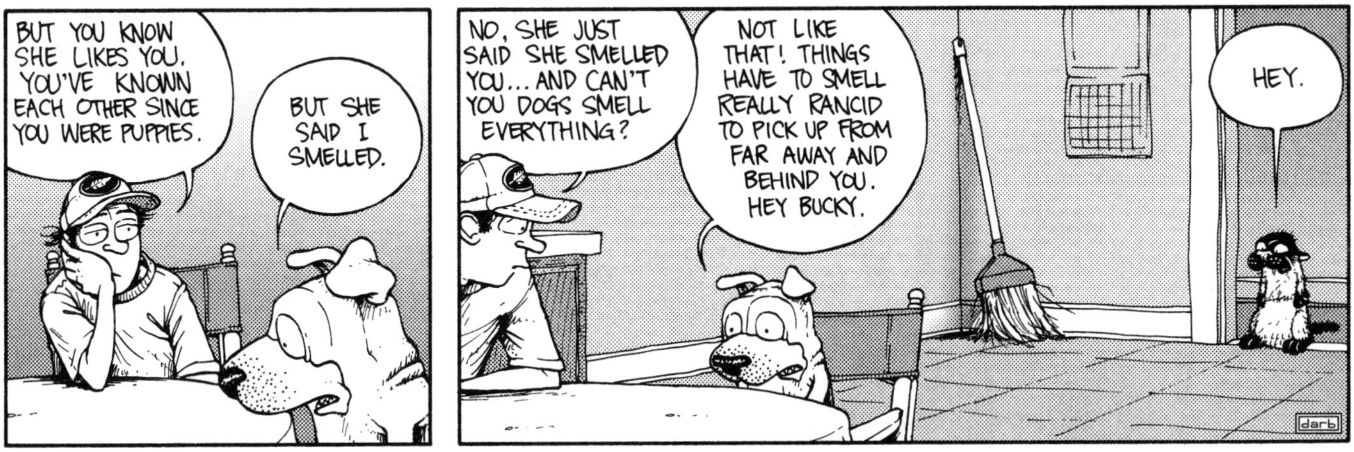
BUT YOU KNOW SHE LIKES YOU. YOU'VE KNOWN EACH OTHER SINCE YOU WERE PUPPIES.
BUT SHE SAID I SMELLED.
NO, SHE JUST SAID SHE SMELLED YOU... AND CAN'T YOU DOGS SMELL EVERYTHING?
NOT LIKE THAT! THINGS HAVE TO SMELL REALLY RANCID TO PICK UP FROM FAR AWAY AND BEHIND YOU. HEY BUCKY.
HEY.
darb

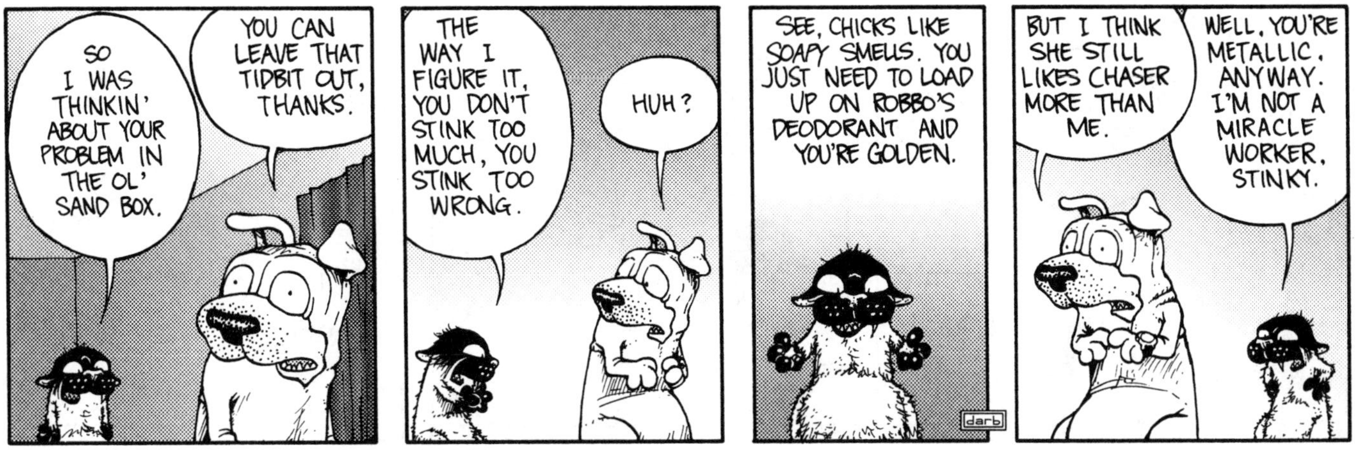
SO I WAS THINKIN' ABOUT YOUR PROBLEM IN THE OL' SAND BOX.
YOU CAN LEAVE THAT TIDBIT OUT, THANKS.
THE WAY I FIGURE IT, YOU DON'T STINK TOO MUCH, YOU STINK TOO WRONG.
HUH?
SEE, CHICKS LIKE SOAPY SMELLS. YOU JUST NEED TO LOAD UP ON ROBBO'S DEODORANT AND YOU'RE GOLDEN.
darb
BUT I THINK SHE STILL LIKES CHASER MORE THAN ME.
WELL, YOU'RE METALLIC. ANYWAY. I'M NOT A MIRACLE WORKER. STINKY.

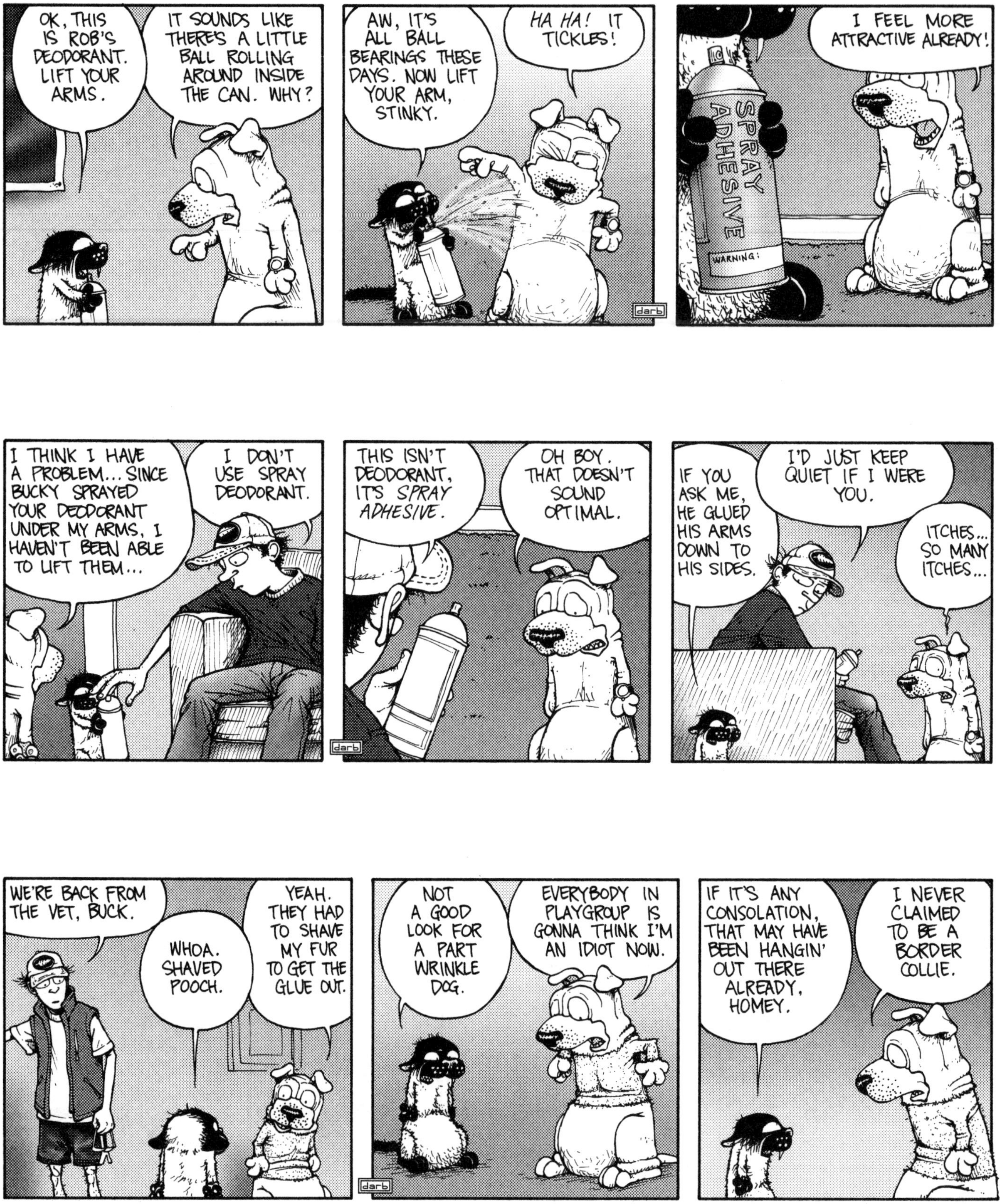
OK, THIS IS ROB'S DEODORANT. LIFT YOUR ARMS.
IT SOUNDS LIKE THERE'S A LITTLE BALL ROLLING AROUND INSIDE THE CAN. WHY?
AW, IT'S ALL BALL BEARINGS THESE DAYS. NOW LIFT YOUR ARM, STINKY.
HA HA! IT TICKLES!
darb
I FEEL MORE ATTRACTIVE ALREADY!
SPRAY ADHESIVE
WARNING:
I THINK I HAVE A PROBLEM... SINCE BUCKY SPRAYED YOUR DEODORANT UNDER MY ARMS, I HAVEN'T BEEN ABLE TO LIFT THEM...
I DON'T USE SPRAY DEODORANT.
darb
THIS ISN'T DEODORANT, IT'S *SPRAY ADHESIVE*.
OH BOY. THAT DOESN'T SOUND OPTIMAL.
IF YOU ASK ME, HE GLUED HIS ARMS DOWN TO HIS SIDES.
I'D JUST KEEP QUIET IF I WERE YOU.
ITCHES... SO MANY ITCHES...
WE'RE BACK FROM THE VET, BUCK.
WHOA. SHAVED POOCH.
YEAH. THEY HAD TO SHAVE MY FUR TO GET THE GLUE OUT.
darb
NOT A GOOD LOOK FOR A PART WRINKLE DOG.
EVERYBODY IN PLAYGROUP IS GONNA THINK I'M AN IDIOT NOW.
IF IT'S ANY CONSOLATION, THAT MAY HAVE BEEN HANGIN' OUT THERE ALREADY, HOMEY.
I NEVER CLAIMED TO BE A BORDER COLLIE.

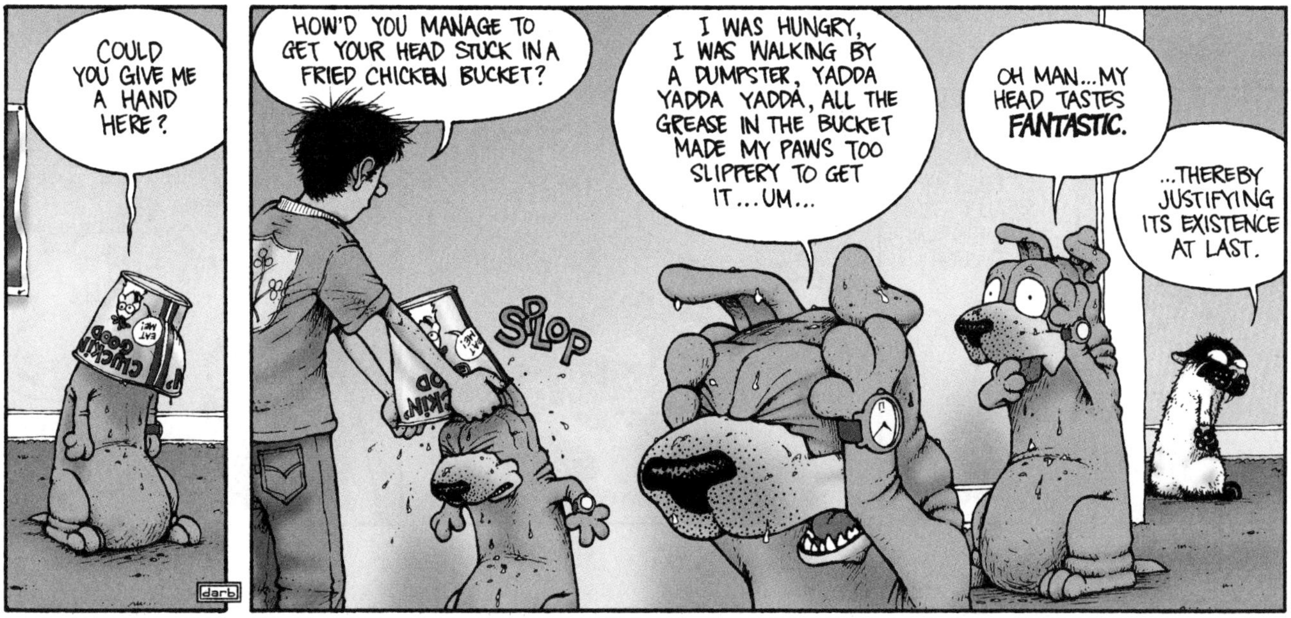
COULD YOU GIVE ME A HAND HERE?
HOW'D YOU MANAGE TO GET YOUR HEAD STUCK IN A FRIED CHICKEN BUCKET?
SPLOP
I WAS HUNGRY, I WAS WALKING BY A DUMPSTER, YADDA YADDA, ALL THE GREASE IN THE BUCKET MADE MY PAWS TOO SLIPPERY TO GET IT... UM...
OH MAN... MY HEAD TASTES **FANTASTIC.**
...THEREBY JUSTIFYING ITS EXISTENCE AT LAST.
darb

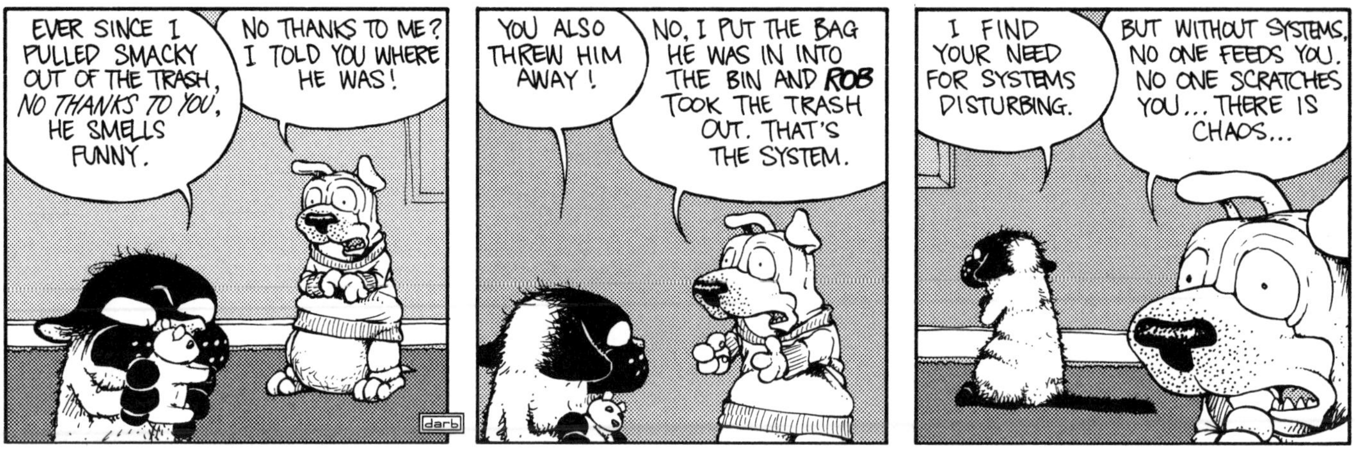
EVER SINCE I PULLED SMACKY OUT OF THE TRASH, *NO THANKS TO YOU*, HE SMELLS FUNNY.
NO THANKS TO ME? I TOLD YOU WHERE HE WAS!
YOU ALSO THREW HIM AWAY!
NO, I PUT THE BAG HE WAS IN INTO THE BIN AND **ROB** TOOK THE TRASH OUT. THAT'S THE SYSTEM.
I FIND YOUR NEED FOR SYSTEMS DISTURBING.
BUT WITHOUT SYSTEMS, NO ONE FEEDS YOU. NO ONE SCRATCHES YOU... THERE IS CHAOS...

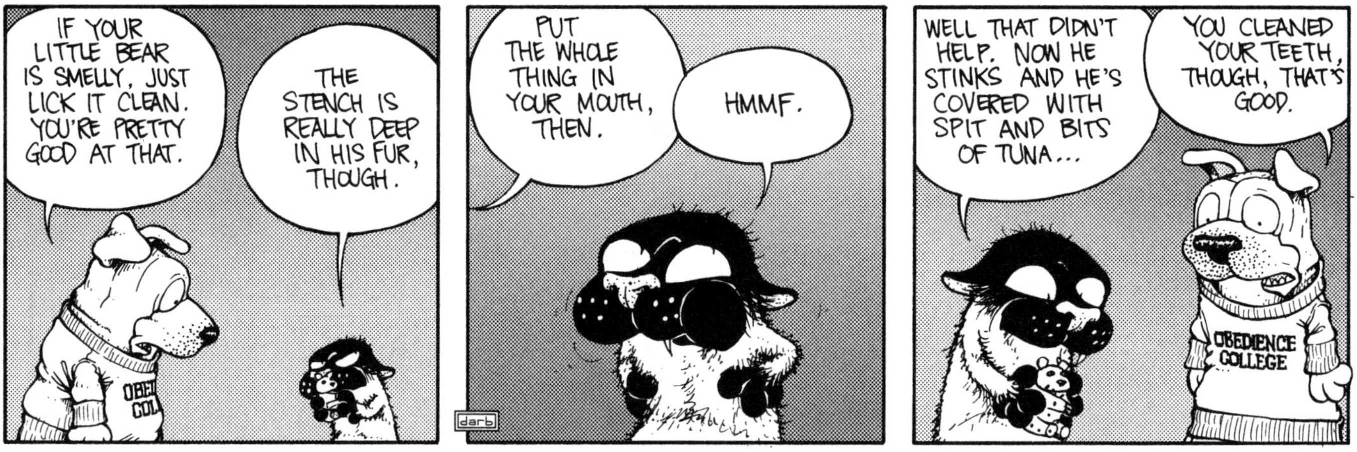
IF YOUR LITTLE BEAR IS SMELLY, JUST LICK IT CLEAN. YOU'RE PRETTY GOOD AT THAT.
THE STENCH IS REALLY DEEP IN HIS FUR, THOUGH.
PUT THE WHOLE THING IN YOUR MOUTH, THEN.
HMMF.
WELL THAT DIDN'T HELP. NOW HE STINKS AND HE'S COVERED WITH SPIT AND BITS OF TUNA...
YOU CLEANED YOUR TEETH, THOUGH, THAT'S GOOD.
OBEDIENCE COLLEGE

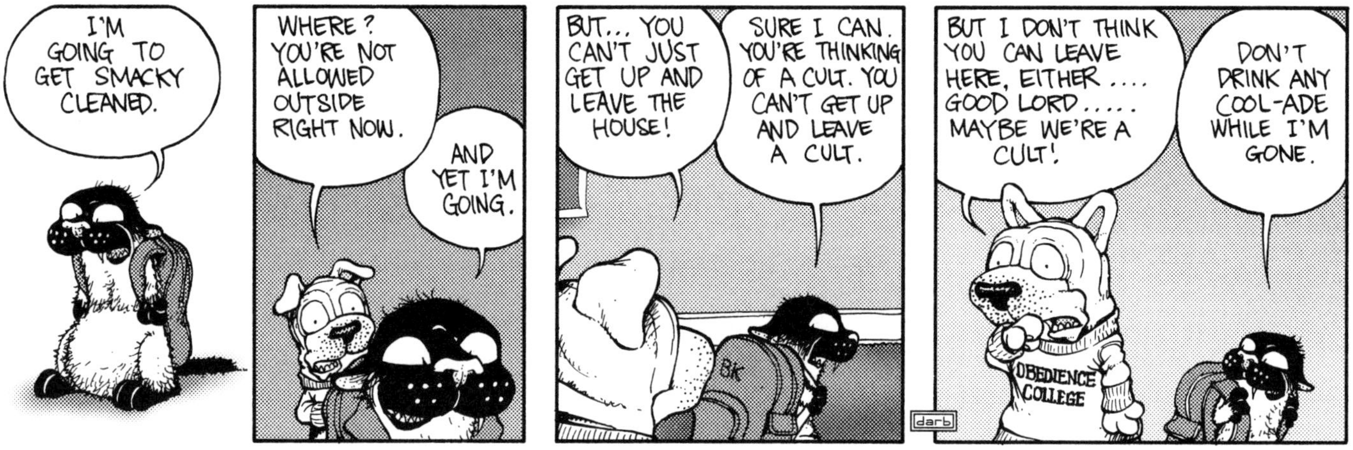
I'M GOING TO GET SMACKY CLEANED.
WHERE? YOU'RE NOT ALLOWED OUTSIDE RIGHT NOW.
AND YET I'M GOING.
BUT... YOU CAN'T JUST GET UP AND LEAVE THE HOUSE!
SURE I CAN. YOU'RE THINKING OF A CULT. YOU CAN'T GET UP AND LEAVE A CULT.
BUT I DON'T THINK YOU CAN LEAVE HERE, EITHER.... GOOD LORD..... MAYBE WE'RE A CULT!
DON'T DRINK ANY COOL-ADE WHILE I'M GONE.
OBEDIENCE COLLEGE

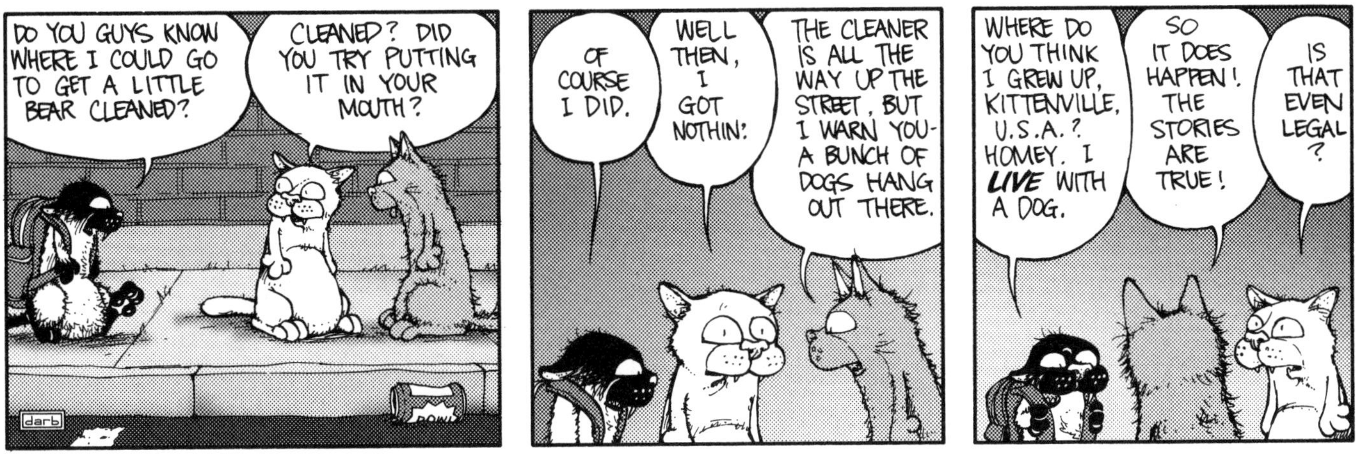
DO YOU GUYS KNOW WHERE I COULD GO TO GET A LITTLE BEAR CLEANED?
CLEANED? DID YOU TRY PUTTING IT IN YOUR MOUTH?
darb
OF COURSE I DID.
WELL THEN, I GOT NOTHIN'.
THE CLEANER IS ALL THE WAY UP THE STREET, BUT I WARN YOU- A BUNCH OF DOGS HANG OUT THERE.
WHERE DO YOU THINK I GREW UP, KITTENVILLE, U.S.A.? HOMEY. I LIVE WITH A DOG.
SO IT DOES HAPPEN! THE STORIES ARE TRUE!
IS THAT EVEN LEGAL?

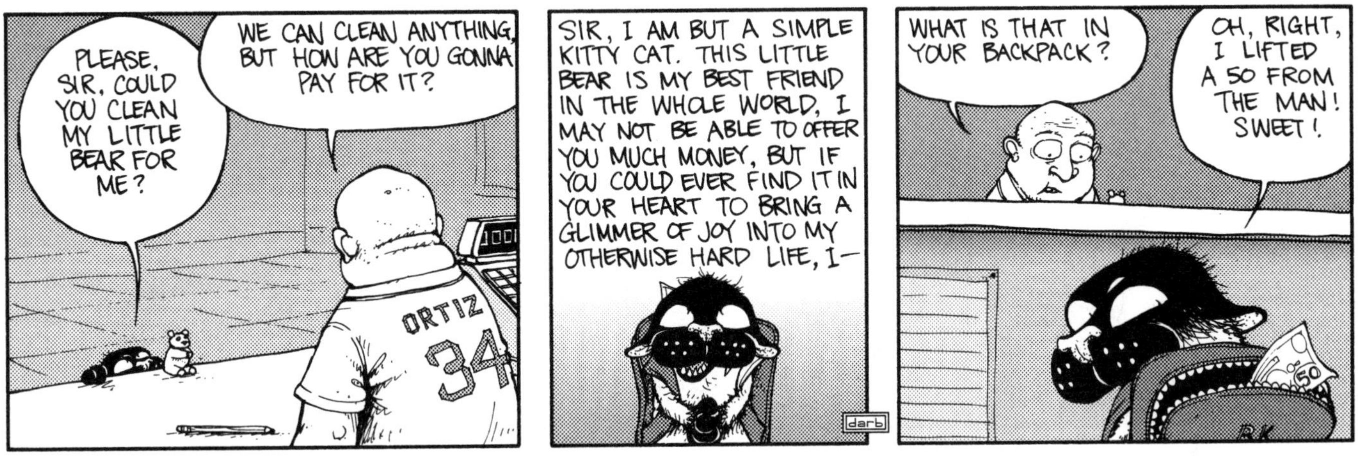
PLEASE, SIR, COULD YOU CLEAN MY LITTLE BEAR FOR ME?
WE CAN CLEAN ANYTHING, BUT HOW ARE YOU GONNA PAY FOR IT?
ORTIZ
34
SIR, I AM BUT A SIMPLE KITTY CAT. THIS LITTLE BEAR IS MY BEST FRIEND IN THE WHOLE WORLD, I MAY NOT BE ABLE TO OFFER YOU MUCH MONEY, BUT IF YOU COULD EVER FIND IT IN YOUR HEART TO BRING A GLIMMER OF JOY INTO MY OTHERWISE HARD LIFE, I—
darb
WHAT IS THAT IN YOUR BACKPACK?
OH, RIGHT, I LIFTED A 50 FROM THE MAN! SWEET!
50

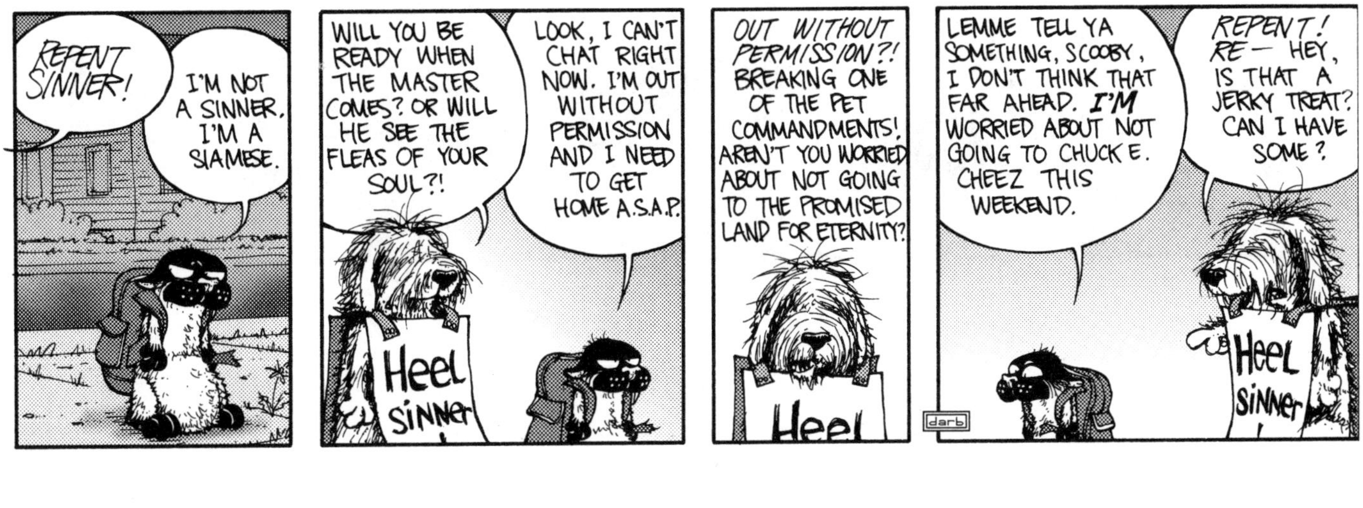
REPENT SINNER!
I'M NOT A SINNER. I'M A SIAMESE.
WILL YOU BE READY WHEN THE MASTER COMES? OR WILL HE SEE THE FLEAS OF YOUR SOUL?!
LOOK, I CAN'T CHAT RIGHT NOW. I'M OUT WITHOUT PERMISSION AND I NEED TO GET HOME A.S.A.P.
Heel sinner
OUT WITHOUT PERMISSION?! BREAKING ONE OF THE PET COMMANDMENTS! AREN'T YOU WORRIED ABOUT NOT GOING TO THE PROMISED LAND FOR ETERNITY?
Heel
darb
LEMME TELL YA SOMETHING, SCOOBY, I DON'T THINK THAT FAR AHEAD. I'M WORRIED ABOUT NOT GOING TO CHUCK E. CHEEZ THIS WEEKEND.
REPENT! RE— HEY, IS THAT A JERKY TREAT? CAN I HAVE SOME?
Heel sinner

I'M GONNA GO MESS WITH THE SCOUT AT THE FRONT DOOR!
DON'T, BUCKY!
WOULD YOU LIKE TO BUY SOME COCONUT OR PEANUT BUTTER COOKIES? JUST $4 A BOX!
YOU GOT RAT?
darb
UM.... WHAT?
I ONLY EAT DEAD RAT COOKIES.
SO IF I PUT A DEAD RAT IN A BOX, YOU'LL BUY IT?
OH, RIGHT. ***THAT***'LL HAPPEN. SURE SNOWFLAKE, GO NUTS. I'LL BUY 'EM ALL.
LATER...
I NEED 400 DOLLARS.

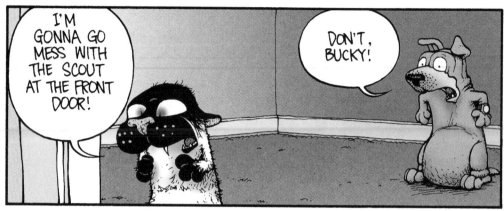

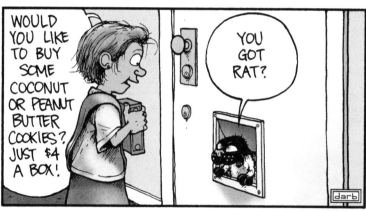

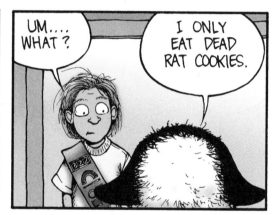

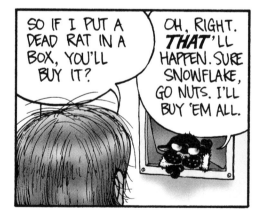

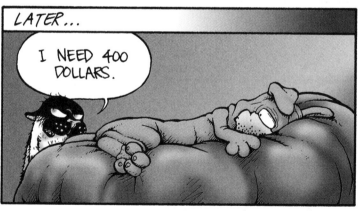

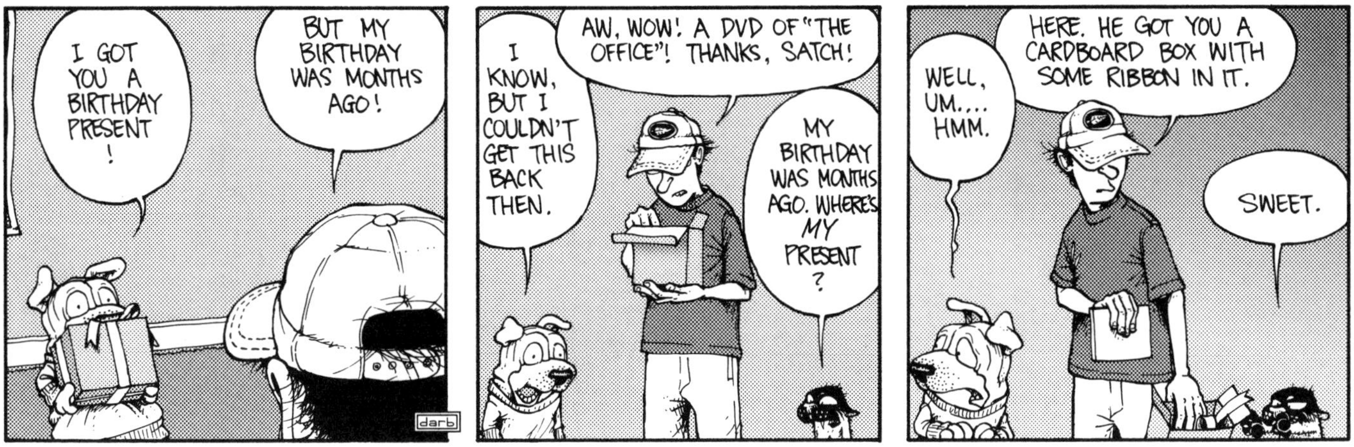
I GOT YOU A BIRTHDAY PRESENT !
BUT MY BIRTHDAY WAS MONTHS AGO!
darb
I KNOW, BUT I COULDN'T GET THIS BACK THEN.
AW, WOW! A DVD OF "THE OFFICE"! THANKS, SATCH!
MY BIRTHDAY WAS MONTHS AGO. WHERE'S *MY* PRESENT ?
WELL, UM.... HMM.
HERE. HE GOT YOU A CARDBOARD BOX WITH SOME RIBBON IN IT.
SWEET.

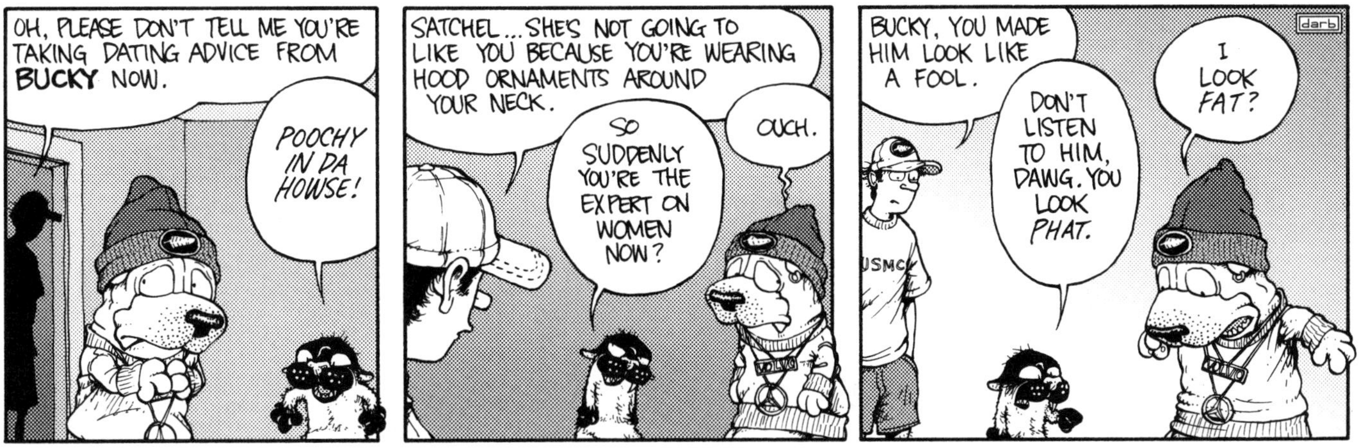
OH, PLEASE DON'T TELL ME YOU'RE TAKING DATING ADVICE FROM **BUCKY** NOW.
POOCHY IN DA HOWSE!
SATCHEL... SHE'S NOT GOING TO LIKE YOU BECAUSE YOU'RE WEARING HOOD ORNAMENTS AROUND YOUR NECK.
SO SUDDENLY YOU'RE THE EXPERT ON WOMEN NOW?
OUCH.
darb
BUCKY, YOU MADE HIM LOOK LIKE A FOOL.
DON'T LISTEN TO HIM, DAWG. YOU LOOK *PHAT.*
I LOOK *FAT?*

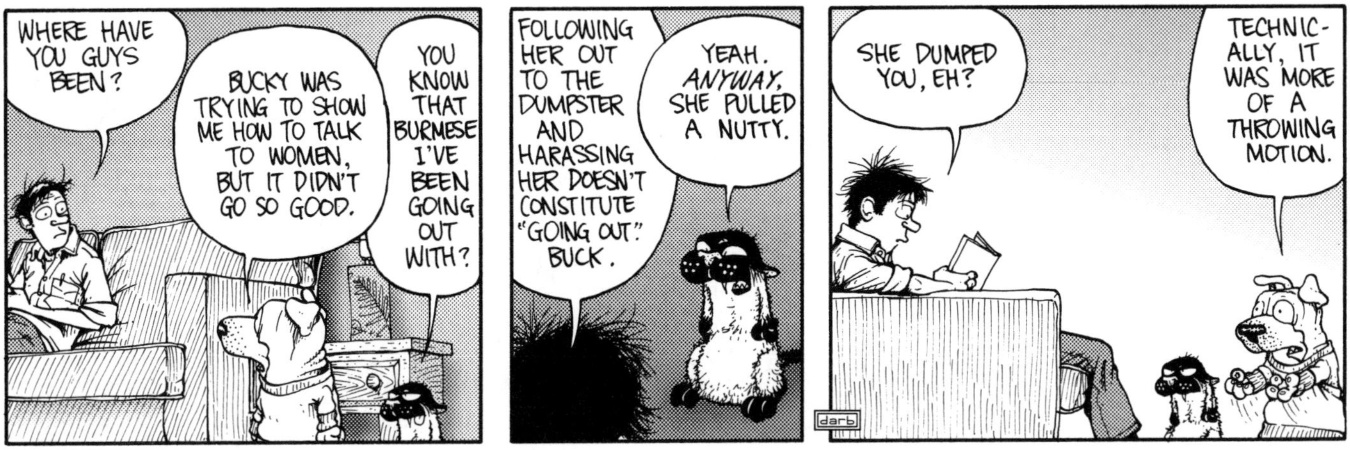
WHERE HAVE YOU GUYS BEEN?
BUCKY WAS TRYING TO SHOW ME HOW TO TALK TO WOMEN, BUT IT DIDN'T GO SO GOOD.
YOU KNOW THAT BURMESE I'VE BEEN GOING OUT WITH?
FOLLOWING HER OUT TO THE DUMPSTER AND HARASSING HER DOESN'T CONSTITUTE "GOING OUT." BUCK.
YEAH. *ANYWAY,* SHE PULLED A NUTTY.
darb
SHE DUMPED YOU, EH?
TECHNIC-ALLY, IT WAS MORE OF A THROWING MOTION.

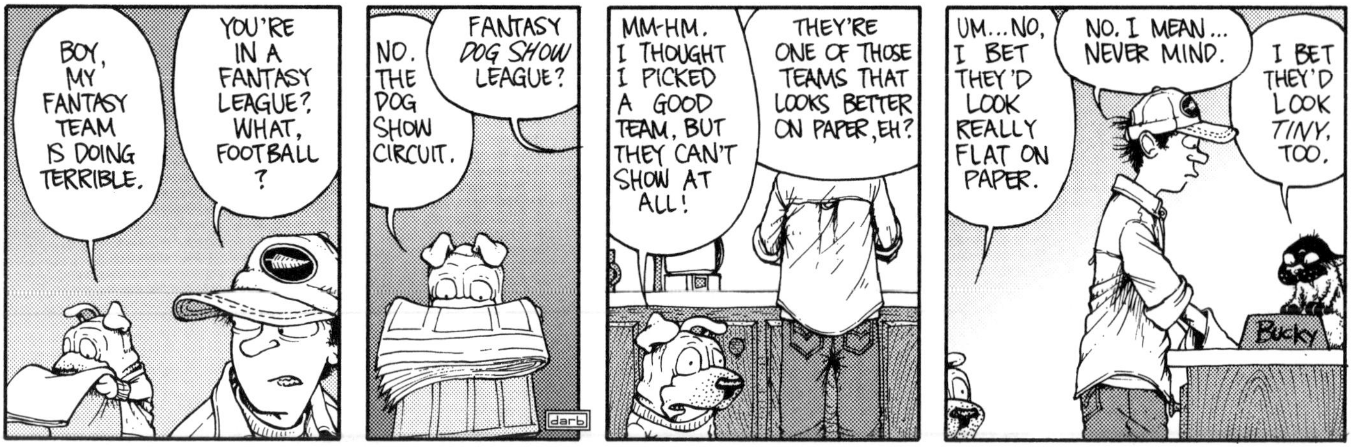

BOY, MY FANTASY TEAM IS DOING TERRIBLE.
YOU'RE IN A FANTASY LEAGUE? WHAT, FOOTBALL?
FANTASY *DOG SHOW* LEAGUE?
NO. THE DOG SHOW CIRCUIT.
MM-HM. I THOUGHT I PICKED A GOOD TEAM, BUT THEY CAN'T SHOW AT ALL!
THEY'RE ONE OF THOSE TEAMS THAT LOOKS BETTER ON PAPER, EH?
UM...NO, I BET THEY'D LOOK REALLY FLAT ON PAPER.
NO. I MEAN... NEVER MIND.
I BET THEY'D LOOK *TINY*, TOO.
Bucky
darb

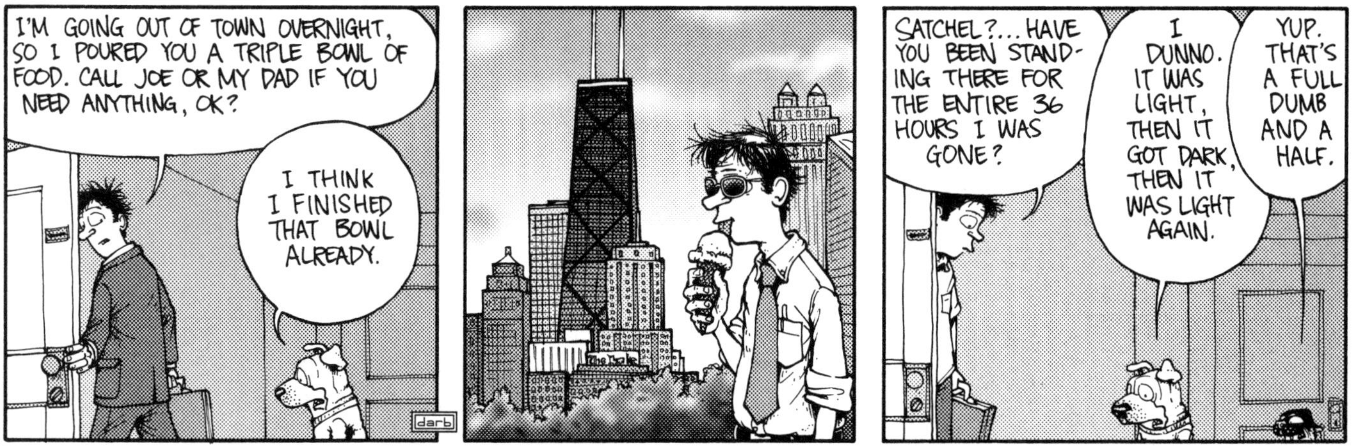

I'M GOING OUT OF TOWN OVERNIGHT, SO I POURED YOU A TRIPLE BOWL OF FOOD. CALL JOE OR MY DAD IF YOU NEED ANYTHING, OK?
I THINK I FINISHED THAT BOWL ALREADY.
darb
SATCHEL?... HAVE YOU BEEN STANDING THERE FOR THE ENTIRE 36 HOURS I WAS GONE?
I DUNNO. IT WAS LIGHT, THEN IT GOT DARK, THEN IT WAS LIGHT AGAIN.
YUP. THAT'S A FULL DUMB AND A HALF.

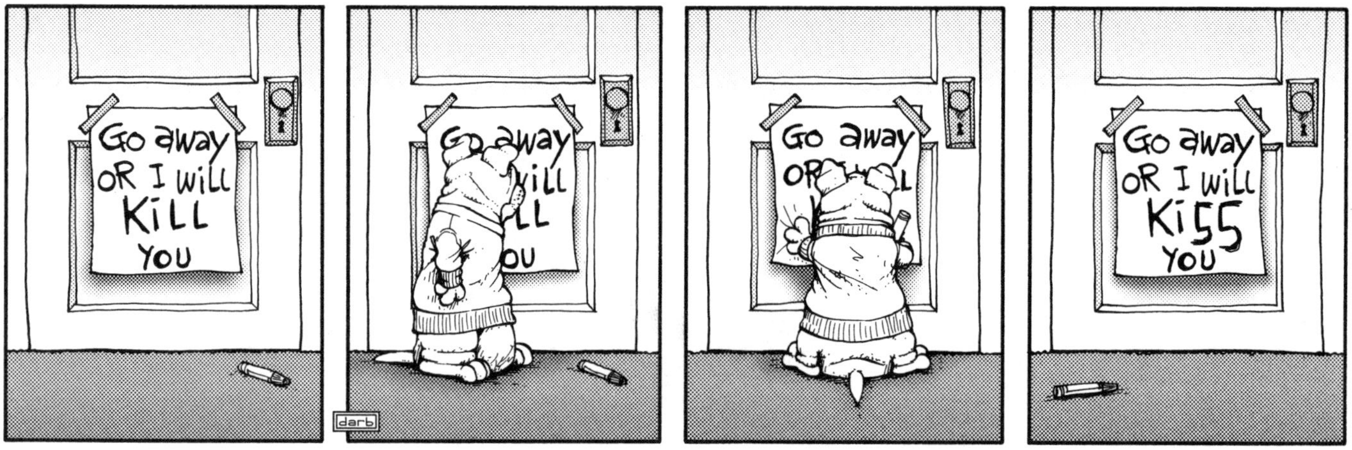

Go away OR I will KiLL YOU
darb
Go away OR I will Ki55 YOU

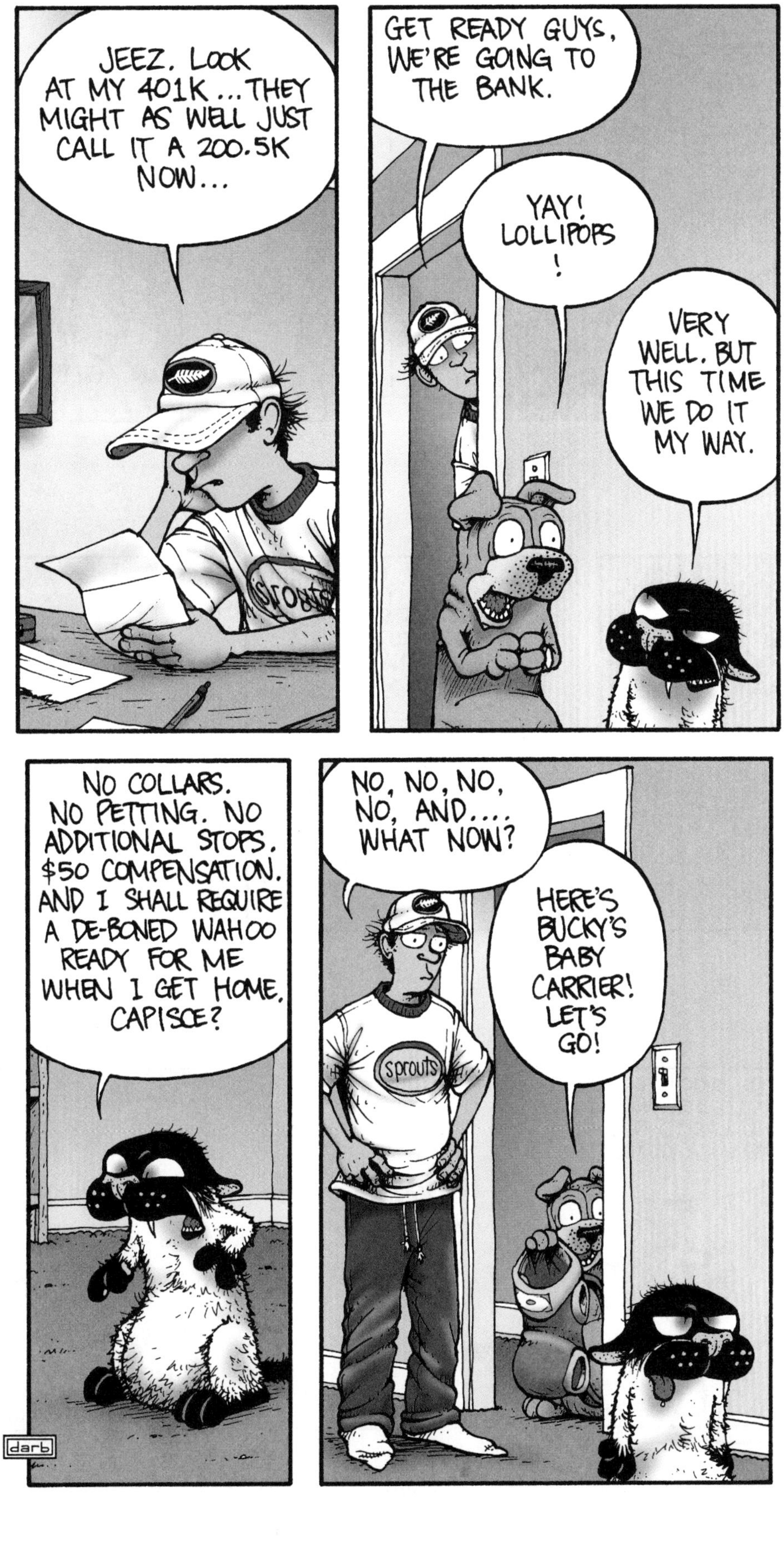
JEEZ. LOOK AT MY 401K...THEY MIGHT AS WELL JUST CALL IT A 200.5K NOW...
GET READY GUYS, WE'RE GOING TO THE BANK.
YAY! LOLLIPOPS!
VERY WELL. BUT THIS TIME WE DO IT MY WAY.
NO COLLARS. NO PETTING. NO ADDITIONAL STOPS. $50 COMPENSATION. AND I SHALL REQUIRE A DE-BONED WAHOO READY FOR ME WHEN I GET HOME, CAPISCE?
NO, NO, NO, NO, AND.... WHAT NOW?
HERE'S BUCKY'S BABY CARRIER! LET'S GO!
darb

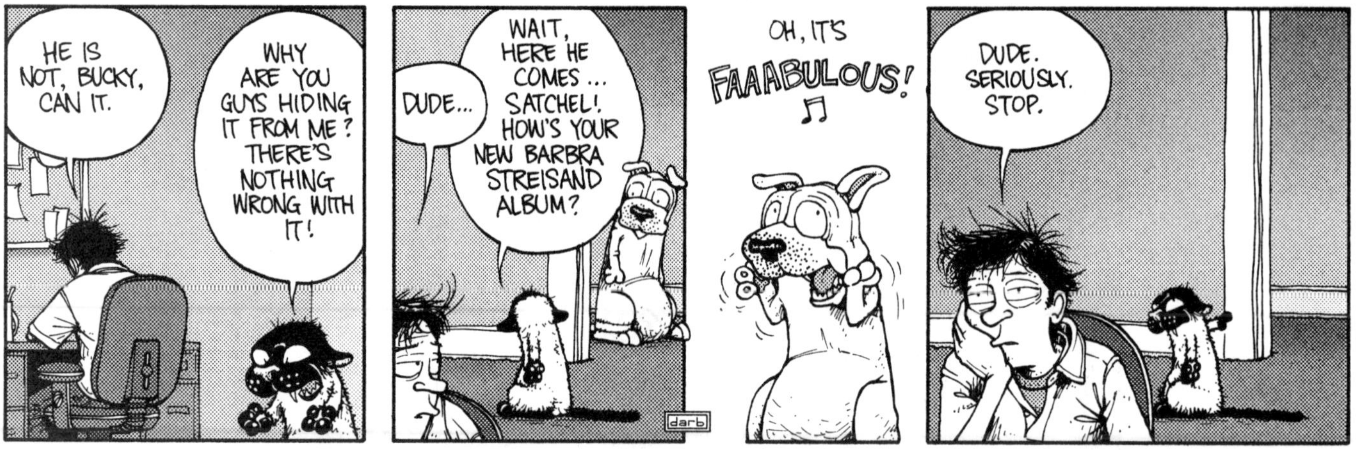
HE IS NOT, BUCKY, CAN IT.
WHY ARE YOU GUYS HIDING IT FROM ME? THERE'S NOTHING WRONG WITH IT!
DUDE...
WAIT, HERE HE COMES... SATCHEL! HOW'S YOUR NEW BARBRA STREISAND ALBUM?
OH, IT'S
FAAABULOUS!
DUDE. SERIOUSLY. STOP.

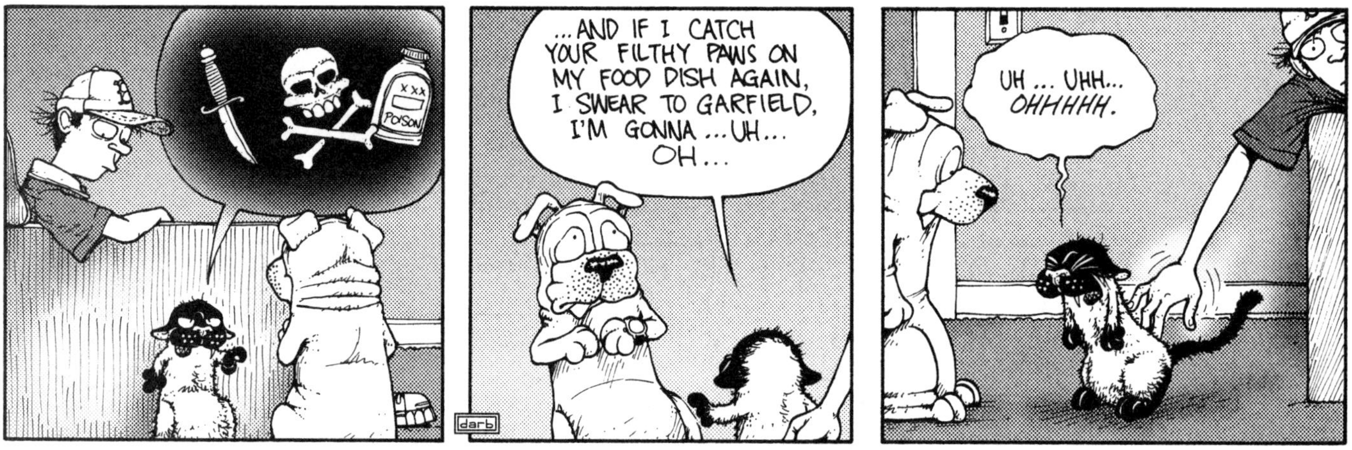
POISON
...AND IF I CATCH YOUR FILTHY PAWS ON MY FOOD DISH AGAIN, I SWEAR TO GARFIELD, I'M GONNA ...UH... OH...
UH ... UHH... OHHHHH.

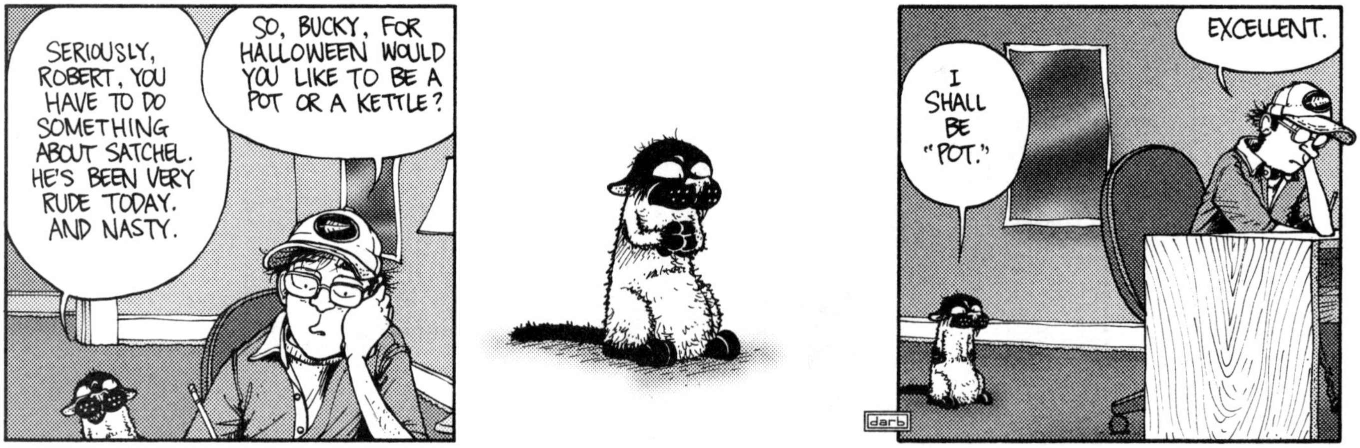
SERIOUSLY, ROBERT, YOU HAVE TO DO SOMETHING ABOUT SATCHEL. HE'S BEEN VERY RUDE TODAY. AND NASTY.
SO, BUCKY, FOR HALLOWEEN WOULD YOU LIKE TO BE A POT OR A KETTLE?
I SHALL BE "POT."
EXCELLENT.

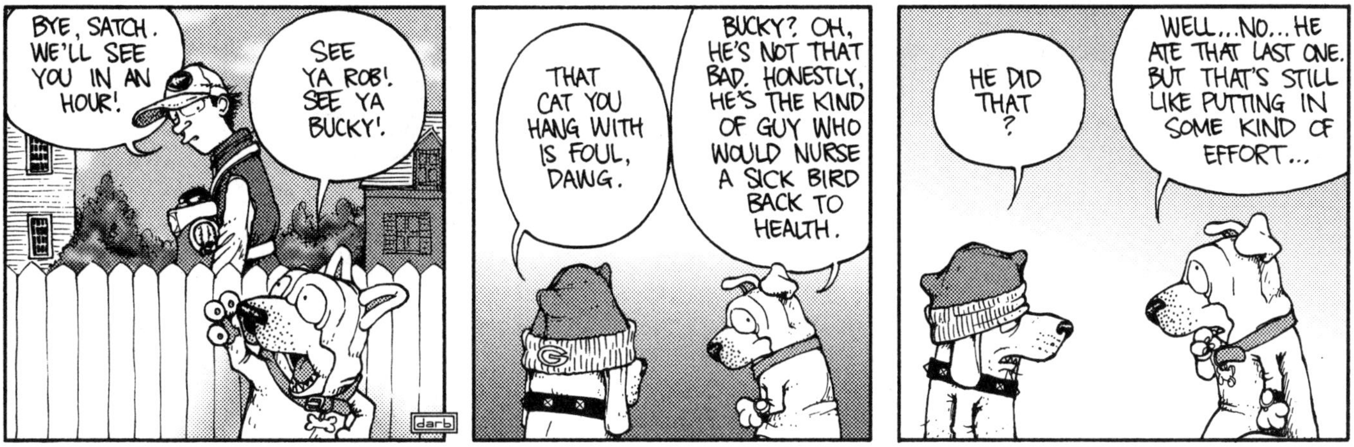
BYE, SATCH. WE'LL SEE YOU IN AN HOUR!
SEE YA ROB! SEE YA BUCKY!
THAT CAT YOU HANG WITH IS FOUL, DAWG.
BUCKY? OH, HE'S NOT THAT BAD. HONESTLY, HE'S THE KIND OF GUY WHO WOULD NURSE A SICK BIRD BACK TO HEALTH.
HE DID THAT?
WELL...NO...HE ATE THAT LAST ONE. BUT THAT'S STILL LIKE PUTTING IN SOME KIND OF EFFORT...
darb

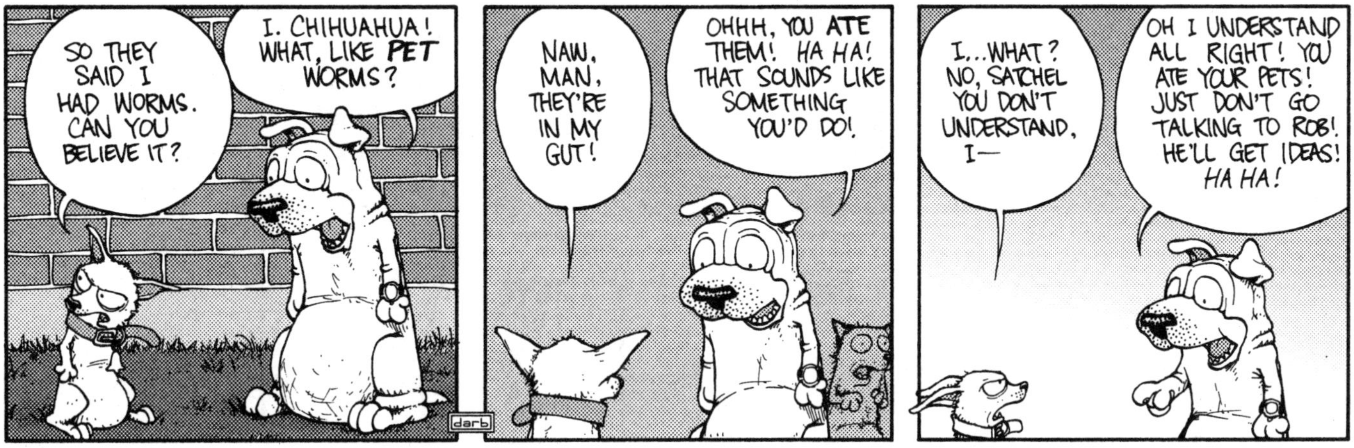
SO THEY SAID I HAD WORMS. CAN YOU BELIEVE IT?
I. CHIHUAHUA! WHAT, LIKE PET WORMS?
NAW, MAN, THEY'RE IN MY GUT!
OHHH, YOU ATE THEM! HA HA! THAT SOUNDS LIKE SOMETHING YOU'D DO!
I...WHAT? NO, SATCHEL YOU DON'T UNDERSTAND, I—
OH I UNDERSTAND ALL RIGHT! YOU ATE YOUR PETS! JUST DON'T GO TALKING TO ROB! HE'LL GET IDEAS! HA HA!
darb

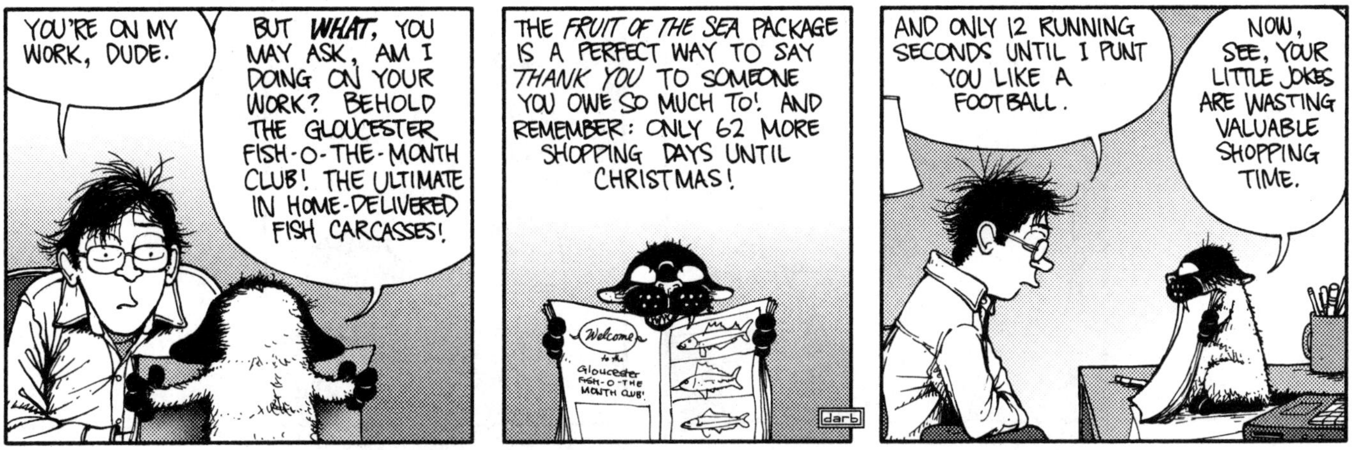
YOU'RE ON MY WORK, DUDE.
BUT WHAT, YOU MAY ASK, AM I DOING ON YOUR WORK? BEHOLD THE GLOUCESTER FISH-O-THE-MONTH CLUB! THE ULTIMATE IN HOME-DELIVERED FISH CARCASSES!
THE FRUIT OF THE SEA PACKAGE IS A PERFECT WAY TO SAY THANK YOU TO SOMEONE YOU OWE SO MUCH TO! AND REMEMBER: ONLY 62 MORE SHOPPING DAYS UNTIL CHRISTMAS!
AND ONLY 12 RUNNING SECONDS UNTIL I PUNT YOU LIKE A FOOTBALL.
NOW, SEE, YOUR LITTLE JOKES ARE WASTING VALUABLE SHOPPING TIME.
darb

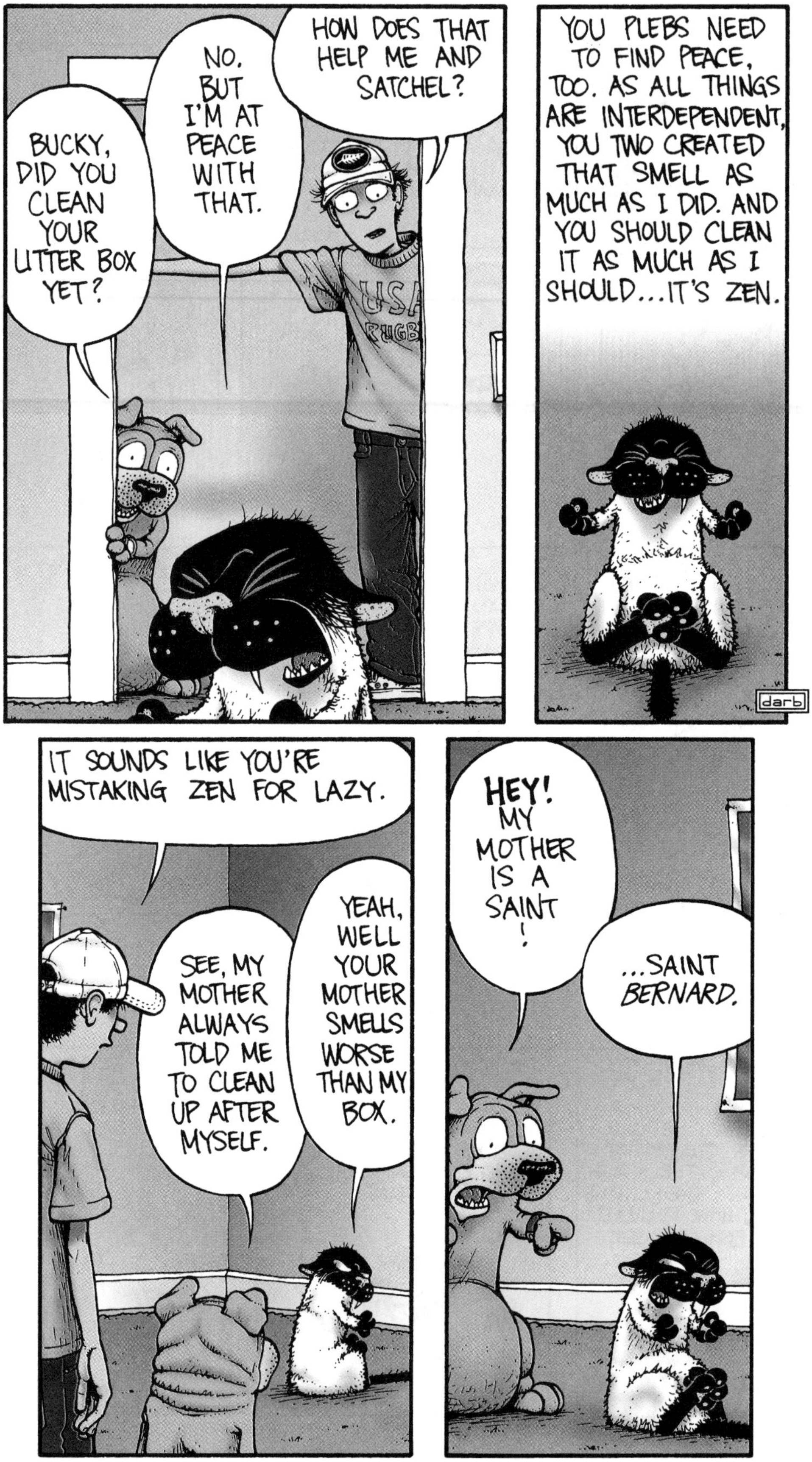

BUCKY, DID YOU CLEAN YOUR LITTER BOX YET?
NO. BUT I'M AT PEACE WITH THAT.
HOW DOES THAT HELP ME AND SATCHEL?
YOU PLEBS NEED TO FIND PEACE, TOO. AS ALL THINGS ARE INTERDEPENDENT, YOU TWO CREATED THAT SMELL AS MUCH AS I DID. AND YOU SHOULD CLEAN IT AS MUCH AS I SHOULD...IT'S ZEN.
darb
IT SOUNDS LIKE YOU'RE MISTAKING ZEN FOR LAZY.
SEE, MY MOTHER ALWAYS TOLD ME TO CLEAN UP AFTER MYSELF.
YEAH, WELL YOUR MOTHER SMELLS WORSE THAN MY BOX.
HEY! MY MOTHER IS A SAINT!
...SAINT *BERNARD*.

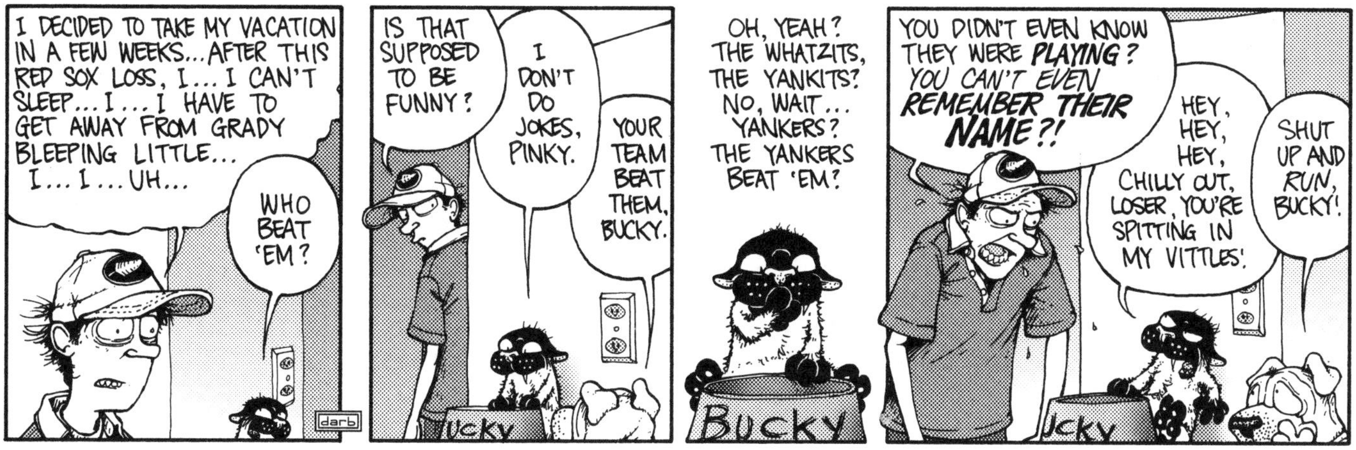
I DECIDED TO TAKE MY VACATION IN A FEW WEEKS... AFTER THIS RED SOX LOSS, I... I CAN'T SLEEP... I... I HAVE TO GET AWAY FROM GRADY BLEEPING LITTLE... I... I... UH...
WHO BEAT 'EM?
darb
IS THAT SUPPOSED TO BE FUNNY?
I DON'T DO JOKES, PINKY.
YOUR TEAM BEAT THEM, BUCKY.
OH, YEAH? THE WHATZITS, THE YANKITS? NO, WAIT... YANKERS? THE YANKERS BEAT 'EM?
BUCKY
YOU DIDN'T EVEN KNOW THEY WERE **PLAYING**? *YOU CAN'T EVEN* **REMEMBER THEIR NAME?!**
HEY, HEY, HEY, CHILLY OUT, LOSER, YOU'RE SPITTING IN MY VITTLES!
SHUT UP AND *RUN*, BUCKY!

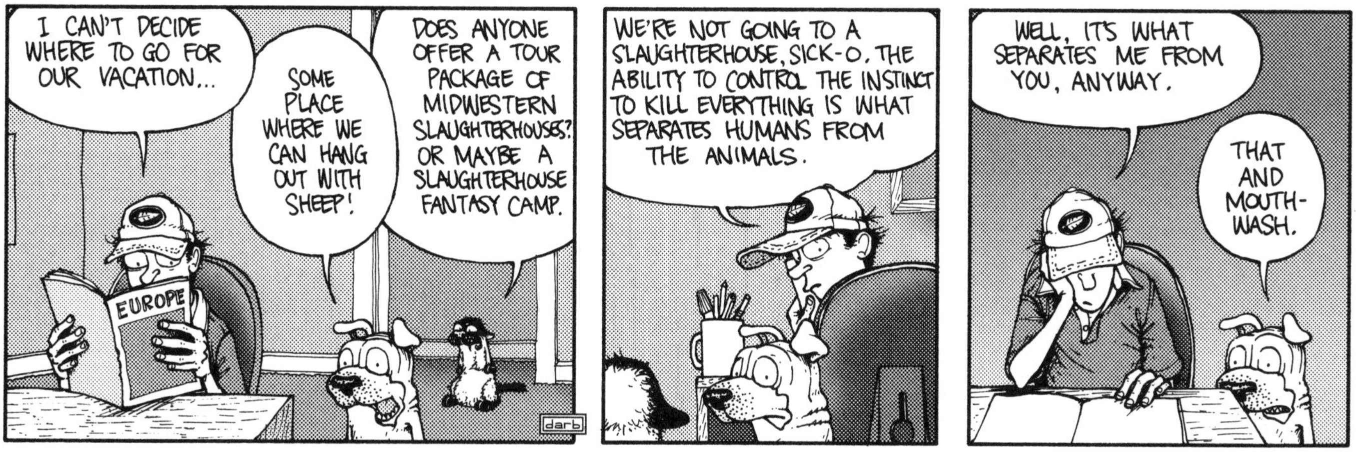
I CAN'T DECIDE WHERE TO GO FOR OUR VACATION...
SOME PLACE WHERE WE CAN HANG OUT WITH SHEEP!
EUROPE
DOES ANYONE OFFER A TOUR PACKAGE OF MIDWESTERN SLAUGHTERHOUSES? OR MAYBE A SLAUGHTERHOUSE FANTASY CAMP.
darb
WE'RE NOT GOING TO A SLAUGHTERHOUSE, SICK-O. THE ABILITY TO CONTROL THE INSTINCT TO KILL EVERYTHING IS WHAT SEPARATES HUMANS FROM THE ANIMALS.
WELL, IT'S WHAT SEPARATES ME FROM YOU, ANYWAY.
THAT AND MOUTH-WASH.

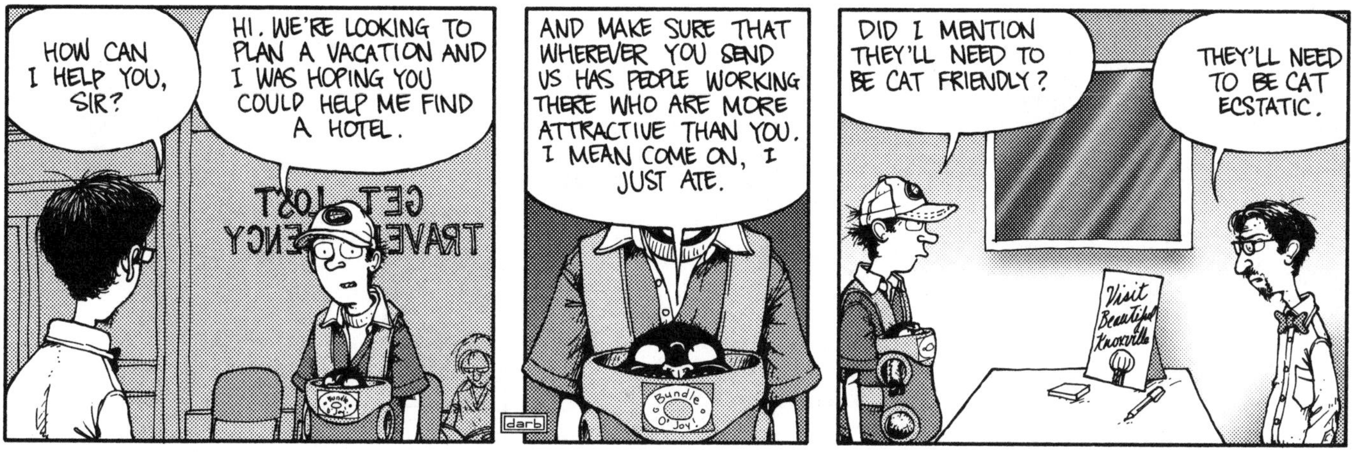
HOW CAN I HELP YOU, SIR?
HI. WE'RE LOOKING TO PLAN A VACATION AND I WAS HOPING YOU COULD HELP ME FIND A HOTEL.
darb
AND MAKE SURE THAT WHEREVER YOU SEND US HAS PEOPLE WORKING THERE WHO ARE MORE ATTRACTIVE THAN YOU. I MEAN COME ON, I JUST ATE.
Bundle O' Joy!
DID I MENTION THEY'LL NEED TO BE CAT FRIENDLY?
THEY'LL NEED TO BE CAT ECSTATIC.
Visit Beautiful Knoxville

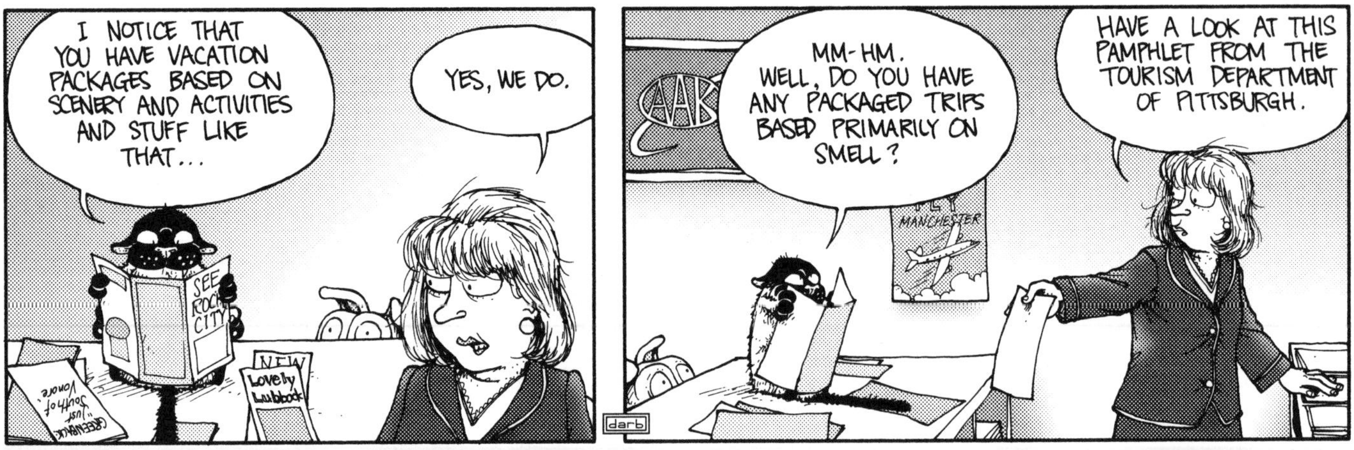
I NOTICE THAT YOU HAVE VACATION PACKAGES BASED ON SCENERY AND ACTIVITIES AND STUFF LIKE THAT...
YES, WE DO.
SEE ROCK CITY
Lovely Lubbock
MM-HM. WELL, DO YOU HAVE ANY PACKAGED TRIPS BASED PRIMARILY ON SMELL?
HAVE A LOOK AT THIS PAMPHLET FROM THE TOURISM DEPARTMENT OF PITTSBURGH.
MANCHESTER
darb

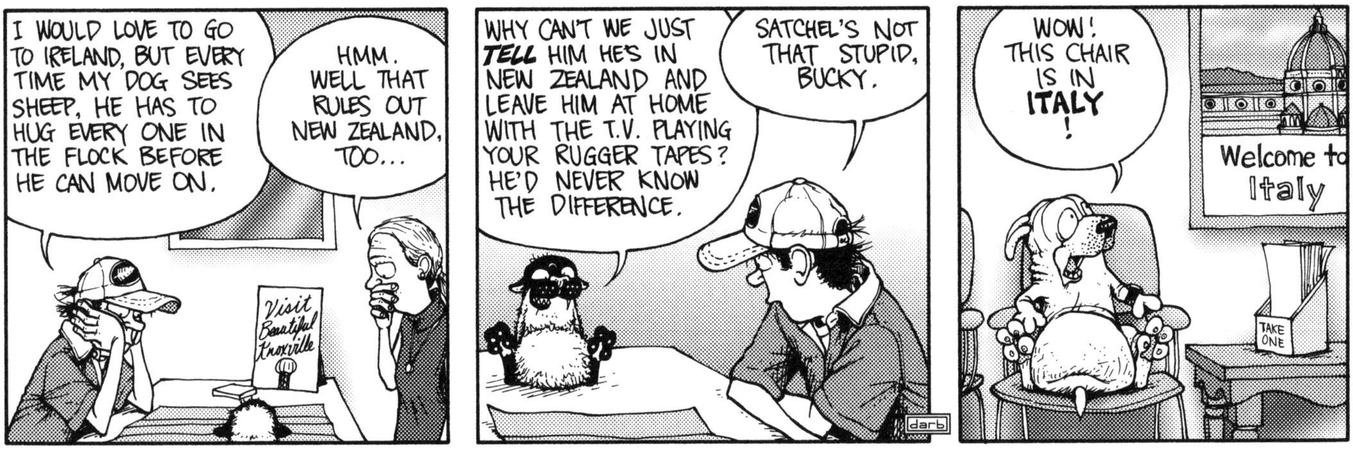
I WOULD LOVE TO GO TO IRELAND, BUT EVERY TIME MY DOG SEES SHEEP, HE HAS TO HUG EVERY ONE IN THE FLOCK BEFORE HE CAN MOVE ON.
HMM. WELL THAT RULES OUT NEW ZEALAND, TOO...
Visit Beautiful Knoxville
WHY CAN'T WE JUST ***TELL*** HIM HE'S IN NEW ZEALAND AND LEAVE HIM AT HOME WITH THE T.V. PLAYING YOUR RUGGER TAPES? HE'D NEVER KNOW THE DIFFERENCE.
SATCHEL'S NOT THAT STUPID, BUCKY.
darb
WOW! THIS CHAIR IS IN **ITALY**!
Welcome to Italy
TAKE ONE

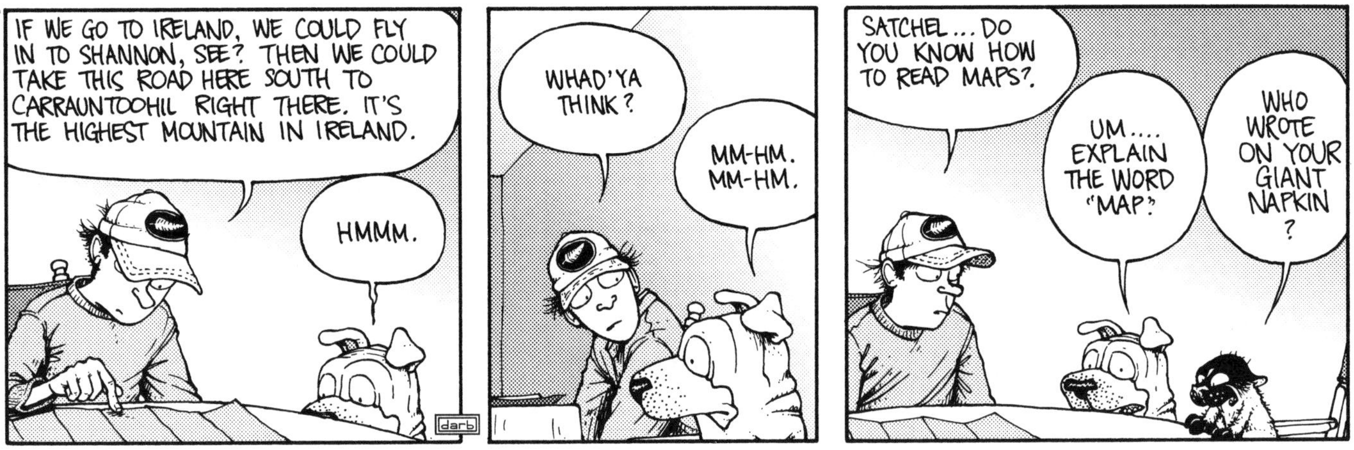
IF WE GO TO IRELAND, WE COULD FLY IN TO SHANNON, SEE? THEN WE COULD TAKE THIS ROAD HERE SOUTH TO CARRAUNTOOHIL RIGHT THERE. IT'S THE HIGHEST MOUNTAIN IN IRELAND.
HMMM.
darb
WHAD'YA THINK?
MM-HM. MM-HM.
SATCHEL... DO YOU KNOW HOW TO READ MAPS?
UM.... EXPLAIN THE WORD "MAP."
WHO WROTE ON YOUR GIANT NAPKIN?

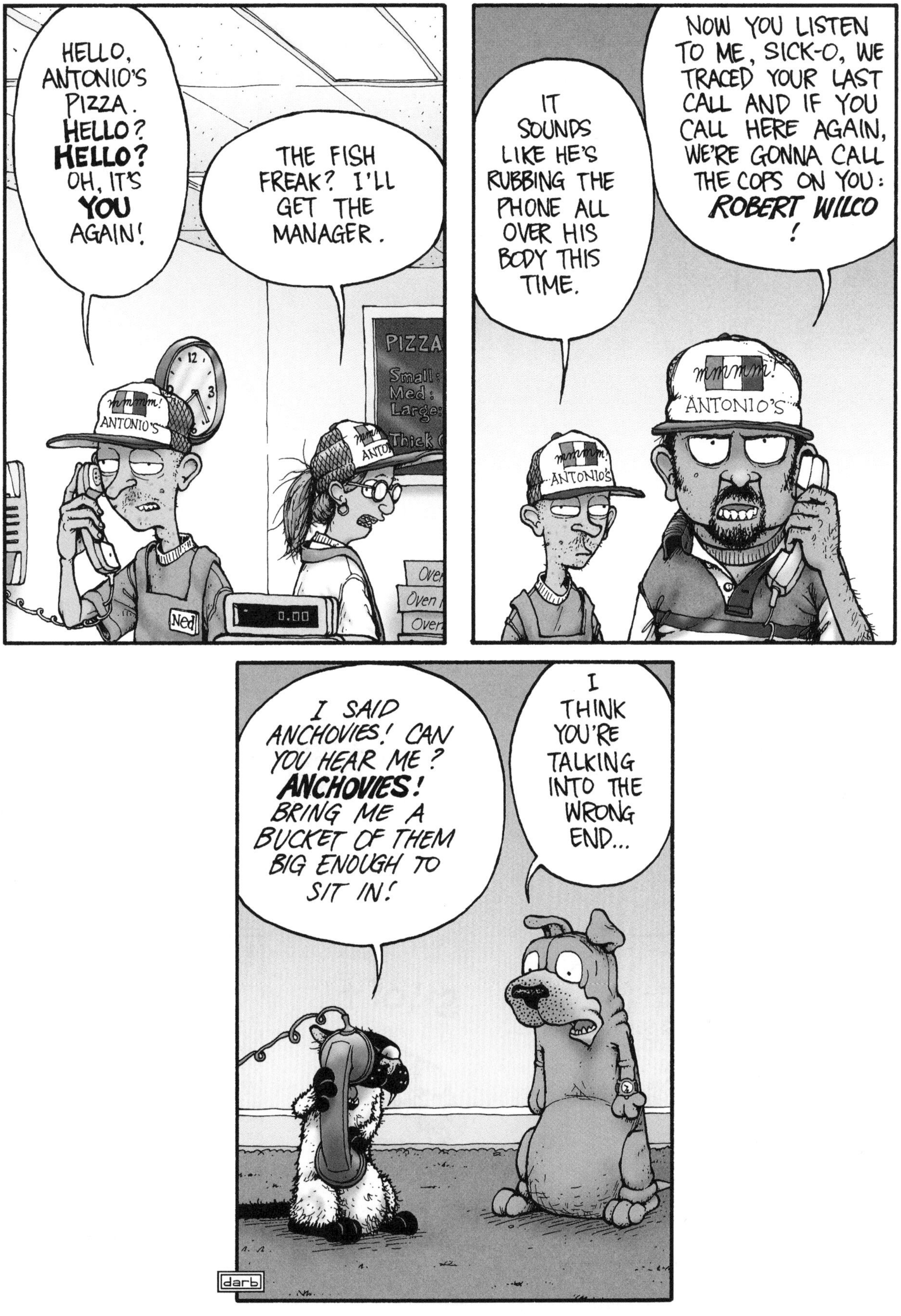

HELLO, ANTONIO'S PIZZA. HELLO? HELLO? OH, IT'S YOU AGAIN!
THE FISH FREAK? I'LL GET THE MANAGER.
PIZZA
Small:
Med:
Large:
Thick
ANTONIO'S
Ned
0.00
IT SOUNDS LIKE HE'S RUBBING THE PHONE ALL OVER HIS BODY THIS TIME.
NOW YOU LISTEN TO ME, SICK-O, WE TRACED YOUR LAST CALL AND IF YOU CALL HERE AGAIN, WE'RE GONNA CALL THE COPS ON YOU: ROBERT WILCO!
I SAID ANCHOVIES! CAN YOU HEAR ME? ANCHOVIES! BRING ME A BUCKET OF THEM BIG ENOUGH TO SIT IN!
I THINK YOU'RE TALKING INTO THE WRONG END...
darb

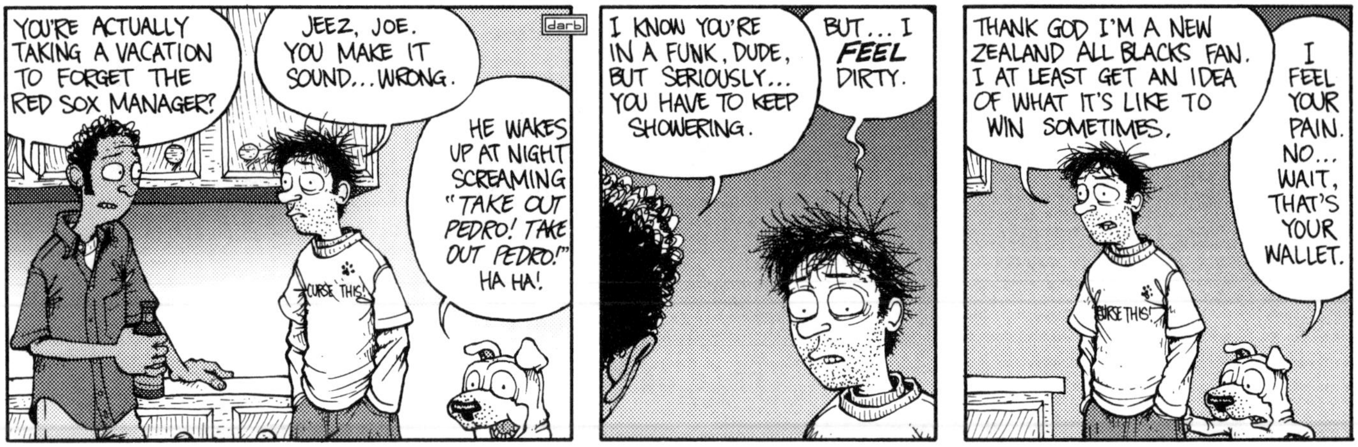
darb
YOU'RE ACTUALLY TAKING A VACATION TO FORGET THE RED SOX MANAGER?
JEEZ, JOE. YOU MAKE IT SOUND... WRONG.
CURSE THIS!
HE WAKES UP AT NIGHT SCREAMING "TAKE OUT PEDRO! TAKE OUT PEDRO!" HA HA!
I KNOW YOU'RE IN A FUNK, DUDE, BUT SERIOUSLY... YOU HAVE TO KEEP SHOWERING.
BUT... I FEEL DIRTY.
THANK GOD I'M A NEW ZEALAND ALL BLACKS FAN. I AT LEAST GET AN IDEA OF WHAT IT'S LIKE TO WIN SOMETIMES.
CURSE THIS!
I FEEL YOUR PAIN. NO... WAIT, THAT'S YOUR WALLET.

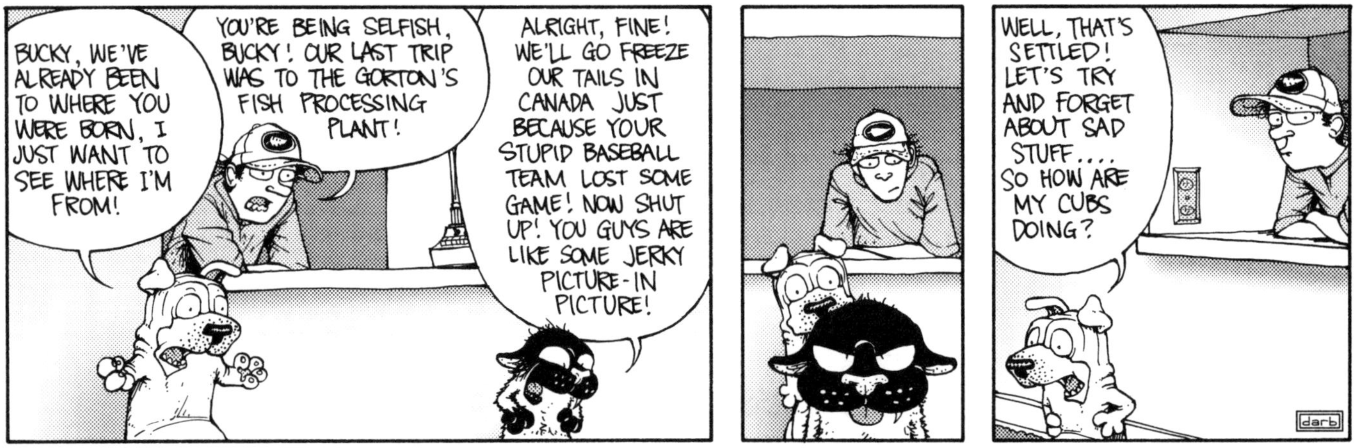
BUCKY, WE'VE ALREADY BEEN TO WHERE YOU WERE BORN, I JUST WANT TO SEE WHERE I'M FROM!
YOU'RE BEING SELFISH, BUCKY! OUR LAST TRIP WAS TO THE GORTON'S FISH PROCESSING PLANT!
ALRIGHT, FINE! WE'LL GO FREEZE OUR TAILS IN CANADA JUST BECAUSE YOUR STUPID BASEBALL TEAM LOST SOME GAME! NOW SHUT UP! YOU GUYS ARE LIKE SOME JERKY PICTURE-IN PICTURE!
WELL, THAT'S SETTLED! LET'S TRY AND FORGET ABOUT SAD STUFF.... SO HOW ARE MY CUBS DOING?
darb

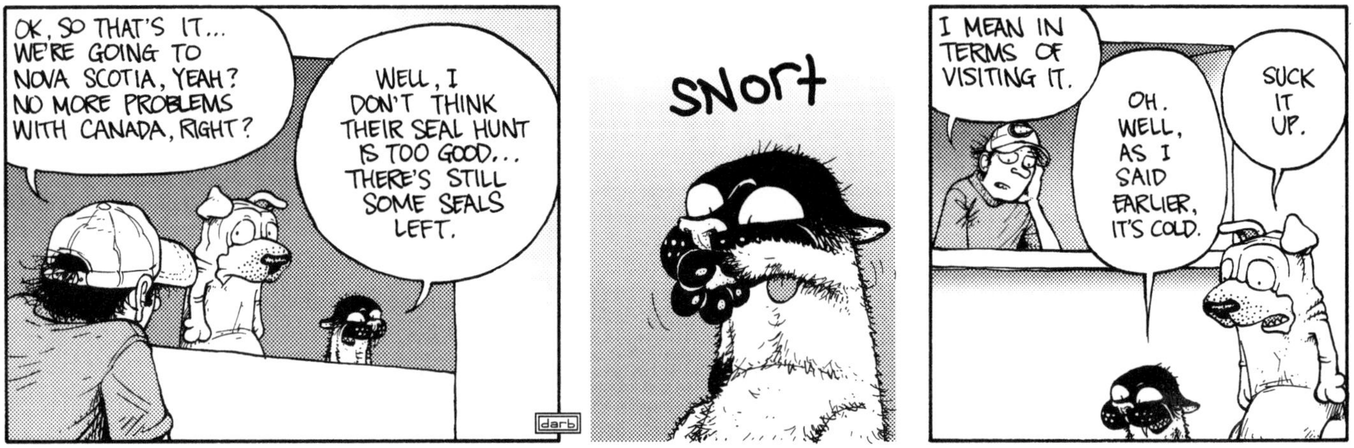
OK, SO THAT'S IT... WE'RE GOING TO NOVA SCOTIA, YEAH? NO MORE PROBLEMS WITH CANADA, RIGHT?
WELL, I DON'T THINK THEIR SEAL HUNT IS TOO GOOD... THERE'S STILL SOME SEALS LEFT.
darb
SNort
I MEAN IN TERMS OF VISITING IT.
OH. WELL, AS I SAID EARLIER, IT'S COLD.
SUCK IT UP.

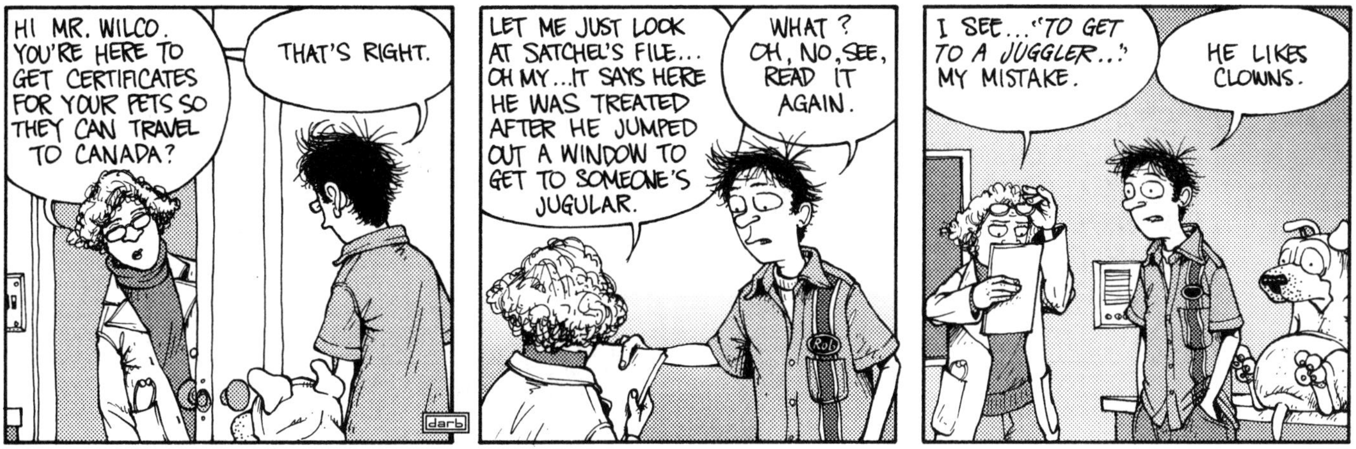
HI MR. WILCO. YOU'RE HERE TO GET CERTIFICATES FOR YOUR PETS SO THEY CAN TRAVEL TO CANADA?
THAT'S RIGHT.
LET ME JUST LOOK AT SATCHEL'S FILE... OH MY...IT SAYS HERE HE WAS TREATED AFTER HE JUMPED OUT A WINDOW TO GET TO SOMEONE'S JUGULAR.
WHAT? OH, NO, SEE, READ IT AGAIN.
I SEE..."TO GET TO A JUGGLER..." MY MISTAKE.
HE LIKES CLOWNS.

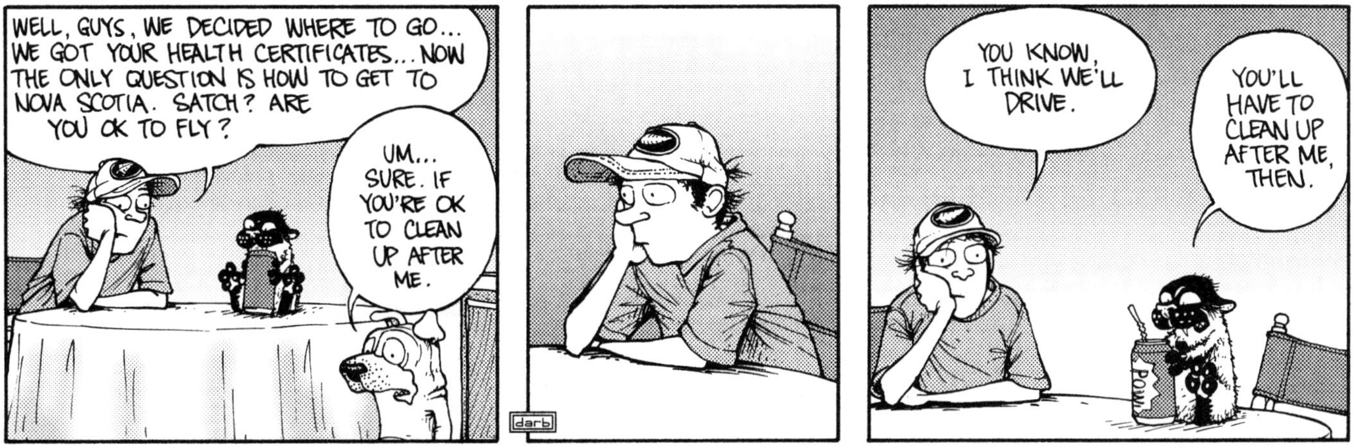
WELL, GUYS, WE DECIDED WHERE TO GO... WE GOT YOUR HEALTH CERTIFICATES... NOW THE ONLY QUESTION IS HOW TO GET TO NOVA SCOTIA. SATCH? ARE YOU OK TO FLY?
UM... SURE. IF YOU'RE OK TO CLEAN UP AFTER ME.
YOU KNOW, I THINK WE'LL DRIVE.
YOU'LL HAVE TO CLEAN UP AFTER ME, THEN.

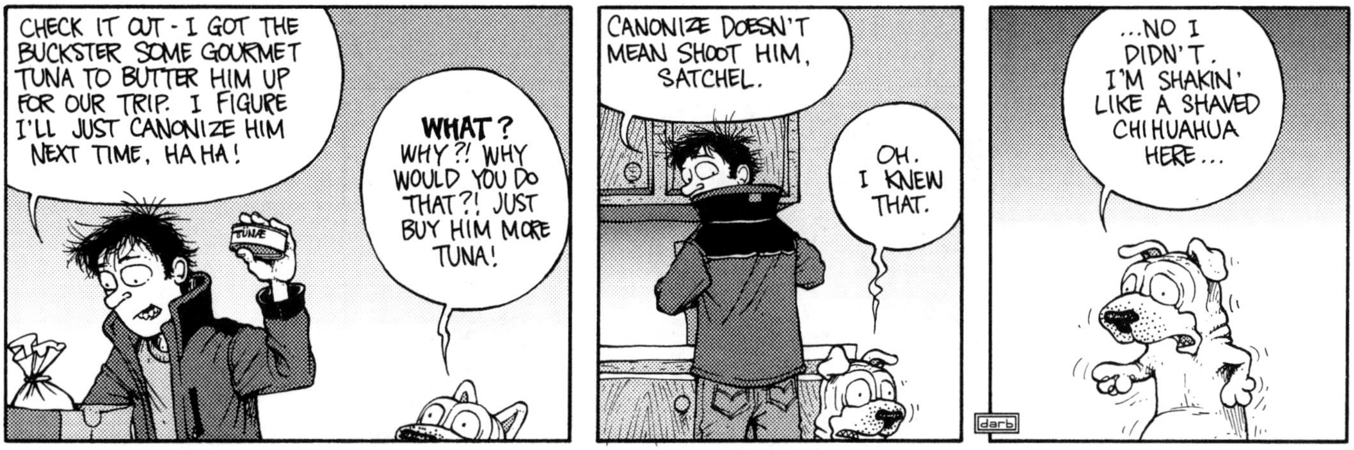
CHECK IT OUT - I GOT THE BUCKSTER SOME GOURMET TUNA TO BUTTER HIM UP FOR OUR TRIP. I FIGURE I'LL JUST CANONIZE HIM NEXT TIME, HA HA!
WHAT? WHY?! WHY WOULD YOU DO THAT?! JUST BUY HIM MORE TUNA!
CANONIZE DOESN'T MEAN SHOOT HIM, SATCHEL.
OH. I KNEW THAT.
...NO I DIDN'T. I'M SHAKIN' LIKE A SHAVED CHIHUAHUA HERE...

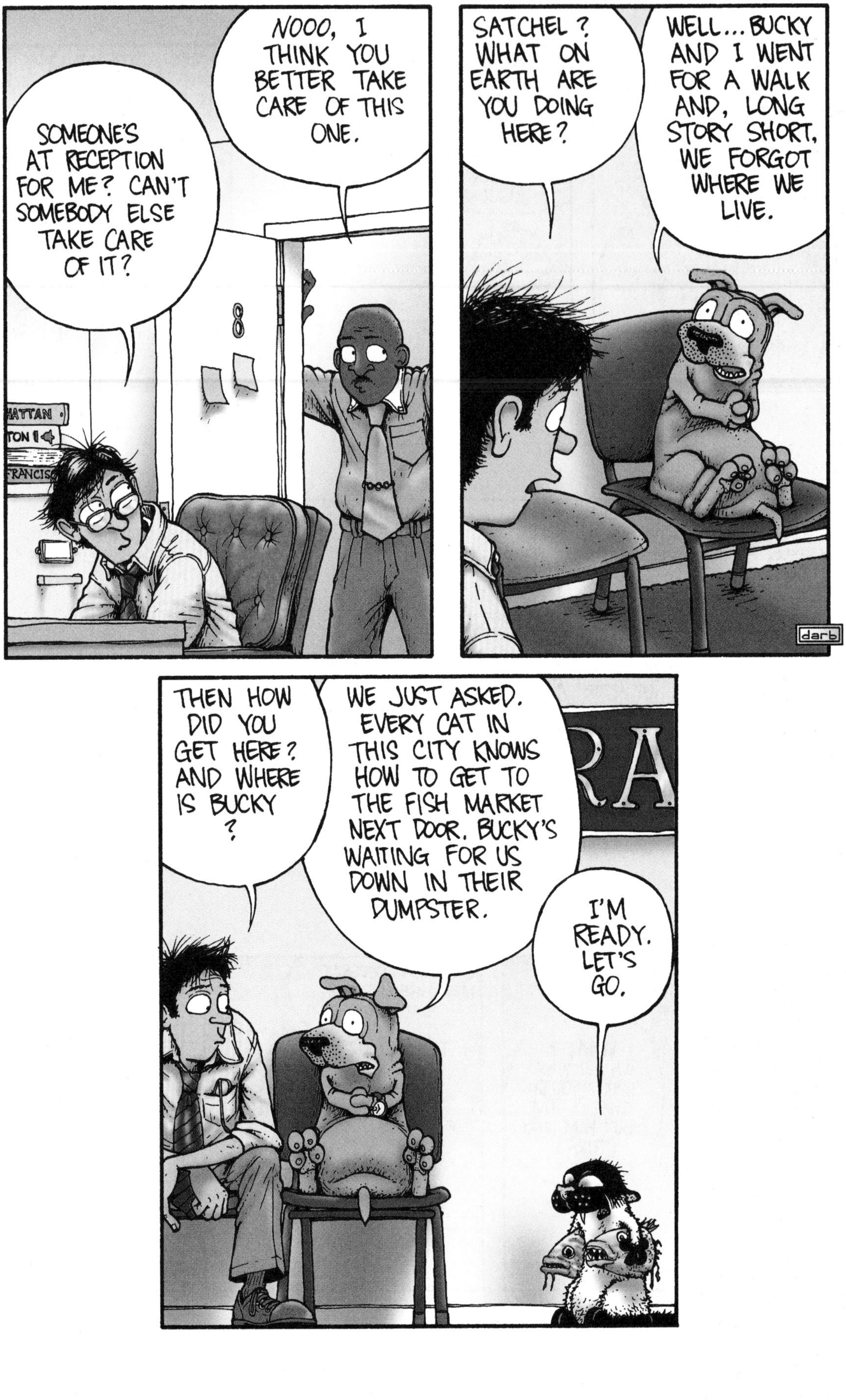
SOMEONE'S AT RECEPTION FOR ME? CAN'T SOMEBODY ELSE TAKE CARE OF IT?
NOOO, I THINK YOU BETTER TAKE CARE OF THIS ONE.
SATCHEL? WHAT ON EARTH ARE YOU DOING HERE?
WELL... BUCKY AND I WENT FOR A WALK AND, LONG STORY SHORT, WE FORGOT WHERE WE LIVE.
darb
THEN HOW DID YOU GET HERE? AND WHERE IS BUCKY?
WE JUST ASKED. EVERY CAT IN THIS CITY KNOWS HOW TO GET TO THE FISH MARKET NEXT DOOR. BUCKY'S WAITING FOR US DOWN IN THEIR DUMPSTER.
I'M READY. LET'S GO.

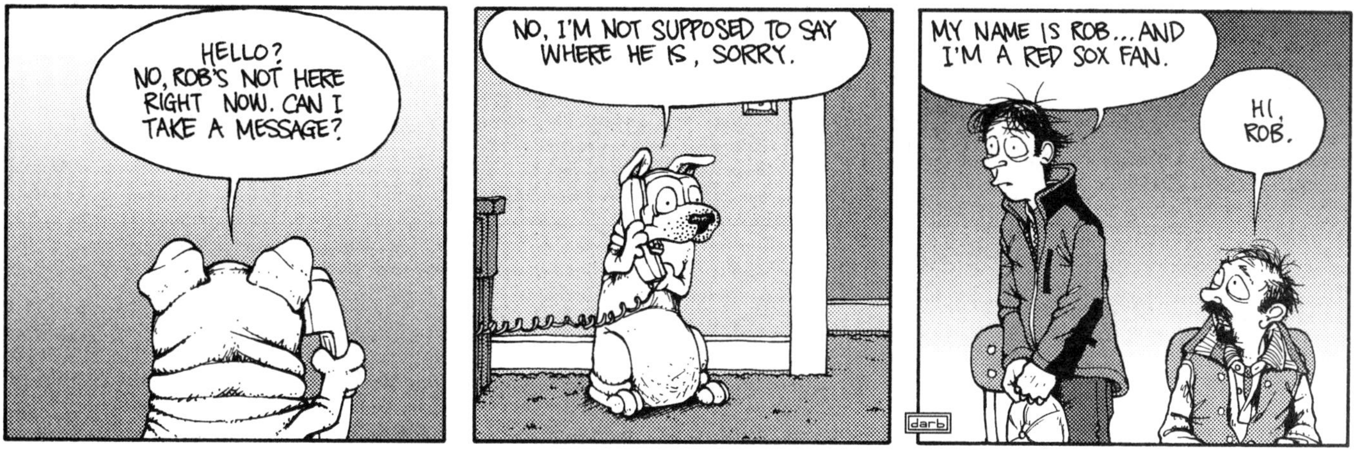
HELLO? NO, ROB'S NOT HERE RIGHT NOW. CAN I TAKE A MESSAGE?
NO, I'M NOT SUPPOSED TO SAY WHERE HE IS, SORRY.
MY NAME IS ROB... AND I'M A RED SOX FAN.
HI, ROB.

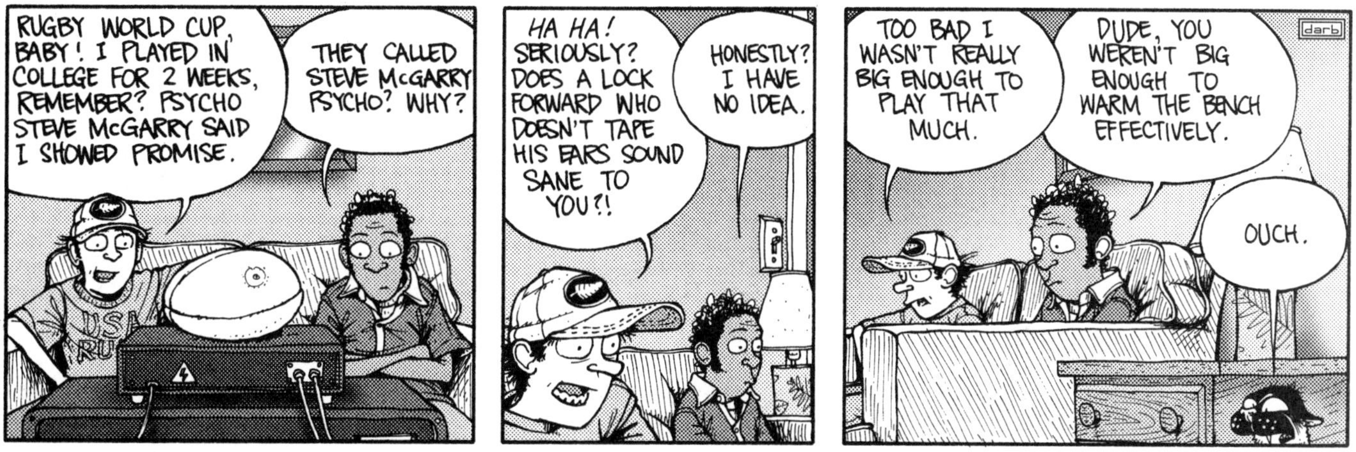
RUGBY WORLD CUP, BABY! I PLAYED IN COLLEGE FOR 2 WEEKS, REMEMBER? PSYCHO STEVE McGARRY SAID I SHOWED PROMISE.
THEY CALLED STEVE McGARRY PSYCHO? WHY?
HA HA! SERIOUSLY? DOES A LOCK FORWARD WHO DOESN'T TAPE HIS EARS SOUND SANE TO YOU?!
HONESTLY? I HAVE NO IDEA.
TOO BAD I WASN'T REALLY BIG ENOUGH TO PLAY THAT MUCH.
DUDE, YOU WEREN'T BIG ENOUGH TO WARM THE BENCH EFFECTIVELY.
OUCH.

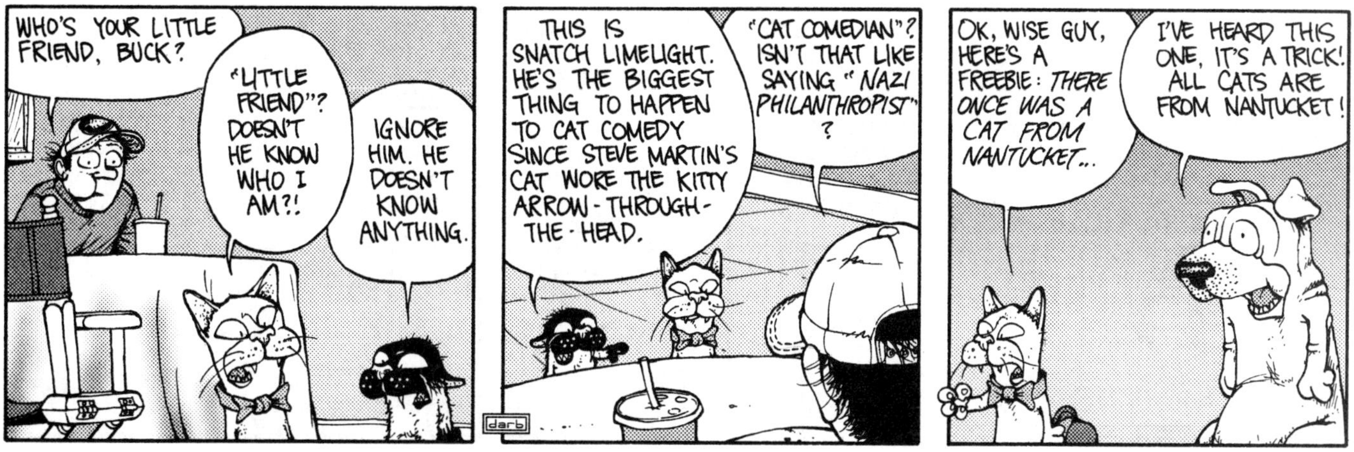
WHO'S YOUR LITTLE FRIEND, BUCK?
"LITTLE FRIEND"? DOESN'T HE KNOW WHO I AM?!
IGNORE HIM. HE DOESN'T KNOW ANYTHING.
THIS IS SNATCH LIMELIGHT. HE'S THE BIGGEST THING TO HAPPEN TO CAT COMEDY SINCE STEVE MARTIN'S CAT WORE THE KITTY ARROW-THROUGH-THE-HEAD.
"CAT COMEDIAN"? ISN'T THAT LIKE SAYING "NAZI PHILANTHROPIST"?
OK, WISE GUY, HERE'S A FREEBIE: THERE ONCE WAS A CAT FROM NANTUCKET...
I'VE HEARD THIS ONE, IT'S A TRICK! ALL CATS ARE FROM NANTUCKET!

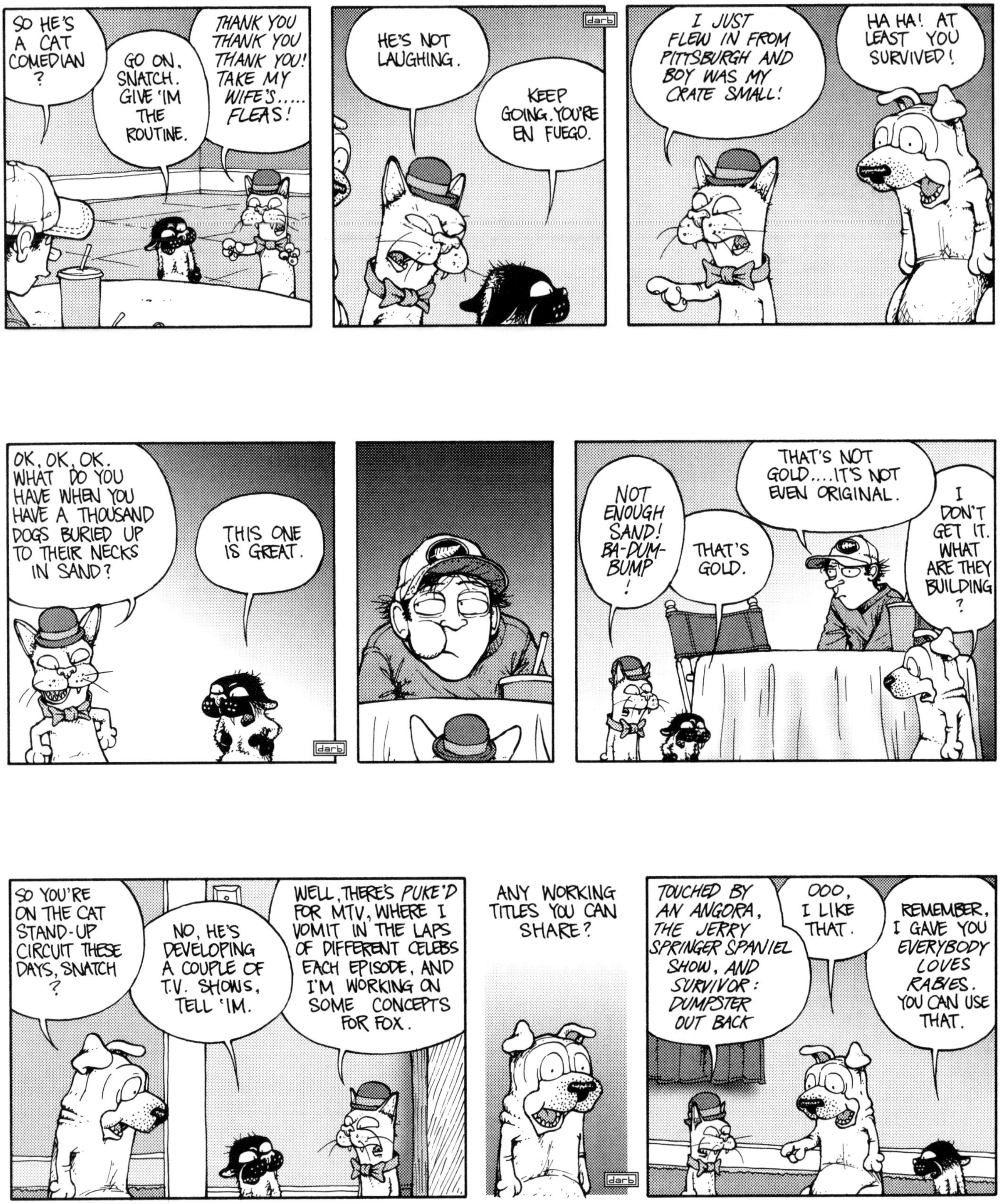
SO HE'S A CAT COMEDIAN ?
GO ON, SNATCH. GIVE 'IM THE ROUTINE.
THANK YOU THANK YOU THANK YOU! TAKE MY WIFE'S..... FLEAS!
darb
HE'S NOT LAUGHING.
KEEP GOING. YOU'RE EN FUEGO.
I JUST FLEW IN FROM PITTSBURGH AND BOY WAS MY CRATE SMALL!
HA HA! AT LEAST YOU SURVIVED!
OK, OK, OK. WHAT DO YOU HAVE WHEN YOU HAVE A THOUSAND DOGS BURIED UP TO THEIR NECKS IN SAND?
THIS ONE IS GREAT.
darb
NOT ENOUGH SAND! BA-DUM-BUMP !
THAT'S GOLD.
THAT'S NOT GOLD....IT'S NOT EVEN ORIGINAL.
I DON'T GET IT. WHAT ARE THEY BUILDING ?
SO YOU'RE ON THE CAT STAND-UP CIRCUIT THESE DAYS, SNATCH ?
NO, HE'S DEVELOPING A COUPLE OF T.V. SHOWS, TELL 'IM.
WELL, THERE'S PUKE'D FOR MTV, WHERE I VOMIT IN THE LAPS OF DIFFERENT CELEBS EACH EPISODE, AND I'M WORKING ON SOME CONCEPTS FOR FOX.
ANY WORKING TITLES YOU CAN SHARE?
darb
TOUCHED BY AN ANGORA, THE JERRY SPRINGER SPANIEL SHOW, AND SURVIVOR: DUMPSTER OUT BACK
OOO, I LIKE THAT.
REMEMBER, I GAVE YOU EVERYBODY LOVES RABIES. YOU CAN USE THAT.

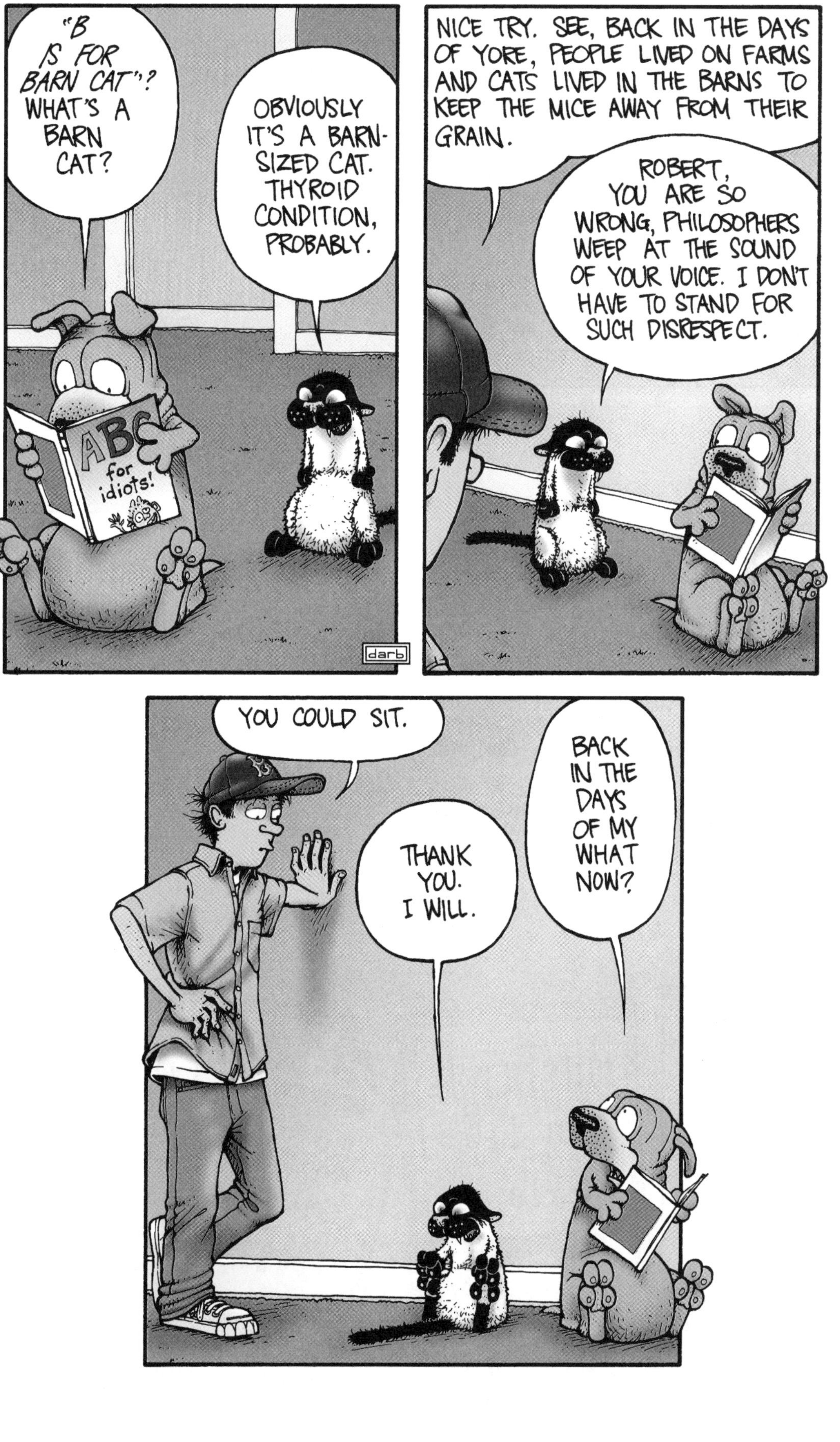
"B IS FOR BARN CAT"? WHAT'S A BARN CAT?
OBVIOUSLY IT'S A BARN-SIZED CAT. THYROID CONDITION, PROBABLY.
ABC for idiots!
darb
NICE TRY. SEE, BACK IN THE DAYS OF YORE, PEOPLE LIVED ON FARMS AND CATS LIVED IN THE BARNS TO KEEP THE MICE AWAY FROM THEIR GRAIN.
ROBERT, YOU ARE SO WRONG, PHILOSOPHERS WEEP AT THE SOUND OF YOUR VOICE. I DON'T HAVE TO STAND FOR SUCH DISRESPECT.
YOU COULD SIT.
THANK YOU. I WILL.
BACK IN THE DAYS OF MY WHAT NOW?

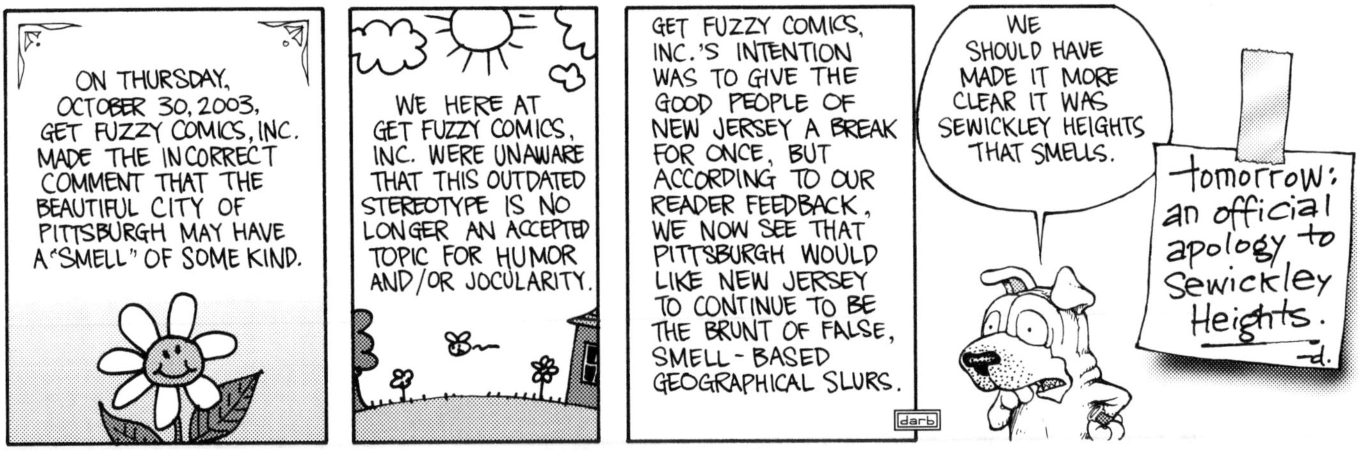
ON THURSDAY, OCTOBER 30, 2003, GET FUZZY COMICS, INC. MADE THE INCORRECT COMMENT THAT THE BEAUTIFUL CITY OF PITTSBURGH MAY HAVE A "SMELL" OF SOME KIND.
WE HERE AT GET FUZZY COMICS, INC. WERE UNAWARE THAT THIS OUTDATED STEREOTYPE IS NO LONGER AN ACCEPTED TOPIC FOR HUMOR AND/OR JOCULARITY.
GET FUZZY COMICS, INC.'S INTENTION WAS TO GIVE THE GOOD PEOPLE OF NEW JERSEY A BREAK FOR ONCE, BUT ACCORDING TO OUR READER FEEDBACK, WE NOW SEE THAT PITTSBURGH WOULD LIKE NEW JERSEY TO CONTINUE TO BE THE BRUNT OF FALSE, SMELL-BASED GEOGRAPHICAL SLURS.
darb
WE SHOULD HAVE MADE IT MORE CLEAR IT WAS SEWICKLEY HEIGHTS THAT SMELLS.
tomorrow: an official apology to Sewickley Heights. -d.

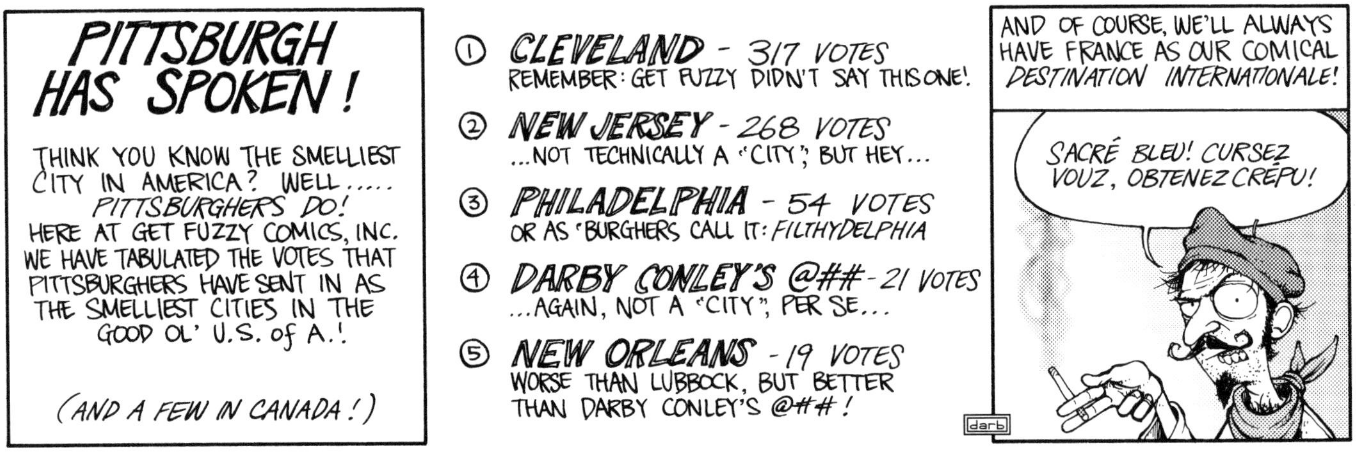
PITTSBURGH HAS SPOKEN!
THINK YOU KNOW THE SMELLIEST CITY IN AMERICA? WELL..... PITTSBURGHERS DO! HERE AT GET FUZZY COMICS, INC. WE HAVE TABULATED THE VOTES THAT PITTSBURGHERS HAVE SENT IN AS THE SMELLIEST CITIES IN THE GOOD OL' U.S. of A.!
(AND A FEW IN CANADA!)
① CLEVELAND - 317 VOTES
REMEMBER: GET FUZZY DIDN'T SAY THIS ONE!
② NEW JERSEY - 268 VOTES
...NOT TECHNICALLY A "CITY", BUT HEY...
③ PHILADELPHIA - 54 VOTES
OR AS 'BURGHERS CALL IT: FILTHYDELPHIA
④ DARBY CONLEY'S @##-21 VOTES
...AGAIN, NOT A "CITY", PER SE...
⑤ NEW ORLEANS - 19 VOTES
WORSE THAN LUBBOCK, BUT BETTER THAN DARBY CONLEY'S @##!
darb
AND OF COURSE, WE'LL ALWAYS HAVE FRANCE AS OUR COMICAL DESTINATION INTERNATIONALE!
SACRÉ BLEU! CURSEZ VOUZ, OBTENEZ CRÉPU!

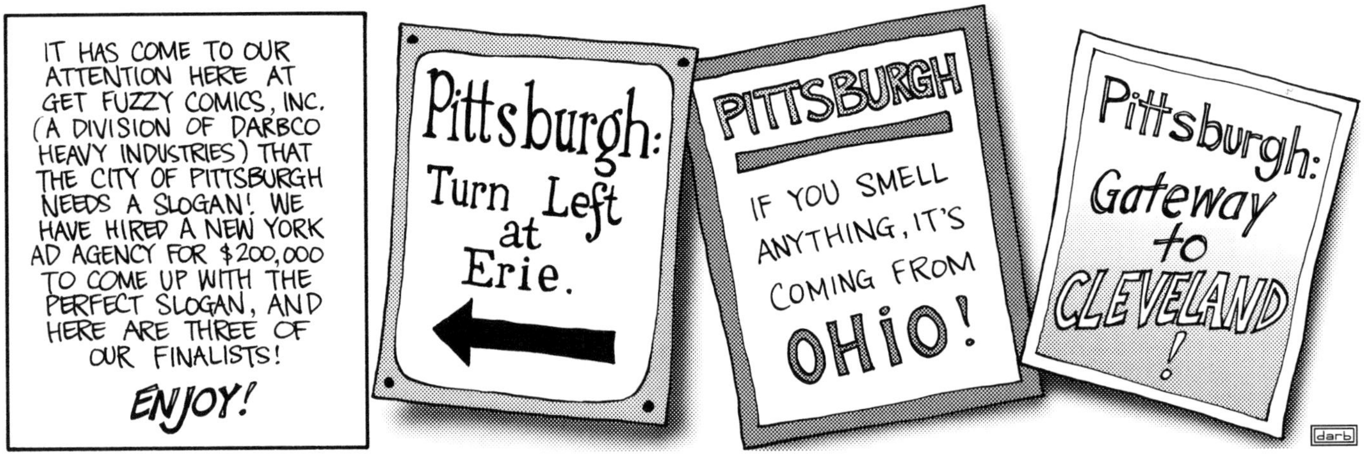
IT HAS COME TO OUR ATTENTION HERE AT GET FUZZY COMICS, INC. (A DIVISION OF DARBCO HEAVY INDUSTRIES) THAT THE CITY OF PITTSBURGH NEEDS A SLOGAN! WE HAVE HIRED A NEW YORK AD AGENCY FOR $200,000 TO COME UP WITH THE PERFECT SLOGAN, AND HERE ARE THREE OF OUR FINALISTS!
ENJOY!
Pittsburgh: Turn Left at Erie.
PITTSBURGH
IF YOU SMELL ANYTHING, IT'S COMING FROM OHIO!
Pittsburgh: Gateway to CLEVELAND!
darb

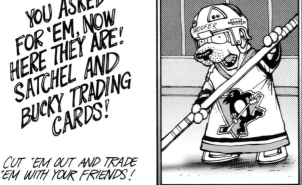

YOU ASKED FOR 'EM, NOW HERE THEY ARE! SATCHEL AND BUCKY TRADING CARDS!

CUT 'EM OUT AND TRADE 'EM WITH YOUR FRIENDS!

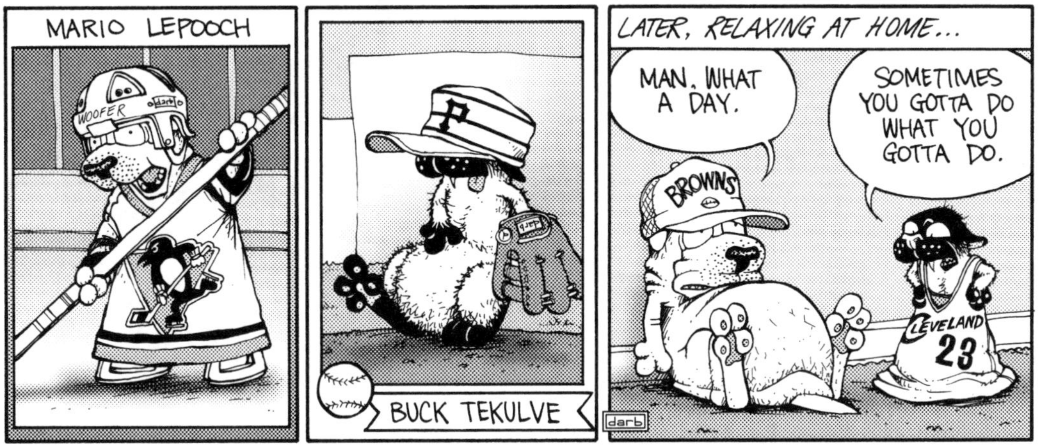

MARIO LEPOOCH
WOOFER
BUCK TEKULVE
LATER, RELAXING AT HOME...
MAN. WHAT A DAY.
SOMETIMES YOU GOTTA DO WHAT YOU GOTTA DO.
BROWNS
CLEVELAND 23
darb

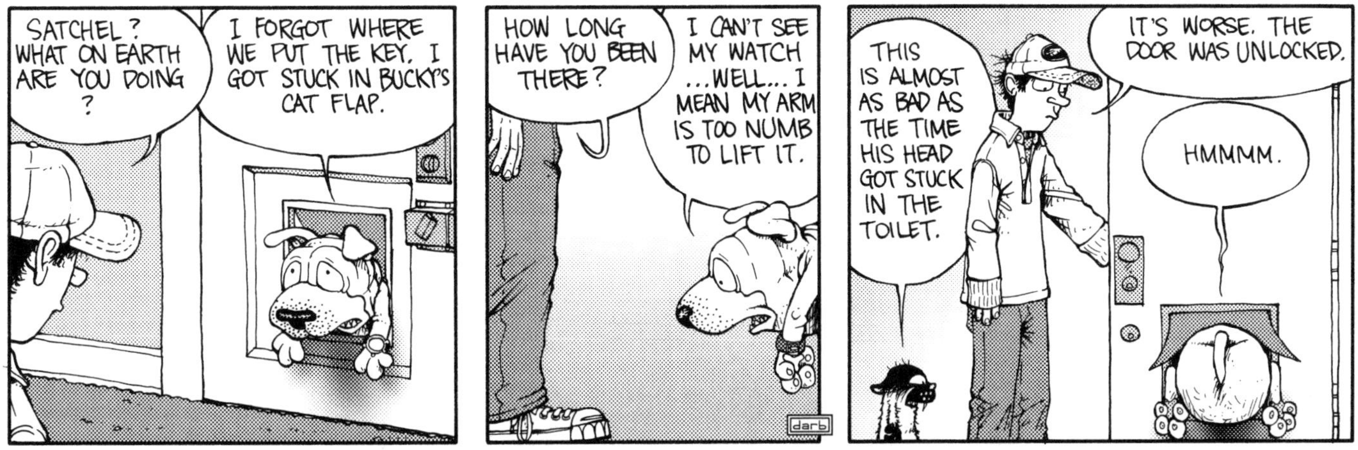

SATCHEL? WHAT ON EARTH ARE YOU DOING?
I FORGOT WHERE WE PUT THE KEY. I GOT STUCK IN BUCKY'S CAT FLAP.
HOW LONG HAVE YOU BEEN THERE?
I CAN'T SEE MY WATCH ...WELL... I MEAN MY ARM IS TOO NUMB TO LIFT IT.
darb
THIS IS ALMOST AS BAD AS THE TIME HIS HEAD GOT STUCK IN THE TOILET.
IT'S WORSE. THE DOOR WAS UNLOCKED.
HMMMM.

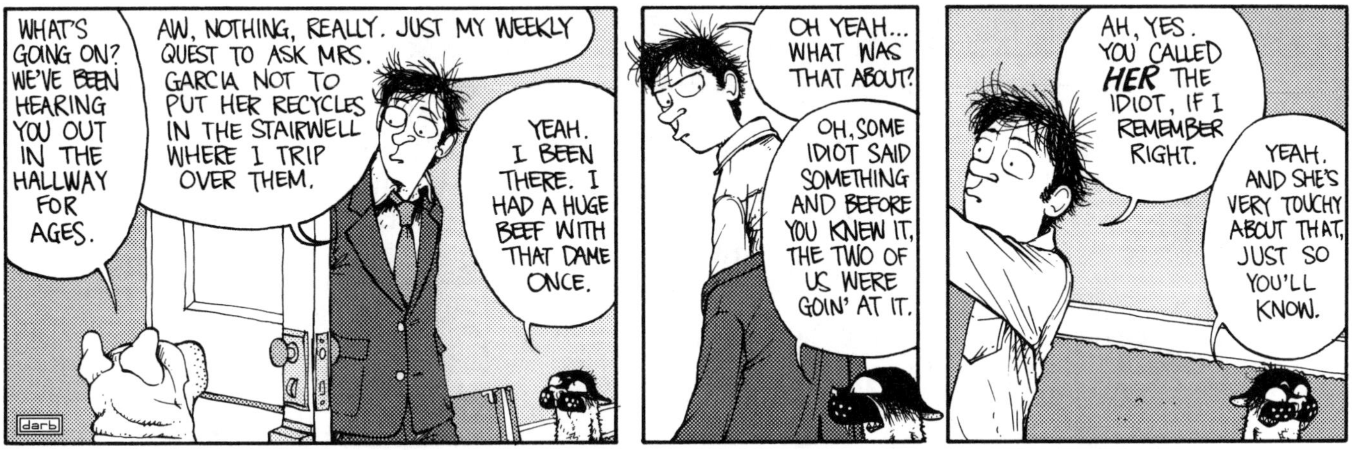

WHAT'S GOING ON? WE'VE BEEN HEARING YOU OUT IN THE HALLWAY FOR AGES.
AW, NOTHING, REALLY. JUST MY WEEKLY QUEST TO ASK MRS. GARCIA NOT TO PUT HER RECYCLES IN THE STAIRWELL WHERE I TRIP OVER THEM.
YEAH. I BEEN THERE. I HAD A HUGE BEEF WITH THAT DAME ONCE.
darb
OH YEAH... WHAT WAS THAT ABOUT?
OH, SOME IDIOT SAID SOMETHING AND BEFORE YOU KNEW IT, THE TWO OF US WERE GOIN' AT IT.
AH, YES. YOU CALLED HER THE IDIOT, IF I REMEMBER RIGHT.
YEAH. AND SHE'S VERY TOUCHY ABOUT THAT, JUST SO YOU'LL KNOW.

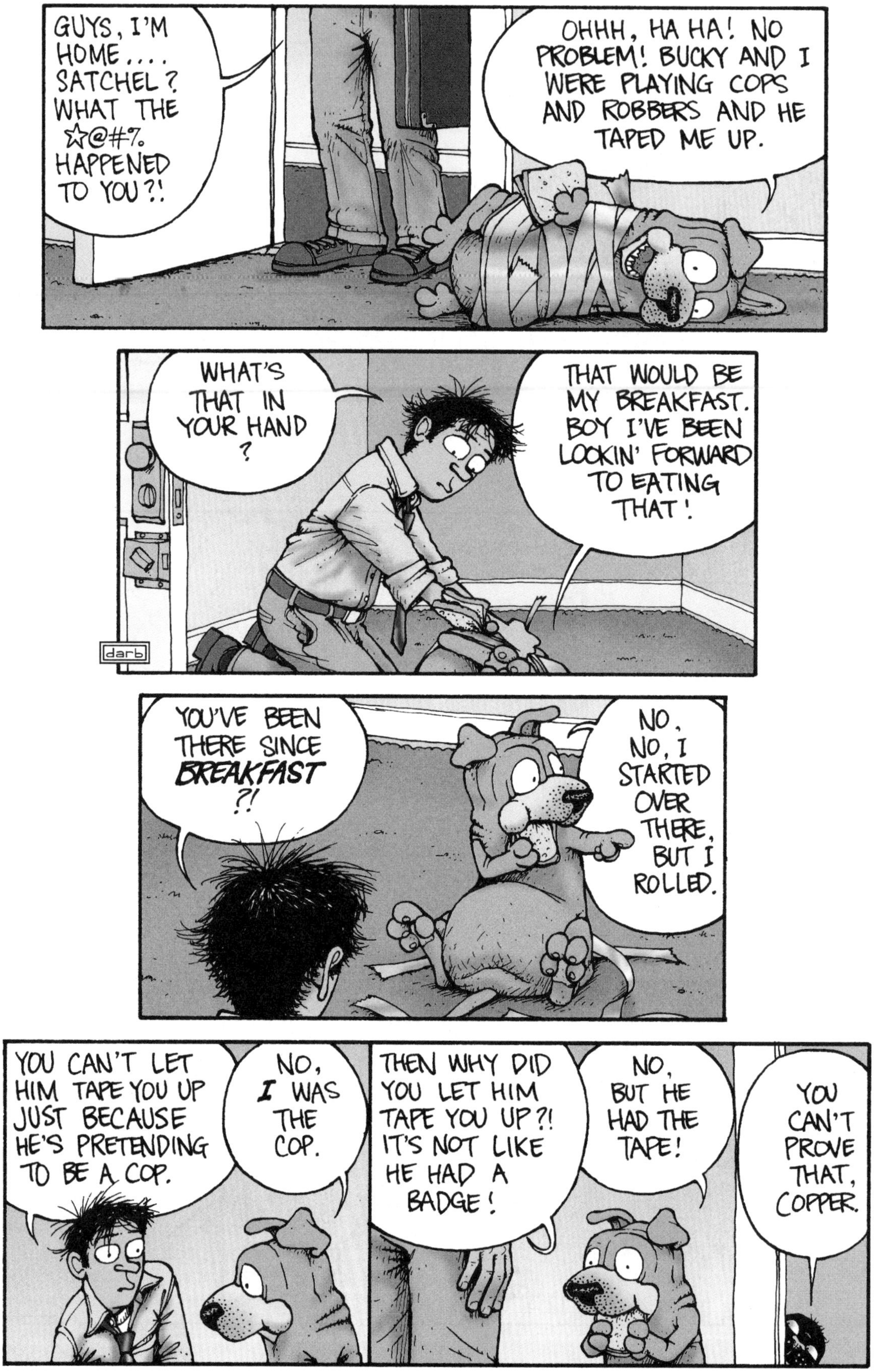
GUYS, I'M HOME.... SATCHEL? WHAT THE ☆@#% HAPPENED TO YOU?!
OHHH, HA HA! NO PROBLEM! BUCKY AND I WERE PLAYING COPS AND ROBBERS AND HE TAPED ME UP.
WHAT'S THAT IN YOUR HAND?
THAT WOULD BE MY BREAKFAST. BOY I'VE BEEN LOOKIN' FORWARD TO EATING THAT!
darb
YOU'VE BEEN THERE SINCE BREAKFAST?!
NO, NO, I STARTED OVER THERE, BUT I ROLLED.
YOU CAN'T LET HIM TAPE YOU UP JUST BECAUSE HE'S PRETENDING TO BE A COP.
NO, I WAS THE COP.
THEN WHY DID YOU LET HIM TAPE YOU UP?! IT'S NOT LIKE HE HAD A BADGE!
NO, BUT HE HAD THE TAPE!
YOU CAN'T PROVE THAT, COPPER.

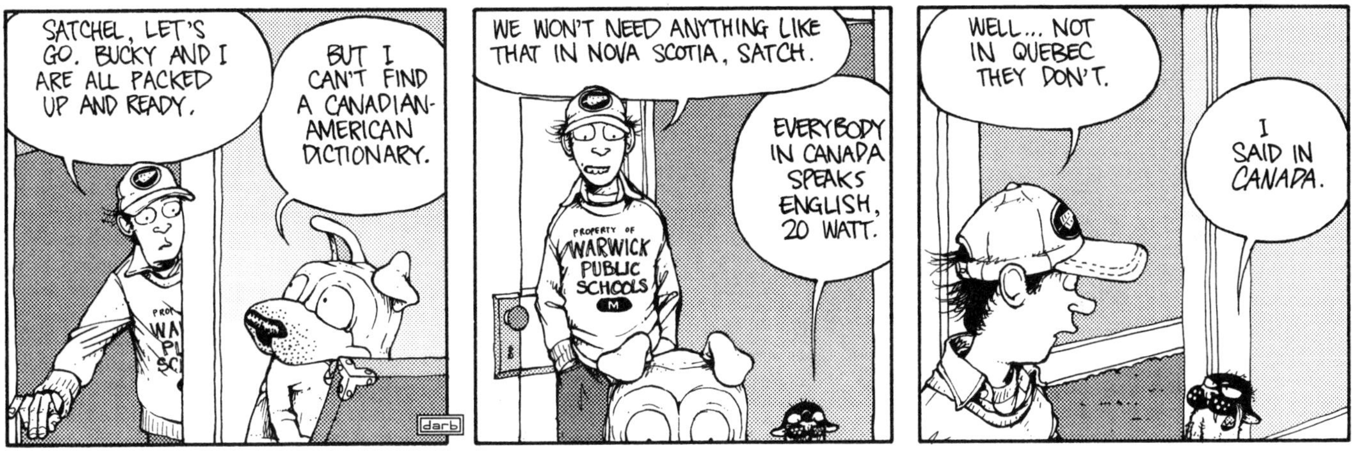
SATCHEL, LET'S GO. BUCKY AND I ARE ALL PACKED UP AND READY.
BUT I CAN'T FIND A CANADIAN-AMERICAN DICTIONARY.
WE WON'T NEED ANYTHING LIKE THAT IN NOVA SCOTIA, SATCH.
PROPERTY OF WARWICK PUBLIC SCHOOLS
EVERYBODY IN CANADA SPEAKS ENGLISH, 20 WATT.
WELL... NOT IN QUEBEC THEY DON'T.
I SAID IN *CANADA*.

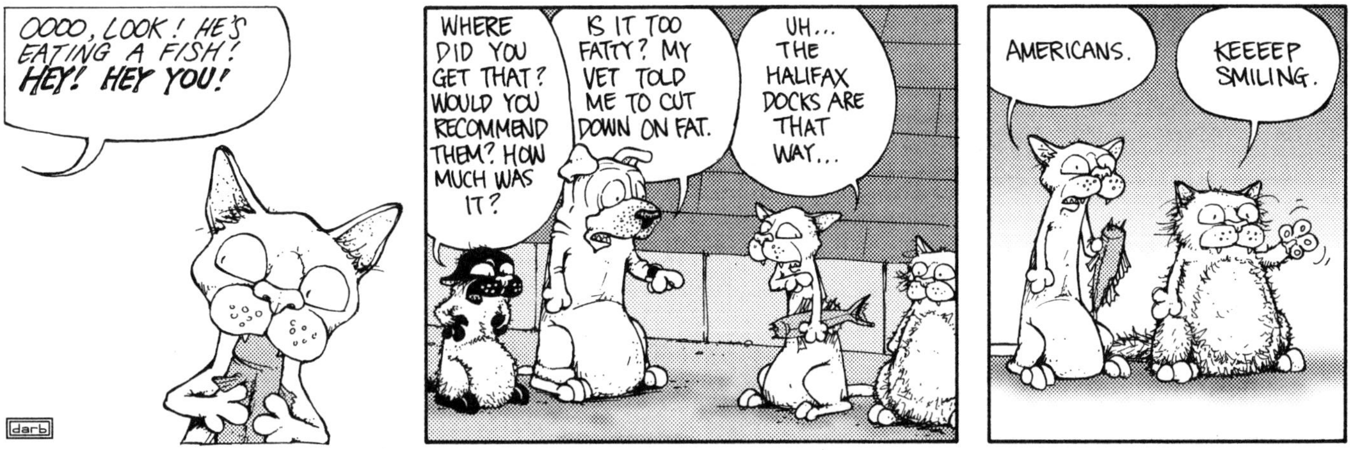
OOOO, LOOK! HE'S EATING A FISH! ***HEY! HEY YOU!***
WHERE DID YOU GET THAT? WOULD YOU RECOMMEND THEM? HOW MUCH WAS IT?
IS IT TOO FATTY? MY VET TOLD ME TO CUT DOWN ON FAT.
UH... THE HALIFAX DOCKS ARE THAT WAY...
AMERICANS.
KEEEEP SMILING.

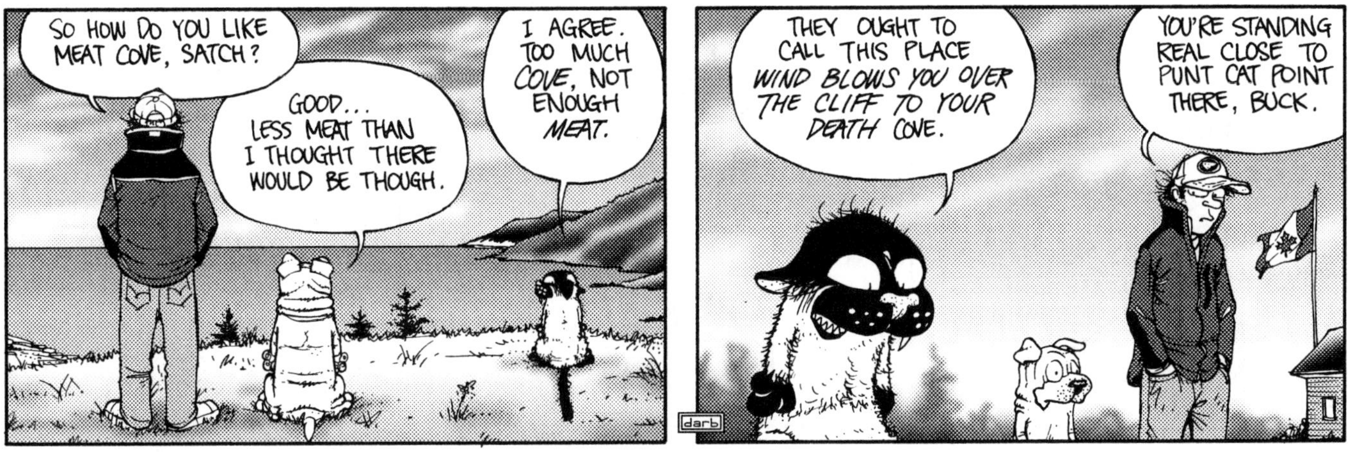
SO HOW DO YOU LIKE MEAT COVE, SATCH?
GOOD... LESS MEAT THAN I THOUGHT THERE WOULD BE THOUGH.
I AGREE. TOO MUCH *COVE*, NOT ENOUGH *MEAT*.
THEY OUGHT TO CALL THIS PLACE *WIND BLOWS YOU OVER THE CLIFF TO YOUR DEATH* COVE.
YOU'RE STANDING REAL CLOSE TO PUNT CAT POINT THERE, BUCK.

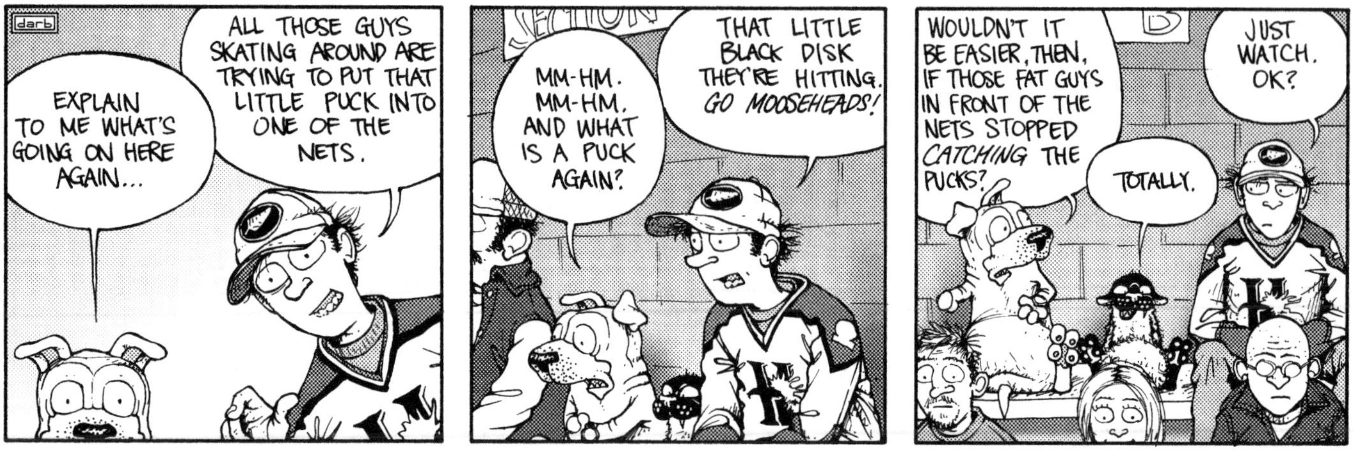
EXPLAIN TO ME WHAT'S GOING ON HERE AGAIN...
ALL THOSE GUYS SKATING AROUND ARE TRYING TO PUT THAT LITTLE PUCK INTO ONE OF THE NETS.
MM-HM. MM-HM. AND WHAT IS A PUCK AGAIN?
THAT LITTLE BLACK DISK THEY'RE HITTING. *GO MOOSEHEADS!*
WOULDN'T IT BE EASIER, THEN, IF THOSE FAT GUYS IN FRONT OF THE NETS STOPPED *CATCHING* THE PUCKS?
JUST WATCH. OK?
TOTALLY.

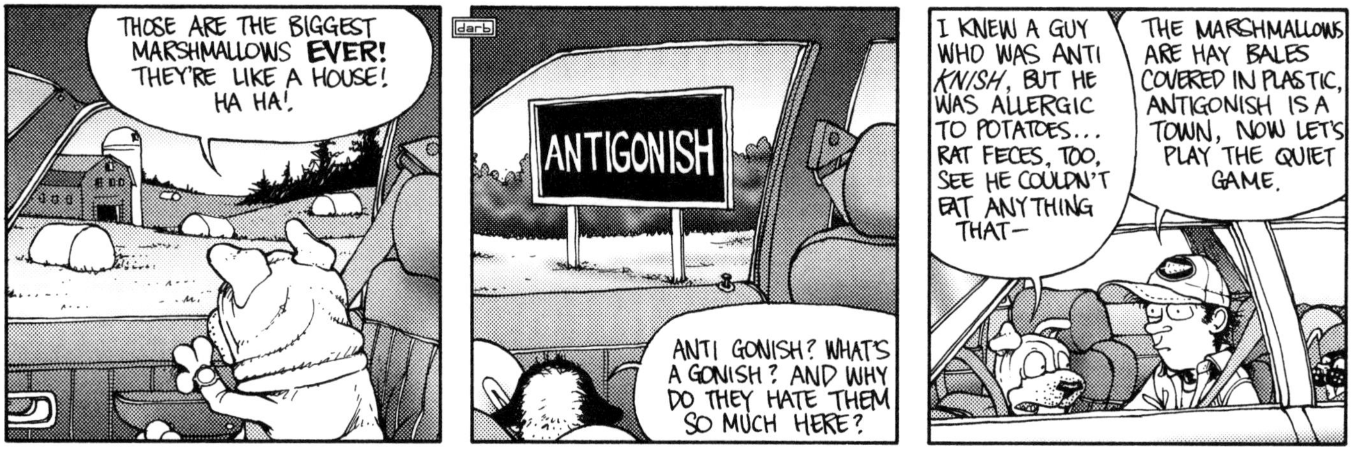
THOSE ARE THE BIGGEST MARSHMALLOWS **EVER!** THEY'RE LIKE A HOUSE! HA HA!
ANTIGONISH
ANTI GONISH? WHAT'S A GONISH? AND WHY DO THEY HATE THEM SO MUCH HERE?
I KNEW A GUY WHO WAS ANTI *KNISH*, BUT HE WAS ALLERGIC TO POTATOES... RAT FECES, TOO, SEE HE COULDN'T EAT ANYTHING THAT—
THE MARSHMALLOWS ARE HAY BALES COVERED IN PLASTIC, ANTIGONISH IS A TOWN, NOW LET'S PLAY THE QUIET GAME.

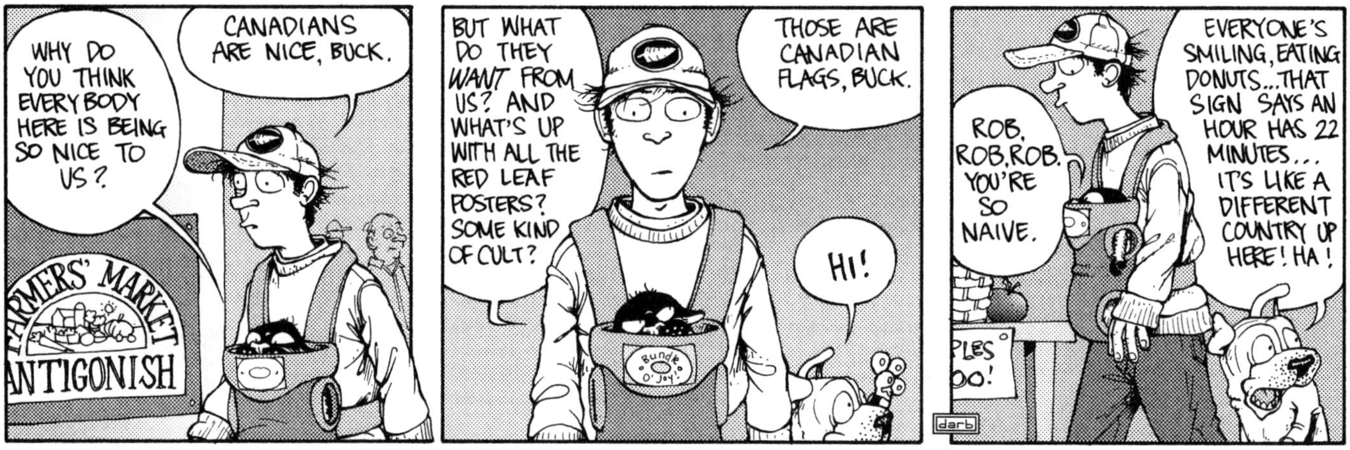
WHY DO YOU THINK EVERYBODY HERE IS BEING SO NICE TO US?
CANADIANS ARE NICE, BUCK.
FARMERS' MARKET ANTIGONISH
BUT WHAT DO THEY *WANT* FROM US? AND WHAT'S UP WITH ALL THE RED LEAF POSTERS? SOME KIND OF CULT?
THOSE ARE CANADIAN FLAGS, BUCK.
HI!
Bundle O' Joy
ROB, ROB, ROB. YOU'RE SO NAIVE.
EVERYONE'S SMILING, EATING DONUTS...THAT SIGN SAYS AN HOUR HAS 22 MINUTES... IT'S LIKE A DIFFERENT COUNTRY UP HERE! HA!

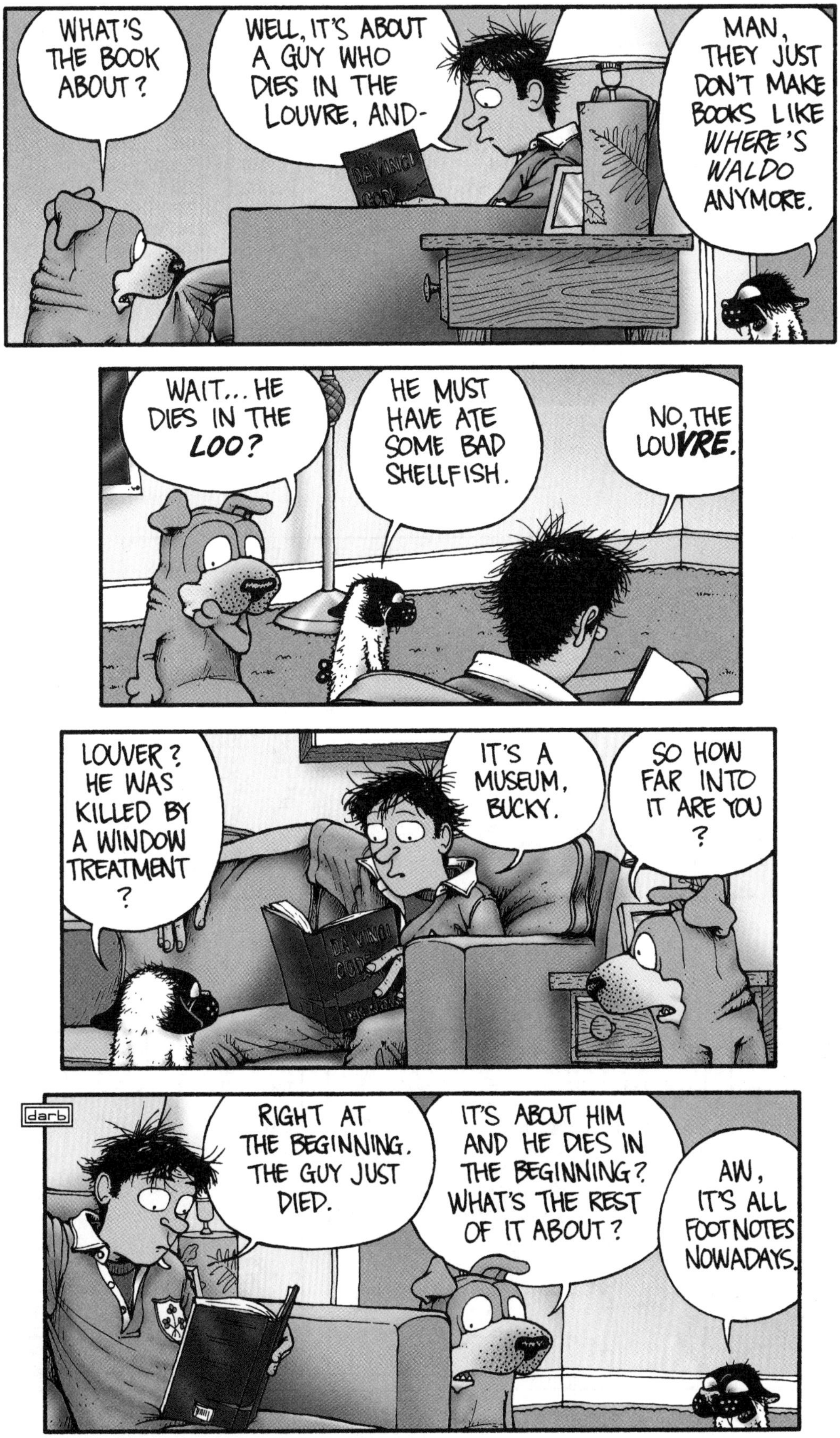
WHAT'S THE BOOK ABOUT?
WELL, IT'S ABOUT A GUY WHO DIES IN THE LOUVRE, AND-
MAN, THEY JUST DON'T MAKE BOOKS LIKE *WHERE'S WALDO* ANYMORE.
WAIT... HE DIES IN THE **LOO?**
HE MUST HAVE ATE SOME BAD SHELLFISH.
NO, THE LOU**VRE**.
LOUVER? HE WAS KILLED BY A WINDOW TREATMENT?
IT'S A MUSEUM, BUCKY.
SO HOW FAR INTO IT ARE YOU?
darb
RIGHT AT THE BEGINNING. THE GUY JUST DIED.
IT'S ABOUT HIM AND HE DIES IN THE BEGINNING? WHAT'S THE REST OF IT ABOUT?
AW, IT'S ALL FOOTNOTES NOWADAYS.

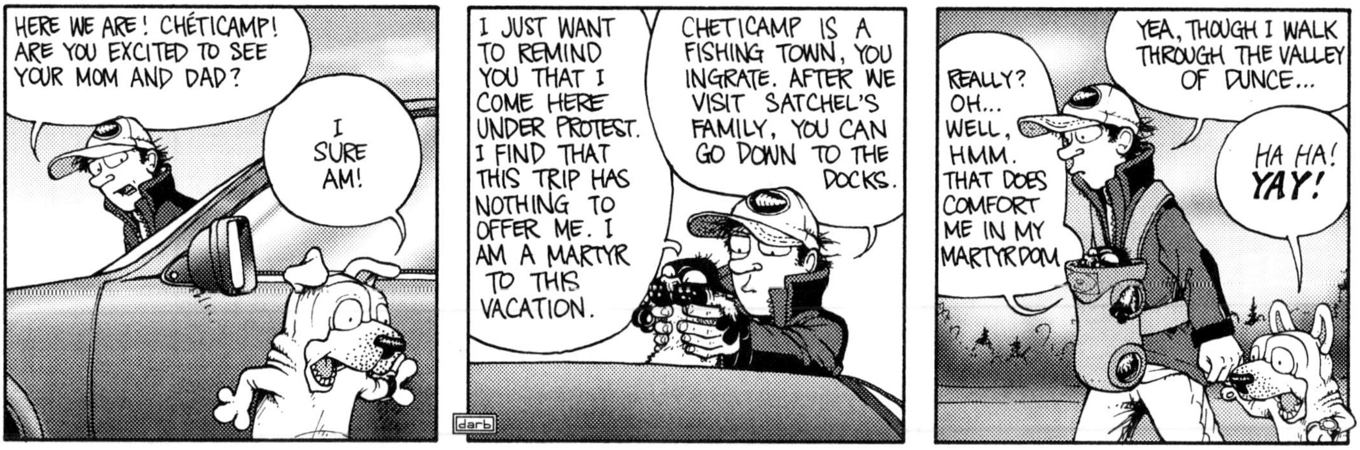
HERE WE ARE! CHÉTICAMP! ARE YOU EXCITED TO SEE YOUR MOM AND DAD?
I SURE AM!
I JUST WANT TO REMIND YOU THAT I COME HERE UNDER PROTEST. I FIND THAT THIS TRIP HAS NOTHING TO OFFER ME. I AM A MARTYR TO THIS VACATION.
CHETICAMP IS A FISHING TOWN, YOU INGRATE. AFTER WE VISIT SATCHEL'S FAMILY, YOU CAN GO DOWN TO THE DOCKS.
REALLY? OH... WELL, HMM. THAT DOES COMFORT ME IN MY MARTYRDOM.
YEA, THOUGH I WALK THROUGH THE VALLEY OF DUNCE...
HA HA! *YAY!*

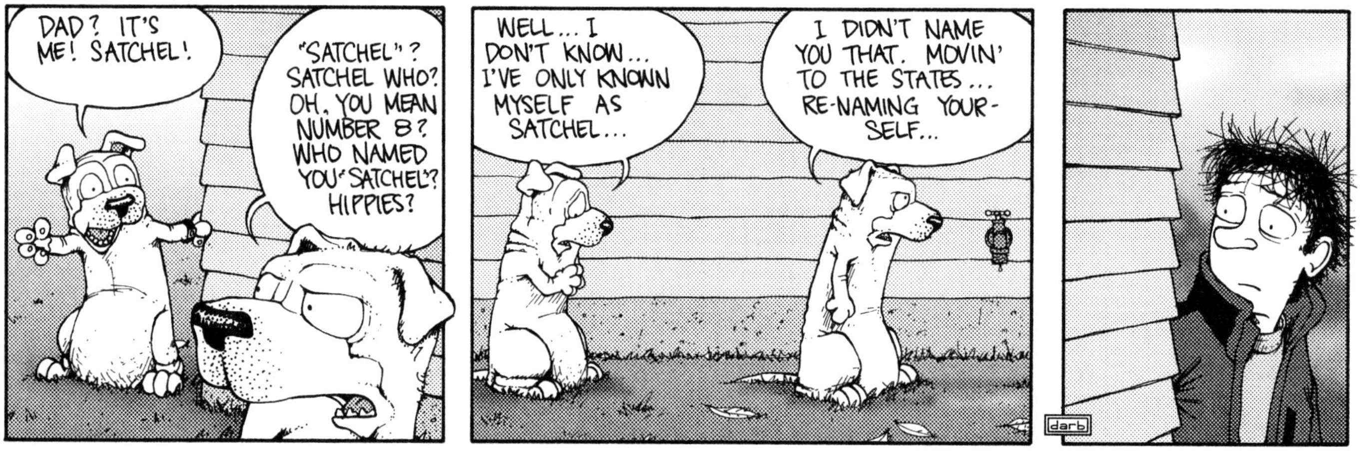
DAD? IT'S ME! SATCHEL!
"SATCHEL"? SATCHEL WHO? OH, YOU MEAN NUMBER 8? WHO NAMED YOU "SATCHEL"? HIPPIES?
WELL... I DON'T KNOW... I'VE ONLY KNOWN MYSELF AS SATCHEL...
I DIDN'T NAME YOU THAT. MOVIN' TO THE STATES... RE-NAMING YOURSELF...

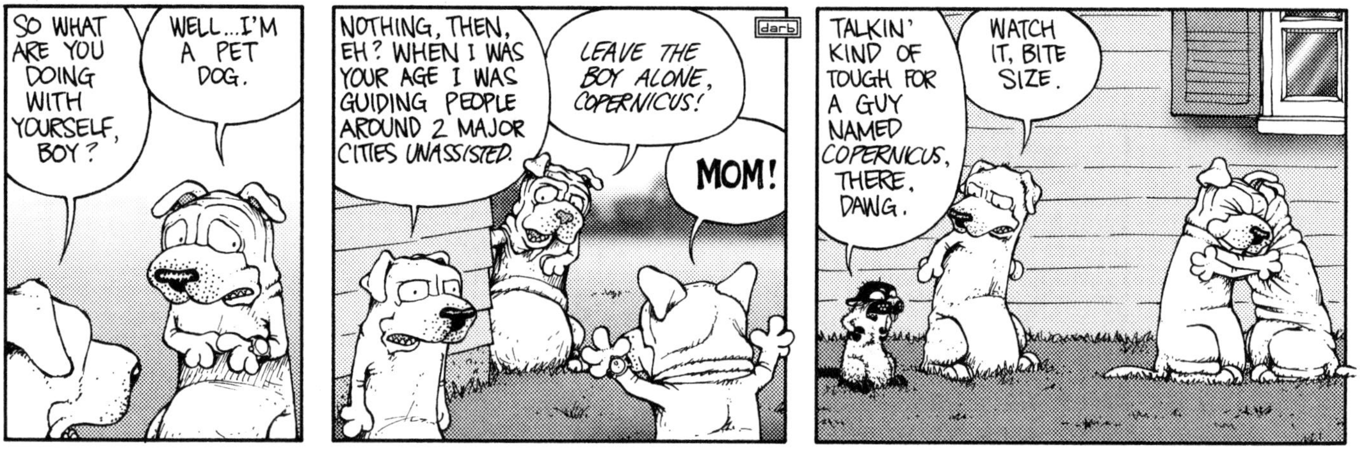
SO WHAT ARE YOU DOING WITH YOURSELF, BOY?
WELL...I'M A PET DOG.
NOTHING, THEN, EH? WHEN I WAS YOUR AGE I WAS GUIDING PEOPLE AROUND 2 MAJOR CITIES *UNASSISTED*.
LEAVE THE BOY ALONE, COPERNICUS!
MOM!
TALKIN' KIND OF TOUGH FOR A GUY NAMED *COPERNICUS*, THERE, DAWG.
WATCH IT, BITE SIZE.

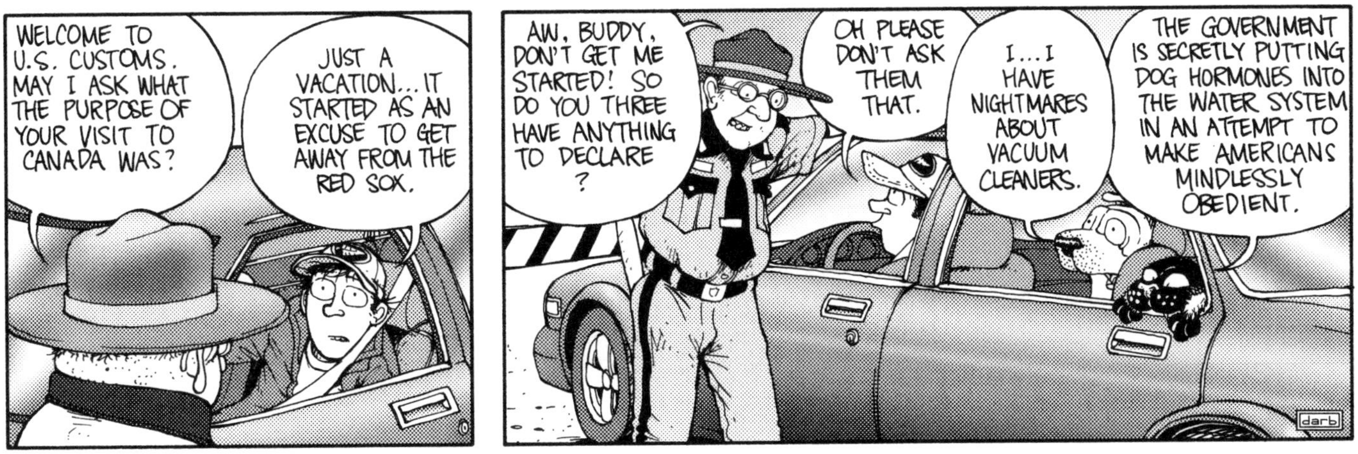
WELCOME TO U.S. CUSTOMS. MAY I ASK WHAT THE PURPOSE OF YOUR VISIT TO CANADA WAS?
JUST A VACATION... IT STARTED AS AN EXCUSE TO GET AWAY FROM THE RED SOX.
AW, BUDDY, DON'T GET ME STARTED! SO DO YOU THREE HAVE ANYTHING TO DECLARE?
OH PLEASE DON'T ASK THEM THAT.
I... I HAVE NIGHTMARES ABOUT VACUUM CLEANERS.
THE GOVERNMENT IS SECRETLY PUTTING DOG HORMONES INTO THE WATER SYSTEM IN AN ATTEMPT TO MAKE AMERICANS MINDLESSLY OBEDIENT.

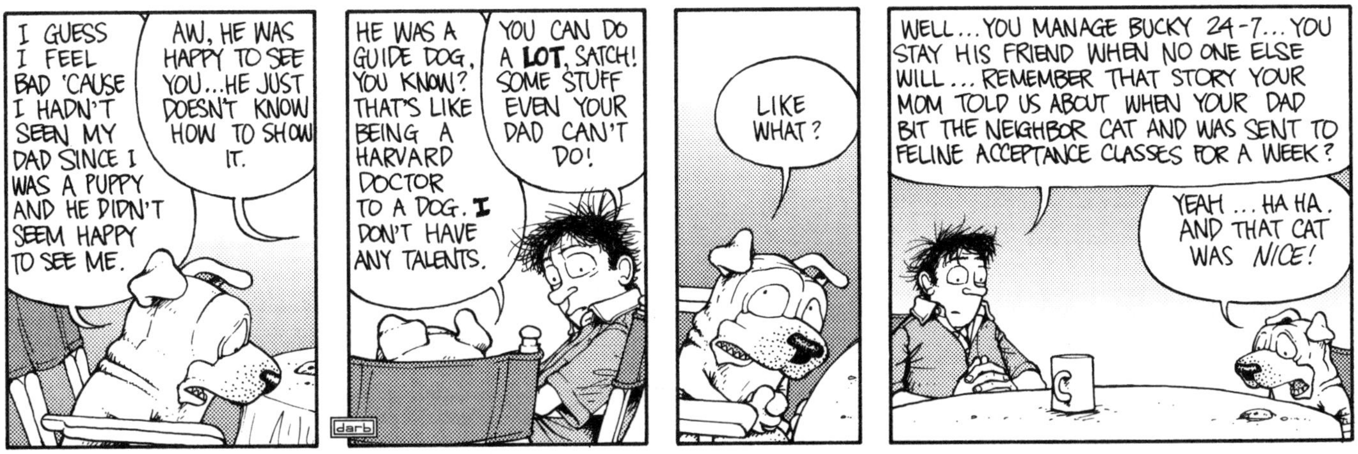
I GUESS I FEEL BAD 'CAUSE I HADN'T SEEN MY DAD SINCE I WAS A PUPPY AND HE DIDN'T SEEM HAPPY TO SEE ME.
AW, HE WAS HAPPY TO SEE YOU... HE JUST DOESN'T KNOW HOW TO SHOW IT.
HE WAS A GUIDE DOG, YOU KNOW? THAT'S LIKE BEING A HARVARD DOCTOR TO A DOG. I DON'T HAVE ANY TALENTS.
YOU CAN DO A **LOT**, SATCH! SOME STUFF EVEN YOUR DAD CAN'T DO!
LIKE WHAT?
WELL... YOU MANAGE BUCKY 24-7... YOU STAY HIS FRIEND WHEN NO ONE ELSE WILL... REMEMBER THAT STORY YOUR MOM TOLD US ABOUT WHEN YOUR DAD BIT THE NEIGHBOR CAT AND WAS SENT TO FELINE ACCEPTANCE CLASSES FOR A WEEK?
YEAH ... HA HA. AND THAT CAT WAS *NICE*!

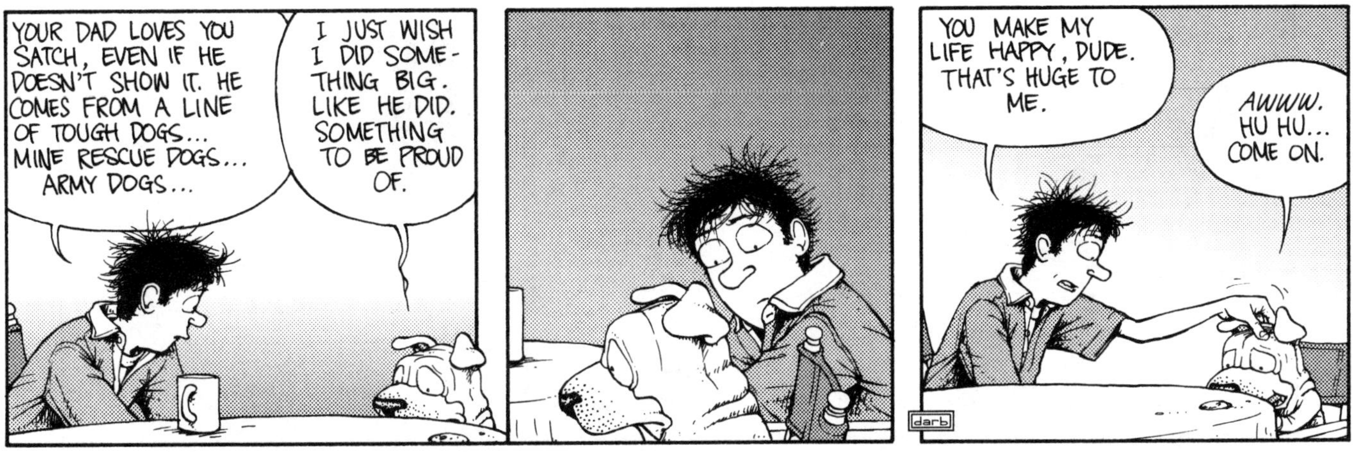
YOUR DAD LOVES YOU SATCH, EVEN IF HE DOESN'T SHOW IT. HE COMES FROM A LINE OF TOUGH DOGS... MINE RESCUE DOGS... ARMY DOGS...
I JUST WISH I DID SOMETHING BIG. LIKE HE DID. SOMETHING TO BE PROUD OF.
YOU MAKE MY LIFE HAPPY, DUDE. THAT'S HUGE TO ME.
AWWW. HU HU... COME ON.

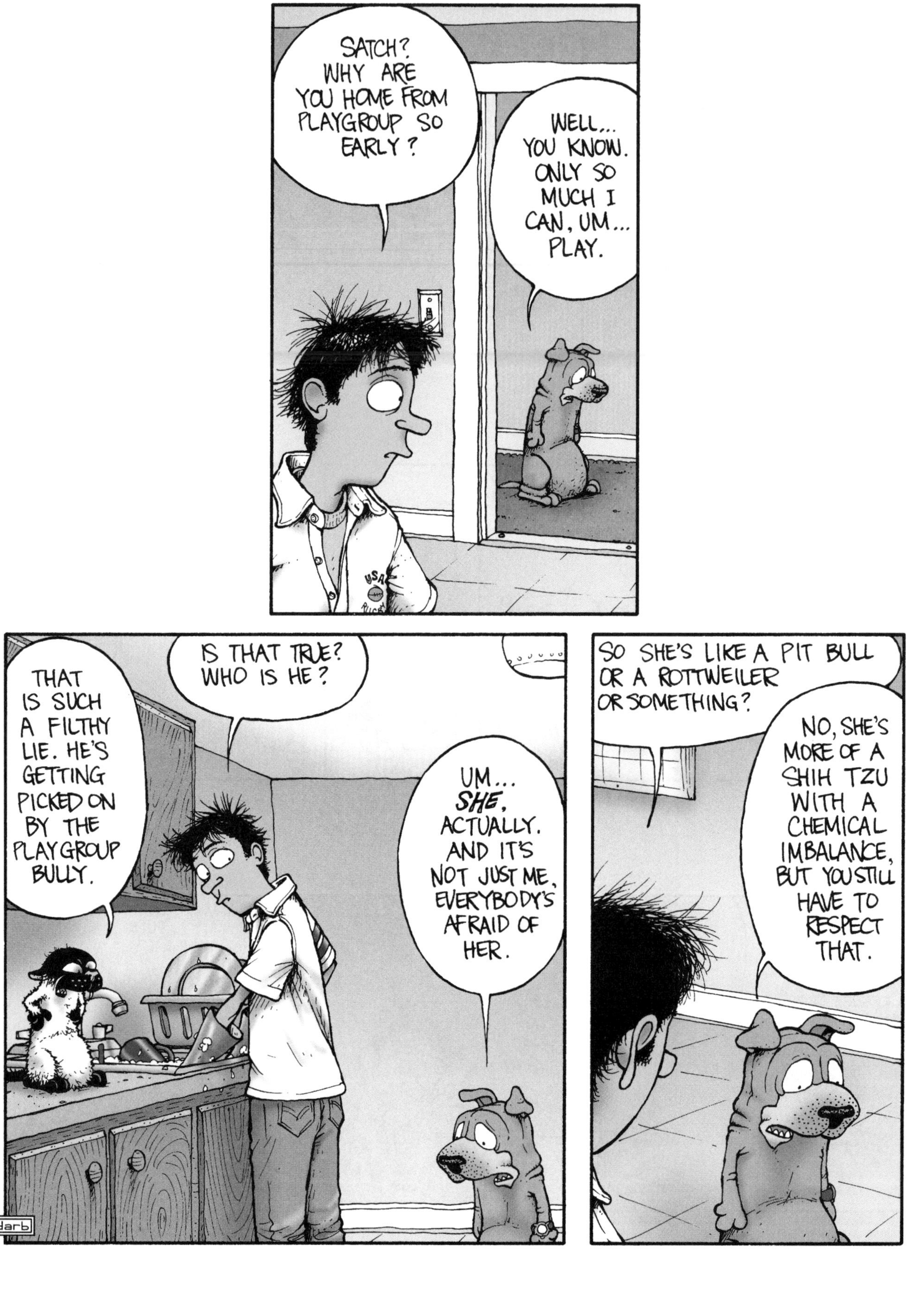
SATCH? WHY ARE YOU HOME FROM PLAYGROUP SO EARLY?
WELL... YOU KNOW. ONLY SO MUCH I CAN, UM... PLAY.
THAT IS SUCH A FILTHY LIE. HE'S GETTING PICKED ON BY THE PLAYGROUP BULLY.
IS THAT TRUE? WHO IS HE?
UM... *SHE*, ACTUALLY. AND IT'S NOT JUST ME, EVERYBODY'S AFRAID OF HER.
SO SHE'S LIKE A PIT BULL OR A ROTTWEILER OR SOMETHING?
NO, SHE'S MORE OF A SHIH TZU WITH A CHEMICAL IMBALANCE, BUT YOU STILL HAVE TO RESPECT THAT.
darb

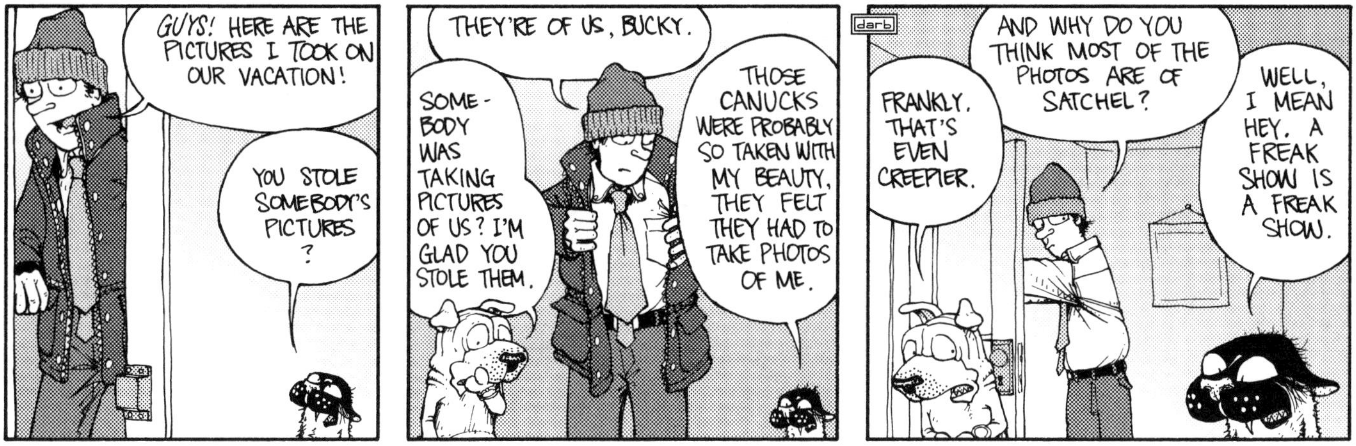
GUYS! HERE ARE THE PICTURES I TOOK ON OUR VACATION!
YOU STOLE SOMEBODY'S PICTURES?
THEY'RE OF US, BUCKY.
SOMEBODY WAS TAKING PICTURES OF US? I'M GLAD YOU STOLE THEM.
THOSE CANUCKS WERE PROBABLY SO TAKEN WITH MY BEAUTY, THEY FELT THEY HAD TO TAKE PHOTOS OF ME.
darb
AND WHY DO YOU THINK MOST OF THE PHOTOS ARE OF SATCHEL?
FRANKLY, THAT'S EVEN CREEPIER.
WELL, I MEAN HEY, A FREAK SHOW IS A FREAK SHOW.

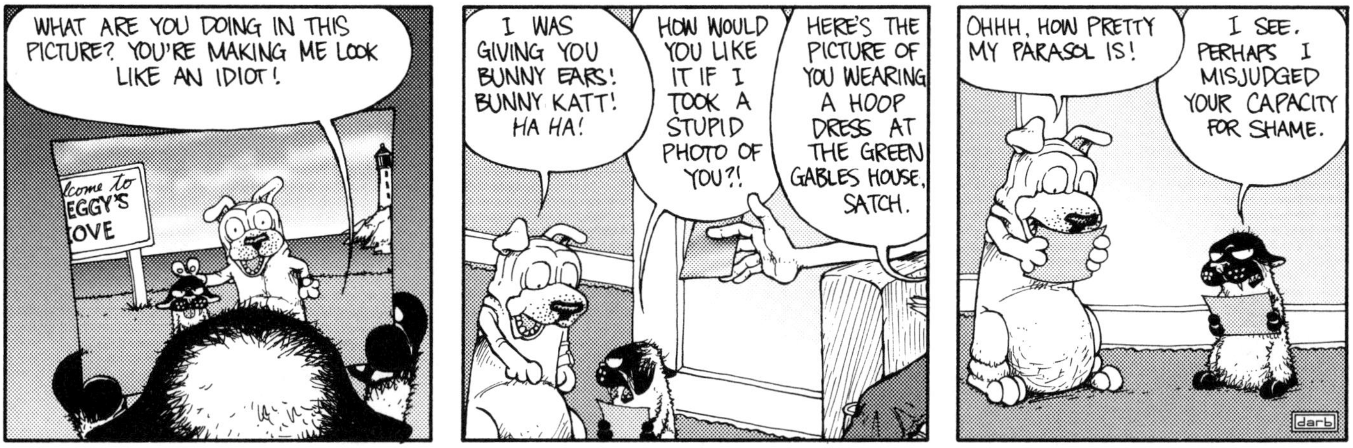
WHAT ARE YOU DOING IN THIS PICTURE? YOU'RE MAKING ME LOOK LIKE AN IDIOT!
I WAS GIVING YOU BUNNY EARS! BUNNY KATT! *HA HA!*
HOW WOULD YOU LIKE IT IF I TOOK A STUPID PHOTO OF YOU?!
HERE'S THE PICTURE OF YOU WEARING A HOOP DRESS AT THE GREEN GABLES HOUSE, SATCH.
OHHH, HOW PRETTY MY PARASOL IS!
I SEE. PERHAPS I MISJUDGED YOUR CAPACITY FOR SHAME.
darb

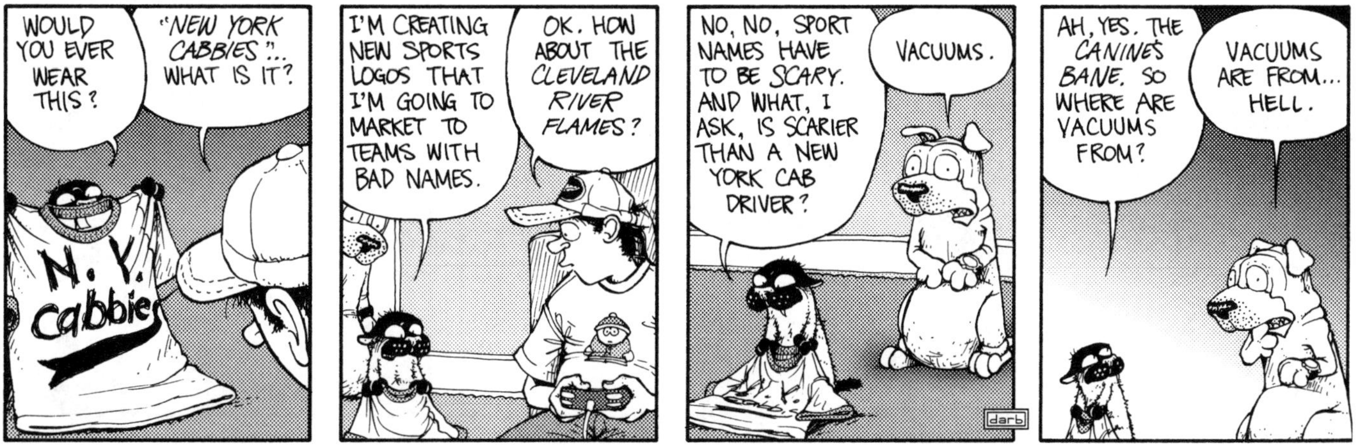
WOULD YOU EVER WEAR THIS?
"*NEW YORK CABBIES*"... WHAT IS IT?
N.Y. Cabbies
I'M CREATING NEW SPORTS LOGOS THAT I'M GOING TO MARKET TO TEAMS WITH BAD NAMES.
OK. HOW ABOUT THE *CLEVELAND RIVER FLAMES*?
NO, NO, SPORT NAMES HAVE TO BE *SCARY*. AND WHAT, I ASK, IS SCARIER THAN A NEW YORK CAB DRIVER?
VACUUMS.
darb
AH, YES. THE *CANINE'S BANE*. SO WHERE ARE VACUUMS FROM?
VACUUMS ARE FROM... HELL.

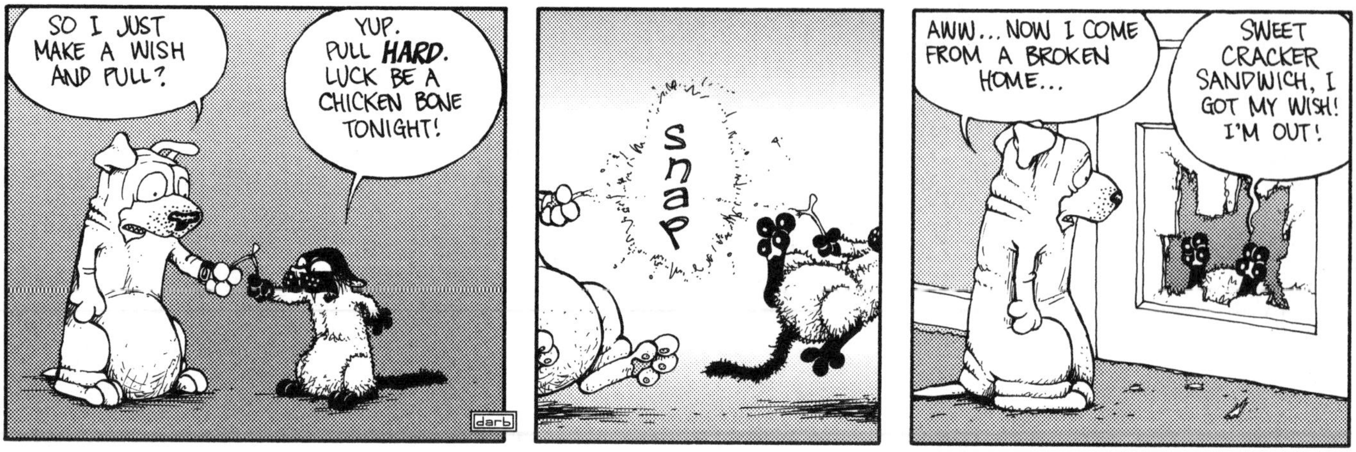

SO I JUST MAKE A WISH AND PULL?
YUP. PULL **HARD**. LUCK BE A CHICKEN BONE TONIGHT!
darb
SNAP
AWW... NOW I COME FROM A BROKEN HOME...
SWEET CRACKER SANDWICH, I GOT MY WISH! I'M OUT!

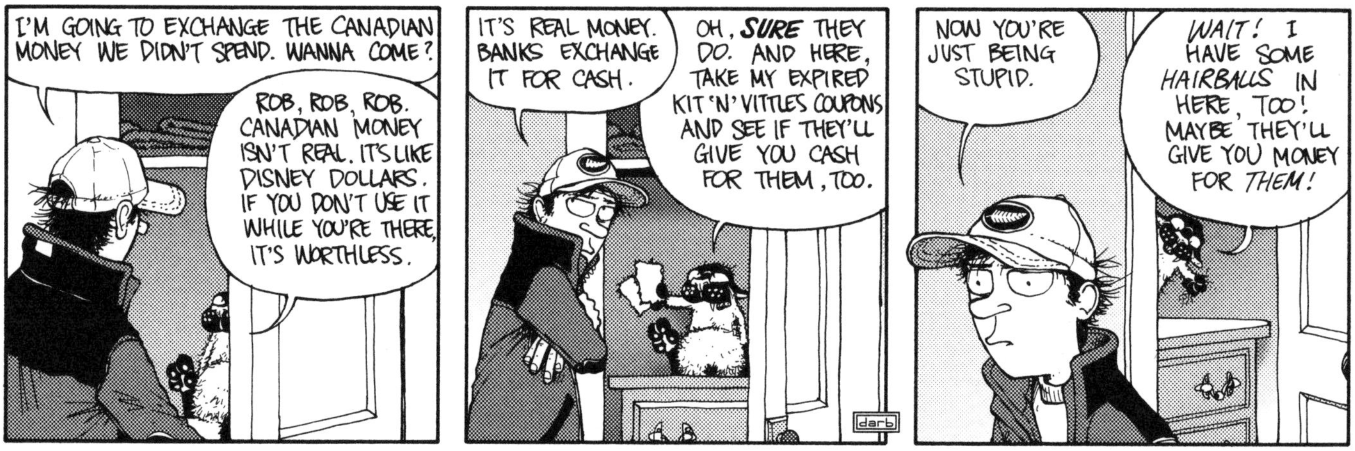

I'M GOING TO EXCHANGE THE CANADIAN MONEY WE DIDN'T SPEND. WANNA COME?
ROB, ROB, ROB. CANADIAN MONEY ISN'T REAL. IT'S LIKE DISNEY DOLLARS. IF YOU DON'T USE IT WHILE YOU'RE THERE, IT'S WORTHLESS.
IT'S REAL MONEY. BANKS EXCHANGE IT FOR CASH.
OH, ***SURE*** THEY DO. AND HERE, TAKE MY EXPIRED KIT 'N' VITTLES COUPONS AND SEE IF THEY'LL GIVE YOU CASH FOR THEM, TOO.
darb
NOW YOU'RE JUST BEING STUPID.
WAIT! I HAVE SOME *HAIRBALLS* IN HERE, TOO! MAYBE THEY'LL GIVE YOU MONEY FOR *THEM*!

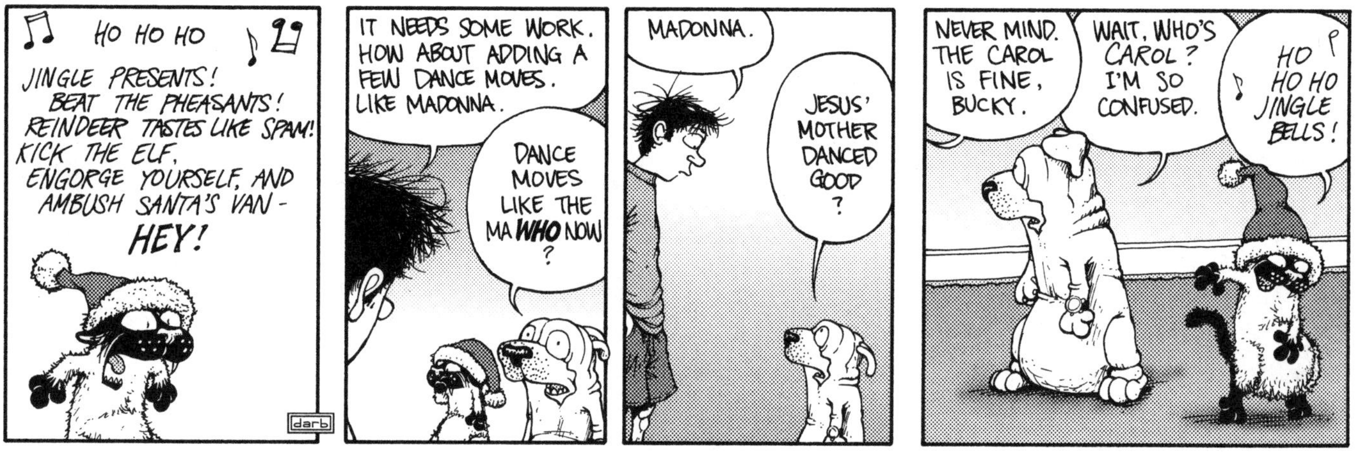

HO HO HO
JINGLE PRESENTS! BEAT THE PHEASANTS! REINDEER TASTES LIKE SPAM! KICK THE ELF, ENGORGE YOURSELF, AND AMBUSH SANTA'S VAN - **HEY!**
darb
IT NEEDS SOME WORK. HOW ABOUT ADDING A FEW DANCE MOVES. LIKE MADONNA.
DANCE MOVES LIKE THE MA ***WHO*** NOW?
MADONNA.
JESUS' MOTHER DANCED GOOD?
NEVER MIND. THE CAROL IS FINE, BUCKY.
WAIT, WHO'S CAROL? I'M SO CONFUSED.
HO HO HO JINGLE BELLS!

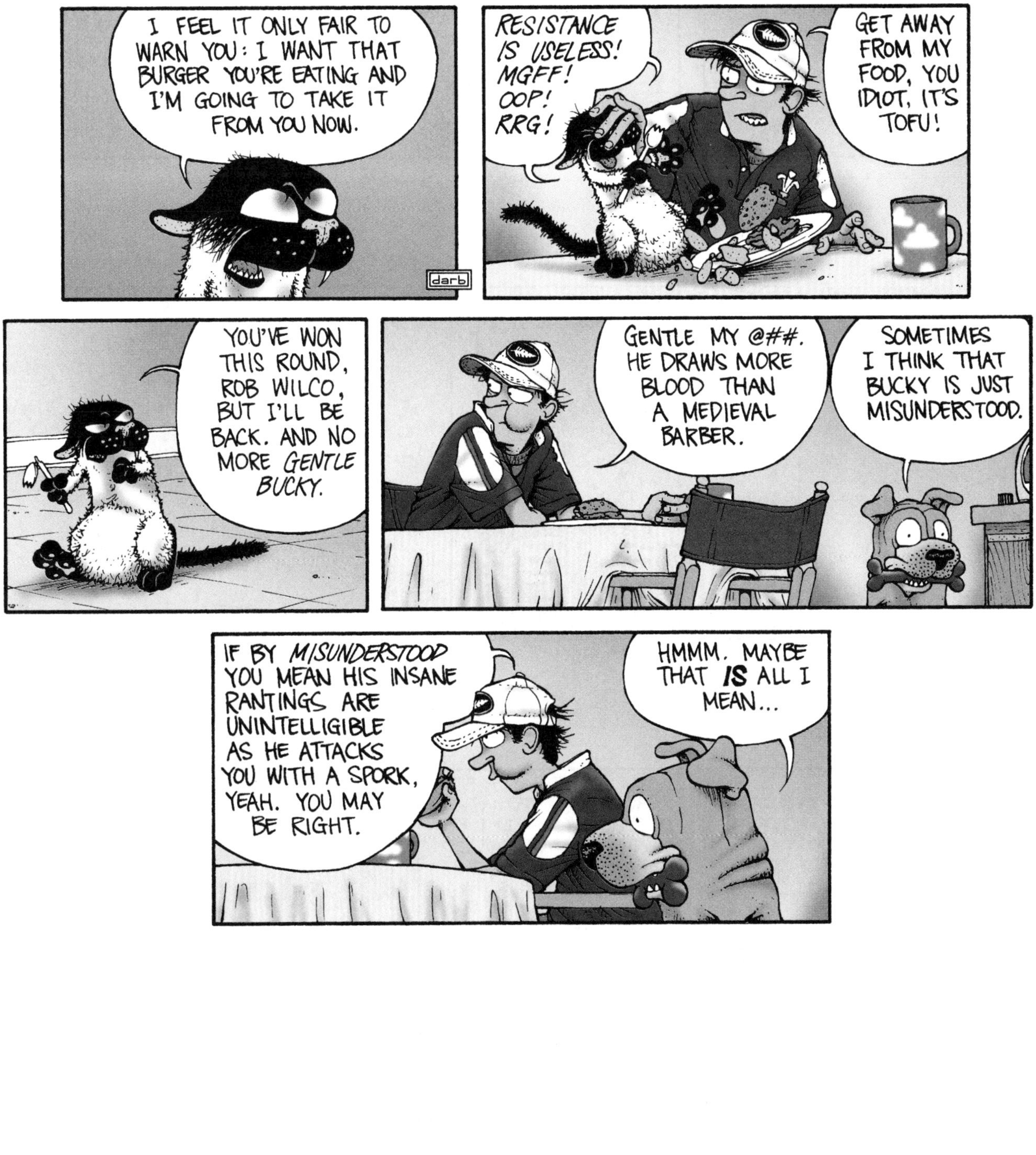
I FEEL IT ONLY FAIR TO WARN YOU: I WANT THAT BURGER YOU'RE EATING AND I'M GOING TO TAKE IT FROM YOU NOW.
darb
RESISTANCE IS USELESS! MGFF! OOP! RRG!
GET AWAY FROM MY FOOD, YOU IDIOT, IT'S TOFU!
YOU'VE WON THIS ROUND, ROB WILCO, BUT I'LL BE BACK. AND NO MORE *GENTLE BUCKY.*
GENTLE MY @##. HE DRAWS MORE BLOOD THAN A MEDIEVAL BARBER.
SOMETIMES I THINK THAT BUCKY IS JUST MISUNDERSTOOD.
IF BY *MISUNDERSTOOD* YOU MEAN HIS INSANE RANTINGS ARE UNINTELLIGIBLE AS HE ATTACKS YOU WITH A SPORK, YEAH. YOU MAY BE RIGHT.
HMMM. MAYBE THAT **IS** ALL I MEAN...

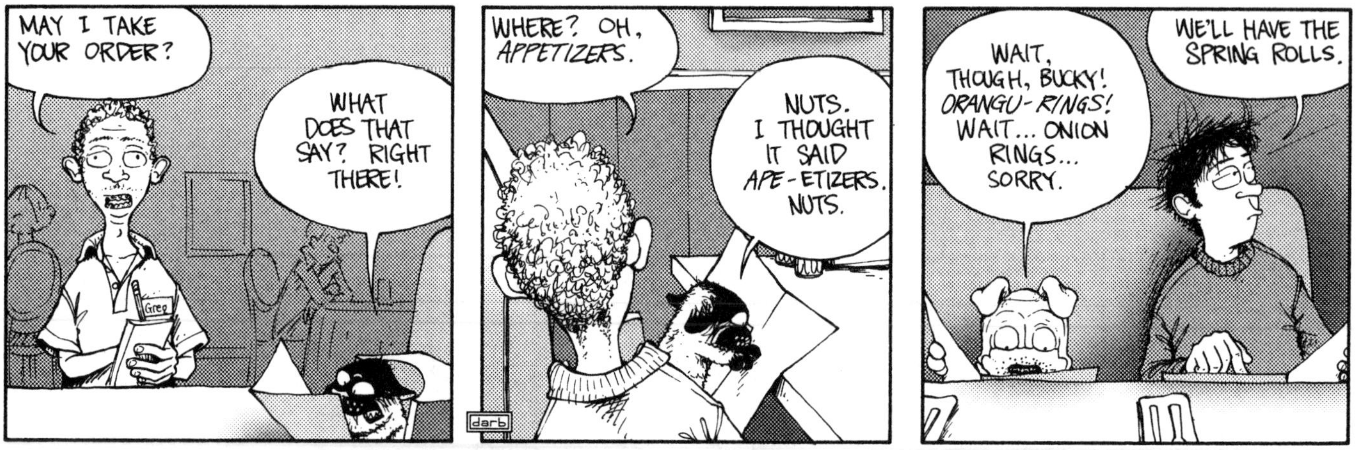
MAY I TAKE YOUR ORDER?
WHAT DOES THAT SAY? RIGHT THERE!
Greg
WHERE? OH, *APPETIZERS*.
NUTS. I THOUGHT IT SAID *APE*-ETIZERS. NUTS.
darb
WAIT, THOUGH, BUCKY! *ORANGU-RINGS!* WAIT... ONION RINGS... SORRY.
WE'LL HAVE THE SPRING ROLLS.

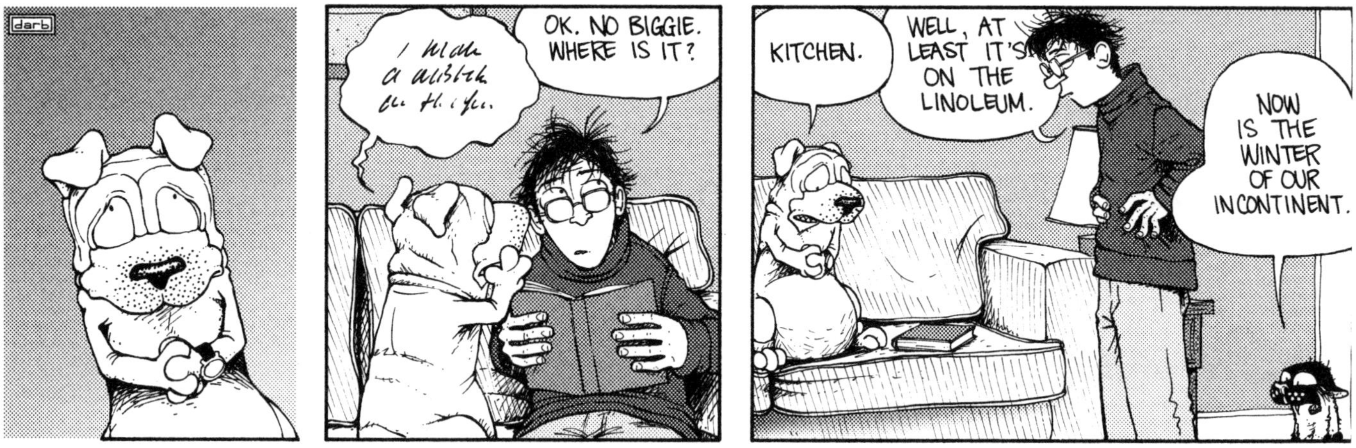
darb
OK. NO BIGGIE. WHERE IS IT?
KITCHEN.
WELL, AT LEAST IT'S ON THE LINOLEUM.
NOW IS THE WINTER OF OUR INCONTINENT.

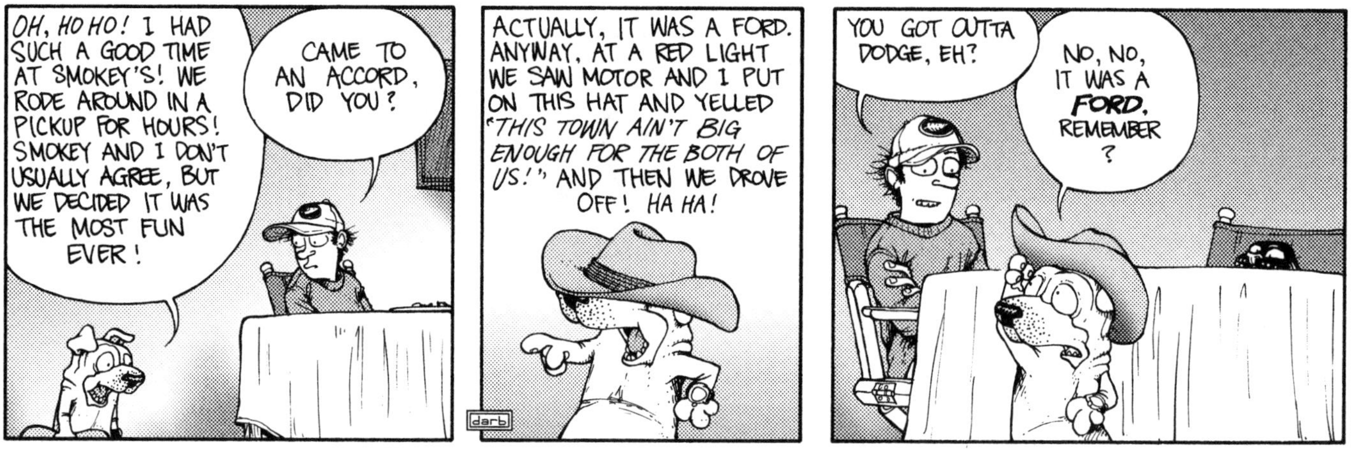
OH, HO HO! I HAD SUCH A GOOD TIME AT SMOKEY'S! WE RODE AROUND IN A PICKUP FOR HOURS! SMOKEY AND I DON'T USUALLY AGREE, BUT WE DECIDED IT WAS THE MOST FUN EVER!
CAME TO AN ACCORD, DID YOU?
ACTUALLY, IT WAS A FORD. ANYWAY, AT A RED LIGHT WE SAW MOTOR AND I PUT ON THIS HAT AND YELLED *"THIS TOWN AIN'T BIG ENOUGH FOR THE BOTH OF US!"* AND THEN WE DROVE OFF! HA HA!
darb
YOU GOT OUTTA DODGE, EH?
NO, NO, IT WAS A **FORD**, REMEMBER?

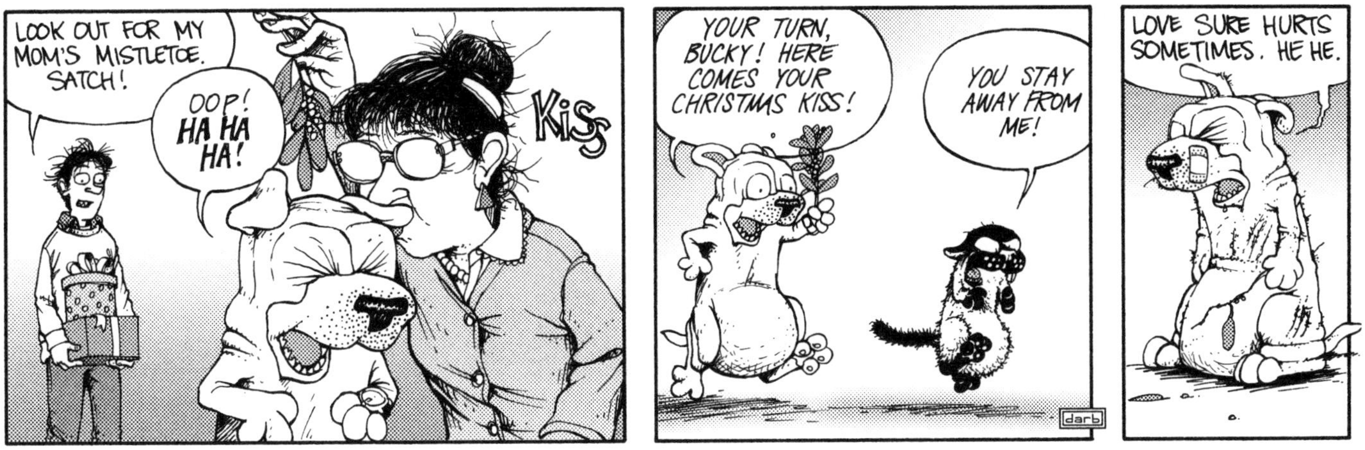
LOOK OUT FOR MY MOM'S MISTLETOE. SATCH!
OOP! HA HA HA!
KISS
YOUR TURN, BUCKY! HERE COMES YOUR CHRISTMAS KISS!
YOU STAY AWAY FROM ME!
LOVE SURE HURTS SOMETIMES. HE HE.

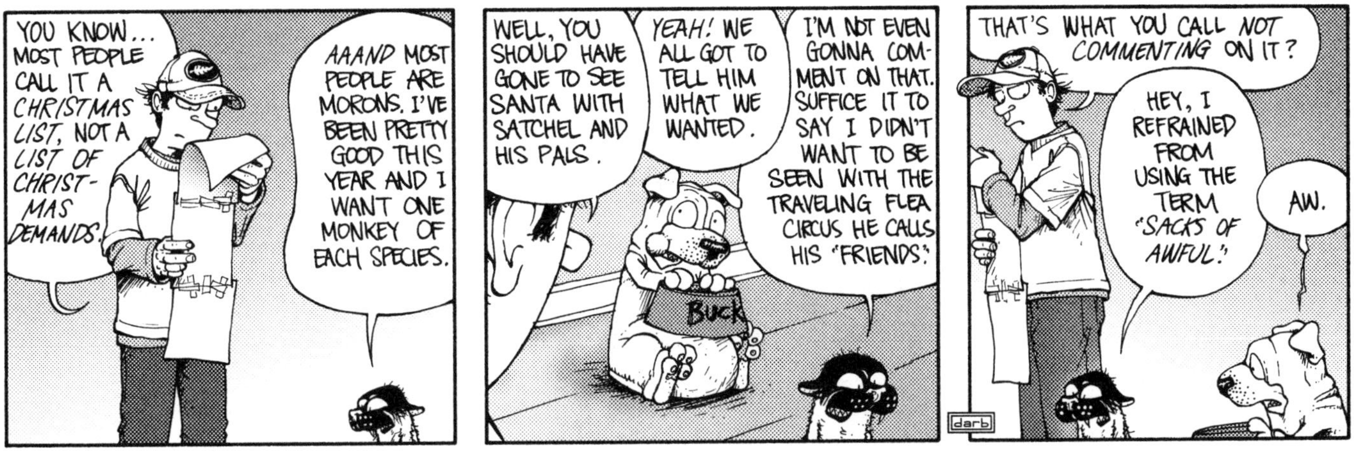
YOU KNOW... MOST PEOPLE CALL IT A CHRISTMAS LIST, NOT A LIST OF CHRISTMAS DEMANDS.
AAAND MOST PEOPLE ARE MORONS. I'VE BEEN PRETTY GOOD THIS YEAR AND I WANT ONE MONKEY OF EACH SPECIES.
WELL, YOU SHOULD HAVE GONE TO SEE SANTA WITH SATCHEL AND HIS PALS.
YEAH! WE ALL GOT TO TELL HIM WHAT WE WANTED.
I'M NOT EVEN GONNA COMMENT ON THAT. SUFFICE IT TO SAY I DIDN'T WANT TO BE SEEN WITH THE TRAVELING FLEA CIRCUS HE CALLS HIS "FRIENDS."
THAT'S WHAT YOU CALL NOT COMMENTING ON IT?
HEY, I REFRAINED FROM USING THE TERM "SACKS OF AWFUL."
AW.

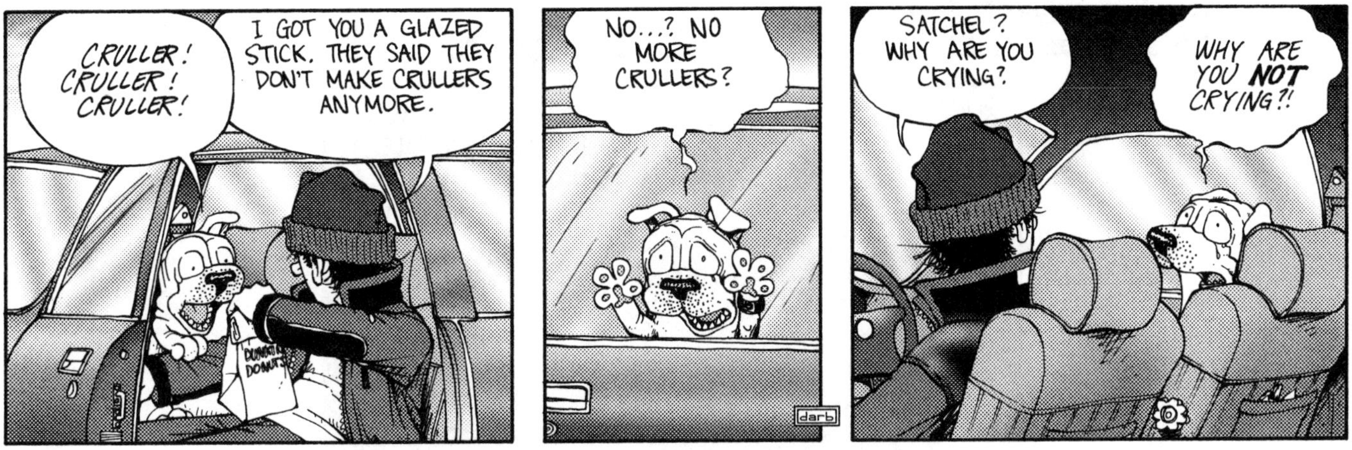
CRULLER! CRULLER! CRULLER!
I GOT YOU A GLAZED STICK. THEY SAID THEY DON'T MAKE CRULLERS ANYMORE.
NO...? NO MORE CRULLERS?
SATCHEL? WHY ARE YOU CRYING?
WHY ARE YOU NOT CRYING?!

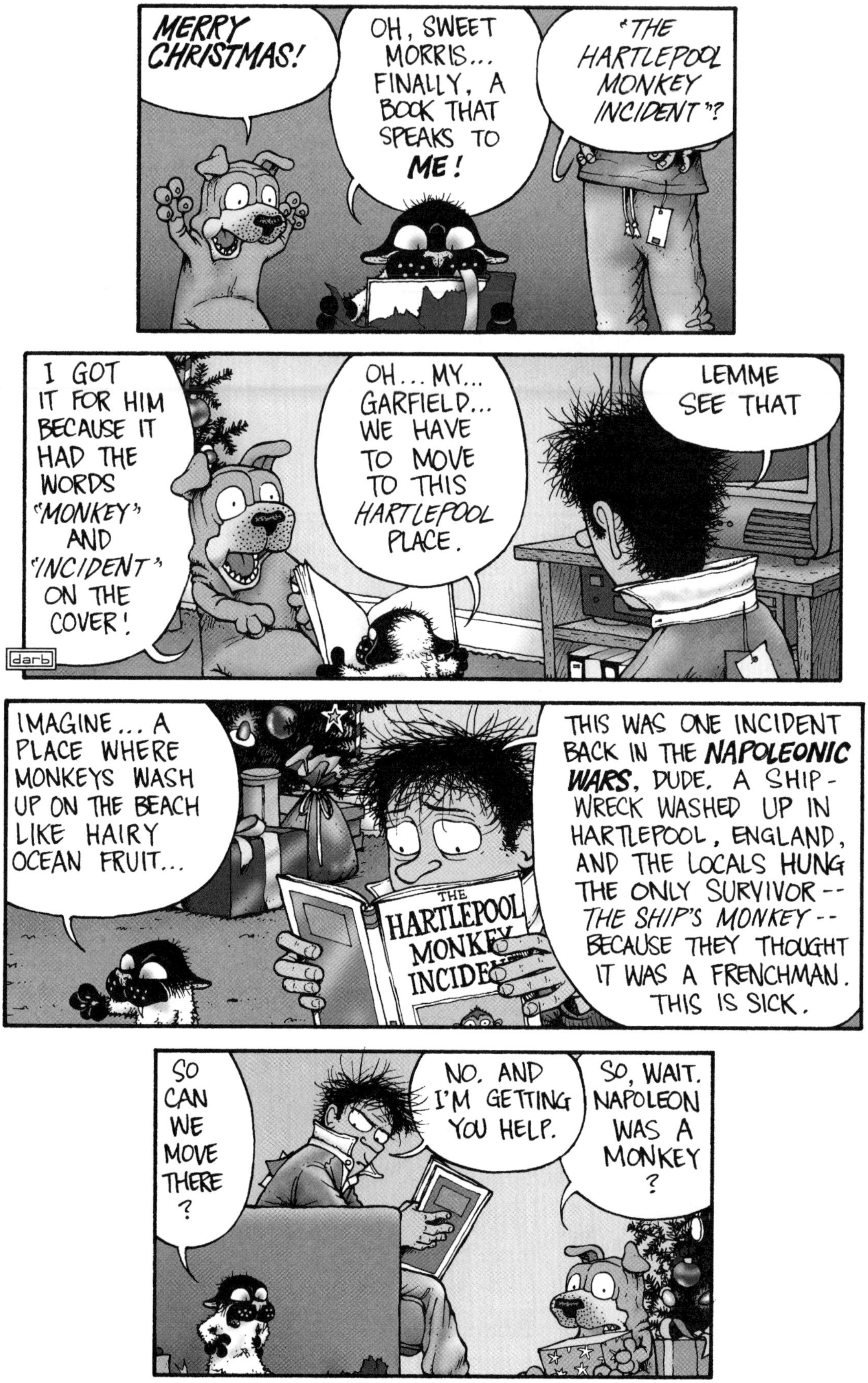
MERRY CHRISTMAS!
OH, SWEET MORRIS... FINALLY, A BOOK THAT SPEAKS TO **ME**!
"THE HARTLEPOOL MONKEY INCIDENT"?
I GOT IT FOR HIM BECAUSE IT HAD THE WORDS "MONKEY" AND "INCIDENT" ON THE COVER!
OH... MY... GARFIELD... WE HAVE TO MOVE TO THIS HARTLEPOOL PLACE.
LEMME SEE THAT
darb
IMAGINE... A PLACE WHERE MONKEYS WASH UP ON THE BEACH LIKE HAIRY OCEAN FRUIT...
THE HARTLEPOOL MONKEY INCIDE
THIS WAS ONE INCIDENT BACK IN THE **NAPOLEONIC WARS**, DUDE. A SHIP-WRECK WASHED UP IN HARTLEPOOL, ENGLAND, AND THE LOCALS HUNG THE ONLY SURVIVOR -- THE SHIP'S MONKEY -- BECAUSE THEY THOUGHT IT WAS A FRENCHMAN. THIS IS SICK.
SO CAN WE MOVE THERE?
SO, WAIT. NAPOLEON WAS A MONKEY?
NO. AND I'M GETTING YOU HELP.

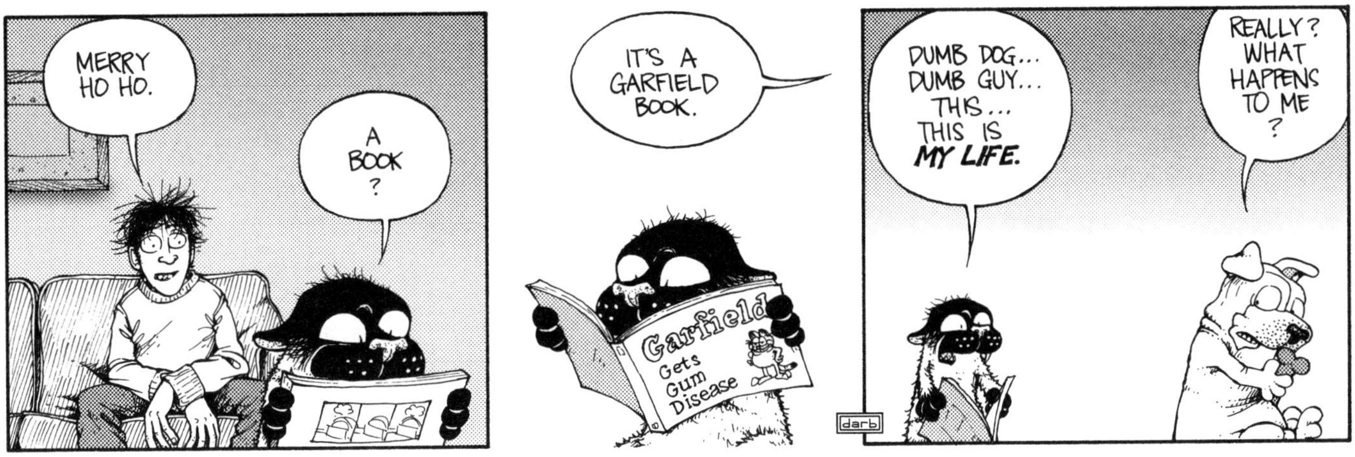
MERRY HO HO.
A BOOK ?
IT'S A GARFIELD BOOK.
Garfield Gets Gum Disease
DUMB DOG... DUMB GUY... THIS... THIS IS **MY LIFE.**
REALLY? WHAT HAPPENS TO ME ?
darb

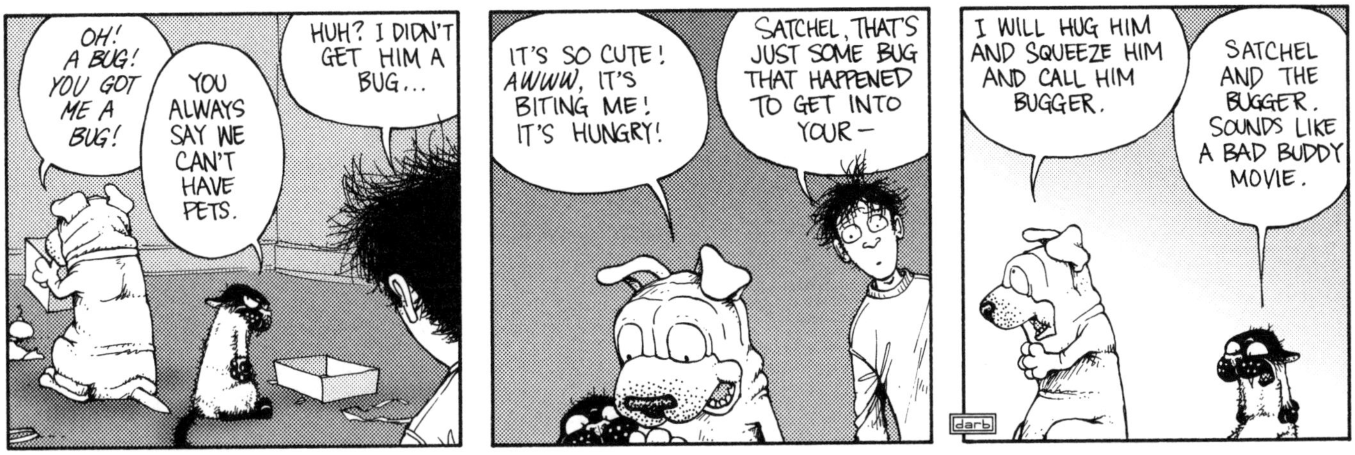
OH! A BUG! YOU GOT ME A BUG!
YOU ALWAYS SAY WE CAN'T HAVE PETS.
HUH? I DIDN'T GET HIM A BUG...
IT'S SO CUTE! *AWWW*, IT'S BITING ME! IT'S HUNGRY!
SATCHEL, THAT'S JUST SOME BUG THAT HAPPENED TO GET INTO YOUR—
I WILL HUG HIM AND SQUEEZE HIM AND CALL HIM BUGGER.
SATCHEL AND THE BUGGER. SOUNDS LIKE A BAD BUDDY MOVIE.
darb

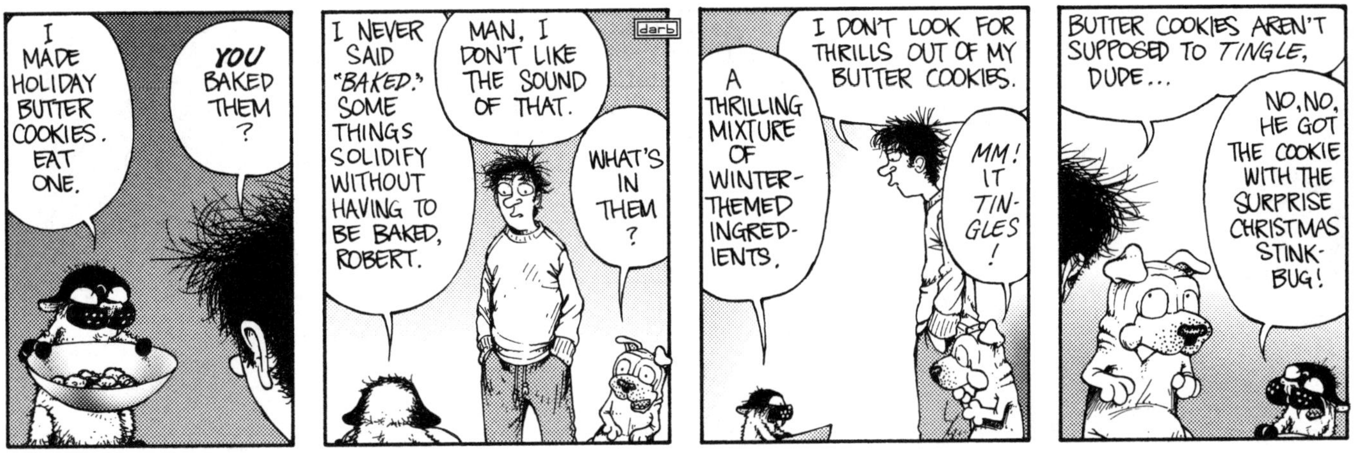
I MADE HOLIDAY BUTTER COOKIES. EAT ONE.
YOU BAKED THEM ?
I NEVER SAID "*BAKED.*" SOME THINGS SOLIDIFY WITHOUT HAVING TO BE BAKED, ROBERT.
MAN, I DON'T LIKE THE SOUND OF THAT.
WHAT'S IN THEM ?
darb
A THRILLING MIXTURE OF WINTER-THEMED INGREDIENTS.
I DON'T LOOK FOR THRILLS OUT OF MY BUTTER COOKIES.
MM! IT *TINGLES*!
BUTTER COOKIES AREN'T SUPPOSED TO *TINGLE*, DUDE...
NO, NO, HE GOT THE COOKIE WITH THE SURPRISE CHRISTMAS STINK-BUG!

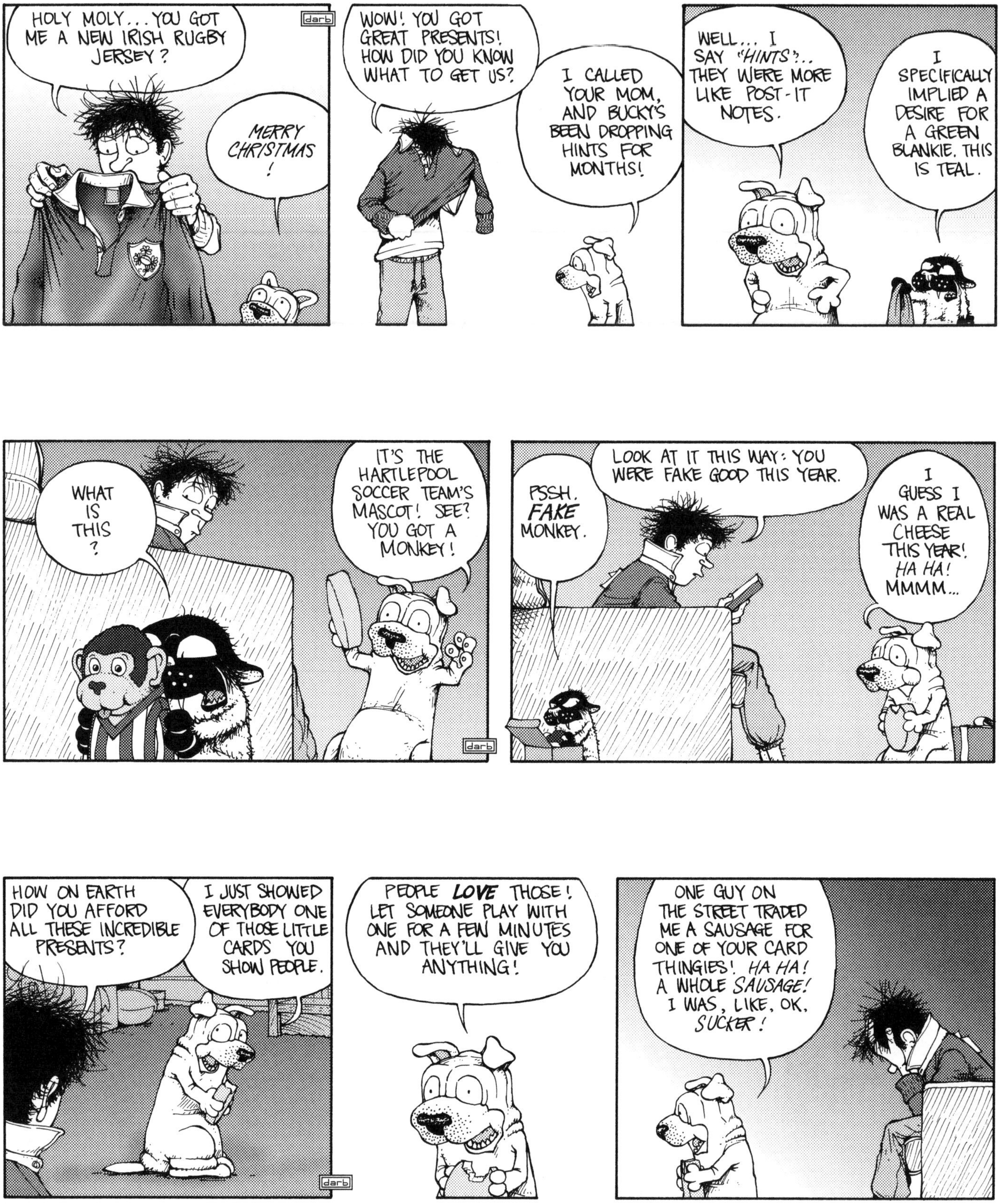

darb
HOLY MOLY... YOU GOT ME A NEW IRISH RUGBY JERSEY?
MERRY CHRISTMAS!
WOW! YOU GOT GREAT PRESENTS! HOW DID YOU KNOW WHAT TO GET US?
I CALLED YOUR MOM, AND BUCKY'S BEEN DROPPING HINTS FOR MONTHS!
WELL... I SAY "HINTS"... THEY WERE MORE LIKE POST-IT NOTES.
I SPECIFICALLY IMPLIED A DESIRE FOR A GREEN BLANKIE. THIS IS TEAL.
WHAT IS THIS?
IT'S THE HARTLEPOOL SOCCER TEAM'S MASCOT! SEE? YOU GOT A MONKEY!
darb
LOOK AT IT THIS WAY: YOU WERE FAKE GOOD THIS YEAR.
PSSH. FAKE MONKEY.
I GUESS I WAS A REAL CHEESE THIS YEAR! HA HA! MMMM...
HOW ON EARTH DID YOU AFFORD ALL THESE INCREDIBLE PRESENTS?
I JUST SHOWED EVERYBODY ONE OF THOSE LITTLE CARDS YOU SHOW PEOPLE.
darb
PEOPLE LOVE THOSE! LET SOMEONE PLAY WITH ONE FOR A FEW MINUTES AND THEY'LL GIVE YOU ANYTHING!
ONE GUY ON THE STREET TRADED ME A SAUSAGE FOR ONE OF YOUR CARD THINGIES! HA HA! A WHOLE SAUSAGE! I WAS, LIKE, OK, SUCKER!

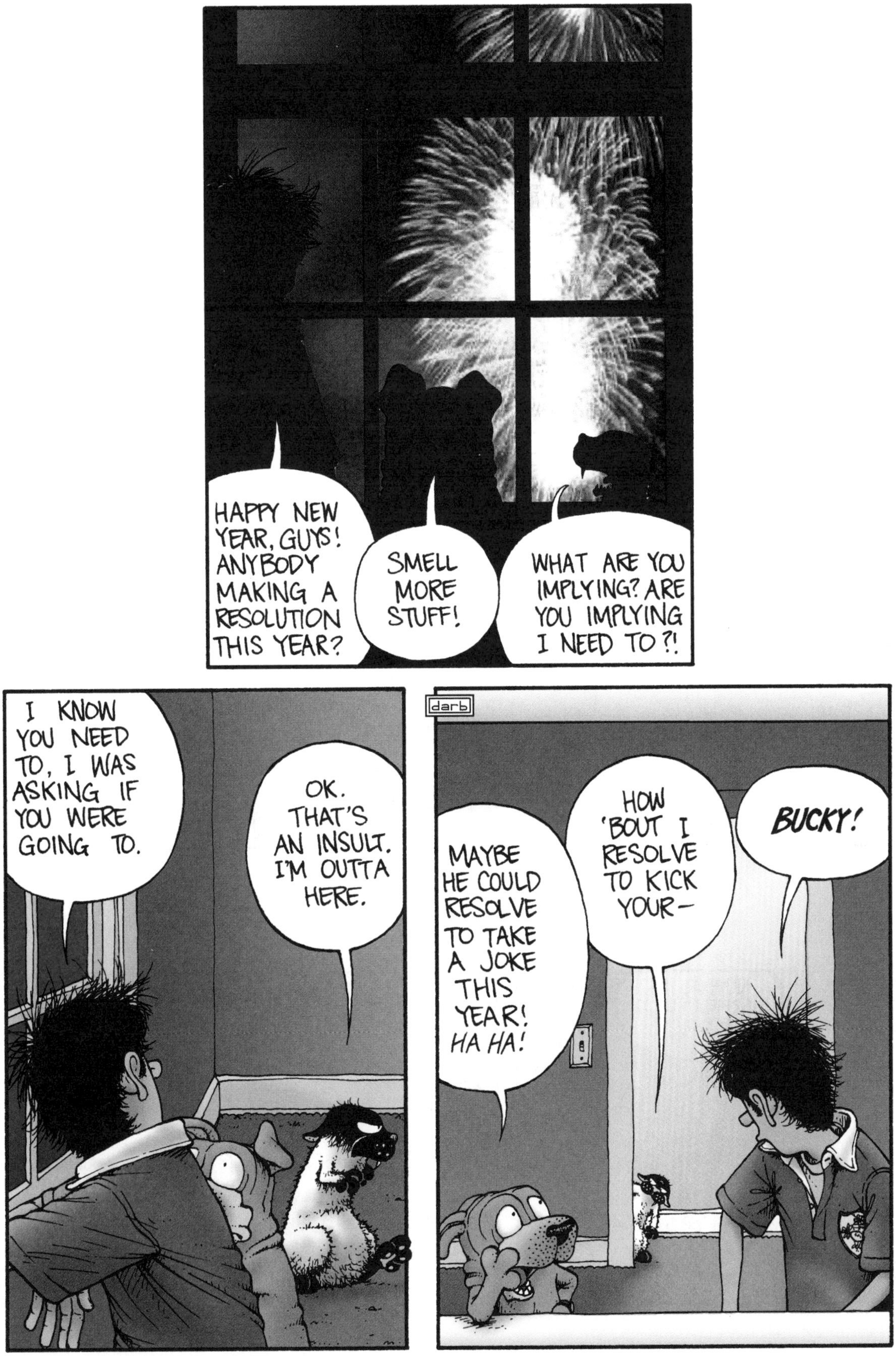
HAPPY NEW YEAR, GUYS! ANYBODY MAKING A RESOLUTION THIS YEAR?
SMELL MORE STUFF!
WHAT ARE YOU IMPLYING? ARE YOU IMPLYING I NEED TO?!
I KNOW YOU NEED TO, I WAS ASKING IF YOU WERE GOING TO.
OK. THAT'S AN INSULT. I'M OUTTA HERE.
darb
MAYBE HE COULD RESOLVE TO TAKE A JOKE THIS YEAR! HA HA!
HOW 'BOUT I RESOLVE TO KICK YOUR—
BUCKY!

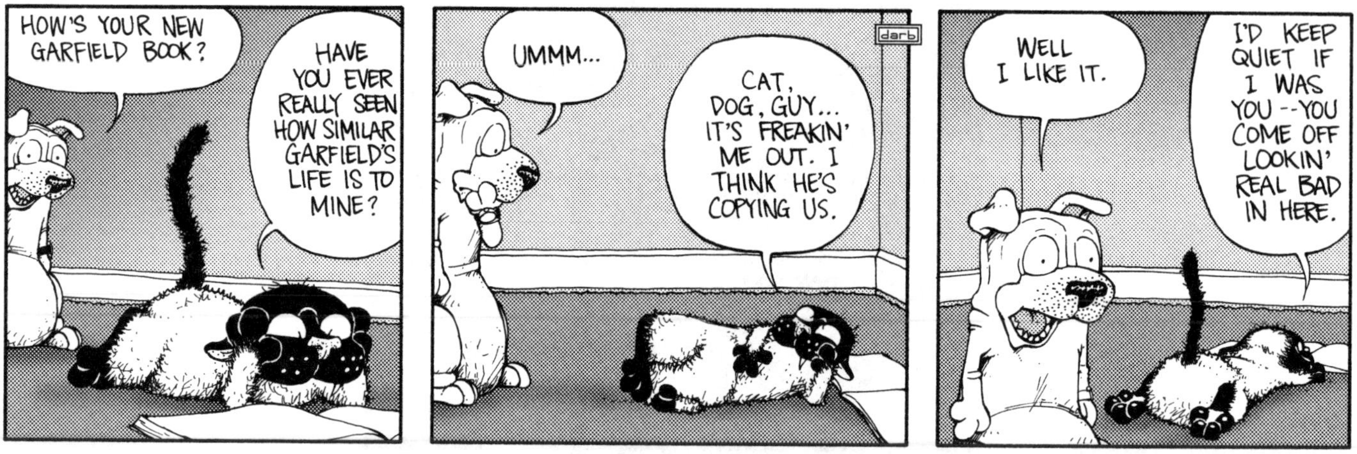
HOW'S YOUR NEW GARFIELD BOOK?
HAVE YOU EVER REALLY SEEN HOW SIMILAR GARFIELD'S LIFE IS TO MINE?
darb
UMMM...
CAT, DOG, GUY... IT'S FREAKIN' ME OUT. I THINK HE'S COPYING US.
WELL I LIKE IT.
I'D KEEP QUIET IF I WAS YOU--YOU COME OFF LOOKIN' REAL BAD IN HERE.

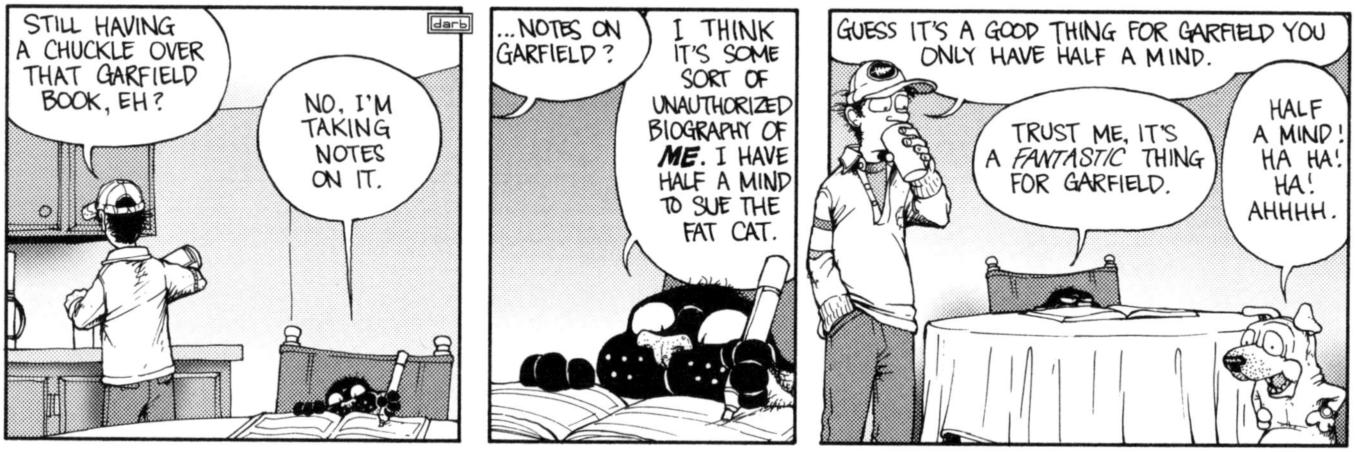
darb
STILL HAVING A CHUCKLE OVER THAT GARFIELD BOOK, EH?
NO, I'M TAKING NOTES ON IT.
...NOTES ON GARFIELD?
I THINK IT'S SOME SORT OF UNAUTHORIZED BIOGRAPHY OF ME. I HAVE HALF A MIND TO SUE THE FAT CAT.
GUESS IT'S A GOOD THING FOR GARFIELD YOU ONLY HAVE HALF A MIND.
TRUST ME, IT'S A FANTASTIC THING FOR GARFIELD.
HALF A MIND! HA HA! HA! AHHHH.

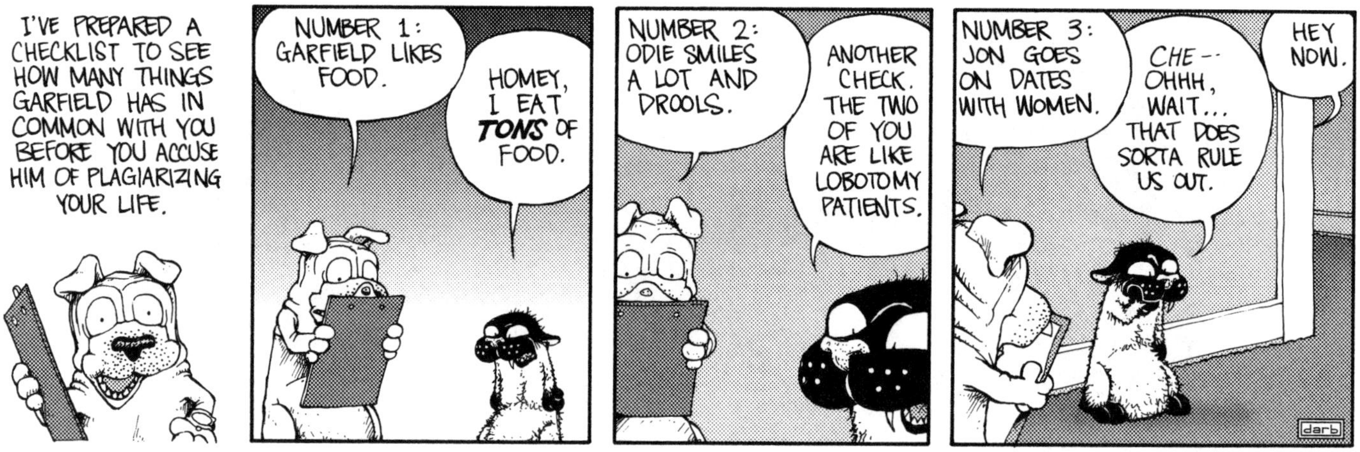
I'VE PREPARED A CHECKLIST TO SEE HOW MANY THINGS GARFIELD HAS IN COMMON WITH YOU BEFORE YOU ACCUSE HIM OF PLAGIARIZING YOUR LIFE.
NUMBER 1: GARFIELD LIKES FOOD.
HOMEY, I EAT TONS OF FOOD.
NUMBER 2: ODIE SMILES A LOT AND DROOLS.
ANOTHER CHECK. THE TWO OF YOU ARE LIKE LOBOTOMY PATIENTS.
NUMBER 3: JON GOES ON DATES WITH WOMEN.
CHE-- OHHH, WAIT... THAT DOES SORTA RULE US OUT.
HEY NOW.
darb

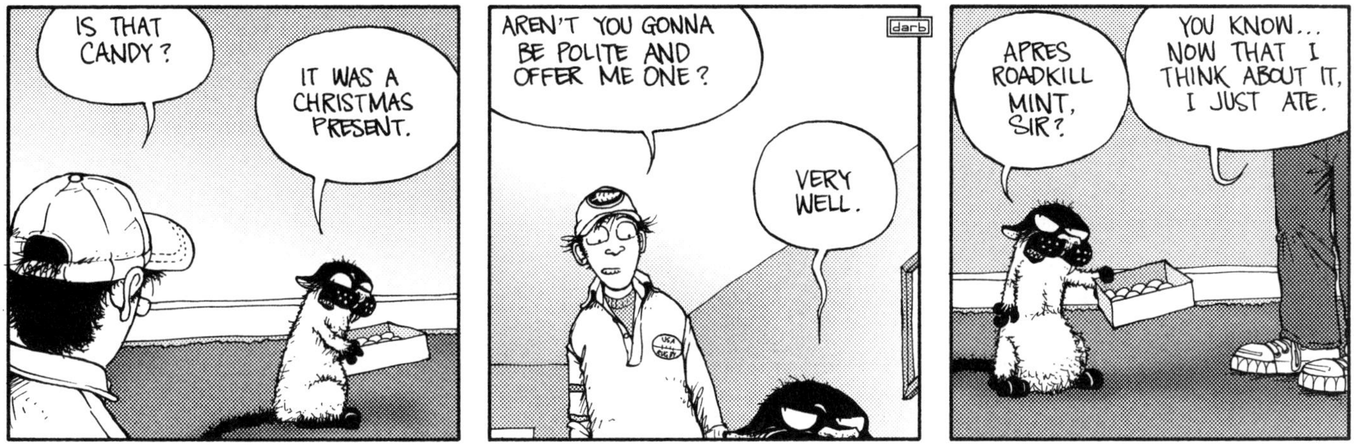
IS THAT CANDY?
IT WAS A CHRISTMAS PRESENT.
AREN'T YOU GONNA BE POLITE AND OFFER ME ONE?
darb
VERY WELL.
APRES ROADKILL MINT, SIR?
YOU KNOW... NOW THAT I THINK ABOUT IT, I JUST ATE.

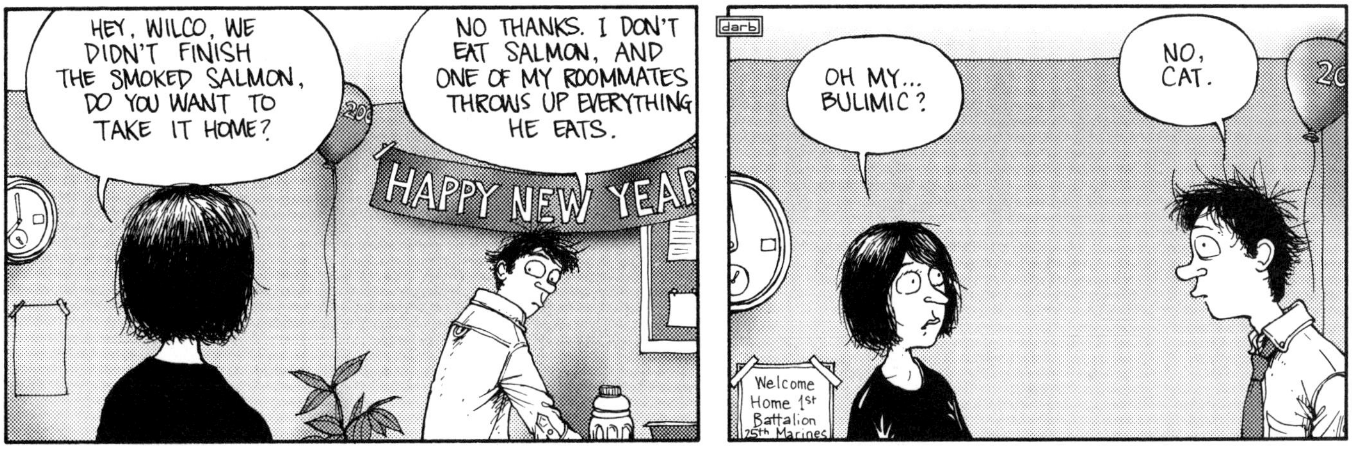
HEY, WILCO, WE DIDN'T FINISH THE SMOKED SALMON, DO YOU WANT TO TAKE IT HOME?
NO THANKS. I DON'T EAT SALMON, AND ONE OF MY ROOMMATES THROWS UP EVERYTHING HE EATS.
HAPPY NEW YEAR
darb
OH MY... BULIMIC?
NO, CAT.
Welcome Home 1st Battalion 25th Marines

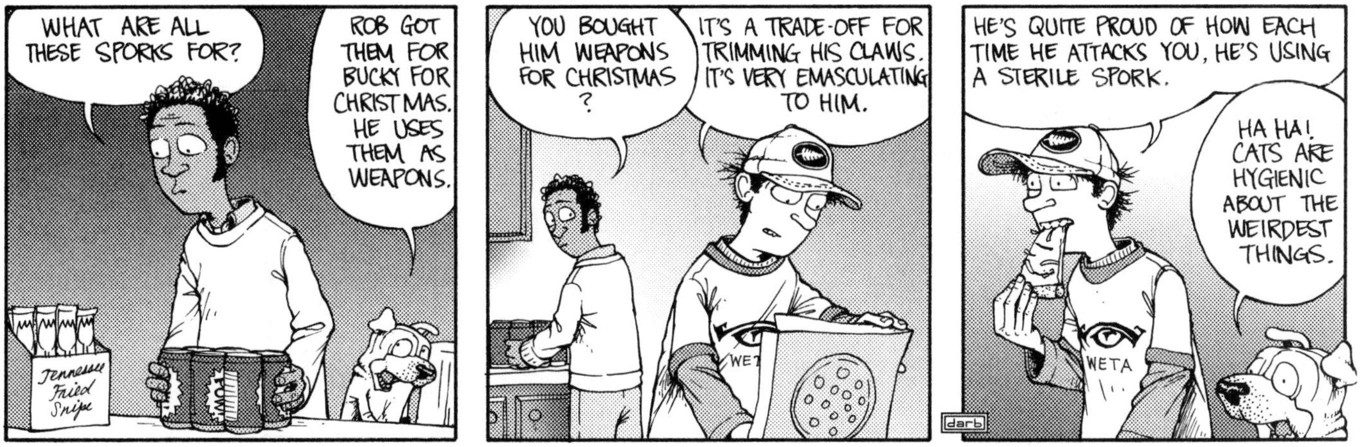
WHAT ARE ALL THESE SPORKS FOR?
ROB GOT THEM FOR BUCKY FOR CHRISTMAS. HE USES THEM AS WEAPONS.
Tennessee Fried Snipe
YOU BOUGHT HIM WEAPONS FOR CHRISTMAS?
IT'S A TRADE-OFF FOR TRIMMING HIS CLAWS. IT'S VERY EMASCULATING TO HIM.
HE'S QUITE PROUD OF HOW EACH TIME HE ATTACKS YOU, HE'S USING A STERILE SPORK.
HA HA! CATS ARE HYGIENIC ABOUT THE WEIRDEST THINGS.
WETA
darb

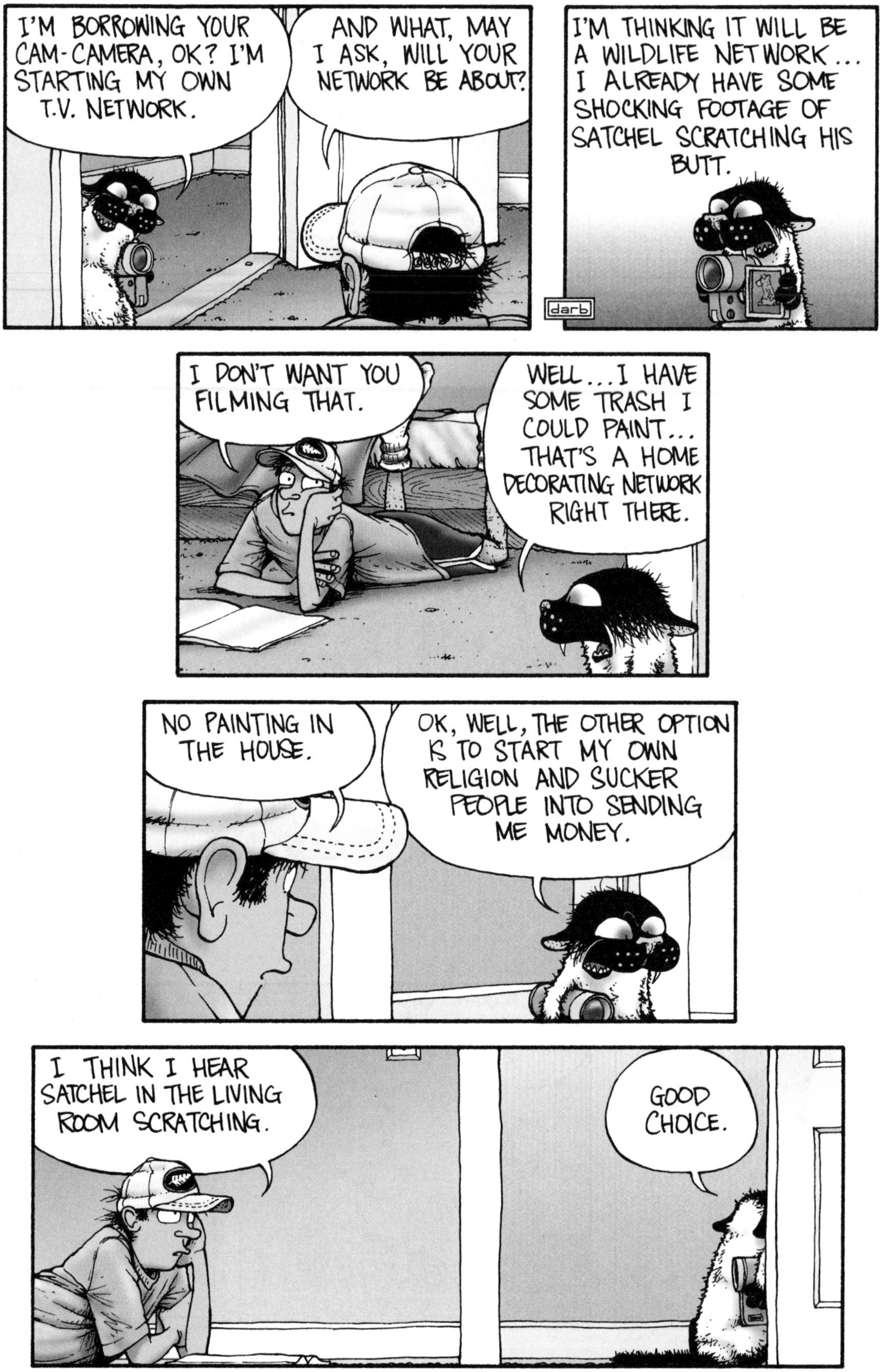
I'M BORROWING YOUR CAM-CAMERA, OK? I'M STARTING MY OWN T.V. NETWORK.
AND WHAT, MAY I ASK, WILL YOUR NETWORK BE ABOUT?
I'M THINKING IT WILL BE A WILDLIFE NETWORK... I ALREADY HAVE SOME SHOCKING FOOTAGE OF SATCHEL SCRATCHING HIS BUTT.
darb
I DON'T WANT YOU FILMING THAT.
WELL... I HAVE SOME TRASH I COULD PAINT... THAT'S A HOME DECORATING NETWORK RIGHT THERE.
NO PAINTING IN THE HOUSE.
OK, WELL, THE OTHER OPTION IS TO START MY OWN RELIGION AND SUCKER PEOPLE INTO SENDING ME MONEY.
I THINK I HEAR SATCHEL IN THE LIVING ROOM SCRATCHING.
GOOD CHOICE.

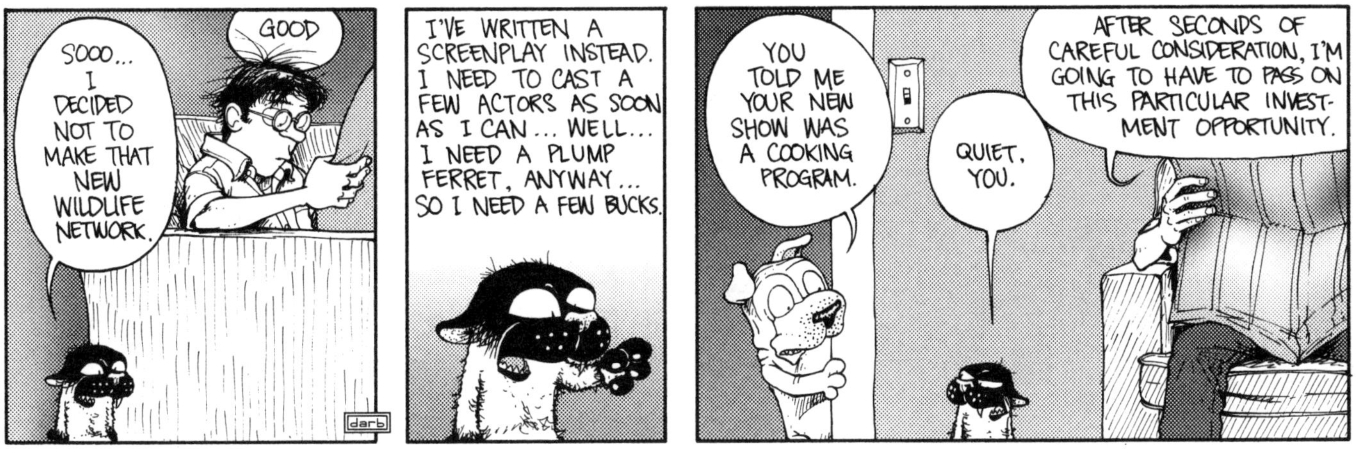
SOOO... I DECIDED NOT TO MAKE THAT NEW WILDLIFE NETWORK.
GOOD
I'VE WRITTEN A SCREENPLAY INSTEAD. I NEED TO CAST A FEW ACTORS AS SOON AS I CAN... WELL... I NEED A PLUMP FERRET, ANYWAY... SO I NEED A FEW BUCKS.
YOU TOLD ME YOUR NEW SHOW WAS A COOKING PROGRAM.
QUIET, YOU.
AFTER SECONDS OF CAREFUL CONSIDERATION, I'M GOING TO HAVE TO PASS ON THIS PARTICULAR INVESTMENT OPPORTUNITY.

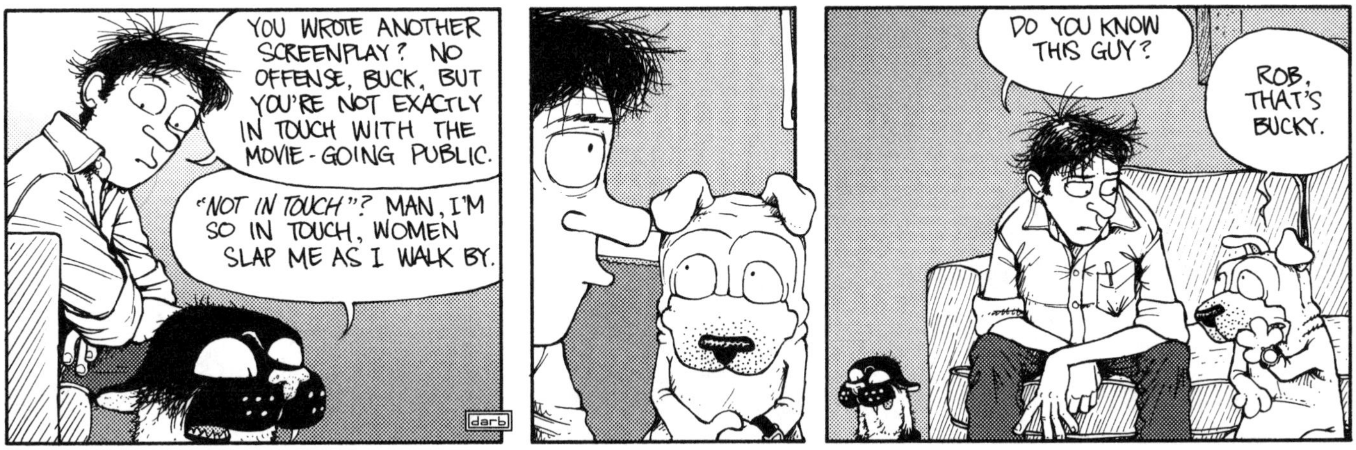
YOU WROTE ANOTHER SCREENPLAY? NO OFFENSE, BUCK, BUT YOU'RE NOT EXACTLY IN TOUCH WITH THE MOVIE-GOING PUBLIC.
"NOT IN TOUCH"? MAN, I'M SO IN TOUCH, WOMEN SLAP ME AS I WALK BY.
DO YOU KNOW THIS GUY?
ROB, THAT'S BUCKY.

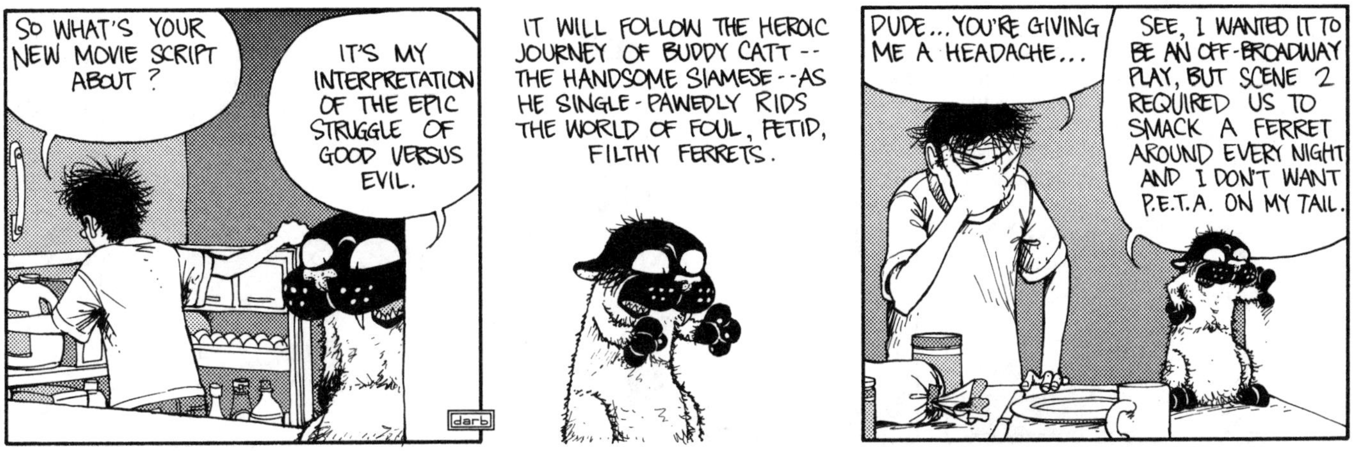
SO WHAT'S YOUR NEW MOVIE SCRIPT ABOUT?
IT'S MY INTERPRETATION OF THE EPIC STRUGGLE OF GOOD VERSUS EVIL.
IT WILL FOLLOW THE HEROIC JOURNEY OF BUDDY CATT -- THE HANDSOME SIAMESE -- AS HE SINGLE-PAWEDLY RIDS THE WORLD OF FOUL, FETID, FILTHY FERRETS.
DUDE... YOU'RE GIVING ME A HEADACHE...
SEE, I WANTED IT TO BE AN OFF-BROADWAY PLAY, BUT SCENE 2 REQUIRED US TO SMACK A FERRET AROUND EVERY NIGHT AND I DON'T WANT P.E.T.A. ON MY TAIL.

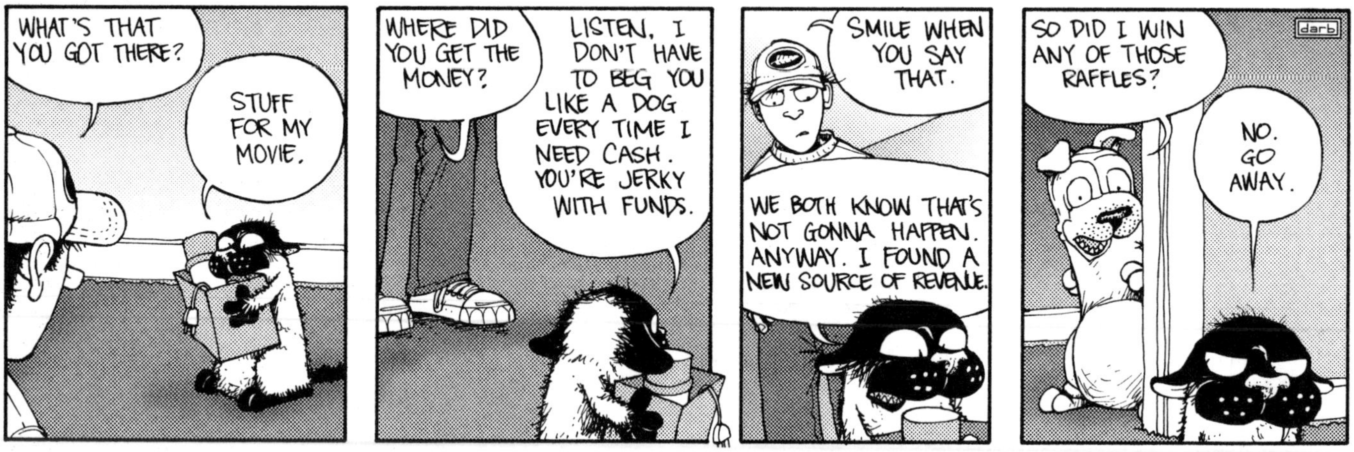
WHAT'S THAT YOU GOT THERE?
STUFF FOR MY MOVIE.
WHERE DID YOU GET THE MONEY?
LISTEN, I DON'T HAVE TO BEG YOU LIKE A DOG EVERY TIME I NEED CASH. YOU'RE JERKY WITH FUNDS.
SMILE WHEN YOU SAY THAT.
WE BOTH KNOW THAT'S NOT GONNA HAPPEN. ANYWAY, I FOUND A NEW SOURCE OF REVENUE.
SO DID I WIN ANY OF THOSE RAFFLES?
NO. GO AWAY.
darb

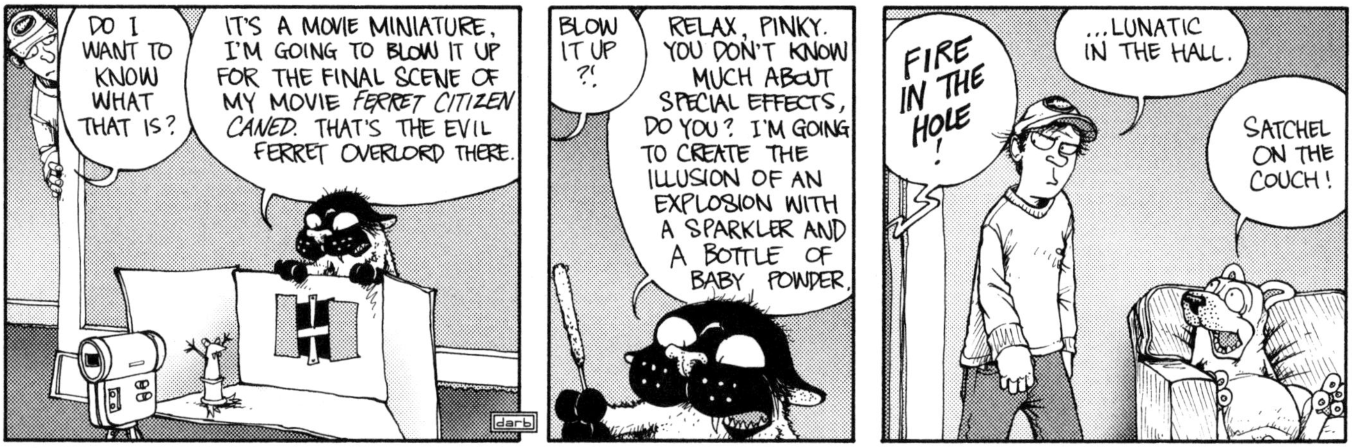
DO I WANT TO KNOW WHAT THAT IS?
IT'S A MOVIE MINIATURE, I'M GOING TO BLOW IT UP FOR THE FINAL SCENE OF MY MOVIE *FERRET CITIZEN CANED*. THAT'S THE EVIL FERRET OVERLORD THERE.
darb
BLOW IT UP ?!
RELAX, PINKY. YOU DON'T KNOW MUCH ABOUT SPECIAL EFFECTS, DO YOU? I'M GOING TO CREATE THE ILLUSION OF AN EXPLOSION WITH A SPARKLER AND A BOTTLE OF BABY POWDER.
FIRE IN THE HOLE!
...LUNATIC IN THE HALL.
SATCHEL ON THE COUCH!

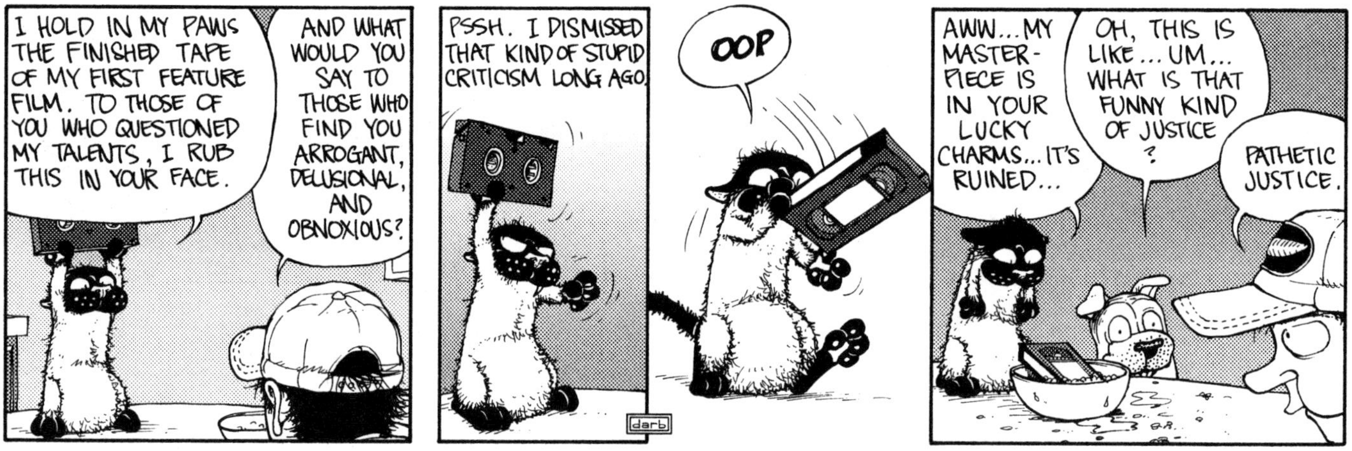
I HOLD IN MY PAWS THE FINISHED TAPE OF MY FIRST FEATURE FILM. TO THOSE OF YOU WHO QUESTIONED MY TALENTS, I RUB THIS IN YOUR FACE.
AND WHAT WOULD YOU SAY TO THOSE WHO FIND YOU ARROGANT, DELUSIONAL, AND OBNOXIOUS?
PSSH. I DISMISSED THAT KIND OF STUPID CRITICISM LONG AGO.
darb
OOP
AWW... MY MASTER-PIECE IS IN YOUR LUCKY CHARMS... IT'S RUINED...
OH, THIS IS LIKE... UM... WHAT IS THAT FUNNY KIND OF JUSTICE ?
PATHETIC JUSTICE.

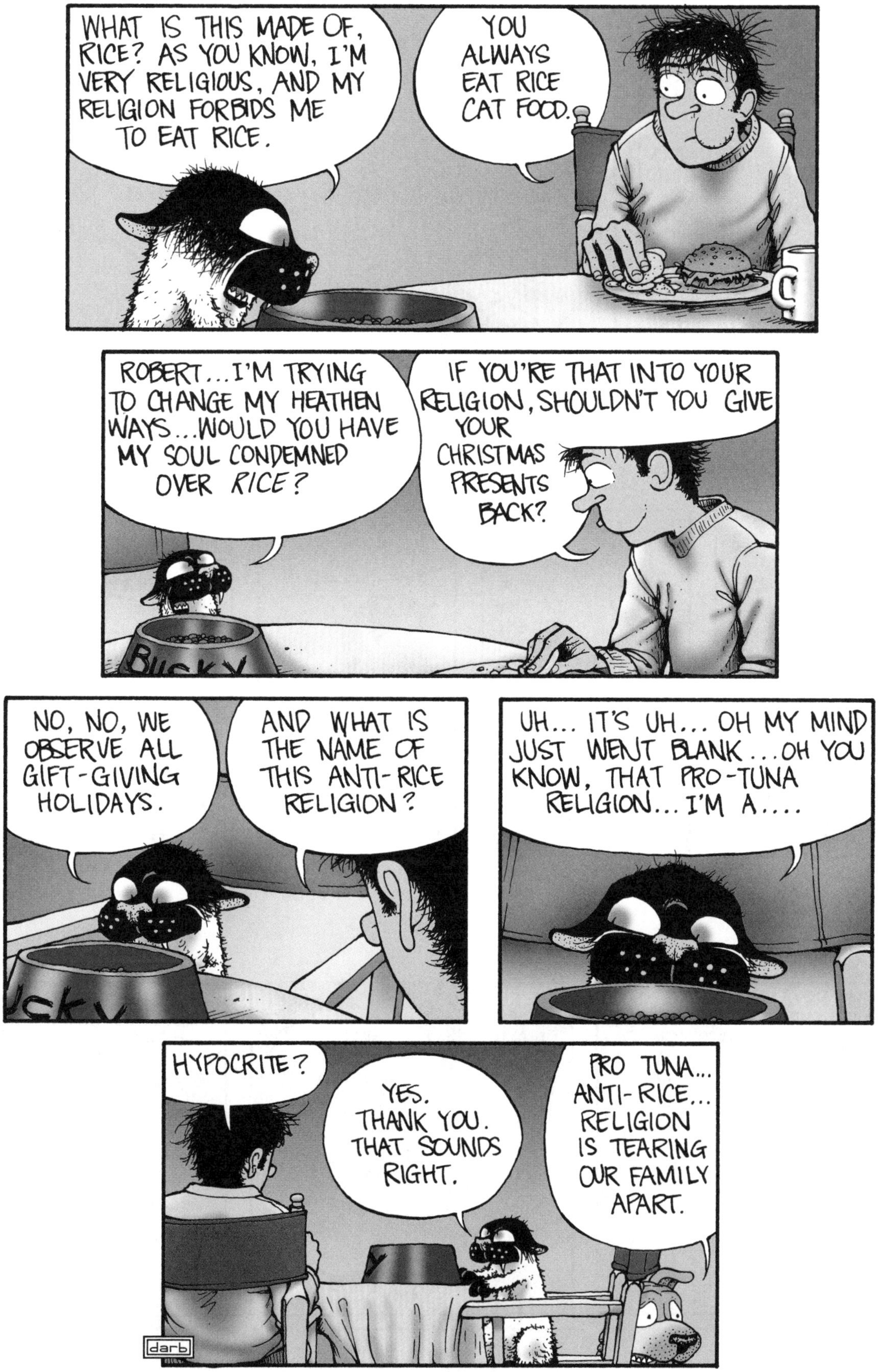
WHAT IS THIS MADE OF, RICE? AS YOU KNOW, I'M VERY RELIGIOUS, AND MY RELIGION FORBIDS ME TO EAT RICE.
YOU ALWAYS EAT RICE CAT FOOD.
ROBERT... I'M TRYING TO CHANGE MY HEATHEN WAYS... WOULD YOU HAVE MY SOUL CONDEMNED OVER *RICE*?
IF YOU'RE THAT INTO YOUR RELIGION, SHOULDN'T YOU GIVE YOUR CHRISTMAS PRESENTS BACK?
BUCKY
NO, NO, WE OBSERVE ALL GIFT-GIVING HOLIDAYS.
AND WHAT IS THE NAME OF THIS ANTI-RICE RELIGION?
UH... IT'S UH... OH MY MIND JUST WENT BLANK... OH YOU KNOW, THAT PRO-TUNA RELIGION... I'M A....
HYPOCRITE?
YES. THANK YOU. THAT SOUNDS RIGHT.
PRO TUNA... ANTI-RICE... RELIGION IS TEARING OUR FAMILY APART.
darb

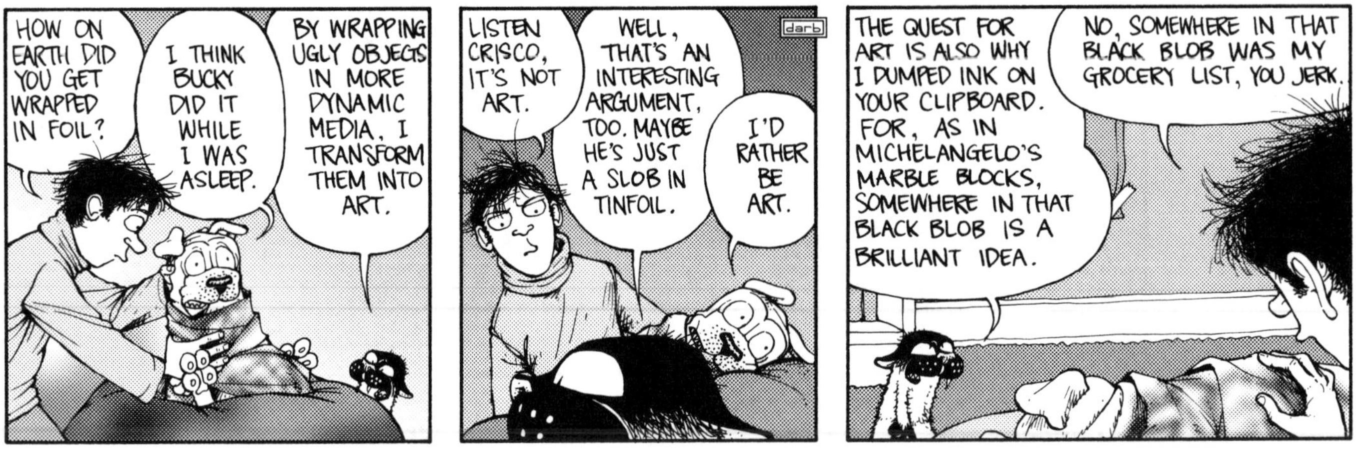
HOW ON EARTH DID YOU GET WRAPPED IN FOIL?
I THINK BUCKY DID IT WHILE I WAS ASLEEP.
BY WRAPPING UGLY OBJECTS IN MORE DYNAMIC MEDIA, I TRANSFORM THEM INTO ART.
LISTEN CRISCO, IT'S NOT ART.
WELL, THAT'S AN INTERESTING ARGUMENT, TOO. MAYBE HE'S JUST A SLOB IN TINFOIL.
I'D RATHER BE ART.
THE QUEST FOR ART IS ALSO WHY I DUMPED INK ON YOUR CLIPBOARD. FOR, AS IN MICHELANGELO'S MARBLE BLOCKS, SOMEWHERE IN THAT BLACK BLOB IS A BRILLIANT IDEA.
NO, SOMEWHERE IN THAT BLACK BLOB WAS MY GROCERY LIST, YOU JERK.

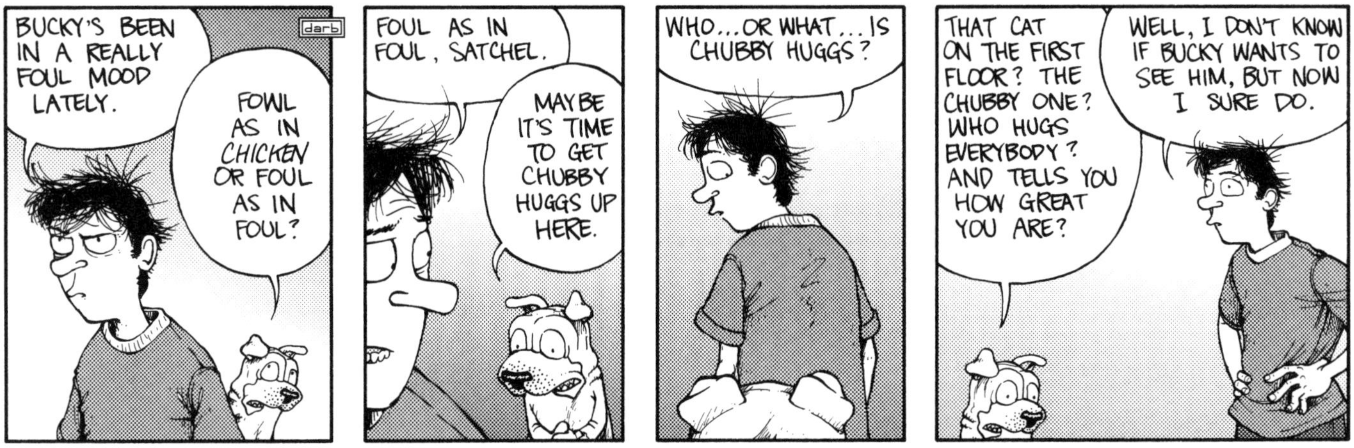
BUCKY'S BEEN IN A REALLY FOUL MOOD LATELY.
FOWL AS IN CHICKEN OR FOUL AS IN FOUL?
FOUL AS IN FOUL, SATCHEL.
MAYBE IT'S TIME TO GET CHUBBY HUGGS UP HERE.
WHO... OR WHAT... IS CHUBBY HUGGS?
THAT CAT ON THE FIRST FLOOR? THE CHUBBY ONE? WHO HUGS EVERYBODY? AND TELLS YOU HOW GREAT YOU ARE?
WELL, I DON'T KNOW IF BUCKY WANTS TO SEE HIM, BUT NOW I SURE DO.

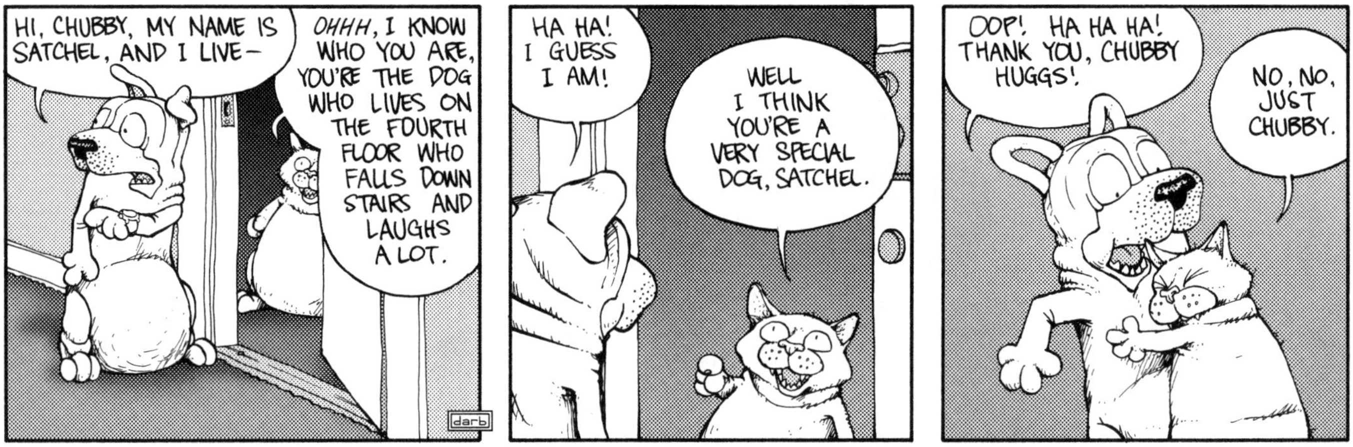
HI, CHUBBY, MY NAME IS SATCHEL, AND I LIVE—
OHHH, I KNOW WHO YOU ARE, YOU'RE THE DOG WHO LIVES ON THE FOURTH FLOOR WHO FALLS DOWN STAIRS AND LAUGHS A LOT.
HA HA! I GUESS I AM!
WELL I THINK YOU'RE A VERY SPECIAL DOG, SATCHEL.
OOP! HA HA HA! THANK YOU, CHUBBY HUGGS!
NO, NO, JUST CHUBBY.

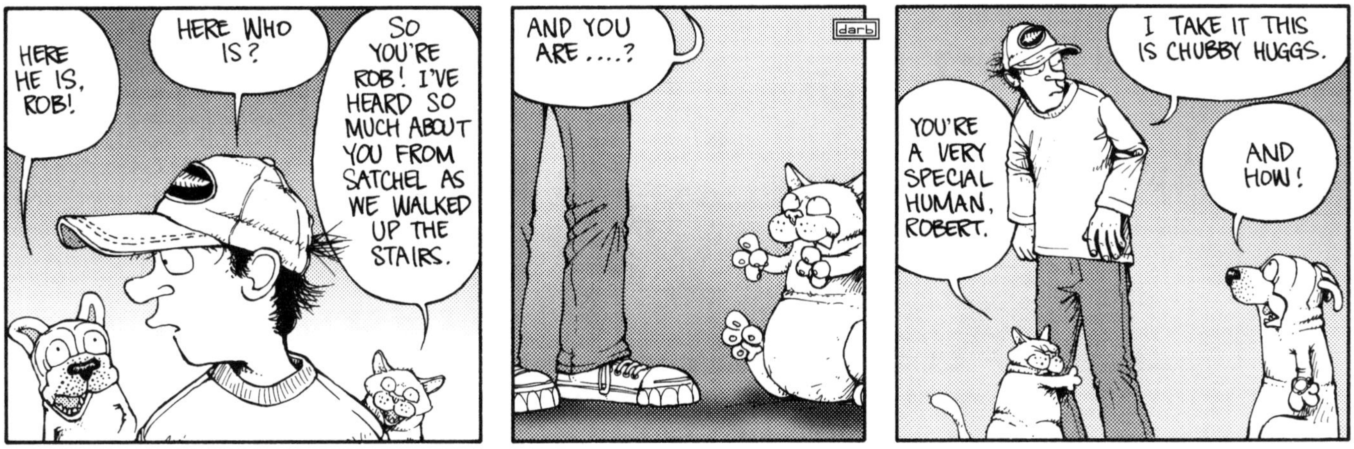
HERE HE IS, ROB!
HERE WHO IS?
SO YOU'RE ROB! I'VE HEARD SO MUCH ABOUT YOU FROM SATCHEL AS WE WALKED UP THE STAIRS.
AND YOU ARE....?
darb
YOU'RE A VERY SPECIAL HUMAN, ROBERT.
I TAKE IT THIS IS CHUBBY HUGGS.
AND HOW!

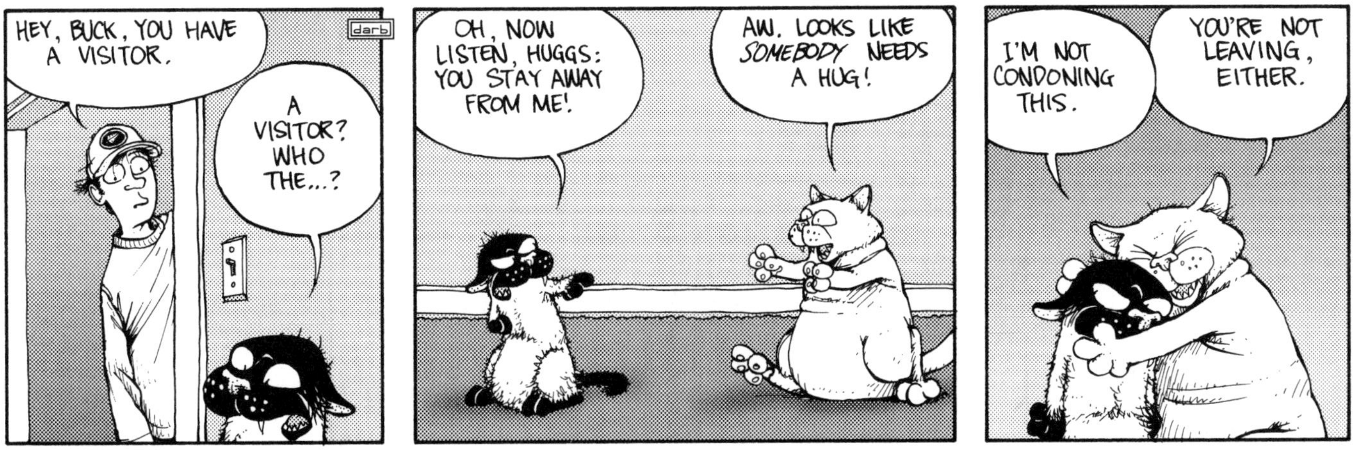
HEY, BUCK, YOU HAVE A VISITOR.
darb
A VISITOR? WHO THE...?
OH, NOW LISTEN, HUGGS: YOU STAY AWAY FROM ME!
AW. LOOKS LIKE *SOMEBODY* NEEDS A HUG!
I'M NOT CONDONING THIS.
YOU'RE NOT LEAVING, EITHER.

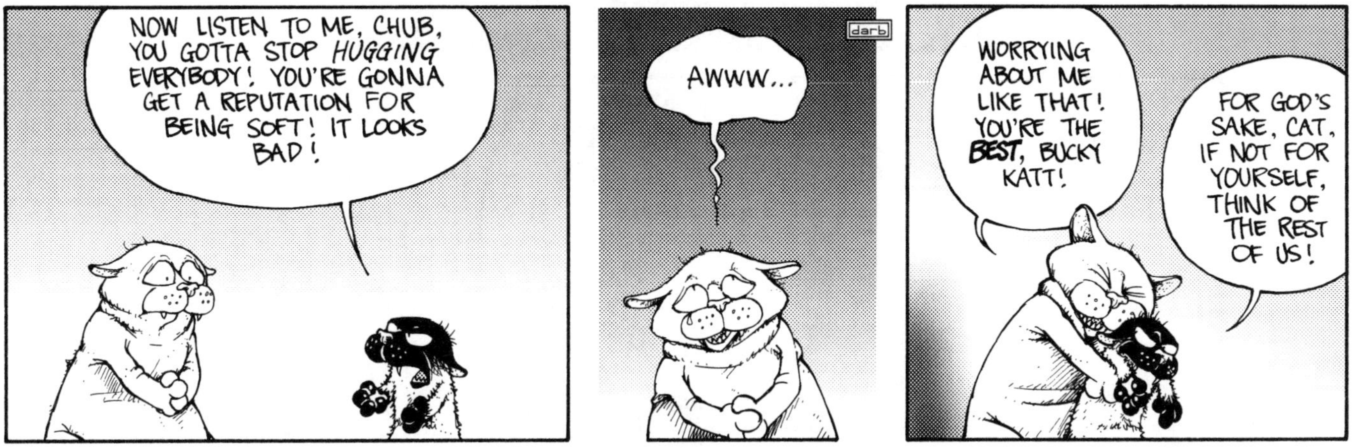
NOW LISTEN TO ME, CHUB, YOU GOTTA STOP *HUGGING* EVERYBODY! YOU'RE GONNA GET A REPUTATION FOR BEING SOFT! IT LOOKS BAD!
darb
AWWW...
WORRYING ABOUT ME LIKE THAT! YOU'RE THE **BEST**, BUCKY KATT!
FOR GOD'S SAKE, CAT, IF NOT FOR YOURSELF, THINK OF THE REST OF US!

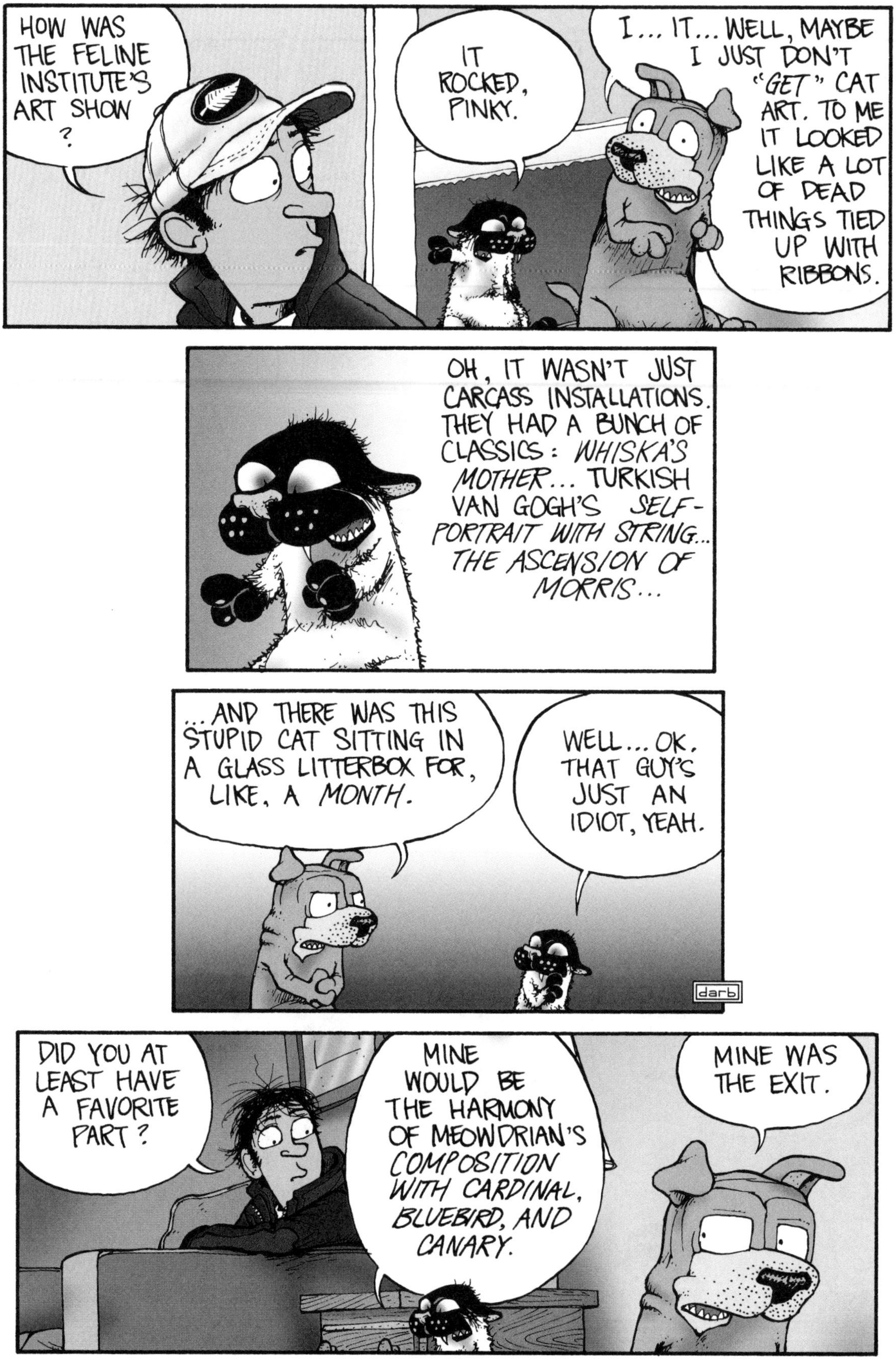
HOW WAS THE FELINE INSTITUTE'S ART SHOW ?
IT ROCKED, PINKY.
I... IT... WELL, MAYBE I JUST DON'T "GET" CAT ART. TO ME IT LOOKED LIKE A LOT OF DEAD THINGS TIED UP WITH RIBBONS.
OH, IT WASN'T JUST CARCASS INSTALLATIONS. THEY HAD A BUNCH OF CLASSICS: WHISKA'S MOTHER... TURKISH VAN GOGH'S SELF-PORTRAIT WITH STRING... THE ASCENSION OF MORRIS...
...AND THERE WAS THIS STUPID CAT SITTING IN A GLASS LITTERBOX FOR, LIKE, A MONTH.
WELL... OK. THAT GUY'S JUST AN IDIOT, YEAH.
darb
DID YOU AT LEAST HAVE A FAVORITE PART ?
MINE WOULD BE THE HARMONY OF MEOWDRIAN'S COMPOSITION WITH CARDINAL, BLUEBIRD, AND CANARY.
MINE WAS THE EXIT.

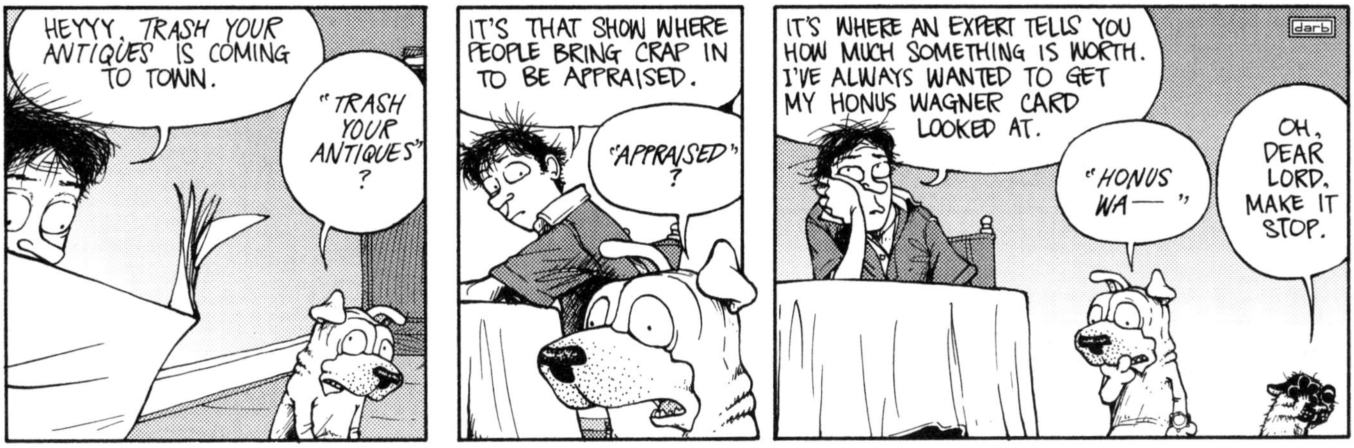
HEYYY, TRASH YOUR ANTIQUES IS COMING TO TOWN.
"TRASH YOUR ANTIQUES"?
IT'S THAT SHOW WHERE PEOPLE BRING CRAP IN TO BE APPRAISED.
"APPRAISED"?
IT'S WHERE AN EXPERT TELLS YOU HOW MUCH SOMETHING IS WORTH. I'VE ALWAYS WANTED TO GET MY HONUS WAGNER CARD LOOKED AT.
"HONUS WA— "
OH, DEAR LORD, MAKE IT STOP.
darb

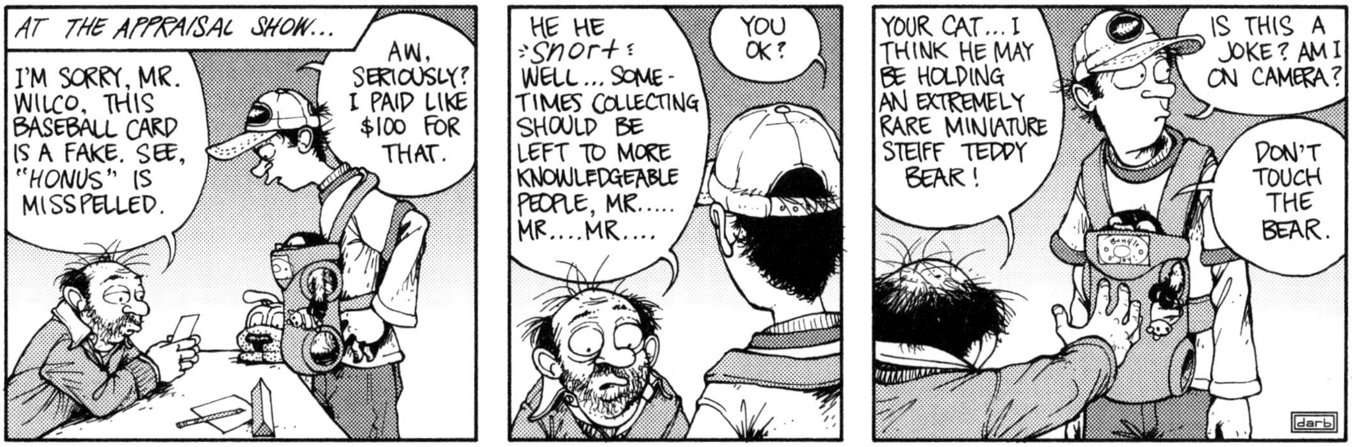
AT THE APPRAISAL SHOW...
I'M SORRY, MR. WILCO, THIS BASEBALL CARD IS A FAKE. SEE, "HONUS" IS MISSPELLED.
AW, SERIOUSLY? I PAID LIKE $100 FOR THAT.
HE HE snort WELL... SOMETIMES COLLECTING SHOULD BE LEFT TO MORE KNOWLEDGEABLE PEOPLE, MR..... MR....MR....
YOU OK?
YOUR CAT... I THINK HE MAY BE HOLDING AN EXTREMELY RARE MINIATURE STEIFF TEDDY BEAR!
IS THIS A JOKE? AM I ON CAMERA?
DON'T TOUCH THE BEAR.
darb

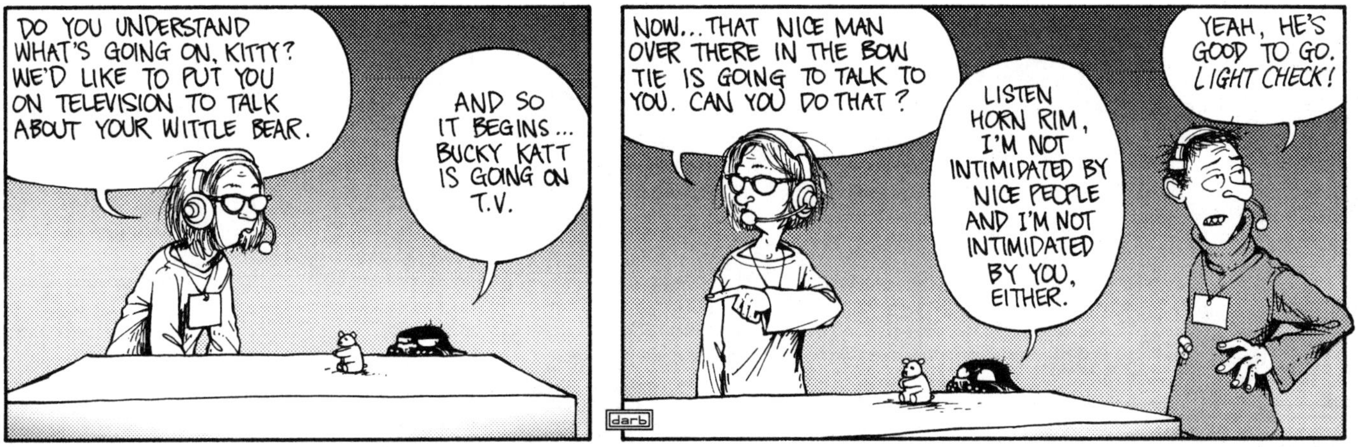
DO YOU UNDERSTAND WHAT'S GOING ON, KITTY? WE'D LIKE TO PUT YOU ON TELEVISION TO TALK ABOUT YOUR WITTLE BEAR.
AND SO IT BEGINS... BUCKY KATT IS GOING ON T.V.
darb
NOW... THAT NICE MAN OVER THERE IN THE BOW TIE IS GOING TO TALK TO YOU. CAN YOU DO THAT?
LISTEN HORN RIM, I'M NOT INTIMIDATED BY NICE PEOPLE AND I'M NOT INTIMIDATED BY YOU, EITHER.
YEAH, HE'S GOOD TO GO. LIGHT CHECK!

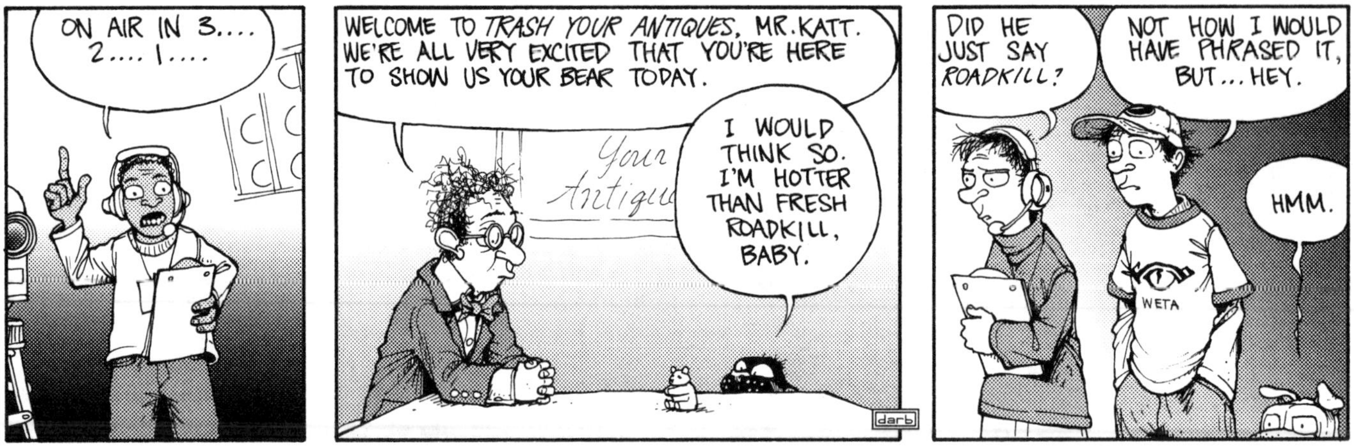
ON AIR IN 3.... 2.... 1....
WELCOME TO *TRASH YOUR ANTIQUES*, MR. KATT. WE'RE ALL VERY EXCITED THAT YOU'RE HERE TO SHOW US YOUR BEAR TODAY.
Your Antiqu
I WOULD THINK SO. I'M HOTTER THAN FRESH ROADKILL, BABY.
darb
DID HE JUST SAY *ROADKILL?*
NOT HOW I WOULD HAVE PHRASED IT, BUT... HEY.
HMM.
WETA

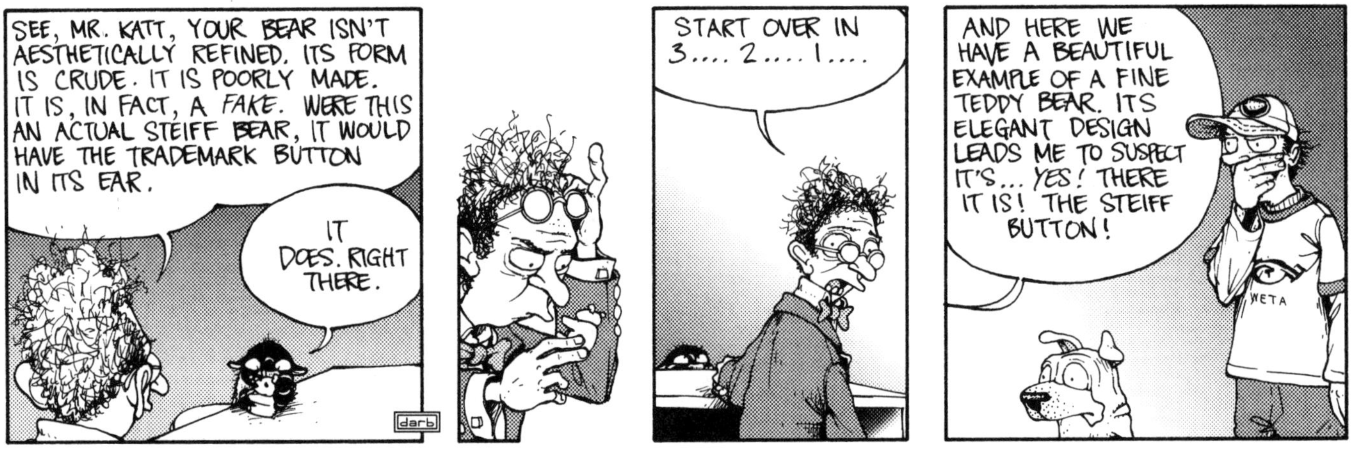
SEE, MR. KATT, YOUR BEAR ISN'T AESTHETICALLY REFINED. ITS FORM IS CRUDE. IT IS POORLY MADE. IT IS, IN FACT, A *FAKE*. WERE THIS AN ACTUAL STEIFF BEAR, IT WOULD HAVE THE TRADEMARK BUTTON IN ITS EAR.
IT DOES. RIGHT THERE.
darb
START OVER IN 3.... 2.... 1....
AND HERE WE HAVE A BEAUTIFUL EXAMPLE OF A FINE TEDDY BEAR. ITS ELEGANT DESIGN LEADS ME TO SUSPECT IT'S... *YES!* THERE IT IS! THE STEIFF BUTTON!
WETA

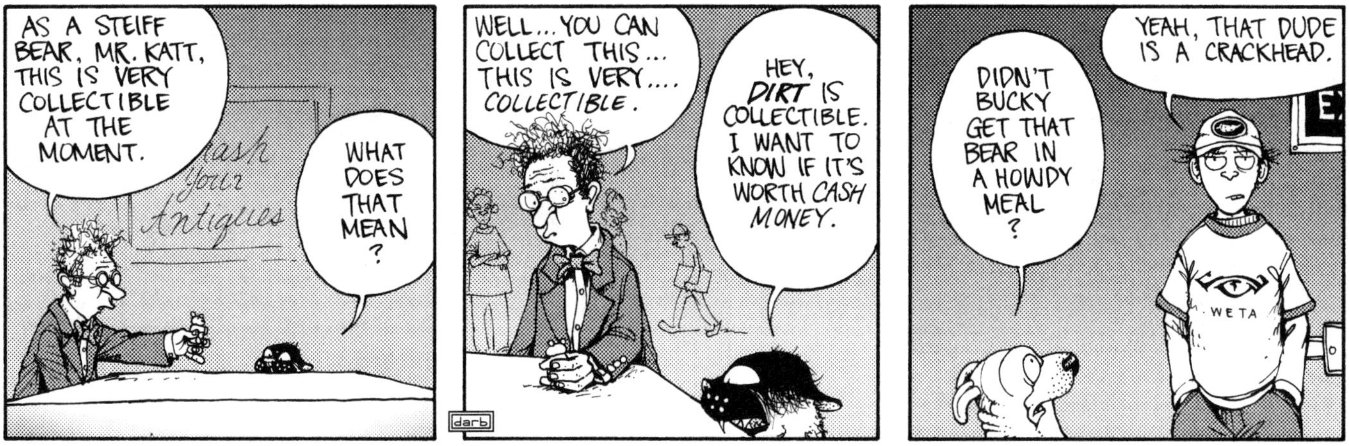
AS A STEIFF BEAR, MR. KATT, THIS IS VERY COLLECTIBLE AT THE MOMENT.
WHAT DOES THAT MEAN?
rash Your Antiques
darb
WELL... YOU CAN COLLECT THIS... THIS IS VERY.... *COLLECTIBLE*.
HEY, ***DIRT*** IS COLLECTIBLE. I WANT TO KNOW IF IT'S WORTH *CASH MONEY*.
YEAH, THAT DUDE IS A CRACKHEAD.
DIDN'T BUCKY GET THAT BEAR IN A HOWDY MEAL?
WETA

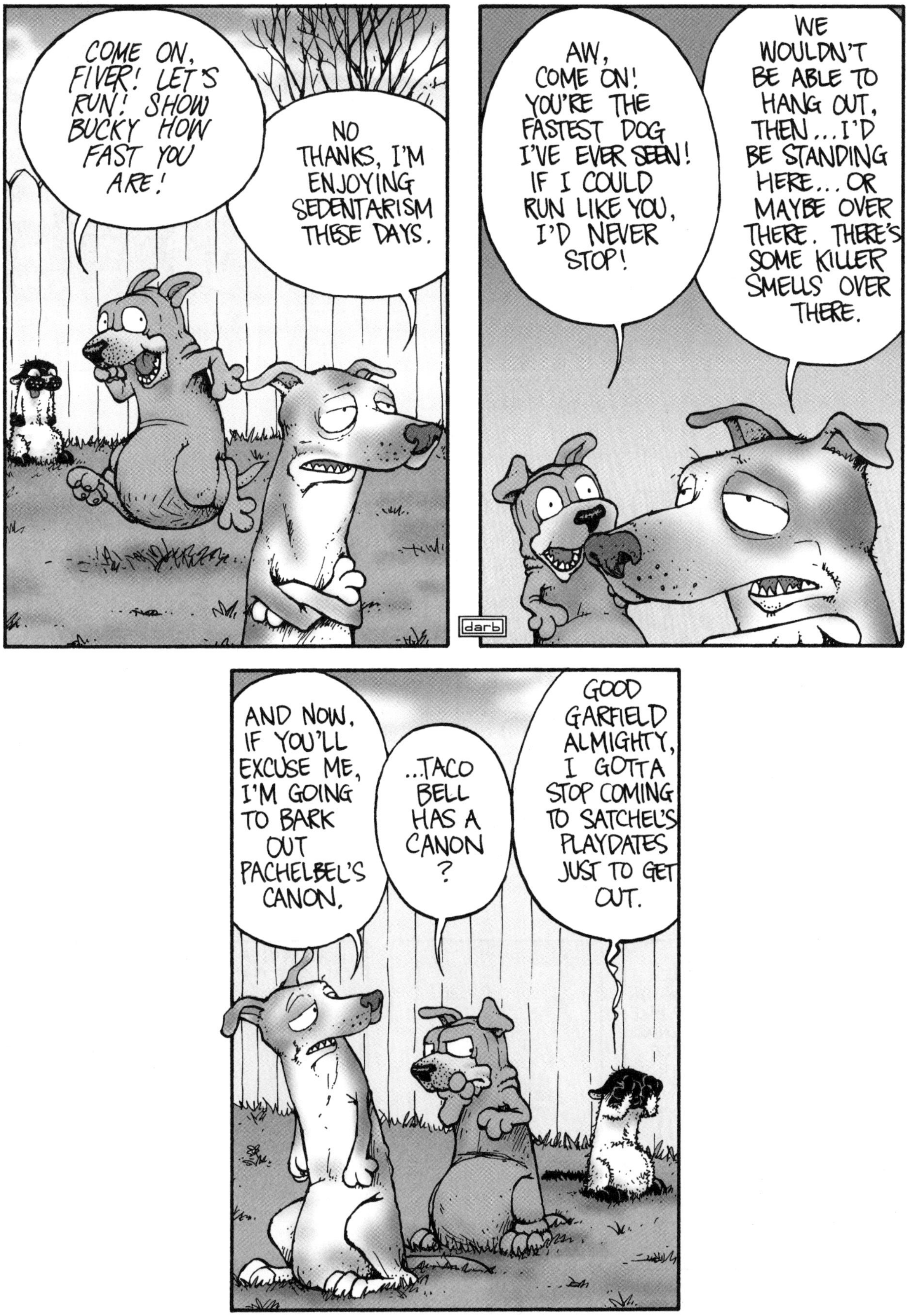
COME ON, FIVER! LET'S RUN! SHOW BUCKY HOW FAST YOU ARE!
NO THANKS, I'M ENJOYING SEDENTARISM THESE DAYS.
AW, COME ON! YOU'RE THE FASTEST DOG I'VE EVER SEEN! IF I COULD RUN LIKE YOU, I'D NEVER STOP!
WE WOULDN'T BE ABLE TO HANG OUT, THEN... I'D BE STANDING HERE... OR MAYBE OVER THERE. THERE'S SOME KILLER SMELLS OVER THERE.
darb
AND NOW, IF YOU'LL EXCUSE ME, I'M GOING TO BARK OUT PACHELBEL'S CANON.
...TACO BELL HAS A CANON ?
GOOD GARFIELD ALMIGHTY, I GOTTA STOP COMING TO SATCHEL'S PLAYDATES JUST TO GET OUT.

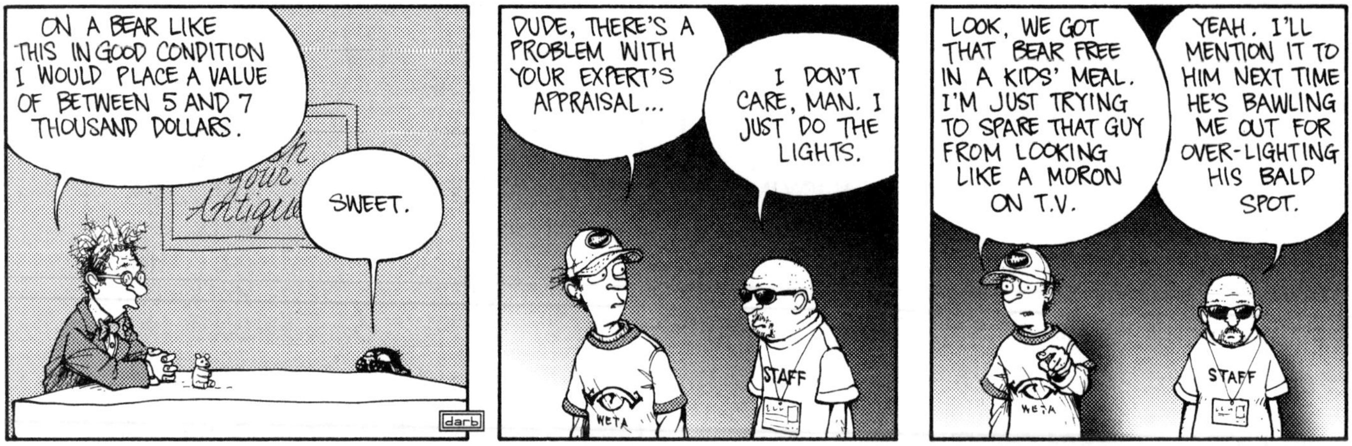

ON A BEAR LIKE THIS IN GOOD CONDITION I WOULD PLACE A VALUE OF BETWEEN 5 AND 7 THOUSAND DOLLARS.
SWEET.
DUDE, THERE'S A PROBLEM WITH YOUR EXPERT'S APPRAISAL...
I DON'T CARE, MAN. I JUST DO THE LIGHTS.
LOOK, WE GOT THAT BEAR FREE IN A KIDS' MEAL. I'M JUST TRYING TO SPARE THAT GUY FROM LOOKING LIKE A MORON ON T.V.
YEAH. I'LL MENTION IT TO HIM NEXT TIME HE'S BAWLING ME OUT FOR OVER-LIGHTING HIS BALD SPOT.

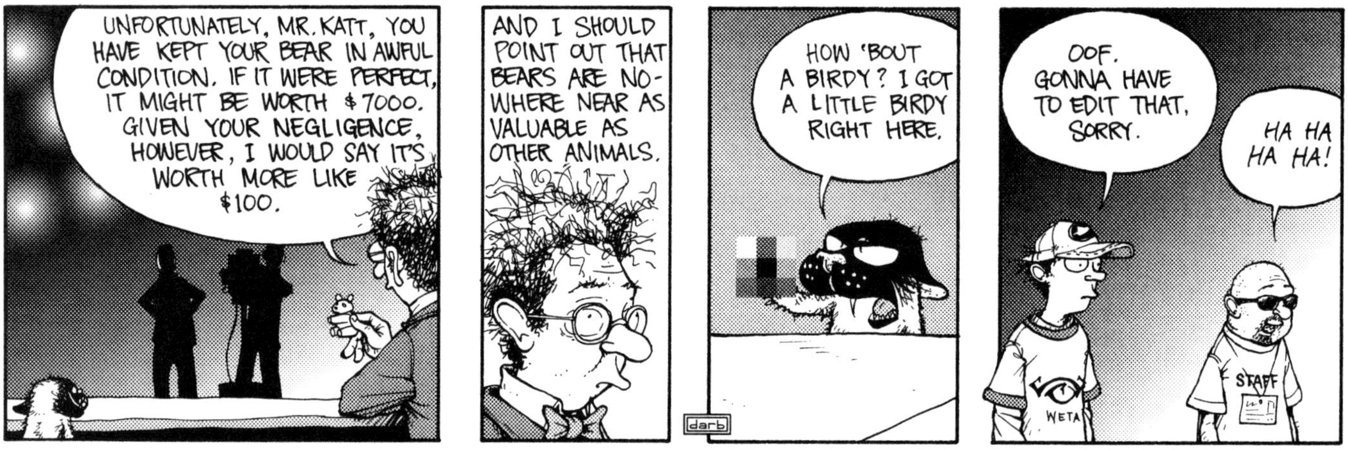

UNFORTUNATELY, MR. KATT, YOU HAVE KEPT YOUR BEAR IN AWFUL CONDITION. IF IT WERE PERFECT, IT MIGHT BE WORTH $7000. GIVEN YOUR NEGLIGENCE, HOWEVER, I WOULD SAY IT'S WORTH MORE LIKE $100.
AND I SHOULD POINT OUT THAT BEARS ARE NO-WHERE NEAR AS VALUABLE AS OTHER ANIMALS.
HOW 'BOUT A BIRDY? I GOT A LITTLE BIRDY RIGHT HERE.
OOF. GONNA HAVE TO EDIT THAT, SORRY.
HA HA HA HA!

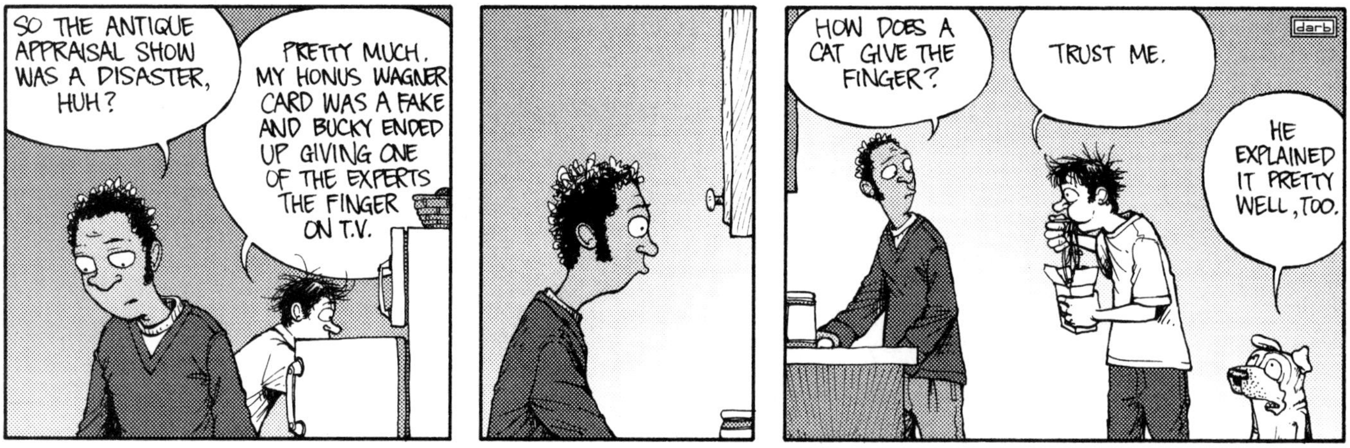

SO THE ANTIQUE APPRAISAL SHOW WAS A DISASTER, HUH?
PRETTY MUCH. MY HONUS WAGNER CARD WAS A FAKE AND BUCKY ENDED UP GIVING ONE OF THE EXPERTS THE FINGER ON T.V.
HOW DOES A CAT GIVE THE FINGER?
TRUST ME.
HE EXPLAINED IT PRETTY WELL, TOO.

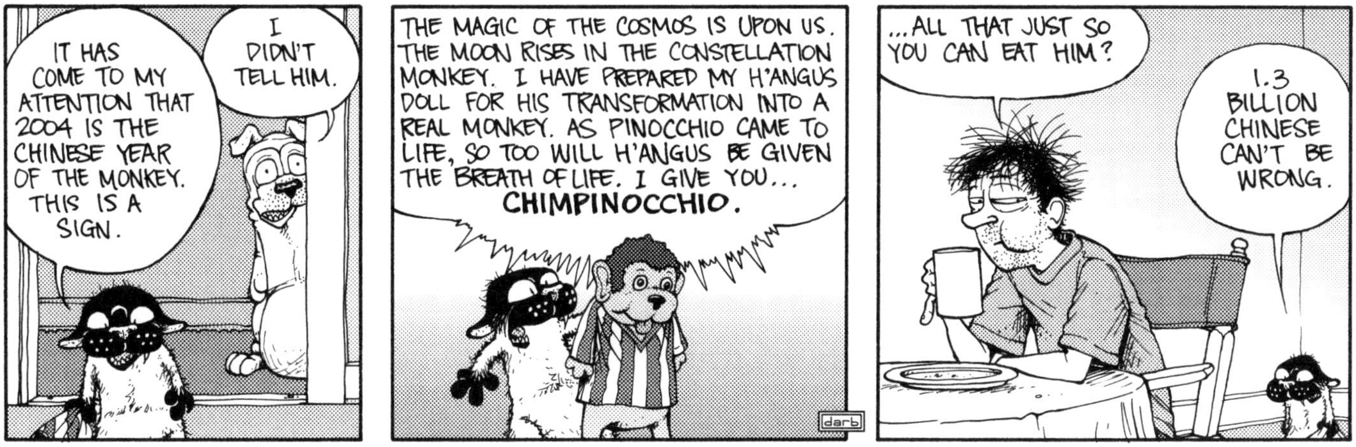
IT HAS COME TO MY ATTENTION THAT 2004 IS THE CHINESE YEAR OF THE MONKEY. THIS IS A SIGN.
I DIDN'T TELL HIM.
THE MAGIC OF THE COSMOS IS UPON US. THE MOON RISES IN THE CONSTELLATION MONKEY. I HAVE PREPARED MY H'ANGUS DOLL FOR HIS TRANSFORMATION INTO A REAL MONKEY. AS PINOCCHIO CAME TO LIFE, SO TOO WILL H'ANGUS BE GIVEN THE BREATH OF LIFE. I GIVE YOU... CHIMPINOCCHIO.
...ALL THAT JUST SO YOU CAN EAT HIM?
1.3 BILLION CHINESE CAN'T BE WRONG.

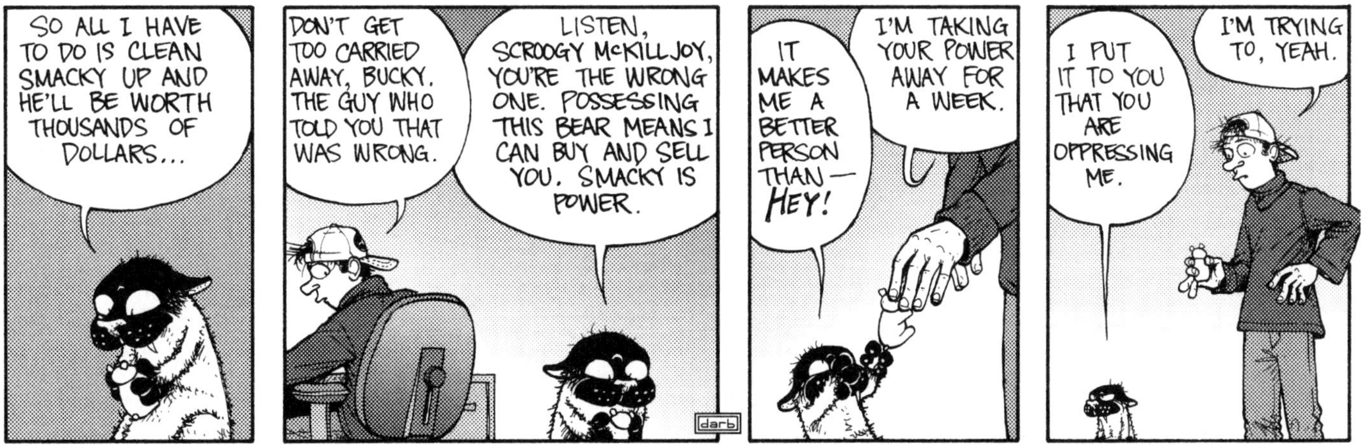
SO ALL I HAVE TO DO IS CLEAN SMACKY UP AND HE'LL BE WORTH THOUSANDS OF DOLLARS...
DON'T GET TOO CARRIED AWAY, BUCKY. THE GUY WHO TOLD YOU THAT WAS WRONG.
LISTEN, SCROOGY McKILLJOY, YOU'RE THE WRONG ONE. POSSESSING THIS BEAR MEANS I CAN BUY AND SELL YOU. SMACKY IS POWER.
IT MAKES ME A BETTER PERSON THAN— HEY!
I'M TAKING YOUR POWER AWAY FOR A WEEK.
I PUT IT TO YOU THAT YOU ARE OPPRESSING ME.
I'M TRYING TO, YEAH.

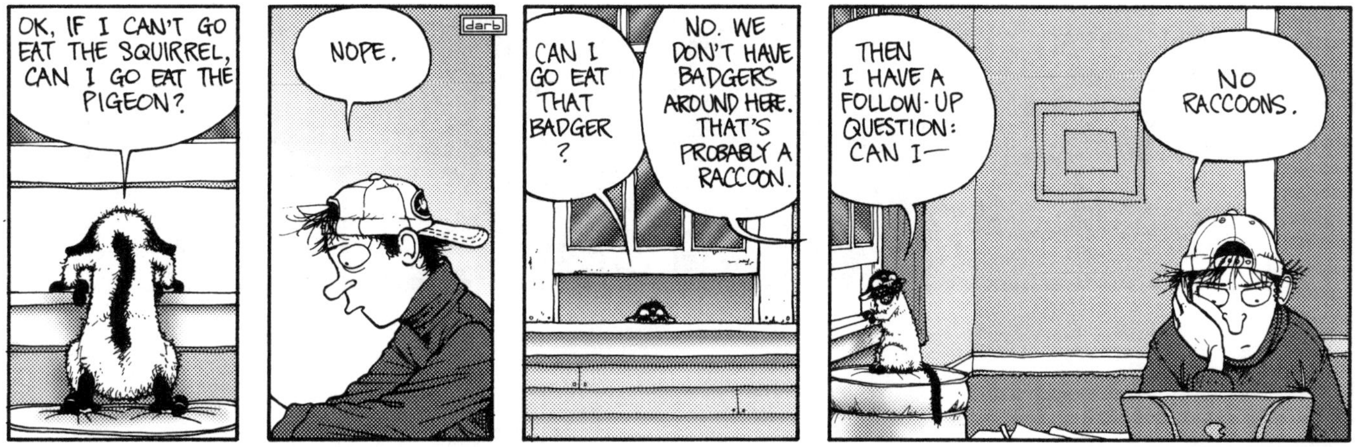
OK, IF I CAN'T GO EAT THE SQUIRREL, CAN I GO EAT THE PIGEON?
NOPE.
CAN I GO EAT THAT BADGER?
NO. WE DON'T HAVE BADGERS AROUND HERE. THAT'S PROBABLY A RACCOON.
THEN I HAVE A FOLLOW-UP QUESTION: CAN I—
NO RACCOONS.

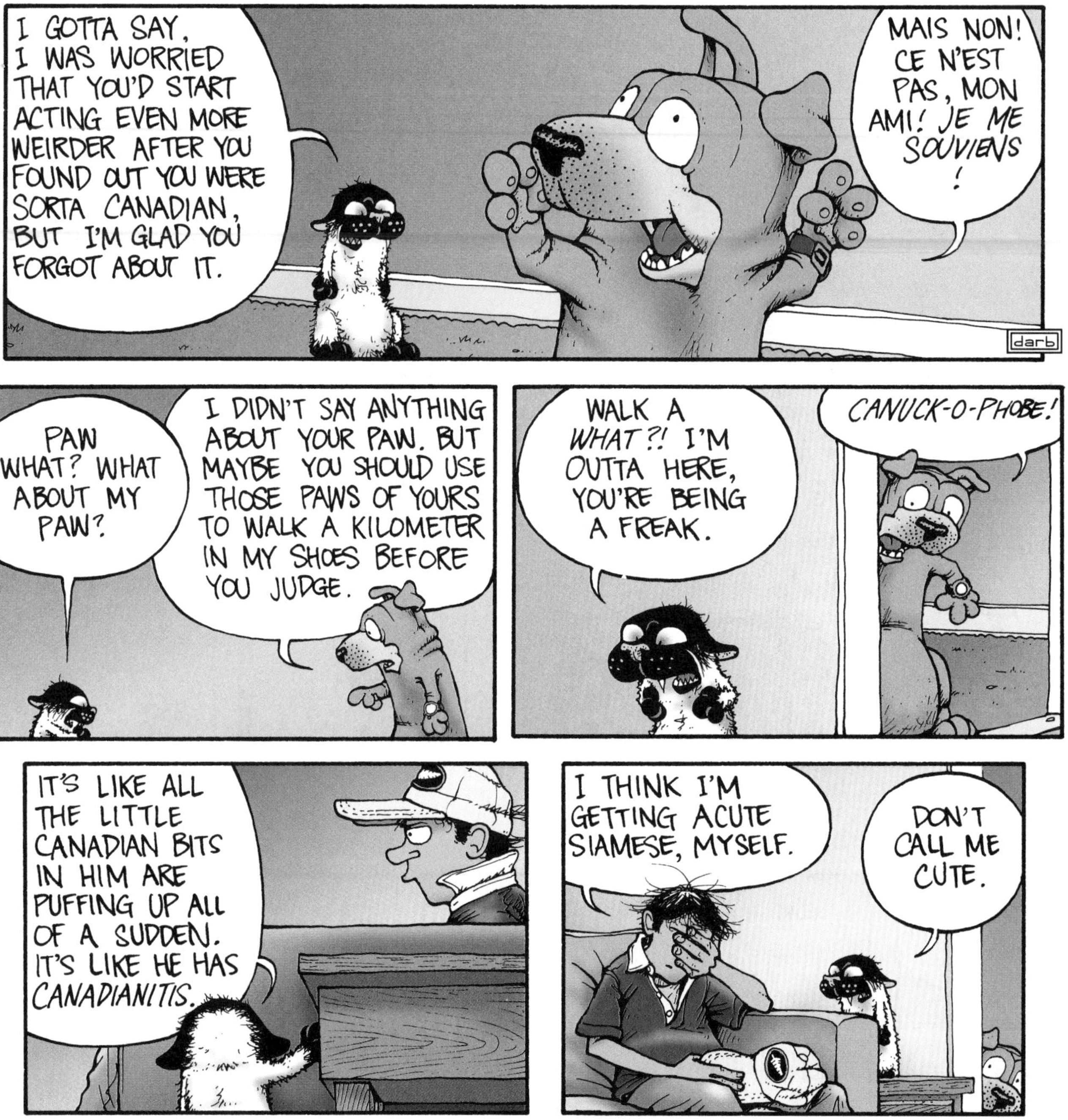
I GOTTA SAY, I WAS WORRIED THAT YOU'D START ACTING EVEN MORE WEIRDER AFTER YOU FOUND OUT YOU WERE SORTA CANADIAN, BUT I'M GLAD YOU FORGOT ABOUT IT.
MAIS NON! CE N'EST PAS, MON AMI! *JE ME SOUVIENS* !
darb
PAW WHAT? WHAT ABOUT MY PAW?
I DIDN'T SAY ANYTHING ABOUT YOUR PAW. BUT MAYBE YOU SHOULD USE THOSE PAWS OF YOURS TO WALK A KILOMETER IN MY SHOES BEFORE YOU JUDGE.
WALK A *WHAT?!* I'M OUTTA HERE, YOU'RE BEING A FREAK.
CANUCK-O-PHOBE!
IT'S LIKE ALL THE LITTLE CANADIAN BITS IN HIM ARE PUFFING UP ALL OF A SUDDEN. IT'S LIKE HE HAS *CANADIANITIS*.
I THINK I'M GETTING ACUTE SIAMESE, MYSELF.
DON'T CALL ME CUTE.

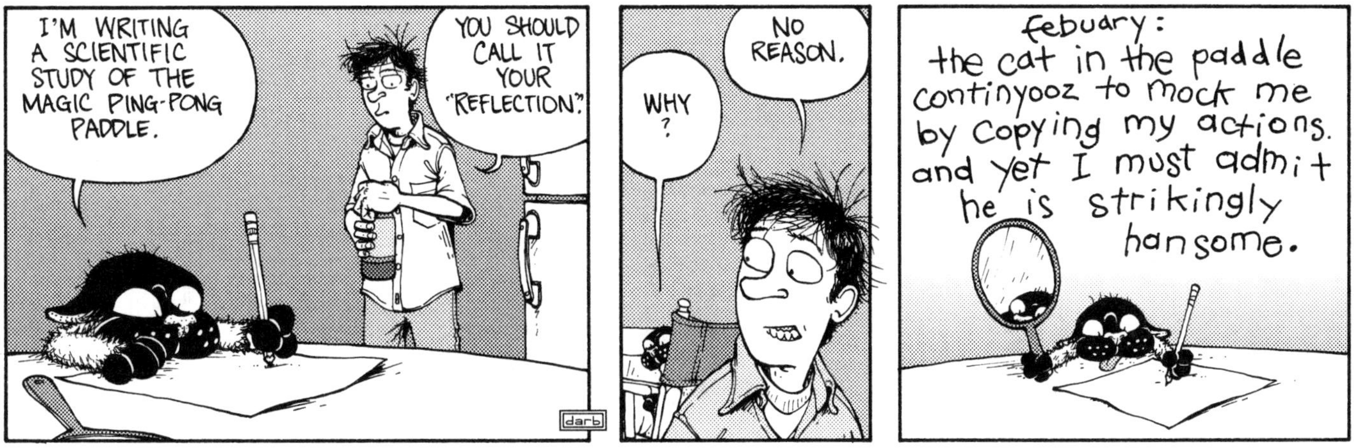
I'M WRITING A SCIENTIFIC STUDY OF THE MAGIC PING-PONG PADDLE.
YOU SHOULD CALL IT YOUR "REFLECTION."
WHY ?
NO REASON.
febuary:
the cat in the paddle continyooz to mock me by copying my actions. and yet I must admit he is strikingly hansome.
darb

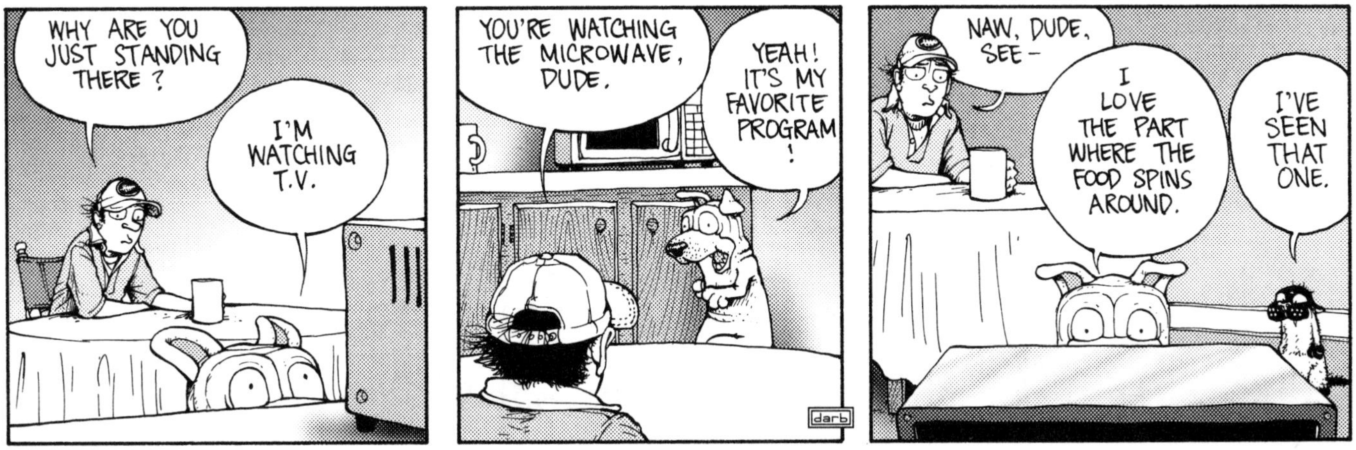
WHY ARE YOU JUST STANDING THERE ?
I'M WATCHING T.V.
YOU'RE WATCHING THE MICROWAVE, DUDE.
YEAH! IT'S MY FAVORITE PROGRAM !
NAW, DUDE, SEE—
I LOVE THE PART WHERE THE FOOD SPINS AROUND.
I'VE SEEN THAT ONE.
darb

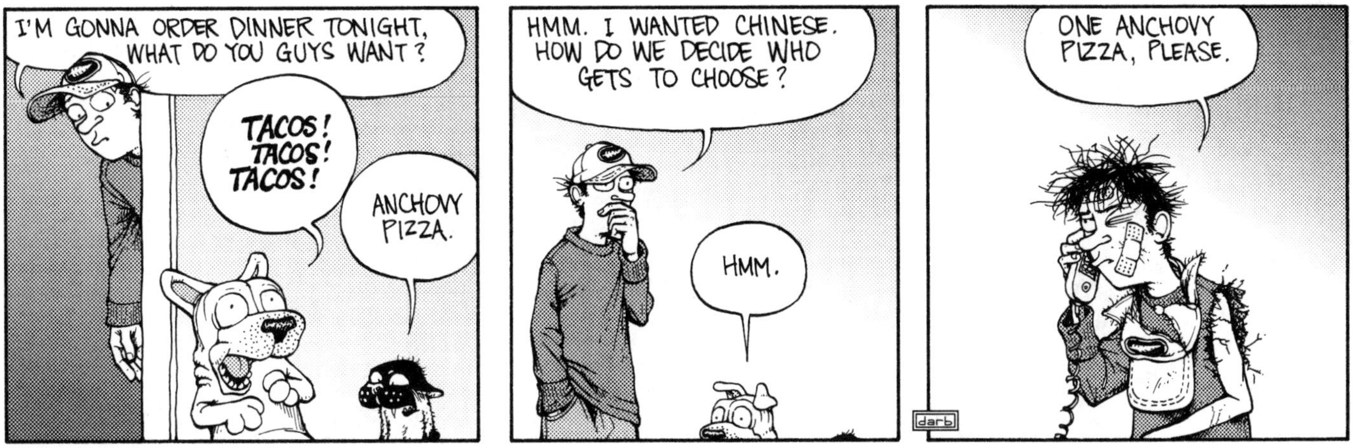
I'M GONNA ORDER DINNER TONIGHT, WHAT DO YOU GUYS WANT ?
TACOS! TACOS! TACOS!
ANCHOVY PIZZA.
HMM. I WANTED CHINESE. HOW DO WE DECIDE WHO GETS TO CHOOSE ?
HMM.
ONE ANCHOVY PIZZA, PLEASE.
darb

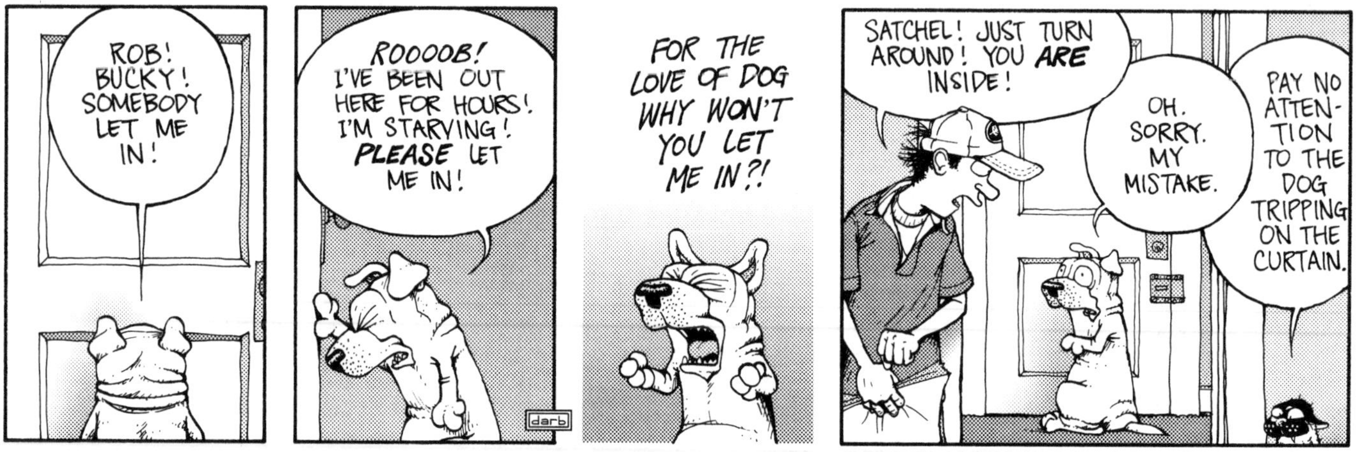
ROB! BUCKY! SOMEBODY LET ME IN!
ROOOOB! I'VE BEEN OUT HERE FOR HOURS! I'M STARVING! PLEASE LET ME IN!
darb
FOR THE LOVE OF DOG WHY WON'T YOU LET ME IN?!
SATCHEL! JUST TURN AROUND! YOU ARE INSIDE!
OH. SORRY. MY MISTAKE.
PAY NO ATTEN-TION TO THE DOG TRIPPING ON THE CURTAIN.

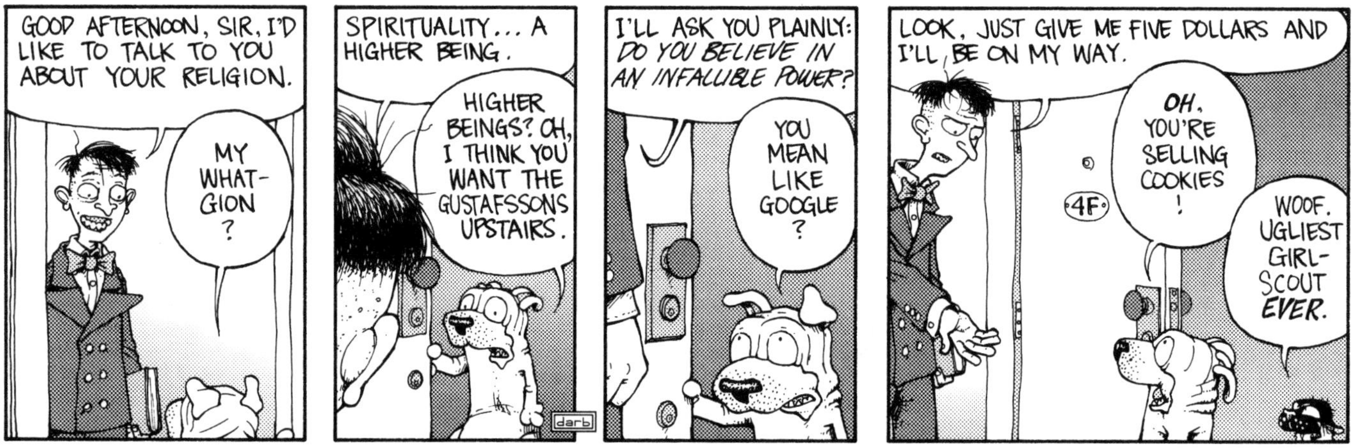
GOOD AFTERNOON, SIR, I'D LIKE TO TALK TO YOU ABOUT YOUR RELIGION.
MY WHAT-GION?
SPIRITUALITY... A HIGHER BEING.
HIGHER BEINGS? OH, I THINK YOU WANT THE GUSTAFSSONS UPSTAIRS.
darb
I'LL ASK YOU PLAINLY: DO YOU BELIEVE IN AN INFALLIBLE POWER?
YOU MEAN LIKE GOOGLE?
LOOK, JUST GIVE ME FIVE DOLLARS AND I'LL BE ON MY WAY.
OH. YOU'RE SELLING COOKIES!
4F
WOOF. UGLIEST GIRL-SCOUT EVER.

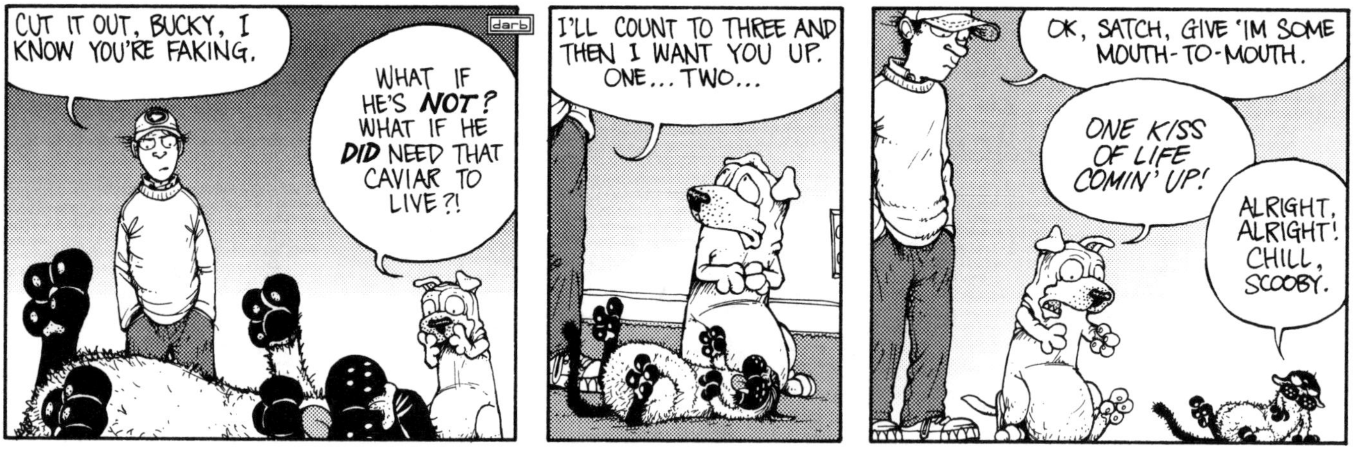
darb
CUT IT OUT, BUCKY, I KNOW YOU'RE FAKING.
WHAT IF HE'S NOT? WHAT IF HE DID NEED THAT CAVIAR TO LIVE?!
I'LL COUNT TO THREE AND THEN I WANT YOU UP. ONE... TWO...
OK, SATCH, GIVE 'IM SOME MOUTH-TO-MOUTH.
ONE KISS OF LIFE COMIN' UP!
ALRIGHT, ALRIGHT! CHILL, SCOOBY.

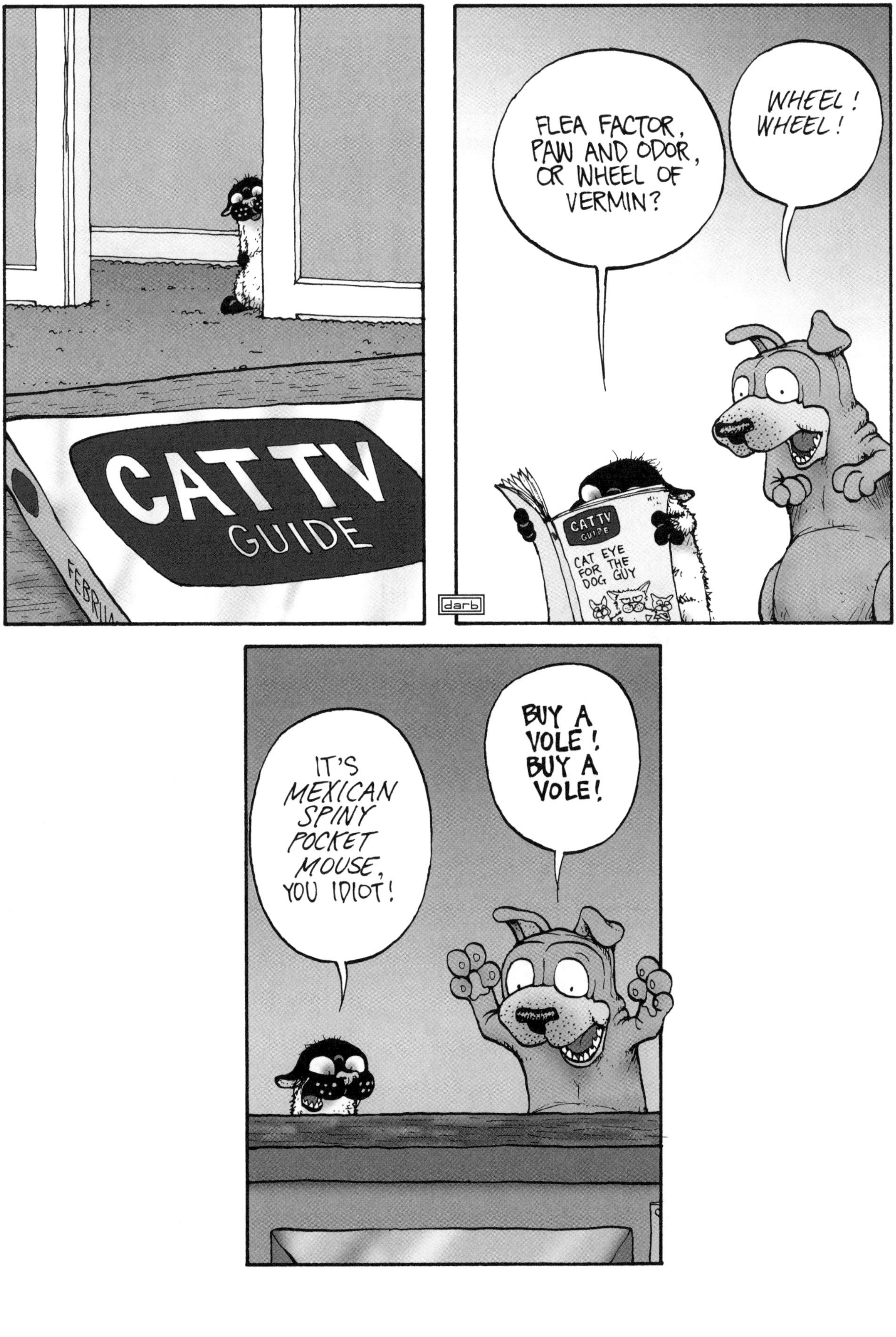
CAT TV
GUIDE
FLEA FACTOR, PAW AND ODOR, OR WHEEL OF VERMIN?
WHEEL! WHEEL!
CAT TV GUIDE
CAT EYE FOR THE DOG GUY
darb
IT'S MEXICAN SPINY POCKET MOUSE, YOU IDIOT!
BUY A VOLE! BUY A VOLE!

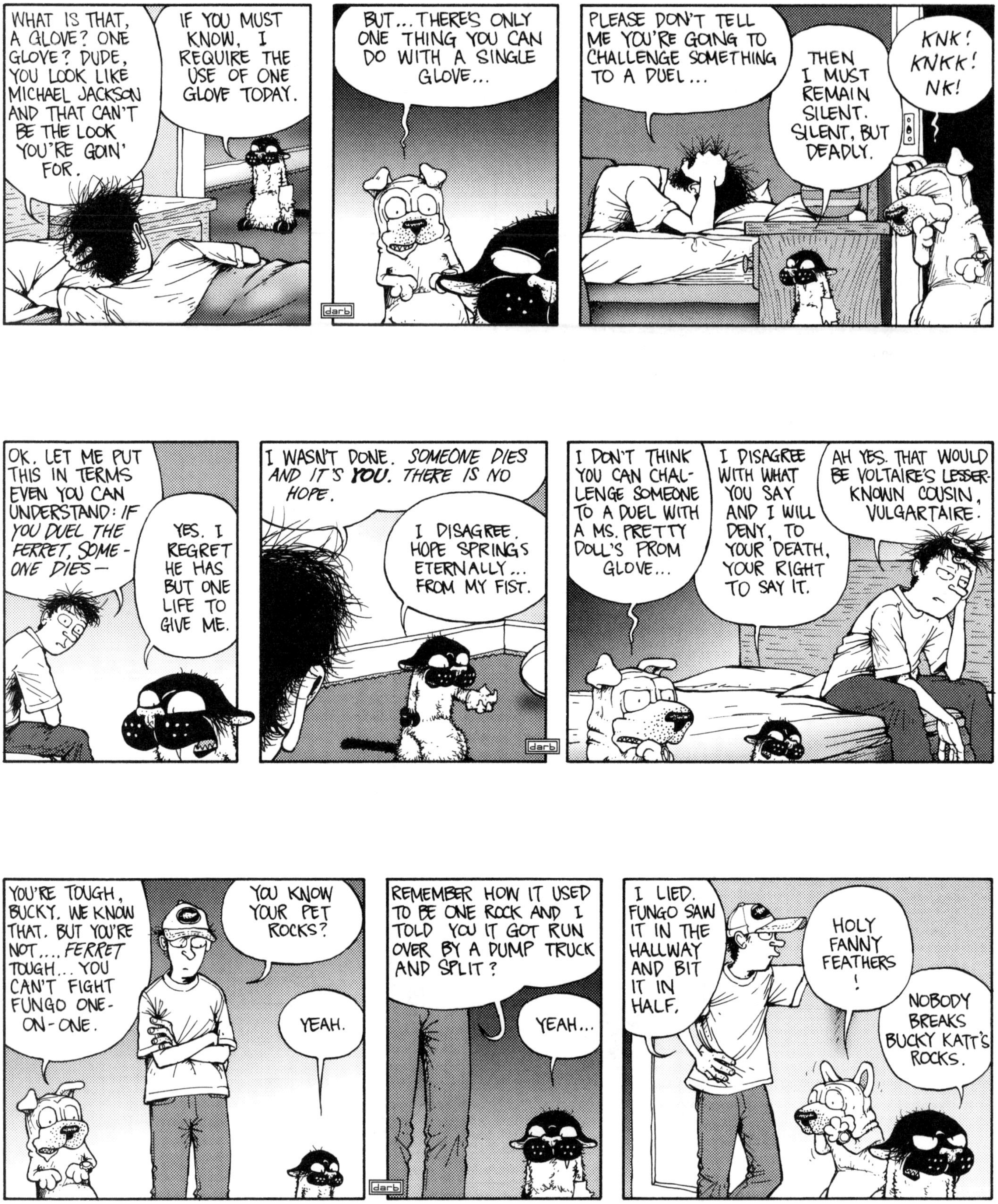
WHAT IS THAT, A GLOVE? ONE GLOVE? DUDE, YOU LOOK LIKE MICHAEL JACKSON AND THAT CAN'T BE THE LOOK YOU'RE GOIN' FOR.
IF YOU MUST KNOW, I REQUIRE THE USE OF ONE GLOVE TODAY.
BUT... THERE'S ONLY ONE THING YOU CAN DO WITH A SINGLE GLOVE...
darb
PLEASE DON'T TELL ME YOU'RE GOING TO CHALLENGE SOMETHING TO A DUEL...
THEN I MUST REMAIN SILENT. SILENT, BUT DEADLY.
KNK! KNKK! NK!
OK. LET ME PUT THIS IN TERMS EVEN YOU CAN UNDERSTAND: IF YOU DUEL THE FERRET, SOMEONE DIES—
YES. I REGRET HE HAS BUT ONE LIFE TO GIVE ME.
I WASN'T DONE. SOMEONE DIES AND IT'S YOU. THERE IS NO HOPE.
I DISAGREE. HOPE SPRINGS ETERNALLY... FROM MY FIST.
darb
I DON'T THINK YOU CAN CHALLENGE SOMEONE TO A DUEL WITH A MS. PRETTY DOLL'S PROM GLOVE...
I DISAGREE WITH WHAT YOU SAY AND I WILL DENY, TO YOUR DEATH, YOUR RIGHT TO SAY IT.
AH YES. THAT WOULD BE VOLTAIRE'S LESSER-KNOWN COUSIN, VULGARTAIRE.
YOU'RE TOUGH, BUCKY. WE KNOW THAT. BUT YOU'RE NOT.... FERRET TOUGH... YOU CAN'T FIGHT FUNGO ONE-ON-ONE.
YOU KNOW YOUR PET ROCKS?
YEAH.
darb
REMEMBER HOW IT USED TO BE ONE ROCK AND I TOLD YOU IT GOT RUN OVER BY A DUMP TRUCK AND SPLIT?
YEAH...
I LIED. FUNGO SAW IT IN THE HALLWAY AND BIT IT IN HALF.
HOLY FANNY FEATHERS!
NOBODY BREAKS BUCKY KATT'S ROCKS.

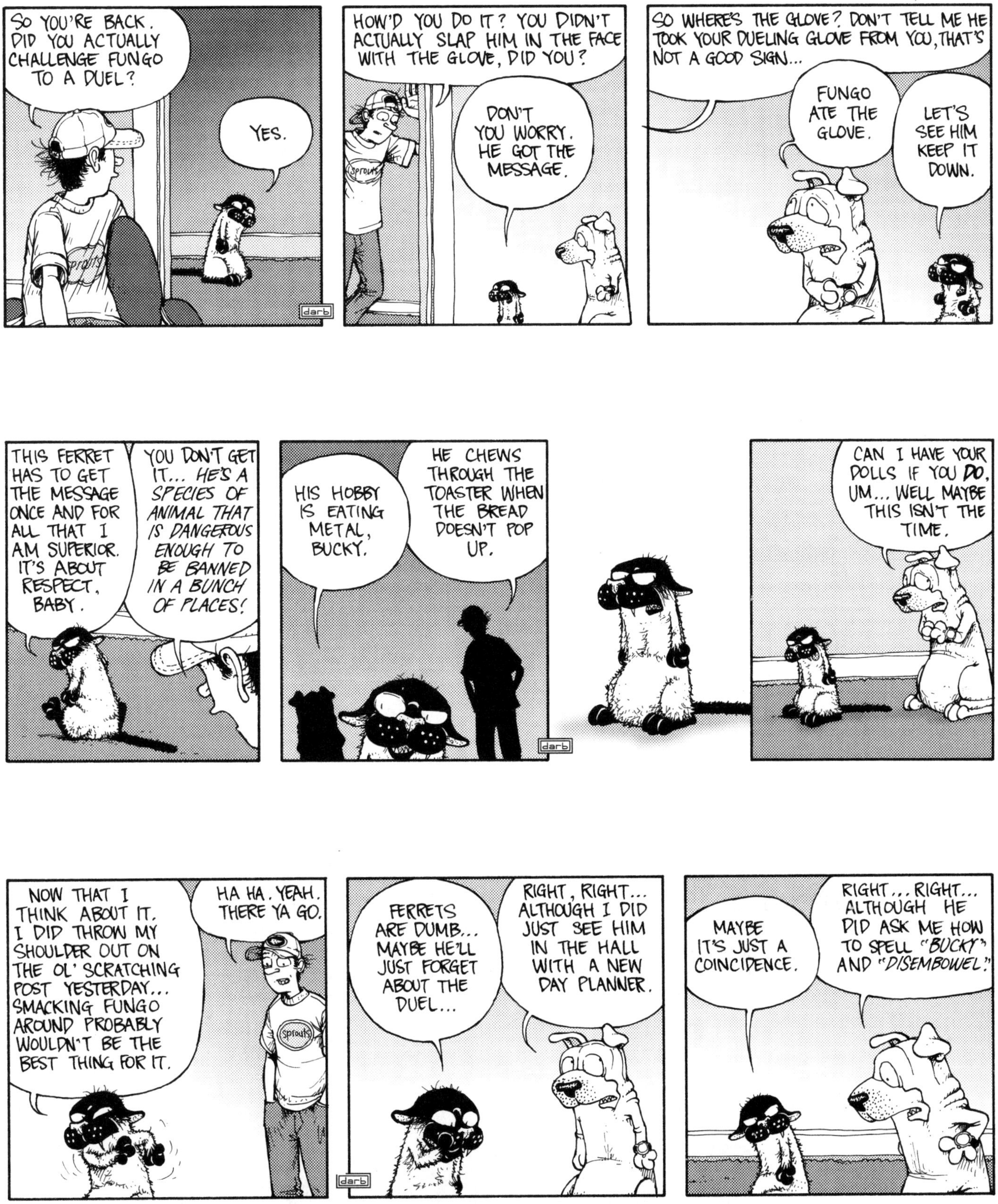
SO YOU'RE BACK. DID YOU ACTUALLY CHALLENGE FUNGO TO A DUEL?
YES.
darb
HOW'D YOU DO IT? YOU DIDN'T ACTUALLY SLAP HIM IN THE FACE WITH THE GLOVE, DID YOU?
DON'T YOU WORRY. HE GOT THE MESSAGE.
SO WHERE'S THE GLOVE? DON'T TELL ME HE TOOK YOUR DUELING GLOVE FROM YOU, THAT'S NOT A GOOD SIGN...
FUNGO ATE THE GLOVE.
LET'S SEE HIM KEEP IT DOWN.
THIS FERRET HAS TO GET THE MESSAGE ONCE AND FOR ALL THAT I AM SUPERIOR. IT'S ABOUT RESPECT, BABY.
YOU DON'T GET IT... HE'S A SPECIES OF ANIMAL THAT IS DANGEROUS ENOUGH TO BE BANNED IN A BUNCH OF PLACES!
HIS HOBBY IS EATING METAL, BUCKY.
HE CHEWS THROUGH THE TOASTER WHEN THE BREAD DOESN'T POP UP.
darb
CAN I HAVE YOUR DOLLS IF YOU DO, UM... WELL MAYBE THIS ISN'T THE TIME.
NOW THAT I THINK ABOUT IT, I DID THROW MY SHOULDER OUT ON THE OL' SCRATCHING POST YESTERDAY... SMACKING FUNGO AROUND PROBABLY WOULDN'T BE THE BEST THING FOR IT.
HA HA. YEAH. THERE YA GO.
darb
FERRETS ARE DUMB... MAYBE HE'LL JUST FORGET ABOUT THE DUEL...
RIGHT, RIGHT... ALTHOUGH I DID JUST SEE HIM IN THE HALL WITH A NEW DAY PLANNER.
MAYBE IT'S JUST A COINCIDENCE.
RIGHT... RIGHT... ALTHOUGH HE DID ASK ME HOW TO SPELL "BUCKY" AND "DISEMBOWEL".

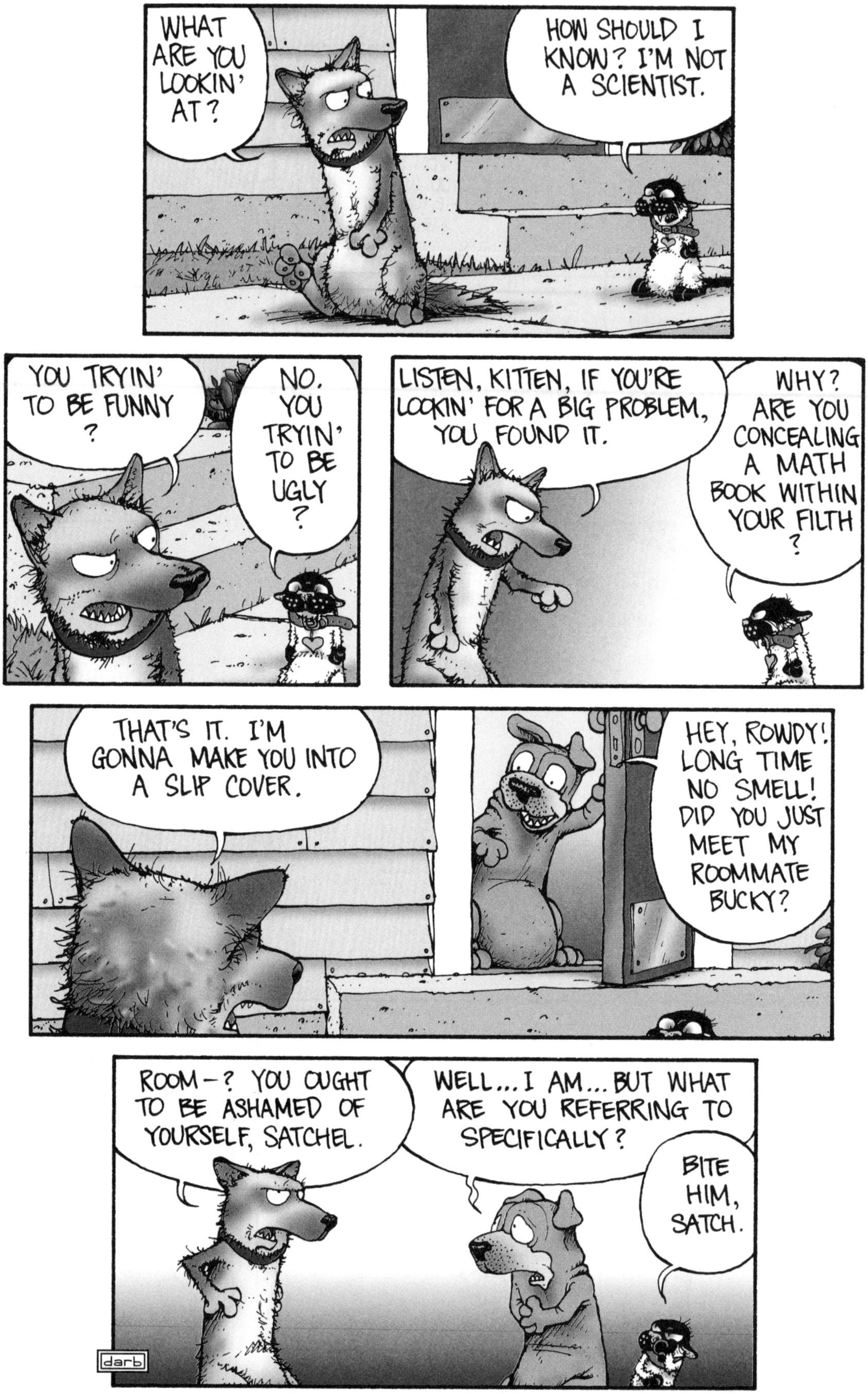
WHAT ARE YOU LOOKIN' AT?
HOW SHOULD I KNOW? I'M NOT A SCIENTIST.
YOU TRYIN' TO BE FUNNY ?
NO. YOU TRYIN' TO BE UGLY ?
LISTEN, KITTEN, IF YOU'RE LOOKIN' FOR A BIG PROBLEM, YOU FOUND IT.
WHY? ARE YOU CONCEALING A MATH BOOK WITHIN YOUR FILTH ?
THAT'S IT. I'M GONNA MAKE YOU INTO A SLIP COVER.
HEY, ROWDY! LONG TIME NO SMELL! DID YOU JUST MEET MY ROOMMATE BUCKY?
ROOM-? YOU OUGHT TO BE ASHAMED OF YOURSELF, SATCHEL.
WELL... I AM... BUT WHAT ARE YOU REFERRING TO SPECIFICALLY?
BITE HIM, SATCH.
darb

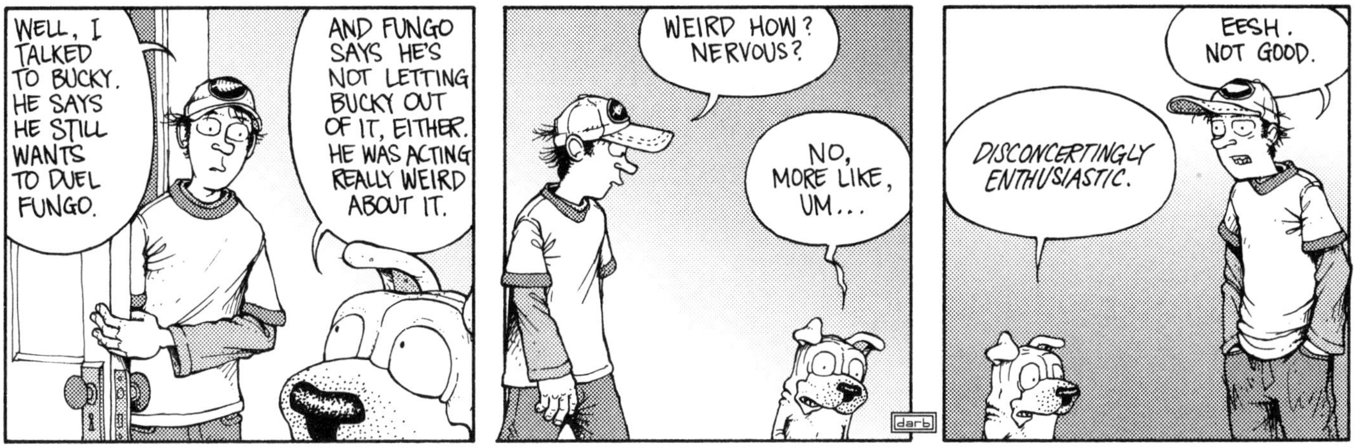
WELL, I TALKED TO BUCKY. HE SAYS HE STILL WANTS TO DUEL FUNGO.
AND FUNGO SAYS HE'S NOT LETTING BUCKY OUT OF IT, EITHER. HE WAS ACTING REALLY WEIRD ABOUT IT.
WEIRD HOW? NERVOUS?
NO, MORE LIKE, UM...
darb
DISCONCERTINGLY ENTHUSIASTIC.
EESH. NOT GOOD.

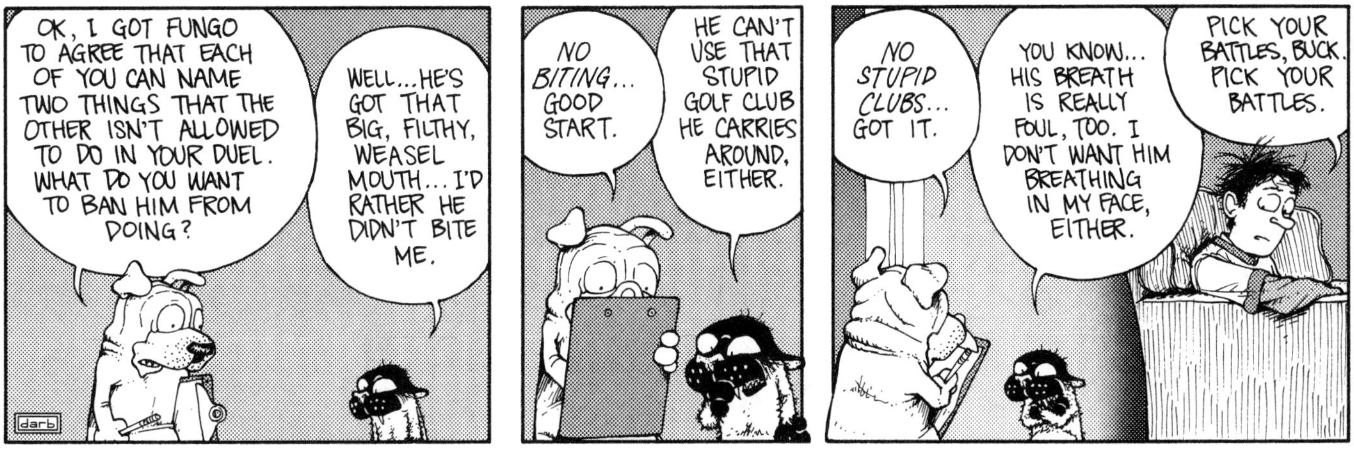
OK, I GOT FUNGO TO AGREE THAT EACH OF YOU CAN NAME TWO THINGS THAT THE OTHER ISN'T ALLOWED TO DO IN YOUR DUEL. WHAT DO YOU WANT TO BAN HIM FROM DOING?
WELL...HE'S GOT THAT BIG, FILTHY, WEASEL MOUTH... I'D RATHER HE DIDN'T BITE ME.
darb
NO BITING... GOOD START.
HE CAN'T USE THAT STUPID GOLF CLUB HE CARRIES AROUND, EITHER.
NO STUPID CLUBS... GOT IT.
YOU KNOW... HIS BREATH IS REALLY FOUL, TOO. I DON'T WANT HIM BREATHING IN MY FACE, EITHER.
PICK YOUR BATTLES, BUCK. PICK YOUR BATTLES.

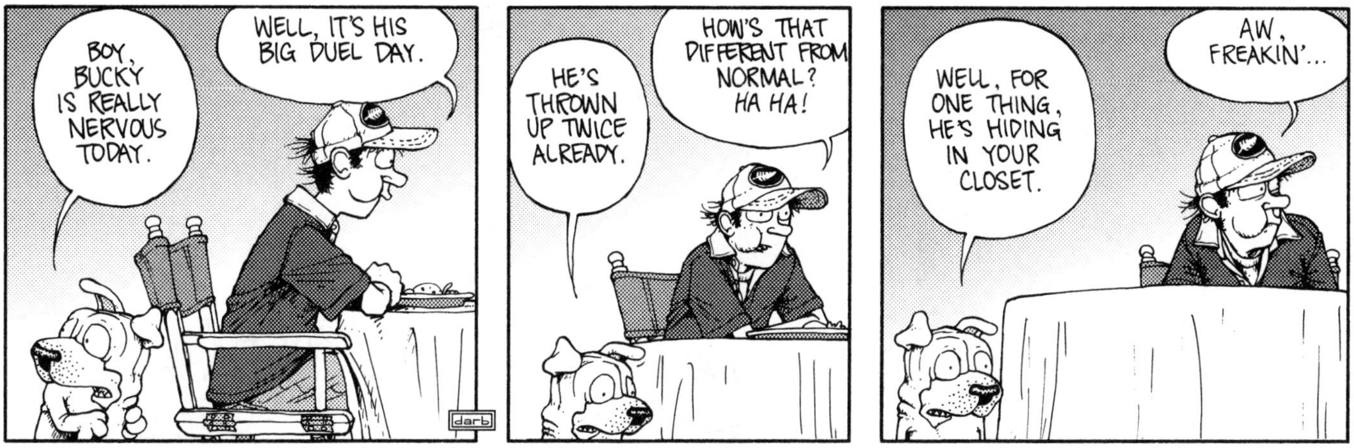
BOY, BUCKY IS REALLY NERVOUS TODAY.
WELL, IT'S HIS BIG DUEL DAY.
darb
HE'S THROWN UP TWICE ALREADY.
HOW'S THAT DIFFERENT FROM NORMAL? *HA HA!*
WELL, FOR ONE THING, HE'S HIDING IN YOUR CLOSET.
AW, FREAKIN'...

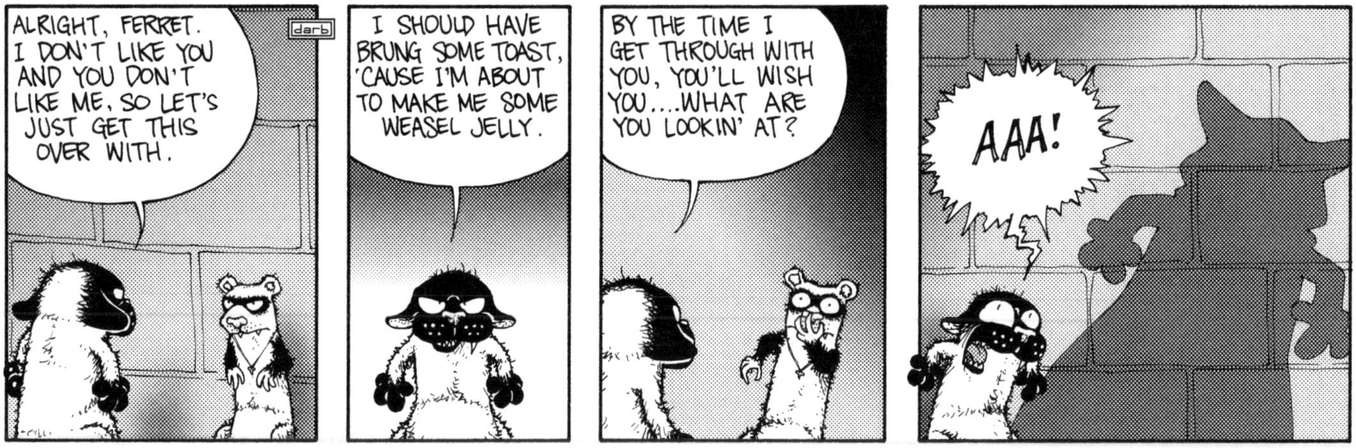

ALRIGHT, FERRET. I DON'T LIKE YOU AND YOU DON'T LIKE ME, SO LET'S JUST GET THIS OVER WITH.
I SHOULD HAVE BRUNG SOME TOAST, 'CAUSE I'M ABOUT TO MAKE ME SOME WEASEL JELLY.
BY THE TIME I GET THROUGH WITH YOU, YOU'LL WISH YOU....WHAT ARE YOU LOOKIN' AT?
AAA!

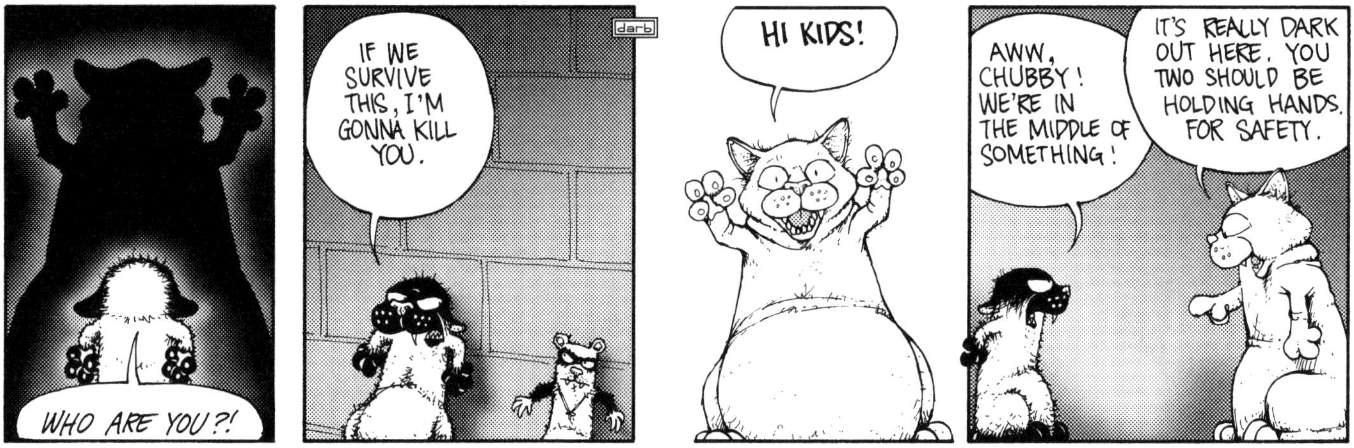

WHO ARE YOU?!
IF WE SURVIVE THIS, I'M GONNA KILL YOU.
HI KIDS!
AWW, CHUBBY! WE'RE IN THE MIDDLE OF SOMETHING!
IT'S REALLY DARK OUT HERE. YOU TWO SHOULD BE HOLDING HANDS. FOR SAFETY.

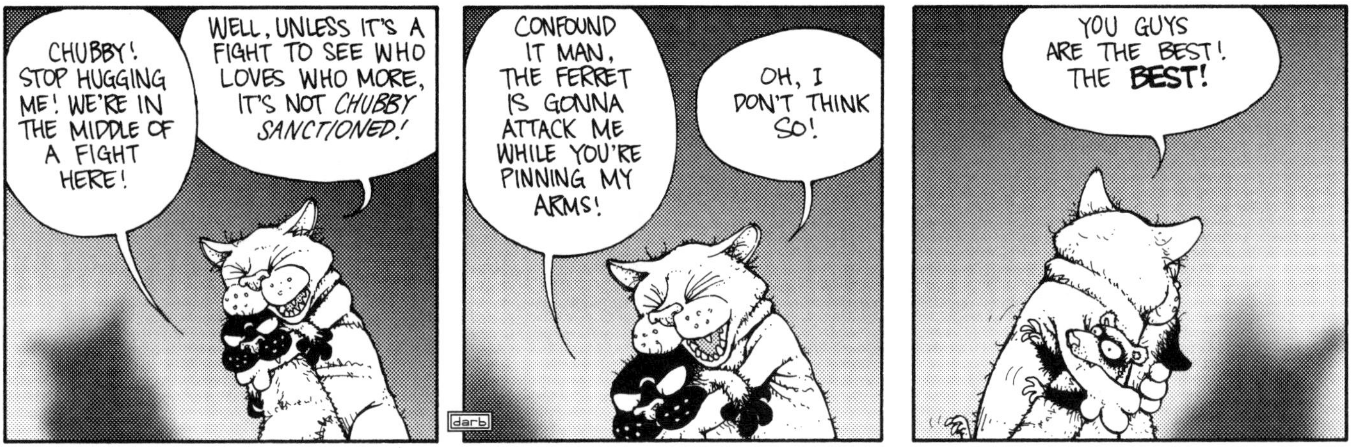

CHUBBY! STOP HUGGING ME! WE'RE IN THE MIDDLE OF A FIGHT HERE!
WELL, UNLESS IT'S A FIGHT TO SEE WHO LOVES WHO MORE, IT'S NOT CHUBBY SANCTIONED!
CONFOUND IT MAN, THE FERRET IS GONNA ATTACK ME WHILE YOU'RE PINNING MY ARMS!
OH, I DON'T THINK SO!
YOU GUYS ARE THE BEST! THE BEST!

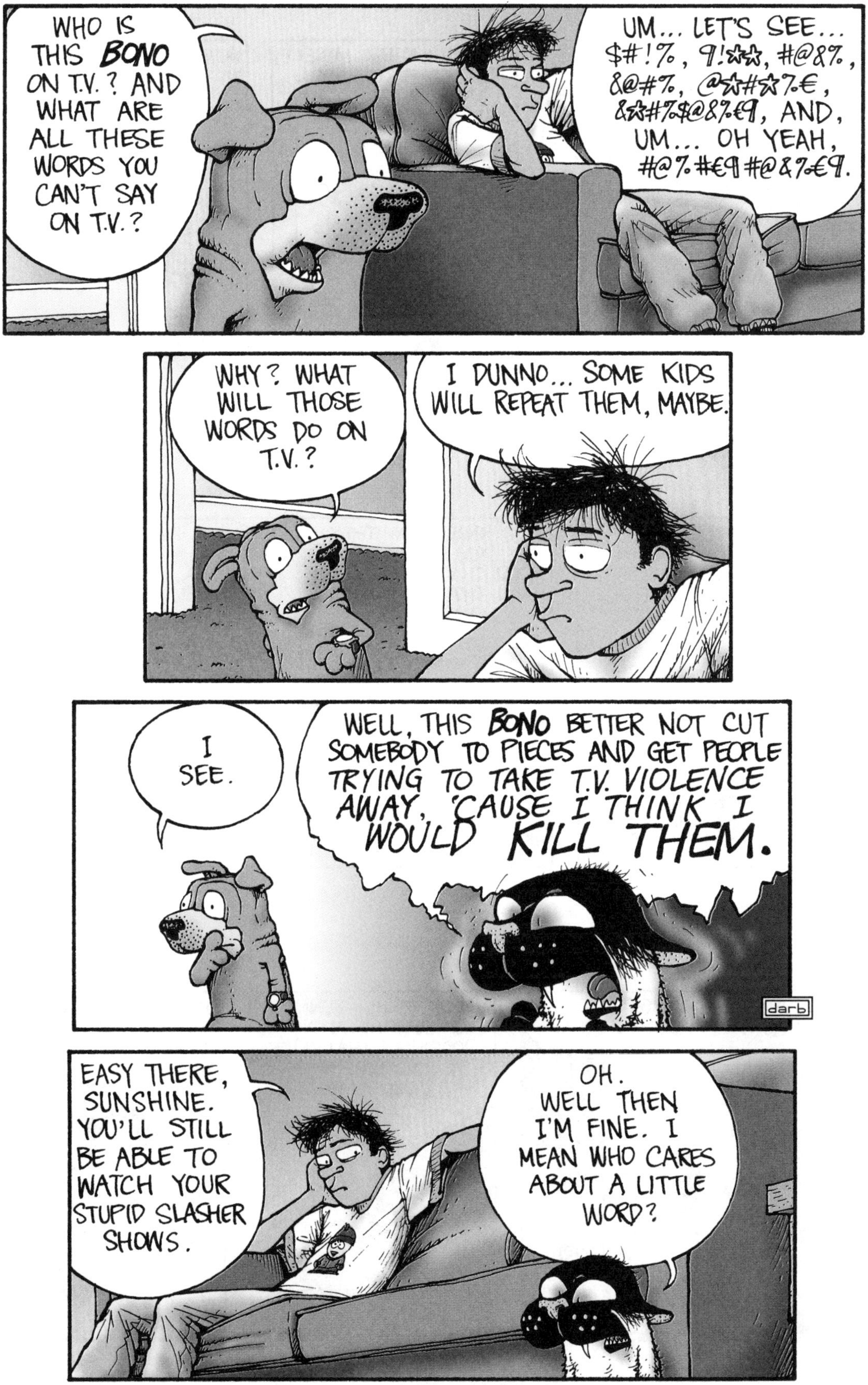
WHO IS THIS BONO ON T.V.? AND WHAT ARE ALL THESE WORDS YOU CAN'T SAY ON T.V.?
UM... LET'S SEE... $#!%, ?!☆☆, #@&%, &@#%, @☆#☆%€, &☆#%$@&%€?, AND, UM... OH YEAH, #@%#€?#@&%€?.
WHY? WHAT WILL THOSE WORDS DO ON T.V.?
I DUNNO... SOME KIDS WILL REPEAT THEM, MAYBE.
I SEE.
WELL, THIS BONO BETTER NOT CUT SOMEBODY TO PIECES AND GET PEOPLE TRYING TO TAKE T.V. VIOLENCE AWAY, 'CAUSE I THINK I WOULD KILL THEM.
darb
EASY THERE, SUNSHINE. YOU'LL STILL BE ABLE TO WATCH YOUR STUPID SLASHER SHOWS.
OH. WELL THEN I'M FINE. I MEAN WHO CARES ABOUT A LITTLE WORD?

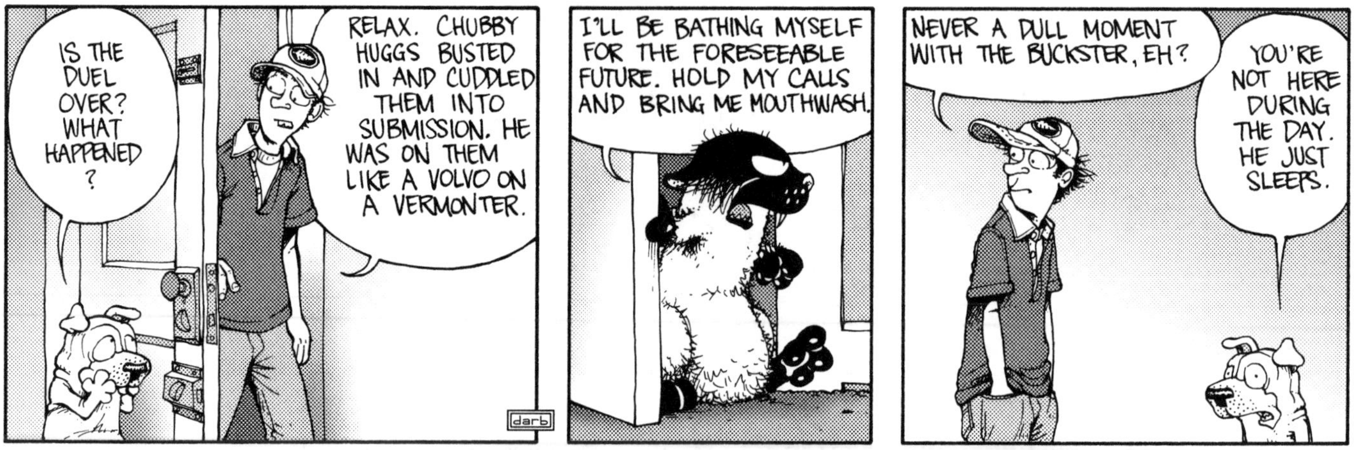
IS THE DUEL OVER? WHAT HAPPENED?
RELAX. CHUBBY HUGGS BUSTED IN AND CUDDLED THEM INTO SUBMISSION. HE WAS ON THEM LIKE A VOLVO ON A VERMONTER.
I'LL BE BATHING MYSELF FOR THE FORESEEABLE FUTURE. HOLD MY CALLS AND BRING ME MOUTHWASH.
NEVER A DULL MOMENT WITH THE BUCKSTER, EH?
YOU'RE NOT HERE DURING THE DAY. HE JUST SLEEPS.
darb

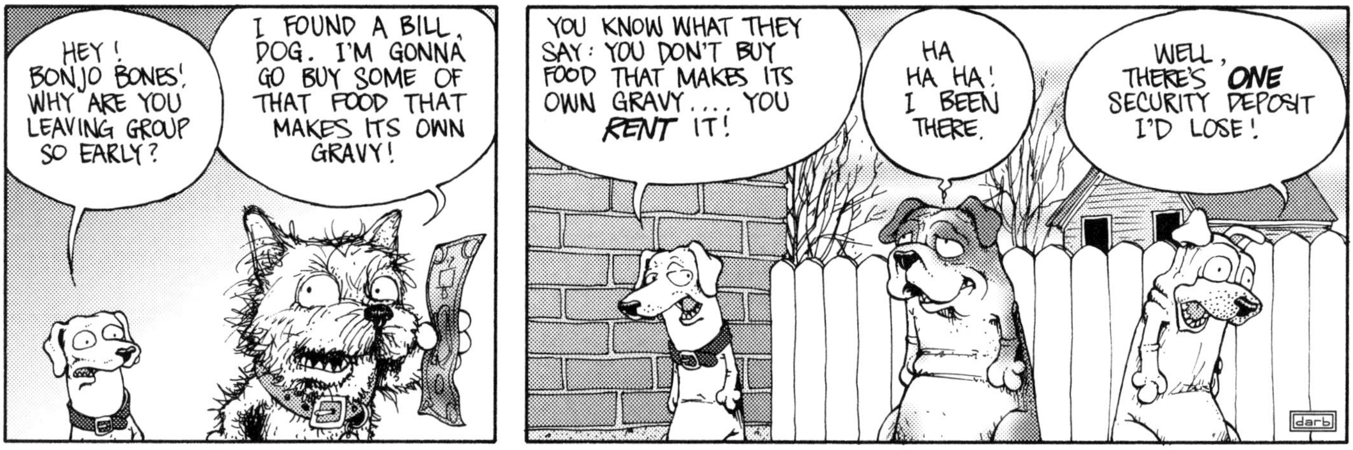
HEY! BONJO BONES! WHY ARE YOU LEAVING GROUP SO EARLY?
I FOUND A BILL, DOG. I'M GONNA GO BUY SOME OF THAT FOOD THAT MAKES ITS OWN GRAVY!
YOU KNOW WHAT THEY SAY: YOU DON'T BUY FOOD THAT MAKES ITS OWN GRAVY.... YOU RENT IT!
HA HA HA! I BEEN THERE.
WELL, THERE'S ONE SECURITY DEPOSIT I'D LOSE!
darb

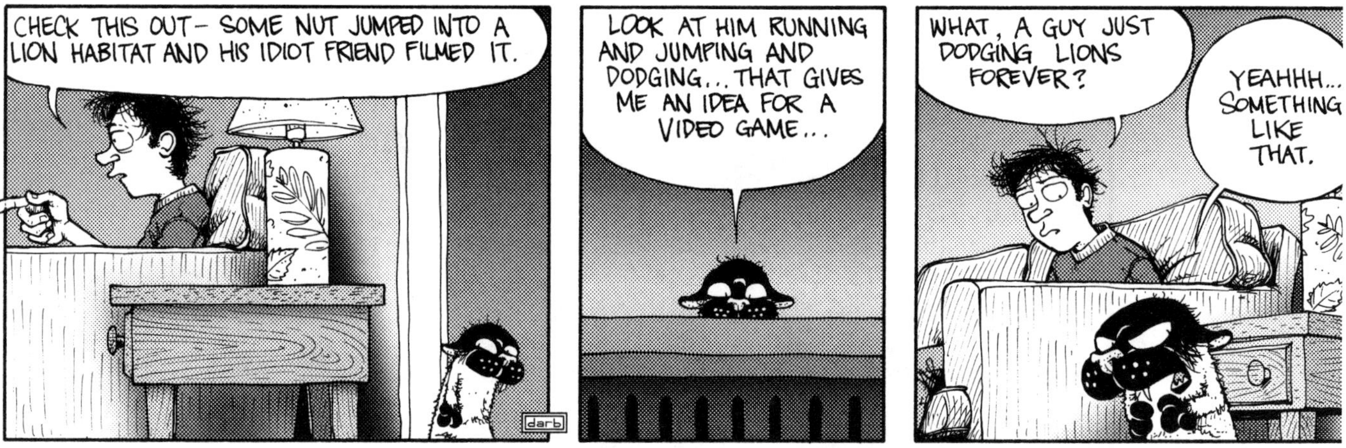
CHECK THIS OUT– SOME NUT JUMPED INTO A LION HABITAT AND HIS IDIOT FRIEND FILMED IT.
LOOK AT HIM RUNNING AND JUMPING AND DODGING... THAT GIVES ME AN IDEA FOR A VIDEO GAME...
WHAT, A GUY JUST DODGING LIONS FOREVER?
YEAHHH... SOMETHING LIKE THAT.
darb

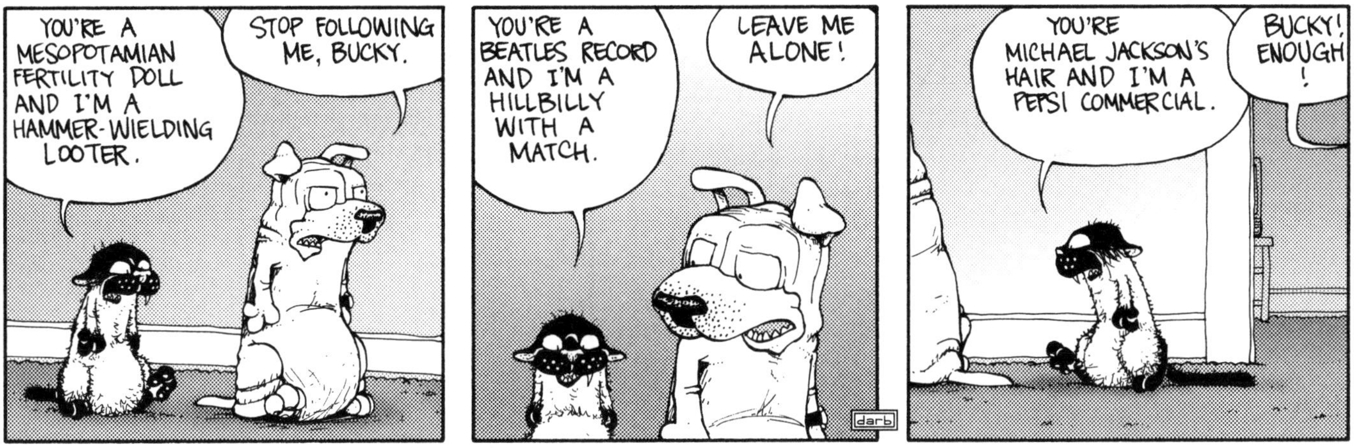
YOU'RE A MESOPOTAMIAN FERTILITY DOLL AND I'M A HAMMER-WIELDING LOOTER.
STOP FOLLOWING ME, BUCKY.
YOU'RE A BEATLES RECORD AND I'M A HILLBILLY WITH A MATCH.
LEAVE ME ALONE!
YOU'RE MICHAEL JACKSON'S HAIR AND I'M A PEPSI COMMERCIAL.
BUCKY! ENOUGH!
darb

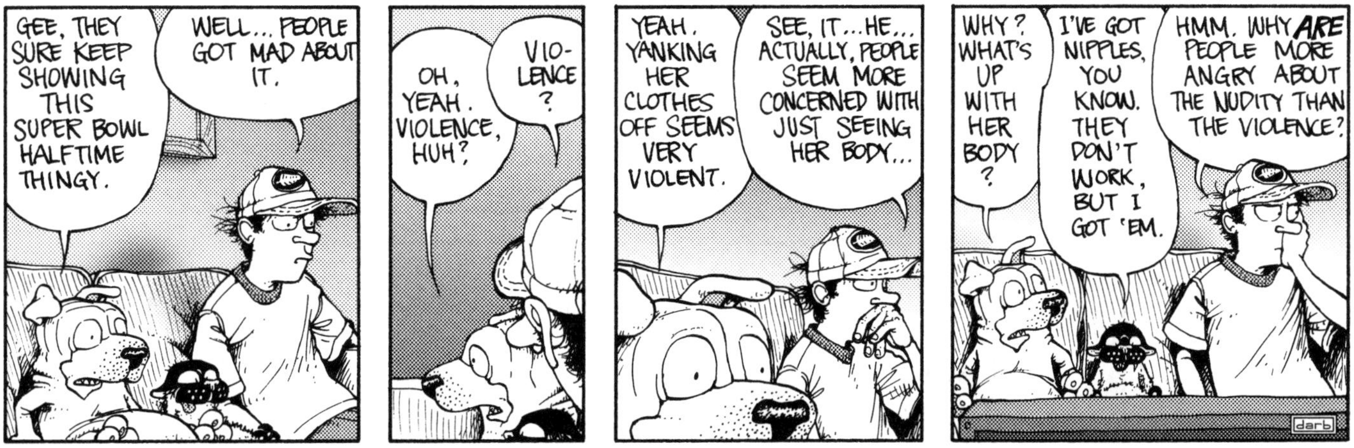
GEE, THEY SURE KEEP SHOWING THIS SUPER BOWL HALFTIME THINGY.
WELL... PEOPLE GOT MAD ABOUT IT.
VIO-LENCE?
OH, YEAH. VIOLENCE, HUH?
YEAH. YANKING HER CLOTHES OFF SEEMS VERY VIOLENT.
SEE, IT... HE... ACTUALLY, PEOPLE SEEM MORE CONCERNED WITH JUST SEEING HER BODY...
WHY? WHAT'S UP WITH HER BODY?
I'VE GOT NIPPLES, YOU KNOW. THEY DON'T WORK, BUT I GOT 'EM.
HMM. WHY ARE PEOPLE MORE ANGRY ABOUT THE NUDITY THAN THE VIOLENCE?
darb

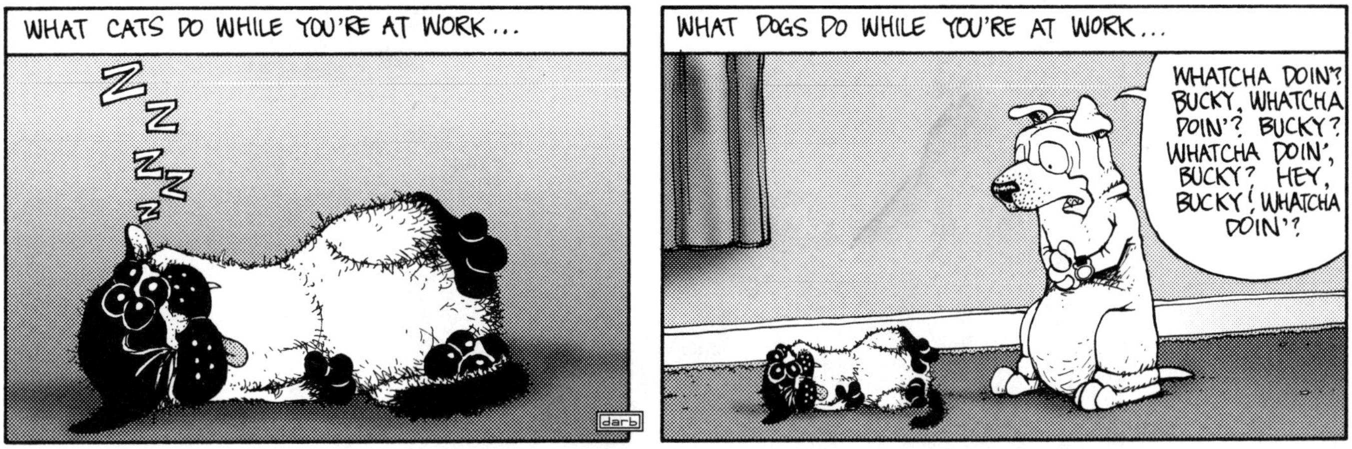
WHAT CATS DO WHILE YOU'RE AT WORK...
Z Z Z Z Z
darb
WHAT DOGS DO WHILE YOU'RE AT WORK...
WHATCHA DOIN'? BUCKY, WHATCHA DOIN'? BUCKY? WHATCHA DOIN', BUCKY? HEY, BUCKY! WHATCHA DOIN'?

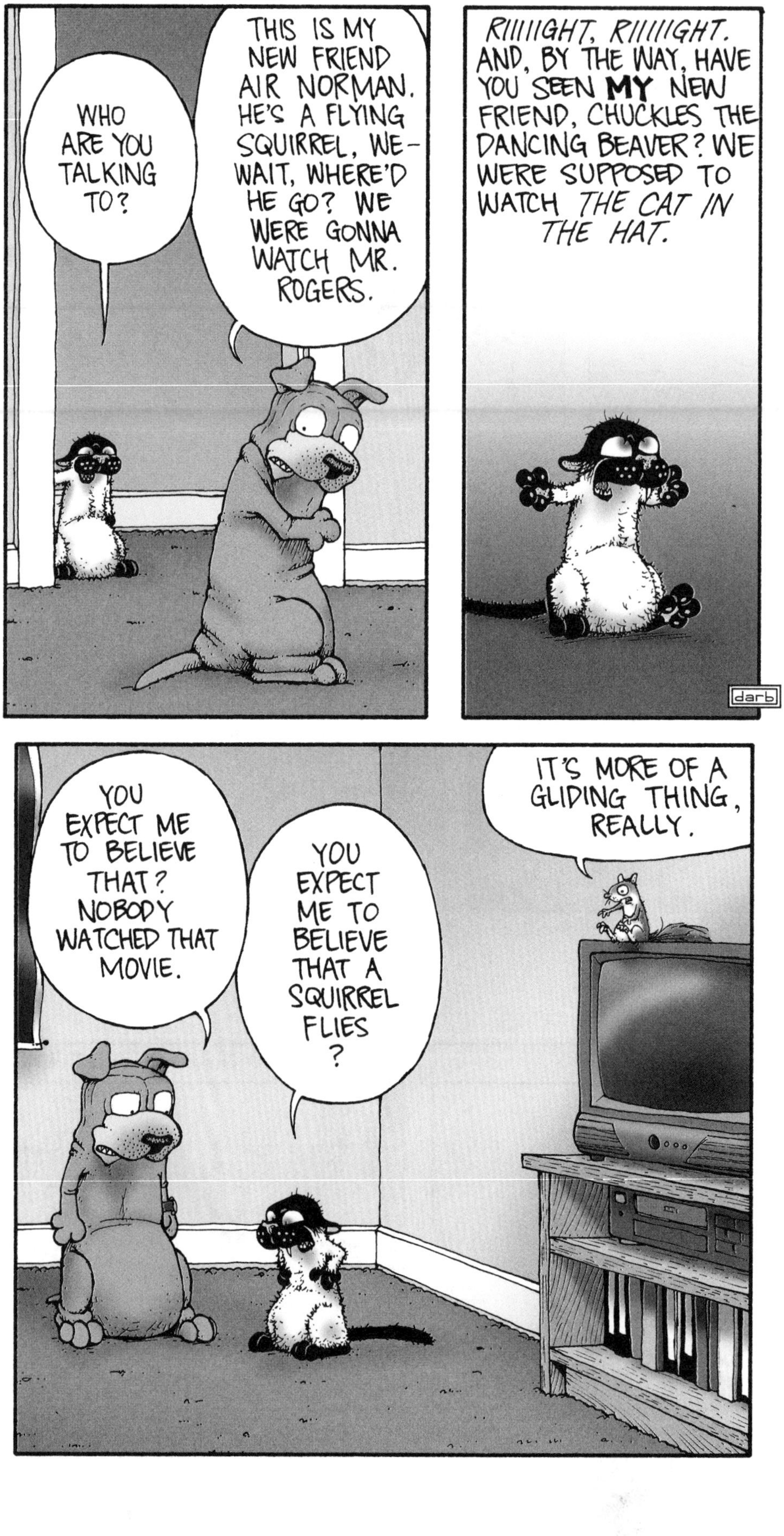
WHO ARE YOU TALKING TO?
THIS IS MY NEW FRIEND AIR NORMAN. HE'S A FLYING SQUIRREL, WE- WAIT, WHERE'D HE GO? WE WERE GONNA WATCH MR. ROGERS.
RIIIIIGHT, RIIIIIGHT. AND, BY THE WAY, HAVE YOU SEEN **MY** NEW FRIEND, CHUCKLES THE DANCING BEAVER? WE WERE SUPPOSED TO WATCH *THE CAT IN THE HAT.*
darb
YOU EXPECT ME TO BELIEVE THAT? NOBODY WATCHED THAT MOVIE.
YOU EXPECT ME TO BELIEVE THAT A SQUIRREL FLIES?
IT'S MORE OF A GLIDING THING, REALLY.

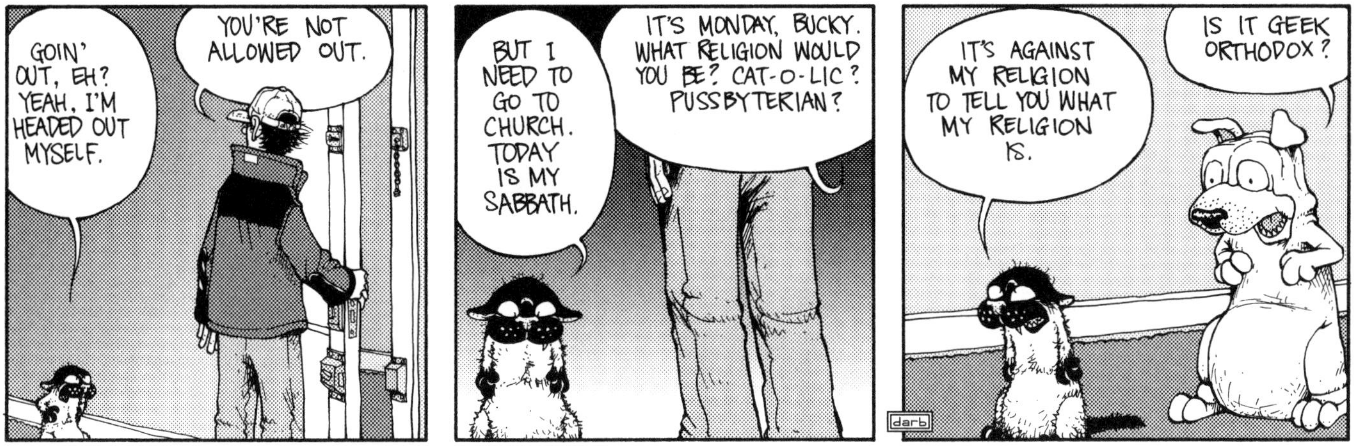
GOIN' OUT, EH? YEAH, I'M HEADED OUT MYSELF.
YOU'RE NOT ALLOWED OUT.
BUT I NEED TO GO TO CHURCH. TODAY IS MY SABBATH.
IT'S MONDAY, BUCKY. WHAT RELIGION WOULD YOU BE? CAT-O-LIC? PUSSBYTERIAN?
IT'S AGAINST MY RELIGION TO TELL YOU WHAT MY RELIGION IS.
IS IT GEEK ORTHODOX?
darb

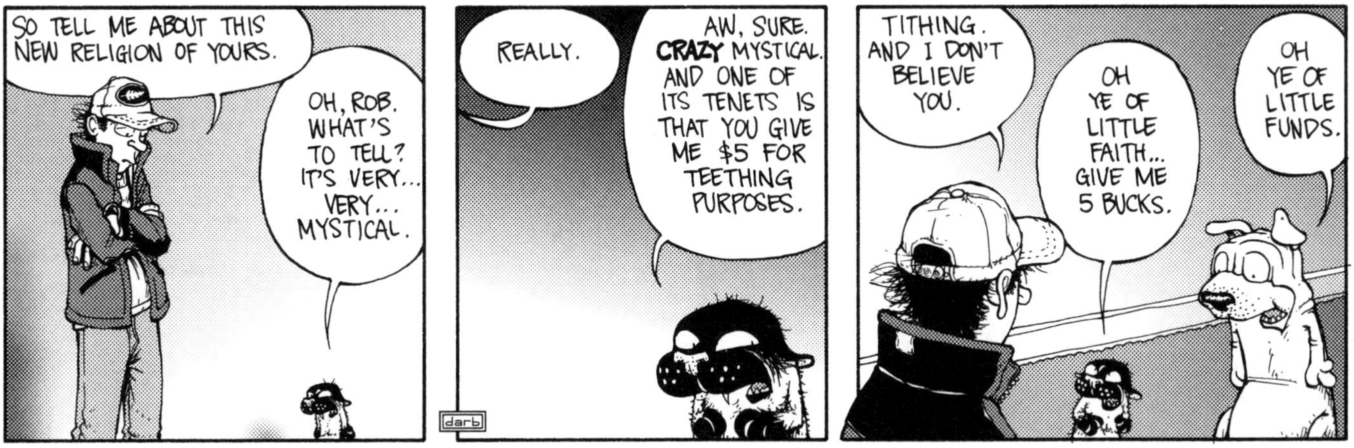
SO TELL ME ABOUT THIS NEW RELIGION OF YOURS.
OH, ROB. WHAT'S TO TELL? IT'S VERY... VERY... MYSTICAL.
darb
REALLY.
AW, SURE. CRAZY MYSTICAL. AND ONE OF ITS TENETS IS THAT YOU GIVE ME $5 FOR TEETHING PURPOSES.
TITHING. AND I DON'T BELIEVE YOU.
OH YE OF LITTLE FAITH... GIVE ME 5 BUCKS.
OH YE OF LITTLE FUNDS.

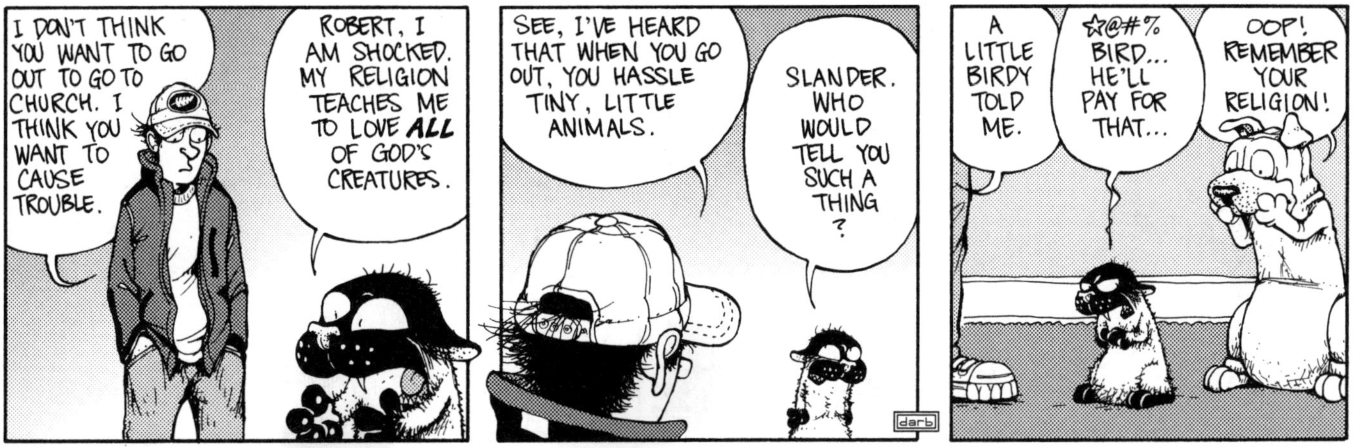
I DON'T THINK YOU WANT TO GO OUT TO GO TO CHURCH. I THINK YOU WANT TO CAUSE TROUBLE.
ROBERT, I AM SHOCKED. MY RELIGION TEACHES ME TO LOVE ALL OF GOD'S CREATURES.
SEE, I'VE HEARD THAT WHEN YOU GO OUT, YOU HASSLE TINY, LITTLE ANIMALS.
SLANDER. WHO WOULD TELL YOU SUCH A THING?
darb
A LITTLE BIRDY TOLD ME.
☆@#% BIRD... HE'LL PAY FOR THAT...
OOP! REMEMBER YOUR RELIGION!

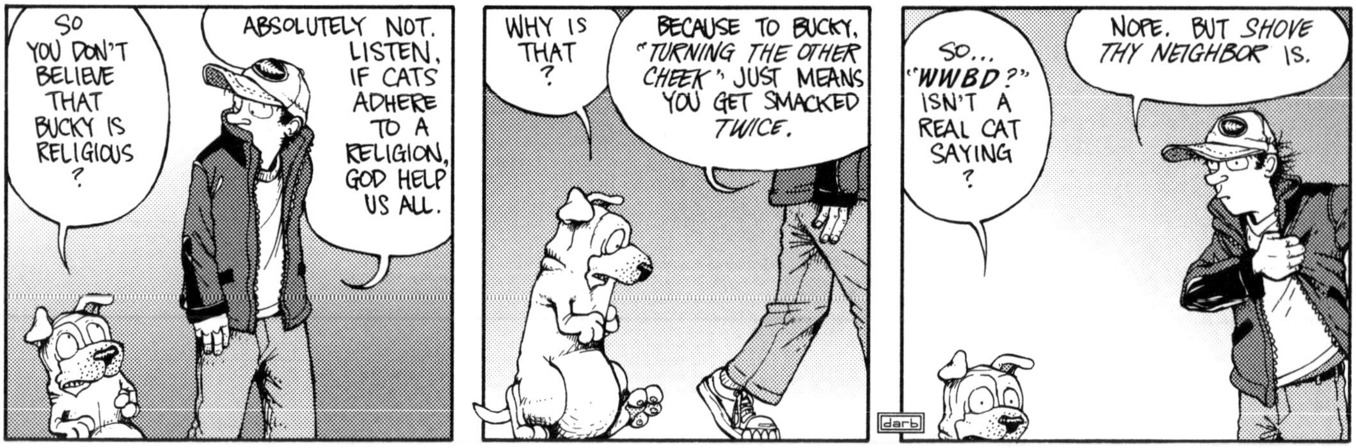
SO YOU DON'T BELIEVE THAT BUCKY IS RELIGIOUS ?
ABSOLUTELY NOT. LISTEN, IF CATS ADHERE TO A RELIGION, GOD HELP US ALL.
WHY IS THAT ?
BECAUSE TO BUCKY, "TURNING THE OTHER CHEEK" JUST MEANS YOU GET SMACKED TWICE.
SO... "WWBD?" ISN'T A REAL CAT SAYING ?
NOPE. BUT SHOVE THY NEIGHBOR IS.
darb

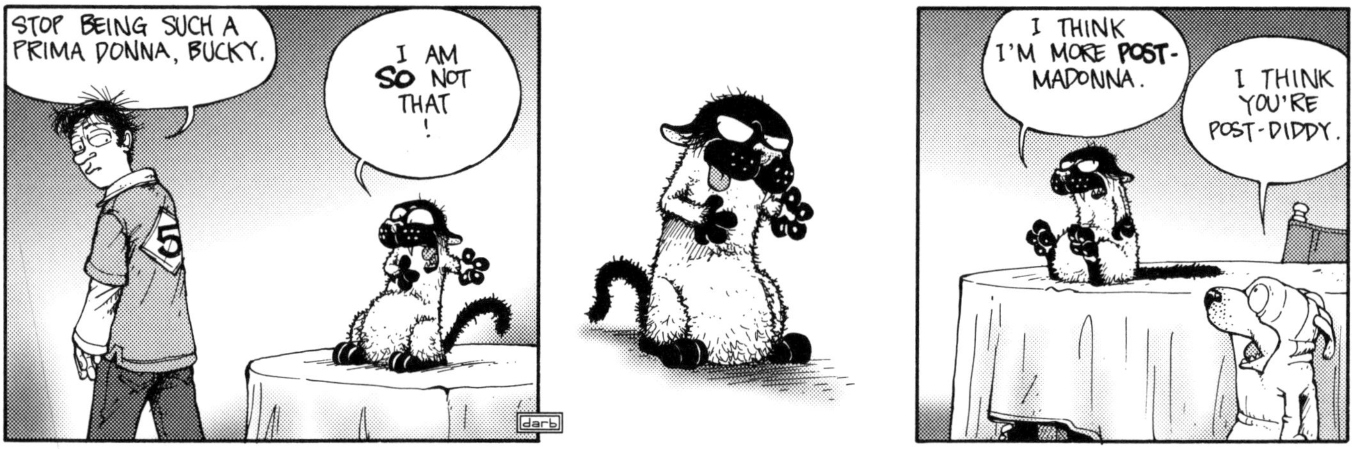
STOP BEING SUCH A PRIMA DONNA, BUCKY.
I AM SO NOT THAT !
darb
I THINK I'M MORE POST-MADONNA.
I THINK YOU'RE POST-DIDDY.

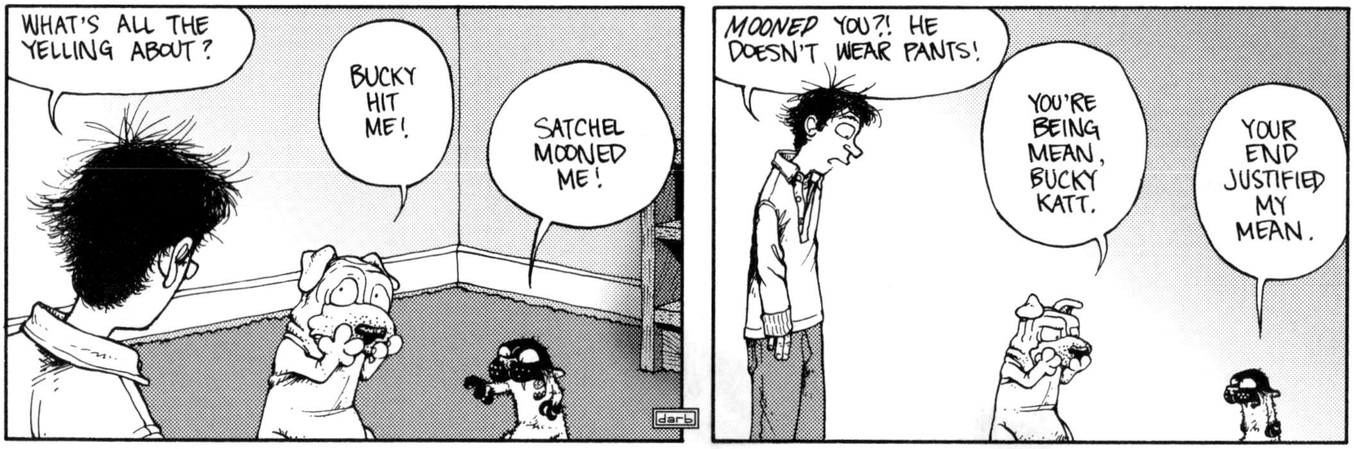
WHAT'S ALL THE YELLING ABOUT?
BUCKY HIT ME!
SATCHEL MOONED ME!
darb
MOONED YOU?! HE DOESN'T WEAR PANTS!
YOU'RE BEING MEAN, BUCKY KATT.
YOUR END JUSTIFIED MY MEAN.

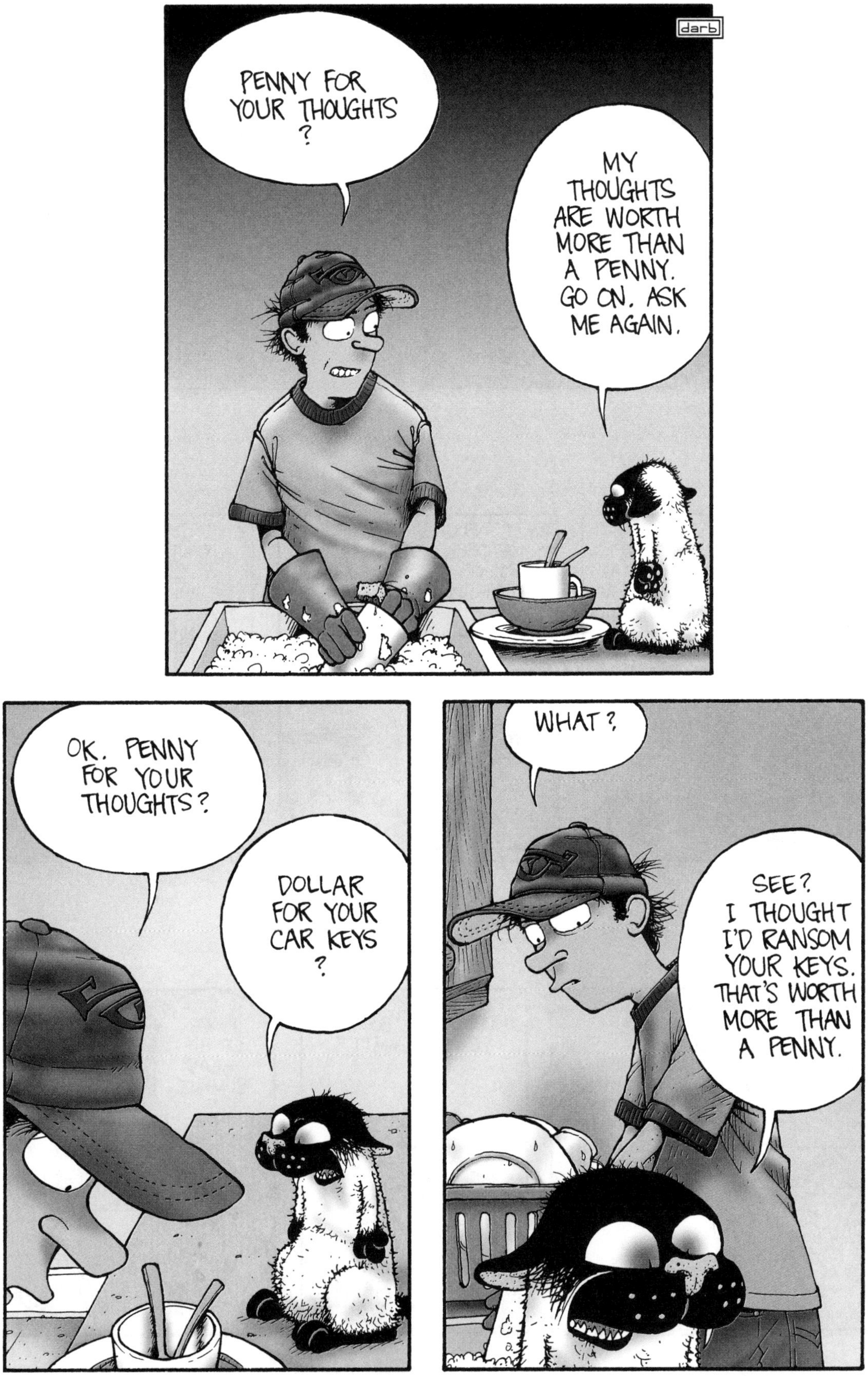
darb
PENNY FOR YOUR THOUGHTS ?
MY THOUGHTS ARE WORTH MORE THAN A PENNY. GO ON. ASK ME AGAIN.
OK. PENNY FOR YOUR THOUGHTS?
DOLLAR FOR YOUR CAR KEYS ?
WHAT?
SEE? I THOUGHT I'D RANSOM YOUR KEYS. THAT'S WORTH MORE THAN A PENNY.

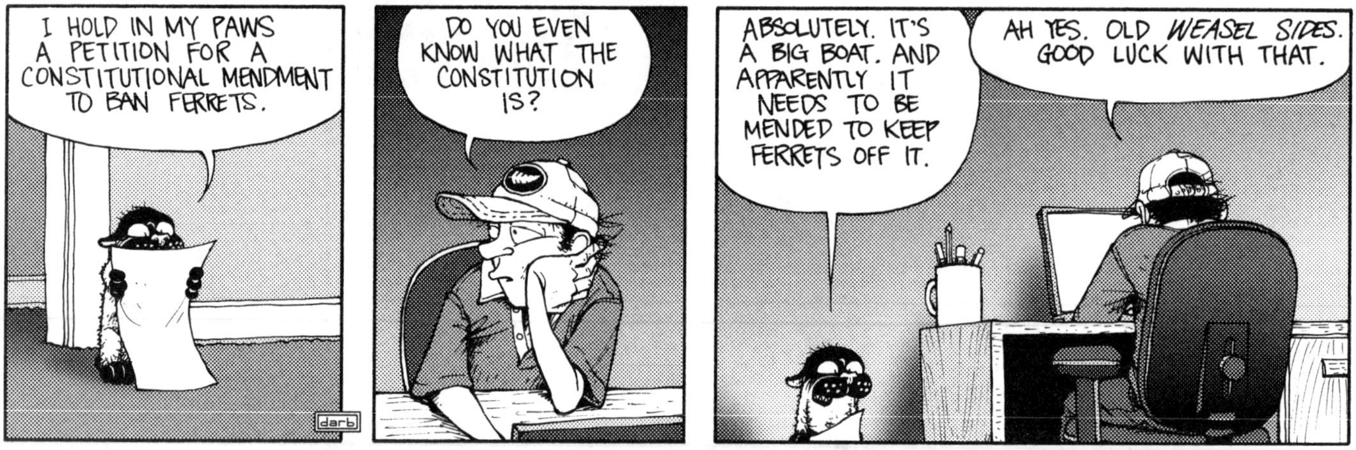
I HOLD IN MY PAWS A PETITION FOR A CONSTITUTIONAL MENDMENT TO BAN FERRETS.
darb
DO YOU EVEN KNOW WHAT THE CONSTITUTION IS?
ABSOLUTELY. IT'S A BIG BOAT. AND APPARENTLY IT NEEDS TO BE MENDED TO KEEP FERRETS OFF IT.
AH YES. OLD *WEASEL SIDES*. GOOD LUCK WITH THAT.

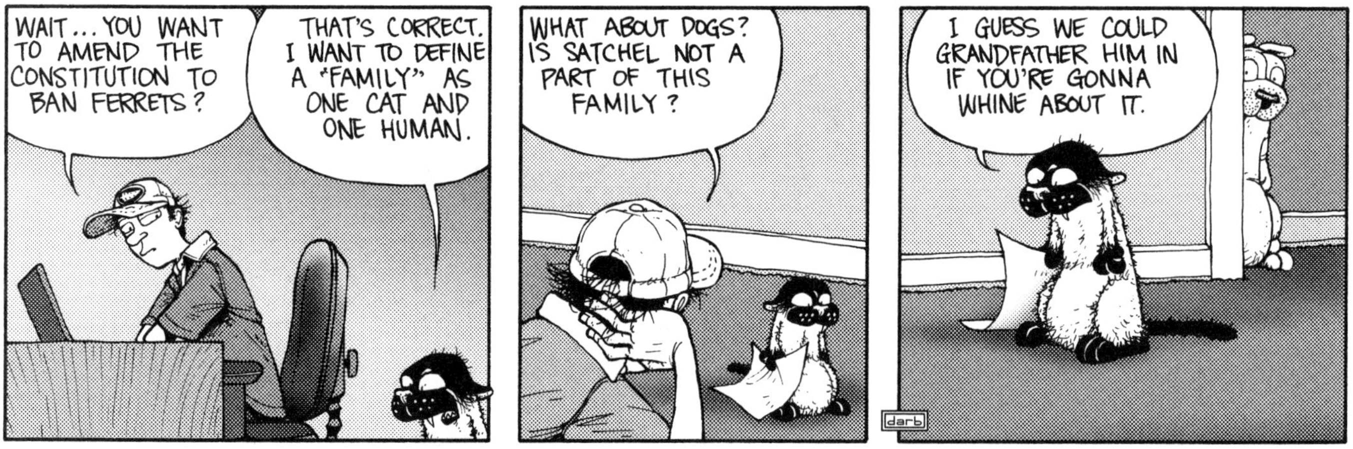
WAIT... YOU WANT TO AMEND THE CONSTITUTION TO BAN FERRETS?
THAT'S CORRECT. I WANT TO DEFINE A "FAMILY" AS ONE CAT AND ONE HUMAN.
WHAT ABOUT DOGS? IS SATCHEL NOT A PART OF THIS FAMILY?
I GUESS WE COULD GRANDFATHER HIM IN IF YOU'RE GONNA WHINE ABOUT IT.
darb

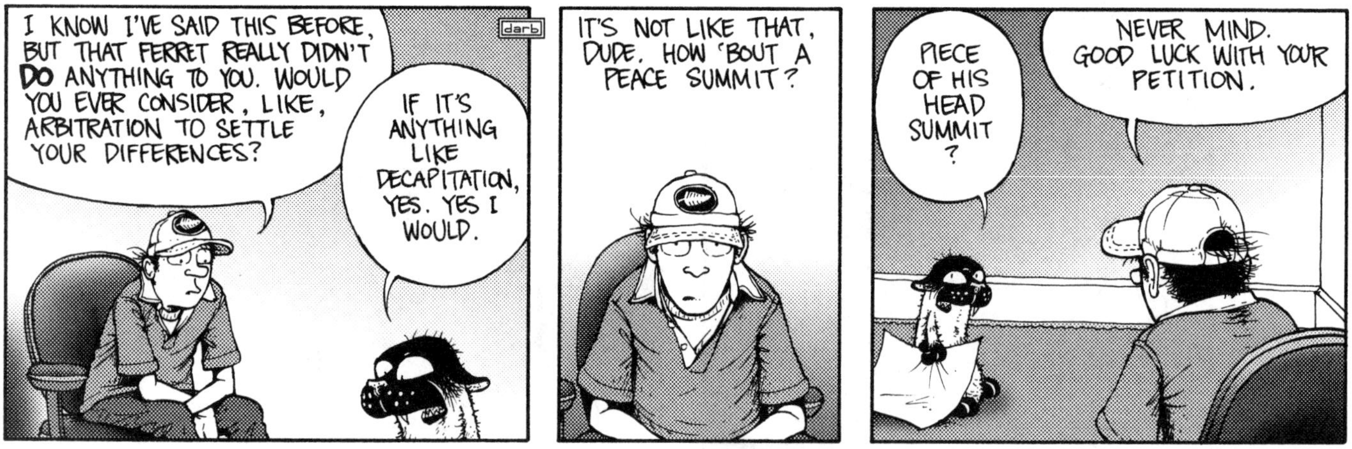
darb
I KNOW I'VE SAID THIS BEFORE, BUT THAT FERRET REALLY DIDN'T **DO** ANYTHING TO YOU. WOULD YOU EVER CONSIDER, LIKE, ARBITRATION TO SETTLE YOUR DIFFERENCES?
IF IT'S ANYTHING LIKE DECAPITATION, YES. YES I WOULD.
IT'S NOT LIKE THAT, DUDE. HOW 'BOUT A PEACE SUMMIT?
PIECE OF HIS HEAD SUMMIT?
NEVER MIND. GOOD LUCK WITH YOUR PETITION.

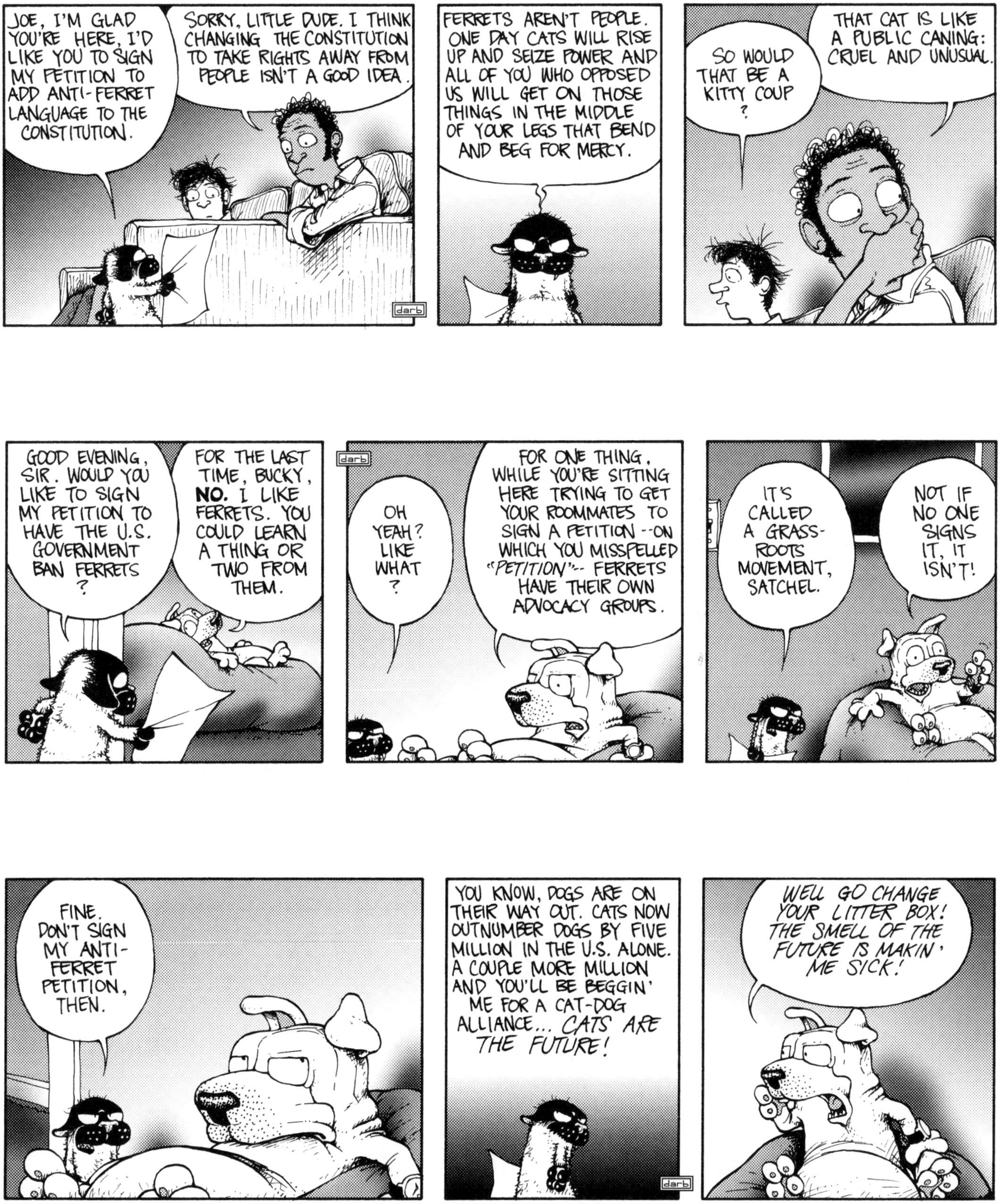
JOE, I'M GLAD YOU'RE HERE, I'D LIKE YOU TO SIGN MY PETITION TO ADD ANTI-FERRET LANGUAGE TO THE CONSTITUTION.
SORRY, LITTLE DUDE. I THINK CHANGING THE CONSTITUTION TO TAKE RIGHTS AWAY FROM PEOPLE ISN'T A GOOD IDEA.
darb
FERRETS AREN'T PEOPLE. ONE DAY CATS WILL RISE UP AND SEIZE POWER AND ALL OF YOU WHO OPPOSED US WILL GET ON THOSE THINGS IN THE MIDDLE OF YOUR LEGS THAT BEND AND BEG FOR MERCY.
SO WOULD THAT BE A KITTY COUP?
THAT CAT IS LIKE A PUBLIC CANING: CRUEL AND UNUSUAL.
GOOD EVENING, SIR. WOULD YOU LIKE TO SIGN MY PETITION TO HAVE THE U.S. GOVERNMENT BAN FERRETS?
FOR THE LAST TIME, BUCKY, NO. I LIKE FERRETS. YOU COULD LEARN A THING OR TWO FROM THEM.
darb
OH YEAH? LIKE WHAT?
FOR ONE THING, WHILE YOU'RE SITTING HERE TRYING TO GET YOUR ROOMMATES TO SIGN A PETITION --ON WHICH YOU MISSPELLED "PETITION"-- FERRETS HAVE THEIR OWN ADVOCACY GROUPS.
IT'S CALLED A GRASS-ROOTS MOVEMENT, SATCHEL.
NOT IF NO ONE SIGNS IT, IT ISN'T!
FINE. DON'T SIGN MY ANTI-FERRET PETITION, THEN.
YOU KNOW, DOGS ARE ON THEIR WAY OUT. CATS NOW OUTNUMBER DOGS BY FIVE MILLION IN THE U.S. ALONE. A COUPLE MORE MILLION AND YOU'LL BE BEGGIN' ME FOR A CAT-DOG ALLIANCE... CATS ARE THE FUTURE!
darb
WELL GO CHANGE YOUR LITTER BOX! THE SMELL OF THE FUTURE IS MAKIN' ME SICK!

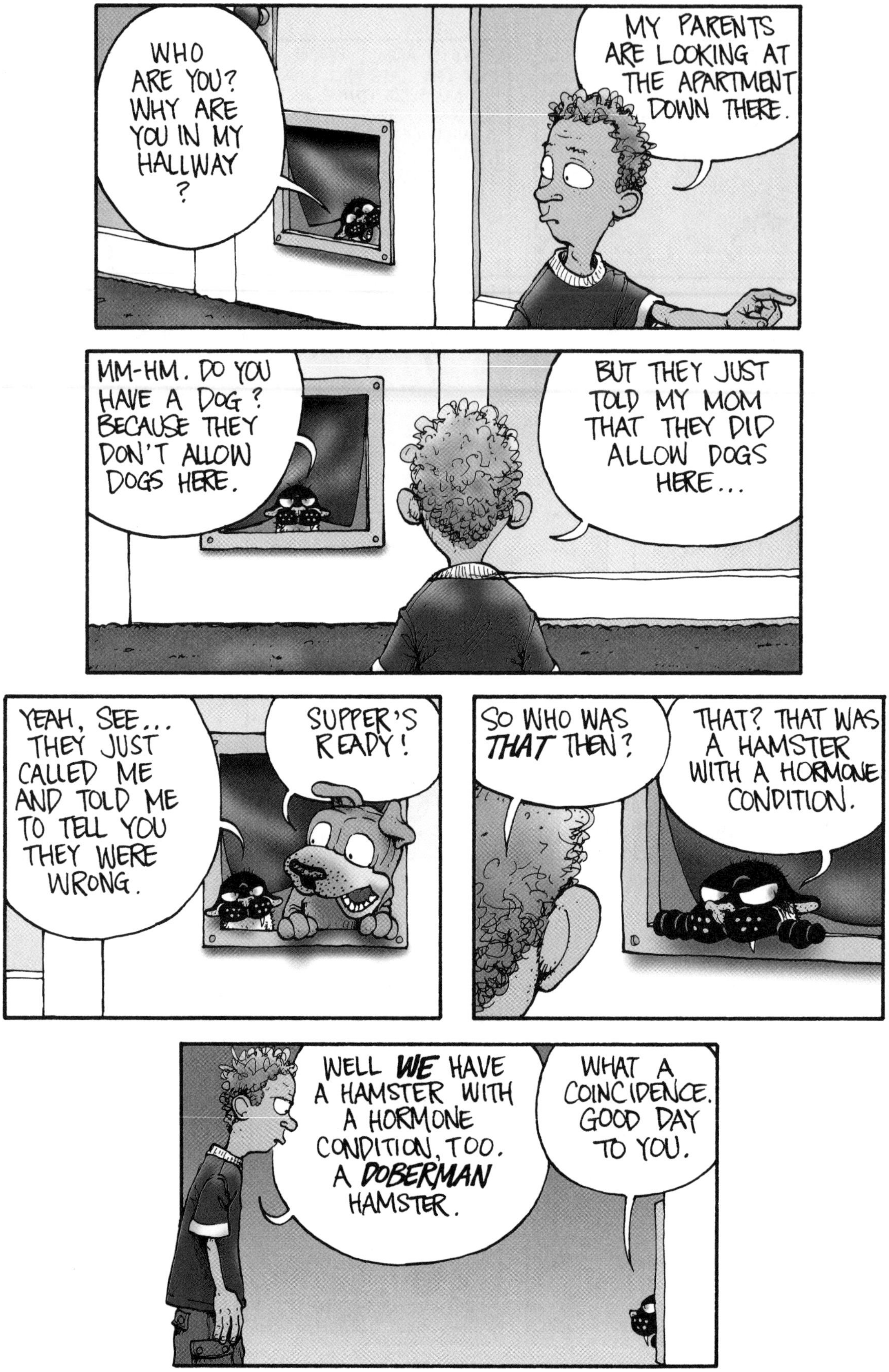
WHO ARE YOU? WHY ARE YOU IN MY HALLWAY?
MY PARENTS ARE LOOKING AT THE APARTMENT DOWN THERE.
MM-HM. DO YOU HAVE A DOG? BECAUSE THEY DON'T ALLOW DOGS HERE.
BUT THEY JUST TOLD MY MOM THAT THEY DID ALLOW DOGS HERE...
YEAH, SEE... THEY JUST CALLED ME AND TOLD ME TO TELL YOU THEY WERE WRONG.
SUPPER'S READY!
SO WHO WAS *THAT* THEN?
THAT? THAT WAS A HAMSTER WITH A HORMONE CONDITION.
WELL **WE** HAVE A HAMSTER WITH A HORMONE CONDITION, TOO. A *DOBERMAN* HAMSTER.
WHAT A COINCIDENCE. GOOD DAY TO YOU.

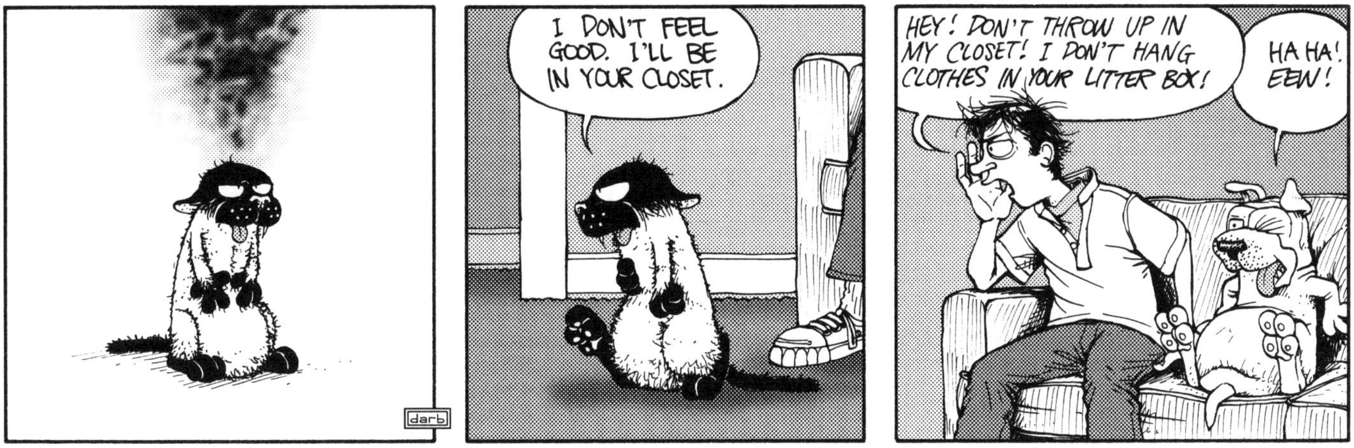
darb
I DON'T FEEL GOOD. I'LL BE IN YOUR CLOSET.
HEY! DON'T THROW UP IN MY CLOSET! I DON'T HANG CLOTHES IN YOUR LITTER BOX!
HA HA! EEW!

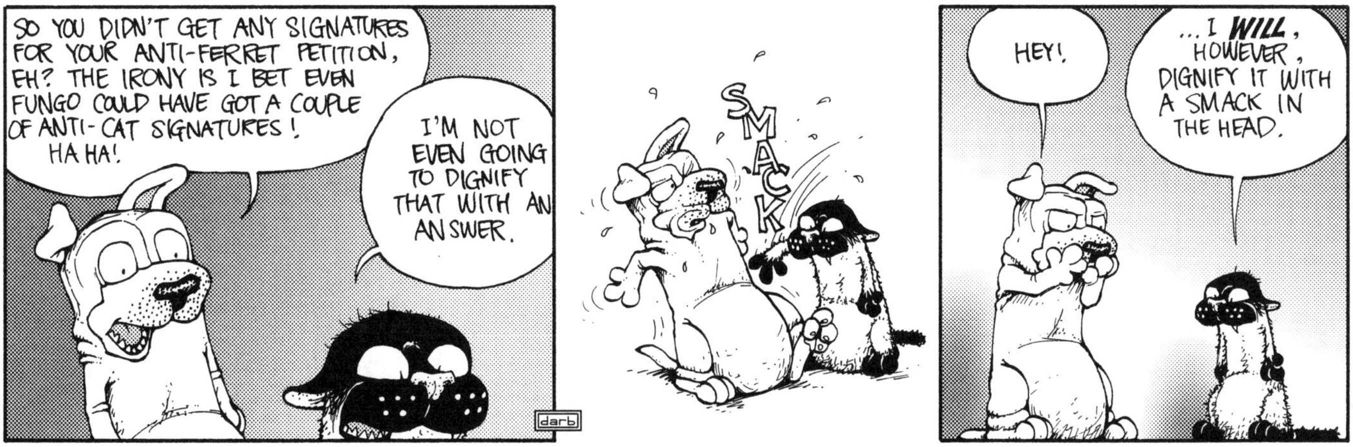
SO YOU DIDN'T GET ANY SIGNATURES FOR YOUR ANTI-FERRET PETITION, EH? THE IRONY IS I BET EVEN FUNGO COULD HAVE GOT A COUPLE OF ANTI-CAT SIGNATURES! HA HA!
I'M NOT EVEN GOING TO DIGNIFY THAT WITH AN ANSWER.
darb
SMACK
HEY!
...I WILL, HOWEVER, DIGNIFY IT WITH A SMACK IN THE HEAD.

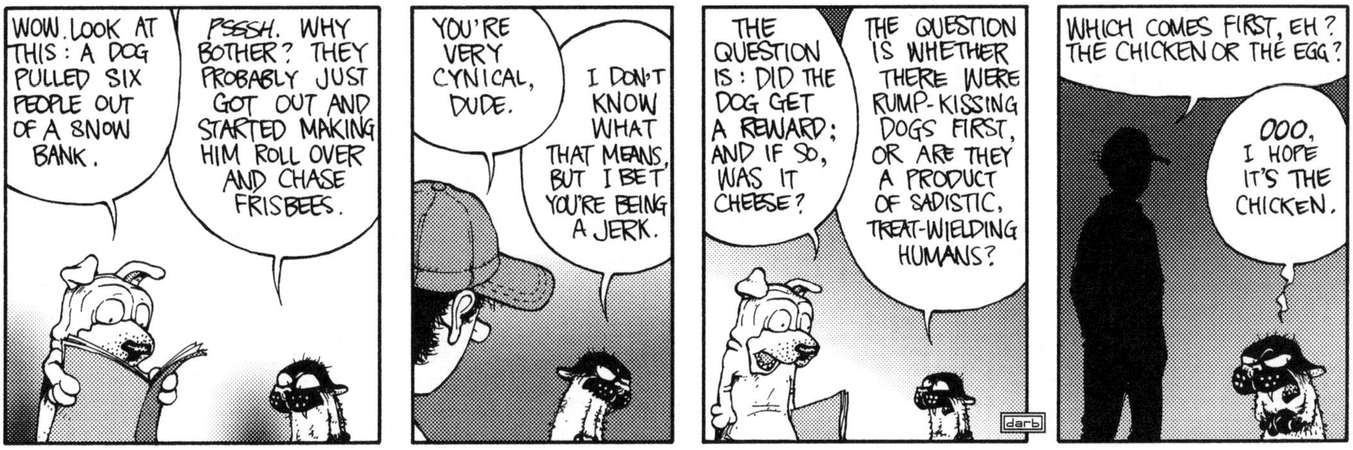
WOW. LOOK AT THIS: A DOG PULLED SIX PEOPLE OUT OF A SNOW BANK.
PSSSH. WHY BOTHER? THEY PROBABLY JUST GOT OUT AND STARTED MAKING HIM ROLL OVER AND CHASE FRISBEES.
YOU'RE VERY CYNICAL, DUDE.
I DON'T KNOW WHAT THAT MEANS, BUT I BET YOU'RE BEING A JERK.
THE QUESTION IS: DID THE DOG GET A REWARD; AND IF SO, WAS IT CHEESE?
THE QUESTION IS WHETHER THERE WERE RUMP-KISSING DOGS FIRST, OR ARE THEY A PRODUCT OF SADISTIC, TREAT-WIELDING HUMANS?
darb
WHICH COMES FIRST, EH? THE CHICKEN OR THE EGG?
OOO. I HOPE IT'S THE CHICKEN.

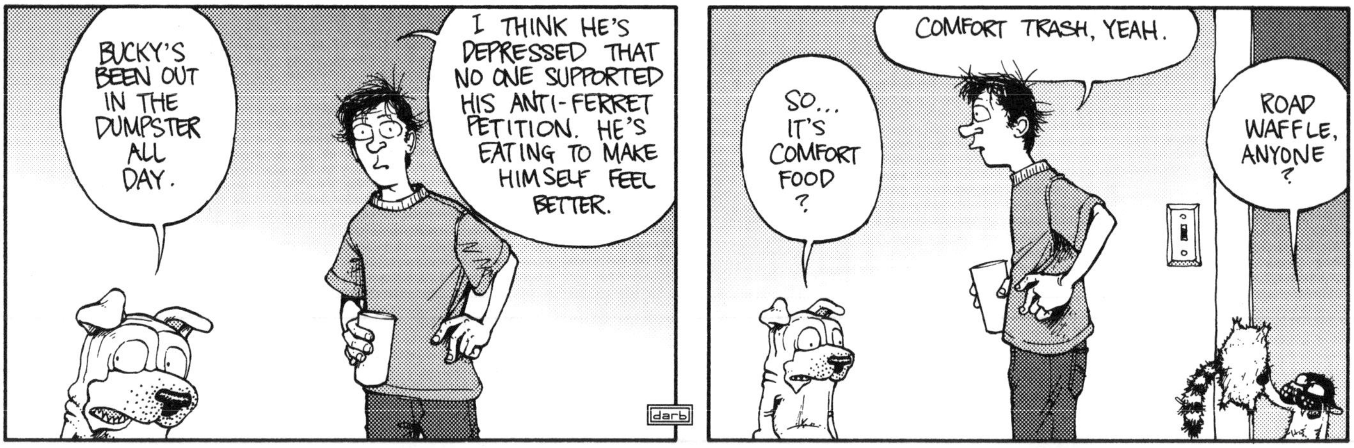
BUCKY'S BEEN OUT IN THE DUMPSTER ALL DAY.
I THINK HE'S DEPRESSED THAT NO ONE SUPPORTED HIS ANTI-FERRET PETITION. HE'S EATING TO MAKE HIMSELF FEEL BETTER.
SO... IT'S COMFORT FOOD?
COMFORT TRASH, YEAH.
ROAD WAFFLE, ANYONE?
darb

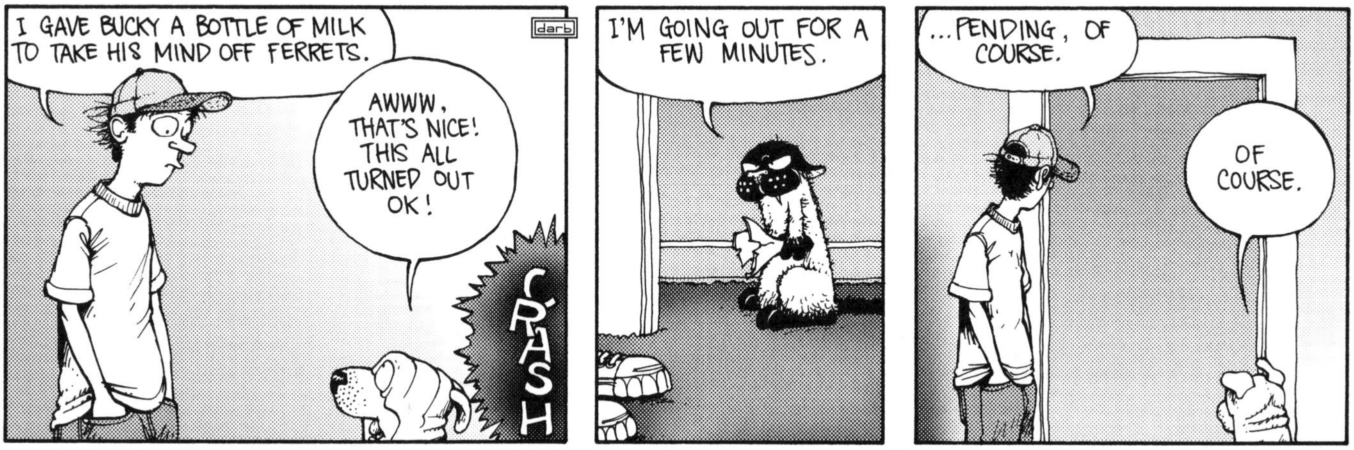
I GAVE BUCKY A BOTTLE OF MILK TO TAKE HIS MIND OFF FERRETS.
AWWW, THAT'S NICE! THIS ALL TURNED OUT OK!
CRASH
I'M GOING OUT FOR A FEW MINUTES.
...PENDING, OF COURSE.
OF COURSE.
darb

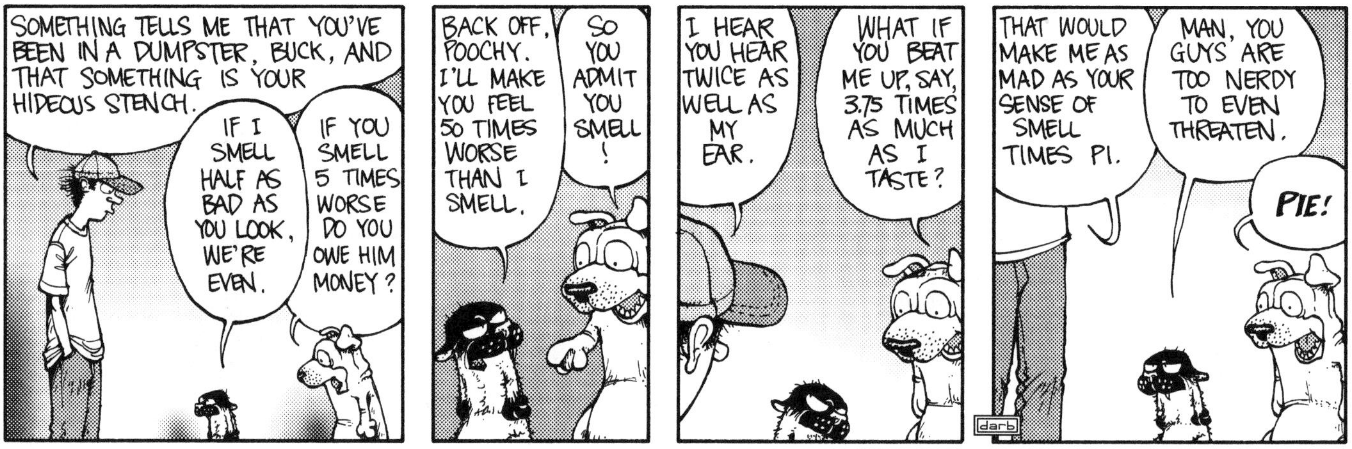
SOMETHING TELLS ME THAT YOU'VE BEEN IN A DUMPSTER, BUCK, AND THAT SOMETHING IS YOUR HIDEOUS STENCH.
IF I SMELL HALF AS BAD AS YOU LOOK, WE'RE EVEN.
IF YOU SMELL 5 TIMES WORSE DO YOU OWE HIM MONEY?
BACK OFF, POOCHY. I'LL MAKE YOU FEEL 50 TIMES WORSE THAN I SMELL.
SO YOU ADMIT YOU SMELL!
I HEAR YOU HEAR TWICE AS WELL AS MY EAR.
WHAT IF YOU BEAT ME UP, SAY, 3.75 TIMES AS MUCH AS I TASTE?
THAT WOULD MAKE ME AS MAD AS YOUR SENSE OF SMELL TIMES PI.
MAN, YOU GUYS ARE TOO NERDY TO EVEN THREATEN.
PIE!
darb

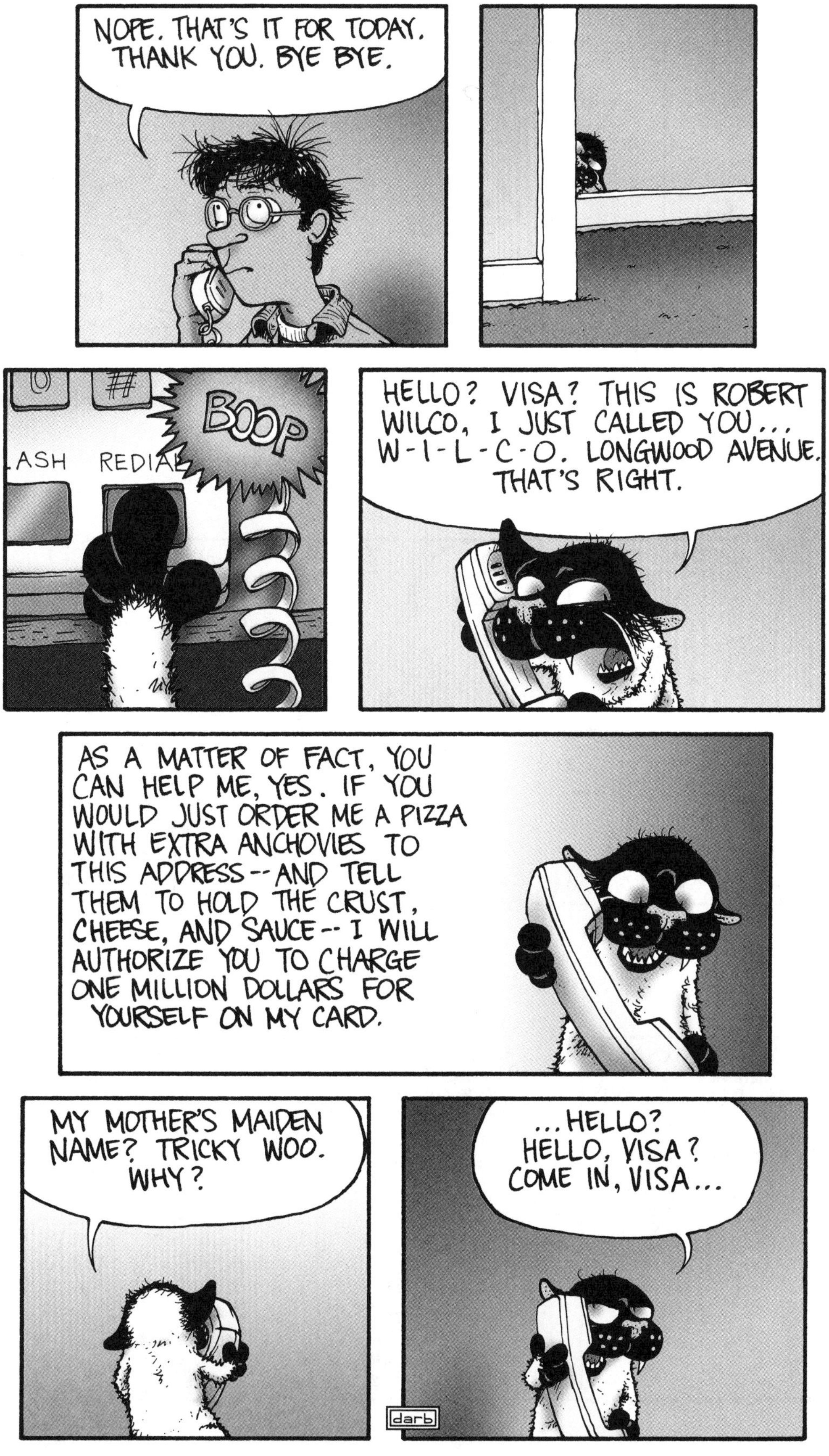
NOPE. THAT'S IT FOR TODAY. THANK YOU. BYE BYE.
BOOP
ASH REDIAL
HELLO? VISA? THIS IS ROBERT WILCO, I JUST CALLED YOU... W-I-L-C-O. LONGWOOD AVENUE. THAT'S RIGHT.
AS A MATTER OF FACT, YOU CAN HELP ME, YES. IF YOU WOULD JUST ORDER ME A PIZZA WITH EXTRA ANCHOVIES TO THIS ADDRESS--AND TELL THEM TO HOLD THE CRUST, CHEESE, AND SAUCE-- I WILL AUTHORIZE YOU TO CHARGE ONE MILLION DOLLARS FOR YOURSELF ON MY CARD.
MY MOTHER'S MAIDEN NAME? TRICKY WOO. WHY?
darb
...HELLO? HELLO, VISA? COME IN, VISA...

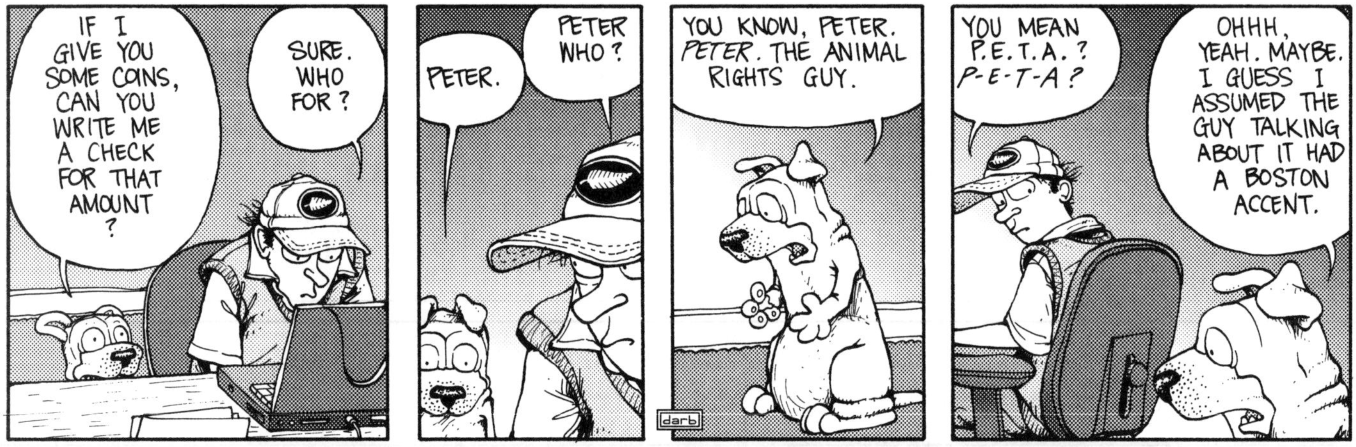
IF I GIVE YOU SOME COINS, CAN YOU WRITE ME A CHECK FOR THAT AMOUNT ?
SURE. WHO FOR ?
PETER.
PETER WHO ?
YOU KNOW, PETER. *PETER*. THE ANIMAL RIGHTS GUY.
YOU MEAN P.E.T.A. ? *P-E-T-A ?*
OHHH, YEAH. MAYBE. I GUESS I ASSUMED THE GUY TALKING ABOUT IT HAD A BOSTON ACCENT.
darb

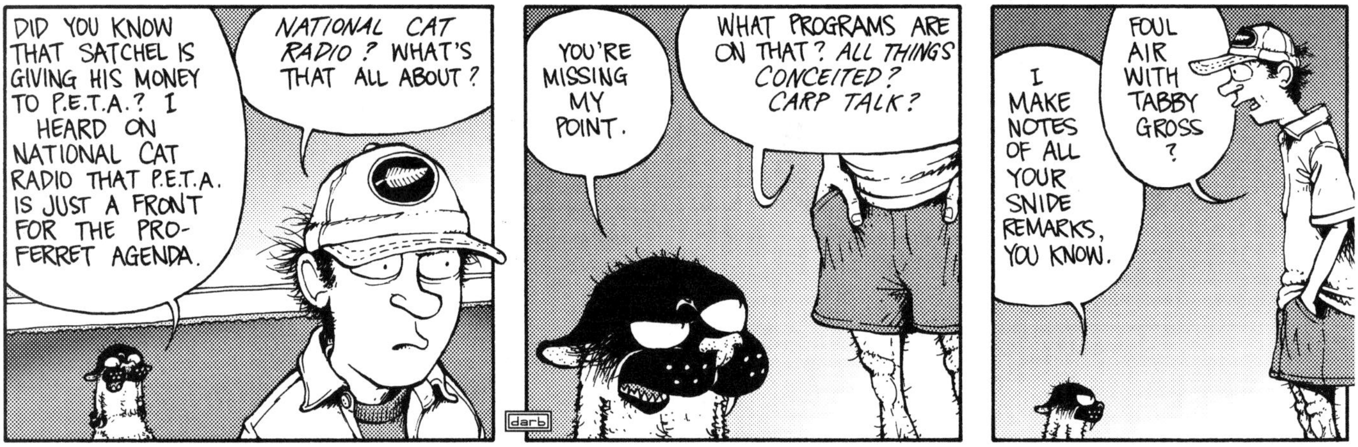
DID YOU KNOW THAT SATCHEL IS GIVING HIS MONEY TO P.E.T.A.? I HEARD ON NATIONAL CAT RADIO THAT P.E.T.A. IS JUST A FRONT FOR THE PRO-FERRET AGENDA.
NATIONAL CAT RADIO ? WHAT'S THAT ALL ABOUT ?
YOU'RE MISSING MY POINT.
WHAT PROGRAMS ARE ON THAT ? *ALL THINGS CONCEITED ? CARP TALK ?*
I MAKE NOTES OF ALL YOUR SNIDE REMARKS, YOU KNOW.
FOUL AIR WITH TABBY GROSS ?
darb

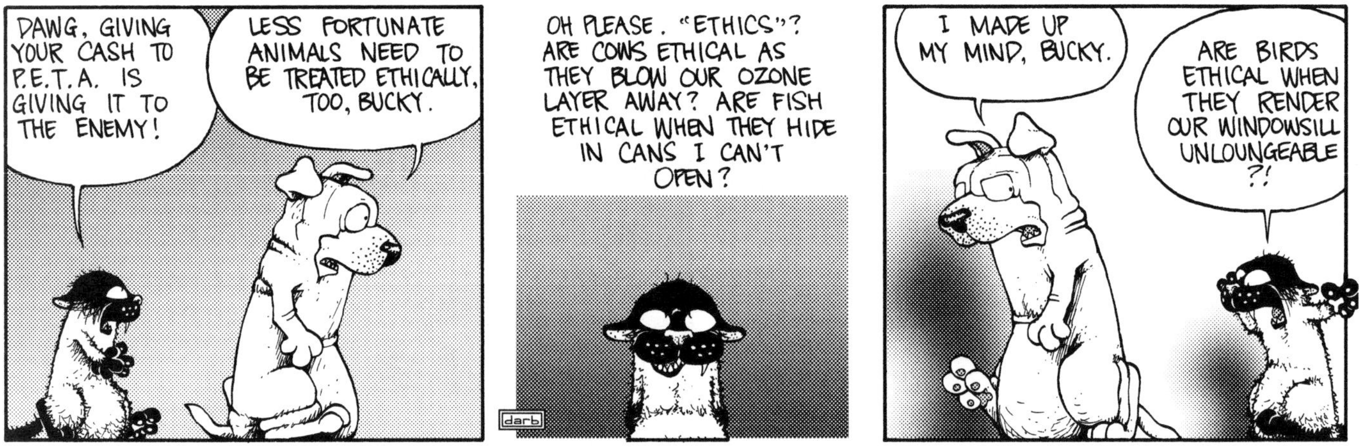
DAWG, GIVING YOUR CASH TO P.E.T.A. IS GIVING IT TO THE ENEMY!
LESS FORTUNATE ANIMALS NEED TO BE TREATED ETHICALLY, TOO, BUCKY.
OH PLEASE. "ETHICS"? ARE COWS ETHICAL AS THEY BLOW OUR OZONE LAYER AWAY? ARE FISH ETHICAL WHEN THEY HIDE IN CANS I CAN'T OPEN?
I MADE UP MY MIND, BUCKY.
ARE BIRDS ETHICAL WHEN THEY RENDER OUR WINDOWSILL UNLOUNGEABLE ?!
darb

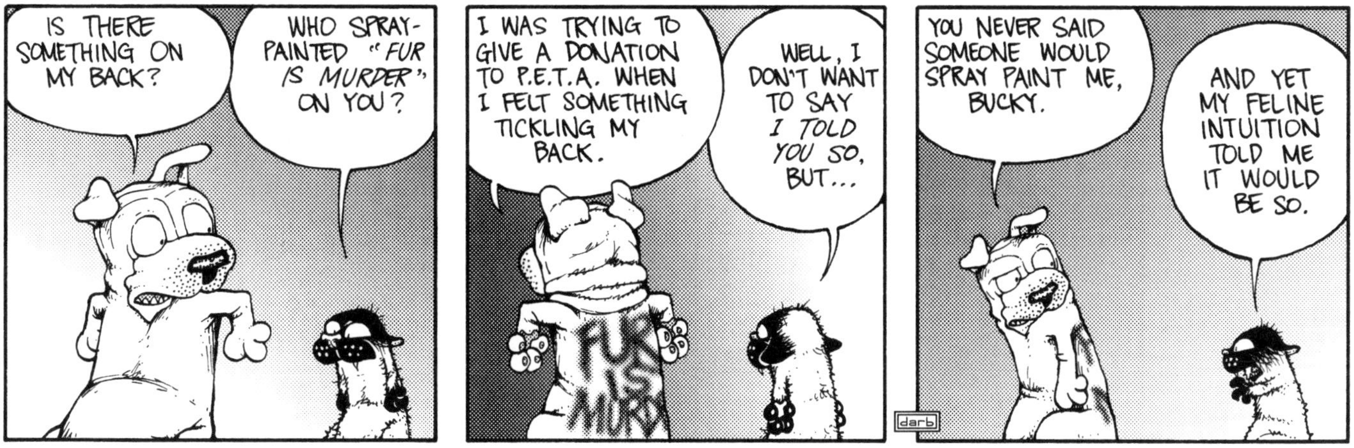
IS THERE SOMETHING ON MY BACK?
WHO SPRAY-PAINTED "FUR IS MURDER" ON YOU?
I WAS TRYING TO GIVE A DONATION TO P.E.T.A. WHEN I FELT SOMETHING TICKLING MY BACK.
WELL, I DON'T WANT TO SAY *I TOLD YOU SO*, BUT...
YOU NEVER SAID SOMEONE WOULD SPRAY PAINT ME, BUCKY.
AND YET MY FELINE INTUITION TOLD ME IT WOULD BE SO.
darb

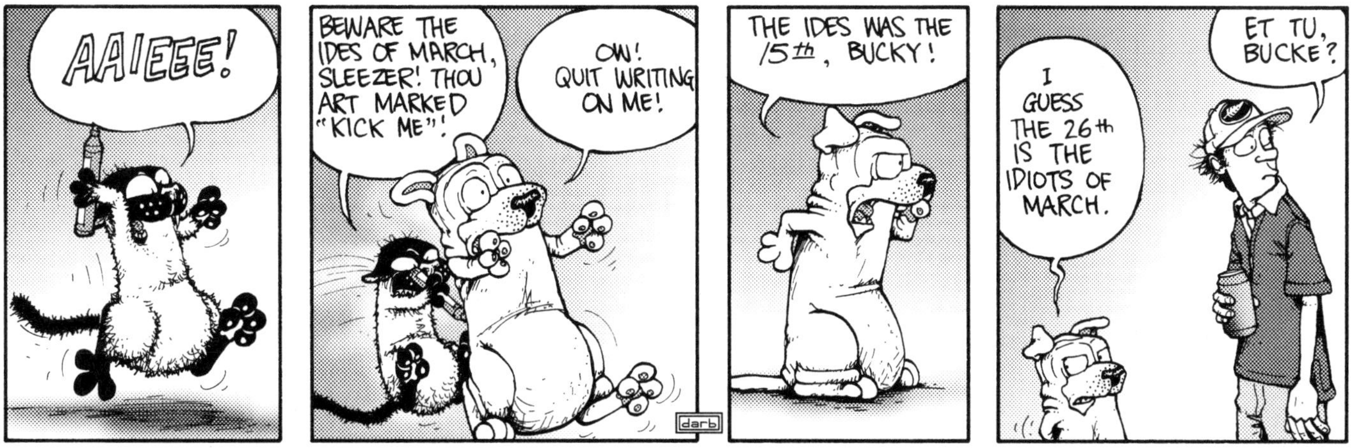
AAIEEE!
BEWARE THE IDES OF MARCH, SLEEZER! THOU ART MARKED "KICK ME"!
OW! QUIT WRITING ON ME!
darb
THE IDES WAS THE 15th, BUCKY!
I GUESS THE 26th IS THE IDIOTS OF MARCH.
ET TU, BUCKE?

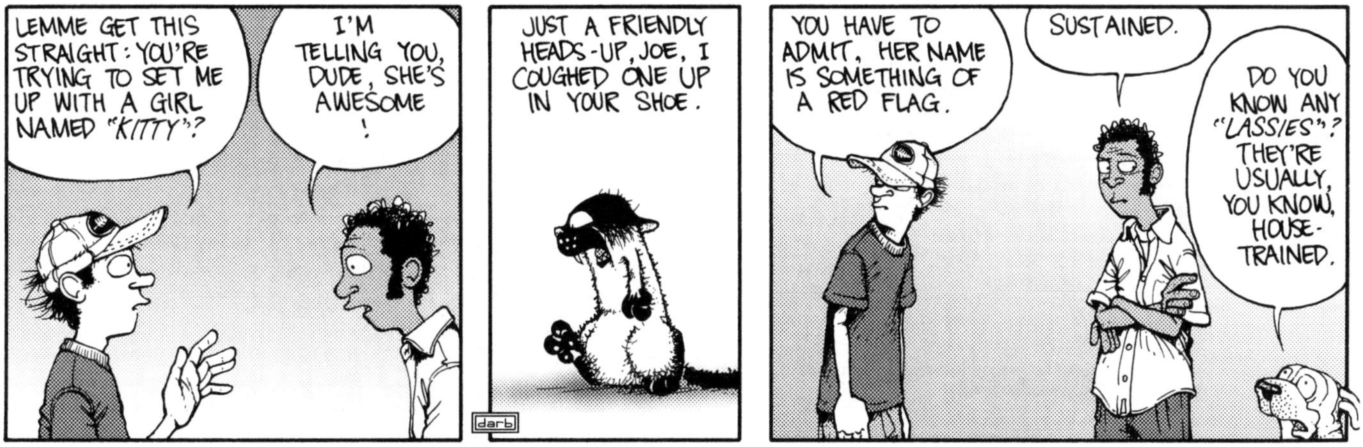
LEMME GET THIS STRAIGHT: YOU'RE TRYING TO SET ME UP WITH A GIRL NAMED "*KITTY*"?
I'M TELLING YOU, DUDE, SHE'S AWESOME!
JUST A FRIENDLY HEADS-UP, JOE, I COUGHED ONE UP IN YOUR SHOE.
darb
YOU HAVE TO ADMIT, HER NAME IS SOMETHING OF A RED FLAG.
SUSTAINED.
DO YOU KNOW ANY "*LASSIES*"? THEY'RE USUALLY, YOU KNOW, HOUSE-TRAINED.

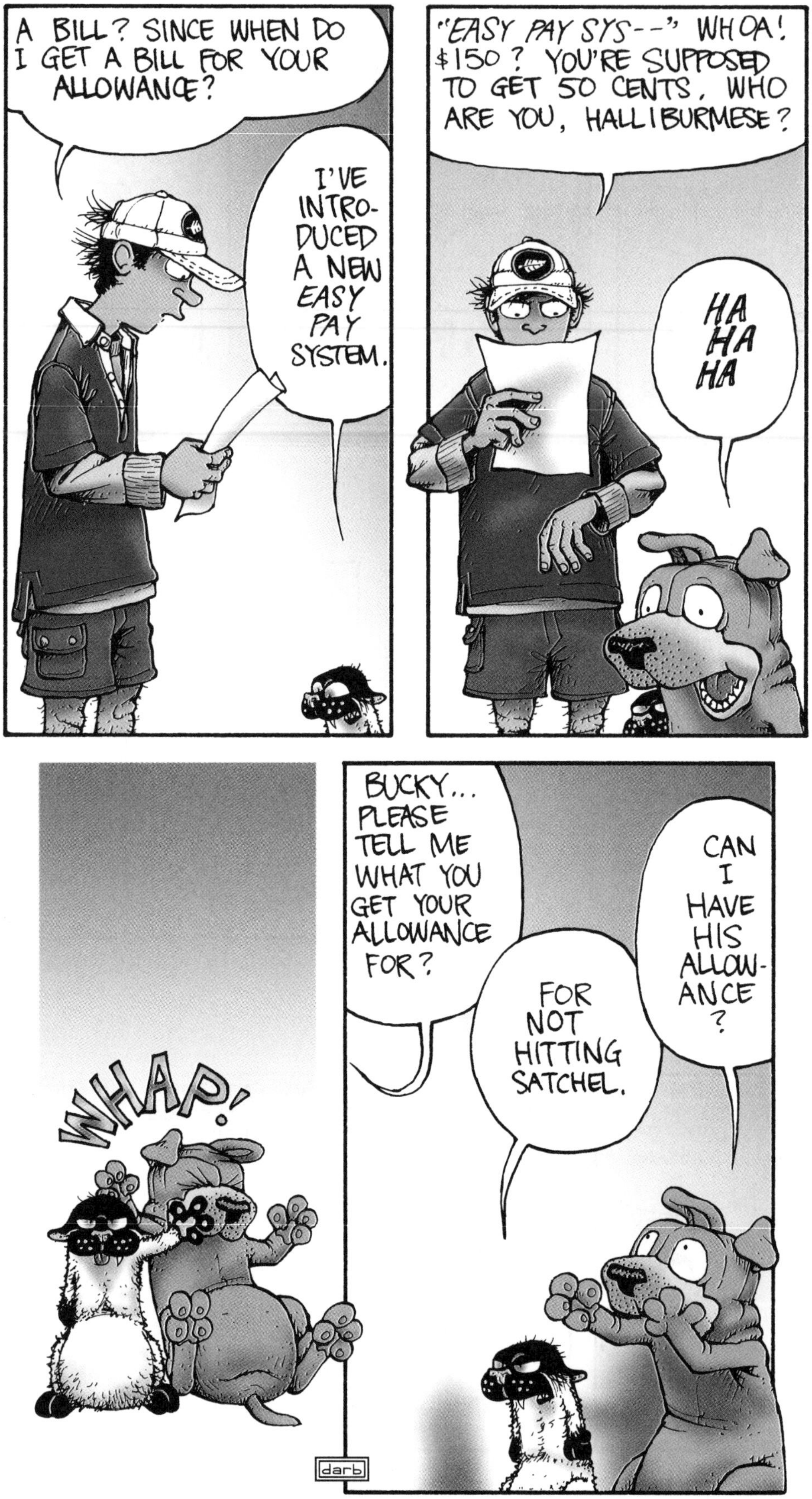
A BILL? SINCE WHEN DO I GET A BILL FOR YOUR ALLOWANCE?
I'VE INTRODUCED A NEW *EASY PAY* SYSTEM.
"*EASY PAY SYS--*" WHOA! $150? YOU'RE SUPPOSED TO GET 50 CENTS. WHO ARE YOU, HALLIBURMESE?
HA HA HA
WHAP!
BUCKY... PLEASE TELL ME WHAT YOU GET YOUR ALLOWANCE FOR?
FOR NOT HITTING SATCHEL.
CAN I HAVE HIS ALLOWANCE?
darb

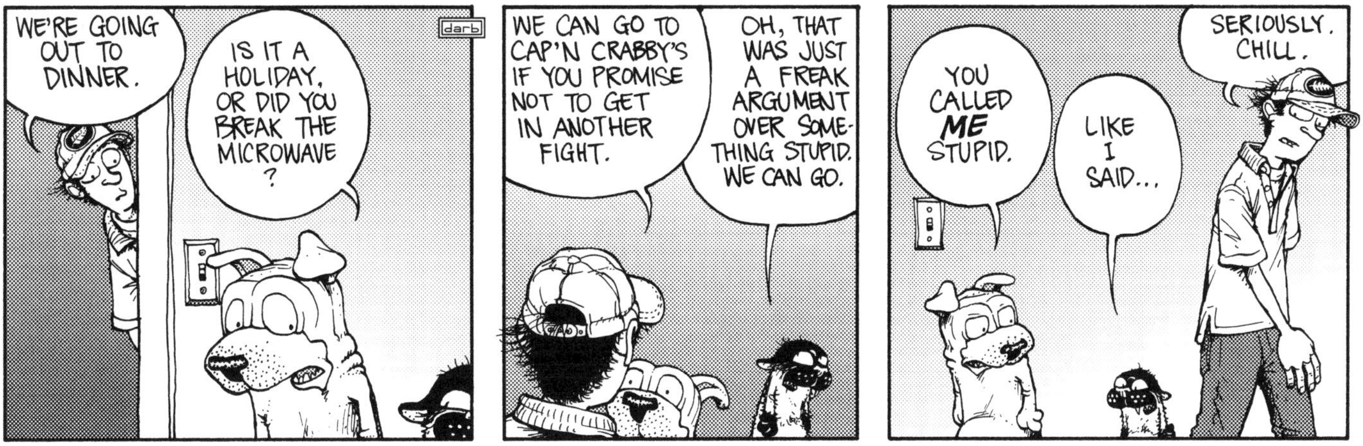
WE'RE GOING OUT TO DINNER.
IS IT A HOLIDAY, OR DID YOU BREAK THE MICROWAVE ?
WE CAN GO TO CAP'N CRABBY'S IF YOU PROMISE NOT TO GET IN ANOTHER FIGHT.
OH, THAT WAS JUST A FREAK ARGUMENT OVER SOMETHING STUPID. WE CAN GO.
YOU CALLED ME STUPID.
LIKE I SAID...
SERIOUSLY. CHILL.

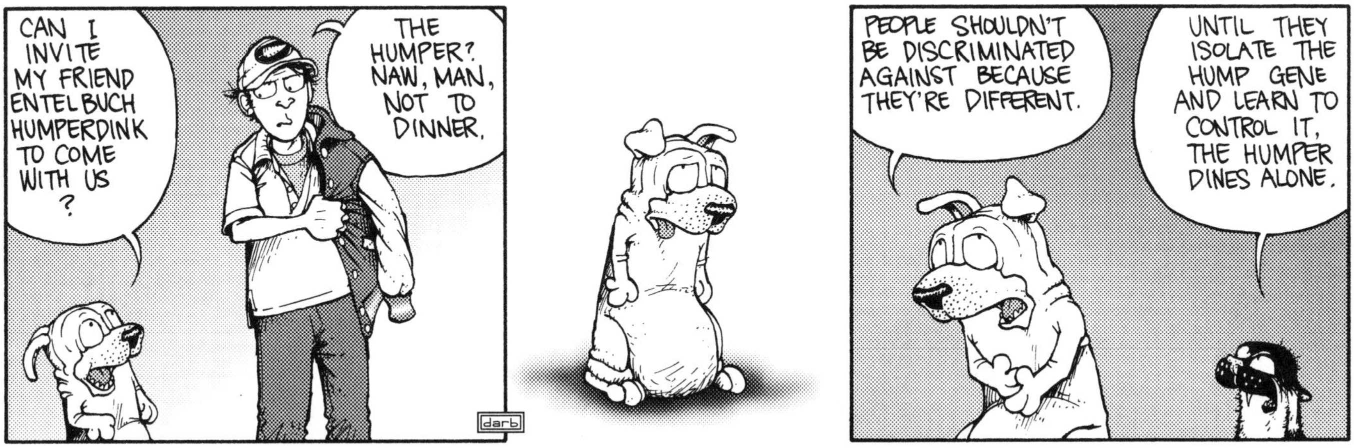
CAN I INVITE MY FRIEND ENTELBUCH HUMPERDINK TO COME WITH US ?
THE HUMPER? NAW, MAN, NOT TO DINNER.
PEOPLE SHOULDN'T BE DISCRIMINATED AGAINST BECAUSE THEY'RE DIFFERENT.
UNTIL THEY ISOLATE THE HUMP GENE AND LEARN TO CONTROL IT, THE HUMPER DINES ALONE.

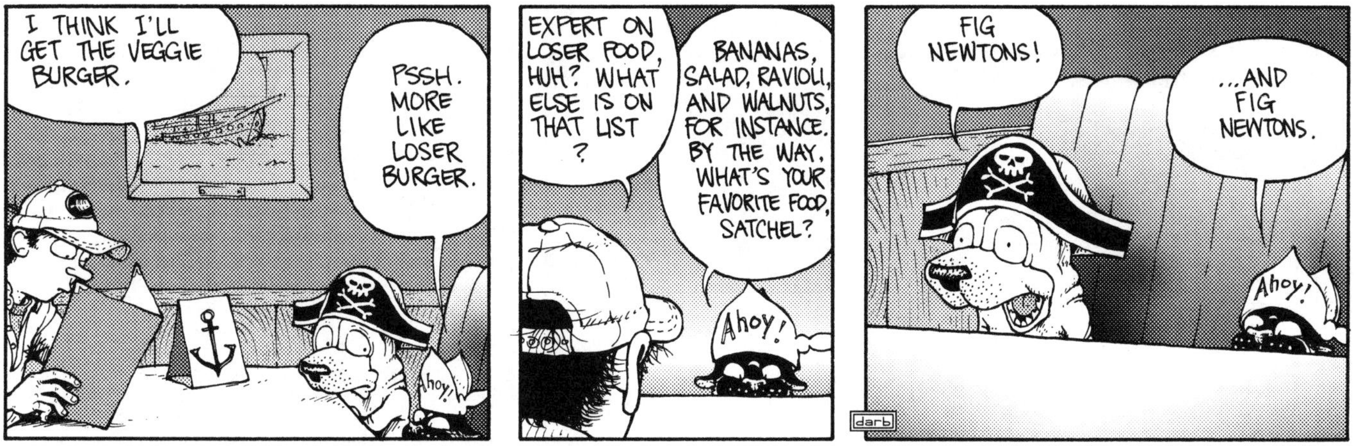
I THINK I'LL GET THE VEGGIE BURGER.
PSSH. MORE LIKE LOSER BURGER.
Ahoy!
EXPERT ON LOSER FOOD, HUH? WHAT ELSE IS ON THAT LIST ?
BANANAS, SALAD, RAVIOLI, AND WALNUTS, FOR INSTANCE. BY THE WAY, WHAT'S YOUR FAVORITE FOOD, SATCHEL?
Ahoy!
FIG NEWTONS!
...AND FIG NEWTONS.
Ahoy!

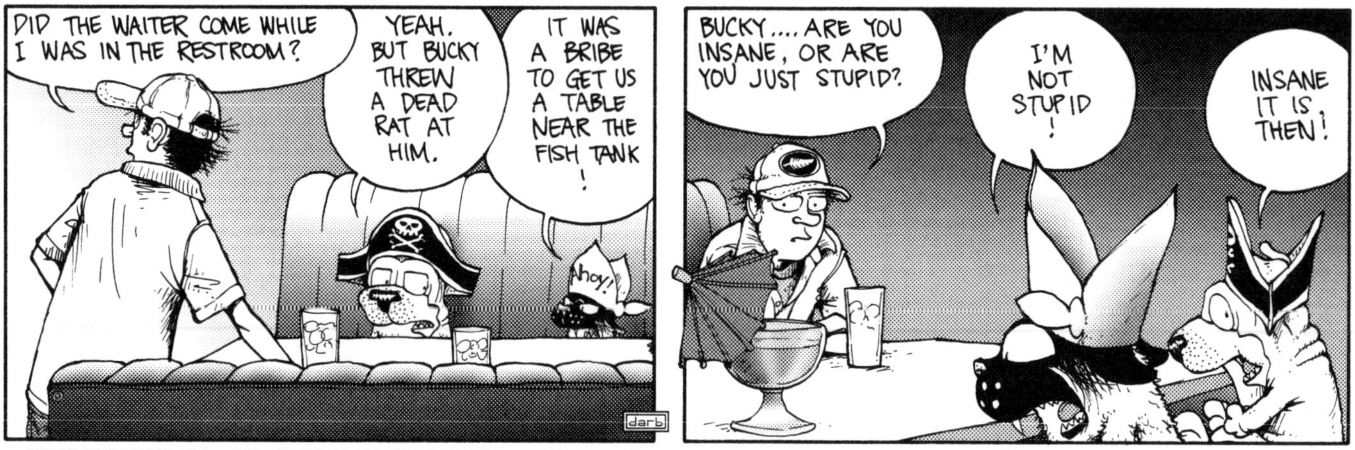
DID THE WAITER COME WHILE I WAS IN THE RESTROOM?
YEAH. BUT BUCKY THREW A DEAD RAT AT HIM.
IT WAS A BRIBE TO GET US A TABLE NEAR THE FISH TANK!
Ahoy!
darb
BUCKY.... ARE YOU INSANE, OR ARE YOU JUST STUPID?
I'M NOT STUPID!
INSANE IT IS, THEN!

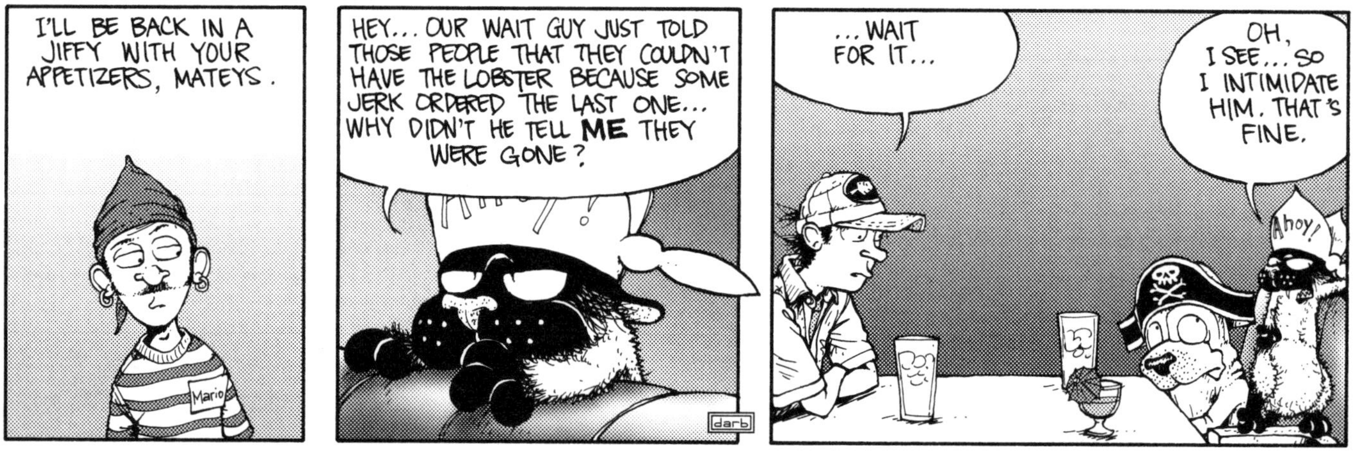
I'LL BE BACK IN A JIFFY WITH YOUR APPETIZERS, MATEYS.
Mario
HEY... OUR WAIT GUY JUST TOLD THOSE PEOPLE THAT THEY COULDN'T HAVE THE LOBSTER BECAUSE SOME JERK ORDERED THE LAST ONE... WHY DIDN'T HE TELL **ME** THEY WERE GONE?
darb
...WAIT FOR IT...
OH, I SEE... SO I INTIMIDATE HIM. THAT'S FINE.
Ahoy!

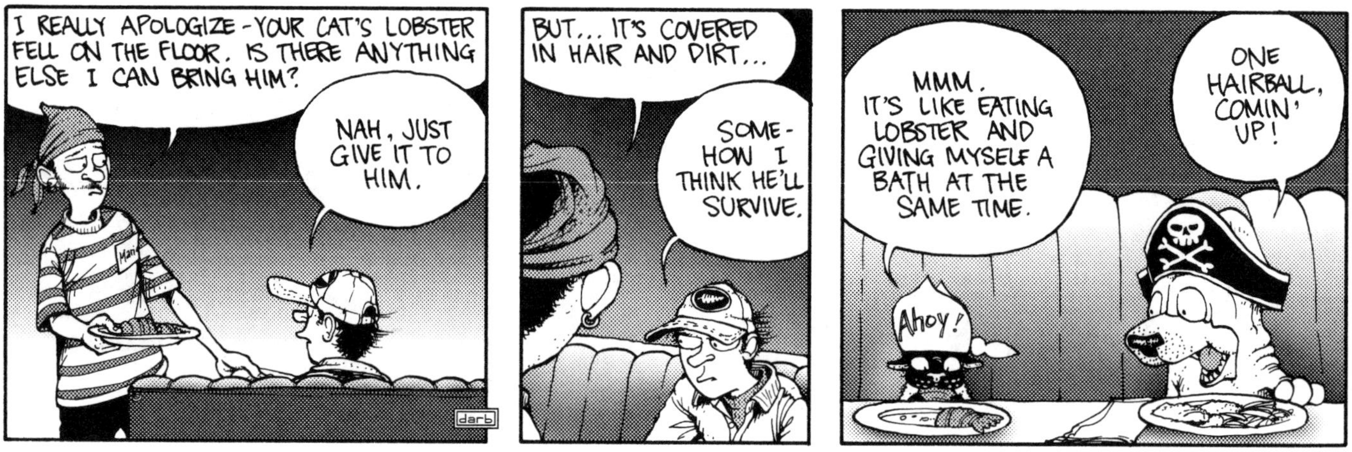
I REALLY APOLOGIZE - YOUR CAT'S LOBSTER FELL ON THE FLOOR. IS THERE ANYTHING ELSE I CAN BRING HIM?
NAH, JUST GIVE IT TO HIM.
darb
BUT... IT'S COVERED IN HAIR AND DIRT...
SOME-HOW I THINK HE'LL SURVIVE.
MMM. IT'S LIKE EATING LOBSTER AND GIVING MYSELF A BATH AT THE SAME TIME.
ONE HAIRBALL, COMIN' UP!
Ahoy!

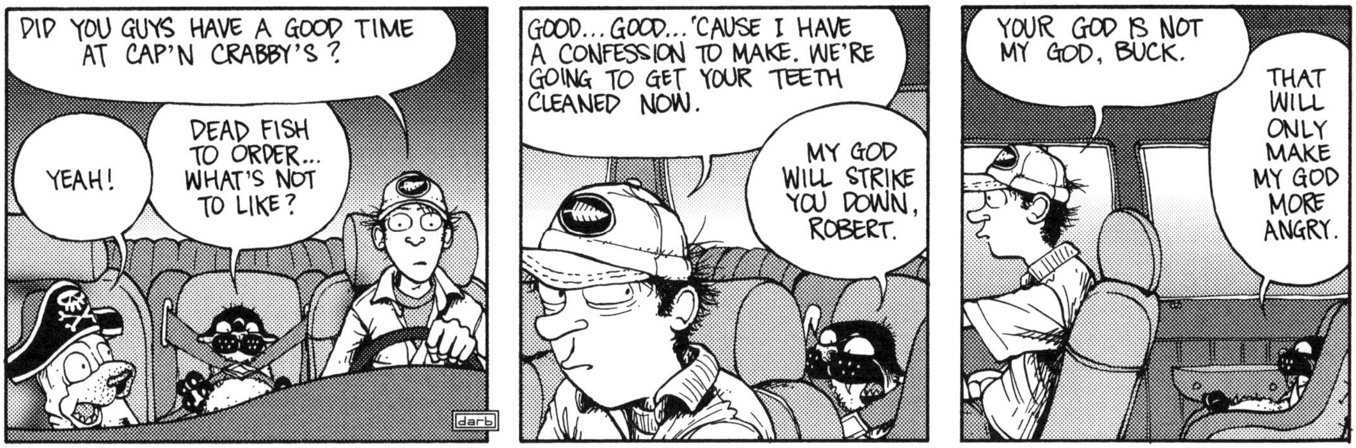
DID YOU GUYS HAVE A GOOD TIME AT CAP'N CRABBY'S?
YEAH!
DEAD FISH TO ORDER... WHAT'S NOT TO LIKE?
GOOD... GOOD... 'CAUSE I HAVE A CONFESSION TO MAKE. WE'RE GOING TO GET YOUR TEETH CLEANED NOW.
MY GOD WILL STRIKE YOU DOWN, ROBERT.
YOUR GOD IS NOT MY GOD, BUCK.
THAT WILL ONLY MAKE MY GOD MORE ANGRY.

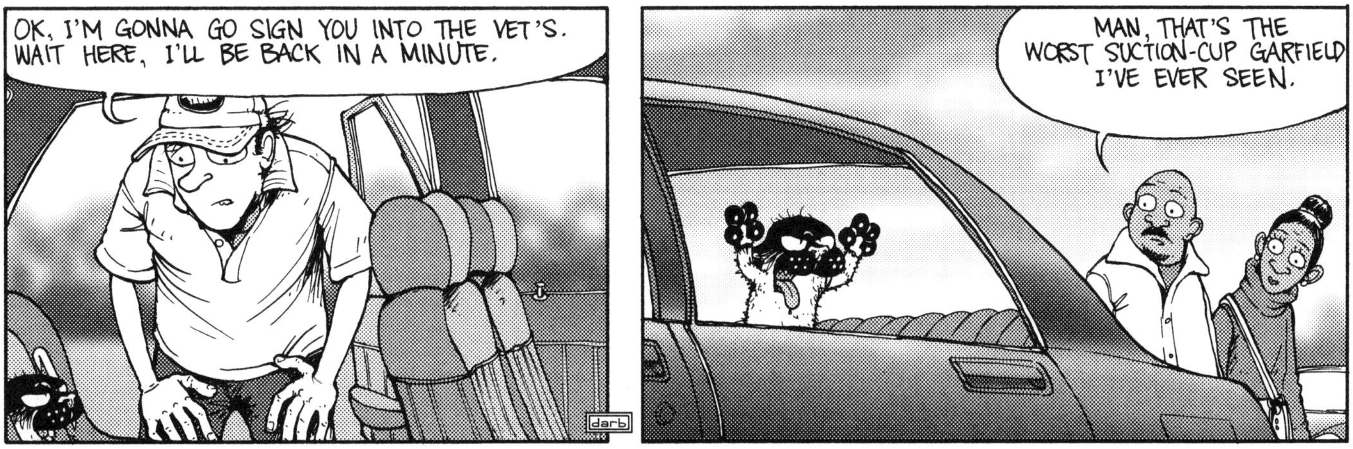
OK, I'M GONNA GO SIGN YOU INTO THE VET'S. WAIT HERE, I'LL BE BACK IN A MINUTE.
MAN, THAT'S THE WORST SUCTION-CUP GARFIELD I'VE EVER SEEN.

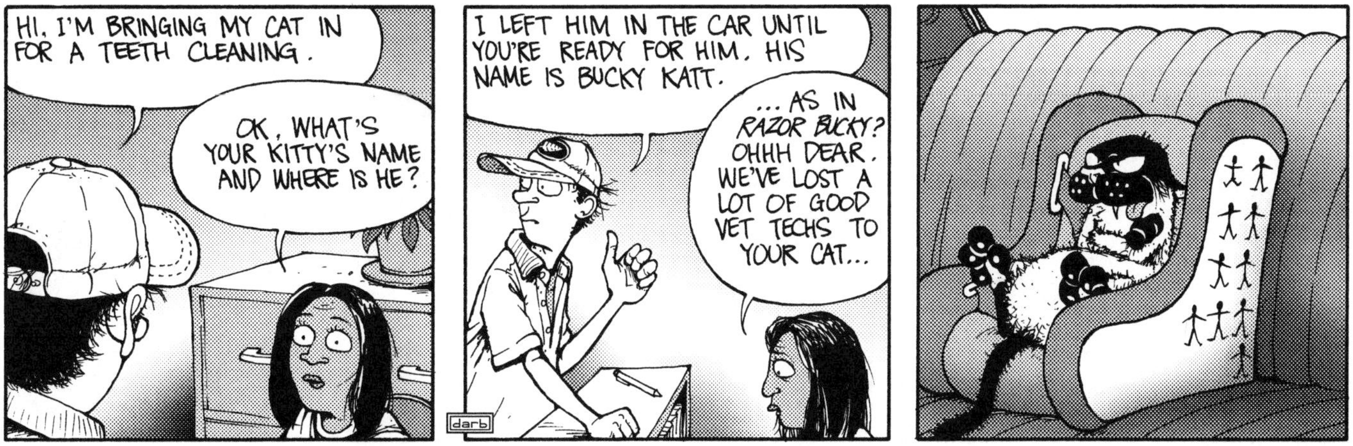
HI. I'M BRINGING MY CAT IN FOR A TEETH CLEANING.
OK, WHAT'S YOUR KITTY'S NAME AND WHERE IS HE?
I LEFT HIM IN THE CAR UNTIL YOU'RE READY FOR HIM. HIS NAME IS BUCKY KATT.
...AS IN *RAZOR BUCKY*? OHHH DEAR. WE'VE LOST A LOT OF GOOD VET TECHS TO YOUR CAT...

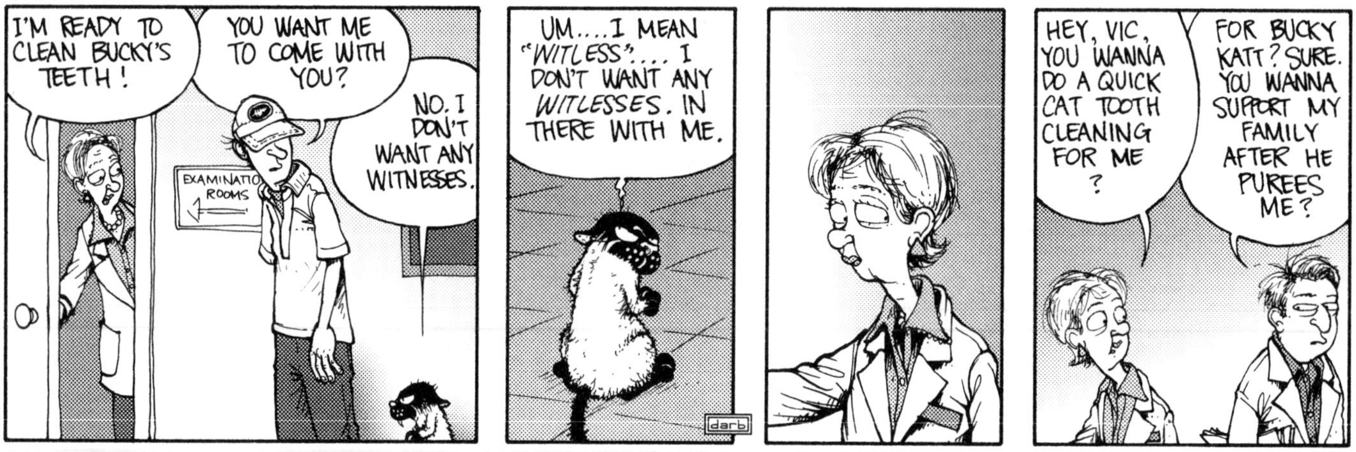
I'M READY TO CLEAN BUCKY'S TEETH!
YOU WANT ME TO COME WITH YOU?
NO. I DON'T WANT ANY WITNESSES.
UM.... I MEAN "WITLESS".... I DON'T WANT ANY WITLESSES. IN THERE WITH ME.
HEY, VIC, YOU WANNA DO A QUICK CAT TOOTH CLEANING FOR ME?
FOR BUCKY KATT? SURE. YOU WANNA SUPPORT MY FAMILY AFTER HE PUREES ME?

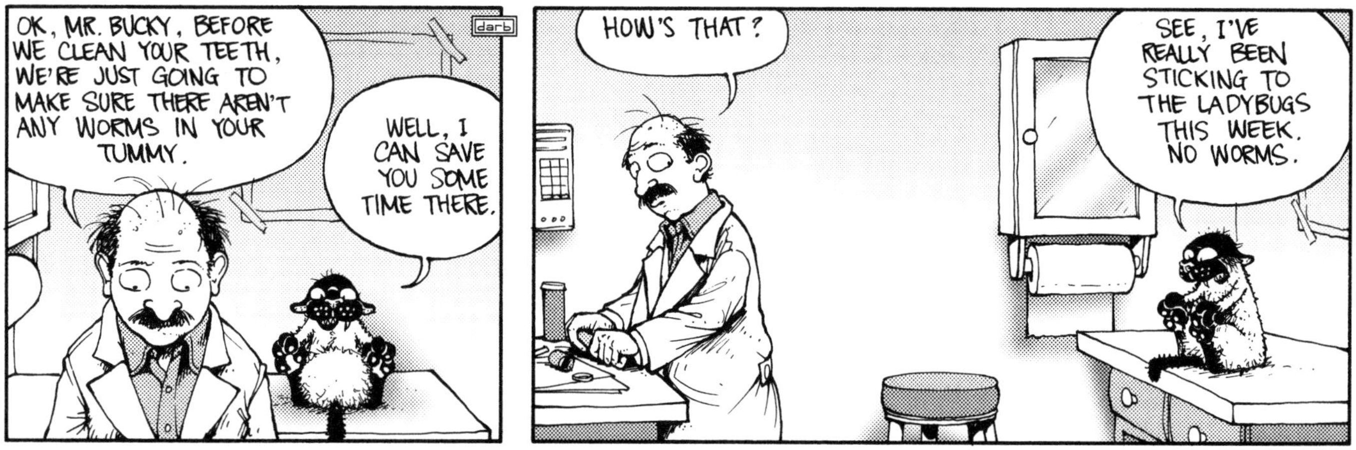
OK, MR. BUCKY, BEFORE WE CLEAN YOUR TEETH, WE'RE JUST GOING TO MAKE SURE THERE AREN'T ANY WORMS IN YOUR TUMMY.
WELL, I CAN SAVE YOU SOME TIME THERE.
HOW'S THAT?
SEE, I'VE REALLY BEEN STICKING TO THE LADYBUGS THIS WEEK. NO WORMS.

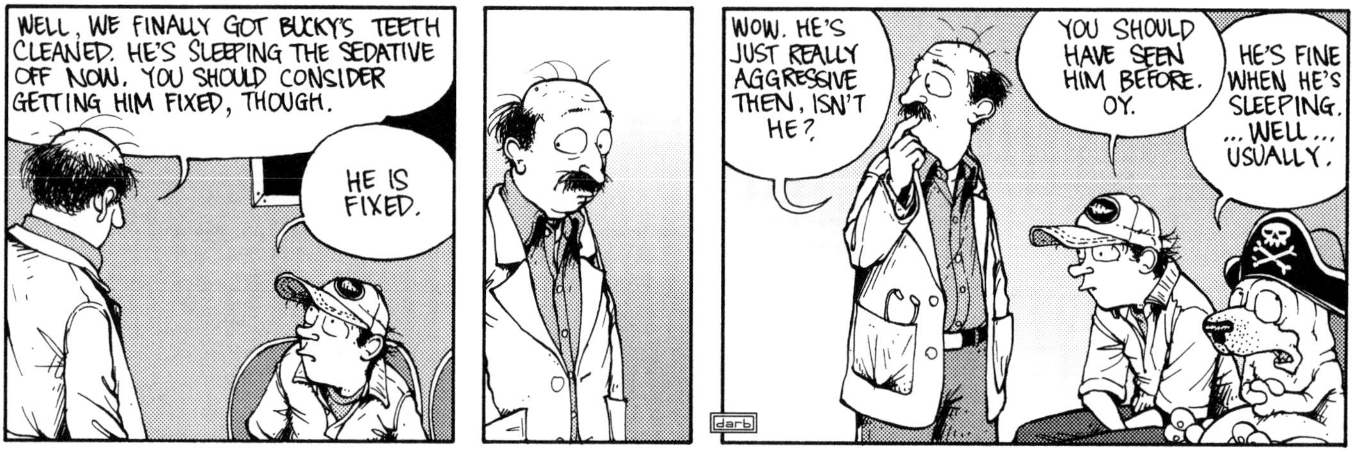
WELL, WE FINALLY GOT BUCKY'S TEETH CLEANED. HE'S SLEEPING THE SEDATIVE OFF NOW. YOU SHOULD CONSIDER GETTING HIM FIXED, THOUGH.
HE IS FIXED.
WOW. HE'S JUST REALLY AGGRESSIVE THEN, ISN'T HE?
YOU SHOULD HAVE SEEN HIM BEFORE. OY.
HE'S FINE WHEN HE'S SLEEPING. ...WELL... USUALLY.

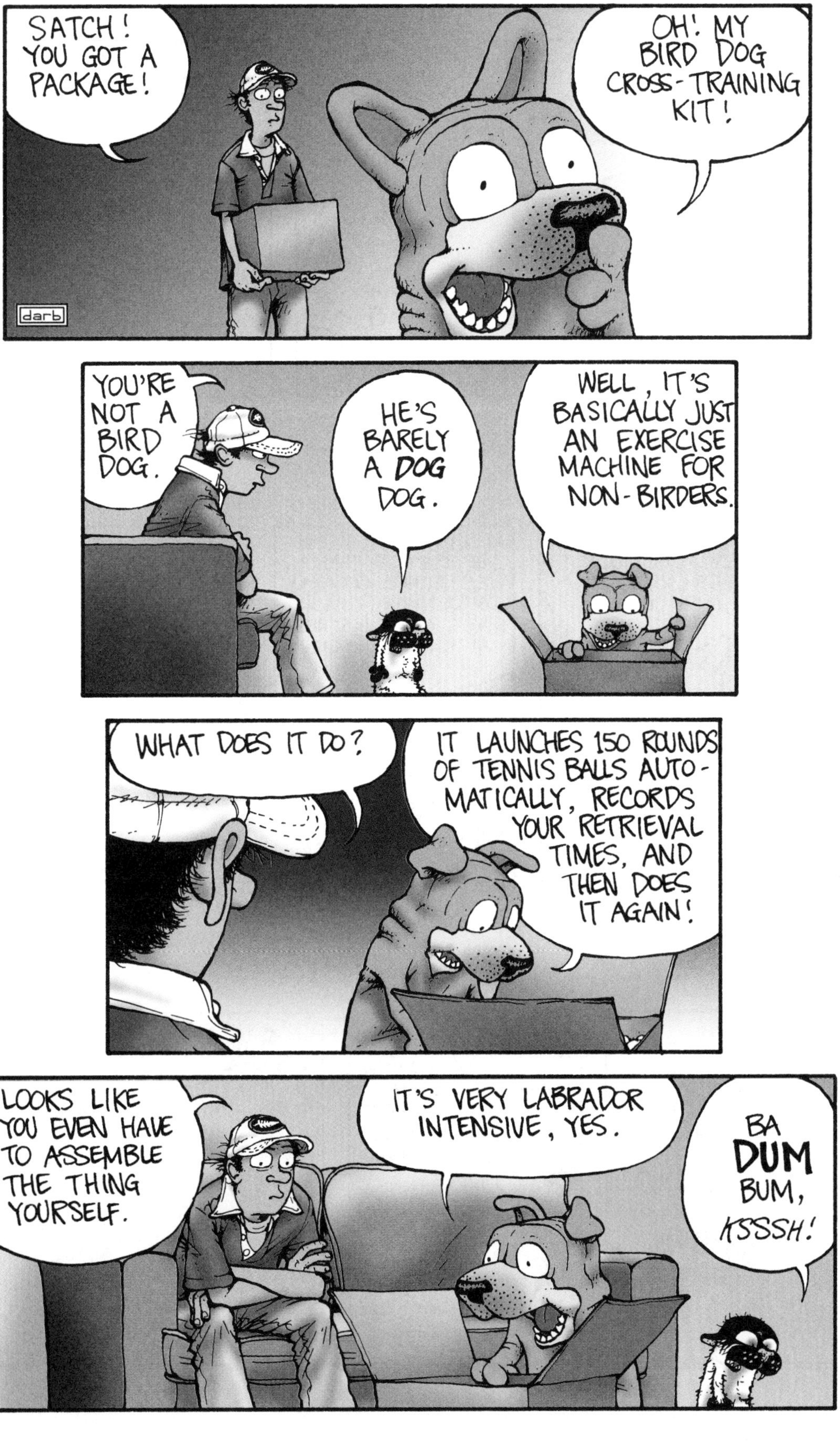
SATCH! YOU GOT A PACKAGE!
OH! MY BIRD DOG CROSS-TRAINING KIT!
darb
YOU'RE NOT A BIRD DOG.
HE'S BARELY A **DOG** DOG.
WELL, IT'S BASICALLY JUST AN EXERCISE MACHINE FOR NON-BIRDERS.
WHAT DOES IT DO?
IT LAUNCHES 150 ROUNDS OF TENNIS BALLS AUTOMATICALLY, RECORDS YOUR RETRIEVAL TIMES, AND THEN DOES IT AGAIN!
LOOKS LIKE YOU EVEN HAVE TO ASSEMBLE THE THING YOURSELF.
IT'S VERY LABRADOR INTENSIVE, YES.
BA **DUM** BUM, *KSSSH!*

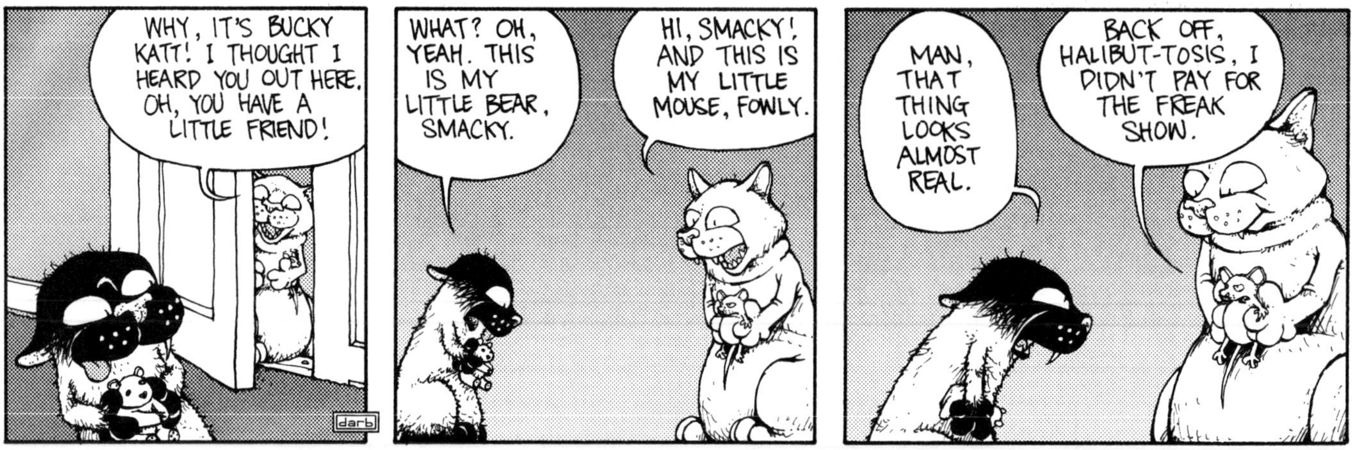
WHY, IT'S BUCKY KATT! I THOUGHT I HEARD YOU OUT HERE. OH, YOU HAVE A LITTLE FRIEND!
WHAT? OH, YEAH. THIS IS MY LITTLE BEAR, SMACKY.
HI, SMACKY! AND THIS IS MY LITTLE MOUSE, FOWLY.
MAN, THAT THING LOOKS ALMOST REAL.
BACK OFF, HALIBUT-TOSIS, I DIDN'T PAY FOR THE FREAK SHOW.

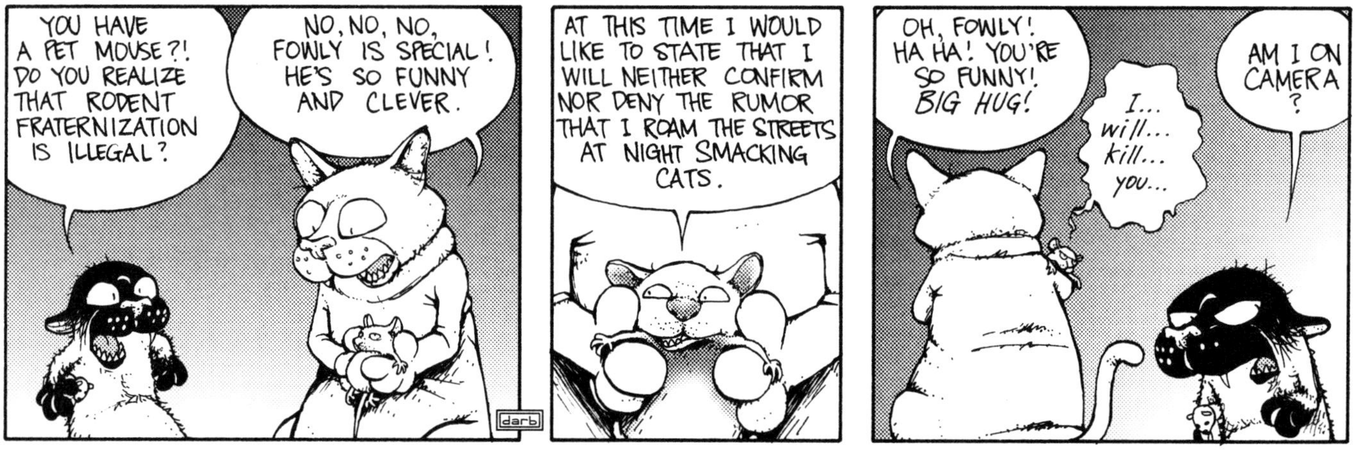
YOU HAVE A PET MOUSE?! DO YOU REALIZE THAT RODENT FRATERNIZATION IS ILLEGAL?
NO, NO, NO, FOWLY IS SPECIAL! HE'S SO FUNNY AND CLEVER.
AT THIS TIME I WOULD LIKE TO STATE THAT I WILL NEITHER CONFIRM NOR DENY THE RUMOR THAT I ROAM THE STREETS AT NIGHT SMACKING CATS.
OH, FOWLY! HA HA! YOU'RE SO FUNNY! *BIG HUG!*
I... will... kill... you...
AM I ON CAMERA?

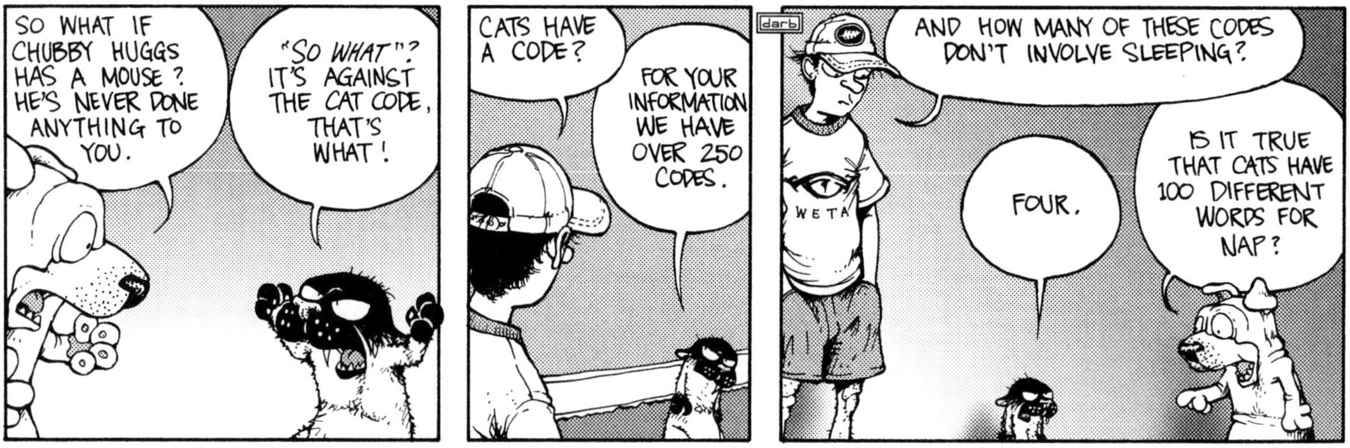
SO WHAT IF CHUBBY HUGGS HAS A MOUSE? HE'S NEVER DONE ANYTHING TO YOU.
"SO *WHAT*"? IT'S AGAINST THE CAT CODE, THAT'S WHAT!
CATS HAVE A CODE?
FOR YOUR INFORMATION WE HAVE OVER 250 CODES.
AND HOW MANY OF THESE CODES DON'T INVOLVE SLEEPING?
FOUR.
IS IT TRUE THAT CATS HAVE 100 DIFFERENT WORDS FOR NAP?

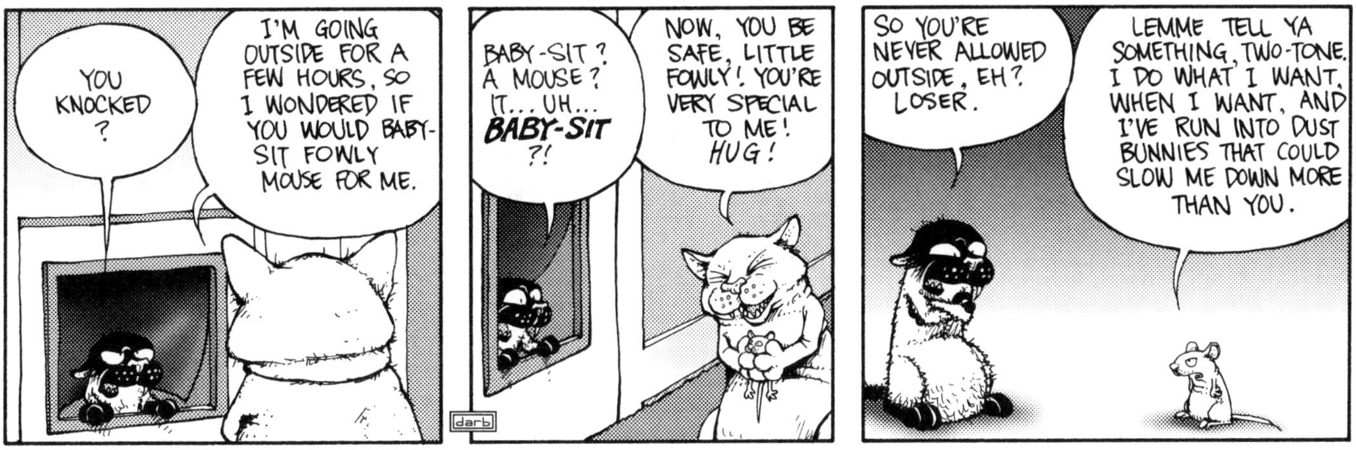
YOU KNOCKED ?
I'M GOING OUTSIDE FOR A FEW HOURS, SO I WONDERED IF YOU WOULD BABY-SIT FOWLY MOUSE FOR ME.
BABY-SIT ? A MOUSE ? IT... UH... BABY-SIT ?!
NOW, YOU BE SAFE, LITTLE FOWLY! YOU'RE VERY SPECIAL TO ME! HUG!
SO YOU'RE NEVER ALLOWED OUTSIDE, EH? LOSER.
LEMME TELL YA SOMETHING, TWO-TONE. I DO WHAT I WANT, WHEN I WANT, AND I'VE RUN INTO DUST BUNNIES THAT COULD SLOW ME DOWN MORE THAN YOU.
darb

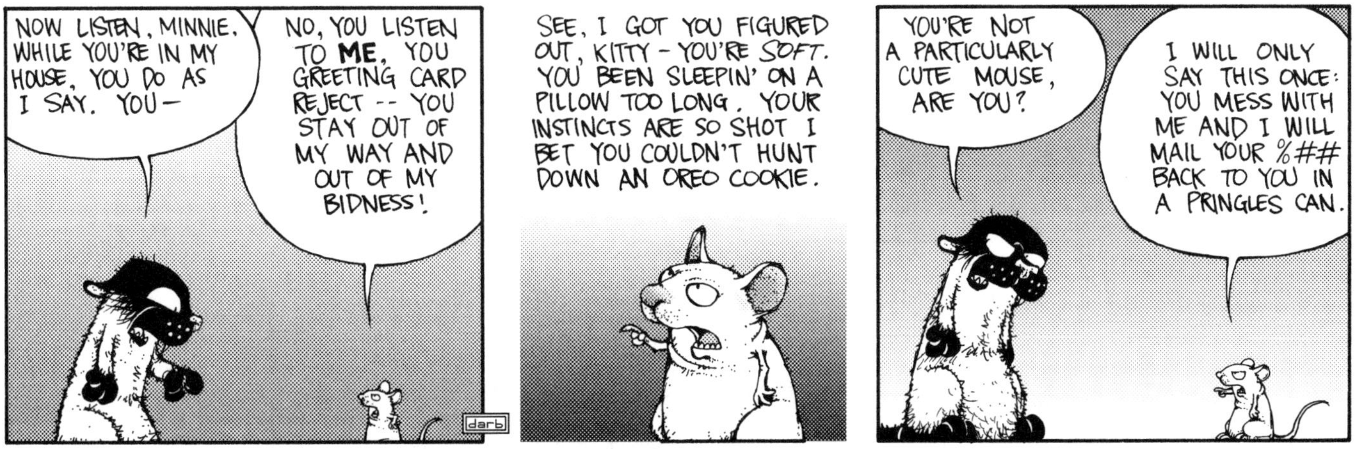
NOW LISTEN, MINNIE. WHILE YOU'RE IN MY HOUSE, YOU DO AS I SAY. YOU—
NO, YOU LISTEN TO ME, YOU GREETING CARD REJECT -- YOU STAY OUT OF MY WAY AND OUT OF MY BIDNESS!
SEE, I GOT YOU FIGURED OUT, KITTY - YOU'RE SOFT. YOU BEEN SLEEPIN' ON A PILLOW TOO LONG. YOUR INSTINCTS ARE SO SHOT I BET YOU COULDN'T HUNT DOWN AN OREO COOKIE.
YOU'RE NOT A PARTICULARLY CUTE MOUSE, ARE YOU?
I WILL ONLY SAY THIS ONCE: YOU MESS WITH ME AND I WILL MAIL YOUR %## BACK TO YOU IN A PRINGLES CAN.
darb

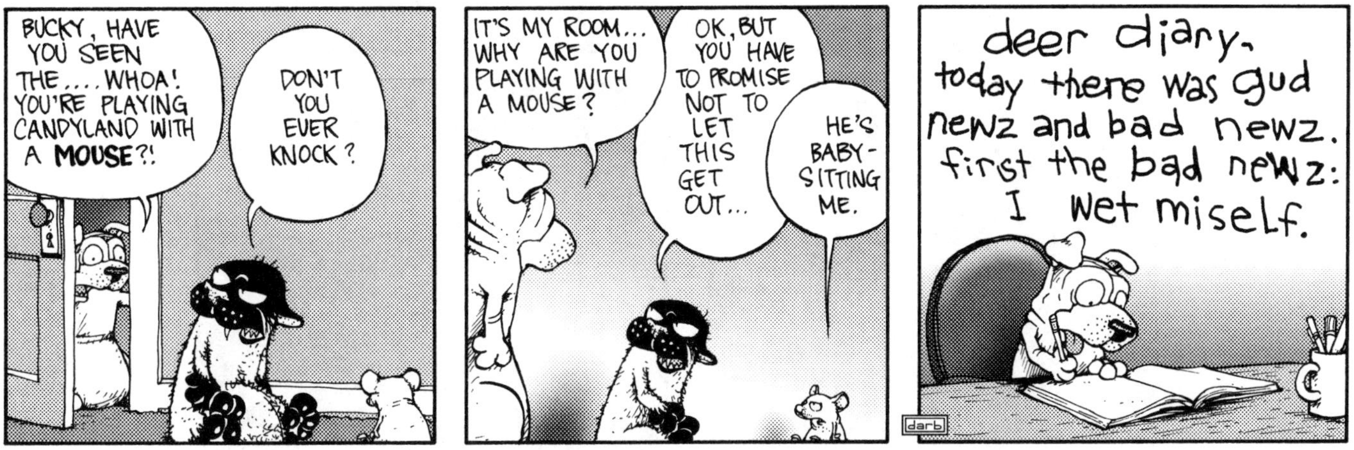
BUCKY, HAVE YOU SEEN THE.... WHOA! YOU'RE PLAYING CANDYLAND WITH A MOUSE?!
DON'T YOU EVER KNOCK ?
IT'S MY ROOM... WHY ARE YOU PLAYING WITH A MOUSE ?
OK, BUT YOU HAVE TO PROMISE NOT TO LET THIS GET OUT...
HE'S BABY-SITTING ME.
deer diary, today there was gud newz and bad newz. first the bad newz: I wet miself.
darb

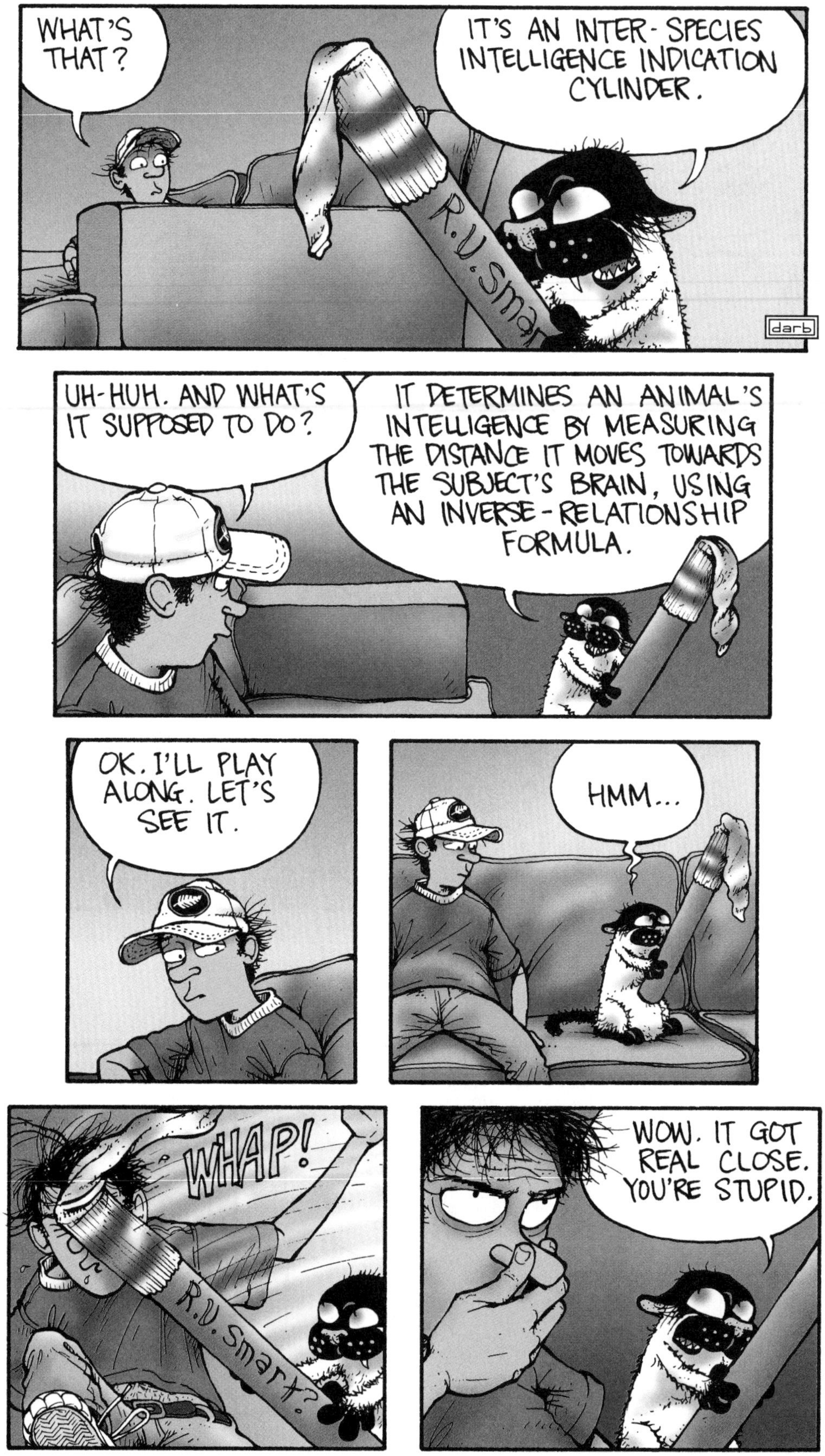
WHAT'S THAT?
IT'S AN INTER-SPECIES INTELLIGENCE INDICATION CYLINDER.
R.U. Smart
darb
UH-HUH. AND WHAT'S IT SUPPOSED TO DO?
IT DETERMINES AN ANIMAL'S INTELLIGENCE BY MEASURING THE DISTANCE IT MOVES TOWARDS THE SUBJECT'S BRAIN, USING AN INVERSE-RELATIONSHIP FORMULA.
OK. I'LL PLAY ALONG. LET'S SEE IT.
HMM...
WHAP!
R.U. Smart?
WOW. IT GOT REAL CLOSE. YOU'RE STUPID.

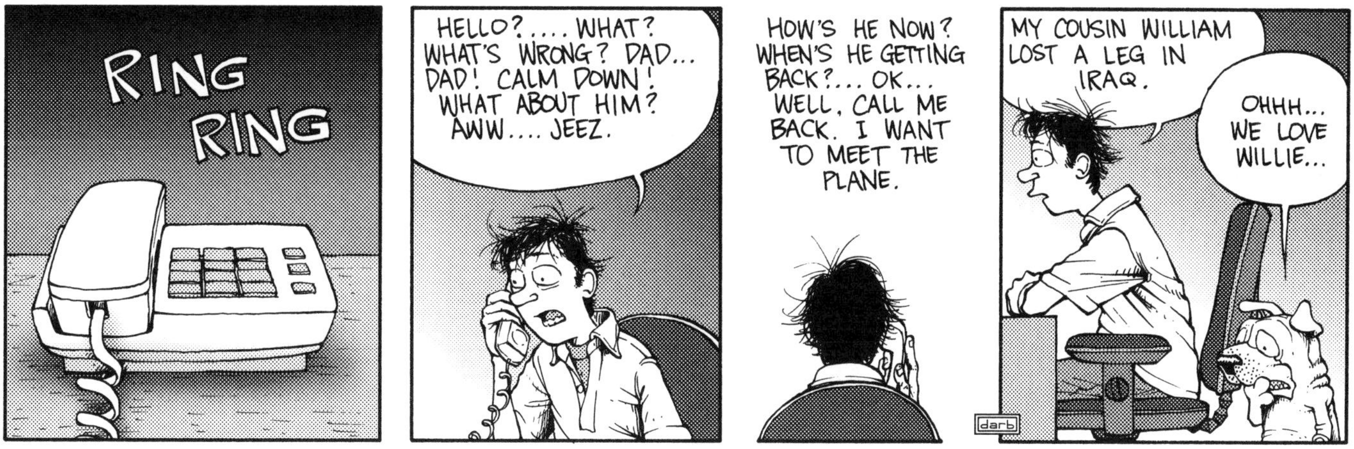
RING
RING
HELLO?.... WHAT? WHAT'S WRONG? DAD... DAD! CALM DOWN! WHAT ABOUT HIM? AWW.... JEEZ.
HOW'S HE NOW? WHEN'S HE GETTING BACK?... OK... WELL, CALL ME BACK. I WANT TO MEET THE PLANE.
MY COUSIN WILLIAM LOST A LEG IN IRAQ.
OHHH... WE LOVE WILLIE...
darb

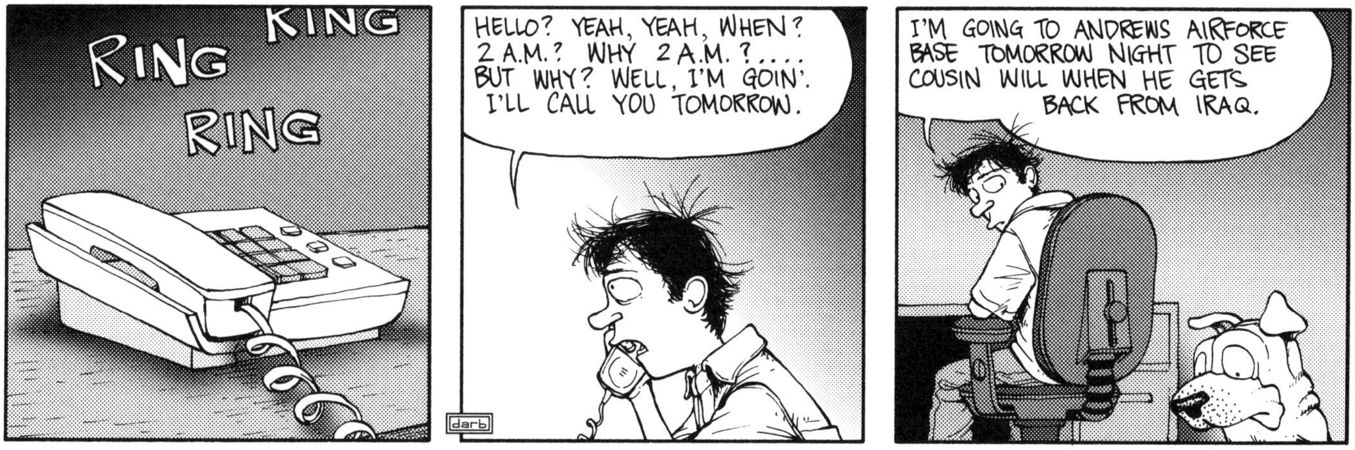
RING
RING
HELLO? YEAH, YEAH, WHEN? 2 A.M.? WHY 2 A.M.?.... BUT WHY? WELL, I'M GOIN'. I'LL CALL YOU TOMORROW.
I'M GOING TO ANDREWS AIRFORCE BASE TOMORROW NIGHT TO SEE COUSIN WILL WHEN HE GETS BACK FROM IRAQ.
darb

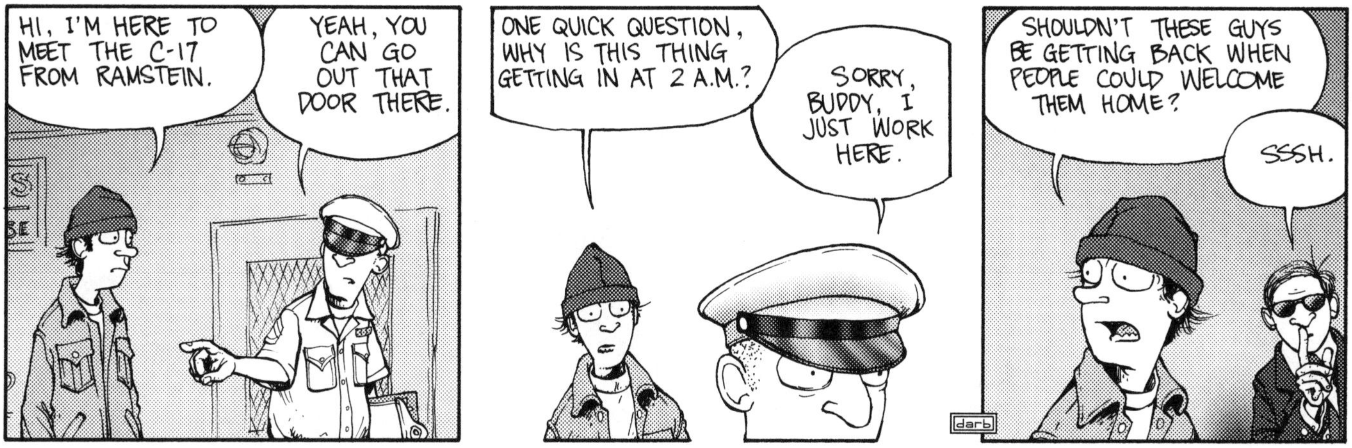
HI, I'M HERE TO MEET THE C-17 FROM RAMSTEIN.
YEAH, YOU CAN GO OUT THAT DOOR THERE.
ONE QUICK QUESTION, WHY IS THIS THING GETTING IN AT 2 A.M.?
SORRY, BUDDY, I JUST WORK HERE.
SHOULDN'T THESE GUYS BE GETTING BACK WHEN PEOPLE COULD WELCOME THEM HOME?
SSSH.
darb

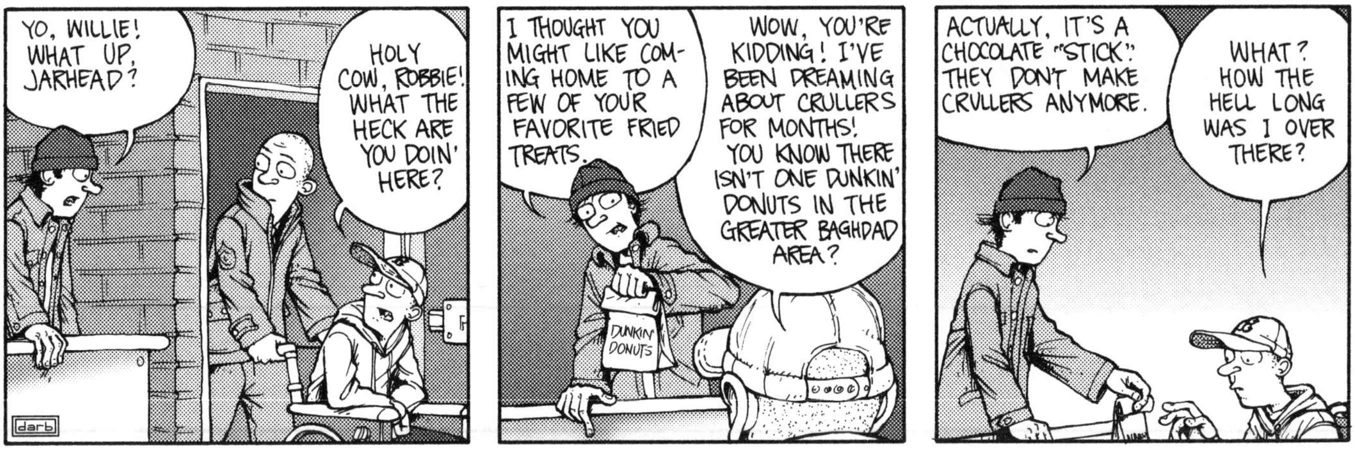
YO, WILLIE! WHAT UP, JARHEAD?
HOLY COW, ROBBIE! WHAT THE HECK ARE YOU DOIN' HERE?
I THOUGHT YOU MIGHT LIKE COMING HOME TO A FEW OF YOUR FAVORITE FRIED TREATS.
WOW, YOU'RE KIDDING! I'VE BEEN DREAMING ABOUT CRULLERS FOR MONTHS! YOU KNOW THERE ISN'T ONE DUNKIN' DONUTS IN THE GREATER BAGHDAD AREA?
DUNKIN' DONUTS
ACTUALLY, IT'S A CHOCOLATE "STICK." THEY DON'T MAKE CRULLERS ANYMORE.
WHAT? HOW THE HELL LONG WAS I OVER THERE?
darb

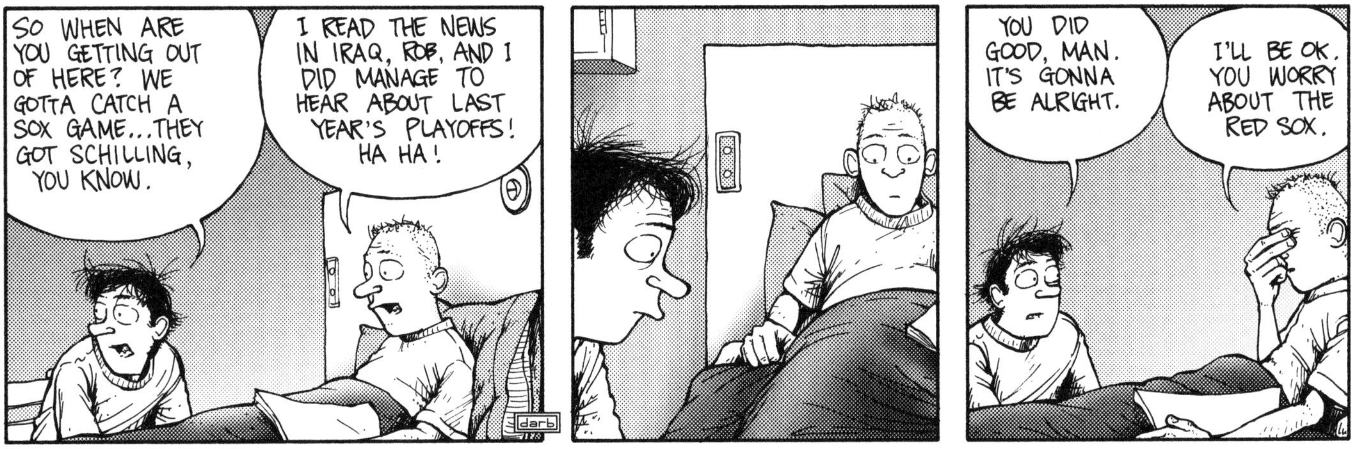
SO WHEN ARE YOU GETTING OUT OF HERE? WE GOTTA CATCH A SOX GAME...THEY GOT SCHILLING, YOU KNOW.
I READ THE NEWS IN IRAQ, ROB, AND I DID MANAGE TO HEAR ABOUT LAST YEAR'S PLAYOFFS! HA HA!
darb
YOU DID GOOD, MAN. IT'S GONNA BE ALRIGHT.
I'LL BE OK. YOU WORRY ABOUT THE RED SOX.

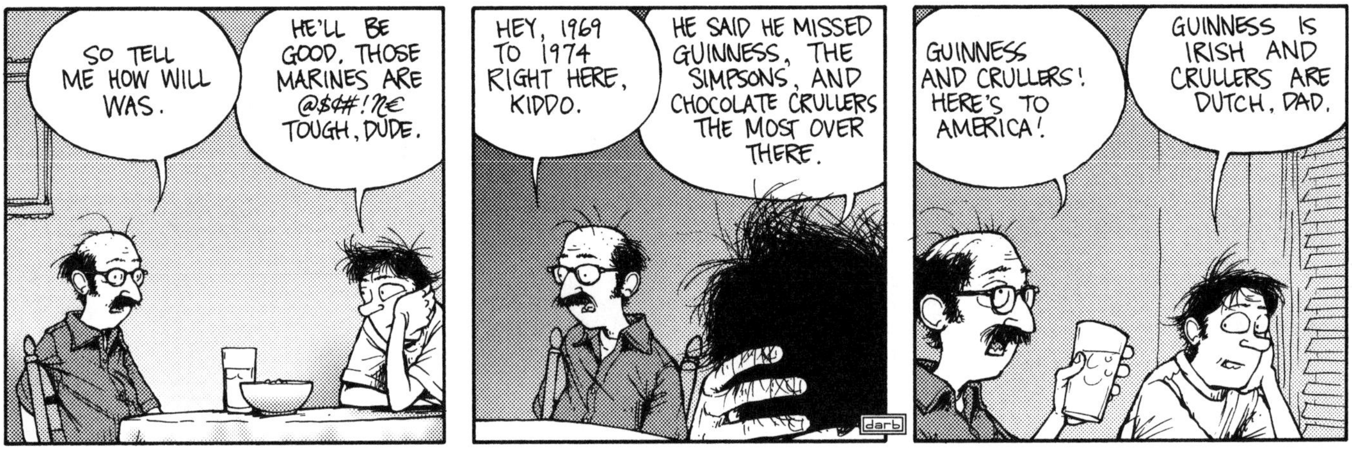
SO TELL ME HOW WILL WAS.
HE'LL BE GOOD. THOSE MARINES ARE @$¢#!№€ TOUGH, DUDE.
HEY, 1969 TO 1974 RIGHT HERE, KIDDO.
HE SAID HE MISSED GUINNESS, THE SIMPSONS, AND CHOCOLATE CRULLERS THE MOST OVER THERE.
darb
GUINNESS AND CRULLERS! HERE'S TO AMERICA!
GUINNESS IS IRISH AND CRULLERS ARE DUTCH, DAD.

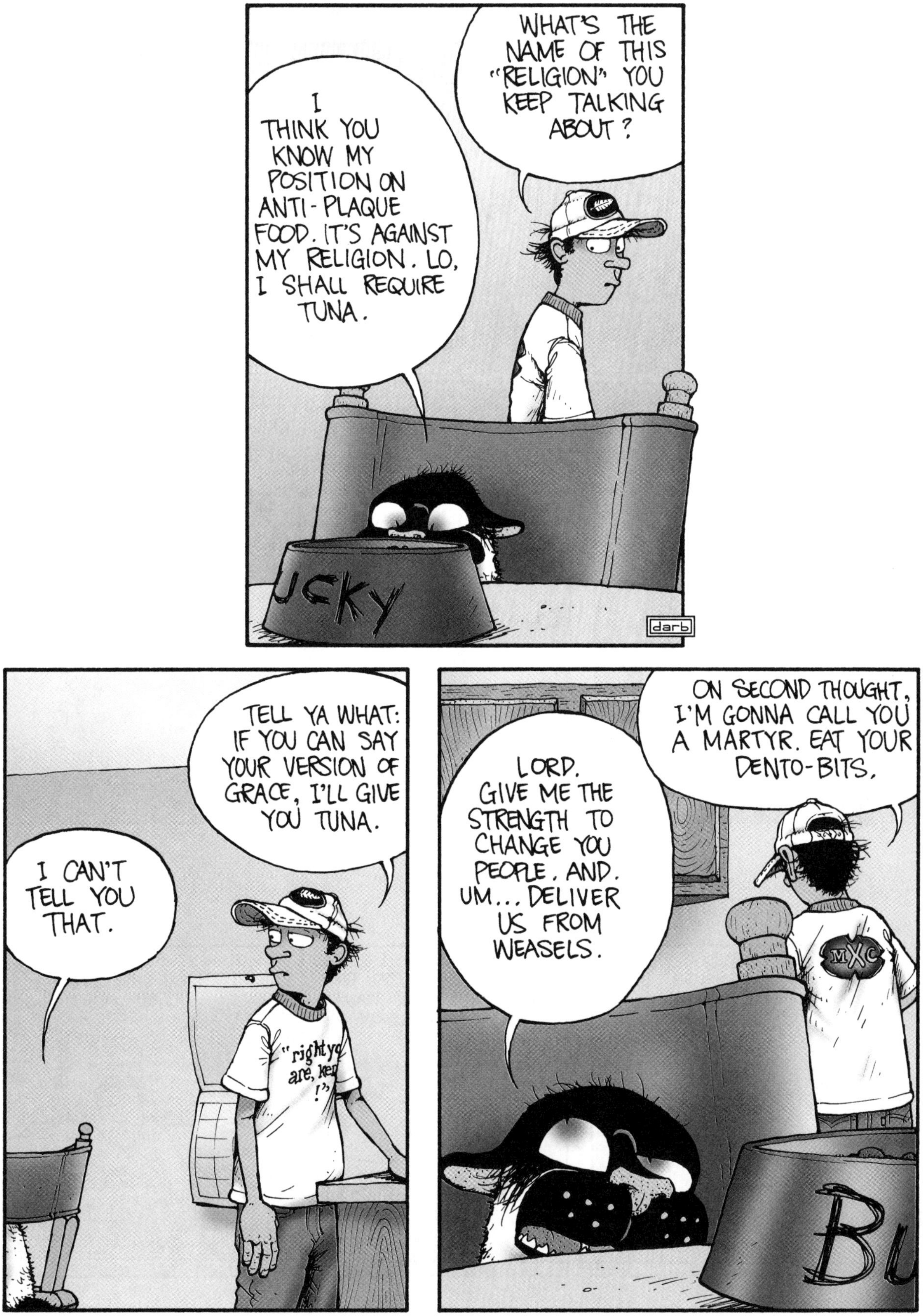
I THINK YOU KNOW MY POSITION ON ANTI-PLAQUE FOOD. IT'S AGAINST MY RELIGION. LO, I SHALL REQUIRE TUNA.
WHAT'S THE NAME OF THIS "RELIGION" YOU KEEP TALKING ABOUT?
TELL YA WHAT: IF YOU CAN SAY YOUR VERSION OF GRACE, I'LL GIVE YOU TUNA.
I CAN'T TELL YOU THAT.
LORD. GIVE ME THE STRENGTH TO CHANGE YOU PEOPLE. AND. UM... DELIVER US FROM WEASELS.
ON SECOND THOUGHT, I'M GONNA CALL YOU A MARTYR. EAT YOUR DENTO-BITS.

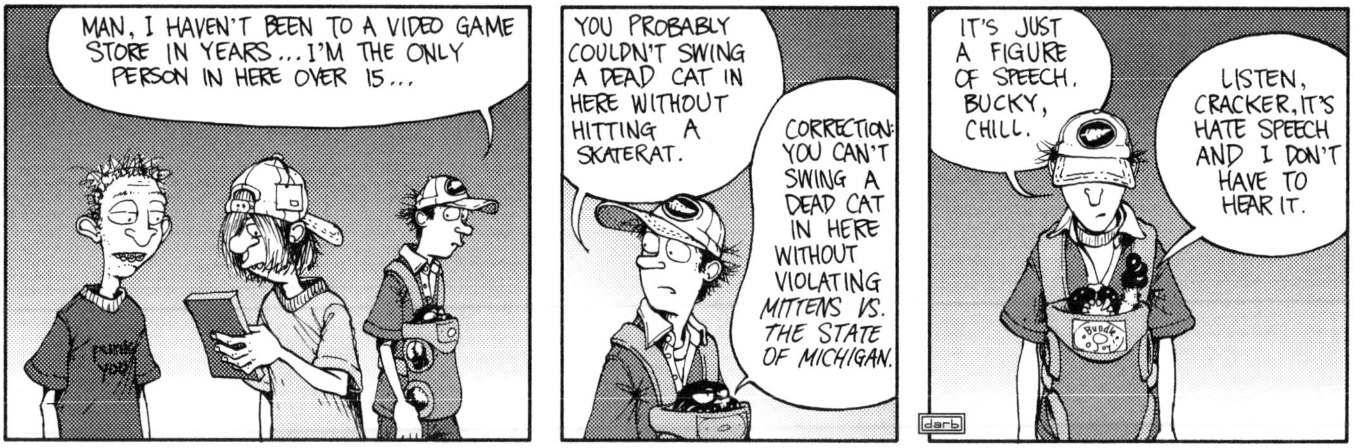
MAN, I HAVEN'T BEEN TO A VIDEO GAME STORE IN YEARS... I'M THE ONLY PERSON IN HERE OVER 15...
YOU PROBABLY COULDN'T SWING A DEAD CAT IN HERE WITHOUT HITTING A SKATERAT.
CORRECTION: YOU CAN'T SWING A DEAD CAT IN HERE WITHOUT VIOLATING MITTENS VS. THE STATE OF MICHIGAN.
IT'S JUST A FIGURE OF SPEECH. BUCKY, CHILL.
LISTEN, CRACKER, IT'S HATE SPEECH AND I DON'T HAVE TO HEAR IT.
darb

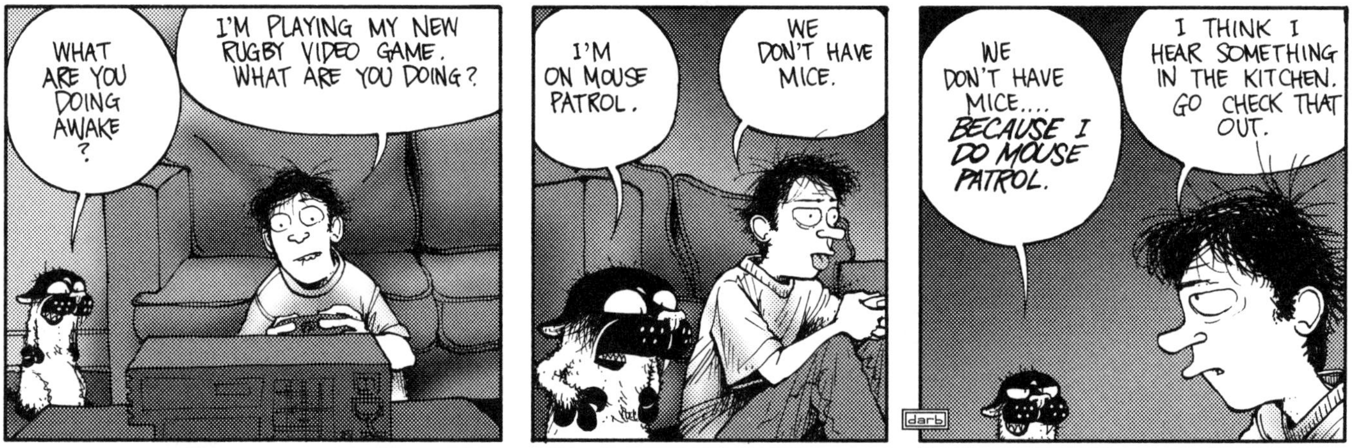
WHAT ARE YOU DOING AWAKE ?
I'M PLAYING MY NEW RUGBY VIDEO GAME. WHAT ARE YOU DOING?
I'M ON MOUSE PATROL.
WE DON'T HAVE MICE.
WE DON'T HAVE MICE.... BECAUSE I DO MOUSE PATROL.
I THINK I HEAR SOMETHING IN THE KITCHEN. GO CHECK THAT OUT.
darb

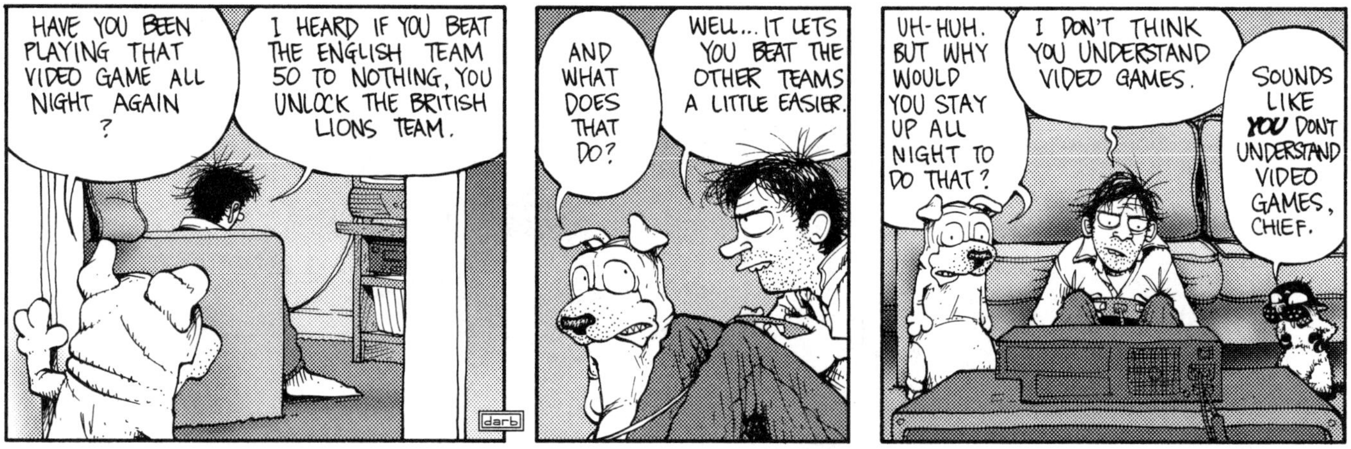
HAVE YOU BEEN PLAYING THAT VIDEO GAME ALL NIGHT AGAIN ?
I HEARD IF YOU BEAT THE ENGLISH TEAM 50 TO NOTHING, YOU UNLOCK THE BRITISH LIONS TEAM.
AND WHAT DOES THAT DO?
WELL... IT LETS YOU BEAT THE OTHER TEAMS A LITTLE EASIER.
UH-HUH. BUT WHY WOULD YOU STAY UP ALL NIGHT TO DO THAT?
I DON'T THINK YOU UNDERSTAND VIDEO GAMES.
SOUNDS LIKE YOU DON'T UNDERSTAND VIDEO GAMES, CHIEF.
darb

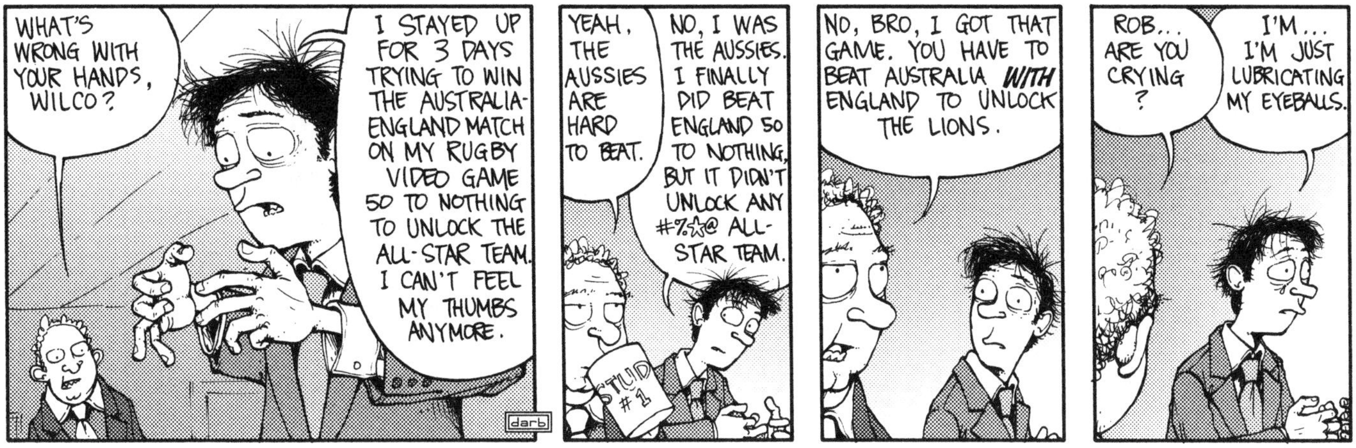
WHAT'S WRONG WITH YOUR HANDS, WILCO?
I STAYED UP FOR 3 DAYS TRYING TO WIN THE AUSTRALIA-ENGLAND MATCH ON MY RUGBY VIDEO GAME 50 TO NOTHING TO UNLOCK THE ALL-STAR TEAM. I CAN'T FEEL MY THUMBS ANYMORE.
darb
YEAH, THE AUSSIES ARE HARD TO BEAT.
NO, I WAS THE AUSSIES. I FINALLY DID BEAT ENGLAND 50 TO NOTHING, BUT IT DIDN'T UNLOCK ANY #%☆@ ALL-STAR TEAM.
STUD #1
NO, BRO, I GOT THAT GAME. YOU HAVE TO BEAT AUSTRALIA *WITH* ENGLAND TO UNLOCK THE LIONS.
ROB... ARE YOU CRYING?
I'M... I'M JUST LUBRICATING MY EYEBALLS.

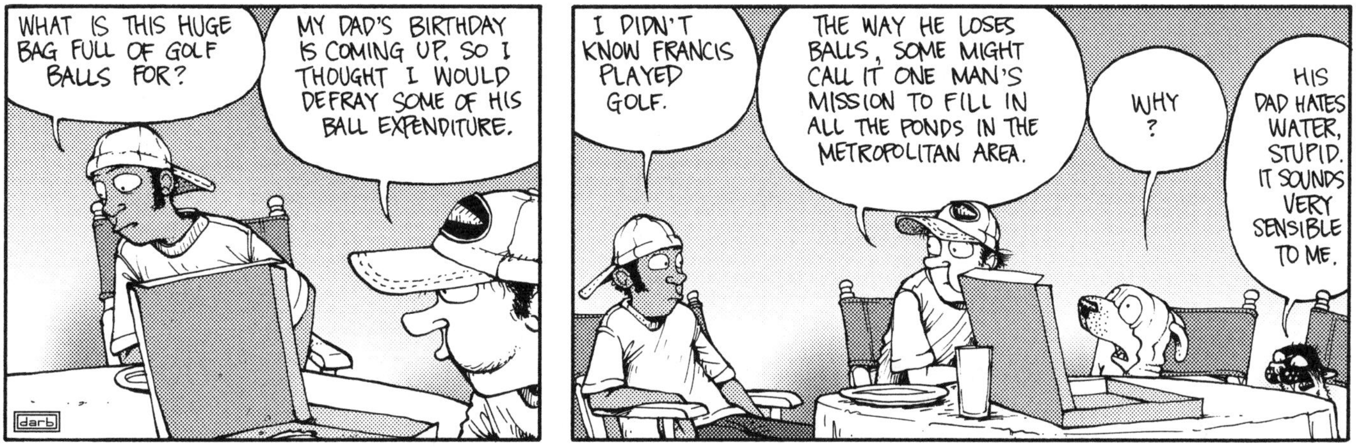
WHAT IS THIS HUGE BAG FULL OF GOLF BALLS FOR?
MY DAD'S BIRTHDAY IS COMING UP, SO I THOUGHT I WOULD DEFRAY SOME OF HIS BALL EXPENDITURE.
darb
I DIDN'T KNOW FRANCIS PLAYED GOLF.
THE WAY HE LOSES BALLS, SOME MIGHT CALL IT ONE MAN'S MISSION TO FILL IN ALL THE PONDS IN THE METROPOLITAN AREA.
WHY?
HIS DAD HATES WATER, STUPID. IT SOUNDS VERY SENSIBLE TO ME.

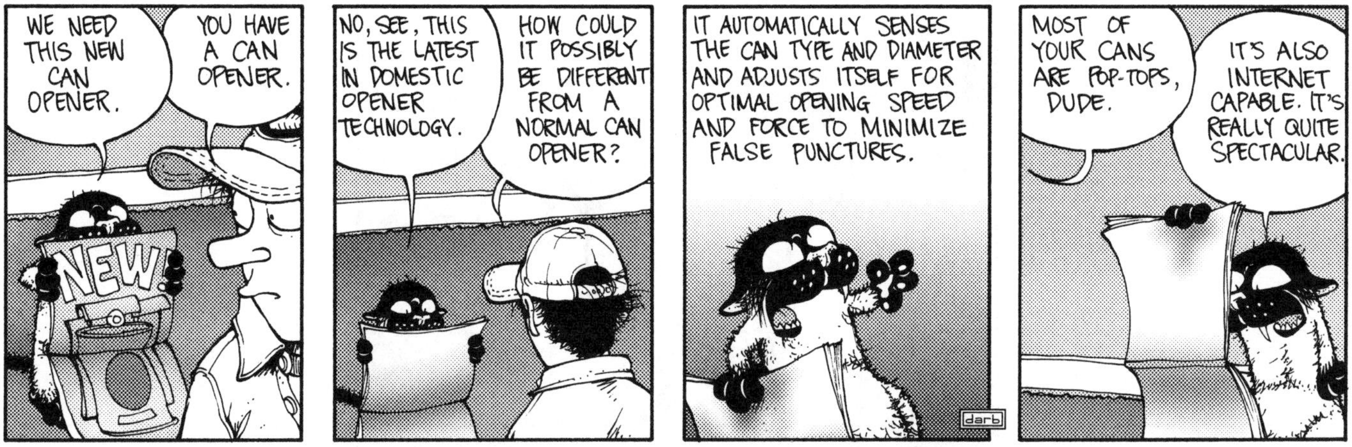
WE NEED THIS NEW CAN OPENER.
YOU HAVE A CAN OPENER.
NEW!
NO, SEE, THIS IS THE LATEST IN DOMESTIC OPENER TECHNOLOGY.
HOW COULD IT POSSIBLY BE DIFFERENT FROM A NORMAL CAN OPENER?
IT AUTOMATICALLY SENSES THE CAN TYPE AND DIAMETER AND ADJUSTS ITSELF FOR OPTIMAL OPENING SPEED AND FORCE TO MINIMIZE FALSE PUNCTURES.
darb
MOST OF YOUR CANS ARE POP-TOPS, DUDE.
IT'S ALSO INTERNET CAPABLE. IT'S REALLY QUITE SPECTACULAR.

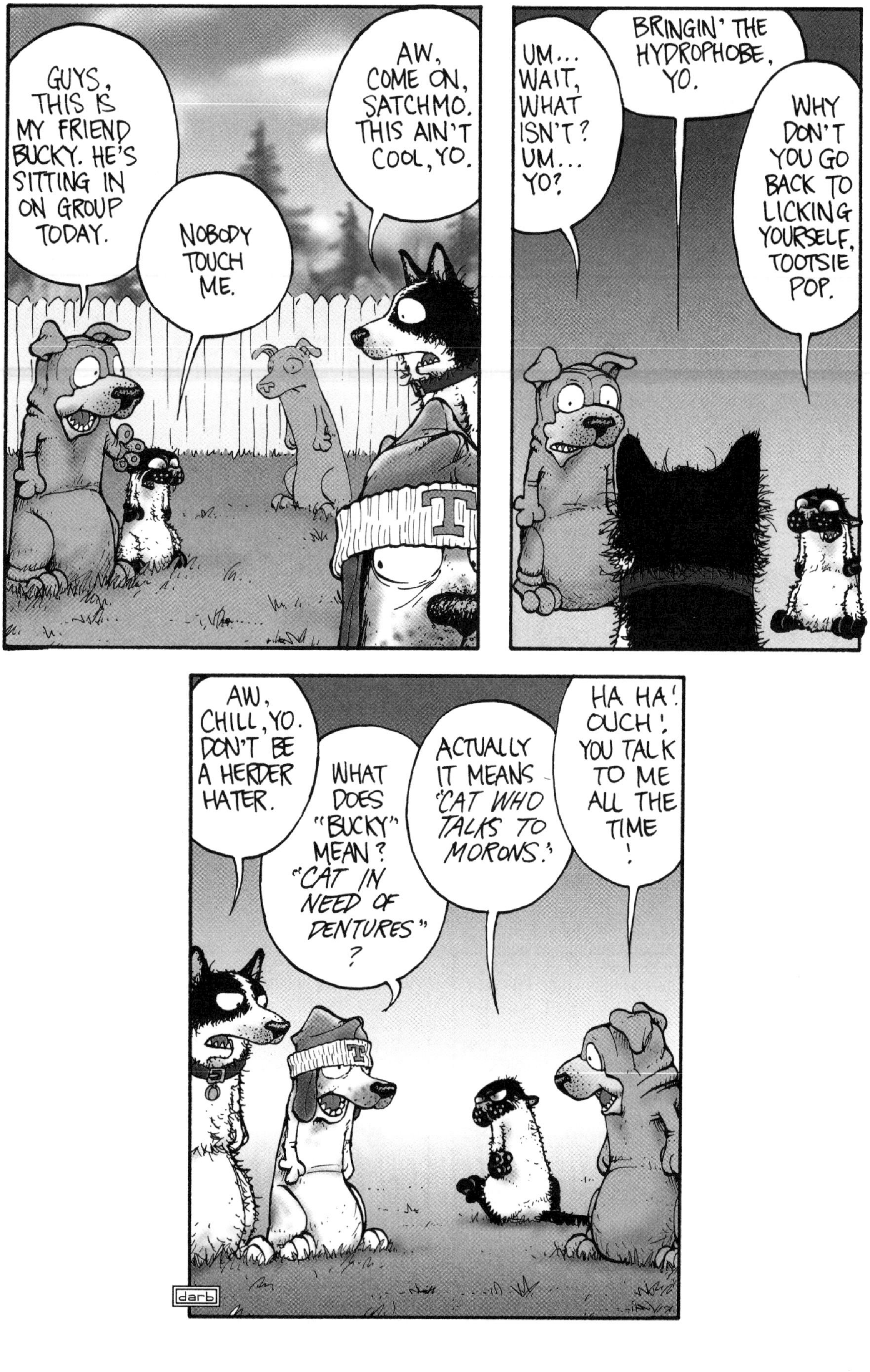
GUYS, THIS IS MY FRIEND BUCKY. HE'S SITTING IN ON GROUP TODAY.
NOBODY TOUCH ME.
AW, COME ON, SATCHMO. THIS AIN'T COOL, YO.
BRINGIN' THE HYDROPHOBE, YO.
UM... WAIT, WHAT ISN'T? UM... YO?
WHY DON'T YOU GO BACK TO LICKING YOURSELF, TOOTSIE POP.
AW, CHILL, YO. DON'T BE A HERDER HATER.
WHAT DOES "BUCKY" MEAN? "CAT IN NEED OF DENTURES"?
ACTUALLY IT MEANS "CAT WHO TALKS TO MORONS."
HA HA! OUCH! YOU TALK TO ME ALL THE TIME!
darb

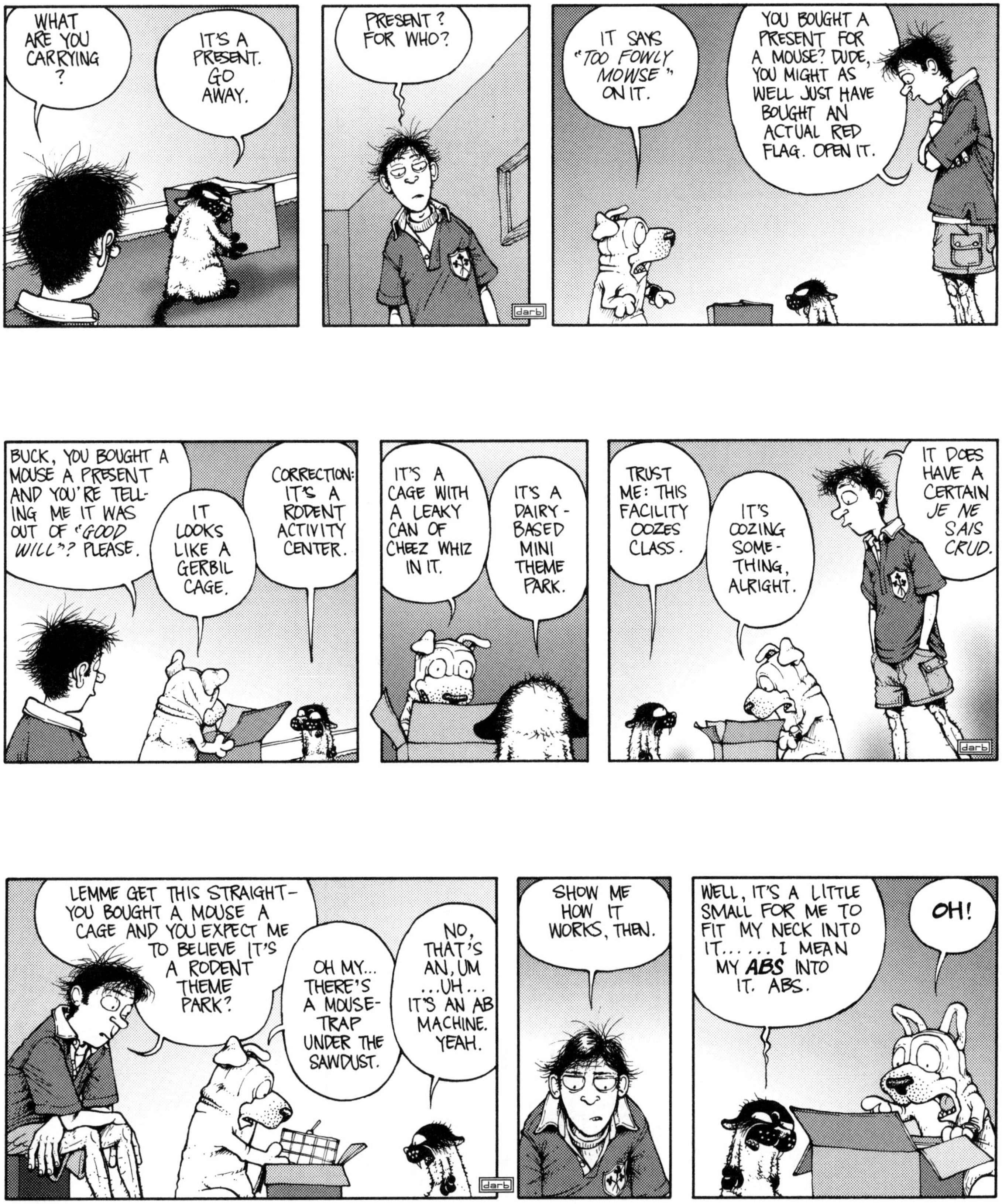
WHAT ARE YOU CARRYING ?
IT'S A PRESENT. GO AWAY.
PRESENT? FOR WHO?
IT SAYS "TOO FOWLY MOWSE" ON IT.
YOU BOUGHT A PRESENT FOR A MOUSE? DUDE, YOU MIGHT AS WELL JUST HAVE BOUGHT AN ACTUAL RED FLAG. OPEN IT.
darb
BUCK, YOU BOUGHT A MOUSE A PRESENT AND YOU'RE TELLING ME IT WAS OUT OF "GOOD WILL"? PLEASE.
IT LOOKS LIKE A GERBIL CAGE.
CORRECTION: IT'S A RODENT ACTIVITY CENTER.
IT'S A CAGE WITH A LEAKY CAN OF CHEEZ WHIZ IN IT.
IT'S A DAIRY-BASED MINI THEME PARK.
TRUST ME: THIS FACILITY OOZES CLASS.
IT'S OOZING SOMETHING, ALRIGHT.
IT DOES HAVE A CERTAIN JE NE SAIS CRUD.
darb
LEMME GET THIS STRAIGHT- YOU BOUGHT A MOUSE A CAGE AND YOU EXPECT ME TO BELIEVE IT'S A RODENT THEME PARK?
OH MY... THERE'S A MOUSE-TRAP UNDER THE SAWDUST.
NO, THAT'S AN, UM ...UH... IT'S AN AB MACHINE. YEAH.
darb
SHOW ME HOW IT WORKS, THEN.
WELL, IT'S A LITTLE SMALL FOR ME TO FIT MY NECK INTO IT...... I MEAN MY ABS INTO IT. ABS.
OH!

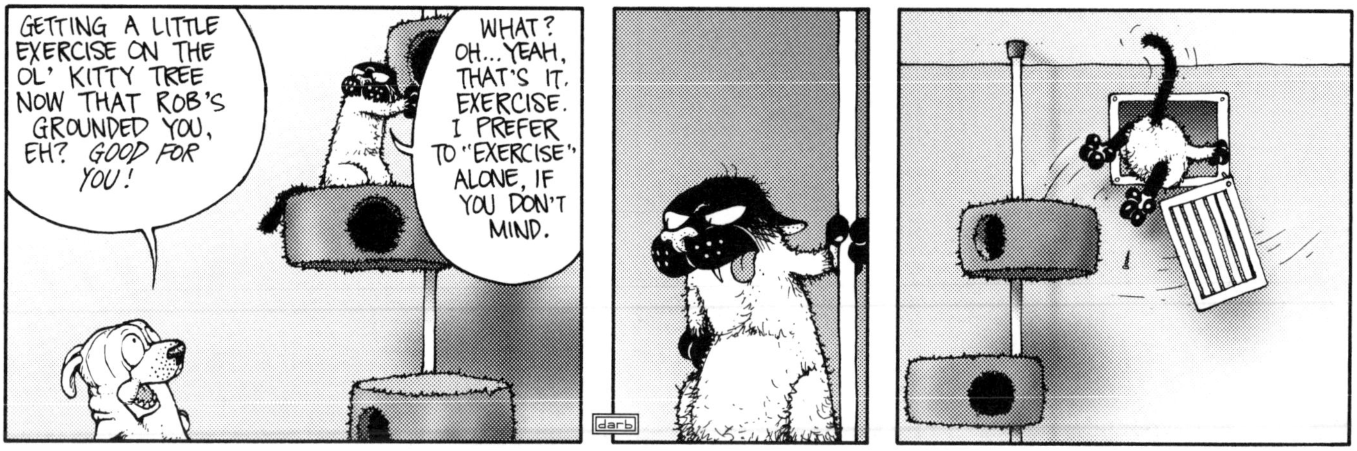
GETTING A LITTLE EXERCISE ON THE OL' KITTY TREE NOW THAT ROB'S GROUNDED YOU, EH? *GOOD FOR YOU!*
WHAT? OH... YEAH, THAT'S IT. EXERCISE. I PREFER TO "EXERCISE" ALONE, IF YOU DON'T MIND.

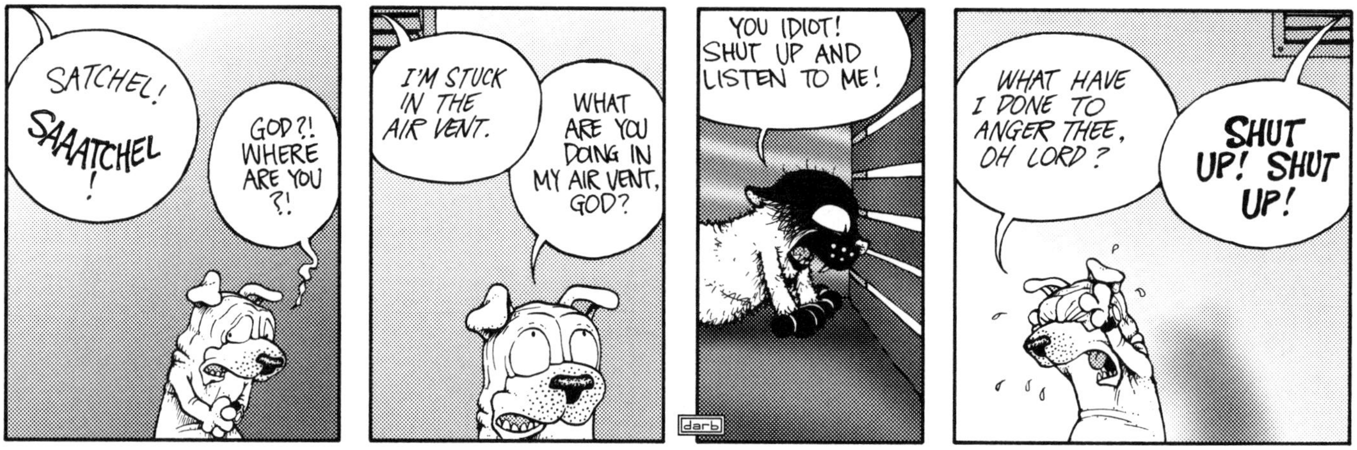
SATCHEL! **SAAATCHEL!**
GOD?! WHERE ARE YOU?!
I'M STUCK IN THE AIR VENT.
WHAT ARE YOU DOING IN MY AIR VENT, GOD?
YOU IDIOT! SHUT UP AND LISTEN TO ME!
WHAT HAVE I DONE TO ANGER THEE, OH LORD?
SHUT UP! SHUT UP!

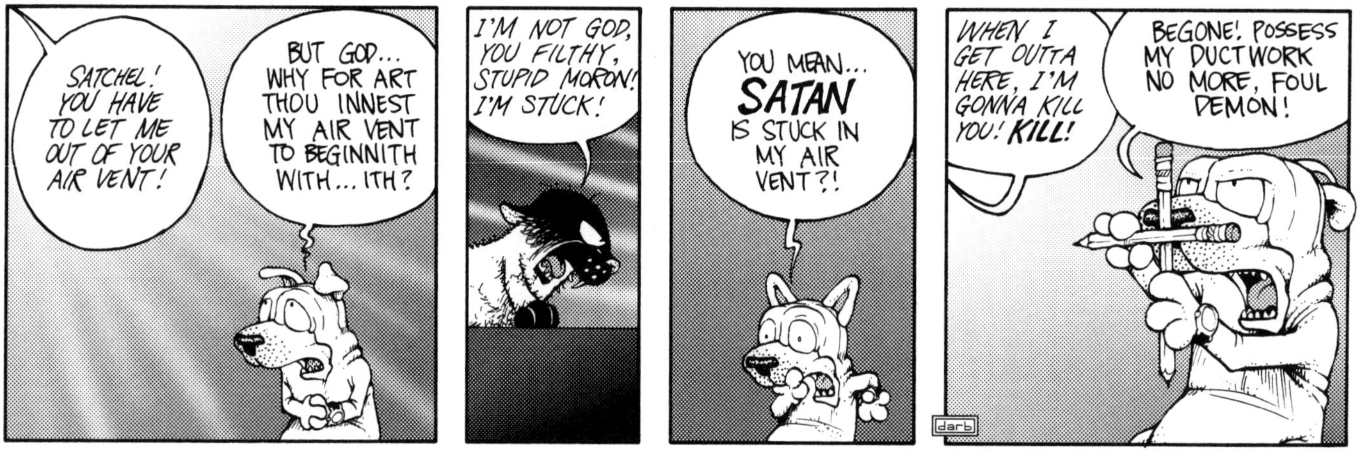
SATCHEL! YOU HAVE TO LET ME OUT OF YOUR AIR VENT!
BUT GOD... WHY FOR ART THOU INNEST MY AIR VENT TO BEGINNITH WITH... ITH?
I'M NOT GOD, YOU FILTHY, STUPID MORON! I'M STUCK!
YOU MEAN... **SATAN** IS STUCK IN MY AIR VENT?!
WHEN I GET OUTTA HERE, I'M GONNA KILL YOU! ***KILL!***
BEGONE! POSSESS MY DUCTWORK NO MORE, FOUL DEMON!

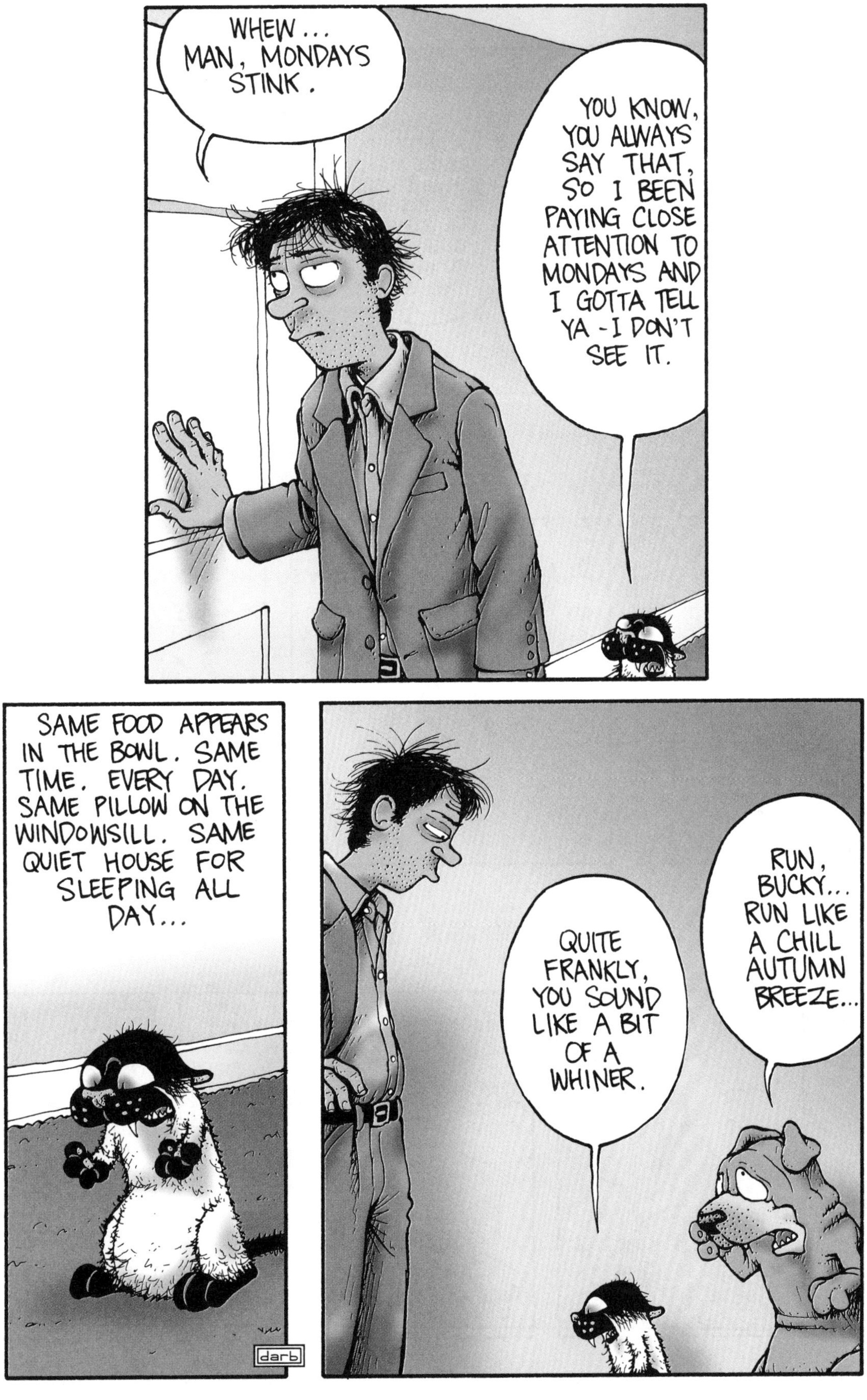
WHEW... MAN, MONDAYS STINK.
YOU KNOW, YOU ALWAYS SAY THAT, SO I BEEN PAYING CLOSE ATTENTION TO MONDAYS AND I GOTTA TELL YA - I DON'T SEE IT.
SAME FOOD APPEARS IN THE BOWL. SAME TIME. EVERY DAY. SAME PILLOW ON THE WINDOWSILL. SAME QUIET HOUSE FOR SLEEPING ALL DAY...
darb
RUN, BUCKY... RUN LIKE A CHILL AUTUMN BREEZE...
QUITE FRANKLY, YOU SOUND LIKE A BIT OF A WHINER.

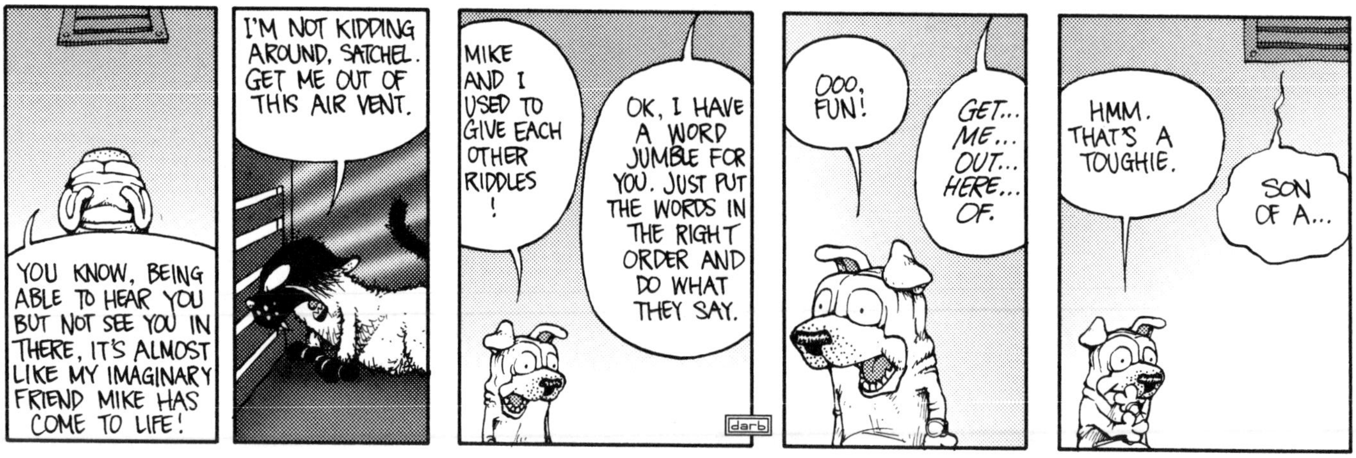
YOU KNOW, BEING ABLE TO HEAR YOU BUT NOT SEE YOU IN THERE, IT'S ALMOST LIKE MY IMAGINARY FRIEND MIKE HAS COME TO LIFE!
I'M NOT KIDDING AROUND, SATCHEL. GET ME OUT OF THIS AIR VENT.
MIKE AND I USED TO GIVE EACH OTHER RIDDLES!
OK, I HAVE A WORD JUMBLE FOR YOU. JUST PUT THE WORDS IN THE RIGHT ORDER AND DO WHAT THEY SAY.
darb
OOO, FUN!
GET... ME... OUT... HERE... OF.
HMM. THAT'S A TOUGHIE.
SON OF A...

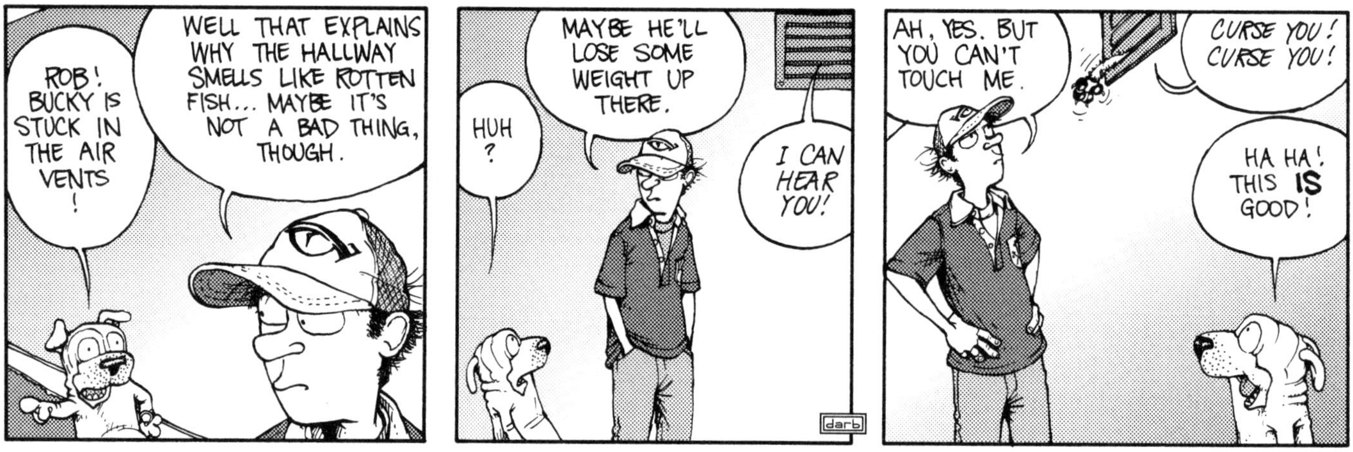
ROB! BUCKY IS STUCK IN THE AIR VENTS!
WELL THAT EXPLAINS WHY THE HALLWAY SMELLS LIKE ROTTEN FISH... MAYBE IT'S NOT A BAD THING, THOUGH.
HUH?
MAYBE HE'LL LOSE SOME WEIGHT UP THERE.
I CAN HEAR YOU!
darb
AH, YES. BUT YOU CAN'T TOUCH ME.
CURSE YOU! CURSE YOU!
HA HA! THIS **IS** GOOD!

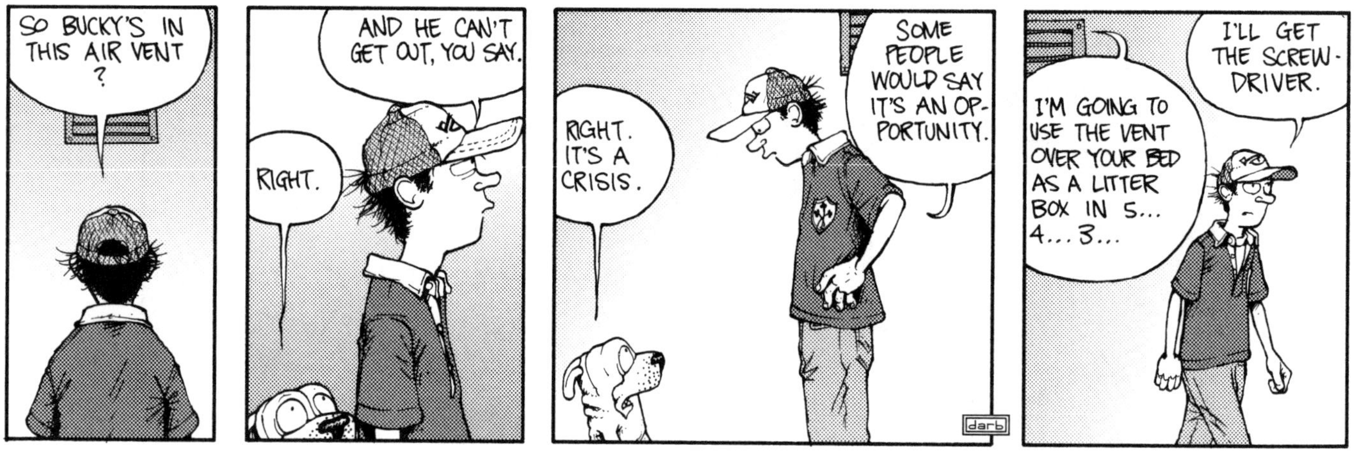
SO BUCKY'S IN THIS AIR VENT?
AND HE CAN'T GET OUT, YOU SAY.
RIGHT.
RIGHT. IT'S A CRISIS.
SOME PEOPLE WOULD SAY IT'S AN OPPORTUNITY.
darb
I'LL GET THE SCREWDRIVER.
I'M GOING TO USE THE VENT OVER YOUR BED AS A LITTER BOX IN 5... 4... 3...

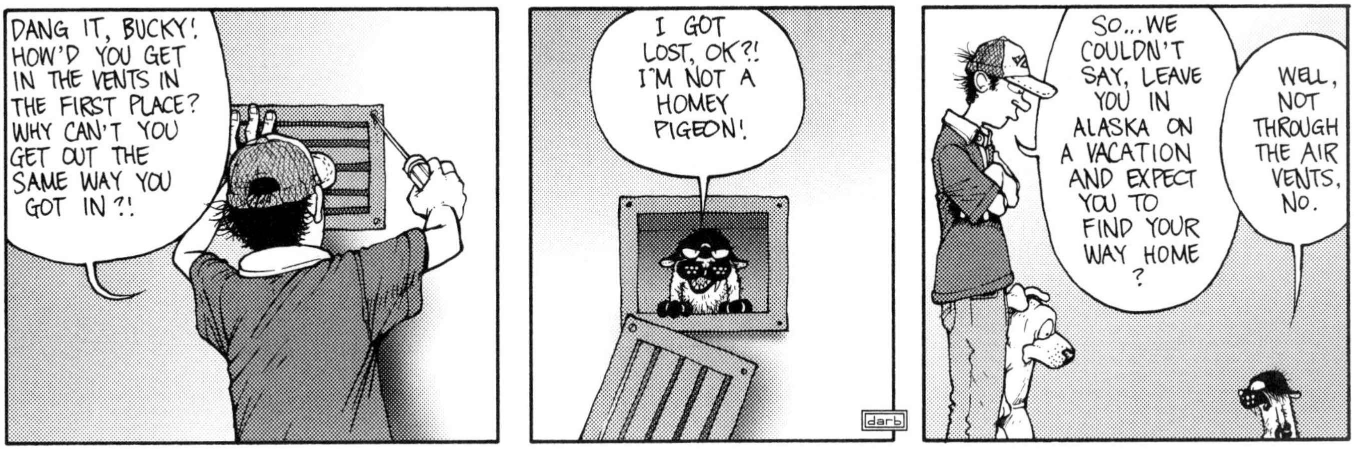
DANG IT, BUCKY! HOW'D YOU GET IN THE VENTS IN THE FIRST PLACE? WHY CAN'T YOU GET OUT THE SAME WAY YOU GOT IN?!
I GOT LOST, OK?! I'M NOT A HOMEY PIGEON!
darb
SO... WE COULDN'T SAY, LEAVE YOU IN ALASKA ON A VACATION AND EXPECT YOU TO FIND YOUR WAY HOME?
WELL, NOT THROUGH THE AIR VENTS, NO.

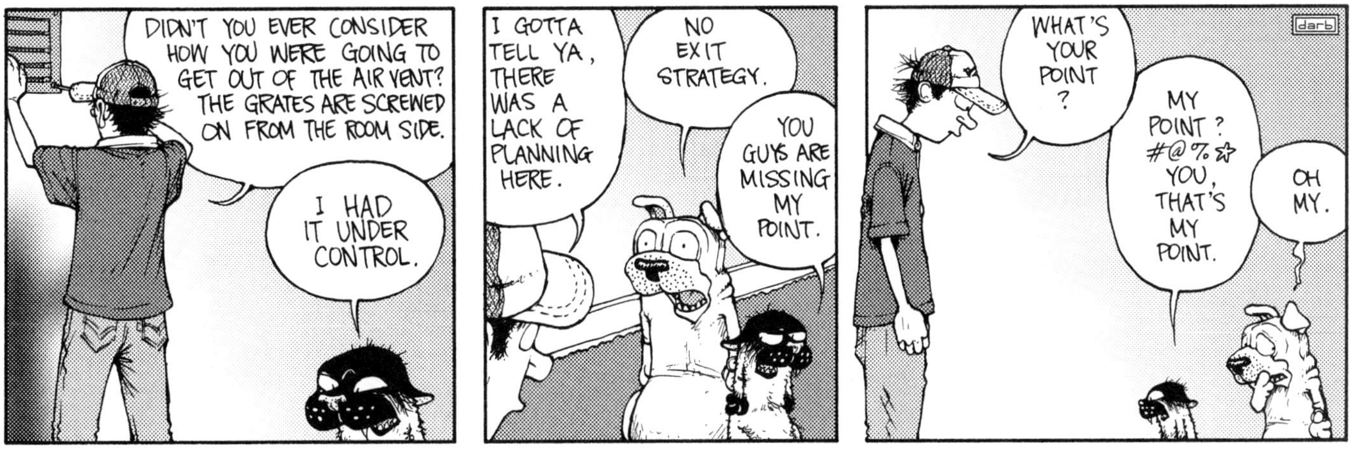
DIDN'T YOU EVER CONSIDER HOW YOU WERE GOING TO GET OUT OF THE AIR VENT? THE GRATES ARE SCREWED ON FROM THE ROOM SIDE.
I HAD IT UNDER CONTROL.
I GOTTA TELL YA, THERE WAS A LACK OF PLANNING HERE.
NO EXIT STRATEGY.
YOU GUYS ARE MISSING MY POINT.
darb
WHAT'S YOUR POINT?
MY POINT? #@%✩ YOU, THAT'S MY POINT.
OH MY.

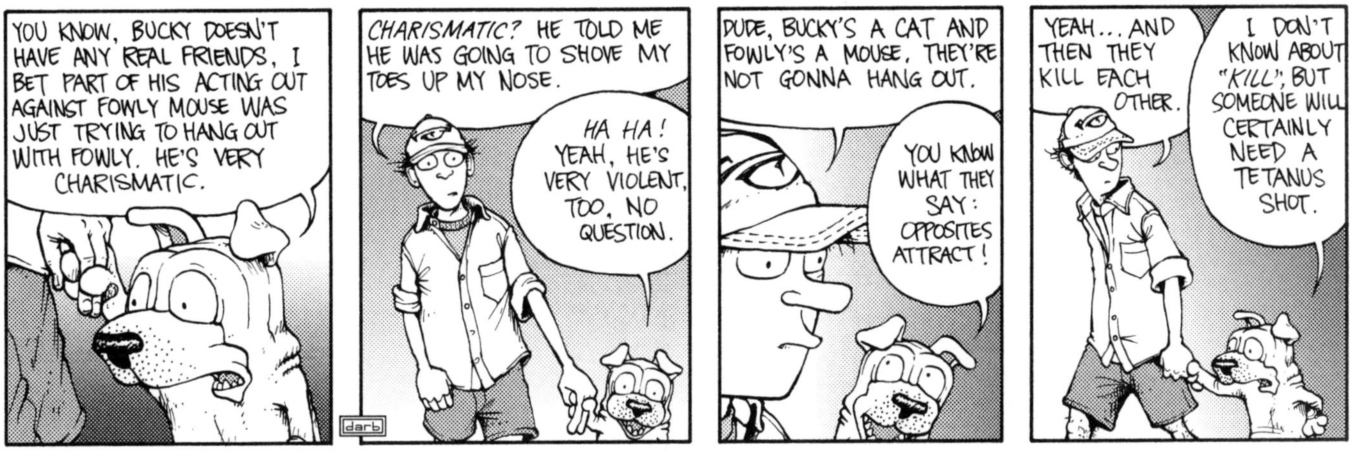
YOU KNOW, BUCKY DOESN'T HAVE ANY REAL FRIENDS, I BET PART OF HIS ACTING OUT AGAINST FOWLY MOUSE WAS JUST TRYING TO HANG OUT WITH FOWLY. HE'S VERY CHARISMATIC.
darb
CHARISMATIC? HE TOLD ME HE WAS GOING TO SHOVE MY TOES UP MY NOSE.
HA HA! YEAH, HE'S VERY VIOLENT, TOO, NO QUESTION.
DUDE, BUCKY'S A CAT AND FOWLY'S A MOUSE. THEY'RE NOT GONNA HANG OUT.
YOU KNOW WHAT THEY SAY: OPPOSITES ATTRACT!
YEAH... AND THEN THEY KILL EACH OTHER.
I DON'T KNOW ABOUT "KILL", BUT SOMEONE WILL CERTAINLY NEED A TETANUS SHOT.

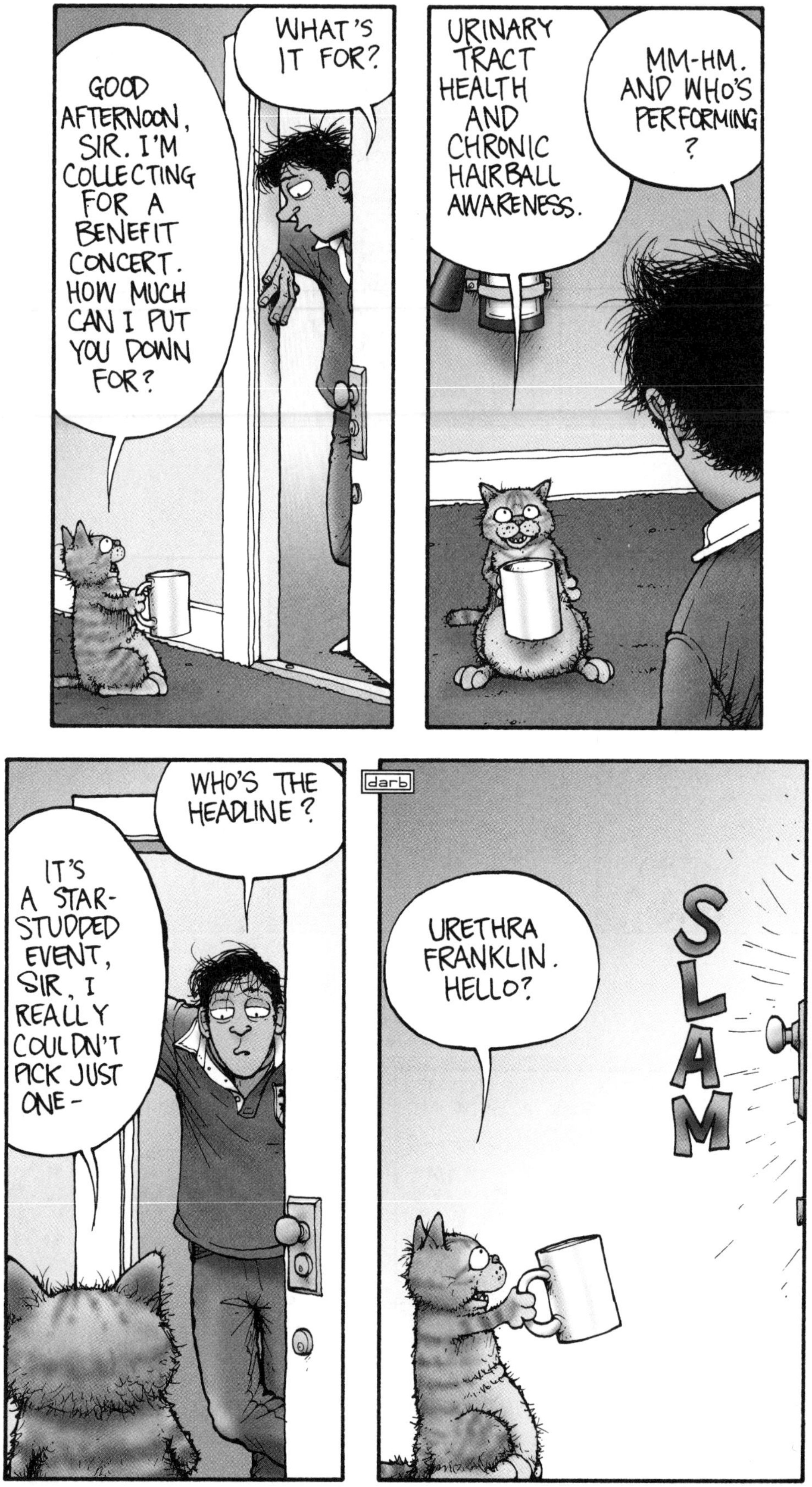
GOOD AFTERNOON, SIR. I'M COLLECTING FOR A BENEFIT CONCERT. HOW MUCH CAN I PUT YOU DOWN FOR?
WHAT'S IT FOR?
URINARY TRACT HEALTH AND CHRONIC HAIRBALL AWARENESS.
MM-HM. AND WHO'S PERFORMING?
WHO'S THE HEADLINE?
IT'S A STAR-STUDDED EVENT, SIR, I REALLY COULDN'T PICK JUST ONE-
darb
URETHRA FRANKLIN. HELLO?
SLAM

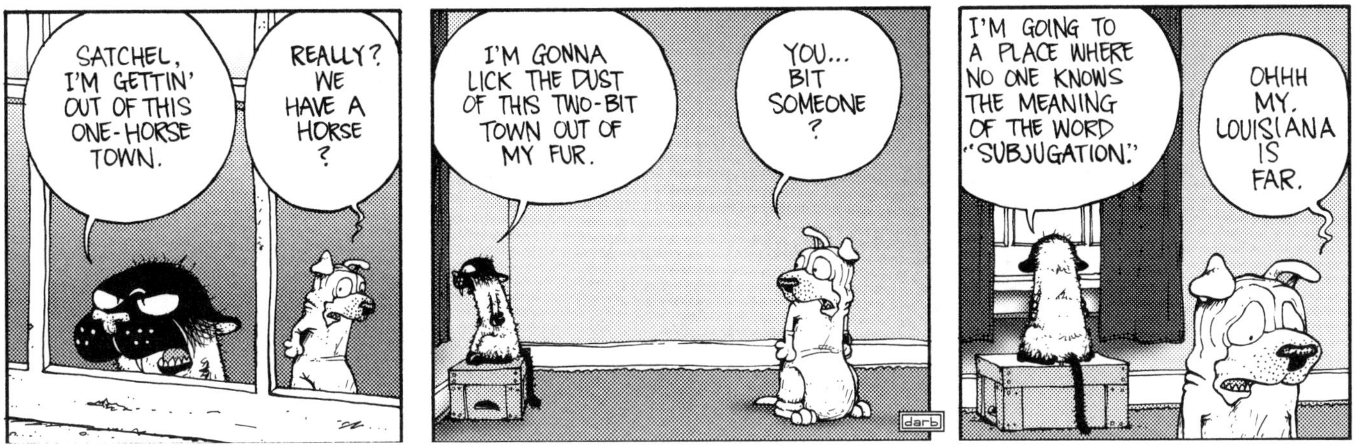
SATCHEL, I'M GETTIN' OUT OF THIS ONE-HORSE TOWN.
REALLY? WE HAVE A HORSE ?
I'M GONNA LICK THE DUST OF THIS TWO-BIT TOWN OUT OF MY FUR.
YOU... BIT SOMEONE ?
I'M GOING TO A PLACE WHERE NO ONE KNOWS THE MEANING OF THE WORD "SUBJUGATION."
OHHH MY. LOUISIANA IS FAR.

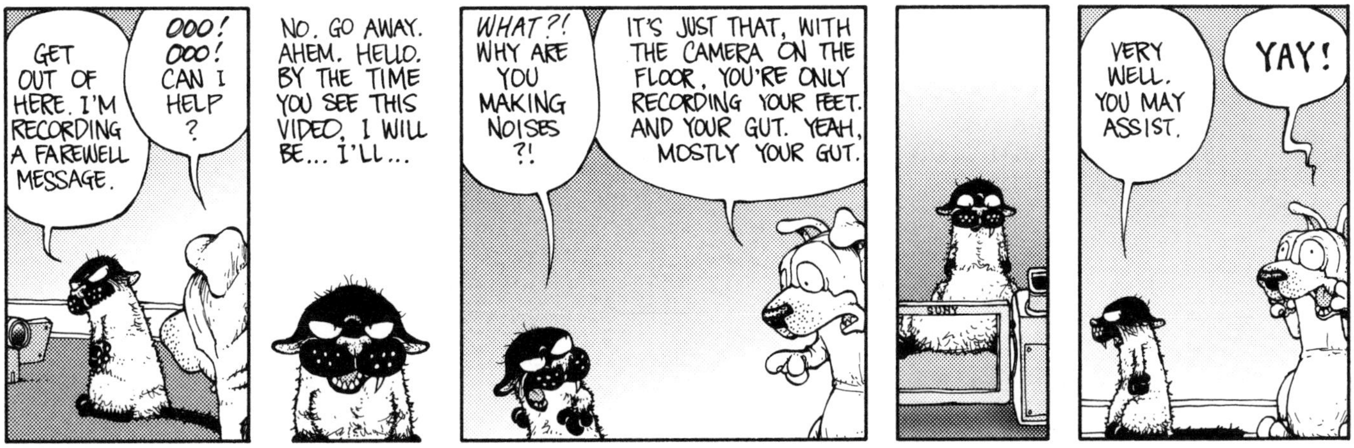
GET OUT OF HERE. I'M RECORDING A FAREWELL MESSAGE.
OOO! OOO! CAN I HELP ?
NO. GO AWAY. AHEM. HELLO. BY THE TIME YOU SEE THIS VIDEO, I WILL BE... I'LL...
WHAT?! WHY ARE YOU MAKING NOISES ?!
IT'S JUST THAT, WITH THE CAMERA ON THE FLOOR, YOU'RE ONLY RECORDING YOUR FEET. AND YOUR GUT. YEAH, MOSTLY YOUR GUT.
SONY
VERY WELL. YOU MAY ASSIST.
YAY!

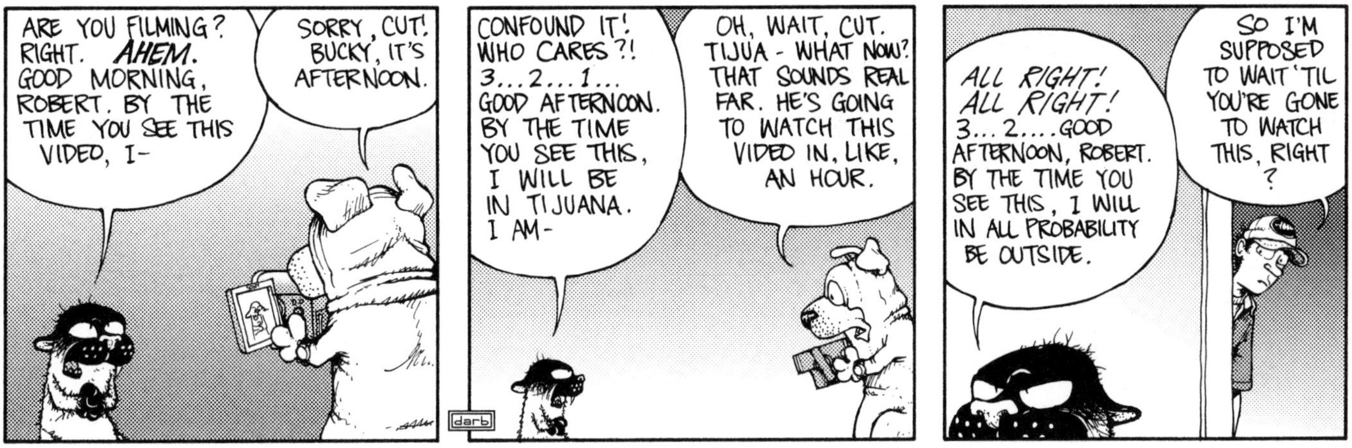
ARE YOU FILMING? RIGHT. AHEM. GOOD MORNING, ROBERT. BY THE TIME YOU SEE THIS VIDEO, I-
SORRY, CUT! BUCKY, IT'S AFTERNOON.
CONFOUND IT! WHO CARES?! 3...2...1... GOOD AFTERNOON. BY THE TIME YOU SEE THIS, I WILL BE IN TIJUANA. I AM-
OH, WAIT, CUT. TIJUA - WHAT NOW? THAT SOUNDS REAL FAR. HE'S GOING TO WATCH THIS VIDEO IN, LIKE, AN HOUR.
ALL RIGHT! ALL RIGHT! 3... 2.... GOOD AFTERNOON, ROBERT. BY THE TIME YOU SEE THIS, I WILL IN ALL PROBABILITY BE OUTSIDE.
SO I'M SUPPOSED TO WAIT 'TIL YOU'RE GONE TO WATCH THIS, RIGHT ?

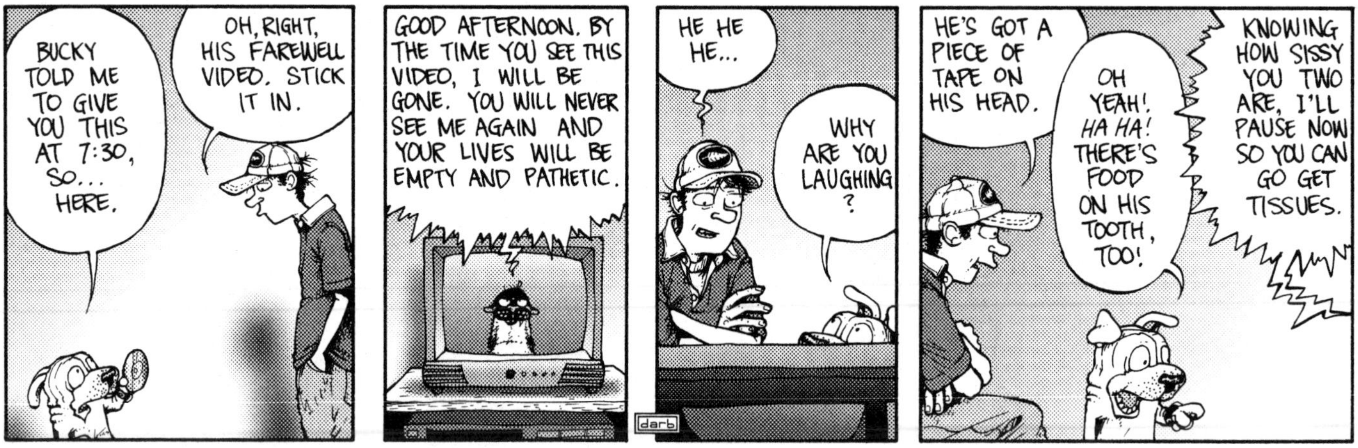
BUCKY TOLD ME TO GIVE YOU THIS AT 7:30, SO... HERE.
OH, RIGHT, HIS FAREWELL VIDEO. STICK IT IN.
GOOD AFTERNOON. BY THE TIME YOU SEE THIS VIDEO, I WILL BE GONE. YOU WILL NEVER SEE ME AGAIN AND YOUR LIVES WILL BE EMPTY AND PATHETIC.
HE HE HE...
WHY ARE YOU LAUGHING?
HE'S GOT A PIECE OF TAPE ON HIS HEAD.
OH YEAH! HA HA! THERE'S FOOD ON HIS TOOTH, TOO!
KNOWING HOW SISSY YOU TWO ARE, I'LL PAUSE NOW SO YOU CAN GO GET TISSUES.

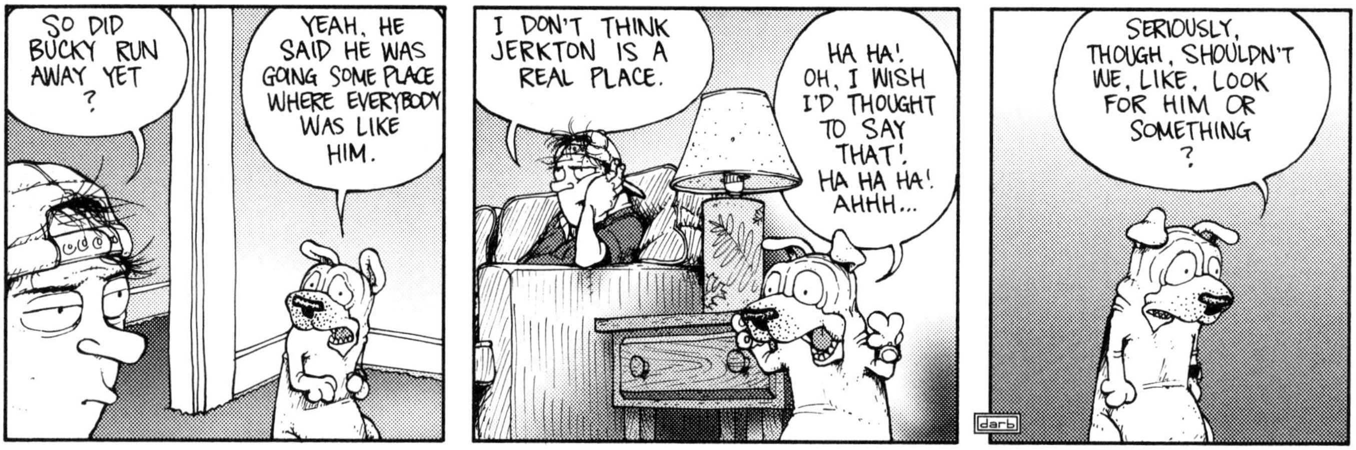
SO DID BUCKY RUN AWAY YET?
YEAH, HE SAID HE WAS GOING SOME PLACE WHERE EVERYBODY WAS LIKE HIM.
I DON'T THINK JERKTON IS A REAL PLACE.
HA HA! OH, I WISH I'D THOUGHT TO SAY THAT! HA HA HA! AHHH...
SERIOUSLY, THOUGH, SHOULDN'T WE, LIKE, LOOK FOR HIM OR SOMETHING?

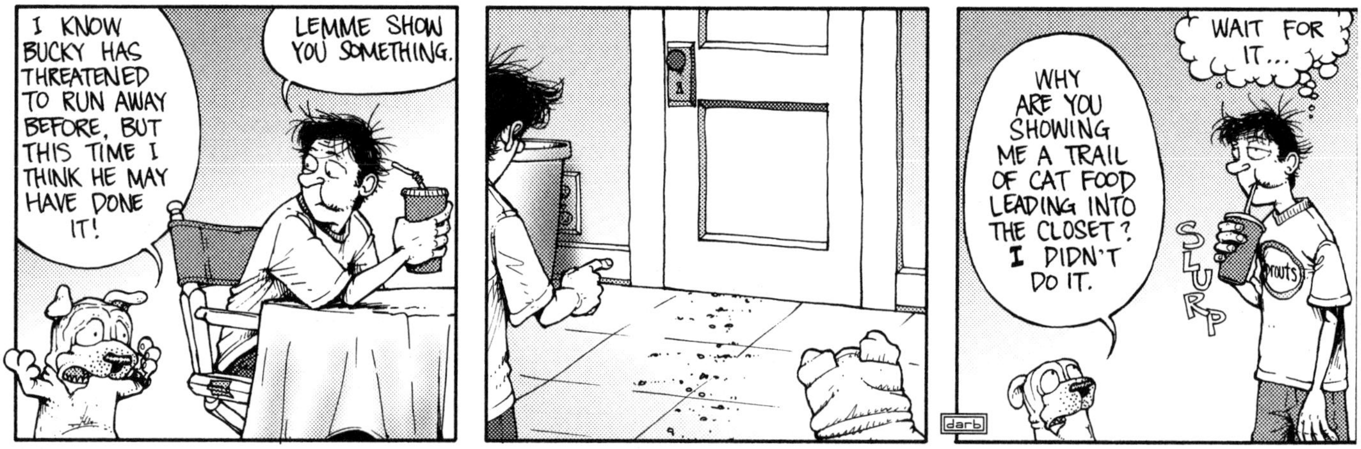
I KNOW BUCKY HAS THREATENED TO RUN AWAY BEFORE, BUT THIS TIME I THINK HE MAY HAVE DONE IT!
LEMME SHOW YOU SOMETHING.
WAIT FOR IT...
WHY ARE YOU SHOWING ME A TRAIL OF CAT FOOD LEADING INTO THE CLOSET? I DIDN'T DO IT.
SLURP

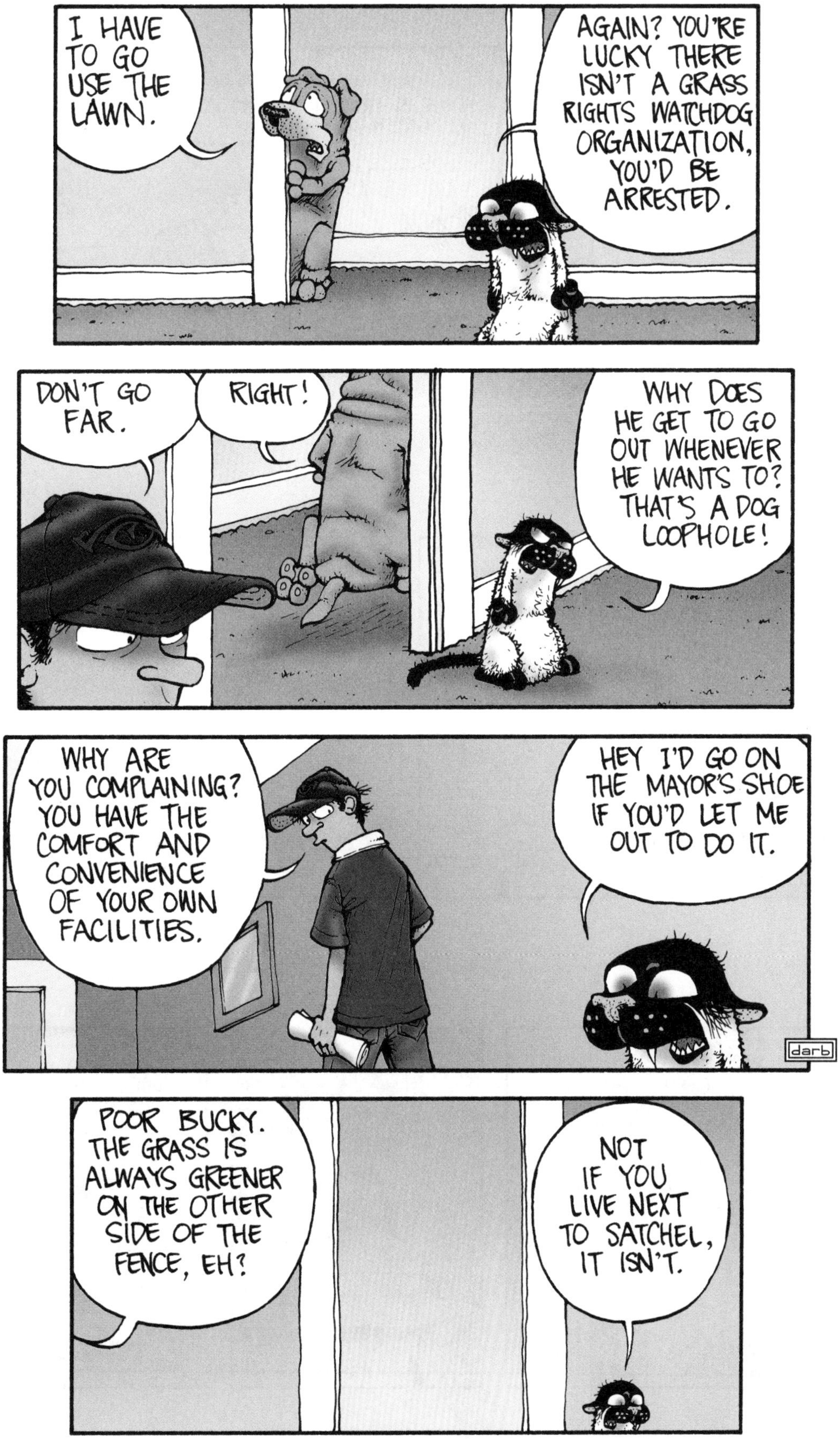
I HAVE TO GO USE THE LAWN.
AGAIN? YOU'RE LUCKY THERE ISN'T A GRASS RIGHTS WATCHDOG ORGANIZATION, YOU'D BE ARRESTED.
DON'T GO FAR.
RIGHT!
WHY DOES HE GET TO GO OUT WHENEVER HE WANTS TO? THAT'S A DOG LOOPHOLE!
WHY ARE YOU COMPLAINING? YOU HAVE THE COMFORT AND CONVENIENCE OF YOUR OWN FACILITIES.
HEY I'D GO ON THE MAYOR'S SHOE IF YOU'D LET ME OUT TO DO IT.
darb
POOR BUCKY. THE GRASS IS ALWAYS GREENER ON THE OTHER SIDE OF THE FENCE, EH?
NOT IF YOU LIVE NEXT TO SATCHEL, IT ISN'T.

HA HA! WHY THE CRAZY GETUP?

I'M CELEBRATING. IT'S CATSMAS.

CATS- WHAT NOW?

CATSMAS. AS IN MERRY CATSMAS.

DO I WANT TO KNOW ABOUT THIS?

PINKY, YOU'RE NOT **ALLOWED** TO KNOW ABOUT IT. I'D HAVE TO KILL YOU.

WOW, WHAT AN EXCITING HOLIDAY!

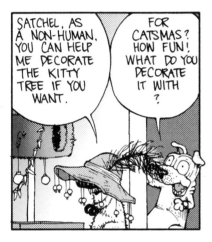

SATCHEL, AS A NON-HUMAN, YOU CAN HELP ME DECORATE THE KITTY TREE IF YOU WANT.

FOR CATSMAS? HOW FUN! WHAT DO YOU DECORATE IT WITH?

YOU KNOW: LIGHTS, ORNAMENTS, TINSEL, MOUSE TOE...

MISTLE- TOE?

NO, MOUSE TOE.

ON SECOND THOUGHT, I HAVE TO UM... NOT BE HERE.

BASHING ON THE SNAKE! WITH A SHOVEL AND A RAKE! O'ER THE RAT WE'LL DRIVE! 'TIL IT'S NOT ALIVE- HO HO HO!

HEY! DON'T YOU HAVE ANY CATSMAS CAROLS THAT AREN'T ABOUT KILLING THINGS?

WELL...

THERE'S A COUPLE ABOUT WOUNDING STUFF...

NAW, MAN. NAW.

240

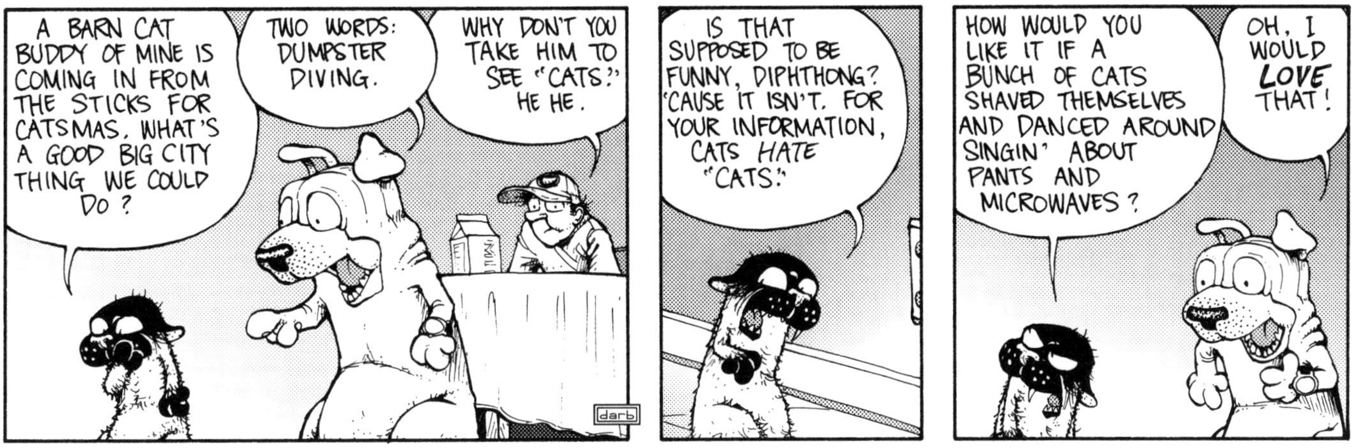
A BARN CAT BUDDY OF MINE IS COMING IN FROM THE STICKS FOR CATSMAS. WHAT'S A GOOD BIG CITY THING WE COULD DO?
TWO WORDS: DUMPSTER DIVING.
WHY DON'T YOU TAKE HIM TO SEE "CATS?" HE HE.
darb
IS THAT SUPPOSED TO BE FUNNY, DIPHTHONG? 'CAUSE IT ISN'T. FOR YOUR INFORMATION, CATS *HATE* "CATS."
HOW WOULD YOU LIKE IT IF A BUNCH OF CATS SHAVED THEMSELVES AND DANCED AROUND SINGIN' ABOUT PANTS AND MICROWAVES?
OH, I WOULD ***LOVE*** THAT!

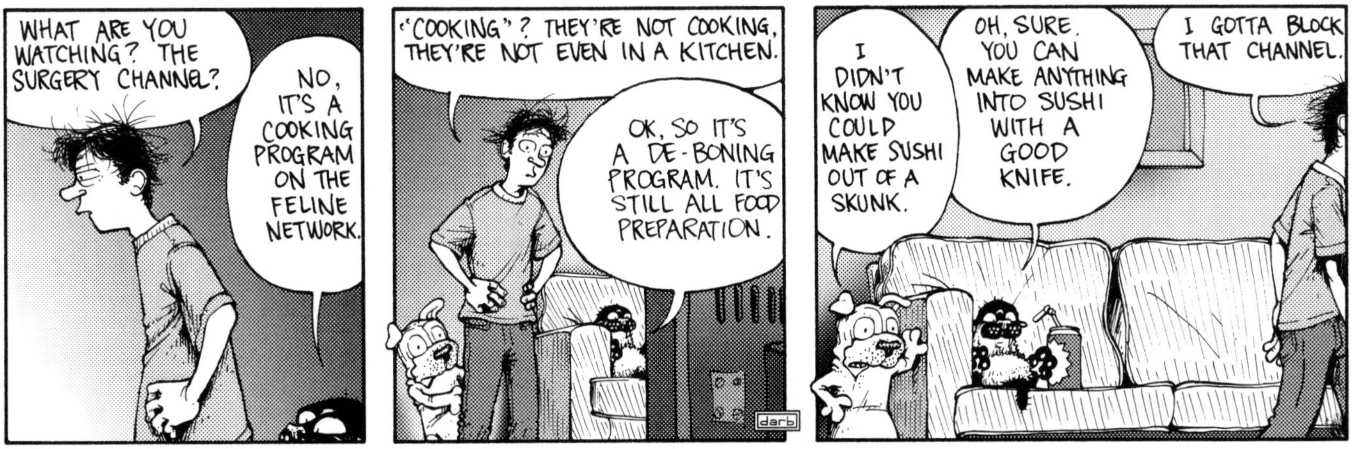
WHAT ARE YOU WATCHING? THE SURGERY CHANNEL?
NO, IT'S A COOKING PROGRAM ON THE FELINE NETWORK.
"COOKING"? THEY'RE NOT COOKING, THEY'RE NOT EVEN IN A KITCHEN.
OK, SO IT'S A DE-BONING PROGRAM. IT'S STILL ALL FOOD PREPARATION.
darb
I DIDN'T KNOW YOU COULD MAKE SUSHI OUT OF A SKUNK.
OH, SURE. YOU CAN MAKE ANYTHING INTO SUSHI WITH A GOOD KNIFE.
I GOTTA BLOCK THAT CHANNEL.

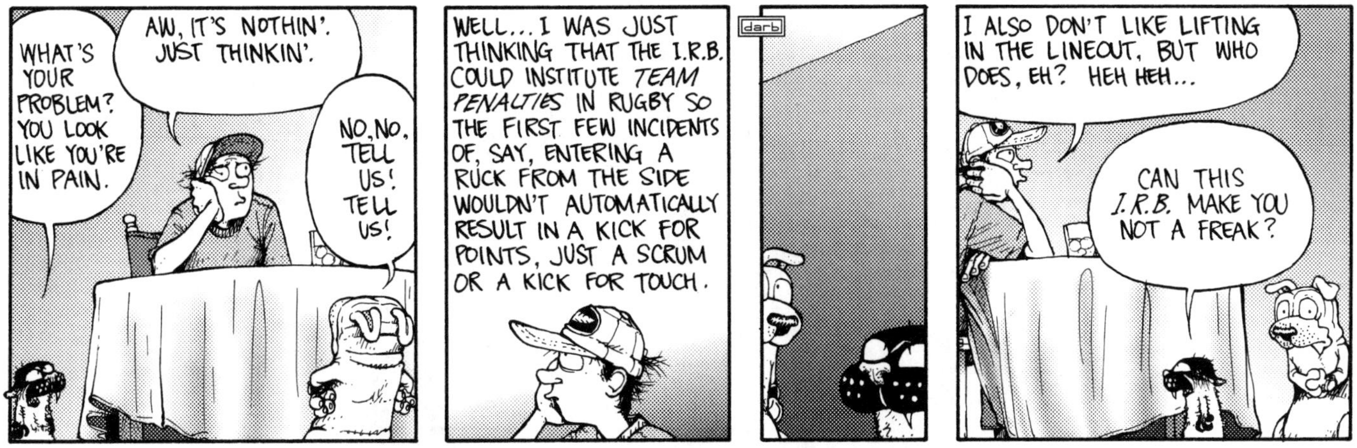
WHAT'S YOUR PROBLEM? YOU LOOK LIKE YOU'RE IN PAIN.
AW, IT'S NOTHIN'. JUST THINKIN'.
NO, NO. TELL US! TELL US!
WELL... I WAS JUST THINKING THAT THE I.R.B. COULD INSTITUTE *TEAM PENALTIES* IN RUGBY SO THE FIRST FEW INCIDENTS OF, SAY, ENTERING A RUCK FROM THE SIDE WOULDN'T AUTOMATICALLY RESULT IN A KICK FOR POINTS, JUST A SCRUM OR A KICK FOR TOUCH.
darb
I ALSO DON'T LIKE LIFTING IN THE LINEOUT, BUT WHO DOES, EH? HEH HEH...
CAN THIS *I.R.B.* MAKE YOU NOT A FREAK?

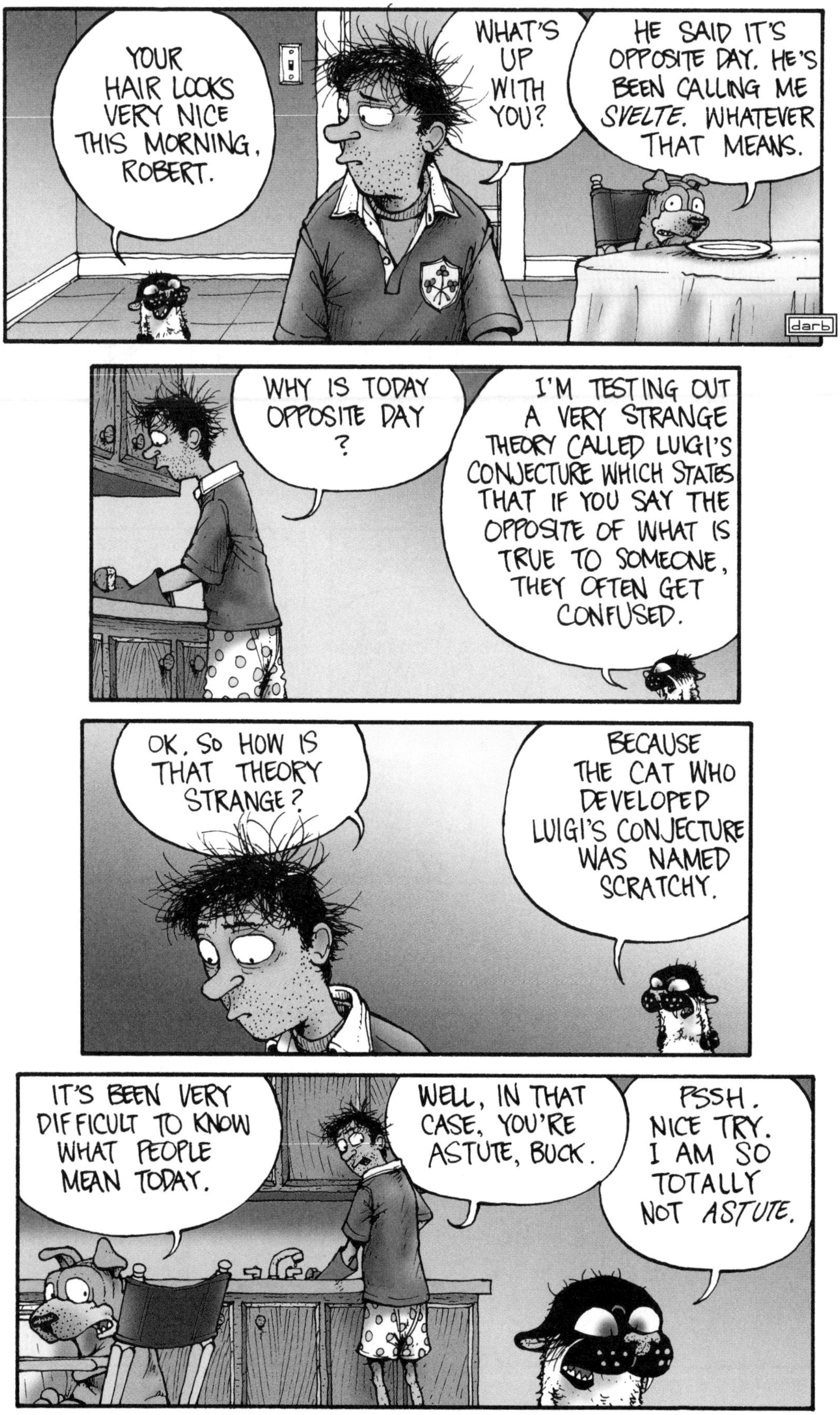
YOUR HAIR LOOKS VERY NICE THIS MORNING, ROBERT.
WHAT'S UP WITH YOU?
HE SAID IT'S OPPOSITE DAY. HE'S BEEN CALLING ME *SVELTE*. WHATEVER THAT MEANS.
darb
WHY IS TODAY OPPOSITE DAY ?
I'M TESTING OUT A VERY STRANGE THEORY CALLED LUIGI'S CONJECTURE WHICH STATES THAT IF YOU SAY THE OPPOSITE OF WHAT IS TRUE TO SOMEONE, THEY OFTEN GET CONFUSED.
OK, SO HOW IS THAT THEORY STRANGE?
BECAUSE THE CAT WHO DEVELOPED LUIGI'S CONJECTURE WAS NAMED SCRATCHY.
IT'S BEEN VERY DIFFICULT TO KNOW WHAT PEOPLE MEAN TODAY.
WELL, IN THAT CASE, YOU'RE ASTUTE, BUCK.
PSSH. NICE TRY. I AM SO TOTALLY NOT *ASTUTE*.

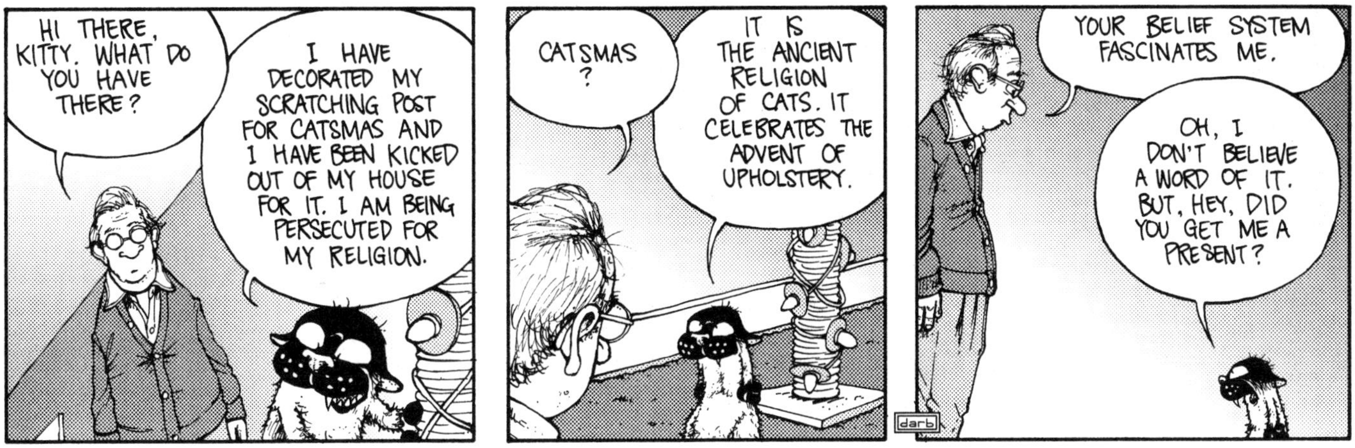
HI THERE, KITTY. WHAT DO YOU HAVE THERE?
I HAVE DECORATED MY SCRATCHING POST FOR CATSMAS AND I HAVE BEEN KICKED OUT OF MY HOUSE FOR IT. I AM BEING PERSECUTED FOR MY RELIGION.
CATSMAS?
IT IS THE ANCIENT RELIGION OF CATS. IT CELEBRATES THE ADVENT OF UPHOLSTERY.
YOUR BELIEF SYSTEM FASCINATES ME.
OH, I DON'T BELIEVE A WORD OF IT. BUT, HEY, DID YOU GET ME A PRESENT?
darb

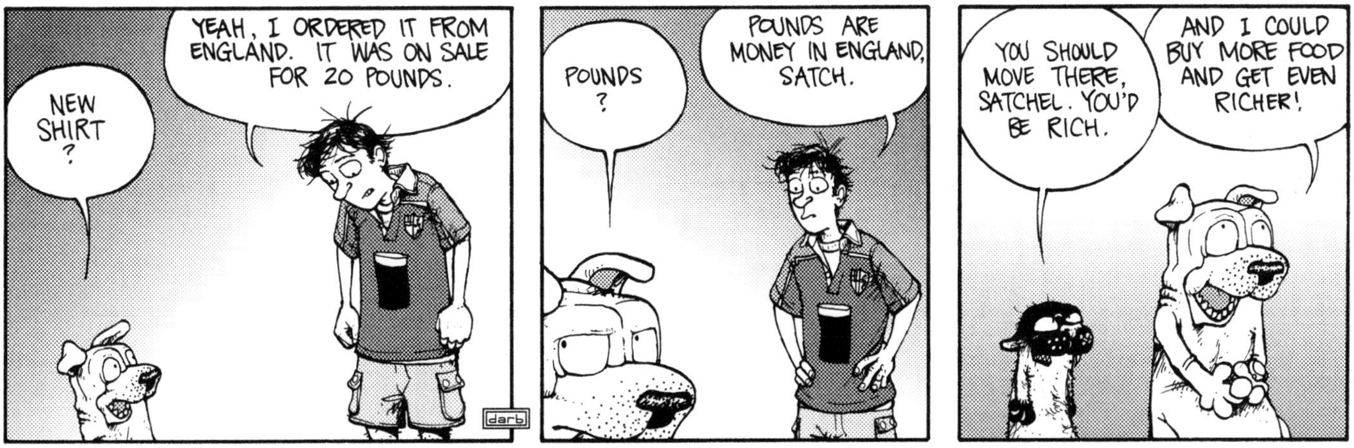
NEW SHIRT?
YEAH, I ORDERED IT FROM ENGLAND. IT WAS ON SALE FOR 20 POUNDS.
darb
POUNDS?
POUNDS ARE MONEY IN ENGLAND, SATCH.
YOU SHOULD MOVE THERE, SATCHEL. YOU'D BE RICH.
AND I COULD BUY MORE FOOD AND GET EVEN RICHER!

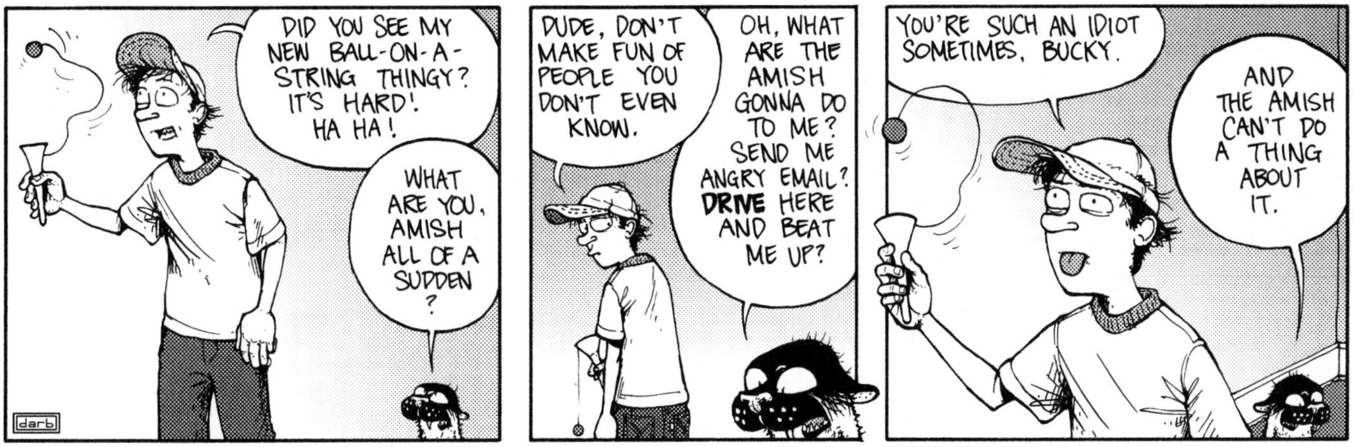
DID YOU SEE MY NEW BALL-ON-A-STRING THINGY? IT'S HARD! HA HA!
WHAT ARE YOU, AMISH ALL OF A SUDDEN?
darb
DUDE, DON'T MAKE FUN OF PEOPLE YOU DON'T EVEN KNOW.
OH, WHAT ARE THE AMISH GONNA DO TO ME? SEND ME ANGRY EMAIL? **DRIVE** HERE AND BEAT ME UP?
YOU'RE SUCH AN IDIOT SOMETIMES, BUCKY.
AND THE AMISH CAN'T DO A THING ABOUT IT.

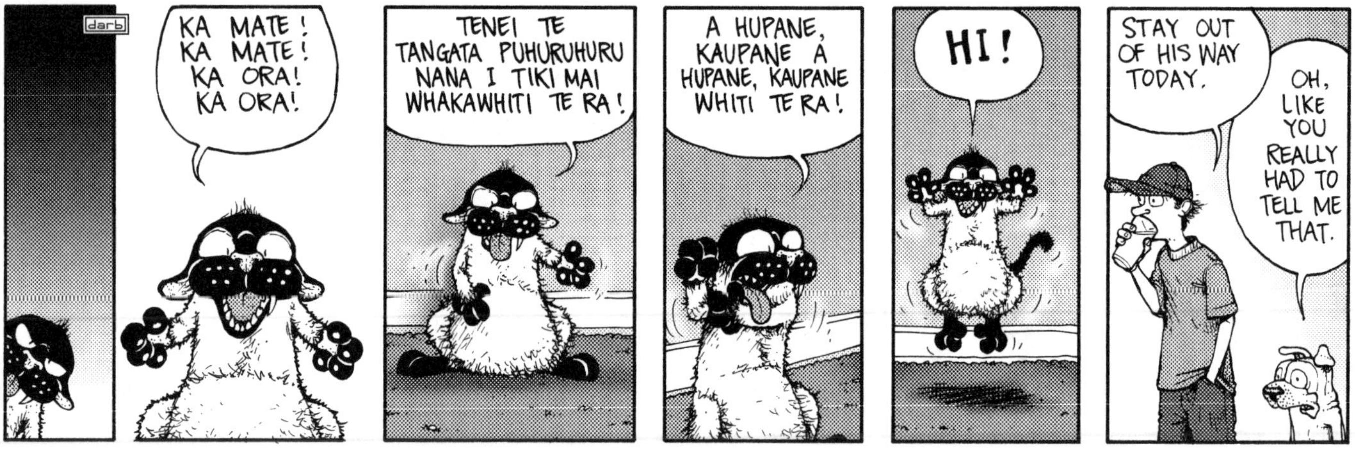
darb
KA MATE! KA MATE! KA ORA! KA ORA!
TENEI TE TANGATA PUHURUHURU NANA I TIKI MAI WHAKAWHITI TE RA!
A HUPANE, KAUPANE A HUPANE, KAUPANE WHITI TE RA!
HI!
STAY OUT OF HIS WAY TODAY.
OH, LIKE YOU REALLY HAD TO TELL ME THAT.

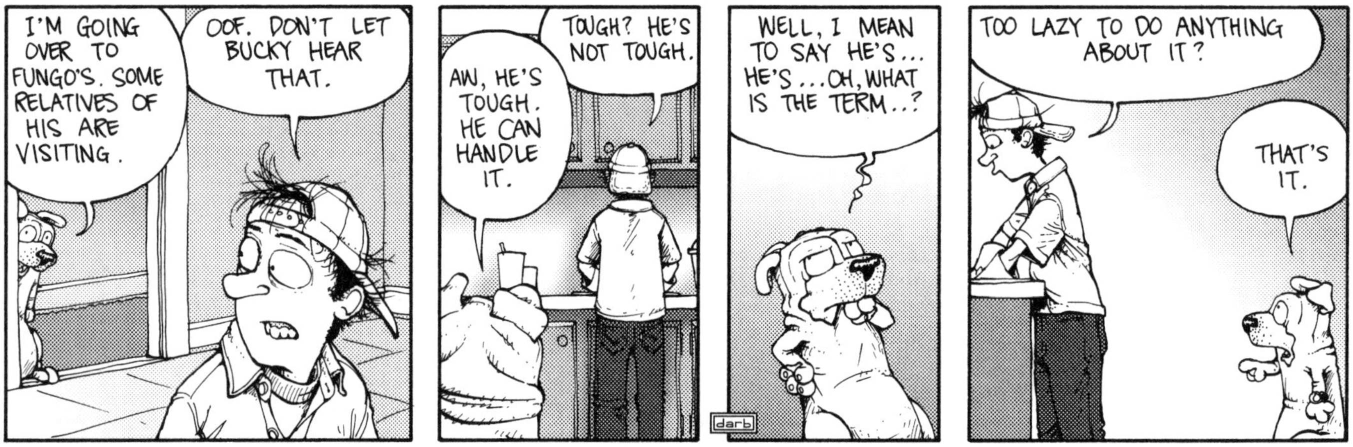
I'M GOING OVER TO FUNGO'S. SOME RELATIVES OF HIS ARE VISITING.
OOF. DON'T LET BUCKY HEAR THAT.
AW, HE'S TOUGH. HE CAN HANDLE IT.
TOUGH? HE'S NOT TOUGH.
darb
WELL, I MEAN TO SAY HE'S... HE'S...OH, WHAT IS THE TERM..?
TOO LAZY TO DO ANYTHING ABOUT IT?
THAT'S IT.

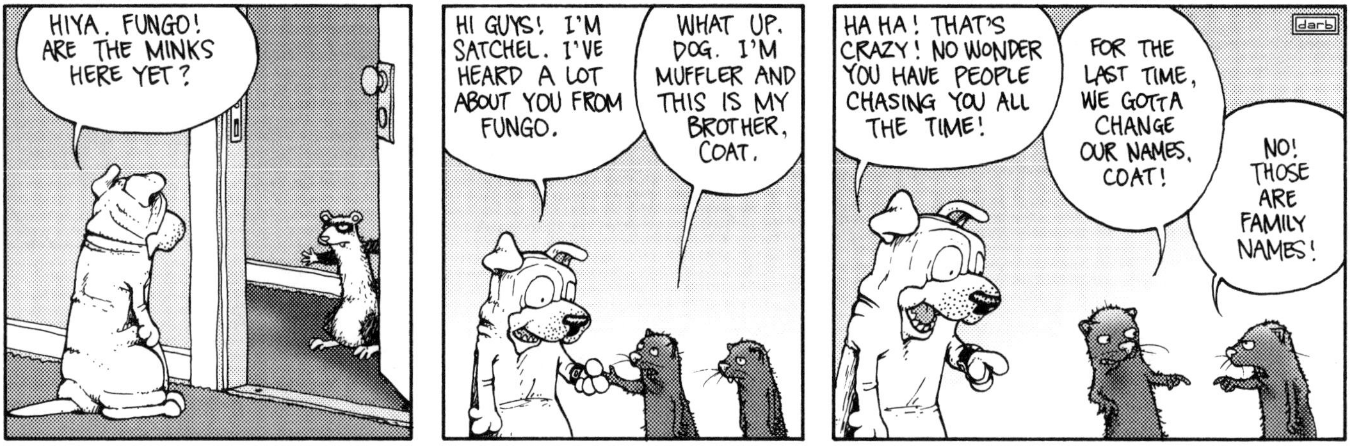
HIYA, FUNGO! ARE THE MINKS HERE YET?
HI GUYS! I'M SATCHEL. I'VE HEARD A LOT ABOUT YOU FROM FUNGO.
WHAT UP, DOG. I'M MUFFLER AND THIS IS MY BROTHER, COAT.
darb
HA HA! THAT'S CRAZY! NO WONDER YOU HAVE PEOPLE CHASING YOU ALL THE TIME!
FOR THE LAST TIME, WE GOTTA CHANGE OUR NAMES, COAT!
NO! THOSE ARE FAMILY NAMES!

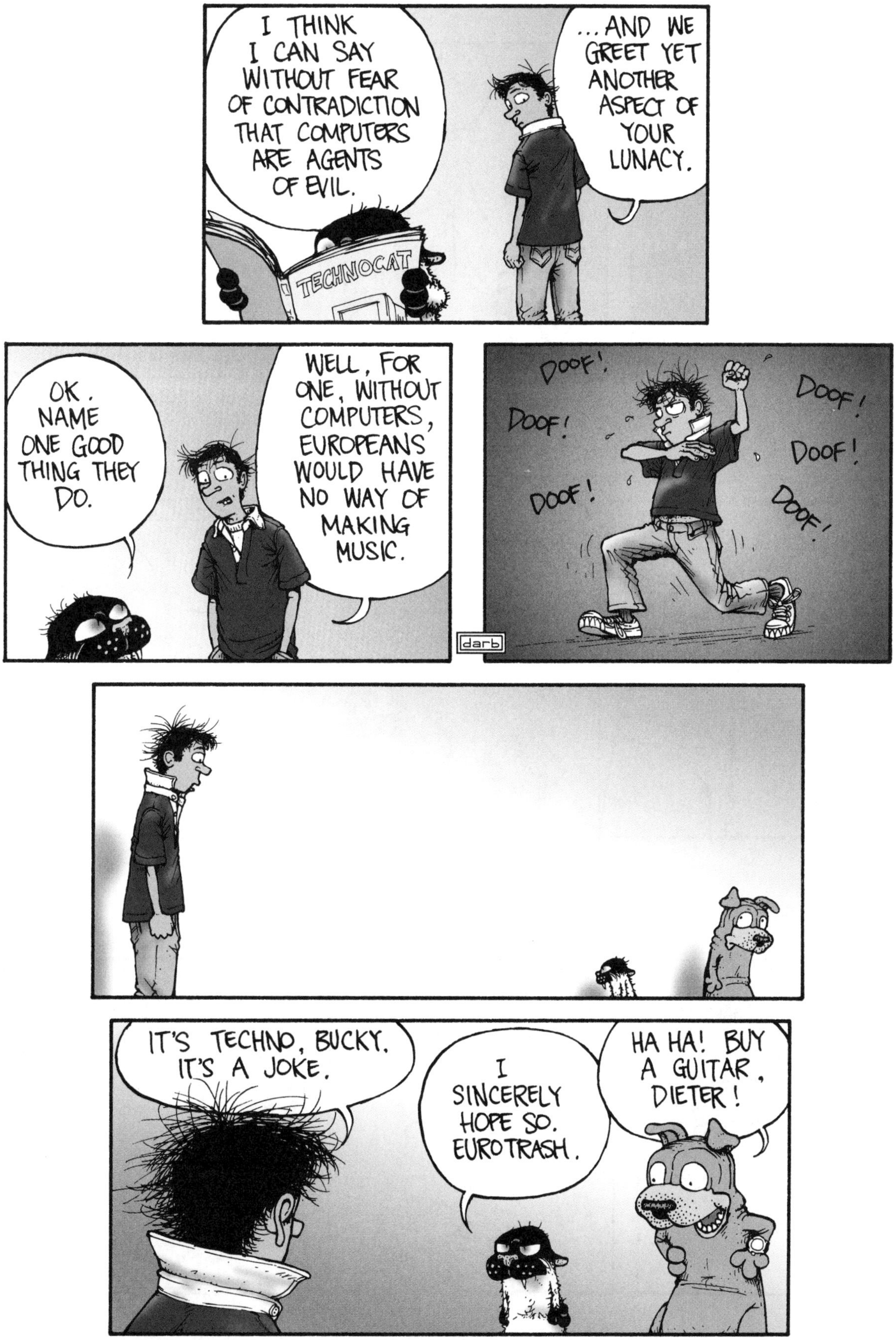
I THINK I CAN SAY WITHOUT FEAR OF CONTRADICTION THAT COMPUTERS ARE AGENTS OF EVIL.
...AND WE GREET YET ANOTHER ASPECT OF YOUR LUNACY.
TECHNOCAT
OK. NAME ONE GOOD THING THEY DO.
WELL, FOR ONE, WITHOUT COMPUTERS, EUROPEANS WOULD HAVE NO WAY OF MAKING MUSIC.
darb
DOOF! DOOF! DOOF! DOOF! DOOF! DOOF!
IT'S TECHNO, BUCKY. IT'S A JOKE.
I SINCERELY HOPE SO. EUROTRASH.
HA HA! BUY A GUITAR, DIETER!

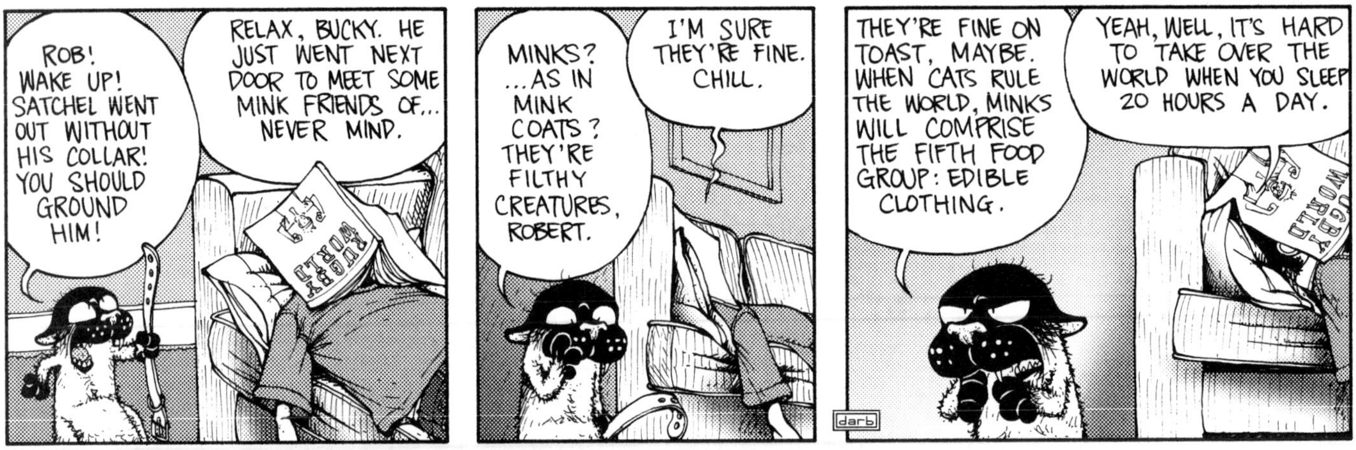
ROB! WAKE UP! SATCHEL WENT OUT WITHOUT HIS COLLAR! YOU SHOULD GROUND HIM!
RELAX, BUCKY. HE JUST WENT NEXT DOOR TO MEET SOME MINK FRIENDS OF... NEVER MIND.
RUGBY WORLD
MINKS? ...AS IN MINK COATS? THEY'RE FILTHY CREATURES, ROBERT.
I'M SURE THEY'RE FINE. CHILL.
THEY'RE FINE ON TOAST, MAYBE. WHEN CATS RULE THE WORLD, MINKS WILL COMPRISE THE FIFTH FOOD GROUP: EDIBLE CLOTHING.
YEAH, WELL, IT'S HARD TO TAKE OVER THE WORLD WHEN YOU SLEEP 20 HOURS A DAY.
darb

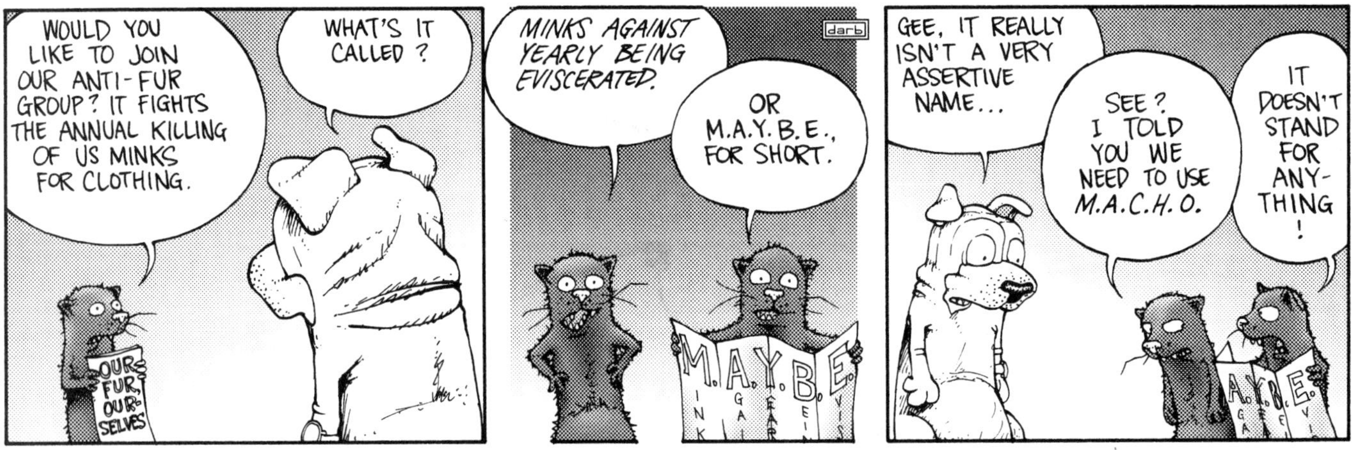
WOULD YOU LIKE TO JOIN OUR ANTI-FUR GROUP? IT FIGHTS THE ANNUAL KILLING OF US MINKS FOR CLOTHING.
OUR FUR, OURSELVES
WHAT'S IT CALLED?
MINKS AGAINST YEARLY BEING EVISCERATED.
OR M.A.Y.B.E., FOR SHORT.
M.A.Y.B.E.
darb
GEE, IT REALLY ISN'T A VERY ASSERTIVE NAME...
SEE? I TOLD YOU WE NEED TO USE M.A.C.H.O.
IT DOESN'T STAND FOR ANY-THING!

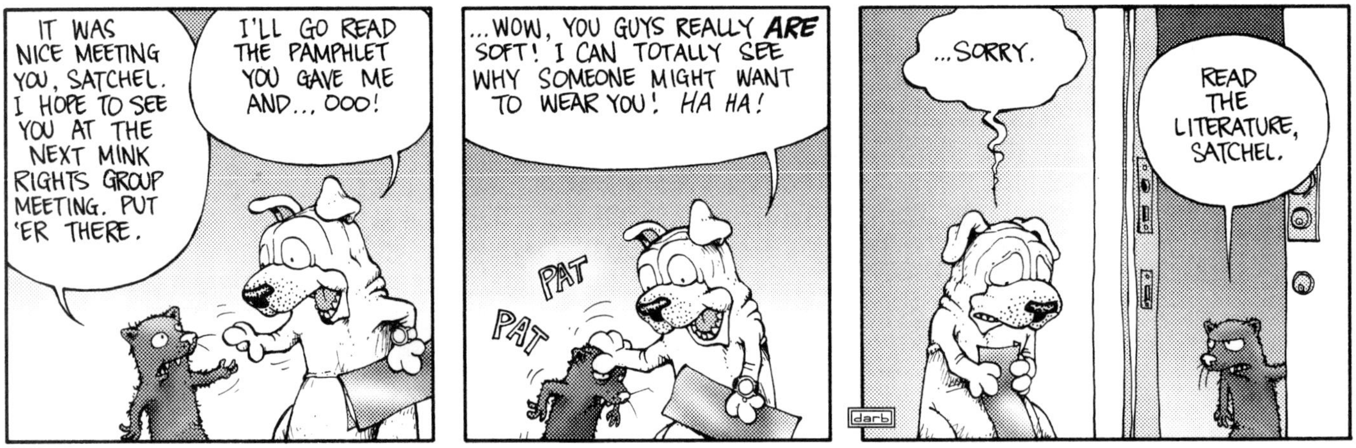
IT WAS NICE MEETING YOU, SATCHEL. I HOPE TO SEE YOU AT THE NEXT MINK RIGHTS GROUP MEETING. PUT 'ER THERE.
I'LL GO READ THE PAMPHLET YOU GAVE ME AND... OOO!
...WOW, YOU GUYS REALLY ARE SOFT! I CAN TOTALLY SEE WHY SOMEONE MIGHT WANT TO WEAR YOU! HA HA!
PAT
PAT
...SORRY.
READ THE LITERATURE, SATCHEL.
darb

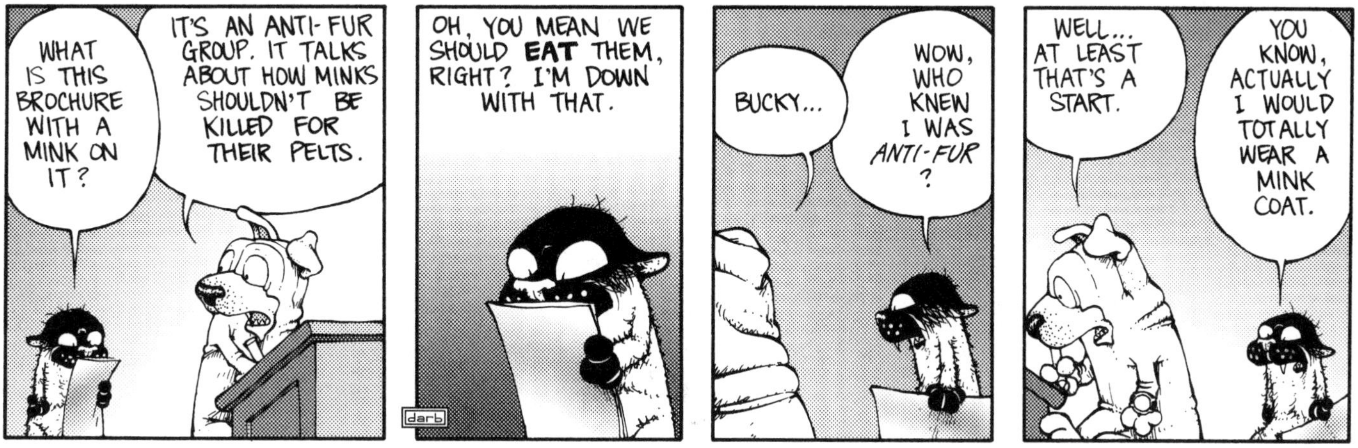
WHAT IS THIS BROCHURE WITH A MINK ON IT?
IT'S AN ANTI-FUR GROUP. IT TALKS ABOUT HOW MINKS SHOULDN'T **BE** KILLED FOR THEIR PELTS.
OH, YOU MEAN WE SHOULD **EAT** THEM, RIGHT? I'M DOWN WITH THAT.
darb
BUCKY...
WOW, WHO KNEW I WAS *ANTI-FUR*?
WELL... AT LEAST THAT'S A START.
YOU KNOW, ACTUALLY I WOULD TOTALLY WEAR A MINK COAT.

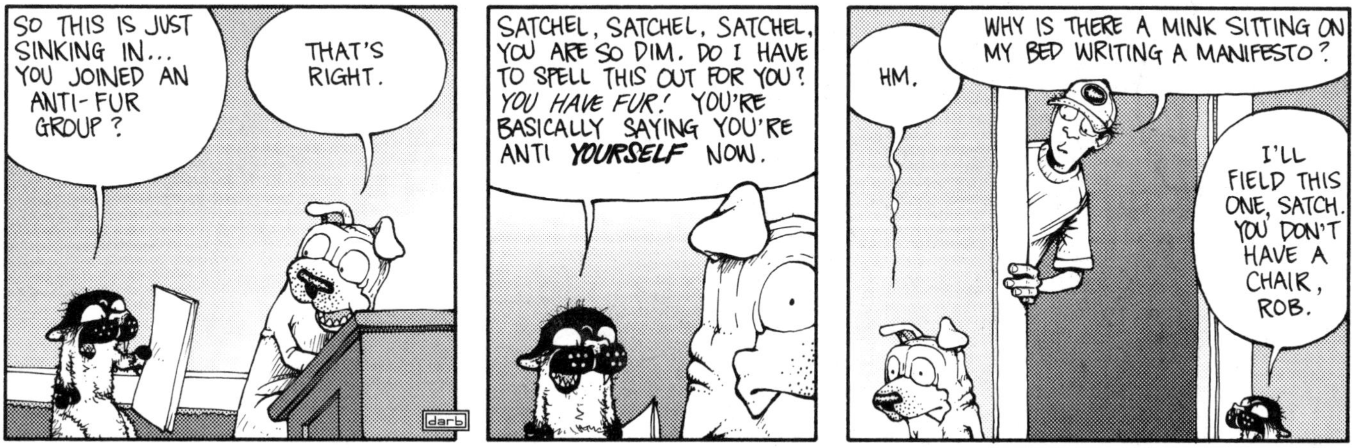
SO THIS IS JUST SINKING IN... YOU JOINED AN ANTI-FUR GROUP?
THAT'S RIGHT.
darb
SATCHEL, SATCHEL, SATCHEL, YOU ARE SO DIM. DO I HAVE TO SPELL THIS OUT FOR YOU? *YOU HAVE FUR!* YOU'RE BASICALLY SAYING YOU'RE ANTI ***YOURSELF*** NOW.
HM.
WHY IS THERE A MINK SITTING ON MY BED WRITING A MANIFESTO?
I'LL FIELD THIS ONE, SATCH. YOU DON'T HAVE A CHAIR, ROB.

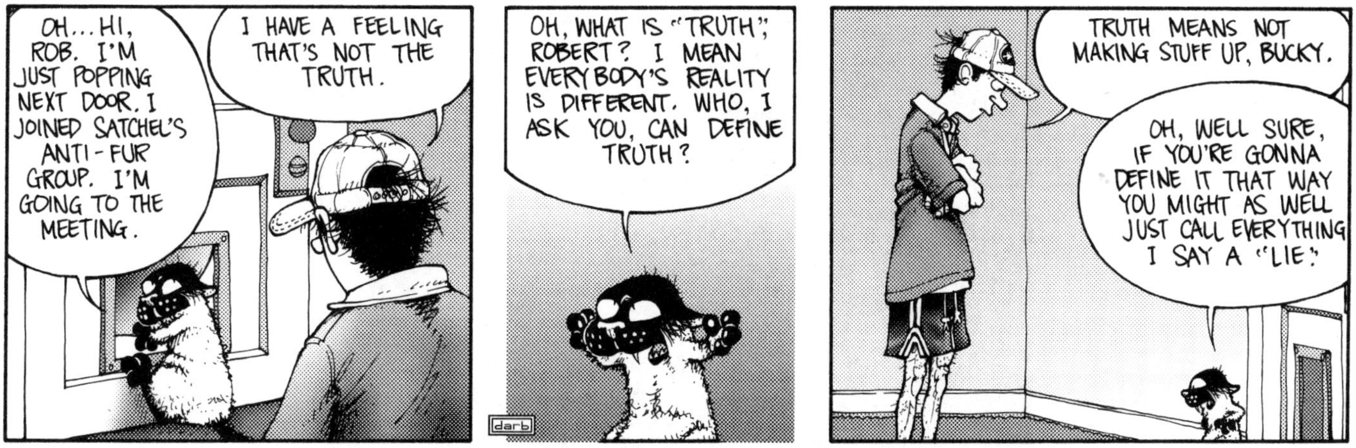
OH... HI, ROB. I'M JUST POPPING NEXT DOOR. I JOINED SATCHEL'S ANTI-FUR GROUP. I'M GOING TO THE MEETING.
I HAVE A FEELING THAT'S NOT THE TRUTH.
OH, WHAT IS "TRUTH," ROBERT? I MEAN EVERYBODY'S REALITY IS DIFFERENT. WHO, I ASK YOU, CAN DEFINE TRUTH?
darb
TRUTH MEANS NOT MAKING STUFF UP, BUCKY.
OH, WELL SURE, IF YOU'RE GONNA DEFINE IT THAT WAY YOU MIGHT AS WELL JUST CALL EVERYTHING I SAY A "LIE."

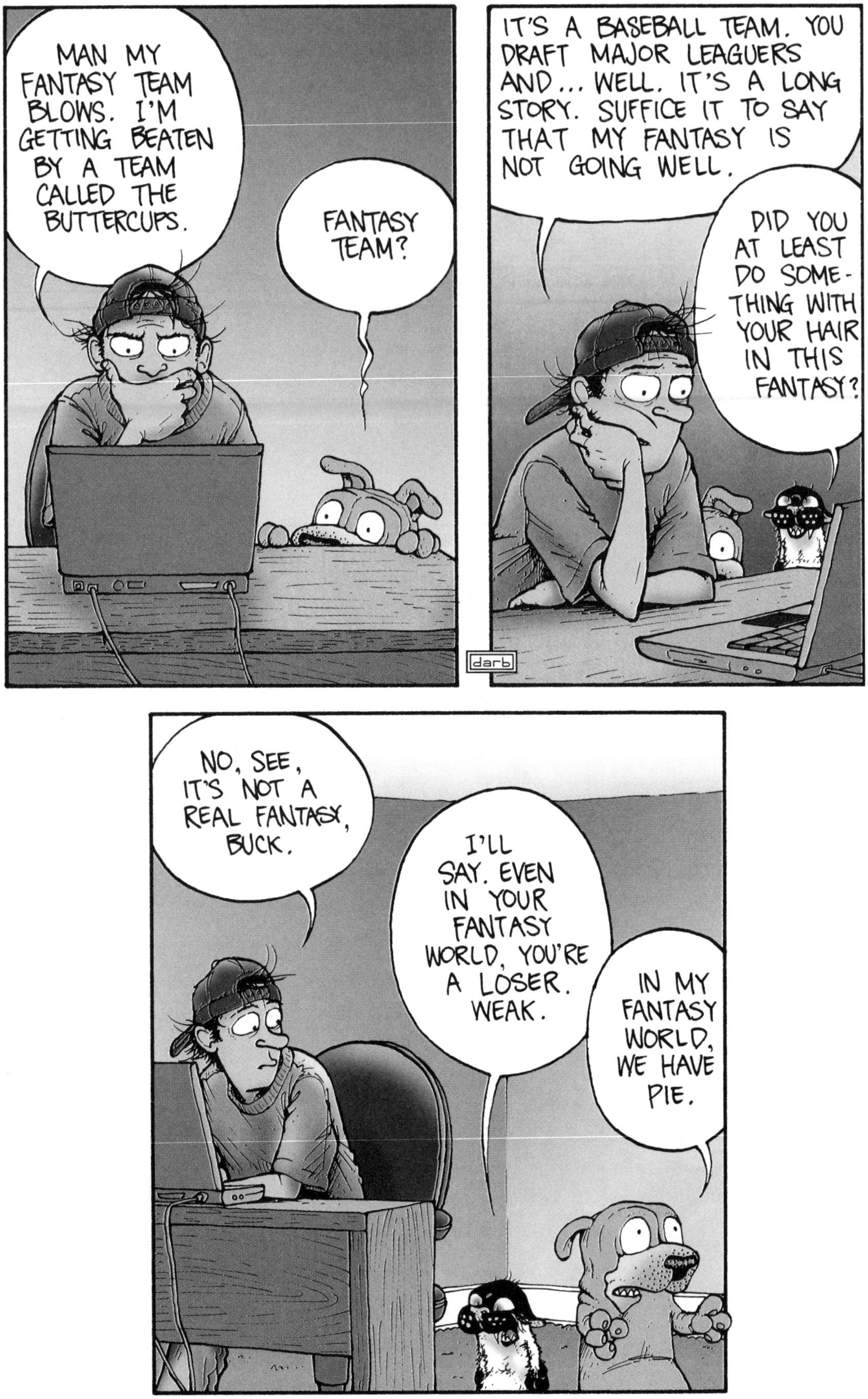
MAN MY FANTASY TEAM BLOWS. I'M GETTING BEATEN BY A TEAM CALLED THE BUTTERCUPS.
FANTASY TEAM?
IT'S A BASEBALL TEAM. YOU DRAFT MAJOR LEAGUERS AND... WELL. IT'S A LONG STORY. SUFFICE IT TO SAY THAT MY FANTASY IS NOT GOING WELL.
DID YOU AT LEAST DO SOME-THING WITH YOUR HAIR IN THIS FANTASY?
darb
NO, SEE, IT'S NOT A REAL FANTASY, BUCK.
I'LL SAY. EVEN IN YOUR FANTASY WORLD, YOU'RE A LOSER. WEAK.
IN MY FANTASY WORLD, WE HAVE PIE.